WASHINGTON DC

SAMANTHA SAULT

CONTENTS

Discover Washington DC.........4

10 Top Experiences.................6

Explore Washington DC..........12

Planning Your Trip.................25

Neighborhoods....................32

■ Sights.............................66

■ Restaurants 105

■ Nightlife.........................139

■ Arts and Culture 160

■ Sports and Activities 187

■ Shops............................203

■ Where to Stay.................224

Day Trips...........................245

Background.......................280

Essentials.........................288

Resources........................299

Index...............................304

MAPS

Neighborhoods

1 National Mall 318

2 Downtown
and Penn Quarter 320

3 Capitol Hill
and Atlas District 322

4 Dupont Circle 324

5 U Street, Shaw,
and Logan Circle 326

6 Adams Morgan 328

7 Georgetown
and Foggy Bottom 330

8 Navy Yard and Anacostia 332

9 Greater Washington DC 334

Day Trips

Day Trips 247

Old Town Alexandria 249

Annapolis 259

Easton 265

Shenandoah National Park 272

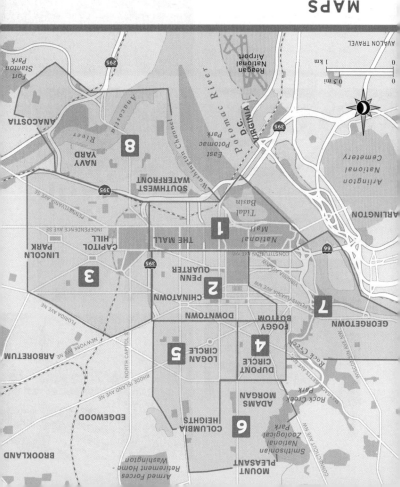

AVALON TRAVEL

1. summer in the Navy Yard (page 56)

2. the 2017 Women's March along the National Mall (page 32)

3. Ben's Chili Bowl on U Street (page 122)

4. *The Spirit of St. Louis* at the National Air and Space Museum (page 72)

5. Union Station (page 89)

6. United States Marine Corps War Memorial (page 103)

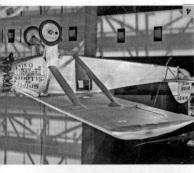

DISCOVER
WASHINGTON DC

The sun sets over the U.S. Capitol, its muscular dome startling in the sky. Fade to the White House, faces outside the gates, calling for change. Pan to the Lincoln Memorial, a reminder of sins and a promise for the future—and an arresting sight, no matter how many times you've seen it.

It's on the news, 24 hours a day. It's on Netflix. But it's not a script. It's real life in the nation's capital.

Generations of changemakers and wonks have chosen a life of "taxation without representation" in this strange, swampy place on the Potomac River, a place that's much more than an average city but not yet a state. Some are trying to make the world a better place. Some are seeking power and influence. Some get caught in a scandal. At the end of the day, they all work hard, and play harder, together, no matter who they voted for.

When you touch down at Reagan National Airport, amid the monuments, you feel that you, too, can touch power. This city is a place where Washington and Jefferson and Lincoln (and JFK and Reagan) became the mythic figures that we know today. Like the cherry blossoms in April, the city explodes with creativity, energy, and passion—not just for politics, but also for food, the arts, and fashion. While those winds may alter the landscape around it, DC can weather any storm.

10 TOP
EXPERIENCES

1 **The White House:** The best-known domicile in America is a must-visit spot for a photo op (page 79).

2 **U.S. Capitol:** Tour the imposing building where lawmakers work (page 84).

3 **Washington Monument:** Get up close to this renowned tribute to the father of the country (page 68).

>>>

IN THIS TEMPLE
AS IN THE HEARTS OF THE PE[...]
FOR WHOM HE SAVED THE UN[...]
THE MEMORY OF ABRAHAM LIN[...]
IS ENSHRINED FOREVER

4 **Lincoln Memorial:** While the awe-inspiring monument to the 16th president lives in the collective consciousness of America, its physical presence remains an inspiration (page 69).

5 **National Mall and Memorials Walk:** How many scenic walks are truly iconic? See some of the most beautiful and moving monuments to the nation's heroes on the mall (page 34).

>>>

6 **The Smithsonian Institution Museums and Galleries:** The Smithsonian offers so many museums of so many different types that you might need to extend your trip to fit them all in (page 70).

<<<

7 **Independence Day:** Head to the nation's capital for the be-all and end-all of Fourth of July celebrations (page 183).

>>>

8 **Arlington National Cemetery:** Pay your respects at the Tomb of the Unknown Solider and JFK's gravesite (page 97).

<<<

9 **Happy Hour:** This is how business gets done in DC, whether in a pub on Capitol Hill or a posh cocktail bar near the White House (page 143).

>>>

10 **Cherry Blossoms:** Spring in DC means an explosion of cherry blossoms. Celebrate the beauty during the **National Cherry Blossom Festival** (page 181) or from a **paddleboat on the Tidal Basin** (page 190).

<<<

EXPLORE
WASHINGTON DC

THE BEST OF WASHINGTON DC

History, politics, power—and the world's best free museums. To experience the best of Washington DC in a few days, stay downtown in a hotel like Penn Quarter's Hotel Monaco, a short walk or just a few Metro stops away from the halls of power and the best restaurants and nightlife. You don't need a car; everything in this itinerary is accessible by Metro, a taxi or ride-share, or walking.

>DAY 1:
DOWNTOWN, PENN QUARTER, AND CAPITOL HILL

Start your day at **Pete's Diner,** one block from the U.S. Capitol. You'll be joined by Hill staffers and perhaps a few lawmakers; former Speaker of the House John Boehner had eggs and coffee here almost every day.

>> **Public Transit:** To get from downtown/Penn Quarter to the U.S. Capitol, take the Metro Blue, Orange, or Silver Line from Metro Center to Capitol South.

Head west on Independence Avenue SE to the **U.S. Capitol.** You

White House from Lafayette Square

BEST VIEWS

U.S. CAPITOL DOME
It's not easy to get a tour of the Capitol building's dome, but it's worth the trouble. You'll have to plan in advance—and perhaps have a close connection in your member of Congress's office—to climb the winding staircase to see the amazing view from the exterior walkway (page 84).

FREDERICK DOUGLASS NATIONAL HISTORIC SITE
The abolitionist spent the last years of his life at his Anacostia mansion, perched on a 51-foot hill offering expansive views all the way to the U.S. Capitol (page 95).

POV
The posh rooftop bar and lounge at the W Hotel overlooks the White House—though you'll pay dearly for the only-in-Washington view, especially if you want a preferred table on the edge (page 141).

TOP OF THE GATE
The Watergate Hotel's huge rooftop bar has 360-degree views, including the Washington Monument, Pentagon, Georgetown, and Potomac River (page 155).

can explore the grounds and see the imposing dome from every angle; get a spectacular up-close selfie on the west side. No matter how many times you've seen photos—or passed by on your way to work—it's always awe-inspiring. If you'd like a tour, reserve one in advance via the **U.S. Capitol Visitor Center** or through your member of Congress; same-day passes are sometimes available at the information desk on the visitor center's lower level, but don't count on it. The visitor center has public exhibits about the Capitol and Congress, as well as a gift shop.

Across from the visitor center entrance on 1st Street, get a glimpse of the **Library of Congress** and the **Supreme Court of the United States.** If you did not take a Capitol tour, you'll have time before lunch to pop inside the **United States Botanic Garden,** a hidden gem on the Capitol grounds full of thousands upon thousands of plant specimens from around the world.

For lunch, go to **Eastern Market** on 7th Street SE between C Street NE and North Carolina Avenue SE, 15 minutes from the Capitol by foot. The crab cake at **Market Lunch,** the casual counter inside the main market building, is one of the best in DC, but if you prefer finer dining, try **Acqua Al 2** across the street. On the weekend, people-watch and shop for local, DC-inspired artwork at the outdoor market; on weekdays, drop by **Bullfeathers** back at 1st Street and D Street for happy hour and political gossip.

>> **Public Transit:** To get from Eastern Market to downtown/Penn Quarter, take the Metro Blue, Orange, or Silver Line from Eastern Market to Metro Center.

Celebrate your first night in the city with the seafood tower at **Old Ebbitt Grill.** Before you sit down, however, detour one block past the restaurant to see the **White House** and **Lafayette Square** during the golden hour. End with a nightcap at the historic **Round Robin Bar** at the **Willard InterContinental.**

>DAY 2: NATIONAL MALL
If you have tickets to the Smithsonian's **National Museum of African American History and**

Culture, grab coffee at **Compass Coffee** on 7th and F Streets NW, then beeline to the museum to be in line a few minutes before your entry time. You'll need the better part of a day to see everything, but it's worth it; start in the basement and work your way up, then have lunch at **Sweet Home Café** before the pop culture exhibits.

>> **Public Transit:** To get from downtown/Penn Quarter to the National Mall, simply walk south on 7th Street or 9th Street to Constitution Avenue. It's 10-20 minutes by foot to the major museums.

If you didn't get tickets, the Smithsonian's **National Museum of American History** and **National Air and Space Museum** are the other must-see museums. If you try to do both, don't miss the Star-Spangled Banner and first ladies' dresses at the former and, of course, the spaceships at the latter. **Mitsitam Native Foods Café** at the **National Museum of the American Indian** is a good option for lunch.

You can stay in the museums if you have foul weather, but otherwise, explore the memorials on the National Mall. Follow the **walking tour** on page 34 to hit the **Washington Monument, Martin Luther King Jr. Memorial, Franklin Delano Roosevelt Memorial, Thomas Jefferson Memorial,** and **Tidal Basin.**

>> **Public Transit:** To get from the memorials on the southwest side of the Mall back to downtown/Penn Quarter, take the Metro Green or Yellow Line from L'Enfant Plaza to Gallery Pl-Chinatown.

Relax before a late dinner at

BEST PEOPLE-WATCHING

LAFAYETTE SQUARE
The park on the north side of the White House is a popular gathering spot for tourists and protesters alike (page 80).

DUPONT CIRCLE
The park at the center of the traffic circle draws all kinds of people to read the paper, picnic, exercise, sunbathe, play chess on the permanent boards—and even get married (page 90).

THE PALM
This famous steakhouse is frankly better for the people-watching than the food, especially during the lunch hour, when the Washington VIPs whose faces are painted on the walls pack the tables (page 119).

MERIDIAN HILL PARK
This historic park is a prime spot for impromptu soccer games, engagement photo shoots, or just relaxing on a blanket. Since the 1970s, every Sunday afternoon around 3pm a drum circle has drawn musicians, dancers, and a crowd of spectators (page 193).

Jaleo, the José Andrés Spanish restaurant that ignited the nation's tapas obsession. After, grab a taxi or ride-share to the **Lincoln Memorial,** which absolutely must be seen at night.

> **DAY 3:**
NATIONAL MALL, U STREET, AND SHAW
Start the day at the **National Gallery of Art.** If you didn't have breakfast, grab coffee and a pastry in the **Pavilion Café** in the **Sculpture Garden.** There's something for every art lover here: Choose the West Building for the French Impressionists and Da Vinci's only painting

on view in the United States, or the East Building for modern art.

When you get hungry, head to CityCenterDC, where you can parse the works over leisurely brunch or lunch at **DBGB Kitchen & Bar,** or grab a healthy juice at **Fruitive.** Here, you can enjoy an afternoon of window shopping the luxury stores, or walk about 15 minutes south to the **Newseum,** which is totally worth the ticket price in the era of "fake news."

>> **Public Transit:** To get from downtown/Penn Quarter to U Street/Shaw, take the Metro Green or Yellow Line from Gallery Place-Chinatown to U Street/African-Amer Civil War Memorial/Cardozo, or grab a taxi/ride-share.

Spend the evening at **U Street and Shaw,** DC's nightlife hub, bustling with trendy restaurants, cocktail and wine bars, and dance clubs. This is the neighborhood to try Ethiopian food—the Washington area has the largest Ethiopian population in the United States, and restaurants here include **Dukem Ethiopian Restaurant** and the more upscale **Etete.** For the definitive DC nightlife experience, catch a show at the **9:30 Club,** followed by a late-night half-smoke (a spicy half-pork/half-beef sausage, served on a bun and smothered in chili) at the famous **Ben's Chili Bowl.**

With More Time

You could spend days—weeks—touring DC's museums and memorials, and if you're visiting for more than a few days, it's worth choosing one or two museums to explore at a more leisurely pace.

With more time, spend a morning in Dupont Circle. Take your coffee in the park at the center of the circle, a great spot to people-watch among locals, and meander to Kramerbooks, one of DC's essential bookstores, stocking top fiction and nonfiction, including the latest political tomes. The Phillips Collection, the country's first modern art museum, is worth a few hours.

Spend an afternoon in Georgetown, shopping top brands and independent boutiques on the brick-lined streets or, in exceptionally beautiful weather, renting a boat on the Potomac River. Enjoy a pre-dinner cocktail at one of the neighborhood's stylish hotels—The Lounge at Bourbon Steak at the Four Seasons and The Observatory at The Graham Georgetown are good bets—before dinner at Fiola Mare, where you should ask for a table in the see-and-be-seen dining room for some of the best Italian seafood in the city.

Before you go, make time for a performance, because DC has a vibrant theater scene on par with the world capitals. Get tickets for anything at The John F. Kennedy Center for the Performing Arts before your Georgetown dinner, or better yet, see a thought-provoking new play at the Woolly Mammoth Theatre Company in Penn Quarter or Studio Theatre in Logan Circle.

THE CITY WITH KIDS

Washington DC is a wonderful city to visit with children, with a plethora of interactive museums and easy-to-use public transportation. And parents won't feel like they're missing out, because the top museums and attractions for kids are among the top museums and attractions in the city, period.

There are lots of family-friendly hotels, but two stand out. Steps from the Smithsonian's National Zoo and the Metro Red Line, the Omni Shoreham Hotel is a quiet hideaway with an outdoor pool and children's amenities; if you want to be closer to the National Mall, the Mandarin Oriental is a surprisingly kid-friendly choice, with a peaceful spa for tired parents.

>DAY 1

Whether you have dinosaur-loving toddlers or hard-to-please teens, the museums and memorials are sure to wow the entire family. Head to **Union Station** for breakfast at one of the many quick-serve restaurants, then pick up the **DC Ducks** tour out front to see the major sights, including the **Washington Monument,** **White House,** and **Thomas Jefferson Memorial** by land and water. The 90-minute tour will take you back to Union Station, from where you can walk to the **National Mall** by heading southeast on Louisiana Avenue past the **U.S. Capitol** and **Reflecting Pool,** or catch the DC Circulator.

>> **Public Transit:** The Metro Red

the Star Spangled Banner exhibit at the National Museum of American History

CAPITAL BY DESIGN

Architecture lovers should first fly into Dulles International Airport in Virginia. The main terminal, designed by Eero Saarinen, evokes flight. Here are just a few of the architectural highlights of the city:

UNION STATION
The city's major railroad station was designed by Daniel Burnham, architect of New York's Flatiron Building. Don't miss the restored Main Hall with soaring granite arches (page 89).

WASHINGTON NATIONAL CATHEDRAL
The imposing, neo-Gothic cathedral is an architectural delight, with 215 stained glass windows and 112 unique gargoyles (page 103).

HIRSHHORN MUSEUM
The circular contemporary art museum is a striking work of art itself, designed by Gordon Bunshaft (page 162).

NATIONAL GALLERY OF ART EAST BUILDING
Reopened in 2016 following an extensive renovation, the gallery's modern art wing was designed by I. M. Pei (page 162).

MARTIN LUTHER KING JR. MEMORIAL LIBRARY
Completed in 1972, DC's flagship library (closed for renovations until 2020) was Mies van der Rohe's last building (page 168).

National Air and Space Museum

aircraft and spacecraft. When hunger pangs strike, skip McDonald's at the latter; the Natural History Museum has a standard food court, with burgers, pizza, and barbecue, or if you're feeling adventurous, try **Mitsitam Native Foods Café** at the **National Museum of the American Indian.** Food trucks often cluster on Constitution Avenue around 15th Street and 17th Street. Round out the day in another museum, or head to the **Franklin Delano Roosevelt Memorial,** a kid favorite with larger-than-life statues and waterfalls.

>> **Public Transit:** To get from the National Mall to Capitol Hill, take the Metro Blue, Orange, or Silver Line from Smithsonian to Capitol South. If you're closer to the FDR Memorial, you can catch the DC Circulator National Mall route from the Lincoln Memorial toward Union Station four stops to Jefferson Drive and 12th Street, then transfer to Metro.

After a long day of sightseeing, have a casual dinner at **Good Stuff Eatery** or **We, the Pizza** on Capitol Hill, serving inexpensive, tasty, kid-approved food with local, farm-raised ingredients (and adult beverages for you). You can walk

Line goes directly to Union Station, where you can walk to the National Mall and Capitol Hill. The DC Circulator National Mall route goes from Union Station to the National Mall; take the bus in the direction of Lincoln Memorial.

The **National Museum of Natural History** is a good choice no matter your kids' interests, with dinosaurs, mummies, and sparkling gems, as is the **National Air and Space Museum,** with amazing

the Berlin Wall Gallery at the Newseum

by the **U.S. Capitol** illuminated in the evening before turning in.

>DAY 2

After breakfast at your hotel, head to **The White House.** You can get a good look, and teach your kids a lesson about the freedom of assembly, from **Lafayette Square,** where you may see (calm, peaceful) protesters on any given day. The **White House Visitor Center** is open to the public daily, though more suitable for older children.

>> **Public Transit:** The Metro stations closest to the White House are Farragut West and McPherson Square, serving the Blue, Orange, and Silver Lines; you can transfer from the Red Line at Metro Center or walk from Farragut North.

A few blocks away, you'll find several good lunch options, including the bustling **Old Ebbitt Grill,** which has an expansive menu that will satisfy even picky eaters,

or **Astro Doughnuts and Fried Chicken,** a fast-casual spot for yummy fried treats. After lunch, choose one of the nearby, highly interactive museums: Try reporting the news during a live shot at the **Newseum,** which has lots of flashy, fun exhibits about free speech and major news events, or go on a spy mission at the **International Spy Museum,** full of super cool spy artifacts. If you're visiting during the holiday season, the magical production of A Christmas Carol at **Ford's Theatre** will appeal to children of all ages, and children at heart.

For dinner, the energetic **Jaleo** is a good restaurant to introduce the family to tapas, especially if you can get one of the glass-topped foosball tables; after all, pan con tomate (grilled bread with tomato), patatas bravas (fried potatoes), and croquetas de pollo (chicken croquettes) are Spanish riffs on kid palate pleasers, and parents can kick back with refreshing gin and tonics or a pitcher of sangria in the famous hot spot.

Open City

>DAY 3

Start your day in Upper Northwest at **Open City,** which serves breakfast all day, plus sandwiches, salads, pizza, and a full bar in a casual, family-filled diner. From there, it's a half-mile, 10-minute walk up Connecticut Avenue to the main entrance of **Smithsonian's National Zoo.** There's tons to explore: giant pandas, the great ape house, and lots of indigenous American beasts, like bald eagles and chipper California sea lions. The zoo has a train and carousel, as well.

>> **Public Transit:** The Metro stations closest to the zoo are Woodley Park-Zoo/Adams Morgan and Cleveland Park, serving the Red

Line. The main entrance is about the same distance from both stations, but it's an uphill walk from the former and a flat walk from the latter.

After relaxing at your hotel, get a taxi or ride-share to Cathedral Heights to see if you can find the Darth Vader gargoyle at the **Washington National Cathedral,** before enjoying D.O.C.-certified pizza at family favorite **2 Amys,** one of the city's best pizza joints.

>DAY 4

If time permits, the day trip to George Washington's home, **Mount Vernon,** is a fantastic family outing, no car required, where you can learn about Washington and how he lived. When visiting with children, don't miss the farm and the 4-D film about life during the American Revolution; the estate frequently hosts story hours and special holiday events.

The best route from DC is by boat; you can take the *Spirit of Washington* **river cruise** from the Southwest Waterfront directly to Mount Vernon from March to October. It's also reachable by car/taxi or public transportation (see the *Day Trips* chapter for details). Detour through **Old Town Alexandria** on the way back to DC for dinner on the waterfront.

PLAYING POLITICS

Whether you have a pet issue you want to discuss, or simply want to say hello, you, too, can play lobbyist for a day and visit your member of Congress. Afterward, see the city like the VIPs do.

>MORNING

If you want to say hello to your **senator** or **representative,** visit their website to get the office location and hours; some host weekly or monthly meet-and-greets for constituents, while others explicitly welcome you to drop by when you're in Washington. Regardless, **Senate** and **House office buildings** are open to the public, and anyone, including international visitors, is free to visit even without an appointment, though there's no guarantee the representative will be available.

If you have a specific issue or bill you want to discuss, contact the office to see if you can arrange a **15-minute meeting** with the member or relevant staffer. If you get a meeting, here are some tips from the pro lobbyists: First, make a clear "ask"—such as how you want them to vote on a bill. If possible, bring a one-page document or other materials with facts to make your case. You may get a vague answer, but follow up with a thank you note. And keep in mind House representatives will be easier to meet than, say, a senator or someone in a leadership position.

If you contact the office in advance, they can arrange a **U.S. Capitol tour** led by an intern, as

Russell Senate Office Building on Capitol Hill

We claim this ground in remembrance of the events of September 11, 2001. To honor the 184 people whose lives were lost, their families, and all who sacrifice that we may live in freedom. We will never forget.

National 9/11 Pentagon Memorial

THE STAR-SPANGLED BANNER
See the original flag that inspired Francis Scott Key to pen the national anthem in the **National Museum of American History** (page 71).

NATIONAL AIR AND SPACE MUSEUM
See the results of America's race to the moon in this must-see museum (page 72).

THE WHITE HOUSE
No matter who's in charge, it's impossible not to feel a swell of patriotic pride when you pass by the White House. You'll have a great view from Lafayette Square (page 79).

NATIONAL 9/11 PENTAGON MEMORIAL
The site of the terrorist attack at the Pentagon on September 11, 2001, is a poignant memorial to the 184 souls killed (page 98).

NATIONAL ARCHIVES MUSEUM
Get an up-close look at several of the nation's founding documents, including the Declaration of Independence, U.S. Constitution, and Bill of Rights (page 163).

well as tours of the **White House, Pentagon,** and other major sights.

An alternate activity for wonks is seeing a **committee hearing** in action. Most are open to the public. (Check www.congress.gov for more information and the congressional schedule.)

›AFTERNOON
Make a reservation for lunch at **The Palm** in Dupont Circle, where lobbyists and reporters go to shake hands with other VIPs whose faces

Mirabelle

Top of the Gate at The Watergate Hotel

are painted on the walls. (Yes, the person at the next table over was probably on CNN earlier.)

Washington is all about who you know, and many lunch meetings turn into happy hour. And Washingtonians can drink, a lot, so don't attempt to keep up. Instead, put on your running shoes and go for a jog (or walk) around the **National Mall** and **monuments,** a favorite activity of DC's active VIPs before the schmoozing resumes in the evening.

›EVENING

Spend your evening in Georgetown, where DC's power set has historically lived and socialized. Start with a cocktail at one of the bars at **The Watergate Hotel,** followed by dinner at **Cafe Milano,** where you may very well see a cabinet secretary or senator enjoying pasta or branzino on any given night. Or, head downtown to **Mirabelle,** one of the newer power spots, helmed by Frank Ruta, a former chef at the White House.

SUMMER IN THE CITY

Washingtonians will tell you to avoid DC during July and August, when the city is feeling the swampiest due to extreme heat and humidity, but don't let the weather deter you from visiting during congressional "recess." When locals go on vacation, enjoy DC's many air-conditioned museums, patios and rooftops, and waterfront views. The only requirement for your hotel? An outdoor pool. The Washington Plaza Hotel in Logan Circle and Liaison Capitol Hill have good ones.

❯MORNING

After coffee by your hotel's pool—the Liaison Capitol Hill has resort-style cabanas and weekend yoga, too—beat the heat in one of the lesser-known (but still air-conditioned) museums. Tourists continue to pack the most popular museums even at the height of summer, but others are far enough off the beaten track to provide respite. Try the Asian art galleries **Freer Gallery of Art and Arthur M. Sackler Gallery** or the Smithsonian's **National Museum of African Art,** the only museum dedicated exclusively to African art in the United States.

❯AFTERNOON

Head to the water. Take the Metro Green Line from L'Enfant Plaza to Navy Yard-Ballpark; you'll have several options for patio dining with a view of the Anacostia River. On the weekend, **Whaley's** serves oysters and rosé from 11am, and **Osteria Morini** has an

Ballpark Boathouse in Navy Yard

excellent, hearty brunch; the latter serves weekday lunch, too.

After, walk west along the river to **Ballpark Boathouse** to rent a kayak or canoe; paddle west toward the Potomac River for monument views.

>EVENING

If it's a game day, stick around to catch the **Washington Nationals** at **Nationals Park,** where concessions serve local foodie favorites like Ben's Chili Bowl half-smokes and DC Brau beers.

On Fridays, however, go back to the National Mall for **Jazz in the Garden** at the National Gallery of Art's **Sculpture Garden.** Washingtonians love to skip out of work early for the free outdoor jazz concert every Friday 5pm-8:30pm. You can bring a blanket and picnic or purchase hors d'oeuvres, sandwiches, and barbecue, plus beer, wine, and sangria from the **Pavilion Café.**

Another favorite summer activity: **outdoor movie screenings.** Throughout the summer, you'll find free, family-friendly, film screenings in several neighborhoods, including Navy Yard; check www.dcoutdoorfilms.com for locations and schedules.

>LATE NIGHT

Head to Shaw for a plethora of rooftops, patios, and beer gardens; the Shaw-Howard U Metro station is just five or six stops on the Green Line from Navy Yard-Ballpark or Waterfront. **Dacha Beer Garden** is a laid-back spot for international craft beer, while

BEST FOR ROMANCE

Deluxe King suite at The Jefferson

LINCOLN MEMORIAL

Conclude your date night at the Lincoln Memorial—the 19-foot statue gives a powerful jolt to your heart when illuminated against the dark backdrop of the National Mall (page 69).

FIOLA MARE

Impress your date at this very fine Italian restaurant in Georgetown, which has a glamorous interior and crowd, plus excellent seafood (page 133).

TINY JEWEL BOX

If you're looking for a special gift, you can't go wrong with something in a red and gold box from the jewelry store where presidents and first ladies have shopped since 1930 (page 207).

THE JEFFERSON

The luxurious Dupont Circle hotel inspired by Thomas Jefferson's estate has gorgeous suites, a Michelin-starred restaurant, and private nooks near the bar for canoodling (page 234).

the roof deck at **Nellie's Sports Bar** is one of the most fun gay bars in the city. Or, grab a seat on the patio at **Maxwell Park,** which has about 50 wines by the glass that rotate every month, plus innovative cocktails.

PLANNING YOUR TRIP

WHEN TO GO

Ask any local when you should visit DC, and they'll likely tell you **spring.** While these months are susceptible to unseasonably cold or hot weather and rain, you'll have plenty of mild, sunshine-filled days to explore the sights and join Washingtonians with "spring fever" on patios and rooftops. The cherry blossoms bloom in March or April, covering the National Mall and memorials in pink, and the **National Cherry Blossom Festival** is a bucket-list event with about three weeks of parades, parties, and special deals. There are two major downsides to visiting in the spring: high hotel prices and large crowds.

The **summer** months are hot, sticky, and jam-packed with tourists, though the **Smithsonian Folklife Festival, Capital Pride,** and, of course, **Independence Day,** are among the reasons to brave the humidity and expensive hotel rooms. The **fall** is crisp and lovely as the leaves begin to change colors and tourists disperse, and **winter** is even quieter, though often very cold.

The **holiday season** is a wonderful time to explore Washington, thanks to the **National Christmas**

Washington DC welcomes the arrival of spring with the National Cherry Blossom Festival.

Tree and lighter crowds, and every four years, January gets busy the week of the **Presidential Inauguration.**

ENTRY REQUIREMENTS

All international visitors are required to have a **valid passport** to enter the United States. Canadian citizens traveling by air need a passport or NEXUS card, but those arriving by land may show an enhanced driver's license/identification card instead. Depending on your country of origin, a visa may be required, or you may be eligible for the Visa Waiver Program (VWP), allowing travel to the United States for business or leisure for 90 days or less without a visa. All visitors and their baggage may be subject to an interview or inspection by U.S. Customs and Border Protection; be prepared to provide details about the purpose of your visit, where you are staying, and when you plan to leave. For more information on entry requirements and restrictions, including prohibited items, visit www.cbp.gov.

TRANSPORTATION

The Washington metropolitan region is served by three airports: **Ronald Reagan Washington National Airport** in Arlington, Virginia; **Washington Dulles International Airport** in Dulles, Virginia; and **Baltimore/Washington International Thurgood Marshall Airport** in Maryland.

Amtrak serves **Union Station,** a convenient travel method between DC, Baltimore, Philadelphia, and New York.

It's not necessary or recommended to rent a car in DC. Public

TOURIST TIPS

- **Stand to the Right:** On Metro escalators, stand to the right and walk to the left. You don't want to get in the path of a late, disgruntled staffer careening down one of the escalators—some of which are more than 200 feet long.

- **Don't Hold the Doors:** Metro train doors are not like elevator doors—they won't slide open again if you stick your arm out when the door is closing. You'll hold up the train and possibly injure yourself.

- **Don't Mind the Sirens:** You may be walking downtown when police cars, motorcycles, and ambulances start barreling down the street, sirens blazing. Stay in place, and don't be alarmed—it's the presidential motorcade. Keep your eyes peeled and you might see the POTUS in "The Beast," an armored black limo with secure communication lines and its own air supply—able to withstand biological, chemical, and nuclear attacks. (The jaded locals around you, however, will likely just roll their eyes and check their phones while waiting for the motorcade to pass.)

- **Prep for Security:** Government buildings and museums require you to pass through a metal detector before entering, while your belongings get X-ray screening. Many items are prohibited, ranging from scissors to food to luggage, so check the building's website if you're unsure whether you can bring something inside.

- **It's Probably Open:** Many sights managed by the U.S. Government or Smithsonian Institution are open daily year-round except Christmas Day; a few sights are closed on major holidays like Thanksgiving Day or New Year's Day, too. While it's probably open, it doesn't hurt to check before showing up at a museum or park on a federal holiday. Most outdoor memorials are accessible 24 hours daily, 365 days per year.

transportation options include Washington Metrorail and Metrobus, DC Circulator, and DC Streetcar service between Union Station and the H Street Corridor/Atlas District; all accept the Metro SmarTrip card, and the streetcar is currently free.

Ride-hailing services like Uber and Lyft are recommended and will take you throughout DC, Maryland, and Virginia.

RESERVATIONS

Washington DC is increasingly a reservations-recommended town. Reservations/tickets are required for **U.S. Capitol and White House tours** as well as the Smithsonian's **National Museum of African American History and Culture.** Generally, if you have the option to reserve a ticket or tour in advance, you should if the sight is on your must-see list. On the other hand, with the exception of special exhibits, most museums are free and don't require tickets, and many tours, especially during non-busy seasons, have walk-up availability. You can usually acquire tickets to theatrical or musical performances a day or two in advance, except for major, one-night-only concerts.

Reserve your hotel as far in advance as possible, especially if you're visiting during cherry blossom season, the first week of July, or inauguration weekend. You can almost always find available rooms, but prices get extremely high during prime tourist seasons or major conferences, and hotels offering good deals always sell out.

Reservations are required for the most popular fine dining restaurants, especially those included in the Michelin Guide, which typically book up 2-3 weeks in advance, though it's possible to score a last-minute table if you're willing to dine early or late. Some exceptionally buzzy restaurants will have their own system for reservations and you'll want to call the first day possible; for example, **minibar by José Andrés** accepts reservations two calendar months at a time, starting at 10am on the first Monday of each month, while **Komi** accepts reservations exactly one month in advance by phone only. For most other restaurants, reservations are recommended a few days in advance, especially on weekends, though not always required. Check **OpenTable** or **Resy** for last-minute availability.

PASSES AND DISCOUNTS

One of the best things about a trip to Washington DC? The majority of the city's sights and museums—including the most exclusive ones, like the U.S. Capitol and White House, are free. Aside from the high cost of hotel accommodations, it's possible to have a relatively inexpensive vacation in DC thanks to dozens of free museums, memorials, and parks, plus excellent fast-casual restaurants and diners. The museums that charge admission fees usually offer discounts for seniors, students, military, and young children, and typically, these museums, like the Newseum and The Phillips Collection, are worth the price.

GUIDED TOURS

There are many options for guided tours of the major sights, including the **Old Town Trolley Tours,**

Pick up tour buses at Union Station or several area hotels.

open-air tours with live guides around DC and Arlington National Cemetery, and **DC Ducks,** 90-minute tours of the National Mall, Capitol Hill, and White House by land and water. Several traditional bus tours depart from Union Station, including double-decker buses, nighttime monuments tours, and day trips; look for (friendly, albeit pushy) uniformed operators at the southwest corner of the station. For something more active, choose a bike or Segway tour, including **Segs in the City,** from Pennsylvania Avenue, or **Bike and Roll** (202/842-2453, www.bikeandrolldc.com; prices vary), with departure points from the National Mall, Capitol Hill, and Old Town Alexandria; both offer guided and self-guided tours. **Smithsonian National Mall Tours** combine the Smithsonian Institution's knowledge with Segway/walking tour operators for educational experiences.

Like many things in DC, some of the best tours are free. The **National Park Service** offers a huge variety of free, ranger-led **walking tours** (www.nps.gov/nama/planyourvisit) around the National Mall and at major monuments and memorials, while guided tours of the U.S. Capitol, White House, and other key buildings are available for free if you plan in advance. In addition, the Smithsonian Institution museums and National Gallery of Art offer free, docent-led tours daily; check the museum's website for the schedule or inquire at the information desk, usually located just after the security screening.

CALENDAR OF EVENTS

JANUARY

Every four years, the city comes together for the **Presidential Inauguration.** Since the second inauguration of FDR in 1937, the swearing-in ceremony has taken

WHAT'S NEW?

If you haven't been to Washington DC in a while, you'll hardly recognize it.

- **Metro Silver Line:** Beginning service in 2014, the Metro Silver Line was the first new line to open in over two decades. When it's complete in 2019, it will connect Washington Dulles International Airport to the city center.

- **National Mall Additions:** In September 2016, the Smithsonian's National Museum of African American History and Culture opened, and the National Gallery of Art's East Building reopened with 12,250 square feet of new exhibition space.

- **CityCenterDC:** This shiny shopping and dining district near Chinatown is home to luxury stores and some of the city's best restaurants.

- **Union Market:** The revitalized historic market in Northeast is home to dozens of local, artisanal vendors, with fine dining and entertainment popping up in nearby warehouses.

- **Ivy City:** Centered around the art deco Hecht Warehouse, this small but growing development is home to a few cool restaurants, shops, and local distilleries.

- **District Wharf:** This mile-long complex on the Potomac River opened in October 2017 and changed the landscape with several new hotels, restaurants, and a concert venue.

- **Michelin Guide:** Known more for fine dining than tires, the French tastemaker published its first Washington DC guide in 2016, recognizing the city's exploding culinary scene.

- **Splashy New Hotels:** The Watergate Hotel, The Darcy, and The LINE are among the many brand-new or fully restored hotels, boasting world-class amenities and destination dining and bars, while POD DC and Hotel Hive bring a new concept for budget-minded travelers.

place on January 20 after an election; if the date falls on a Sunday, the public ceremony occurs on Monday, January 21. Details on how to obtain tickets for festivities including the swearing-in ceremony, parade, and balls are usually available within a few weeks after the November election.

Dr. King had an enormous impact on Washington, which celebrates **Martin Luther King Jr. Day** (www.mlkholidaydc.org) with special events, including the Memorial Peace Walk and parade through Southeast DC.

Beat the January doldrums with the winter edition of the **Metropolitan Washington Restaurant Week** (www.ramw.org/restaurantweek), during which hundreds of local restaurants offer prix fixe menus for brunch ($22), lunch ($22), and dinner ($35) for one week in late January.

MARCH-APRIL

For 3-4 weeks in March and April, the **National Cherry Blossom Festival** (www.nationalcherryblossomfestival.org) celebrates the cherry trees, given to the United States by Japan in 1912. (The festival is timed to coincide with peak bloom, though it can be unpredictable if winter is unusually long or unusually warm.) The festival includes tons of free events like a parade, kite festival, Japanese street festival, fireworks, special exhibits and museum events, and of course, the main event: the magnificent pink and white blossoms around the Tidal Basin and National Mall.

On Easter Monday, the **White House Easter Egg Roll** (www. whitehouse.gov/easter-egg-roll) welcomes more than 20,000 people to the South Lawn for children's egg-rolling races as well as celebrity performances, arts and crafts, and meet-and-greets with high-level officials. The free tickets are available approximately one month in advance by online lottery.

Every spring, the White House opens the gardens and grounds to the public for just two days in April for the **White House Spring Garden Tours** (www.whitehouse. gov), allowing you to explore the Jacqueline Kennedy Garden, Rose Garden, White House Kitchen Garden, and South Lawn. The White House announces the date and ticket information approximately 3-4 weeks in advance, and free, timed tickets are distributed first-come, first-served the morning of the tours.

MAY

The Sunday before Memorial Day, the free **National Memorial Day Concert** (www.pbs.org/national-memorial-day-concert) takes place on the U.S. Capitol West Lawn, featuring celebrity performers, military heroes, the National Symphony Orchestra, and several U.S. military bands and choral groups. On Memorial Day, the **National Memorial Day Parade** runs along Constitution Avenue NW; check local news outlets for details.

JUNE

One of the largest pride festivals in the country, **Capital Pride** (www. capitalpride.org) is a colorful parade and street festival through Dupont Circle with more than 180 floats, entertainers, and participating groups. In recent years,

the event has expanded to include a festival and concert with major stars, including Miley Cyrus, The Pointer Sisters, and the Gay Men's Chorus in 2017. The Dupont Circle neighborhood stays alive into the evening as parade-goers continue the celebration.

JULY-AUGUST

Independence Day in Washington DC is a bucket-list event. It begins with the **National Independence Day Parade** (www.july4thparade. com) on Constitution Avenue NW before crowds move to the U.S. Capitol West Lawn for **A Capitol Fourth** (www.pbs.org/a-capitol-fourth), the free, patriotic concert with celebrity guests, including The Beach Boys and Trace Adkins in 2017. The concert ends with the iconic **fireworks at the Washington Monument,** which are best-viewed from the National Mall but can be seen from rooftops and vistas across the city.

Starting late July, tennis fans make their way to the Rock Creek Park Tennis Center in Upper Northwest for **Citi Open** (www. citiopentennis.com; $15-100), one of the first open tennis tournaments in the United States. The outdoor event features

Capital Pride 2017

professional men and women players from around the world.

The summer edition of the bi-annual **Metropolitan Washington Restaurant Week** (www.ramw.org/restaurantweek) provides a great opportunity to try the DC culinary scene with prix fixe menus for brunch ($22), lunch ($22), and dinner ($35) at hundreds of restaurants.

SEPTEMBER

In early September, the Library of Congress organizes the annual **National Book Festival** (www.loc.gov/bookfest), a free, one-day event at the Walter E. Washington Convention Center where more than 100 authors and illustrators across genres read and sign their books and participate in panel discussions.

OCTOBER

As the foliage changes colors, the White House opens the gardens and grounds to the public for the annual **White House Fall Garden Tours** (www.whitehouse.gov), allowing you to explore the Jacqueline Kennedy Garden, Rose Garden, White House Kitchen Garden, and South Lawn. The White House announces the date and ticket information approximately 3-4 weeks in advance, and free, timed tickets

are distributed first-come, first-served the morning of the tours.

NOVEMBER

Veterans Day is a somber day in the capital as visitors pay respects at war memorials throughout DC and Virginia. The **wreath-laying ceremony at Arlington National Cemetery** (www.arlingtoncemetery.mil) on November 11 is open to the public.

DECEMBER

For nearly 100 years, the president of the United States and First Family have hosted the **National Christmas Tree Lighting** (www.thenationaltree.org) on the Ellipse, kicking off the holiday season in Washington DC with a festive performance featuring A-list celebrities. The free, coveted tickets are available by lottery beginning in October; check in late September for details. The tree is lit daily through January 1, along with 56 trees representing the states and territories.

Every Chanukah, politicians and Jewish community leaders light the **National Menorah** (www.nationalmenorah.org), the largest in the world at 30 feet tall. The ceremony features Jewish performers; free tickets are required and available online in advance.

NEIGHBORHOODS

National Mall

Map 1

The National Mall is America's lawn, where people gather for major events like Independence Day and presidential inaugurations, as well as festivals, concerts, and protests for every issue imaginable. In addition to being the location of the **national monuments and memorials,** it's a national park with more than 1,000 acres of **green space** and photo-op-worthy areas for picnics, jogging, biking, and boating. The National Mall is also home to many of the **Smithsonian Institution museums and galleries,** which are free and open to the public every day except Christmas Day.

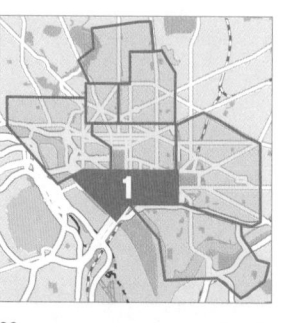

TOP SIGHTS

- Washington Monument (page 68)
- Lincoln Memorial (page 69)
- National Museum of American History (page 71)
- National Museum of African American History and Culture (page 72)
- National Air and Space Museum (page 72)
- National Museum of Natural History (page 73)

TOP RESTAURANTS

- Mitsitam Native Foods Café (page 107)

TOP ARTS AND CULTURE

- Hirshhorn Museum and Sculpture Garden (page 162)
- National Gallery of Art (page 162)
- United States Holocaust Memorial Museum (page 162)

TOP SPORTS AND ACTIVITIES

- Tidal Basin Paddleboats (page 190)

GETTING THERE AND AROUND

- Metro lines: Blue, Green, Orange, Silver, Yellow
- Metro stations: Federal Center SW, L'Enfant Plaza, Smithsonian
- Major bus routes: DC Circulator National Mall

NATIONAL MALL AND MEMORIALS WALK

TOTAL DISTANCE: 3.1 miles (5 kilometers)
WALKING TIME: 1 hour and 15 minutes

For a history lesson on foot, head to the west side of the National Mall, where you'll find a maze of memorials set among idyllic grassy areas. It's possible to power through this walk in less than two hours, but it's better to budget up to three hours to fully take in the grandeur of the monuments (and take plenty of photos). To avoid crowds, try the walk in the early morning or dusk. Taking this walk during peak cherry blossom bloom, usually around late March to early April, should be on your travel bucket list—though you'll need to add at least one hour to your walking time to get around the Tidal Basin, which will be packed with tourists.

Start this walk at the corner of **17th Street NW and Constitution Avenue NW.** It's easily accessible by foot from downtown and Dupont Circle.

1 Walking south, you'll pass the **Lockkeeper's House** on your right, the small stone house for the lockkeeper who raised and lowered the

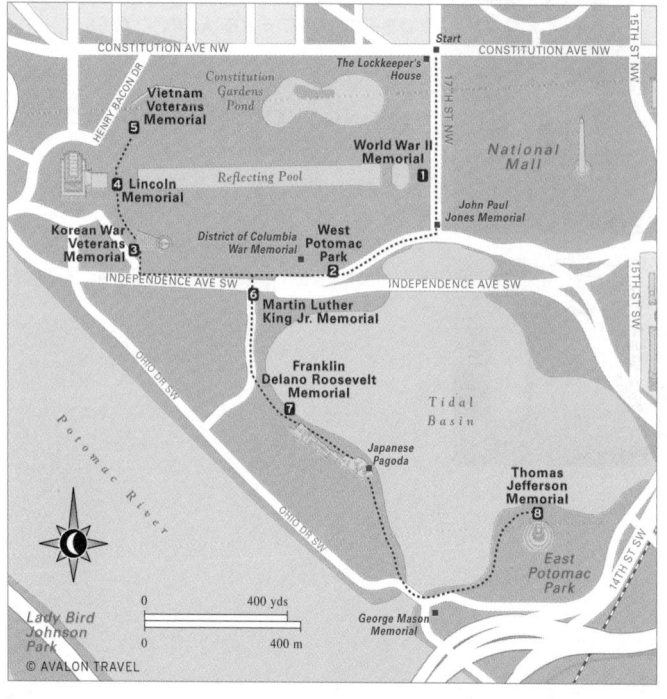

Franklin Delano Roosevelt Memorial

C&O Canal lock, and the oldest structure on the National Mall. Walk two minutes down this block to approach the **World War II Memorial** on your right; you can't miss the 56 stone columns. You'll have a great view of the Washington Monument to the east and the Lincoln Memorial to the west, but keep walking southwest on the sidewalk along Homefront Drive SW. To your left is the **John Paul Jones Memorial,** a statue honoring the Revolutionary War hero considered the "Father of the U.S. Navy."

2 Homefront Drive runs into Independence Avenue SW. Keep heading west on Independence; you're in the heart of **West Potomac Park.** On the right you'll pass a circular, marble structure, the **District of Columbia War Memorial,** honoring the 499 Washington DC residents who died serving in World War I.

3 To see the Vietnam and Korean War memorials, along with a closer look at the Lincoln Memorial, continue west on Independence Avenue SW for about five minutes. The **Korean War Veterans Memorial** will be on your right at the stoplight near David French Memorial Drive SW. Take in the 19 figures representing soldiers from all branches of the country's military. Get up close and you'll see for yourself the stunning detail imbued in each statue.

4 Take the path leading northwest to reach the **Lincoln Memorial.** Climb the steps to get an up-close view of the iconic statue of a seated Abraham Lincoln gazing toward the Reflecting Pool.

5 Next, take one of the paths headed northeast to reach the **Vietnam Veterans Memorial.** (If you get disoriented, look for rectangular gray signs pointing you toward major sights as well as tourist information and facilities.) Absorb the scale of the Vietnam War as you scan the 58, 315 names of the Americans killed or missing in action that are engraved on the Memorial Wall. Retrace your steps to Independence Avenue, then head east until you reach West Basin Drive SW, about five minutes.

6 At West Basin Drive SW, cross the street to head south to the **Martin Luther King Jr. Memorial.** Keep walking south, through the "mountain of despair" to the "stone of hope," structures that represent a line from Dr. King's "I Have A Dream" speech. Stand as close as you can to the sculpture of MLK to feel the enormous impact he had on our nation, then walk back to the railing at the Tidal Basin to see him emerging from the mountains.

Martin Luther King Jr. Memorial

7 From here, continue walking south just under half a mile on the path around the Tidal Basin to reach the **Franklin Delano Roosevelt Memorial,** where you can spend time exploring and taking photos of the life-size statues of FDR and First Lady Eleanor Roosevelt. Walk up the stone steps to enter the memorial at Room One, which represents Roosevelt's first presidential term, during the Great Depression. (Backtrack a bit to visit the Prologue Room, which was added later to accommodate a statue of FDR in a wheelchair. It's to the right by the visitor center once you're inside.) Continue south through the memorial, which guides you chronologically through each of Roosevelt's four terms and his death.

8 Exit the memorial on the south end to return to the Tidal Basin path. Look for the **Japanese Pagoda,** a 17th-century stone structure given to the United States by the mayor of Yokohama, Japan, in 1957. It symbolizes the friendship between the two nations. Keep along the asphalt path around the Tidal Basin for views of the Washington Monument and the Thomas Jefferson Memorial glimmering on the water. During cherry blossom season, this path is covered in pink blooms—and people. Cross the bridge at Ohio Drive SW and approach the **George Mason Memorial,** honoring a lesser-known Founding Father who did not sign the Declaration of Independence because it did not contain a bill of rights or abolish slavery. It's looking a little worse for the wear, but you

the Thomas Jefferson Memorial

can relax on the benches under the trellis, next to the bronze statue of George Mason. From here, walk east on East Basin Drive SW and turn left to approach the **Thomas Jefferson Memorial.** Walk counterclockwise around the memorial to approach the stone steps and enter the open-air memorial, where you'll see the 19-foot statue of Jefferson and quotations from his writings.

From here, you have options: Walk back to the east side of the National Mall for an afternoon at a museum, or go southeast to **East Potomac Park** and **Hains Point** for a scenic walk. If you do head to the park, stop at the **East Potomac Golf Course and Driving Range** for a bottle of water if you plan to walk the 1.8 miles to Hains Point.

Downtown and Penn Quarter

Map 2

Downtown is where the city's movers and shakers eat, work, and play . . . oh, yes, and the president of the United States lives here, too. It's the **ideal home base,** with easy access to the rest of the city by public transportation, as well as **beautiful hotels, fine restaurants,** and **historic cocktail bars** to enjoy at the end of a long day of sightseeing.

Downtown is home to Penn Quarter and **Chinatown,** the bustling home of the Capital One Arena and several theaters, as well as City-

CenterDC, a **luxury shopping** and dining development.

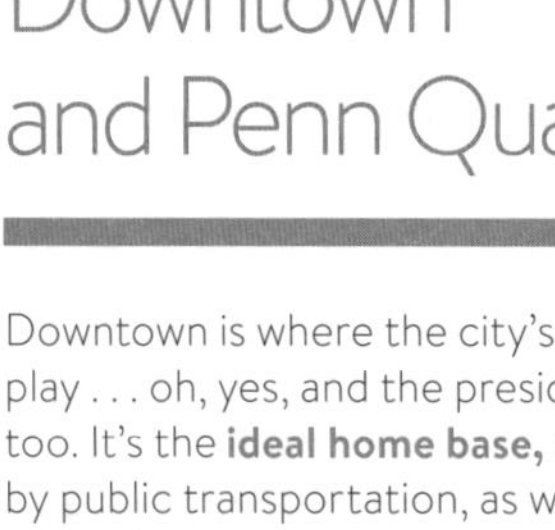

TOP SIGHTS
- The White House (page 79)

TOP RESTAURANTS
- Mirabelle (page 110)
- Jaleo (page 112)

TOP NIGHTLIFE
- POV (page 141)
- Round Robin Bar (page 141)

TOP ARTS AND CULTURE
- Newseum (page 164)
- Woolly Mammoth Theatre Company (page 166)

TOP SHOPS
- Tiny Jewel Box (page 207)
- White House Visitor Center Shop (page 208)

TOP HOTELS
- The Hay-Adams (page 229)
- Sofitel Washington DC Lafayette Square (page 229)
- Kimpton Hotel Monaco Washington DC (page 231)
- The Mayflower (page 232)

GETTING THERE AND AROUND
- Metro lines: Blue, Green, Orange, Red, Silver, Yellow
- Metro stations: Archives-Navy Memorial-Penn Quarter, Farragut North, Farragut West, Federal Triangle, Gallery Place-Chinatown, Judiciary Square, McPherson Square, Metro Center
- Major bus routes: DC Circulator Georgetown-Union Station, Woodley Park-Adams Morgan-McPherson Square Metro

Capitol Hill and Atlas District

Map 3

In addition to being the location of two of the three branches of government, Capitol Hill is home to **cozy restaurants** and **dive bars,** where you can enjoy reasonably priced meals and get the legislative gossip during happy hour.

In the nearby Atlas District, **trendy restaurants, cafés,** and **bars** line popular **H Street NE,** where you'll mix with hipsters and millennials for a casual night out.

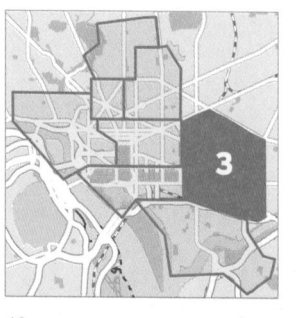

TOP SIGHTS
- U.S. Capitol (page 84)

TOP RESTAURANTS
- Garrison (page 114)
- Charlie Palmer Steak (page 115)

TOP SPORTS AND ACTIVITIES
- DC Ducks (page 192)

TOP SHOPS
- Hill's Kitchen (page 212)

TOP HOTELS
- Liaison Capitol Hill (page 232)

GETTING THERE AND AROUND
- Metro lines: Blue, Orange, Red, Silver
- Metro stations: Capitol South, Eastern Market, Union Station
- Major bus routes: DC Circulator Union Station-Navy Yard, DC Circulator Potomac Ave Metro-Skyland via Barracks Row, DC Streetcar H/Benning

Dupont Circle

Map 4

Washington comes together at Dupont Circle, the traffic circle and urban park where a mix of locals—intellectuals, activists, young families, and the homeless—congregate to have a bite, play chess, protest injustice, or even say their wedding vows. The spokes of the circle lead to **abundant dining and nightlife options,** The Phillips Collection and niche galleries, and the historic center of the city's **gay culture,** with beloved gay bars and events like Capital Pride in June and the High Heel Drag Race at Halloween. With several hotels set on leafy, residential streets, blocks from the grand foreign embassies, Dupont Circle is the ideal base for experiencing DC like a local.

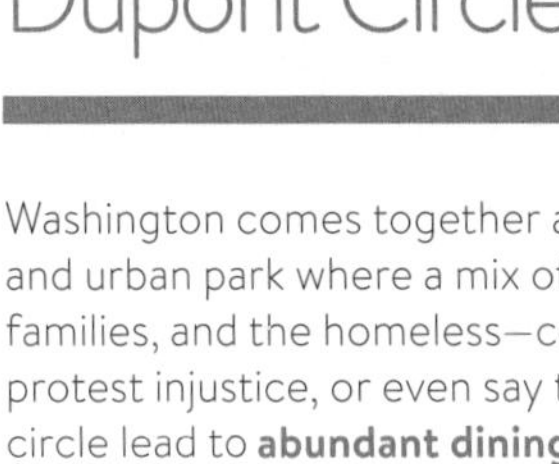

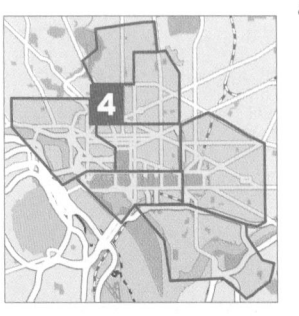

TOP RESTAURANTS
- Hank's Oyster Bar (page 119)
- Bagels Etc. (page 121)

TOP NIGHTLIFE
- Eighteenth Street Lounge (page 146)
- JR's Bar (page 147)

TOP ARTS AND CULTURE
- The Phillips Collection (page 170)

TOP SHOPS
- Kramerbooks (page 213)

TOP HOTELS
- The Jefferson (page 234)
- The Carlyle (page 235)

GETTING THERE AND AROUND
- Metro lines: Red
- Metro stations: Dupont Circle
- Major bus routes: DC Circulator Dupont Circle-Georgetown-Rosslyn

DUPONT CIRCLE WALK

TOTAL DISTANCE: 1.6 miles (2.6 kilometers)
WALKING TIME: 40 minutes

Any tour of Dupont Circle must include the circular park that lends its name—but the neighborhood is so much more than a traffic circle. Travel beyond the spokes to explore the rich history of this northwest DC neighborhood, and get to know the eclectic residents: diplomats, aristocrats, and even homeless chess players.

1 Start with carbs. **Bagels Etc.** has the closest thing you can get to a New York bagel in DC. The cash-only shop is cheap and fast; if you don't want breakfast, get a deli sandwich or pizza bagel. Take it to go, and walk east on P Street NW for about two blocks toward Dupont Circle.

2 Go to the center of **Dupont Circle** to eat on one of the benches surrounding the beaux arts fountain, a memorial to Admiral Samuel Francis Du Pont. On the northeast side of the circle, watch chess

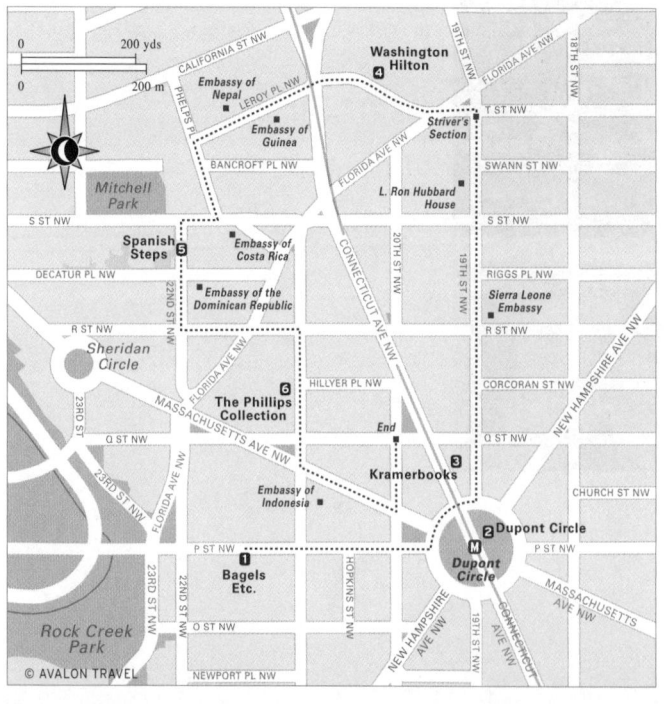

experts play—and don't be offended if you're asked to pay a small fee, because that's how some of the players make their living.

3 Head north toward Starbucks and walk half a block up Connecticut Avenue NW to **Kramerbooks.** Everyone has shopped here—including Monica Lewinsky, whose purchases were subpoenaed by Kenneth Starr to determine if she had bought gifts for President Bill Clinton. After you've browsed a bit, continue northwest to Q Street NW, where you'll turn east (right), then take a quick left to head north on 19th Street NW. Walk north about four blocks, passing the **Sierra Leone embassy.** You'll approach the **L. Ron Hubbard House** on your left, where its namesake lived when he founded the Church of Scientology in 1955.

4 Keep heading north for six blocks. The area from 19th Street eastward to 16th Street was once called **Strivers' Section.** This is where upper-middle-class African Americans, including Frederick Douglass and Langston Hughes, lived at the turn of the 20th century. Turn left at T Street NW. The **Washington Hilton** looms ahead. The curving, concrete, brutalist structure is nicknamed the Hinckley Hilton, because it's where John Hinckley Jr. shot President Reagan in 1981. Today, it's the location of the White House Correspondents' Association Dinner.

5 Continue west to Connecticut Avenue, then cross the street to Leroy Place NW and pass the **embassies of Guinea and Nepal.** Turn south (left) on Phelps Place NW and walk about two blocks; the **embassy of Costa Rica** will be ahead. Turn west (right) on S Street NW, then take a quick left to go south on 22nd Street NW. Keep your eyes peeled for the **Spanish Steps.** Meander down them and continue south on 22nd Street NW, past the **embassy of the Dominican Republic.**

6 When you reach R Street NW, turn east (left) and continue two blocks to 21st Street NW and turn south (right). You'll run into **The Phillips Collection,** America's first modern art museum, a great stopping point for a few hours. When you're ready to leave Dupont Circle, take 21st Street NW south for just over a block to Massachusetts Avenue NW toward the **Indonesian embassy,** also called the Walsh-McLean House for the wealthy owners. (How wealthy, you ask? *Washington Post* heir Edward McLean once purchased a special gift for his wife, Evalyn Walsh—the Hope Diamond.) If you're taking the Metro, walk 1.5 blocks to Q and 20th Streets NW to the station entrance. A quote from Walt Whitman's poem "The Wound-Dresser" envelops you as you enter. It was carved in the station's stone entrance in 2007 to recognize the AIDS crisis, which particularly affected this historic gay neighborhood.

U Street, Shaw, and Logan Circle

Map 5

The historic center of the city's **African American arts and culture** for much of the 20th century, U Street and Shaw are home to the African American Civil War Memorial and Howard University, as well as several restored institutions along "Black Broadway," like **The Howard Theatre** and **The Lincoln Theatre.** These neighborhoods, along with nearby Logan Circle, have become the **trendy hub** for **nightlife** and culture, as the city's young professionals with disposable income fill the **restaurants, cocktail bars,** and nightclubs that have exploded here in the last two decades.

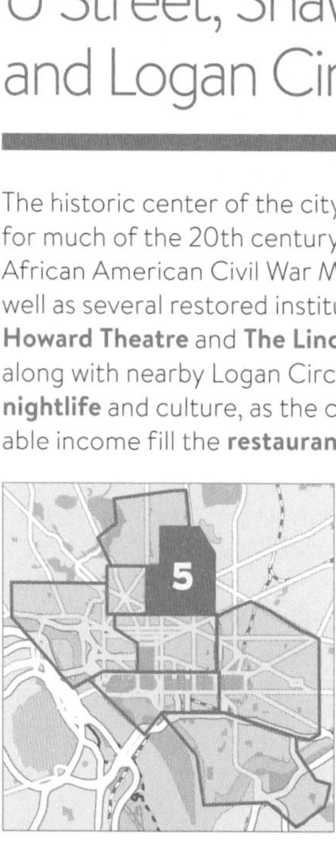

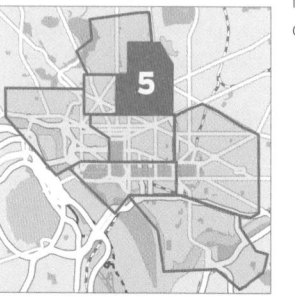

TOP RESTAURANTS

- Ben's Chili Bowl (page 122)
- Dukem Ethiopian Restaurant (page 125)
- Busboys and Poets (page 127)

TOP NIGHTLIFE

- Black Cat (page 151)
- 9:30 Club (page 151)
- Nellie's Sports Bar (page 152)

TOP ARTS AND CULTURE

- The Howard Theatre (page 173)

TOP SHOPS

- Violet (page 215)
- Miss Pixie's (page 216)
- Union Kitchen Grocery (page 217)

TOP HOTELS

- Kimpton Mason & Rook Hotel (page 237)
- Washington Plaza Hotel (page 238)

GETTING THERE AND AROUND

- Metro lines: Green, Yellow
- Metro stations: Shaw-Howard U, U Street/
  African-Amer Civil War Memorial/Cardozo
- Major bus routes: DC Circulator
  Woodley Park-Adams Morgan-
  McPherson Square Metro

U STREET AND SHAW WALK

TOTAL DISTANCE: 1.8 miles (2.9 kilometers)
WALKING TIME: 35 minutes

Take a walk through U Street and Shaw, a center of African-American life and culture for much of the 20th century, and the childhood home of Duke Ellington, who later played at the jazz clubs around U Street, known as "Black Broadway." The neighborhood was decimated during the riots in April 1968, after the assassination of Martin Luther King Jr. The neighborhood eventually began to rebuild. Today, you'll find rejuvenated landmarks like The Howard Theatre and markers for the self-guided African American Heritage Trail, as well as booming growth and development, with new restaurants and shops popping up seemingly every day.

To experience the joy of the neighborhood, take this walk on a weekend afternoon, when locals flock to the streets for late brunches that turn into early cocktails and dinner. If you're taking the Metro to the neighborhood, the starting point of the walk, Ben's Chili Bowl, is directly across the street from the 13th Street and U

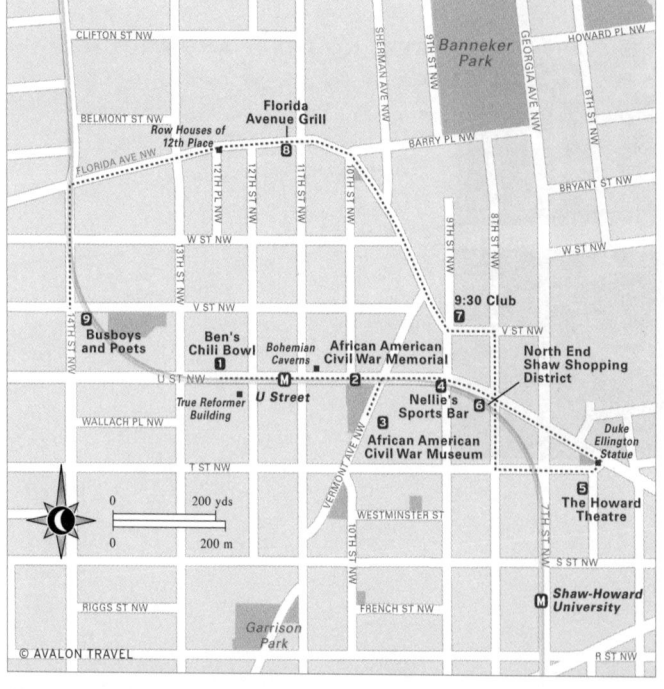

African American Civil War Memorial

Street entrance of the U Street/African-Amer Civil War Memorial/ Cardozo Metro station.

1 The tour begins at one of the must-visit restaurants in DC: **Ben's Chili Bowl,** which stayed open late to serve half-smokes (spicy half-pork/half-beef sausages, served on buns and smothered in chili) to law enforcement and activists following the 1968 race riots. Have a bite at the old-fashioned counter, or at least peek at the walls covered with photos of famous diners visiting the restaurant, including President Obama. And don't miss the mural on the outside wall; it was redone in June 2017 to add Harriet Tubman, Dave Chappelle, and the Obamas.

2 Head east on U Street, busy with brunchers and shoppers and fitness fanatics on a weekend afternoon. On the right before 12th Street, look for the **True Reformer Building,** the classical revival and Romanesque building designed in 1903 by John Anderson Lankford, the first registered African American architect in Washington DC. Now the headquarters of the Public Welfare Foundation, the building originally housed organizations that helped African Americans set up businesses and access social services in the early 1900s. Keep walking east to 11th Street to **Bohemian Caverns,** DC's oldest jazz club, which operated for 90 years before it closed in 2016. Turn north onto 11th Street NW to see the gorgeous blue and purple mural depicting jazz legends (on the north side of the building). Return to U Street, then walk 1.5 blocks toward Vermont Avenue. Enter the plaza on your right at the Metro station to view the **African American Civil War Memorial.**

3 Continue southwest on Vermont Avenue to tour the **African American Civil War Museum,** across the street from the memorial. This museum is packed with educational displays about African Americans who fought in the Civil War. History buffs could easily spend a few hours diving in. If you have relatives who served in the Civil War, look up your family tree in the museum's registry.

4 Double back to U Street NW and walk two short blocks east to **Nellie's Sports Bar,** where a crowd has likely gathered on the roof if the weather's nice. On weekends, this popular gay bar is a hot spot from brunch into the evening. Head south on 9th Street NW, the heart of Shaw and DC's Little Ethiopia.

5 Walk south one block on 9th Street, then go east on T Street NW for about three short blocks to reach **The Howard Theatre.** The box office is open Tuesday through Sunday. If one of DC's go-go bands is on the schedule, be sure to get tickets to hear Washington's home-grown music tradition, which was popularized by the late Chuck Brown in the 1970s and 1980s. Half a block northeast of the theater at T Street NW and Florida Avenue NW, the 20-foot stainless steel **Duke Ellington statue** pays homage to the musician, who grew up in Shaw and began his career in the jazz clubs of "Black Broadway."

Le Diplomate

6 Walk northwest on Florida Avenue NW three blocks to 9th Street. You'll notice shiny new buildings as you enter the **North End Shaw shopping district,** which has several niche, high-end apparel, accessories, and beauty retailers.

7 When you're done shopping, head north on 9th Street NW two blocks to approach the **9:30 Club** at the corner of 9th and V Street NW. It looks like a nondescript warehouse from the outside, but this is the city's top music venue, rated one of the best in the country by *Rolling Stone.* The box office is open Monday through Friday, plus weekends when there's a show. Check the lineup, because if something catches your eye, a show at the 9:30 Club is must-experience nightlife.

8 Turn back the way you came on V Street NW and veer slightly northwest on Florida Avenue NW. Enjoy this quiet, mostly residential area, and walk for about four long blocks (10 minutes) to reach **Florida Avenue Grill** at the corner of Florida and 11th Street NW. If you didn't eat at Ben's, you can stop for a hearty meal at the oldest soul food restaurant in the world. Otherwise, continue west for another 2.5 blocks on Florida Avenue and peek at the rainbow of **row houses** on 12th Place.

Busboys and Poets

9 Continue west along Florida Avenue for two long blocks (about five minutes) to reach 14th Street NW. Turn south on 14th Street, where you'll have a plethora of options for a cocktail or, if you're ready to eat, a late lunch or early dinner. At 14th Street NW and V Street NW, stop at neighborhood icon **Busboys and Poets,** where you can eat, drink, and shop in the on-site bookstore specializing in books about social justice issues and DC life and history.

To get back to the Metro and your starting point, walk another block south on 14th Street and go east on U Street for one long block (about four minutes). Or continue south on 14th Street, where the options for shopping and nightlife continue for six bustling blocks all the way to Logan Circle. Highlights include **Le Diplomate, Café Saint-Ex,** and **Pearl Dive Oyster Palace,** as well as **Miss Pixie's** and **Salt & Sundry** for cool housewares and local souvenirs.

Adams Morgan   Map 6

With a large immigrant population, Adams Morgan has historically been one of DC's most **ethnically diverse** neighborhoods and a center for social activism. It's known for a young, **rowdy bar scene,** but it's also the place to go for good, affordable **ethnic food** and **neighborhood restaurants, live music** and **dive bars,** and community-focused **shops.**

Nearby, **Columbia Heights** draws locals to **Meridian Hill Park** and **hipster bars** on weekends. For a different side of DC, **Mount Pleasant** offers **small-town charm** and cheap Mexican and Latin American food.

TOP RESTAURANTS
- Johnny's Half Shell (page 128)
- The Diner (page 128)

TOP NIGHTLIFE
- Jack Rose Dining Saloon (page 153)

TOP SPORTS AND ACTIVITIES
- Meridian Hill Park (page 193)

TOP SHOPS
- Mercedes Bien Vintage (page 218)

GETTING THERE AND AROUND
- Metro lines: Green, Red, Yellow
- Metro stations: Columbia Heights, Woodley Park-Zoo/Adams Morgan
- Major bus routes: DC Circulator Woodley Park-Adams Morgan-McPherson Square Metro

Georgetown and Foggy Bottom

Map 7

Washington's rich and famous have always lived in Georgetown, but the quiet **cobblestone streets** with a college-town feel welcome more visitors lately thanks to several **fine restaurants** and **luxury hotels.**

Home to the U.S. Department of State and many government and hospital offices, Foggy Bottom is a quiet maze of concrete on weekends but well worth visiting to enjoy **world-class theater,** music, and dance at **The John F. Kennedy Center for the Performing Arts**

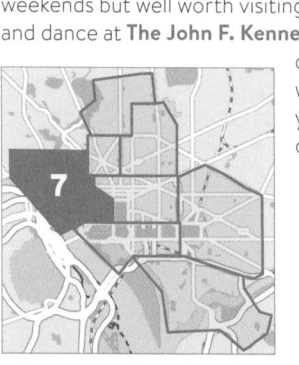

or drinks at **The Watergate Hotel,** with a mod design that will transport you to the neighborhood's heyday during the Nixon scandal.

TOP RESTAURANTS

- Cafe Milano (page 133)
- Fiola Mare (page 133)

TOP NIGHTLIFE

- The Lounge at Bourbon Steak (page 155)
- Top of the Gate (page 155)

TOP ARTS AND CULTURE

- The John F. Kennedy Center for the
  Performing Arts (page 177)

TOP SPORTS AND ACTIVITIES

- Theodore Roosevelt Island (page 193)

TOP SHOPS

- Curio Concept (page 220)

TOP HOTELS

- The Watergate Hotel (page 239)

GETTING THERE AND AROUND

- Metro lines: Blue, Orange, Silver
- Metro stations: Foggy Bottom-GWU
- Major bus routes: DC Circulator
  Dupont Circle-Georgetown-Rosslyn,
  Georgetown-Union Station

Navy Yard and Anacostia   Map 8

Southwest Washington, just a quick Metro ride from the city center, is home to **The District Wharf.** Appealing to visiting foodies and fun seekers, this waterfront complex features several **mega restaurants, hotels,** and **entertainment venues.**

In Navy Yard, watch a game at **Nationals Park,** one of the greenest baseball stadiums in the country. Nearby, the **Anacostia Riverwalk Trail,** boating facilities, and green space make up for the neighborhood's lack of charm as **high-rise buildings** dominate the skyline.

On the other side of the river, **culturally rich** Anacostia is a neigh-

borhood in transition. It boasts the Smithsonian's **Anacostia Community Museum,** which chronicles the city's history. Visit the **Frederick Douglass National Historic Site,** where the famed abolitionist once lived, or check out **art galleries** displaying the work of emerging artists.

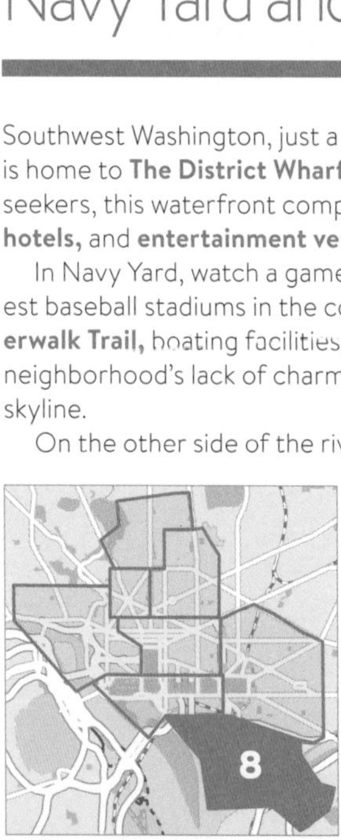

TOP SIGHTS
- Frederick Douglass National Historic Site (page 95)

TOP ARTS AND CULTURE
- Arena Stage (page 179)

TOP SPORTS AND ACTIVITIES
- Anacostia Riverwalk Trail (page 196)
- Washington Nationals (page 197)

GETTING THERE AND AROUND
- Metro lines: Green
- Metro stations: Navy Yard-Ballpark, Waterfront, Anacostia
- Major bus routes: DC Circulator Union Station-Navy Yard, Potomac Ave Metro-Skyland via Barracks Row

NAVY YARD WALK

TOTAL DISTANCE: 1.3 miles (2.1 kilometers)
WALKING TIME: 30 minutes

This riverfront community was once the city's busiest port and the U.S. Navy's largest and longest-operating shipbuilding facility in the country, from 1799 until the 1960s. While shipbuilding activities have ceased, thousands of U.S. Navy administrative staff and federal employees work here today in the shadow of new apartment and condo buildings, restaurants, and Nationals Park. Here, you can pick up hiking trails or rent a boat, or just enjoy the view of the water; by the time you read this book, there's likely to be even more development, including more restaurants, bars, and shops, in this rapidly growing neighborhood.

The starting point for this walk is the **Navy Yard/Ballpark Metro station.**

1 When you get off the Metro, take the Department of Transportation exit to enter the heart of Navy Yard. Walk southeast (right) on New Jersey Avenue SE, with the 2.1-million-square-foot U.S. Department

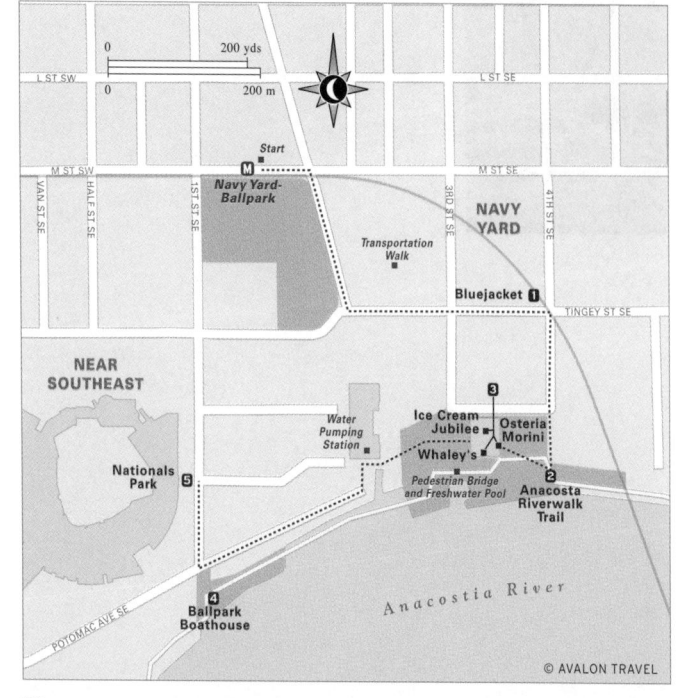

of Transportation on your left. After about a block and a half, turn left to enter the **Transportation Walk,** a two-block, outdoor museum about transportation milestones and leaders in America along the south side of the DOT's main building. Check out the old-fashioned gas pumps and a restored electrical substation, and informational signs about Sally Ride and the Lewis and Clark Expedition. Continue for just over a block to 4th Street SE, and go south (right). On your right, **Bluejacket** is a good place to stop for a beer and a bite in a former Navy Yard factory.

2 Cross Tingey Street SE and continue south on 4th Street SE. If beer isn't your cup of tea, you have several options on this block for refreshments, like The Juice Laundry, serving organic pressed juices and smoothies, or District Winery, DC's first commercial winery which opened in 2017 with a tasting bar and full restaurant, to much critical acclaim. Keep heading toward the Anacostia River to reach the **Anacostia Riverwalk Trail,** a 20-mile paved path riverside path that connects DC and Maryland. You'll soon be in the heart of Yards Park.

3 Head west along the boardwalk (part of the Anacostia Riverwalk Trail). You'll pass by several good options for waterfront dining for brunch or dinner, including **Whaley's** and **Osteria Morini,** or you can grab a locally made cone at **Ice Cream Jubilee** to enjoy on the grass. Cross the sculptural steel **pedestrian bridge,** or if the weather is nice, dip your toes into the **freshwater pool** directly underneath the bridge, an area that's busy with families splashing around on hot days.

4 Keep heading west on the waterfront trail, which is busy with runners and cyclists year-round. You'll quickly come upon DC's historic **water pumping station,** the Beaux Arts structure that's been pumping wastewater since 1905. Today, it pumps 400 million gallons per day. After you check out the short exhibit about the DC Clean Rivers Project and the work that goes into cleaning up the pollution in the river, keep walking west on the bridge to reach **Ballpark Boathouse,** where you can rent kayaks or canoes seasonally.

5 When you reach **Nationals Park,** head north on First Street SE, with the stadium on your left. If you want to get tickets to a ballgame, walk about three blocks to the main box office on N Street SE; otherwise, keep walking to M Street SE and head east one block to return to the Navy Yard-Ballpark Metro station. From here, the Green Line offers several choices for your next adventure: Go one stop south, where you can start the Anacostia walking tour on page 60. Take the Metro one stop north to the Waterfront station and check out the dining and entertainment options at the District Wharf. Or take a slightly longer ride: It's four stops to Gallery Place-Chinatown and the heart of downtown.

ANACOSTIA WALK

TOTAL DISTANCE: 1.4 miles (2.25 kilometers)
WALKING TIME: 30 minutes

Among DC's neighborhoods, Anacostia has the most interesting and challenging history. It was incorporated in 1854 to be an affordable suburb for working-class families, but time—and the Civil War, segregation, and the 1968 riots after the assassination of Dr. Martin Luther King Jr.—brought turmoil and saw growth in drugs, gangs, and crime.

This has changed. Anacostia is a neighborhood in transition, one where residents, community organizations, and businesses are coming together to help Anacostia embrace the boom in DC while maintaining its historic character and culture. Note that some areas covered by this walking tour may feel desolate even during the day. You're advised to take the walk during the daytime and stick to the areas covered here unless you're familiar with the area.

This walk, which takes you through the Anacostia Historic District (listed on the National Register of Historic Places) to the Frederick Douglass National Historic Site, is a lovely way to learn about the

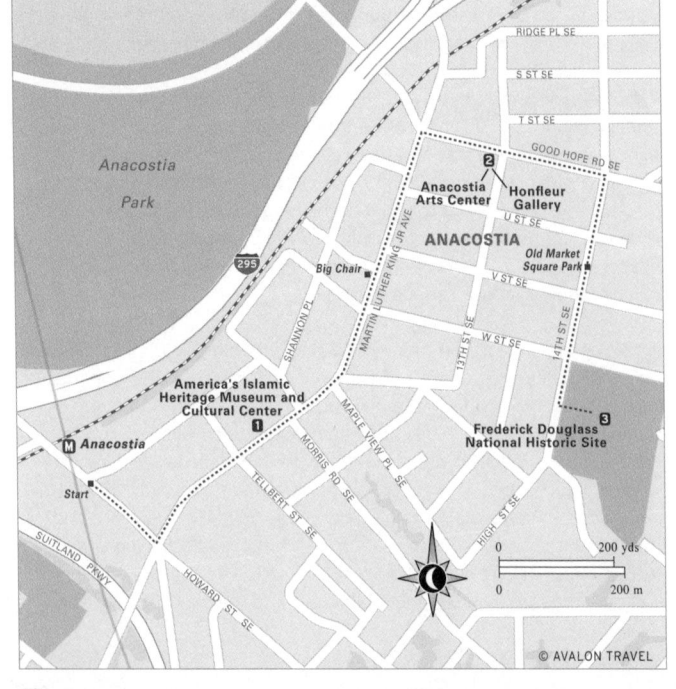

Anacostia Arts Center

neighborhood's rich history, and bright future. The Anacostia Historic District is easily accessible by Metro; take the Green Line to **Anacostia Station** and exit at Howard Road.

1 From the Metro station, walk southeast on Howard Road for approximately one block, then head northeast on Martin Luther King Jr. Avenue SE. Along this route, you'll see several of the 20 numbered signs of the Anacostia Heritage Trail, which Cultural Tourism DC launched in 2015 to showcase the history of the community; get to know prominent African Americans who lived here, like John A. Moss, who escaped slavery

and became the neighborhood's first lawyer, Solomon Brown, the first African American to work at the Smithsonian Institution, and of course, Frederick Douglass. After about a block and a half, **America's Islamic Heritage Museum and Cultural Center** will be on the left. This museum has displays, rife with text and photographs, which traveled with the U.S. State Department before finding a permanent home in Anacostia. It's worth spending an hour or two here if you want to dig into the stories of American Muslims that you may not have known before.

directional sign in Anacostia

Frederick Douglass National Historic Site

2 Keep going northeast on Martin Luther King Avenue SE for about 2.5 blocks. You can't miss the 19.5-foot **Big Chair** on your left, a mahogany chair sculpture built in 1959 to advertise Curtis Bros. Furniture Company, an Anacostia business. Located between W Street SE and V Street SE, it's an iconic neighborhood landmark. Walk northeast another two blocks to Good Hope Road SE. To your left at the intersection, a strip of buildings containing a drugstore and hydroponics supply shop sports the famous "Anacostia" neon sign. (If you were to keep heading north, you'd come to the 11th Street Bridge, which was part of John Wilkes Booth Jr.'s escape route after he assassinated President Abraham Lincoln.) From here, go east (right) on Good Hope Road SE for less than a block to get to the **Anacostia Arts Center** and **Honfleur Gallery.** In addition to housing art exhibitions, the Arts Center is a good place to stop for a cup of coffee or a snack and browse the boutiques that share the space.

the Big Chair

3 Walk east another block on Good Hope Road SE and head south on 14th Street SE. The median between U Street SE and V Street SE, surrounded by several churches, is **Old Market Square Park,** built in 1913; it's been an

Anacostia neon sign

important community meeting spot for decades, though it was recently renovated with new benches and landscaping. Walk south on 14th Street SE another block, then go east on W Street SE. The **Frederick Douglass National Historic Site** is ahead high on the hill; pass by the stairs leading up to the mansion and start your tour in the visitors center.

4 To get back to the Metro, head west on W Street SE for about three blocks, then go south on Martin Luther King Jr. Avenue SE for four blocks to Howard Road SE. Turn north (right) onto Howard; the Metro station will be on your left in one block. If you haven't yet explored Navy Yard, take the Metro Green Line from Anacostia Station one stop north to Navy Yard/Ballpark Station, then follow the Navy Yard walking tour on page 58.

Greater Washington DC   Map 9

True to Pierre Charles L'Enfant's original plan, DC has **four quadrants** around the U.S. Capitol: Northeast, Southeast, Northwest, and Southwest. Many of the top attractions and neighborhoods for dining, shopping, and accommodations are centered around the White House and business districts in Northwest and the Capitol in Southeast, but there are destination sights, restaurants, and shopping in all four quadrants, ranging from **historic homes** and **parks** in Upper Northwest to the culinary delights of **Union Market** and **local distillers** in Northeast, to parks with water views in Southwest. And although not technically located in the District of Columbia, two of the top sights are just over the border in Virginia: **Arlington National Cemetery** and the **National 9/11 Pentagon Memorial,** both accessible by Metro.

TOP SIGHTS

- Arlington National Cemetery (page 97)
- National 9/11 Pentagon
  Memorial (page 98)
- Smithsonian's National Zoo (page 99)

TOP RESTAURANTS

- Masseria (page 137)

TOP ARTS AND CULTURE

- Hillwood Estate, Museum &
  Gardens (page 180)

TOP SPORTS AND ACTIVITIES

- East Potomac Park and Hains
  Point (page 199)
- U.S. National Arboretum (page 199)

TOP SHOPS

- New Columbia Distillers (page 223)

TOP HOTELS

- Omni Shoreham Hotel (page 243)

SIGHTS

National Mall 68
Downtown and Penn Quarter 79
Capitol Hill and Atlas District 84
Dupont Circle 90
U Street, Shaw, and Logan Circle 91
Georgetown and Foggy Bottom 92
Navy Yard and Anacostia 95
Greater Washington DC 97

Do you want to feel the magnitude of the moon walk? Hear arguments before the U.S. Supreme Court? Stand at Lincoln's feet? It's all possible—and for the most part, free—in Washington DC.

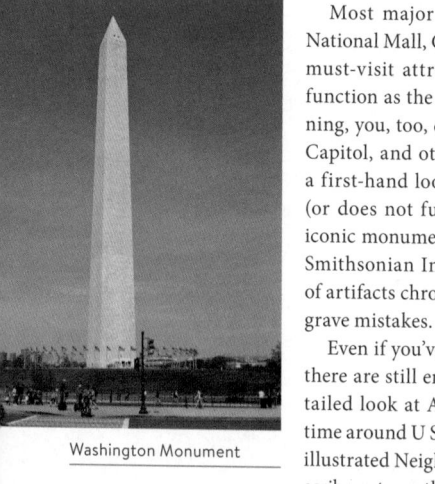

Washington Monument

Most major sights are situated around the National Mall, Capitol Hill, and downtown. Here, must-visit attractions play a role in the city's function as the nation's capital. With some planning, you, too, can tour the White House or U.S. Capitol, and other government buildings to get a first-hand look at how government functions (or does not function). It's essential to see the iconic monuments and memorials, as well as the Smithsonian Institution's unbeatable collection of artifacts chronicling the nation's triumphs and grave mistakes.

Even if you've already done the National Mall, there are still endless sights to explore. For a detailed look at African American history, spend time around U Street, Shaw, and Anacostia, where illustrated Neighborhood Heritage Trail signs describe noteworthy residents and cultural moments. In Georgetown, see remnants of DC's earliest history. And don't miss more far-flung neighborhoods, from Northwest's majestic embassies to Northeast's Union market to Arlington National Cemetery and the National 9/11 Pentagon Memorial in Virginia.

HIGHLIGHTS

✪ **MOST PROMINENT MONUMENT:** You can't miss the **Washington Monument** dominating the city skyline (page 68).

✪ **MOST STIRRING SIGHT:** The **Lincoln Memorial** is awe-inspiring and best seen when illuminated at night (page 69).

✪ **BEST FOR AMERICAN NOSTALGIA:** View the flag that inspired the national anthem, among other artifacts from American history and pop culture, at the **National Museum of American History** (page 71).

✪ **MUSEUM WORTH SPENDING THE ENTIRE DAY:** If you get tickets to the **National Museum of African American History and Culture,** go early and stay late—it's worth seeing everything inside the five-story museum (page 72).

✪ **BEST PLACE TO GET YOUR GEEK ON:** The **National Air and Space Museum** has the largest collection of history-making aircraft, from the 1903 Wright Flyer to Lunar Module 2 (page 72).

✪ **BEST FOR KIDS:** Children of all ages love seeing dinosaurs, mummies, and the Hope Diamond at the **National Museum of Natural History** (page 73).

✪ **MOST EXCLUSIVE ADDRESS:** Don't miss a photo op in front of **The White House,** the residence of every U.S. president except George Washington (page 79).

✪ **BEST PLACE TO SEE HISTORY IN THE MAKING:** Tour the **U.S. Capitol,** the imposing building where laws are made (page 84).

✪ **HIDDEN BLACK HISTORY GEM:** It's easy to reserve tickets to tour the **Frederick Douglass National Historic Site,** where the abolitionist lived at the end of his life (page 95).

✪ **MOST INTERESTING BURIAL GROUNDS:** The burial site of more than 400,000 veterans, **Arlington National Cemetery** is where you can see the Tomb of the Unknown Soldier and JFK's gravesite (page 97).

✪ **MOST MOVING MEMORIAL:** The **National 9/11 Pentagon Memorial** pays tribute to the 184 people who were killed in the attack on the Department of Defense headquarters (page 98).

✪ **BEST PLACE TO CATCH PANDA FEVER:** **Smithsonian's National Zoo** is home to hundreds of cuddly creatures, but the giant pandas on loan from the People's Republic of China are an adorable highlight (page 99).

National Mall

Map 1

✪ Washington Monument

The Washington Monument dominates the horizon, but the tribute to George Washington is worth an up-close look. At 555 feet tall and comprising 36,000 stones, it's the world's tallest obelisk and the tallest structure in DC, excluding radio towers. Though it invites jokes about the Founding Fathers' Napoleon complexes, the enormity will nonetheless take your breath away.

The monument to the first U.S. president took more than three decades to complete. Construction began on July 4, 1848; Congressman Abraham Lincoln was among those who attended the ceremony to lay the cornerstone. But construction was delayed due to a lack of funding and the Civil War. You'll notice the top two-thirds are a different color, because the original marble could not be matched when it was finally completed in 1888.

While visitors can walk around the grounds 24 hours a day, the interior is closed until at least spring 2019 while the elevator is refurbished. When the monument reopens, you'll be able to see the statue of George Washington in the lobby and take the elevator to the observation deck inside the pyramidion for an unmatched view of the capital. Timed entry tickets are required to go inside the monument; purchase them online up to three months in advance, though a limited number of same-day tickets are

Washington Monument

available starting at 8:30am at the visitor building in front of the monument on 15th Street NW.

MAP 1: 15th St. NW and Madison Dr. NW, 202/426-6841, www.nps.gov/wamo; grounds 24 hours daily, elevator access 9am-5pm daily Labor Day-Memorial Day, 9am-10pm daily Memorial Day-Labor Day, visitors center 8am-8:30pm daily; timed entry tickets required, $1.50 fee/ticket

NEARBY:

- Appreciate some of the country's most iconic objects at the National Museum of American History (page 71).
- Plan ahead to get an entry pass to the newest and best Smithsonian, the National Museum of African American History and Culture (page 72).
- See where paper currency gets printed at the Bureau of Engraving and Printing (page 74).
- Enjoy Southern and creole dishes at Sweet Home Café, in the Museum of African American History and Culture (page 107).
- Experience the United States Holocaust Memorial Museum, a must for any traveler (page 162).
- Explore the mall on foot or by

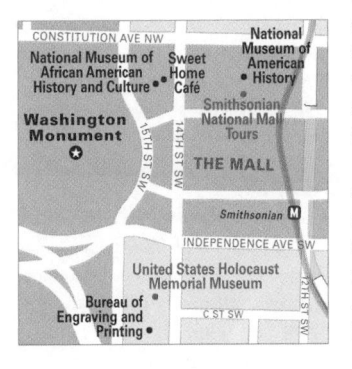

Segway with Smithsonian National Mall Tours (page 189).

TOP EXPERIENCE

✪ Lincoln Memorial

"In this temple, as in the hearts of the people for whom he saved the Union, the memory of Abraham Lincoln is enshrined forever." *New York Herald Tribune* art critic Royal Cortissoz wrote these words, carved directly above the 19-foot sculpture of a seated President Lincoln inside the Lincoln Memorial, located in a former swampy area at the west end of the National Mall. The memorial was not completed until 50 years after Lincoln's assassination, but the awe-inspiring result was worth the wait—and it's most magnificent at night, after the crowds have dispersed and interior lights cast a dramatic glow on the 16th U.S. president as he gazes across the 2,029-foot-long Reflecting Pool, which stretches from the Lincoln Memorial to the Washington Monument.

Examine the symbolic details that architect Henry Bacon and sculptor Daniel Chester French thoughtfully placed throughout. As you climb the steps, you'll notice the 36 columns, which represent the 36 states in the Union when Lincoln died. Above the columns, 48 garland carvings represent the 48 states when the memorial was completed in 1922. These details symbolize his dedication to keeping the Union intact.

Inside, the texts of two of Lincoln's most important speeches are etched on either side of the statue: to the left, the 1863 Gettysburg Address, and to the right, the 1865 Second Inaugural Address, which he delivered months before his death. The 60- by 12-foot

THE SMITHSONIAN INSTITUTION MUSEUMS AND GALLERIES

There are more Smithsonian museums and galleries than most people can visit in one trip. This list outlines all of DC's Smithsonians and will help you choose the ones that are perfectly suited to your tastes, as well as give you the must-see exhibits at each spot.

NATIONAL MUSEUM OF AMERICAN HISTORY (PAGE 71)
Best for: Fans of American nostalgia and pop culture
Don't Miss: The Star-Spangled Banner; first ladies' dresses

NATIONAL MUSEUM OF AFRICAN AMERICAN HISTORY AND CULTURE (PAGE 72)
Best for: People looking to immerse themselves in a museum for an entire day
Don't Miss: History Galleries, including "Paradox of Liberty," about the slaves at Monticello; interactive lunch counter with stools from the 1960 Greensboro Woolworth sit-ins

NATIONAL AIR AND SPACE MUSEUM (PAGE 72)
Best for: Space geeks
Don't Miss: *The Spirit of St. Louis*, Friendship 7, Lunar Module 2

NATIONAL MUSEUM OF NATURAL HISTORY (PAGE 73)
Best for: Kids of all ages
Don't Miss: Hope Diamond and other gems; dinosaur fossils

HIRSHHORN MUSEUM AND SCULPTURE GARDEN (PAGE 162)
Best for: Lovers of cool contemporary art
Don't Miss: The latest temporary exhibition; Sculpture Garden

NATIONAL MUSEUM OF THE AMERICAN INDIAN (PAGE 164)
Best for: Those seeking a quiet, educational experience

murals above each speech depict Lincoln's values, with the Angel of Truth freeing slaves above the Gettysburg Address and uniting figures representing the North and the South above the Second Inaugural.

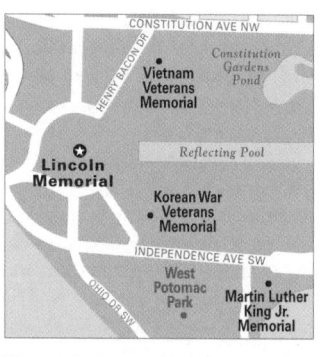

(And if you're a grammar nerd, see if you can spot the spelling error in the Second Inaugural text.)

The most recent addition to the memorial was etched in 2003, on the 18th step below the top landing, marking the spot where Martin Luther King Jr. delivered his "I Have A Dream" speech on August 28, 1963.

MAP 1: 2 Lincoln Memorial Circle NW, 202/426-6841, www.nps.gov/linc; 24 hours daily, visitors center 9am-6pm daily; free

NEARBY:

- Visit the **Korean War Veterans Memorial** and its extremely detailed figures representing soldiers from the three branches of the U.S. military (page 75).

Don't Miss: The tipi-like sculptures and native landscape on the grounds; Mitsitam Native Foods Café

FREER GALLERY OF ART AND ARTHUR M. SACKLER GALLERY (PAGE 163)
Best for: Asian art and decor aficionados
Don't Miss: Whistler's Peacock Room

NATIONAL MUSEUM OF AFRICAN ART (PAGE 163)
Best for: Admirers of traditional and contemporary African art
Don't Miss: Disney-Tishman Collection ceramics; healing arts in the entryway

NATIONAL PORTRAIT GALLERY (PAGE 166)
Best for: Those looking for a new view of American history
Don't Miss: The only complete collection of U.S. presidential portraits outside the White House

RENWICK GALLERY (PAGE 166)
Best for: American crafts and decorative arts buffs
Don't Miss: Larry Fuente's *Game Fish*; jewelry

SMITHSONIAN AMERICAN ART MUSEUM (PAGE 166)
Best for: American modern folk art enthusiasts
Don't Miss: New Deal art; Jonathan Borofsky's *Man with Briefcase*

NATIONAL POSTAL MUSEUM (PAGE 168)
Best for: Folks who want to kill some time near the U.S. Capitol
Don't Miss: William H. Gross Stamp Gallery; vintage mail planes

ANACOSTIA COMMUNITY MUSEUM (PAGE 177)
Best for: People who love getting off the beaten path
Don't Miss: Temporary exhibitions about local communities; film screenings and lectures

- Take in the striking **Martin Luther King Jr. Memorial,** with its 30-foot carving of Dr. King (page 76).
- Pay your respects at the Memorial Wall at the **Vietnam Veterans Memorial** (page 77).
- Wander through **West Potomac Park** and you'll be able to see many of the national memorials (page 189).

✪ National Museum of American History

This museum has a heavy focus on American pop culture, technology, medicine, and media—but very little examination of some of the more painful, and frankly shameful, aspects of American history.

(Thankfully, the National Museum of the American Indian and the new, incredible National Museum of African American History and Culture cover those issues in detail.) Still, it's worth a visit to appreciate great American icons, offering educational but fun exhibits appropriate for all ages. If the museum is not too busy, you can hit the highlights in a couple hours, or spend more time digging into the best museum for American nostalgia.

The must-see exhibit is the **Star-Spangled Banner,** the 200-year-old flag that inspired Francis Scott Key to write the poem that would become the national anthem. This is the very flag that the U.S. troops raised after defeating the British at Fort McHenry in Baltimore during the War of 1812, turning the tide of the war. Today, the flag is kept in a climate-controlled chamber that still allows you to get a close look at the detail.

Other beloved exhibits include the first ladies' dresses, Julia Child's kitchen from her Massachusetts home, and the 26,000-square-foot America on the Move hall, containing historical trains and automobiles.

MAP 1: 1300 Constitution Ave. NW between 12th St. NW and 14th St. NW, 202/633-1000, http://americanhistory.si.edu; 10am-5:30pm daily; free

✪ National Museum of African American History and Culture

The newest and by far the best Smithsonian museum, the National Museum of African American History and Culture, deserves several days to fully explore the magnitude of information and artifacts contained in 12 exhibitions over five floors—but you'll likely only have entry passes for one day, so plan to spend the better part of a day here, if you can. Since the museum opened in September 2016, the timed entry passes have been snapped up almost as soon as they are released each month. (See *The Hottest Ticket in Town* on page 73 for details on how to obtain passes.)

Beeline for the concourse level to tour the History Galleries. When you step off the elevator in the basement, you'll immediately sense the doom and terror one would have felt when being shackled in a slave ship to the New World; the low-ceilinged galleries are designed to feel this way. The horrifying facts of the journey, and what awaited the survivors, are described in overwhelming detail. Plan to spend at least two hours climbing the ramps in the galleries from the

Civil War through segregation and the civil rights movement to present day, alternately distraught by the treatment of African Americans by their fellow Americans and elated at the triumphs, culminating with the election of America's first black president.

After decompressing by the indoor rain-shower waterfall in the Contemplative Court, save time for the upper levels, which are dedicated to art and culture. Don't miss the celebratory Musical Crossroads, where you can see and hear African Americans' influence on music through the decades, with objects like Chuck Berry's red Cadillac as well as outfits worn by Marian Anderson, Michael Jackson, Whitney Houston, and Public Enemy.

MAP 1: 1400 Constitution Ave. NW between 14th St. NW and 15th St. NW, 844/750-3012, http://nmaahc.si.edu; 10am-5:30pm daily; free

✪ National Air and Space Museum

The soaring ceilings of the Smithsonian's National Air and Space Museum accommodate the world's largest collection of real aircraft and spacecraft, including the Wright brothers' 1903 plane and SpaceShipOne, the first private spacecraft in history to reach space and return, plus commercial and military aircraft.

Enter the museum at the Jefferson Drive entrance to get an immediate look at many of the must-sees in the Boeing Milestones of Flight Hall: *The Spirit of St. Louis,* which Charles Lindbergh flew on the first solo flight across the Atlantic Ocean in 1927; Mercury Friendship 7, in which John Glenn Jr. orbited Earth in 1962 during the Space Race with the Soviet Union; and Lunar Module 2, which was used

THE HOTTEST TICKET IN TOWN

Since opening in September 2016, the Smithsonian's **National Museum of African American History and Culture** (1400 Constitution Ave. NW between 14th St. NW and 15th St. NW, 844/750-3012, http://nmaahc.si.edu; 10am-5:30pm daily; free) has welcomed more than 2.5 million visitors. While admission is free, as with every Smithsonian museum, timed entry passes are required—and you'll need an alarm clock to get one.

If you're planning your trip at least three months in advance, check the museum's website to see when the next batch of passes will be released. The passes will be available on a certain date starting at 9am ET, and they're typically snapped up within a few hours.

A limited number of same-day passes are available. The museum releases same-day passes online every day at 6:30am ET, and they're usually gone within 15 minutes. Depending on capacity, there are a limited number of walk-up passes available on weekdays only at 1pm at the entrance on Madison Drive.

If you're lucky enough to score a timed entry pass in advance, you don't need to show up more than a few minutes early, because you won't be permitted to go in before your entry time. If you're running late, don't panic; you can still enter after your time slot, though you may need to wait if the museum is already at capacity.

for testing before the Apollo moon landing. This museum is extremely popular and crowded, especially during the summer; depending on your interest, you can see the ground floor's highlights in an hour or two, or geek out for half a day or longer.

When it's hot and sticky during DC's infamous summers, the museum is a great place to relax in the dark. The Albert Einstein Planetarium offers a free live show at 10:30am daily, while the immersive, five-story Lockheed Martin IMAX Theater shows several different films each day.

MAP 1: 600 Independence Ave. SW at 6th St. SW, 202/633-1000, http://airandspace.si.edu; 10am-5:30pm daily; free

✪ National Museum of Natural History

It's no surprise that the National Museum of Natural History is the most-visited natural history museum in the world. After all, the big elephant, the big dinosaurs, and the big diamond—the Hope Diamond—all live in the building, making the museum a must-visit for families with children. But don't let the museum's popularity deter you; it's the size of 18 football fields, with more than 300,000 square feet of exhibition space, so there's plenty of room for everyone to enjoy the natural wonders inside.

This is one of the oldest museums on the National Mall. In 1910, the U.S. National Museum opened in this space to showcase the national science, art, and history collections, including items from the 126 million artifacts collected during the United States Exploring Expedition, when the U.S. Congress authorized six naval ships and a group of civilian scientists to survey the Pacific from 1832-1842. As the collections grew, multiple museums were needed. In 1969, it was renamed the National Museum of Natural History, devoted to botany, geology, paleontology, and zoology.

In addition to the 14-foot elephant from Angola in the rotunda and the rare gems, highlights include human and animal mummies from Egypt and the high-tech Sant Ocean Hall, which will make you feel like you're deep underwater with some of the rarest specimens of the sea. The fossil hall will reopen in 2019 with the most complete *T. rex* skeleton in the world; in the meantime, you can see

the National Museum of Natural History

The Last American Dinosaurs, featuring recently unearthed fossils from Hell Creek Formation, North Dakota. If you want to explore a few exhibits, budget 3-4 hours minimum, especially during the summer, when there can be winding lines to view the jewels and other popular exhibits.

MAP 1: 1000 Constitution Ave. NW at 10th St. NW, 202/633-1000, http://naturalhistory. si.edu; 10am-5:30pm daily; free

Bureau of Engraving and Printing

See, kids, money doesn't grow on trees—it's printed at the U.S. Treasury's Bureau of Engraving and Printing, which prints paper banknotes as well as other government documents, like official invitations and military commissions and awards. It's not to be confused with the United States Mint, which produces coins. During the week, tour the production floor via glass windows from a gallery above, where you can see money being printed—and destroyed. The quick guided tours are free, but the required tickets are distributed first-come, first-served at the booth outside the bureau, so plan ahead if you want to visit. Large groups may make reservations for a tour.

MAP 1: 14th St. SW and C St. SW, 202/874-2330, www.moneyfactory.gov/ washingtondctours.html; 8:30am-7pm Mon.-Fri. Mar. 20-Sept.1, 8:30am-3pm Mon.-Fri. Sept. 2-Mar. 19.; free, tickets required

Franklin Delano Roosevelt Memorial

"The only thing we have to fear is fear itself." Spoken by President Franklin Delano Roosevelt during his first inaugural address in 1933, these words are carved in commanding stone at the beginning of one of the National Mall's gems, the Franklin Delano Roosevelt Memorial, which tells the story of the 32nd president's impact on the nation. Many Washingtonians say this is their favorite memorial, a tranquil space for reflection away from the crowds (if you avoid cherry

WE MUST SCRUPULOUSLY
GUARD THE CIVIL RIGHTS
AND CIVIL LIBERTIES OF
ALL CITIZENS, WHATEVER
THEIR BACKGROUND.
WE MUST REMEMBER THAT
ANY OPPRESSION, ANY
INJUSTICE, ANY HATRED, IS
A WEDGE DESIGNED TO
ATTACK OUR CIVILIZATION.

Franklin Delano Roosevelt Memorial

blossom season) and a memorial worthy of the president who championed national parks.

The memorial is set up like an outdoor museum, with "rooms" about FDR's presidency containing life-size statues of FDR and Eleanor Roosevelt (it's the only presidential memorial that includes a first lady). Stone walls with engraved quotations are interspersed with peaceful waterfalls. Each room covers one of his four terms: The Great Depression (1933-1937), The New Deal (1937-1941), The Second World War (1941-1945), and Legacy, about his final term, cut short when he died in 1945. The Prologue Room was added to the beginning of the memorial in 2001 to show FDR in his wheelchair, after the National Organization on Disability criticized the memorial for not accurately depicting Roosevelt as he was—paralyzed by polio.

Access the memorial, located on the west side of the Tidal Basin, from West Basin Drive SW or by walking through the Martin Luther King Jr. Memorial to the path along the Tidal Basin.

MAP 1: 400 W. Basin Dr. SW at Ohio Dr. SW, 202/426-6841, www.nps.gov/frde; 24 hours daily, visitors center and bookstore 9am-6pm daily; free

Korean War Veterans Memorial

The Korean War Veterans Memorial is dedicated to the American soldiers who helped South Korea fight North Korea from 1950 to 1953. On the west end of the National Mall, the memorial shows the human face of war, and it's even more stirring when you consider the United States' ongoing tensions with North Korea.

In the triangular memorial grounds, directly southeast of the Lincoln Memorial, stand 19 stainless steel figures representing soldiers from the Air Force, Army, Marines, and Navy, sculpted with striking detail by World War II veteran Frank Gaylord. If you get close enough, you'll see stunning detail that renders each figure into an individual. Be sure not

statues of soldiers at the Korean War Veterans Memorial

to miss the three that are partially hidden in the trees.

On the south side of the triangle is a 164-foot-long black granite wall, with more than 2,500 images from the war etched on the surface. The triangle points to the **Pool of Remembrance,** where you'll find lists of the number of American and United Nations soldiers killed, wounded, missing in action, or taken prisoner during the war. Near the pool, another low wall has a simple but important reminder: "Freedom Is Not Free."

MAP 1: 10 Daniel French Dr. SW at Independence Ave. SW, 202/426-6841, www.nps.gov/kowa; 24 hours daily; free

Martin Luther King Jr. Memorial

On the western banks of the Tidal Basin is the newest memorial on the Mall, the Martin Luther King Jr. Memorial, which was officially dedicated on August 28, 2011, the 48th anniversary of Dr. King's "I Have A Dream" speech. It's the first and only memorial on the National Mall dedicated to an African American, and the fourth dedicated to an individual who did not serve as U.S. president.

The centerpiece is a striking 30-foot carving of Dr. King, seemingly emerging from a block of stone, an incredible likeness created by Chinese master sculptor Lei Yixin. Behind the sculpture is a broken stone mountain, symbolizing a line from Dr. King's famous speech: "With this faith, we will be able to hew out of the mountains of despair a stone of hope." This is paraphrased on the side of the sculpture.

Surrounding the sculptures is a 450-foot-long granite wall inscribed with 14 of Dr. King's most memorable quotes, including one from his sermon at the Washington National Cathedral (3101 Wisconsin Ave. NW, 202/537-6200, www.cathedral.org) just four days before his assassination: "We shall overcome because the arc of the moral universe is long, but it bends towards justice." This metaphor originated with 19-century Unitarian minister Theodore Parker, and Dr. King used it several times in his sermons and speeches.

It's worth braving the crowds to pay your respects near the anniversary of Dr. King's death, April 4, because the cherry blossom trees that surround the memorial are often in full, glorious bloom.

MAP 1: 1964 Independence Ave. SW at W. Basin Dr. SW, 202/426-6841, www.nps.gov/mlkm; 24 hours daily; free

Thomas Jefferson Memorial

Thomas Jefferson was a complex man. On the one hand, the third U.S. president wrote the Declaration of Independence and led our nation to democracy. On the other, he owned more than 600 slaves, even while he was calling for equal rights to life, liberty, and the pursuit of happiness.

Designed in 1929 by John Russell Pope, who also designed the National Archives (Constitution Ave. NW between 7th St. NW and 9th St. NW, 202/357-5000, www.archives.gov) and the National Gallery of Art (Constitution Ave. NW between 3rd St. NW and 9th St. NW, 202/737-4215, www.nga.gov), this neoclassical memorial is inspired by the Pantheon in Rome. Jefferson loved this architectural style; similar columns and domes appear on Monticello, his estate in Charlottesville, Virginia, as well as the University of Virginia, which he founded in 1819.

Located on the southeast bank of the Tidal Basin, it's just far enough from the National Mall's most beaten paths to make it a little less crowded than the Lincoln Memorial during prime tourist season. Stand on the banks of the Tidal Basin to get the best photo op of the imposing, iconic structure from the outside, then go inside to see the 19-foot bronze statue of the man himself, surrounded by his words and looking toward the White House.

MAP 1: 701 E. Basin Dr. SW, adjacent to the Tidal Basin, 202/426-6841, www.nps.gov/thje; 24 hours daily, visitors center 9am-6pm daily; free

Vietnam Veterans Memorial

Visiting the Vietnam Veterans Memorial is an emotional experience. The focus is the Memorial Wall, comprising two 246-foot-long black granite walls carved with the names of the 58,318 Americans who were killed or missing in action during the long, controversial war. As you run your fingers over the sharply etched, seemingly infinite list of names, the shiny wall mirrors your reflection. The names are listed first by day of death or disappearance, then alphabetically within each day. Search for the location of a specific name at the Vietnam Veterans Memorial Fund website (www.vvmf.org).

Amazingly, this poignant site is not the work of a venerable architect. The wall was the creation of Maya Lin, a 21-year-old architecture student at Yale University when she beat out more than 1,400 other applicants to have her design chosen for the memorial.

Two statues were added to the memorial grounds after the wall was built. *The Three Soldiers*, depicting three men—one white, one African American, and one Latino—looking at the wall, was added in 1984. The Vietnam Women's Memorial, showing three uniformed women helping a wounded soldier, was added in 1993 to honor the 265,000 women who served in Vietnam.

MAP 1: 5 Henry Bacon Dr. NW at Constitution Ave. NW, 202/426-6841, www.nps.gov/vive; 24 hours daily

wreaths at the Memorial Wall of the Vietnam Veterans Memorial

World War II Memorial

Honoring the 16 million Americans who served during World War II and the 400,000 who died, the World War II Memorial sits on 7.4 acres of prime National Mall real estate, on the west side of the Washington Monument. The memorial's 56 stone pillars—one for each of the 48 U.S. states during the war, plus eight U.S. territories—are arranged in a circle around the Rainbow Pool, which was built in 1923 and incorporated into the memorial's design. Each pillar has a bronze and granite wreath, and between the pillars are detailed panels depicting various battles and scenes of soldiers preparing to go to war. By the entrance on 17th Street, two flagpoles emblazoned with the seals of each branch of the military welcome visitors.

From a distance, the memorial is massive. Inside, it's engulfing. In fact, some critics say the architecture is reminiscent of Fascist construction, its 17-foot utilitarian pillars feeling a little too similar to Albert Speer's Third Reich headquarters.

The memorial is not completely stone-cold. Look for the engravings of "Kilroy was here" graffiti, the bald cartoon man peeking over a fence. American soldiers scribbled this everywhere they went, a sign for those who would come after them.

MAP 1: 1750 Independence Ave. SW at 17th St. SW, 202/426-6841, www.nps.gov/wwii; 24 hours daily

Downtown and Penn Quarter

Map 2

✪ The White House

America's most iconic home has served as the residence of every U.S. president except George Washington. Built in 1792-1800, the white neoclassical mansion made of painted sandstone includes the Executive Residence as well as the offices of the president in the West Wing, and reception rooms and the offices of the first lady in the East Wing. While George Washington oversaw the construction, John Adams was the first president to occupy it, writing in a letter to his wife, "I pray Heaven to bestow the best of blessings on this House, and all that shall hereafter inhabit it. May none but honest and wise men ever rule under this roof." (FDR had this line carved on the mantel in the State Dining Room.) Every first family has lived in the White House, with a few exceptions—like James Madison, who moved out after the British burned the structure in 1814, and Harry S. Truman, because the building was in disrepair and required its most extensive architectural renovation to date in 1949-1951.

Very little has changed since the 1950s, except the decor; First Lady Jackie Kennedy famously redecorated it with American antiques and artifacts to reflect the history of the nation and the office, and she had the

view of the White House from Lafayette Square

White House declared a museum to ensure the building and everything inside would be preserved for future generations.

There's an excellent photo op of the White House on Pennsylvania Avenue in **Lafayette Square**, a favorite gathering spot of protestors. Considered a part of the White House grounds, Lafayette Square provides a head-on view of the White House and North Lawn through a security fence. Usually, you can easily walk through the square and right up to the fence. However, the square is occasionally blocked off for high-level diplomatic events, such as a state dinner, or the inauguration, as it's part of the day's parade route.

Visit the **White House Visitor Center** (1450 Pennsylvania Ave. NW, 202/208-1631, www.nps.gov/whho; 7:30am-4pm daily), a few blocks away, to see nearly 100 artifacts and exhibits about the White House's history, architecture, and social events.

As you're planning your trip to DC, you may be wondering how to get inside the White House. Before your trip, you can request a free, self-guided tour of the East Wing from your member of Congress's office (see *Touring the White House* on page 81 for more details).

MAP 2: 1600 Pennsylvania Ave. NW, 202/456-7041, www.whitehouse.gov

NEARBY:

- Get a photo-worthy view of the White House from **Lafayette Square** (page 80).
- Dine in the plush setting of **Joe's Seafood, Prime Steak & Stone Crab** (page 109).
- Soak in the old-fashioned atmosphere at **Old Ebbitt Grill** as you devour a salad or sandwich (page 110).
- Enjoy excellent, yet unpretentious French fare at **Mirabelle** (page 110).
- Lounge away the evening at **POV**, a covered rooftop bar (page 141).
- Sip DC-inspired cocktails at **Off the Record** (page 142).
- Appreciate the collection of contemporary American craft at the **Renwick Gallery** (page 166).

Lafayette Square

Lafayette Square, on the north side of the White House, is named for French general Gilbert du Motier, Marquis de Lafayette, who helped the colonists defeat the British during the Revolutionary War. The park contains five statues: General Andrew Jackson, Lafayette, and other military leaders from France, Poland, and Prussia who aided the Continental Army during the American Revolution.

The park is surrounded by powerful players: the U.S. Treasury, the Eisenhower Executive Office Building, where many Executive Branch employees work, and Blair House, the president's guest house for visiting dignitaries. St. John's Episcopal Church, where many U.S. presidents have worshipped since 1816, is to the north across H Street NW.

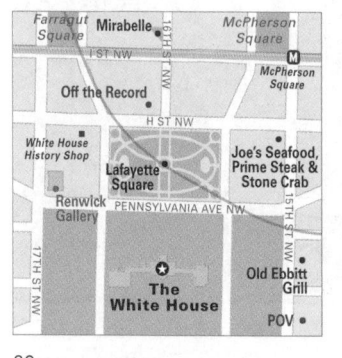

tourists at the White House

It's possible to get a glimpse inside the White House on a tour, but it requires planning ahead.

U.S. citizens must submit tour requests through the office of their senator or representative (www.senate.gov/senators/contact or www.house.gov/representatives/find). Requests should be submitted between three months and 21 days in advance. Submit your request as early as possible. If you want to see the holiday decorations in December, submit your request in September.

The free, self-guided tours are generally available 7:30am-11:30am Tuesday through Thursday and 7:30am-1:30pm Friday and Saturday, though they may be cancelled depending on the White House schedule and security concerns.

The tour takes approximately 30-60 minutes to complete. You won't have much choice of the day or time slot, but you will get to see the parlors that were meticulously restored by First Lady Jackie Kennedy as well as the State Dining Room. The tour also gives you a look at a few of the rooms in the East Wing and the ground floor of the residence, including the China Room, showcasing glassware used by First Families, and the East Room, with the iconic portraits of George Washington and John F. Kennedy. Secret Service agents stand ready to answer your questions about the building's history and artifacts. (If you want a tour of the West Wing, you generally need to have a friend in the White House to be admitted to the Oval Office, Press Room, and Rose Garden.)

For two days in the spring and fall, you can tour the White House gardens and grounds; check www.whitehouse.gov in early April and early October for tour dates and ticket information.

Tours for international visitors may be restricted. Contact your country's embassy in Washington for more information. Non-U.S. citizens may still schedule tours of the U.S. Capitol.

For more information on tours, contact the White House's 24-hour information hotline at 202/456-7041.

Don't be surprised if you run into a celebration or a peaceful protest here. The square is occasionally blocked off for security purposes.

MAP 2: Pennsylvania Ave. NW and H Street NW between 15th St. NW and 17th St. NW; 24 hours daily

President's Park and the Ellipse

President's Park is an 82-acre national park that includes must-see sights like the White House and Lafayette Square, as well as historic trails and public green spaces. Two of the park's trails allow access to many

the J. Edgar Hoover Building, headquarters of the Federal Bureau of Investigation

monuments and memorials north and south of the White House. Pick them up from the **White House Visitor Center** (1450 Pennsylvania Ave. NW, 202/208-1631, www.nps.gov/whho).

Inside President's Park, south of the White House, the Ellipse is a 52-acre circular park that's a popular meeting spot for events ranging from protests to official White House events. In 1932, President Calvin Coolidge lit the first national Christmas tree in the center of the Ellipse. Today, it continues to be the site for the National Christmas Tree Lighting, as well as the National Menorah and Christmas trees decorated for every state and U.S. territory. **MAP 2:** Between 15th St. NW and 17th St. NW, H Street NW and Constitution Ave. NW, 202/208-1631, www.nps.gov/whho; 24 hours daily (hours may be limited for security purposes)

Federal Bureau of Investigation (FBI)

Inside the FBI headquarters, the FBI Experience is a 60- to 90-minute self-guided tour showcasing the history and mission of the agency. But don't expect to just show up. U.S. citizens must contact their senator or representative (and foreign citizens should contact their country's embassy in DC) between four weeks and five months in advance to make a reservation. You'll be notified about two weeks before your requested date whether you've been cleared for the tour, which features real crime-solving equipment and artifacts from historic cases, sure to be a hit with slightly older children who want to be police officers or federal agents when they grow up.

Even if you don't take the tour, it's worth passing by one of the most imposing—and one of the ugliest—buildings in DC. The **J. Edgar Hoover Building,** named for the agency's first director, received strong mixed reactions when it was completed in 1975. Many architecture critics considered the brutalist, "Orwellian" building a blight on the city, but others said the two-million-plus-square-foot concrete structure was perfect for the agency tasked with capturing the most dangerous criminals.

MAP 2: 935 Pennsylvania Ave. NW, 202/324-3000, www.fbi.gov; tours 9am-3pm Mon.-Thurs. by reservation only; free

Ford's Theatre

During the Civil War, Ford's Theatre was a popular entertainment venue among Washingtonians, including President Abraham Lincoln, who attended the theater nearly a dozen times. On April 14, 1865, Lincoln was shot by John Wilkes Booth during a performance of *Our American Cousin*. The next morning, the president died in Petersen House, the boarding house across the street.

The theater was shuttered, but it reopened in 1968 and today shows American plays and musicals like *Ragtime* and *Death of a Salesman*. The highlight is the annual production of *A Christmas Carol*, which the theater has produced every holiday season since 1979.

The historic site is a popular attraction, with 30- to 45-minute guided tours ($3) of the theater and Lincoln's private box, which has been carefully restored to look like it did on the night he died. Tour tickets include a self-guided tour of Petersen House and entrance to the on-site museum, which features exhibits about Lincoln's presidency and assassination. While same-day tickets may be available at the box office, it's recommended to reserve your timed entry tickets online in advance.

MAP 2: 511 10th St. NW, 202/347-4833, www.fords.org; tours 9am-4:30pm daily, box office 8:30am-5pm daily and until 8pm on performance days; tours $3

Friendship Archway in Chinatown

Friendship Archway

DC's Chinatown was established in the 1880s by Chinese residents around present-day Federal Triangle. They were later displaced by construction, and in the 1930s, the community moved northeast and eventually spanned G Street NW north to Massachusetts Avenue NW, between 5th Street and 8th Street NW. Alas, the 1968 riots caused an exodus to the suburbs, and the neighborhood continued to shrink through the 1990s with the construction of the massive Capital One Arena.

One of the most prominent landmarks of Chinatown is the Friendship Archway, an elaborate, 60-foot structure crossing H Street. Built in 1986, the colorful tiled archway incorporates elements of traditional Chinese architecture and symbolizes the friendship between Washington DC and Beijing. On the surrounding streets are a few residences that house the bulk of the neighborhood's Chinese community, as well as a dozen or so tired Chinese restaurants and shops. Look for the Chinese characters on fast-food restaurants and drugstores in the vicinity. During Chinese New Year, a traditional parade makes its way under the archway through what remains of the neighborhood.

MAP 2: H St. NW between 6th Street NW and 7th St. NW

Capitol Hill and Atlas District

Map 3

TOP EXPERIENCE

✪ U.S. Capitol

While this imposing white neoclassical dome is visible for miles, rising 288 feet into the Washington skyline, the U.S. Capitol, where Congress makes laws—or not, but who's keeping track?—is worth seeing up close.

If you plan ahead, it's relatively easy to take the free, 45-minute guided tour of the Capitol, either by contacting the office of your senator or representative or by reserving tickets online through the **U.S. Capitol Visitor Center** (1st St. SE and E. Capitol St. NE, 202/226-8000, www.visitthecapitol.gov). (For more information on tours, see *Booking a Tour of the Capitol* on page 87.)

The tour is the only way to see some of the Capitol's historic areas that are still in use. The highlight is the **rotunda,** the 96-foot-wide circular room under the dome that connects the House and Senate sides of the Capitol. Look up to see the magnificent fresco *The Apotheosis of George Washington,* painted by Italian artist Constantino Brumidi in 1865, depicting the first president as a god-like figure. (Want to go a little higher? It's possible to tour the **top of the dome,** if you're accompanied by a member of Congress. You'll climb 300 spiraling steps to get an up-close look at the dome and an expansive view from an exterior walkway. It's hard to nab a spot, but it's worth asking when you request a tour of the Capitol.)

The tour also takes visitors

inside the U.S. Capitol dome

directly underneath the rotunda, to the **crypt**, with 40 Doric columns supporting the dome and a star marking the spot from which the city's quadrants and streets are laid out. The architects intended for George Washington to be buried under the star, though he chose to remain at home at Mount Vernon. Another stop is the **statuary hall**, where Congress hosts the luncheon for the newly inaugurated president. It contains 35 statues from the Capitol's collection of 100 influential Americans, two from every state; the remainder are located throughout the rotunda, crypt, and visitor center.

The **visitor center**, underneath the Capitol's east plaza, is open to the public and contains historical artifacts and exhibits about the history of Congress. The visitor center has two gift shops on the upper level with exclusive Capitol merchandise, as well as a large **cafeteria** (8:30am-4pm Mon.-Sat.) on the lower level, where you can try the famous Senate Bean Soup, which has been served in Senate dining rooms every day since the early 1900s.

All visitors must pass through airport-style security to enter the visitor center; expect waits up to 45 minutes during peak tourist season. Leave yourself plenty of time—your tour won't wait for you. (Tip: Visit the Capitol after you've toured the Library of Congress. From the LOC, there's an underground tunnel leading to the U.S. Capitol Visitor Center, with lines that are often shorter than at the main entrance.)

The Capitol is nestled in a 58-acre park between Constitution Avenue NW and Independence Avenue SE at 1st Street, though the entire U.S. Capitol grounds cover about 270 acres. On the west side of the Capitol, explore the verdant grounds and see the dome and Capitol Reflecting Pool. To access the grounds, head southwest on Delaware Avenue NE through the Lower and Upper Senate Parks, and just keep heading toward the dome.

MAP 3: U.S. Capitol Visitor Center, 1st St. SE and E. Capitol St. NE, 202/226-8000, www.visitthecapitol.gov; 8:30am-4:30pm Mon.-Sat.; grounds 24 hours daily

NEARBY:

- Get yourself a Reader Identification Card and cozy up in the Main Reading Room of the **Library of Congress** (page 87).
- Visit the **Supreme Court of the United States,** where you can even watch oral arguments if court is in session (page 88).
- Sink your teeth into a burger from **Good Stuff Eatery** (page 115).
- Head to friendly **Pete's Diner** for breakfast or lunch (page 118).
- Hang out with the locals at **Tune Inn,** one of DC's last remaining dive bars (page 145).
- Stop into **Bullfeathers** for a cold beer and listen in on political gossip (page 145).
- Attend one of Shakespeare's plays at **Folger Theatre** (page 169).

Eastern Market

Eastern Market is the longest-running public market in DC, part of urban planner Pierre L'Enfant's idea to have three such markets in the capital. Originally located near Navy Yard, it moved to its current location after the Civil War. The market building, completed in 1873, has survived riots and fire, and it remains an important part of local life and a destination for excellent food, shopping, and people-watching, especially on weekends, when it's buzzing with activity.

The historic building includes **South Hall,** from which merchants sell produce, meat, dairy, flowers, and prepared food and baked goods, as well as **North Hall,** now an events space with picnic tables and an area for kids to run around. On Saturdays and Sundays, dozens of local farmers and artisans set up stands surrounding the building's exterior to sell antique and refinished furniture, art and photography, jewelry, produce, and snacks. Spend a few hours on a beautiful weekend afternoon having brunch in the market building—try the crab cakes or blueberry pancakes at **Market Lunch,** or a strudel from the bakery—then browsing the vendors for unique souvenirs. For a one-of-a-kind piece of contemporary Americana, look for artist Robert Jaxson around 7th Street and C Street SE, who paints brightly colored American and DC flags and jazz scenes on pieces of wood.

Eastern Market

BOOKING A TOUR OF THE CAPITOL

inside the U.S. Capitol Visitor Center

It's much easier to schedule a tour of the U.S. Capitol than the White House, though you'll still want to plan ahead. There are two options for public tours.

Option 1: Schedule a free, guided tour through the U.S. Capitol Visitor Center online (www.visitthecapitol.gov), up to three months in advance. Generally, the 45-minute tours depart every 10 minutes during opening hours. Schedule your tour at least a few weeks in advance, especially if you're traveling in the spring and summer, but same-day passes are sometimes available at the information desk on the visitor center's lower level. On the tour, you'll see the crypt, rotunda, and statuary hall.

Option 2: Contact your senator or representative to schedule a tour led by a staff member or intern in the office. Visit www.senate.gov/senators/contact or www.house.gov/representatives/find for contact information, and contact the office as far in advance as possible. While these tours may be harder to get, they have advantages, including smaller groups as well as the possibility of seeing some areas of the Capitol that are not usually open to the public. In addition, the office can get you passes to enter the Senate or House gallery to see Congress in action. (International visitors can inquire about gallery passes at the House and Senate Appointment Desks in the visitor center.)

For more information, including details on exhibits at the visitor center and items you cannot bring through security, visit www.visitthecapitol.gov.

MAP 3: 225 7th St. SE, 202/698-5253, www.easternmarket-dc.org; indoor market 7am-7pm Tues.-Fri., 7am-6pm Sat., 9am-5pm Sun., outdoor market 7am-6pm Sat., 9am-5pm Sun.

Library of Congress

For voracious readers, there's no better souvenir than the **Library of Congress Reader Identification Card,** your key to the largest library in the world. You can register for your card in person with government identification; it will provide access to the library's Main Reading Room, where you can read, write, reflect, or dig into some of the 150 million books, recordings, photographs, and other materials in the collections with the help of the expert librarians.

Even without the card, you can visit the library's public rooms and exhibits, which occupy three buildings. Most of the must-see exhibits are located in the **Thomas Jefferson Building,** the magnificent main structure completed in 1897, and the entrance to the complex; it connects

Library of Congress

to the **James Madison Memorial Building** and the **John Adams Building,** which contain specialized reading rooms. Free, one-hour **guided tours** (hourly, 10:30am-3:30pm Mon.-Fri., 10:30am-2:30pm Sat.) of the Thomas Jefferson Building are available, or you can download a self-guided tour booklet or pick one up at the information desks inside. Thomas Jefferson Building highlights include the handwritten Giant Bible of Mainz (circa 1452-1453), the first map to use the word "America" (circa 1507), and a replica of Jefferson's personal library, containing the 6,000-plus books he sold to the government after the British burned the Library of Congress in 1814. To see what else is on view from the library's collections, visit www.loc.gov/exhibits.

From the Library of Congress, you can access the **U.S. Capitol Visitor Center** (1st St. and E. Capitol St. SE) via underground tunnel. This entry to the U.S. Capitol often has a shorter wait time than the main entrance.

MAP 3: 10 1st St. SE, 202/707-8000, www.loc.gov; 8:30am-4:30pm Mon.-Sat.

Supreme Court of the United States

The Supreme Court of the United States is the highest authority on the law in the land, and yet even today, you can't watch the proceedings on television. (Who says newspapers are obsolete?) If you're visiting Washington DC while court is in session, you can watch the oral arguments in person at 10am and 1pm. (Check online for the court calendar.) Two lines for first-come, first-served seating at the 10am argument begin forming around 8am, earlier for major, headline cases; you can choose to wait for seating for the entire argument, or to pop in for three minutes.

Even when court is not in session, the building is open to the public via the main steps. While the Supreme Court does not offer guided tours, you can nonetheless take advantage of 30-minute, docent-led lectures

Union Station

about the Supreme Court and the architecture of the building, available every 30 minutes 9:30am-3:30pm on weekdays when court is not in session, and after court adjourns at 3pm when in session. You're free to explore most of the first and ground floors, where you'll find busts of every former chief justice, as well as special exhibits.

MAP 3: 1 1st St. NE, 202/479-3030, www.supremecourt.gov; 9am-4:30pm Mon.-Fri. daily, visitor access may change when court is in session

Union Station

If you're traveling to Washington DC via Amtrak, you'll pass through Union Station, the city's major railroad station, which opened in 1908. The three-level transportation hub (and Amtrak's second-busiest station in the country) is worth a visit to explore the beaux arts architecture designed by Daniel Burnham, architect of the Flatiron Building in New York City. On the outside, you'll recognize the neoclassical arches reminiscent of the Arch of Constantine in Rome. Inside the 96-foot-high Main Hall, beautifully restored again in 2012-2016 following an earthquake, soaring white granite arches inlaid with 23-karat gold leaf welcome about 40 million visitors and travelers each year.

In addition to providing access to Amtrak, Metro, local and national bus services, and several city tours, including DC Ducks (866/754-5039, www.dcducks.com; $28-42), Union Station contains dozens of casual and fast-food restaurants and shops on the departures level as well as in the basement food court.

MAP 3: 50 Massachusetts Ave. NE, 202/289-1908, www.unionstationdc.com; food court 6am-9pm Mon.-Fri., 9am-9pm Sat., 7am-6pm Sun., retail 10am-9pm Mon.-Sat., noon-6pm Sun.

Dupont Circle Map 4

Dupont Circle

Built in 1871 to honor Union Navy rear admiral Samuel Francis Du Pont, Dupont Circle is the heart of one of DC's most prestigious neighborhoods. At the center is a classical white marble fountain designed by beaux arts architect Henry Bacon and sculptor Daniel Chester French, best known for creating the Lincoln Memorial.

The park is an important rendezvous point for residents, protesters, yogis, young professionals with bagel and newspaper in hand, homeless men and women, and groups mingling over chess games at the permanent boards on the northeast side of the circle. The spokes lead to neighborhood must-sees: majestic embassies on Massachusetts Avenue, dining and shopping on Connecticut Avenue, and, during Capital Pride in June, a party on P Street.

On Sundays, head to 20th Street for the **Freshfarm Dupont Circle Market** (20th St. NW between Massachusetts Ave. and Hillyer Pl., www.freshfarm.org/dupont-circle), where residents shop for local produce, meat, dairy, baked goods, and more year-round. The market is small but robust, with options for picnics (everything from breakfast tacos and pizzas to dumplings and gourmet popsicles) and tasty souvenirs.

MAP 4: Intersection of Massachusetts Ave. NW, Connecticut Ave. NW, New Hampshire Ave. NW, P St. NW, and 19th St. NW

Spanish Steps

Spanish Steps

For urban-planning geeks, Dupont Circle's Spanish Steps are worth a stop. The steps were built in 1911 during the City Beautiful movement, an urban architecture philosophy in which city planners built beautiful spaces in the inner cities of DC, Chicago, Cleveland, and Detroit to promote virtue and civic engagement. Inspired by the Spanish Steps in Rome, the steep, stone staircase leading to a small fountain is an idyllic place to enjoy your coffee and scroll through your iPhone camera roll. But, don't tell too many of your friends—Dupont Circle locals like to believe the steps, which are hidden among the embassies and homes around 22nd Street, are a secret spot.

MAP 4: 22nd St. NW and Decatur Pl. NW

U Street, Shaw, and Logan Circle

Map 5

African American Civil War Memorial and Museum

The small but moving African American Civil War Memorial honors the 200,000 African Americans who served in the Union Army and Navy during the Civil War. Located in the heart of one of DC's historic African American neighborhoods and "Black Broadway," the center of African American arts and culture in the 20th century, the memorial includes a nine-foot bronze sculpture (sculptor Ed Hamilton) of several soldiers with the names of those who served on the walls surrounding it. Across the street from the memorial, the informative African American Civil War Museum (1925 Vermont Ave. NW, 202/667-2667, www.afroamcivilwar.org; 10am-5pm Mon., 10am-6:30pm Tues.-Fri., 10am-4pm Sat., noon-4pm Sun.) tells the stories of these soldiers through photographs, stories, and artifacts, and allows descendants of those who served to register and research their family members.

MAP 5: Vermont Ave. at 10th St. and U St. NW, 202/426-6841, www.nps.gov/afam; 24 hours daily

Howard University

Generations of black leaders have graduated from Howard University, the top-ranked historically black university founded in 1867. The university is named for Union Army general Oliver Otis Howard, who led the Freedman's Bureau and helped freed blacks assimilate after the Civil War. The list of prominent graduates is a who's-who of trailblazers in government, law, education, and the arts, including the first African American Supreme Court justice, Thurgood Marshall, civil rights activist Stokely Carmichael, U.S. Senator Kamala Harris, Sean "Puffy" Combs, and author Toni Morrison, as well as local icons like former DC mayor Adrian Fenty and Ben Ali, founder of Ben's Chili Bowl. The campus has played an important role in the black community of DC. Even as early as the 1940s, Howard students organized sit-ins around the segregated city.

Located just northeast of Shaw's growing business and nightlife center, the campus has several points of interest, including the Gothic Andrew

African American Civil War Memorial

Rankin Memorial Chapel, built in 1894-1895, where renowned preachers, activists, and political leaders including Frederick Douglass, Martin Luther King Jr., and JFK have spoken. Howard continues to bring distinguished speakers to the campus, though the public Sunday service has outgrown the chapel and now congregates in the 1,500-seat Cramton Auditorium.

Howard University Homecoming is another popular event, with a parade, fashion show, and parties at bars and clubs citywide every October. Prospective students may tour the campus at 10am, noon, and 2pm Monday through Friday when classes are in session.

MAP 5: 2400 6th St. NW, 202/806-6100, www.howard.edu

Georgetown and Foggy Bottom

Map 7

Diplomatic Reception Rooms of the Department of State

The U.S. Department of State is a sprawling complex in one of the swampiest parts of the city—hence the name Foggy Bottom. For the most part, it's closed to the public. However, you can tour the most splendid rooms in the building: the Diplomatic Reception Rooms, which are used for official meetings such as the signing of treaties or summits with foreign leaders. Located on the eighth floor of the State Department's headquarters, the rooms look like a colonial mansion and contain one of the finest collections of American art, furniture, and decorative arts, including some 5,000 objects from 1750 to 1825. Highlights include the desk on which Benjamin Franklin, John Jay, and John Adams signed the Treaty of Paris in 1783, ending the Revolutionary War, as well as silver made by Paul Revere and portraits of Jefferson, Franklin, Adams, and Henry Clay. You must register for the tour at least 90 days in advance on the U.S. Department of State website or through your member of Congress; the 45-minute guided tour is recommended for visitors age 12 and up.

MAP 7: 21st St. NW and C St. NW, 202/647-3241, http://receptiontours.state. gov; tours 9:30am, 10:30am, 2:45pm Mon.-Fri. by appointment

George Washington University

George Washington University breeds public servants, particularly in the post-grad programs in international affairs, business, and law, which are popular among young DC staffers who want to get ahead. Notable grads include senators, representatives, governors, diplomats, and media personalities, including General Colin Powell, U.S. Senator Harry Reid, First Lady Jackie Onassis Kennedy, and CNN's Dana Bash, to name a few. Founded in 1821 by an act of Congress and named for the president who hoped to establish a national university in the nation's capital, this private university is DC's largest, with 25,000 undergraduate and graduate students across three regional campuses, including the main campus in Foggy Bottom, just a few blocks from the White House and U.S. State Department. Places of note include The George Washington University Museum and The Textile Museum, which are open to the public daily, as well as The George Washington University Hospital, the most centrally located hospital for most visitors to DC, which is affiliated with the university's medical school. The Lisner Auditorium (730 21st St. NW, 202/994-6800, http://lisner.gwu. edu) is a 1,500-seat theater where you can attend discussions with politicians, authors, and media personalities ranging from Hillary Clinton to Alec Baldwin. Prospective students may register for a campus tour at the Admissions Welcome Center (800 21st St. NW, 202/994-6602).

MAP 7: 2121 Eye St. NW, 202/994-1000, www.gwu.edu

Georgetown University

Founded in 1789 by John Carroll, the first Catholic bishop in the United States, Georgetown University is the oldest Catholic and Jesuit institution of higher education in the nation. It's consistently ranked among the top universities, with a highly selective admissions process. Georgetown's elite alumni include President Bill Clinton (who lost his 1967 race for student council president), Supreme Court Justice Antonin Scalia, General John F. Kelly, and royals from Spain, Saudi Arabia, Jordan, and Greece.

The most iconic building on campus is the neo-medieval Healy Hall, which looks like something out of the Harry Potter movies and bears the name of Patrick Francis Healy, the first African American president of a non-historically black college or university; Healy Hall was prominently featured in *The Exorcist,* the 1973 horror film based on the novel of the same name by William Peter Blatty, class of 1950. Sports fans may want to catch 1985 grad and former New York Knicks starter Patrick Ewing coaching the Georgetown Hoyas Division I men's basketball team, which has won several NCAA titles and plays home games at the **Capital One Arena** from November to March. Download a self-guided tour map (http://uadmissions.georgetown.edu) of the idyllic, 104-acre main campus, nestled on a hill high above the Georgetown shopping streets.

MAP 7: 37th St. NW and O St. NW, 202/687-0100, www.georgetown.edu

Old Stone House

You might miss the unremarkable granite and fieldstone building entirely on your way to the boutiques or C&O Canal. However, the Old Stone House, smack in the middle of the M Street shopping district, is worth a stop for a snapshot of life in early Washington DC. Built in 1765, it's the oldest structure on its original foundation in the city. When the National Park Service purchased the house in 1953, then a used car dealership, it was thought to be the location where George Washington met with city planner Pierre Charles L'Enfant to discuss plans for the federal city; historians discovered the men actually met at a tavern a few blocks away, but the house had already been preserved and opened for tours. Take a guided tour of the inside to see how a middle-class family in the 18th century would have furnished their home, or stop for a shopping break in the Colonial Revival garden, a lovely spot to enjoy a treat from one of the neighborhood's excellent coffee shops.

MAP 7: 3051 M St. NW, 202/895-6000, www.nps.gov/places/old-stone-house.htm;

This staircase was a filming location for *The Exorcist*.

house 11am-6pm daily, garden dawn-dusk daily; free

The Exorcist Stairs

Washington politics can be pretty frightening, but the most horrifying movie ever filmed in DC has nothing to do with political intrigue. In 1949, William Peter Blatty was attending Georgetown University when he heard a story in class about a real-life exorcism of a teen boy, which inspired him to write his bestseller *The Exorcist*. Many key scenes were filmed in Georgetown, notably the dramatic ending in which Father Damien Karras, momentarily possessed by the demon he has been trying to exorcise from Regan MacNeil, leaps out of the girl's bedroom window and tumbles down the steep staircase to his death. You can see the real house, and climb those terrifying steps, at the corner of Prospect Street NW and 36th Street NW. Don't try to count them, because you'll get a different number every time.

MAP 7: 3600 Prospect St. NW, 24 hours daily; free

District Wharf

Since opening in October 2017, this 24-acre development—the largest new development in Washington DC in decades—has dramatically changed the landscape of the Southwest quadrant's waterfront. This once quiet stretch along the Potomac River, cut off from the city center by a major highway, is now a destination with three major hotels, four residence buildings, two office buildings, four recreation and transportation piers, and dozens of restaurants, bars, and shops, including some of the most influential names in dining and nightlife in DC.

This shiny, mile-long complex is not authentically cool, but it is impressive in scale—and when the newness wears off and the neighborhood finds its role in the rhythms of daily life in DC, District Wharf will surely become an essential part of the city. Already, there are reasons to visit, notably the most exciting new nightlife venue in the city, The Anthem (901 Wharf St., 202/888-0020, tickets 877/435-9849, www.theanthemdc.com), the 6,000-capacity club from the owners of the storied 9:30 Club. In addition, District Wharf has several much-hyped, multi-story restaurants—providing dining options before or after a performance at nearby Arena Stage—including Del Mar (791 Wharf St. SW, 202/525-1402, www.delmardc.com), serving coastal Spanish cuisine by Fabio Trabocchi of Georgetown's Fiola Mare, and Kith & Kin (202/878-8566, http://kithandkindc.com), featuring Kwame Onwuachi's African-Caribbean fusion, as well as an outpost of Hank's Oyster Bar (202/817-3055, http://hanksoysterbar.com). And, of course, the piers provide recreation opportunities, including sailing lessons, rentals, and charters at DC Sail (202/547-1250, www.dcsail.org) and a seasonal ice skating rink. For an authentic taste of the waterfront of yore, don't miss the Maine Avenue Fish Market, which opened in 1805 and remains the oldest continually operating fish market in the country. The open-air market has been incorporated into the west end of District Wharf, and it remains an authentic choice for fresh seafood, including crabs, shrimp, oysters, and fish, which you can enjoy right on the water, or take home to prepare.

While District Wharf seems distant from the city's primary tourist areas, it's actually quite convenient, less than 10 minutes by foot from the Waterfront and L'Enfant Plaza Metro stations, and less than 20 minutes by foot from the National Mall. A free shuttle (7th St. and Independence Ave. SW; 6:30am-11:30pm Mon.-Thurs., 6:30am-1am Fri., 9am-1am Sat., 9am-11pm Sun.) is available from the National Mall daily. From the Transit Pier, catch water taxis ($10-$18 adults, $7-$12.60 children) to Georgetown and Old Town Alexandria.

MAP 8: Maine Ave. SW from 6th St. SW west toward L'Enfant Plaza, www.wharfdc.com; 24 hours/daily, individual merchant hours vary

✪ Frederick Douglass National Historic Site

While the new National Museum of African American History and Culture has been getting so much

Frederick Douglass National Historic Site

attention, the National Park Service has been quietly preserving the legacy of one of the country's most important abolitionists—and you won't need to wait for hours to see it. Located in Anacostia, the Frederick Douglass National Historic Site is also known as Cedar Hill. It's the estate where Douglass lived from 1877, when he was appointed U.S. Marshall by President Rutherford B. Hayes, until his death in 1895. The tour of this restored Victorian mansion offers a glimpse of life at the turn of the 20th century. See rooms containing many of Douglass's personal belongings in the exact spots they would have been while he was alive, as well as artwork and photographs of the Douglass family. The home is only accessible by

guided tour with a park ranger, who will point out fascinating artifacts and relate tidbits about the man who was born a slave and would eventually become a renowned (and mostly self-educated) abolitionist, author, and speaker. Tickets for the six daily, 30-minute tours are readily available if you reserve them online at least a few days in advance. Arrive early to catch the 19-minute film about Douglass, and when you finish the tour, take in the view from his porch, located high above the city on a 51-foot hill and offering expansive views all the way to the U.S. Capitol.

MAP 8: 1411 W St. SE, 202/426-5961, www. nps.gov/frdo; 9am-5pm daily Apr.-Oct., 9am-4:30pm daily Nov.-Mar.; $1.50 for reserved ticket

✪ Arlington National Cemetery

More than 400,000 veterans and their immediate family members are buried at Arlington National Cemetery, the country's largest military cemetery, located across the Potomac in Arlington, Virginia. Inside, the seemingly endless sea of white headstones is a reminder of the high price of serving the country, a price that continues to be paid today.

After the security screening, stop by the welcome center for an introduction and map. There are dozens of memorials and historical sites to explore; plan to spend a minimum of 2-3 hours if you want to walk in the cemetery,

and wear comfortable walking shoes and weather-appropriate clothing. Alternatively, you can take the official bus tour (866/754-9014, www.arlingtontours.com; $13.50 adults, $10 seniors, $6.75 children 3-11, free for children under 3, discounts for military/groups), which is operated by Old Town Trolley Tours (202/796-2606, www.trolleytours.com).

The two most prominent sites at Arlington are the Tomb of the Unknown Soldier, the memorial to unidentified American soldiers who died in battle, which is guarded 24/7 by the Army's 3rd U.S. Infantry Regiment, and President John F. Kennedy's gravesite, where a flame has been burning since he was buried on November 25, 1963; Jacqueline

Tomb of the Unknown Soldier at Arlington National Cemetery

Kennedy Onassis was buried next to him in 1994.

Other notable locations include the **gravesite of President William Howard Taft,** the only person to serve as both president and chief justice of the Supreme Court, and **Arlington House,** the mansion once occupied by Confederate general Robert E. Lee. During the Civil War, the Union Army chose the site for the cemetery in part to ensure that Lee, who had resigned from the U.S. Army when Virginia seceded, could never again live in the mansion. **Section 27** houses the graves of more than 3,000 former slaves who could not afford to buy burial plots, as well as about 1,500 African Americans who fought in the Civil War.

To find a specific grave, download the ANC Explorer app or visit http://ancexplorer.army.mil/publicwmv. The Arlington National Cemetery Metro station is located by the main entrance and welcome center. Paid parking is available in a garage at Memorial Avenue, but you cannot drive inside the cemetery unless you are attending a funeral. Arlington is an important historical site, but keep in mind it's also an operating cemetery, with funerals taking place Monday through Saturday.

MAP 9: Entrance at Arlington Memorial Bridge and Memorial Ave. or Arlington National Cemetery Metro station (Virginia), 877/907-8585, www.arlingtoncemetery.mil; 8am-7pm daily Apr.-Sept., 8am-5pm daily Oct.-Mar.; free

NEARBY:

- Be inspired by the 16th president's legacy at the **Lincoln Memorial,** just across the Potomac (page 69).

- Pay your respects at the **National**

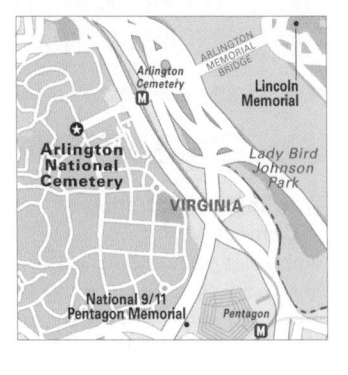

9/11 Pentagon Memorial (page 98).

✪ National 9/11 Pentagon Memorial

On September 11, 2001, at 9:37:46am, hijackers flew American Airlines Flight 77 into the Pentagon in Arlington, Virginia, killing the 59 passengers and crew on board as well as 125 people working in the U.S. Department of Defense headquarters.

Located on the southwest side of the building, where the plane hit, the National 9/11 Pentagon Memorial is accessible 24/7. The contemporary design is a place for calm reflection. The memorial consists of 184 cantilevered stainless steel and granite benches, representing the 184 individuals killed in the attack. Each bench has the name of one victim, and by looking at the name, you can determine where they died; if you see the Pentagon in your line of vision, the victim died in the building, but if you see the sky, the person was a passenger on the flight. An illuminated pool of water is underneath each bench.

The memorial is surrounded by a wall that rises from 3 inches, representing the youngest passenger killed, age 3, to 71 inches, representing the

A lioness plays with a ball at the Smithsonian's National Zoo.

oldest. Planted among the benches are 85 crape myrtles, which will provide a cooling canopy when they are fully grown. Dedicated and opened to the public on September 11, 2008, it was the first national 9/11 memorial completed in the United States.

Tours of the Pentagon are also available; reservations are required and must be booked 14-90 days in advance online (http://pentagontours.osd.mil). On the tour, you'll glean insight on the DOD's branches and activities, as well as see the indoor memorial near the crash site.

From the Pentagon Metro station, follow the signs to the memorial; visitor parking is not available at the Pentagon, but you may park at the nearby shopping mall, the Fashion Centre at Pentagon City, about a five-minute walk from the memorial through a pedestrian tunnel.

MAP 9: 1 N. Rotary Rd., Arlington (Virginia), 301/740-3388, www. pentagonmemorial.org; 24 hours daily, facilities 7am-10pm daily; free

✪ Smithsonian's National Zoo

Washington has panda fever, due to the three famous giant pandas at the Smithsonian's National Zoo, on loan from the People's Republic of China until at least 2020. But they're not the only cuddly critters inside the sprawling, 163-acre park (officially part of Rock Creek Park). At the zoo, you'll find hundreds of animal residents, including the fascinating primates in the Great Ape House, the majestic great cats, and elephants. In the American Trail exhibit you can see California sea lions and bald eagles.

In addition to the animals, attractions include a carousel ($3.50), a children's choo-choo train ($3), and animal demonstrations and feedings, as well as a free, two-hour guided tour of the highlights, which departs from the visitor center at 9:45am daily, no reservations required. The zoo is an outdoor park situated on hilly terrain, and many animal exhibits are outdoors, so wear comfortable walking shoes and weather-appropriate clothing. Refreshments are available for purchase throughout the park, but you are welcome to bring your own food and nonalcoholic beverages; water is recommended if you're visiting during the summer. Plan to spend 2-3 hours minimum to see the major exhibits; if you want to guarantee you'll spot pandas Mei Xiang, Tian Tian, and their child Bei Bei, your best bet is to visit the exhibit as early in the day as possible, when the crowds are lighter and the pandas are more likely to be playing outside.

The zoo's main entrance is in residential Woodley Park, approximately 10 minutes by foot from both the Woodley Park-Zoo/Adams Morgan Metro station and Cleveland Park Metro station. There are two pedestrian- and bike-friendly entrances a short walk from Adams Morgan and Mount Pleasant, as well, where you can check out excellent ethnic restaurants and dive bars after your visit.

MAP 9: 3001 Connecticut Ave. NW, 202/633-4888, http://nationalzoo.si.edu; exhibit buildings 9am-6pm daily Apr.-Sept., 9am-4pm daily Oct.-Mar., grounds 8am-7pm daily; free

American University

In 1917, the U.S. government took over parts of the American University campus, located near Tenleytown, to train soldiers and begin extensive chemical weapons testing and research. The campus was divided into Camp American University, where construction crews found bombs and contamination underground as late as the 1990s, and Camp Leach, where military researchers developed camouflage techniques. Today, this private (and now bomb-free) university enrolls more than 13,000 undergraduate and graduate students; alumni of the Schools of International Service, Communication, and Public Affairs often go on to work in federal government, political management, or media, and several AU students receive the prestigious Presidential Management Fellowship every year. Of note, the American University Museum at the Katzen Arts Center (4400 Massachusetts Ave. NW, 202/885-1300, www.american.edu/cas/museum) has 30,000 square feet of exhibition space for contemporary art exhibits featuring political art as well as works by DC artists. Prospective students may register for campus tours (www.american.edu/admissions) during the fall and spring semesters.

MAP 9: 4400 Massachusetts Ave. NW, 202/885-1000, www.american.edu

Basilica of the National Shrine of the Immaculate Conception

Walk in the pious footsteps of three popes, Mother Teresa, and one million annual pilgrims at the largest Roman Catholic church in North America. Serving The Catholic University of America and United States Conference of Catholic Bishops, the Byzantine-Romanesque structure honors the Virgin Mary in an enormous, uniquely American way, with 70 chapels and the largest collection of contemporary religious art in the world, including more than 75,000 square feet of mosaics. Close to the Brookland-CUA Metro station, the basilica offers free guided tours daily, along with six Masses and five hours of Confession; check the website for feast day schedules and special events.

MAP 9: 400 Michigan Ave. NE, 202/526-8300, www.nationalshrine.com; 7am-7pm daily Apr.-Oct., 7am-6pm daily Nov.-Mar.; free

Embassy Row

Crossing through several neighborhoods, Embassy Row is the stretch of Massachusetts Avenue NW lined with the stately international embassies and diplomatic missions where foreign ambassadors to the United States live and work. Beginning at Scott Circle, with the embassies of Australia and the Philippines, it heads northwest through Dupont Circle to the United States Naval Observatory, where the vice president lives. The buildings start getting really impressive just past the embassy of India in Dupont Circle, marked by a bronze Gandhi statue. The limestone Chinese embassy, designed by I. M. Pei, and imposing Japanese chancery building look like spy movie sets. Don't miss the former **embassy of Iran** (3003-3005 Massachusetts Ave. NW), known for some of the most lavish parties in Washington (think caviar, alcohol, and drugs, according to accounts by guests) before diplomatic ties were severed in 1980; the shuttered building is still owned by Tehran but maintained by the U.S. State Department. The embassies are generally closed to the public, but every May, they open their doors for **Passport DC**, when you can go inside dozens of the mansions to experience the countries' art, culture, and food.

MAP 9: Massachusetts Ave. NW from Scott Circle northwest to the United States Naval Observatory

President Lincoln's Cottage

The Old Soldiers' Home served as a refuge for wounded and retired military veterans, as well as a summer retreat for four U.S. presidents in the 19th century. President Lincoln loved it so much that he spent about a quarter of his presidency at the 34-room cottage on a secluded hill three miles

former embassy of Iran on Embassy Row

from the White House and found respite with his family from the stress of the Civil War. It's called "The Cradle of the Emancipation Proclamation" because he drafted his groundbreaking speech there.

Located in Petworth on the grounds of the still-operating Armed Forces Retirement Home, the cottage dives deeper into President Lincoln's ideas and presidency. Start at the visitor center, where you can explore exhibits about DC during the Civil War and Lincoln's experience at the Old Soldiers' Home, then depart on a lively, one-hour guided tour of the cottage, where you'll learn more about Lincoln's life and work. To protect the privacy of the retirement home's residents, you can only access the cottage by the guided tour, so advance tickets are recommended, especially on weekends.

MAP 9: 140 Rock Creek Church Rd. NW, 202/829-0436, www.lincolncottage.org; 9:30am-4:30pm Mon.-Sat., 10:30am-4:30pm Sun.; $15 adults, $12 military ID, $7.50 members, $5 children 6-12, free for children under 6

The Catholic University of America

Founded in 1887 by a charter from Pope Leo XII, The Catholic University of America is the national university of the Catholic Church—and the only university in the country to have been visited by three popes, including Pope Francis in 2015. Catholic teachings and rituals are part of daily life on the Northeast DC campus, where the majority of the 6,000 undergraduate and graduate students identify as Catholic. In addition to schools for the Arts and Sciences, Law, and Business, among others, CUA has the only university music school in Washington DC, considered one of the top among Catholic colleges and universities, as well as the only school of Catholic canon law in the country. For visitors, the highlight is the **Basilica of the National Shrine of the Immaculate Conception,** the largest Roman Catholic church in North America, with the largest collection of contemporary religious art in the world. Prospective students may register for **campus tours** (www.catholic.edu/admission) at 10am and 2pm most weekdays and select Saturdays.

MAP 9: 620 Michigan Ave. NE, 202/319-5000, www.catholic.edu

Union Market

Union Terminal Market opened in Northeast in 1931, and for decades it was the center of food wholesale and distribution in the District. Over the years, however, the market declined. Eventually, the main market building reopened as Union Market, a bright, airy food hall with tons of space for food vendors and artisans. The market is leading the revitalization of this industrial part of town, serving as a home base for many food and beverage startups inside the main market building and surrounding warehouses.

Some advice: Go hungry. Union Market has about 40 vendors, permanent restaurants, and takeout stalls serving innovative cuisine, ranging from local pickles, fast-casual Ethiopian, and gluten-free Venezuelan arepas to an outpost of the kitchen supplies and gift store **Salt & Sundry** (202/556-1866, www.shopsaltandsundry.com), to Harvey's, the family-owned butcher and market mainstay that has been operating since 1931. If you'd like to stay awhile, have a bagel and egg cream at **Buffalo & Bergen**

(202/543-2549, www.buffalobergendc.com), or try **Rappahannock Oyster Co.** (202/544-4702, www.rroysters.com). Outside the main building, one of DC's best Italian restaurants, **Masseria** (1340 4th St. NE, 202/608-1330, www.masseria-dc.com), is hidden among the warehouses and graffiti-filled alleys.

MAP 9: 1309 5th St. NE, 301/347-3998, www.unionmarketdc.com; 11am-8pm Tues.-Fri., 8am-8pm Sat.-Sun., vendor hours may vary

United States Air Force Memorial

You can't miss the three stainless steel spires rising 402 feet into the sky. This memorial is designed to look like the Air Force Thunderbirds, the branch's exhilarating demonstration jets, taking off in the bomb-burst formation. In this case, there are just three jets, instead of four, signifying the Missing Man Formation, used during funerals in honor of the 54,000 airmen and airwomen who died in combat. Four eight-foot bronze statues of members of the Air Force Honor Guard stand near the spires. Two 56-foot-long granite walls name members who have received the Medal of Honor. Completed in 2006, it has a slick, postmodern design by James Ingo Freed, a contemporary of I. M. Pei. In the summer, the Air Force Bands perform free concerts at the memorial.

MAP 9: 1 Air Force Memorial Dr., Arlington, Virginia, 703/462-4093, www.airforcememorial.org; 9am-9pm daily Apr.-Sept., 8am-8pm daily Oct.-Mar.; free

United States Marine Corps War Memorial

Known simply as "Iwo Jima," the United States Marine Corps War Memorial is a monument to the Marines who have died in battle since 1775, though it depicts one iconic day in history: February 23, 1945. The staggering memorial is a bronze replica of the Pulitzer Prize-winning photograph of six U.S. Marines raising the second American flag on Mount Suribachi on Iwo Jima, Japan's island base for kamikaze attacks, which the United States had seized. Taken by the Associated Press's Joe Rosenthal, the photograph became one of the defining images of World War II—depicting the obscenely bloody battle in which more than 6,800 Americans and 23,000 Japanese died, including three of the soldiers pictured.

The American flag has flown at the memorial every single day since the dedication by President Dwight D. Eisenhower in 1954. Visit during the summer to see one of the sunset parades, featuring the United States Marine Drum and Bugle Corps.

MAP 9: 1 U.S. Marine Memorial Circle, Arlington, Virginia, 703/289-2500, www.nps.gov/gwmp; 6am-midnight daily; free

Washington National Cathedral

During times of war, terror, and strife in the United States, Northwest's Washington National Cathedral has served has a gathering place for people of all faiths. And the cathedral's walls have witnessed quite a bit of consequential history since President William McKinley attended the first service in 1898—perhaps most notably, Reverend Dr. Martin Luther King Jr.'s last Sunday sermon on March 31, 1968, days before he was assassinated. Inside, 215 stained-glass windows mix with statues of historical figures, including Dr. King and past U.S. presidents; on the outside, more than 1,000 gargoyles and grotesques keep watch, including some original to the building and others added later, like

Washington National Cathedral

the Darth Vader gargoyle, added to the northwest tower on the "dark side" of the building in 1980. Tours of the highlights inside the cathedral are included with the price of admission; behind-the-scenes tours, gargoyle tours, and climbs up the 333-step Central Tower to see one of the highest views in the city are available for an additional fee. On Sundays, the cathedral holds worship services open to all, regardless of faith, with free admission.

MAP 9: 3101 Wisconsin Ave. NW, 202/537-6200, www.cathedral.org; 10am-5pm Mon.-Fri., 10am-4pm Sat., 8am-4pm Sun.; admission and highlights tour $12 adults, $8 children 5-17, students and teachers with ID, seniors, active military, and veterans, free for children under 5, free on Sun.

RESTAURANTS

National Mall 107
Downtown and Penn Quarter 109
Capitol Hill and Atlas District 114
Dupont Circle 119
U Street, Shaw, and Logan Circle 122
Adams Morgan 128
Georgetown and Foggy Bottom 132
Navy Yard and Anacostia 134
Greater Washington DC 136

Washington DC once was a city where steakhouses were the only options for a nice meal out—and where lunch was more about who you schmoozed with than the food. In recent years, however, it's emerged as a culinary capital with something for every palate and budget, from filets and Chesapeake Bay crab cakes in old-school dining rooms, to innovative fusion cuisine and extravagant tasting menus by celebrity and rising-star chefs, to authentic fare from Ethiopia, Afghanistan, and the Philippines, to American Southern and soul food traditions. And with new restaurants opening practically every week and recognition by Michelin Guides and *Bon Appétit*, it's clear people are now moving to DC to open restaurants, not just to regulate them.

Old Ebbitt Grill

So, what's good? Around the White House and U.S. Capitol, you'll find steakhouses, oyster bars, and other buzzy spots teeming with power players.

U Street and Shaw are home to the essential Washington flavors—half-smokes at Ben's Chili Bowl, soul food, Ethiopian—as well as hip eateries favored by 20- and 30-somethings with disposable income to drop on creative small plates and strong cocktails. And foodies looking for something new will have much to explore, from José Andrés' empire in Penn Quarter, to the international flavors in Adams Morgan and Columbia Heights, where you can taste how DC is a global melting pot.

105

HIGHLIGHTS

✪ **BEST MUSEUM CAFÉ: Mitsitam Native Foods Café** at the National Museum of the American Indian serves native foods from throughout the Western Hemisphere (page 107).

✪ **FIT FOR FANCY FRANCOPHILES: Mirabelle** raises the bar for fine French dining (page 110).

✪ **BEST CHEF:** Of José Andrés's many DC restaurants, **Jaleo** is the best choice for excellent tapas in an energetic environment (page 112).

✪ **BEST SEASONAL MENU: Garrison** serves seasonally changing dishes made with local, farm-fresh ingredients (page 114).

✪ **BEST PLACE TO SPOT A SENATOR:** You're likely to see members of Congress enjoying steak and American wine at **Charlie Palmer Steak** (page 115).

✪ **BEST LATE-NIGHT DINING:** It's a tie: The half-price raw bar from 10pm to midnight at **Hank's Oyster Bar** can't be beat, but **The Diner** serves the latest—24 hours a day, in fact (pages 119 and 128).

✪ **BEST BREAKFAST ON THE GO:** Line up with the locals at **Bagels Etc.,** then take your food along as you explore Dupont Circle (page 121).

✪ **ESSENTIAL LOCAL FLAVOR:** Your trip to Washington isn't complete without a late-night half-smoke at **Ben's Chili Bowl** (page 122).

✪ **BEST ETHIOPIAN:** Ask anyone who loves Ethiopian food where to go and they'll tell you **Dukem Ethiopian Restaurant** (page 125).

✪ **HUB FOR ACTIVISTS: Busboys and Poets** has responsible, affordable American food and a history of activism (page 127).

✪ **BEST CRAB CAKE:** The Maryland-style crab cake at **Johnny's Half Shell** has long been the city's best (page 128).

✪ **MOST ROMANTIC:** Take your date to the sexy **Fiola Mare** for superb seafood on the waterfront, or **Masseria** at Union Market, to experience the Michelin-starred menu in the starry courtyard (pages 133 and 137).

✪ **BEST WAY TO DINE WITH DC'S ELITE: Cafe Milano** is the place to see and be seen, serving Italian fare to cabinet secretaries, ambassadors, and socialites (page 133).

PRICE KEY

$	Entrées less than $15
$ $	Entrées $15-25
$ $ $	Entrées more than $25

NATIVE AMERICAN

✪ Mitsitam Native Foods Café $$

Meaning "let's eat!" in the Delaware and Piscataway native language, Mitsitam at the National Museum of the American Indian is the best of DC's museum cafés and a good choice for lunch on the National Mall—which has few dining options, and even fewer healthy ones. The cafeteria-style restaurant serves seasonal native foods from across the Western Hemisphere, such as buffalo burgers and chili on fry bread from the Great Plains, pork *pibil* tacos from Mesoamerica, and salmon from the Northwest Coast, as well as soups and healthy veggie options. Beverage options include beer, wine, and Mexican Coca-Cola, and the espresso bar (10am-5pm daily) around the corner serves coffee roasted by native peoples, as well as Mexican hot chocolate and snacks. **MAP 1:** National Museum of the American Indian, 4th St. SW and Independence Ave. SW, 202/633-6644, www.mitsitamcafe. com; 11am-5pm Memorial Day-Labor Day, 11am-3pm daily early Sept.-late May

SOUTHERN AND SOUL FOOD

Sweet Home Café $

Nominated for the James Beard Best New Restaurant in 2017, Sweet Home Café at the National Museum of African American History and Culture is worth waiting in the long lunch line for if you're already inside the museum. Executive chef Jerome

Try the pork pibil tacos at Mitsitam Native Foods Café.

Grant prepares African American recipes from across the country, including tasty Southern and creole standards like shrimp and Anson Mills grits, and some of the best fried chicken in DC. But try something new, like the oyster pan roast inspired by Thomas Downing, a free African American who owned a famous oyster house in New York City and helped slaves traveling the Underground Railroad.

MAP 1: National Museum of African American History and Culture, 1400 Constitution Ave. NW, 844/750-3012, http://nmaahc.si.edu; 10am-5pm daily

CAFÉS AND LIGHT BITES

Cascade Café $

Among the National Mall's limited options, you'll find the most choice at Cascade Café, the elegant food court at the National Gallery of Art's East Building. Set by the magnificent cascading waterfall, stations include reasonably priced sandwiches and pizzas, hot entrées, a salad bar, and free-range chicken and sides, plus coffee, pastries, and beer and wine.

MAP 1: National Gallery of Art East Building, 4th St. NW and Constitution Ave. NW, 202/842-6679, www.nga.gov; 11am-3pm Mon.-Sat., 11am-4pm Sun.

Garden Café $$

Dine in the marble halls of the National Gallery of Art's West Building at Garden Café, the only table-service restaurant in a Smithsonian museum. Nestled among the exhibits, it's a lovely spot for a lunch or brunch date. Start with a glass of brut then share a cheese plate and French pastries, or indulge in the weekend brunch buffet. Reservations are recommended for groups of four or more.

MAP 1: National Gallery of Art West Building, 6th St. NW and Constitution Ave. NW, 202/842-6716, www.nga.gov; 11:30am-3pm Mon.-Sat., noon-4pm Sun.

Pavilion Café $

Grab a bite at Pavilion Café, which offers indoor and outdoor seating in the National Gallery of Art's Sculpture Garden. The menu features seasonal sandwiches, salads, soups, and pizzas, as well as coffee, pastries, beer, and wine. During Jazz in the Garden, held Friday evenings in the summer, the café serves hors d'oeuvres and grilled sausages as well as sangria and beer by the glass or pitcher. During the winter, later hours accommodate skaters at the ice rink.

MAP 1: National Gallery of Art Sculpture Garden, 7th St. NW and Constitution Ave. NW, 202/289-3361, www.pavilioncafe.com; 10am-4pm Mon.-Sat., 11am-5pm Sun. mid-Mar.-Memorial Day; 10am-6pm Mon.-Thurs., 10am-8:30pm Fri., 10am-6pm Sat., 11am-6pm Sun. Memorial Day-Labor Day; 10am-4pm Mon.-Sat., 11am-5pm Sun. Labor Day-mid-Nov.; 10am-7pm Mon.-Thurs., 10am-9pm Fri.-Sat., 11am-7pm Sun. mid-Nov.-mid-Mar.

NEW AMERICAN

minibar by José Andrés $$$

This avant-garde restaurant has two Michelin stars and serves 20-plus courses of whimsical dishes that look like science experiments, in which unconventional cooking techniques, tools, and ingredients (like foam and liquid nitrogen) are employed. To reserve one of the 12 counter seats or the chef's table, purchase tickets on the website two months in advance. There are two seatings available each night, with arrival times preset at 5:45pm, 6:15pm, 8:15pm, and 8:45pm. A counter seat costs $275 per person (not including beverages), while the chef's table for six is $565 per person. Next door, barmini (202/393-4451) is billed as a cocktail lab where you can enjoy a similarly creative take on cocktail flights ($75 pp) as well as an à la carte menu ($15 deposit pp) of cocktails, beer, wine, and snacks. Reservations for the bar are strongly recommended but not always required.

MAP 2: 855 E St. NW, 202/393-0812, www.minibarbyjoseandres.com; 5:45pm-1am Tues.-Sat.

Woodward Table $$

Jeffrey Buben, who won a James Beard Award in 1999, has cooked contemporary American fare at DC-area restaurants since the early 1990s. Woodward Table, his current restaurant, showcases seasonal, regional ingredients for breakfast, lunch, dinner, and weekend brunch in a casually refined space with a big bar and patio. Portions are large; two could share a starter (like the house-made charcuterie) and the delicious pork chop with pimento cheese grits.

MAP 2: 1426 H St. NW, 202/347-5353, www.woodwardtable.com; 11:30am-10:30pm Mon.-Fri., 11am-10:30pm Sat.-Sun.

STEAK AND SEAFOOD

BLT Steak $$$

While you have many options for steak downtown, BLT Steak is one of the best for atmosphere and food. The modern dining room and long bar are dark but inviting, and buzzy but not too loud. Make a reservation for lunch or dinner and enjoy perfectly cooked high-quality steaks, served sizzling on individual cast-iron skillets, or specials like American Wagyu and raw bar items.

MAP 2: 1625 I St. NW, 202/689-8999, www.bltrestaurants.com/blt-steak; 11:30am-2:30pm and 5:30pm-10:30pm Mon.-Thurs., 11:30am-2:30pm and 5:30pm-11pm Fri., 5:30pm-11pm Sat.

Joe's Seafood, Prime Steak & Stone Crab $$$

Whether you're wining and dining a client or a date, you can't go wrong with the DC outpost of this South Beach institution, where you can feel power pulsing through the shiny marble floors. Have an important conversation in one of the plush booths in the dining room—where you may very well spot a diplomat or hot-shot lobbyist—or flirt over champagne and a slice of house-made pie at the high-ceilinged bar. Either way, the service and the seafood will be impeccable.

MAP 2: 750 15th St. NW, 202/489-0140, www.joes.net/dc; 11:30am-11pm Mon.-Thurs., 11:30am-midnight Fri.-Sat., 11:30am-10pm Sun.

CLASSIC AMERICAN
Crimson $

Whether you want an early breakfast before sightseeing or late-night bites after an event at the Capital One Arena, this smart diner and coffee bar specializes in Southern fare, serving breakfast all day (with every entrée under $15), as well as burgers, salads, and dinner plates like shrimp and grits. Crimson also houses a spacious no-reservations whiskey bar and a no-reservations rooftop bar, which provides monument views and cocktails sans elevated price tag.

MAP 2: Pod DC, 627 H St. NW, 202/847-4459, www.crimson-dc.com; 7am-midnight Mon.-Thurs., 7am-1am Fri.-Sat., 7am-midnight Sun.

PUBS
Old Ebbitt Grill $$

In 1856, innkeeper William Ebbitt founded a boarding house and saloon in the neighborhood, a favorite of Teddy Roosevelt and Ulysses S. Grant. While the saloon closed in the early 20th century, this restaurant honors the original, with mahogany wood and Victorian-style decor, as well as a few antiques salvaged from the Ebbitt of yore. Steps from the White House, it's beloved by federal employees and lobbyists, who fill the booths day and night for reliable sandwiches, salads, steaks, and snacks. The expansive menu will please the pickiest eaters, though locals will tell you to order the Orca Platter, the seafood tower with dozens of oysters, clams, shrimp, and crab, plus a whole lobster.

MAP 2: 675 15th St. NW, 202/347-4800, www.ebbitt.com; 7:30am-1am Mon.-Fri., 8:30am-1am Sat.-Sun.

Harry's $

In the heart of downtown, Harry's is a reliable spot for late-night grub like buffalo wings, sandwiches, and really good burgers. The slightly grungy pub is located in the Hotel Harrington, a historic spot that's seen better days, but it's easy on the wallet.

MAP 2: 436 11th St. NW, 202/624-0053, www.harryssaloon.com; 11am-2am Sun.-Thurs., 11am-3am Fri.-Sat.

FRENCH
✪ Mirabelle $$$

Mirabelle has raised the bar for fine dining in DC. Helmed by Frank Ruta, who worked as a White House chef for three presidents, the glamorous restaurant's French cuisine is very good but unpretentious—food you actually want to eat, like a perfect strip loin with potatoes, fresh seafood, and caviar. Here, many wines come by the glass. It's pricey—the talked-about Belleburger (lunch only), topped with onions and gruyère, is $28, while dinner entrées run $40 and up—but worth it for a special date in one of the half-moon leather booths.

MAP 2: 900 16th St. NW, 202/506-3833, www.mirabelledc.com; 11:30am-2pm and 5:30pm-9:30pm Mon.-Fri., 5:30pm-10pm Sat., 5:30pm-9pm Sun.

DBGB Kitchen & Bar $$$

After cooking his acclaimed Lyonnaise cuisine around the world, famed French chef Daniel Boulud opened this restaurant in CityCenterDC in 2014. Standouts at this modern, boisterous bistro include house-made pâté and sausages, juicy burgers, and the famous coq au vin, which really is as good as you've heard. Don't skip dessert: The baked Alaska will please a celebratory crowd, and the melt-in-your-mouth raspberry soufflé is the stuff of dreams.

MAP 2: 931 H St. NW, 202/695-7660, www.dbgb.com/dc; 11:30am-10pm Mon.-Thurs., 11:30am-11pm Fri., 11am-11pm Sat., 11am-10pm Sun.

INDIAN
The Bombay Club $$$

The preeminent Indian restaurant in DC, The Bombay Club has served distinguished Indian cuisine to politicians, celebrities, and epicures since 1988. It's classic fine dining: white tablecloths, impeccable service, and live piano music during dinner. Enjoy recipes by Nilesh Singhvi from across India, including Mumbai, Goa, and the southern coast, for lunch, dinner, and Sunday brunch. Singhvi was the top chef at several five-star hotels in India and Nepal before coming to DC.

MAP 2: 815 Connecticut Ave. NW, 202/659-3727, www.bombayclubdc.com; 11:30am-2:30pm and 5:30pm-10:30pm Mon.-Thurs., 11:30am-2:30pm and 5:30pm-11pm Fri., 5:30pm-11pm Sat., 11:30am-2:30pm and 5:30pm-9:30pm Sun.

ITALIAN
Centrolina $$$

Escape the hustle and bustle for superb house-made pasta in this cozy but posh restaurant. Start with a Negroni or Aperol spritz, then enjoy James Beard nominee Amy Brandwein's cooking: slurpy *tagliolini* (ribbon pasta), light and buttery chicken tortelloni, or wood-fired meats and fish. It's connected to a market (8am-9pm daily) where you can grab breakfast at the small counter and purchase fresh pasta and sauce, local produce, and Italian goodies.

Mirabelle

MAP 2: 974 Palmer Alley, 202/898-2426, www.centrolinadc.com; 11:30am-2:30pm and 5pm-10pm Mon.-Thurs., 11:30am-2:30pm and 5pm-midnight Fri., 5pm-midnight Sat., 10:30am-2:30pm and 5pm-10pm Sun.

MEDITERRANEAN
Zaytinya $$

José Andrés is behind this bustling meze restaurant, which provides a trip around the Mediterranean via small plates. Many of the dishes—hummus with ground lamb, *shish taouk* (marinated chicken shish kebab), and spanakopita—are made in the classic style, though there are often unique specials on offer, especially in the spring, when Greek Easter and the city's cherry blossoms provide inspiration for the menu. The modern dining room has glass windows, high ceilings, and an excruciating din on busy nights; grab a seat at the bar for a more intimate, though still lively, experience.

MAP 2: 701 9th St. NW, 202/638-0800, www.zaytinya.com; 11am-10pm Sun.-Mon., 11am-11pm Tues.-Thurs., 11am-midnight Fri.-Sat.

MEXICAN
Oyamel Cocina Mexicana $$

Another must-try in the José Andrés empire, Oyamel shows off the variety that can be found south of the border with authentic small plates as colorful as the restaurant's cheery decor. Start with guacamole prepared tableside, then try Mexican street food like ceviche and tacos, including the famous sautéed grasshopper taco. The margaritas are good, but a tequila or mezcal tasting is better.

MAP 2: 401 7th St. NW, 202/628-1005, www.oyamel.com; 11am-midnight Sun.-Wed., 11am-2am Thurs.-Sat.

PAN-ASIAN
The Source by Wolfgang Puck $$$

Within sight of the Capitol, Wolfgang Puck's Asian fusion restaurant located in the Newseum is pricey, but satisfying. Celebrate something special in the sleek dining room with the whole roasted duck for two—or if you're lucky enough to get invited to a glitzy party in the museum, drop by the bar afterward for spicy tuna ice cream cones and a variety of dumplings.

MAP 2: 575 Pennsylvania Ave. NW, 202/637-6100, www.wolfgangpuck.com; 11:30am-10pm Tues.-Thurs., 11:30am-11pm Fri.-Sat.

SPANISH
✪ Jaleo $$

This tapas restaurant made José Andrés a culinary hero when he became the first chef to import prized *jamón ibérico* (Iberian ham), made from the black-footed pigs of Spain, to the United States. And while new restaurants open in DC practically every week, the veteran Jaleo holds up. The *jamón* is a must, especially with tangy Manchego cheese and *pan con tomate* (grilled bread with tomato), as well as sautéed shrimp, spicy *patatas bravas* (fried potatoes), and *piquillo* peppers bursting with goat cheese. The sangrias and Spanish wines are noteworthy, but the tapas are best paired with a gin and tonic like you'd get on the coast in Spain. This colorful, energetic restaurant is good for groups who aren't afraid to share dishes. If you come with kids, try to get one of the glass-topped foosball tables.

MAP 2: 480 7th St. NW, 202/628-7949, www.jaleo.com; 11am-10pm Mon., 11am-11pm Tues.-Thurs., 11am-midnight Fri., 10am-midnight Sat., 10am-10pm Sun.

VEGETARIAN AND VEGAN

Elizabeth's Gone Raw $$$

Elizabeth's Gone Raw proves raw vegan dining can be bold, flavorful, and filling. Founded by Elizabeth Petty, who turned to a raw vegan diet when she was diagnosed with breast cancer, the restaurant serves a seven-course plant-based tasting menu ($75 pp, wine pairing additional $55 pp) featuring raw, vegan variations on pasta, ice cream, and even meat and shellfish made entirely with gluten-free, dairy-free, and seasonal ingredients. The townhouse-style restaurant is open Friday nights only—it's a catering company and private-event venue the rest of the week—but you can usually get a reservation a week in advance.

MAP 2: 1341 L St. NW, 202/347-8349, www.elizabethsgoneraw.com; reservations 5pm-9pm Fri.

Fruitive $

Trying to eat healthier? Try Fruitive, the CityCenterDC storefront serving organic, plant-based breakfast and lunch. Think super-grain bowls and wraps, avocado toast, and an avocado cucumber sandwich with greens and a sprinkling of sea salt, as satisfying as it is clean. For something light on the go, try a "liquid meal" or bottled juice; the restaurant also serves espresso drinks. Plan to grab and go, or eat at one of the handful of indoor counter seats or outdoor tables.

MAP 2: 1094 Palmer Alley NW, 202/836-7749, www.fruitive.com; 7am-8pm Mon.-Fri., 9am-7pm Sat.-Sun.

BREAKFAST AND BRUNCH

Astro Doughnuts and Fried Chicken $

This fast-casual restaurant founded by two native Washingtonians who

Jaleo

played for the Washington Capitals serves affordable comfort food close to the major sights. You don't have to choose between crispy fried chicken or a fresh-baked doughnut—just get your fried chicken sandwich on a savory doughnut. But save room: Many foodies consider the crème brûlée doughnut one of the best sweet treats in the city.
MAP 2: 1308 G St. NW, 202/809-5565, www.astrodoughnuts.com; 7:30am-5:30pm Mon.-Fri., 9am-5pm Sat., 9am-3pm Sun.

BAKERIES
RareSweets $
It's always throwback Thursday at RareSweets, where French Culinary Institute-trained Meredith Tomason bakes treats from her family recipes and historical American cookbooks, made with seasonal, farm-fresh ingredients. The bakery is known for beautiful cakes—like a perfectly simple yellow cake with chocolate sour cream frosting, or classic carrot cake in the fall—as well as ice cream, sweet and savory pastries, and an irresistible chewy lemon cookie. Take a shopping break with a slice of cake and La Colombe coffee at one of the sidewalk tables.
MAP 2: 963 Palmer Alley NW, 202/499-0077, www.raresweets.com; 7am-7pm Mon.-Thurs., 7am-8pm Fri., 9am-8pm Sat., 9am-5pm Sun.

Capitol Hill and Atlas District   Map 3

NEW AMERICAN
✪ Garrison $$$
Garrison has earned well-deserved praise for seasonal and simple—yet never boring—cuisine. Chef Rob Weland cooked at a few beloved restaurants before opening his own on Barracks Row, a cozy, candlelit spot where you can actually hear your date swoon over the exquisite meal. The menu changes seasonally and features local meat and seafood as well as an abundance of farm-fresh vegetables; a typical dinner might include Atlantic porgy, Gilfeather turnip, and a delightful strawberry, fava bean, and goat cheese salad.
MAP 3: 524 8th St. SE, 202/506-2445, www.garrisondc.com; 5pm-10pm Tues.-Thurs., 5pm-11pm Fri., 11am-2:30pm and 5pm-11pm Sat., 11am-2:30pm and 5pm-10pm Sun.

Pineapple and Pearls $$$
Critics have bestowed many accolades upon this fine-dining establishment by Aaron Silverman. It's one of three regional restaurants to earn two stars from Michelin in 2016. The $325 per head, 13-course tasting menu and beverage pairing is served in the understated dining room, or you can dine at the bar for $225 per person (beverages not included). The coveted reservations are released Monday mornings online, four weeks in advance. The restaurant offers two seatings per night, one at 5pm and the second at 8pm.
MAP 3: 715 8th St. SE, 202/595-7375, www.pineappleandpearls.com; 5pm-9:30pm Tues.-Fri., plus select Sat. Nov.-Dec.

Rose's Luxury $$$
It's tough to get a table at the no-reservations Rose's Luxury, an Aaron

Silverman Michelin-starred restaurant that's credited with making DC a dining destination. However, the casual but creative American cuisine is worth the inevitable wait in line to put your name on the list; get in line early and/or on a weekday to guarantee a table. Dine with fellow foodies and order several plates to share, including at least one pasta.

MAP 3: 717 8th St. SE, 202/580-8889, www.rosesluxury.com; 5pm-10pm Mon.-Sat.

STEAK AND SEAFOOD
✪ Charlie Palmer Steak $$$

Want to dine like the movers and shakers of Capitol Hill? Head to this white-tablecloth restaurant just a few blocks from the Capitol. The elegant dining room is packed with lobbyists who lunch on USDA-certified Angus steaks and local seafood—and you'll likely spot a member of Congress or two, as well. Whatever your politics, you can't go wrong when choosing the wine, because every bottle on the extensive list is American.

Charlie Palmer Steak

MAP 3: 101 Constitution Ave. NW, 202/547-8100, www.charliepalmer.com; 11:30am-10pm Mon.-Fri., 5pm-10:30pm Sat.

CLASSIC AMERICAN
Good Stuff Eatery $

Don't feel guilty giving in to your burger craving. Spike Mendelsohn, of the fourth season of Bravo's *Top Chef*, along with his restaurateur family, founded this fast-casual chain committed to supporting local farms. Sink your teeth into the best burgers in DC—like the Prez Obama Burger (farm-raised beef topped with Roquefort and bacon) or the Michelle Melt (made with free-range turkey)—as well as hand-cut fries and a toasted marshmallow shake that tastes like the real thing. Get your fix at the Capitol Hill flagship or in Georgetown (3291 M St. NW, 202/337-4663).

MAP 3: 303 Pennsylvania Ave. SE, 202/543-8222, www.goodstuffeatery.com; 11am-10pm Mon.-Sat.

BALKAN
Ambar $$

Think you've tried every international flavor in DC? Ambar offers something unique: authentic Balkan cuisine, with a focus on simply prepared but high-quality meats and vegetables. (It really is authentic; the sister restaurant is in Belgrade, Serbia.) Choose from dozens of small plates, including charcuterie and cheeses, spreads and flatbreads, and grilled meat and seafood—or try them all with unlimited small plates and house cocktails for $49 per person during dinner or $39 per person during brunch. The beverage list features wines from Armenia, Croatia, Macedonia, and Slovenia, among others, plus cocktails and flights using *rakia*, a fruit brandy popular in Eastern Europe.

MAP 3: 523 8th St. SE, 202/813-3039, www.ambarrestaurant.com; 11am-2pm and 4pm-10pm Mon.-Thurs., 11am-2pm and 4pm-11pm Fri., 10am-3:30pm and 4:30pm-11pm Sat., 10am-3:30pm and 4:30pm-10pm Sun.

BELGIAN
Granville Moore's $$

Grab a stool at the wooden bar and enjoy Belgian fare and beers in a casual environment before a night out at the nearby bars of the H Street Corridor. Granville Moore's has been a destination for some of the best mussels in DC since 2007, even before H Street became a nightlife destination. Whether you go for classic mussels *marinière* (with white wine, garlic, and herbs) or something more adventurous, like mussels with blue cheese and pork belly, don't skip the *frites* (fries). Tip: Come on a Monday, when the mussels are only $12 (regularly $19).

MAP 3: 1238 H St. NE, 202/399-2546, www.granvillemoores.com; 5pm-10pm Mon.-Thurs., 5pm-11pm Fri., 11am-11pm Sat., 11am-10pm Sun., bar open until midnight Sun.-Thurs., until 1am Fri.-Sat.

ETHIOPIAN
Ethiopic $$

The H Street Corridor has not traditionally been a destination for Ethiopian cuisine, but Ethiopic ably competes with the restaurants in Shaw's Little Ethiopia by offering classic cooking with an elegant ambience more suitable for fine dining. Named for the group of languages spoken in Ethiopia and Eritrea, the restaurant is known for the superb quality of meat used in the *tibs* (sautéed meat, usually beef or lamb) and *kitfo* (spicy minced beef usually served raw), as well as

their selection of Ethiopian beers and wines.

MAP 3: 401 H St. NE, 202/675-2066, www.ethiopicrestaurant.com; 5pm-10pm Tues.-Thurs., noon-10pm Fri.-Sun.

ITALIAN
Acqua Al 2 $$$

Ask any Hill rat, including House Minority Leader Nancy Pelosi, where to find the best Italian food in DC, and they'll point you to this cozy, brick-walled Eastern Market eatery inspired by a restaurant in Florence of the same name. (Yes, there's a chance you'll see Pelosi when you visit.) Can't decide between rigatoni or a perfectly cooked strip steak with arugula? Go with a group and try a few *assaggios*, chef's tastings of 3-5 salads, pastas, steaks, or desserts, to sample the best of the menu.

MAP 3: 212 7th St. SE, 202/525-4375, www.acquaal2.com; 5:30pm-10:30pm Mon., 11:30am-2:30pm and 5:30pm-10:30pm Tues.-Thurs., 11:30am-2:30pm and 5:30pm-11:30pm Fri.-Sat., 11:30am-2:30pm and 5:30pm-10:30pm Sun.

JAPANESE
Sushi Capitol $$$

Located a few blocks from the Capitol, Sushi Capitol is tiny, but it's no hole-in-the-wall. You'll find your favorite *maki, nigiri,* and tempura on the menu, but you'd be wise to let the chefs choose for you. At $50 per person, the *omakase* (chef's choice) is a steal given the quality, quantity, and variety of fish. Chef Minoru Ogawa learned the art of sushi from his master-chef father in Tokyo. Call in advance for a reservation.

MAP 3: 325 Pennsylvania Ave. SE, 202/627-0325, www.sushicapitol.com; noon-2:30pm and 5pm-9:30pm Mon.-Fri., 5pm-9:30pm Sat.

BEST BUDGET EATS

Food trucks line Farragut Square on weekdays.

Washington has the third-highest cost of living in the United States—and it's getting more and more expensive to dine out, as Michelin-starred tasting menus can top $150 per person and $15 cocktails are the norm. However, it's possible to enjoy DC's culinary scene on a budget, without sacrificing flavor or a local experience.

Some of DC's most famous flavors are among the best budget eats. **Ben's Chili Bowl** (page 122) is a late-night must, but you can go anytime for the $6 half-smoke (spicy half-pork/half-beef sausage) with chili, $7.50 salad bowl, and cheap, hearty breakfasts. Mount Pleasant is known for Salvadoran cuisine, and **Pupuseria San Miguel** (page 130) will leave you stuffed for under $15 per person. For something lighter, José Andrés's local chain **Beefsteak** (page 121) serves veggie bowls under $10, plus the beefsteak tomato "burger" for $5.

For a higher-end but still budget-friendly option, **Busboys and Poets** (page 127) serves clean, sustainable meals in several locations, with sandwiches and salads ranging $10-15, less for breakfast. A burger, fries, and shake at **Good Stuff Eatery** (page 115) will set you back $15-20, but you won't be hungry for a while. Pizzas start at $9 at **2 Amys** (page 138). If you want a crab cake, head to **Market Lunch** (page 118), the Eastern Market counter where the $16 platter comes with two sides.

When sightseeing, **food trucks** are some of your best options for a reasonably priced gourmet lunch. You'll find the largest gatherings of trucks around the major museums daily, as well Farragut Square, L'Enfant Plaza, and Union Station. For the truck list and daily map, visit www.foodtruckfiesta.com.

PAN-ASIAN
Maketto $$

Maketto—part restaurant, part café, and part store—is the cool kid on H Street NE, with clean, minimalist spaces and lots of natural light. The ground floor restaurant serves Cambodian and Taiwanese fare—noodle soups, rice bowls, pork *bao* (stuffed buns), and fried chicken—for lunch and dinner, as well as Sunday dim sum brunch. Upstairs, the naturally lit café buzzes morning to evening with locals on their laptops, enjoying Vigilante Coffee, snacks, and the much-Instagrammed matcha latte, served in a picture-perfect ceramic bowl. Before you leave, browse an edited selection of streetwear and accessories from labels like Comme des Garçons and Adidas designer collaborations at the retail shop by the entrance.

MAP 3: 1351 H St. NE, 202/627-0325, www.maketto1351.com; 11:30am-2:30pm and

5pm-10pm Mon.-Thurs., 11:30am-2:30pm and 5pm-midnight Fri.-Sat., 11:30am-3pm Sun.

BREAKFAST AND BRUNCH

Bullfrog Bagels $

The house-baked bagels and bialys at Bullfrog Bagels are slightly pricier than your average bagel shop, starting at $3 for one with plain cream cheese and going up to $8-plus for house-smoked salmon or Baltimore-style beef brisket. But, the ingredients are fresh and the sandwiches are filling fuel for a day browsing the nearby Eastern Market artisans. The tiny shop has a line on weekends, but it moves quickly; there's plenty of seating upstairs, including a few chairs on the sunny balcony overlooking the market. There's another location nearby on H Street NE.

MAP 3: 317 7th St. SE, 202/494-5615, www.bullfrogbagels.com; 7am-2pm Mon.-Fri., 8am-3pm Sat.-Sun.

Market Lunch $

Since 1979, this Eastern Market counter-service vendor has been serving some of the best crab cakes in DC—along with breakfast plates and Benedicts, burgers, and yummy blueberry buckwheat pancakes, all prepared with locally sourced ingredients. Make sure you have money before you get in the long, snaking line during Sunday brunch hours, because it's cash only. Enjoy your food at the communal table (if you don't mind dining surrounded by people waiting in line) or take it

to one of the tables in the market's North Hall.

MAP 3: 225 7th St. SE, 202/547-8444, www.marketlunchdc.com; 7:30am-2:30pm Tues.-Fri., 8am-3pm Sat., 9am-3pm Sun.; cash only

Pete's Diner $

An easy walk from the sights on Capitol Hill and the National Mall, Pete's is perhaps the most authentic diner in the District. Former Speaker of the House John Boehner visited almost every morning for eggs and sausage served by the friendly staff; Hill staffers and residents continue to fill the counter and booths for cheap breakfast platters and pancakes, as well as grilled cheese, patty melts, and simple salads at lunch. Skip your usual Starbucks; Pete's has great coffee, too.

MAP 3: 212 2nd St. SE, 202/544-7335; 6am-3pm Mon.-Fri., 7am-3pm Sat.-Sun.

PIZZA

We, the Pizza $

Whether you order by the slice or whole pie, your purchase at this fast-casual pizza joint helmed by *Top Chef*'s Spike Mendelsohn supports community organizations that provide nutritional and educational services to local families. You can't go wrong with cheese or pepperoni, but For The Greek In Us, cooked Sicilian-style in a cast-iron skillet and topped with feta and veggies, is a fresh alternative. Pair your pie with a homemade soda or $5 beer.

MAP 3: 305 Pennsylvania Ave. SE, 202/544-4008, www.wethepizza.com; 11am-11pm daily

STEAK AND SEAFOOD
The Palm $$$

The Palm is the place to be seen at lunch, especially for the politicos, journalists, and talking heads whose caricatures are painted on the walls. And you'll spot many who go nearly every day for the consistent seafood cocktails, steak salads, and burgers, along with the latest gossip in the bustling dining room.

MAP 4: 1225 19th St. NW, 202/293-9091, www.thepalm.com; 11:30am-10pm Mon.-Thurs., 11:30am-10:30pm Fri., 5:30pm-10:30pm Sat., 5pm-9pm Sun.

✪ Hank's Oyster Bar $$

For more than a decade, Dupont Circle residents have been frequenting this neighborhood spot for market-fresh seafood, comfort-food suppers, and excellent cocktails. The brunch is particularly good, especially the shrimp and grits on the sunny patio, but the best time to go is 10pm-midnight, when the raw bar is half off. If you're visiting the Capitol, you'll find a similar menu at Hank's on the Hill (633 Pennsylvania Ave. SE, 202/733-1971, 11:30am-11pm Mon.-Thurs., 11:30am-midnight Fri., 11am-midnight Sat., 11am-10pm Sun.).

MAP 4: 1624 Q St. NW, 202/462-4865, www.hanksoysterbar.com; 11:30am-1am Mon.-Tues., 11:30am-2am Wed.-Fri., 11am-2am Sat., 11am-1am Sun.

CLASSIC AMERICAN
Tabard Inn $$$

Tucked inside Dupont Circle's charming Tabard Inn is an equally charming restaurant serving cuisine that's anything but standard hotel fare. It's a good bet any time of day but most satisfying at lunch, when you can enjoy sandwiches, salads, and excellent pork shoulder tacos on the idyllic hidden patio away from the crowded dining room. The famous brunch books up weeks in advance, and while it can feel a bit rushed during the prime Sunday hours, the cinnamon sugar donuts are worth it.

MAP 4: 1739 N St. NW, 202/785-1277, www.tabardinn.com; 7am-9:30pm Sun.-Wed., 7am-10pm Thurs.-Sat.

Afterwords Café $$

It's the quintessential DC first date: Shop for the latest news-making political tome in Kramerbooks, then pop into this adjoining café and bar. The menu features hearty classics: chicken pot pie, crab cakes served several ways, and mac-and-cheese. And the literary cocktails will spark conversation as you decide whether you're more The Gin Gatsby or Lord of the Pimms. Don't worry if you get lost in the aisles for hours; the café serves food and drinks late every night of the week.

MAP 4: 1517 Connecticut Ave. NW, 202/387-3825, www.kramers.com/cafe; 7:30am-1am Sun.-Thurs., 7:30am-3am Fri.-Sat.

The Riggsby $$

From the outside, The Riggsby at The Carlyle looks like an unassuming hotel restaurant, but inside, it's a gem. The elegant dining room and inviting bar make it feel more like a private club, where you can enjoy James Beard winner Michael Schlow's supper club favorites, like deviled eggs, classic Caesar salad, and lobster fra diavolo.

The avocado toast with crab—available during lunch, brunch, and the well-priced happy hour—is simple perfection, as are the classic cocktails, served in vintage-style Nick and Nora glasses.

MAP 4: 1731 New Hampshire Ave. NW, 202/787-1500, www.theriggsby.com; 7:30am-10:30pm Mon.-Fri., 8am-10:30pm Sat.-Sun.

FRENCH
Bistrot du Coin $$

The District is home to several flashy bistros, but Bistrot du Coin is one of the most authentic—albeit with friendlier service than you'll find on the Champs-Élysées. You can't go wrong with le steak maison (steak served with fries and Béarnaise sauce), but the large menu is full of bistro standards like salade Niçoise, boeuf bourguignon (beef stew in red wine sauce), cassoulet, and gooey tartines (open-faced sandwiches). Grab a big round table with your friends after happy hour—they're open late and don't mind noise.

MAP 4: 1738 Connecticut Ave. NW, 202/234-6969, www.bistrotducoin. com; 11:30am-midnight Mon.-Wed., 11:30am-1am Thurs.-Fri., noon-1am Sat., noon-midnight Sun.

SOUTHERN AND SOUL FOOD
Henry's Soul Café $

Henry's Soul Café has been baking the best sweet potato pie in the region since 1968. The tiny storefront is best for takeout—there are only a few stools—but you can order ahead online on your way to a picnic in Meridian Hill Park (16th St. and W St. NW). The menu features Southern favorites like lip-smacking barbecue chicken and ribs, as well as traditional soul food recipes like chitterlings,

served with sides and a choice of bread (get the cornbread). Don't forget a slice of the pie.

MAP 4: 1704 U St. NW, 202/265-3336, www.henryssoulcafe.com; 11:30am-8:30pm Tues.-Sat., 11am-5pm Sun.

JAPANESE
Sushi Taro $$$

The only Asian restaurant in DC to earn a Michelin star, and a favorite of Japanese diplomats, Sushi Taro offers the most authentic and pricey omakase (chef's menu) in the region. You can choose one of several tasting dinner experiences; for $155 per person, try suppon, the soft-shell snapping turtle soup believed to have medicinal properties, or for $245 per person, enjoy "surf and turf" with lobster and Wagyu beef. On a budget? The restaurant also offers an à la carte menu—or, go for one of DC's best lunch deals, the $15 bento box.

MAP 4: 1503 17th St. NW, 202/462-8999, www.sushitaro.com; 11:30am-2pm and 5:30pm-10pm Mon.-Fri., 5:30pm-10pm Sat.

MEDITERRANEAN
Komi $$$

If you're celebrating a special occasion during your trip, drop everything now and call Komi. Although Johnny Monis's exquisite Mediterranean cuisine has topped Best Restaurant lists for more than a decade, it remains one of the toughest tables to get. The $150 per person set menu changes regularly, but you can expect about a dozen dishes, including small bites, pasta (typically with seafood), and a hearty Greek-style meat course. The restaurant does not serve cocktails, but the optional $75 wine pairing pulls from a lauded wine list.

MAP 4: 1509 17th St. NW, 202/332-9200, www.komirestaurant.com; reservations from 5:30pm Tues.-Sat.

THAI
Little Serow $$$

It's no surprise you didn't get a table at Komi, but you can still try Johnny Monis's cooking at its more egalitarian sibling, Little Serow. The no-reservations foodie favorite serves a northern Thai set menu for $49 per person. Line up by 4pm to put your name on the list for the evening. The restaurant accommodates only parties of four or fewer. Is it worth it? Absolutely, if you like seafood and a lot of spice.

MAP 4: 1511 17th St. NW, no phone, www.littleserow.com; 5:30pm-10pm Tues.-Thurs., 5:30pm-10:30pm Fri.-Sat.

VEGETARIAN
Beefsteak $

José Andrés of Jaleo fame got in on the fast-casual craze with Beefsteak, serving exciting vegetarian-friendly meals. The signature item is the Beefsteak Burger, made with beefsteak tomato or marinated beet instead of ground beef, but you can also choose from an assortment of hot bowls or salads, or make your own. The vegetables are shockingly fresh, and the lavender lemonade is dreamy. You also can get your veggie fix in Foggy Bottom (800 22nd St. NW, 202/296-1421).

MAP 4: 1528 Connecticut Ave. NW, 202/986-7597, www.beefsteakveggies.com; 10:30am-10pm daily

BREAKFAST AND BRUNCH
✪ Bagels Etc. $

Don't let the line snaking out the door on weekend mornings deter you, because this cash-only shop makes the best bagels in DC. You can't go wrong with a classic bacon-egg-cheese rapidly cooked to order, though the health conscious who drop by after their bike rides in nearby Rock Creek Park will find sprouts on everything wheat bagels as well.

MAP 4: 2122 P St. NW, 202/466-7171, www.bagelsetc.net; 6am-4pm Mon.-Sat., 6am-3pm Sun.

Bagels Etc. in Dupont Circle

U Street, Shaw, and Logan Circle

Map 5

CLASSIC AMERICAN

✪ Ben's Chili Bowl $

Ben's Chili Bowl has been serving its famous chili half-smokes for 60 years—including during the 1968 race riots, when the restaurant got special permission to stay open late to ensure activists and law enforcement had something to eat while they worked to restore the neighborhood. Today, celebrities, politicians, and locals drop by for the spicy half-pork/half-beef sausages, served on buns and smothered in beef or vegetarian chili. This brightly lit, counter-serve diner has traditional hot dogs, burgers, and great milk shakes, too, along with breakfast items. There's another location on H Street NE.

MAP 5: 1213 U St. NW, 202/667-0058, www.benschilibowl.com; 6am-2am Mon.-Thurs., 6am-4am Fri., 7am-4am Sat., 11am-midnight Sun.

Ben's Chili Bowl

NEW AMERICAN

Hazel $$

Near the 9:30 Club, this beautifully lit restaurant with an outdoor garden feels like a hidden secret, but local gastronomes know to book in advance to enjoy the creative cuisine at Hazel, one of the darlings of the DC food scene. The medium-size plates are trendy but tasty; bring a friend and share 3-5, including the addictive sticky-crunchy ribs and warm zucchini bread with foie gras mousse.

MAP 5: 808 V St. NW, 202/847-4980, www.hazelrestauarant.com; 5pm-10:30pm Mon.-Sat., 11am-2pm and 5pm-10:30pm Sun.

SEAFOOD

Siren by RW $$$

The eclectic seafood menu and swish surroundings will lure you to Siren by RW, Robert Wiedmaier's restaurant inside The Darcy. It's big and loud—especially when the jazz band is playing Thursday through Saturday evenings—but it's a glam night out, especially if you're ready to splurge on a raw bar tower or caviar.

MAP 5: 1515 Rhode Island Ave. NW, 202/521-7171, www.sirenbyrw.com; 4pm-midnight Mon.-Fri., 10:30am-midnight Sat., 11am-midnight Sun.

Pearl Dive Oyster Palace $$

Part of chef Jeff Black's local restaurant empire known for sustainable seafood, Pearl Dive Oyster Palace serves Gulf Coast flavors in a rustic hangout in the heart of Logan Circle. There are several types of oysters on offer,

Old Ebbitt Grill

If you see people with dark suits and earpieces crowding the doorway of one of these hot spots, keep your eyes peeled, because the town's top VIP may be chowing down nearby.

The Obamas enjoyed dining at some of DC's most exclusive restaurants, including **Komi** (page 120), **Fiola Mare** (page 133), and, on more than one occasion, **Cafe Milano** (page 133), a favorite of Washington power players and Hollywood celebrities. And days before he took office, Barack Obama stopped by **Ben's Chili Bowl** (page 122), which memorialized him in their mural on the outside wall. (Other famous diners at the late-night spot known for half-smokes include former French president Nicolas Sarkozy and his wife Carla Bruni, Anthony Bourdain, and many DC politicians.)

Other longtime favorites of White House occupants continue to welcome VIPs, staffers, and lobbyists today. **Old Ebbitt Grill** (page 110), just a few blocks from the White House, hosted McKinley, Grant, Johnson, Cleveland, Teddy Roosevelt, and Harding. In 1953, Senator John F. Kennedy proposed to Jackie Bouvier in booth 3 at **Martin's Tavern** (page 133), which has served every POTUS from Truman to George W. Bush. **The Palm** (page 119), where caricatures of its most famous regulars adorn the walls, opened after United Nations ambassador George H. W. Bush urged his favorite New York steakhouse to open a location in DC.

but try the Old Black Salt Oysters, a salty variety Black helped to develop in Chincoteague, Virginia; they're best enjoyed at the bustling outdoor bar counter on 14th Street.

MAP 5: 1612 14th St. NW, 202/319-1612, www.pearldivedc.com; 5pm-10pm Mon., 5pm-11pm Tues.-Thurs., 11am-11pm Fri.-Sat., 11am-10pm Sun.

SOUTHERN AND SOUL FOOD
The Dabney $$$

Jeremiah Langhorne cut his teeth at the critically acclaimed McCrady's in Charleston before opening The Dabney, where reservations are snapped up quicker than you can say "Michelin star." (It has one.) The

LITTLE ETHIOPIA

Dukem Ethiopian Restaurant

In the 1970s and 1980s, thousands of Ethiopians fled civil war to Washington DC, building the largest Ethiopian community outside Africa. While skyrocketing rents have led to many moving to suburbs like Silver Spring, Maryland, and Alexandria, Virginia, dozens of Ethiopian businesses remain in Adams Morgan and Shaw, and the area around 9th Street and U Street NW is known as Little Ethiopia, home to restaurants like **Dukem Ethiopian Restaurant** (page 125) and **Etete** (page 125). Today, Ethiopian food is an essential part of the District's culinary landscape.

No, the server didn't forget your fork. Instead of utensils, the family-style dishes are traditionally served with *injera*, a spongy, nutrient-dense, gluten-free flatbread used to scoop meats, vegetables, and spices from a communal platter. (Many restaurants will provide utensils if you ask.)

Ethiopian cuisine is often spicy, served with *berbere*, a dark red mixture of chilies, garlic, and a host of other spices, which you can add to taste. If it's too hot, ask for a side of homemade cottage cheese.

The must-try dishes for a newbie include *doro wat,* a spicy chicken stew, and *tibs,* sautéed beef or lamb. If you love steak tartare, try the *kitfo,* spicy minced raw beef. (Dukem will cook it, if you prefer.) And don't forget to order a colorful vegetarian platter, which usually includes lentils, peas, carrots, and greens. Many restaurants, including Dukem, serve traditional dishes, while others, like Etete, serve Ethiopian-inspired dishes, like an *injera* taco.

young, Virginia-born chef showcases the best of the Mid-Atlantic—soft-shell crabs and catfish, local produce, Anson Mill grits—in a rustic-chic row house in Shaw. Reservations are available at noon two weeks in advance of the date, by phone or online.
MAP 5: 122 Blagden Alley NW, 202/450-1015, www.thedabney.com; 5:30pm-10pm Tues.-Thurs., 5:30pm-11pm Fri.-Sat., 5pm-10pm Sun.

Florida Avenue Grill $

The oldest soul food restaurant in the world, Florida Avenue Grill was founded in 1944 by Lacey C. Wilson Sr., a shoeshine on Capitol Hill who saved his tips to pursue his dream of opening a restaurant that would be open to everyone, especially the black community. The old-fashioned diner is still in the original spot, having survived the 1968 riots, and serves soul food favorites like fried chicken, ribs, pig's feet, and fried Atlantic croaker, as well as all-day breakfast.

MAP 5: 1100 Florida Ave. NW, 202/265-1586, www.floridaavenuegrill.com; 8am-9pm Tues.-Sat., 8am-4:30pm Sun.

CHINESE
Kyirisan $$$

Tim Ma combines his French Culinary Institute training with Chinese flavor for an interesting fusion that earned a Michelin Bib Gourmand nod. Once you get a handle on the menu—choose from dishes "In the Ground," "On the Ground," and "Under the Water"—you'll enjoy exciting cuisine, like memorable foraged mushrooms with tomato and goat cheese, or an exceptionally decadent bone marrow, served in a cool, casual space.

MAP 5: 1924 8th St. NW, 202/525-2383, www.kyirisandc.com; 5:30pm-10pm Mon.-Fri., 10:30am-2:30pm and 5:30pm-10pm Sat., 10:30am-2:30pm and 5:30pm-9pm Sun.

ETHIOPIAN
✪ Dukem Ethiopian Restaurant $$

Ask any local who loves Ethiopian cuisine—whether they're a lobbyist or a taxi driver—where to get the best *doro wat* (chicken stew) and *kitfo* (steak tartare), and they'll tell you this casual corner restaurant near the heart of DC's Little Ethiopia. Don't let the grungy interior deter you, because you'll enjoy friendly service and plentiful, flavorful, authentic food that you'll eat exclusively with *injera* flatbread and your hands.

MAP 5: 1114-1118 U St. NW, 202/667-8735, www.dukemrestaurant.com; 9am-midnight Sun.-Thurs., 9:30am-1am Fri.-Sat.

Etete $$

This mainstay of DC's Little Ethiopia recently reopened with modern decor and a refreshed menu that reinvents West African cuisine for contemporary palates. Chef Christopher Roberson, who cooked at several beloved restaurants around the city, specializes in small plates based on recipes by the owners' mother, Tiwaltengus "Etete" Shenegelgn—like an *injera* flatbread taco and *kitfo* (beef tartare).

MAP 5: 1942 9th St. NW, 202/232-7600, www.eteterestaurant.com; 5pm-10pm Mon.-Thurs., 5pm-11pm Fri.-Sat.

FRENCH
Le Diplomate $$$

Stephen Starr's Le Diplomate looks like the France Pavilion at Epcot in Disney World, but that doesn't stop the crowds from packing the large, festive dining room and patio tables every night of the week for gourmet, if a bit pricey, bistro classics. The decadent brunch with its own dessert menu is perfect for a Sunday funday celebration; the Burger Américain is considered one of the best in DC.

MAP 5: 1601 14th St. NW, 202/332-3333, www.lediplomatedc.com; 5pm-11pm Tues.-Thurs., 5pm-midnight Fri., 9:30am-midnight Sat., 9:30am-11pm Sun.

MEDITERRANEAN
Maydan $$$

Tucked in an alley next to the Manhattan Laundry building, Maydan's sultry environment and phenomenal food will transport you to Beirut or Tangier. The Mediterranean, Middle Eastern, and North African flavors are inspired by owner Rose Previte's travels (and her Lebanese mother's cooking): flavorful spreads with bread, grilled meat and fresh vegetables, and cooling cocktails and wines

Le Diplomate

to cut the spice. If you don't mind the smoke lingering on your clothes, eat at the bar to watch the action on the showpiece grill. To find Maydan, look for the large, unmarked wooden door.

MAP 5: 1346 Florida Ave. NW, 202/370-3696, www.maydandc.com; 5pm-11pm Mon.-Sat., 5pm-10pm Sun.

MEXICAN
Taqueria Nacional $

You'll find the best tacos in DC on a side street in the 14th Street Corridor, but don't take my word for it. Both *Bon Appétit* and the Mexican embassy have praised this casual taqueria, known for authentic tacos, quesadillas, and tostadas made with locally sourced, farm-fresh ingredients. (Seriously, you might see the farmer when he brings the pork delivery.)

MAP 5: 1409 T St. NW, 202/299-1122, www.taquerianacional.co; noon-10pm Mon.-Wed., noon-11pm Thurs.-Fri., 10am-11pm Sat., 10am-9pm Sun.

SPANISH
ANXO Cidery & Pintxos Bar $$

DC's first cidery is more than a bar; it's an authentic Basque restaurant, too, with a full menu of *pintxos* (snacks) like salty anchovies imported from Spain, as well as a tender rib-eye for two, one of the best steaks in the city. It's often packed, so if you have the choice, reserve a place at the nine-seat dining bar instead of a table so bartenders can help you pair your meal with a tart Spanish cider *(sidra)*, a sparkly rosé cider, or one of their own, made in the District in Brightwood Park. Reservations are recommended for the second-floor dining room; the ground-floor bar by the huge cider barrels is first-come, first-served.

MAP 5: 300 Florida Ave. NW, 202/986-3795, www.anxodc.com; 5pm-midnight Mon.-Thurs., 5pm-1am Fri., 10am-1am Sat., 10am-midnight Sun., kitchen closes two hours prior to closing

CAFÉS AND LIGHT BITES
Slipstream $$

If you prefer to eat something more substantial than a pastry with your coffee, try Slipstream. (Quite a bit of this book was written at the bar with jasmine tea and avocado toast, poached egg added.) The friendly café attracts chatty entrepreneurs and students with laptops who enjoy coffee by day, cocktails by night, and good food, including breakfast and lunch sandwiches, toasts, and a daily soup. Another Slipstream is located at Navy Yard (82 I St. SE, 202/560-5095).

MAP 5: 1333 14th St. NW, 202/450-2216, www.slipstreamdc.com; 7am-10pm Mon.-Fri., 8am-10pm Sat., 8am-8pm Sun.

✪ Busboys and Poets $

Inspired by Langston Hughes, who worked as a busboy in a Washington hotel in the 1920s, Busboys and Poets is where progressive activists meet for breakfast before a march, where artists and poets ruminate on political and cultural issues, and where locals enjoy good, affordable food made with organic, hormone-free, and fair-trade ingredients. This busy, casual restaurant is covered in art inspired by its progressive, community-focused mission. Choose from standard dining tables or cozy couches where you can have coffee or tea while you work on your laptop. After your meal, enjoy a poetry reading or browse the on-site bookshop specializing in social justice issues and DC life and history. In addition to the 14th and V flagship, there are several other locations throughout the city.

MAP 5: 2021 14th St. NW, 202/387-7638, www.busboysandpoets.com; 8am-midnight Mon.-Thurs., 24 hours Fri.-Sat., until midnight Sun.

BAKERIES
Buttercream Bakeshop $

The cupcake craze jumped the shark years ago, but Buttercream Bakeshop is the exception; the almond cupcake with raspberry jam and creamy Chambord frosting will entice even those who claim they don't like sweets. The tiny storefront also sells baked-from-scratch cakes (whole or by the slice), cookies, bars, pies, and fritters, plus breakfast items and Compass Coffee. Grab one of a few stools, or take your treats to go.

MAP 5: 1250 9th St. NW, 202/735-0102, www.buttercreammdc.com; 7am-2pm Mon., 7am-7pm Tues.-Thurs., 7am-8pm Fri., 8am-8pm Sat., 9am-7pm Sun.

COFFEE AND TEA
The Wydown $$

An espresso drink and snack could set you back $15 at this hip coffee shop, but you won't feel ripped off by the smiling staff. The drip coffee is brewed to order, and the matcha latte with almond milk is one of DC's best. Pair it with a pastry or raw, organic juice by District Juicery–but plan to take it to go, because the shop is tiny. There's a more spacious outpost in the Atlas District (600 H St. NE, 202/846-7986).

MAP 5: 1924 14th St. NW, 202/507-8411, www.thewydown.com; 7am-10:30pm daily

Calabash Tea & Café $

Trying to lose weight or cure a stomachache? Get pregnant? Fall in love? This Shaw café brews teas and tonics for dozens of ailments, organized by type (herbal, green, oolong, chai, etc.) with detailed descriptions of the flavors and properties on the menu board, plus *kombucha* (sweetened, fermented tea) on tap, organic coffee, and vegan snacks. The colorful café has hippie vibes and space to lounge or work.

MAP 5: 1847 7th St. NW, 202/525-5386, www.calabashdc.com; 9am-8pm daily

Compass Coffee $

If you haven't found your perfect cup, try this local chain founded by two former Marines who developed an easy-to-decipher matrix with nine bean blends organized by flavor profile and roast darkness. The shops brew single-origin roasts, espresso drinks, and nitro cold brew, too. The Shaw roastery and flagship has lots of space to work and relax. This growing chain has many locations citywide, including one in Chinatown (650 F St. NW, no phone).

MAP 5: 1535 7th St. NW, no phone, www.compasscoffee.com; 6am-8pm daily

Adams Morgan   Map 6

SEAFOOD
✪ Johnny's Half Shell $$

James Beard winner Ann Cashion has found a good home in Adams Morgan for her beloved seafood. Here, you'll find her superb Chesapeake Bay-style crab cakes, barbecue shrimp, and of course, oysters on the half shell. Don't let the foodies' accolades and exposed brick fool you into thinking this is a haughty hot spot; it's a friendly neighborhood restaurant through and through, with a big bar packed with regulars and staff who will make you feel like welcome guests in the home of a friend who loves to cook and does it exceedingly well.

MAP 6: 1819 Columbia Rd. NW, 202/506-5257, www.johnnyshalfshell.net; 5pm-9pm Sun.-Mon., 5pm-10pm Tues.-Thurs., 5pm-11pm Fri.-Sat., oyster bar from 4pm daily

BARBECUE
Federalist Pig $

Does this Adams Morgan joint have the best 'cue in DC? The long line out the door and the fact that the tender cuts of brisket and pork spare ribs sell out almost every night strongly indicate yes. Go early, or place your takeout order in advance, to ensure your choice of wood-smoked meats and fresh vegetarian sides, or wrap your mitts around one of the big sandwiches, which local food critics adore. Seating inside is limited and cramped; grab a spot at one of the outdoor communal tables or take your meal to Meridian Hill Park, about a five-minute walk away.

MAP 6: 1654 Columbia Rd. NW, 202/827-4400, www.federalistpig.com; 5pm-10pm Wed.-Fri., noon until sold out Sat.-Sun.

CLASSIC AMERICAN
✪ The Diner $$

This Adams Morgan institution is one of the few DC restaurants open 24/7—but you won't sacrifice flavor for the convenience. Go for classic diner breakfasts (served day and night), a comforting grilled cheese with tater tots, fresh salads and veggie Reubens, or just a cup of coffee or boozy milk shake. The old-school diner is bright and bustling in the daytime, but darker and quieter at night, so you can linger over a cocktail on

The Diner in Adams Morgan

one of the retro stools overlooking the open kitchen.

MAP 6: 2453 18th St. NW, 202/232-8800, www.dinerdc.com; 24 hours daily

Duplex Diner $$

It's not gourmet, but it's fun. This friendly neighborhood hangout serves classic American diner fare (including healthy salads) and strong, fruity cocktails until late; on weekends, it's busy with regulars who come for the simple, well-priced brunch, including omelets and Benedicts under $15 plus mimosa pitchers and a bottomless French rosé. It's known for gay-friendly late-night events, too, like the High Heel Drag Queen Race after-party in October. Don't miss the Madonna-themed bathroom.

MAP 6: 2004 18th St. NW, 202/265-7828, www.duplexdiner.com; 6pm-11pm Mon.-Wed., 6pm-2am Thurs.-Fri., 11am-2am Sat., 11am-11pm Sun.

FILIPINO
Bad Saint $$

Prepare to wait to dine at one of the top-rated restaurants in America; the teeny 24-seat Bad Saint doesn't take reservations, and the line starts forming as early as 3pm, even on weekdays. But if you do wait—or hire someone to wait in line for you on TaskRabbit, as many locals do—you'll be rewarded with transporting Filipino fare, including standards like *lumpia* (spring rolls) and chicken adobo as well as more inventive dishes, cooked in the open kitchen fenced in by the lucky diners.

MAP 6: 3226 11th St. NW, no phone, www.badsaintdc.com; 5:30pm-10pm Mon. and Wed.-Thurs., 5:30pm-11pm Fri., 5pm-11pm Sat., 5pm-10pm Sun.

Purple Patch $

There's room enough for two excellent Filipino restaurants in this town—and unlike its competitor, Bad Saint, Mount Pleasant's Purple Patch takes reservations. Owner Patrice Cleary was born in the Philippines to a Filipino mother and American father, and she cooks her mother's recipes as well as some innovative fusion, such as adobo chicken wings and beef sliders topped with papaya salad and banana ketchup.

MAP 6: 3155 Mt. Pleasant St. NW, 202/299-0022, www.purplepatchdc.com; 6pm-10:30pm Mon.-Thurs., 6pm-11pm Fri., 11am-3pm and 5pm-11pm Sat., 11am-3pm and 5pm-10:30pm Sun., bar 5pm-1am daily

LAOTIAN
Thip Khao $

After fleeing Laos during the Vietnam War as a child, Seng Luangrath lived in a refugee camp in Thailand, where she learned how to cook. She now runs this Michelin Bib Gourmand pick with her son, who graduated from the Culinary Institute of America and honed his craft at restaurants like minibar by

José Andrés. Named for the baskets that hold sticky rice, this bright, modern restaurant serves flavorful cuisine, with many dishes coming with warnings about the spice.

MAP 6: 3462 14th St. NW, 202/387-5426, www.thipkhao.com; 5pm-10pm Mon., 5pm-10pm Wed.-Thurs., noon-3pm and 5pm-11pm Fri.-Sat., noon-3pm and 5pm-10pm Sun.

MEDITERRANEAN
Tail Up Goat $$

Bubbly and down-to-earth staff, mid-century modern decor, and Marvin Gaye on the speakers—Tail Up Goat is no ordinary Michelin-starred establishment. Start with a cocktail and one of the open-faced sandwiches on homemade sourdough. For one, two, or four, the lamb ribs will be enough—and yes, eat them with your hands. Make your next reservation on the way out—or don't, because they'll welcome you at the bar regardless.

MAP 6: 1827 Adams Mill Rd. NW, 202/986-9600, www.tailupgoat.com; 5:30pm-10pm Mon.-Thurs., 5pm-10pm Fri.-Sun.

MIDDLE EASTERN
Lapis $$

Founded by a local restaurateur family, who fled Afghanistan after the Soviets invaded more than 30 years ago, this white-walled bistro combines family history with contemporary style, serving traditional Afghan recipes and craft cocktails in a light, modern space decorated with Afghan textiles. The family matriarch, Shamin Popal, cooks kebabs, stews, and Afghan dumplings, as well as a large selection of vegetarian and vegan dishes, which earned a Michelin Bib Gourmand nod.

MAP 6: 1847 Columbia Rd. NW, 202/299-9630, www.lapisdc.com; 5:30pm-10pm Mon.-Thurs., 5:30pm-11pm Fri., 10am-4pm and 5:30pm-11pm Sat., 10am-4pm and 5:30pm-10pm Sun.

Amsterdam Falafelshop $

When feeding your late-night hunger pangs, skip the greasy pizza joints that line the Adams Morgan nightlife streets and opt for vegetarian-friendly falafel pitas and fries. Now a national chain, Amsterdam Falafelshop started in this Adams Morgan row house and remains one of Washington's top picks for cheap falafel and shawarma with fresh toppings. You can also get your falafel fix near 14th and U Streets NW (1830 14th St. NW) and L'Enfant Plaza (429 L'Enfant Plaza SW).

MAP 6: 2425 18th St. NW, 202/234-1969, www.falafelshop.com; 11am-midnight Sun.-Mon., 11am-2:30am Tues.-Wed., 11am-3am Thurs., 11am-4am Fri.-Sat.

SALVADORAN
Pupuseria San Miguel $

Mount Pleasant is known for Mexican and Latin American cuisine, including several joints serving traditional Salvadoran *pupusas*, or corn tortillas stuffed with a combination of cheese, beans, and pork and fried golden and crispy. This dim basement hole-in-the-wall has some of the best in the neighborhood, if not the entire Washington area, priced just $1.50-2 each. The menu features fajitas, tacos, and other regional specialties. It's not fine dining, but you'll leave with a full wallet and belly.

MAP 6: 3110 Mt. Pleasant St. NW, 202/387-5410, no website; 9am-10pm Sun.-Mon., 10am-midnight Tues.-Thurs., 10am-11pm Fri.-Sat.

VEGETARIAN AND VEGAN

JRINK Juicery $

Wake Me Up, a spicy carrot and citrus juice from JRINK Juicery, is the perfect post-run fuel, pressed locally in Falls Church, Virginia, along with other concoctions with names like Pick Me Up, Cheer Me Up, Relax, and Detox. In addition to single bottles and cleanse kits, the shop serves smoothies and superfood bowls. The Adams Morgan location is bright and spacious; others include Logan Circle (1630 14th St. NW, 202/459-7785) and Foggy Bottom (1922 I St. NW, 202/290-3193).

MAP 6: 1800 Wyoming Ave. NW, 202/415-2660, www.jrink.com; 7am-6pm Mon.-Fri., 9am-4pm Sat.-Sun.

Sticky Fingers Sweets & Eats $

Have your cake and eat it, too, sans milk and eggs. This vegan bakery serves tasty treats even non-vegans will love—after all, founder Doron Petersan won two seasons of the Food Network's *Cupcake Wars*. Try the famous sticky bun or moist cupcakes. The café also serves diner-style vegan sandwiches, burgers, and weekend brunch in a space inspired by retro diners.

MAP 6: 1370 Park Rd. NW, 202/299-9700, www.stickyfingersbakery.com; 8am-8pm Tues.-Thurs., 8am-9pm Fri., 9am-9pm Sat., 9am-8pm Sun.

CAFÉS AND LIGHT BITES

The Potter's House $

Founded in 1960, The Potter's House is a nonprofit café and bookstore dedicated to social justice issues—and you can feel good about your purchases, because the shop is known for paying workers above-average wages and offering a pay-what-you-can soup to the needy. In addition to coffee and tea, the café serves breakfast, sandwiches, and salads; stay a while and grab a book about current social and cultural issues, or hear guest authors and musicians.

MAP 6: 1658 Columbia Rd. NW, 202/232-5483, www.pottershousedc.org; 8am-8pm daily

Tryst $

It's like the 1990s all over again at this spacious Adams Morgan coffee shop—especially on weekends, because they turn off the Wi-Fi between 7pm Friday and 7pm Sunday. (Did Ross and Rachel just walk in?) This homey hangout serves Durham-based Counter Culture Coffee as well as tea, smoothies, and a full bar, morning until late. If you get hungry, enjoy all-day brunch, as well as sandwiches, salads, and bakery items.

MAP 6: 2459 18th St. NW, 202/232-5500, www.trystdc.com; 7am-midnight Sun.-Thurs., 7am-1am Fri.-Sat.

Georgetown and Foggy Bottom

Map 7

NEW AMERICAN

Blue Duck Tavern $$$

Blue Duck Tavern feels like a cozy neighborhood restaurant—albeit with destination-worthy, Michelin-starred cuisine in a chic atmosphere. The restaurant is warm and rustic, but modern—just like the menu, which features locally sourced, seasonal meats and produce cooked in the open kitchen. The brunch is one of the best; celebrate anything, or nothing at all, with the pecan sticky buns and a bottle of champagne on the patio.

MAP 7: 1201 24th St. NW, 202/419-6755, www.blueducktavern.com; 6:30am-10:30pm Sun.-Thurs., 6:30am-11pm Fri.-Sat.

1789 $$$

This formal restaurant recognizes an important year in Washington history: 1789, the year Georgetown University was established and the United States Constitution came into force. Located in a Federal period townhouse near the top of *The Exorcist* stairs, the restaurant's six dining rooms are decorated with historical American treasures and prints. The menu's seasonal dishes, like fish, duck, and venison paired with produce from local farms, are served in four, five, or six courses ($83-107 per person).

MAP 7: 1226 36th St. NW, 202/965-1789, www.1789restaurant.com; 6pm-10pm Mon.-Thurs., 6pm-11pm Fri., 5:30pm-11pm Sat., 5:30pm-10pm Sun.

ETHIOPIAN

DAS Ethiopian Cuisine $$

If you're new to Ethiopian food, DAS Ethiopian Cuisine in Georgetown's shopping district is a good place to start. The smart, white-tablecloth dining room and sunny patio serve all the traditional dishes—like beef tartare *(kitfo)*, tibs (sautéed meat), and hearty vegetable platters—but with utensils if you're unsure of how to eat with your hands. You'll get freshly baked *injera* bread with every order, too, in case you're a pro.

MAP 7: 1201 28th St. NW, 202/333-4710, www.dasethiopian.com; 11am-11pm daily

INDIAN

Rasika West End $$$

Try innovative Indian cuisine at the sleek sister restaurant of The Bombay Club (815 Connecticut Ave. NW, 202/659-3727, www.bombayclubdc.com). Start with a cocktail flavored with chili, cardamom, or masala chai in the light-filled bar, then move to the modern dining room for classic recipes with contemporary flair. The tandoori lamb chops are memorable, but the menu has plenty of options for vegetarians, too. There's another location downtown (633 D St. NW, 202/637-1222) near the Woolly Mammoth Theatre Company.

MAP 7: 1190 New Hampshire Ave. NW, 202/466-2500, www.rasikarestaurant.com/westend; 11:30am-2:30pm and 5:30pm-10:30pm Mon.-Thurs., 11:30am-2:30pm and 5pm-11pm Fri., 5pm-11pm Sat., 11:30am-2:30pm and 5pm-10pm Sun.

ITALIAN

✪ Cafe Milano $$$

Since 1992, senators, cabinet secretaries, ambassadors, and even First Families have chosen buzzy Cafe Milano when they want to see and be seen during lunch or dinner. (In fact, it's the restaurant the Iranians plotted to blow up in 2011 while the Saudi ambassador was eating one of his frequent meals there.) Georgetown is no longer the hippest part of town, but the house-made pasta, simply prepared sea bass, and flavorful *panzanella* salad continue to attract movers, shakers, and visiting celebrities to the white-tablecloth dining room.

MAP 7: 3251 Prospect St., 202/333-6183, www.cafemilano.com; 11:30am-midnight Mon.-Tues., 11:30am-1am Wed.-Sat., 11am-11pm Sun., bar open late

✪ Fiola Mare $$$

Fiola Mare is such a good date night, even Barack and Michelle lingered for three hours when celebrating the former POTUS's 55th birthday. The sexy interior—dark hardwood, leather chairs, two marble bars—complements the superb seafood towers, caviar, lobster ravioli, and fresh fish, while a prosecco cocktail on the riverside patio will make you feel like you've escaped to Positano.

MAP 7: 3050 K St. NW, 202/628-0065, www.fiolamaredc.com; 5pm-10pm Mon., 11:30am-10pm Tues.-Thurs., 11:30am-10:30pm Fri.-Sat., 11am-10pm Sun.

PUBS

Martin's Tavern $$

To enjoy a family meal or to watch the big game in historical surroundings, Georgetown residents choose the cozy wooden booths at this warm tavern, which has welcomed U.S. presidents and members of Congress since 1933—including John F. Kennedy, who proposed to Jacqueline Bouvier in booth 3 in 1953. The reasonably priced pub menu features Irish favorites, a nod to the founder, William S. Martin, who immigrated to the United States from Galway in the 1890s.

MAP 7: 1264 Wisconsin Ave. NW, 202/333-7370, www.martinstavern.com; 11am-1:30am Mon.-Thurs., 11am-2:30am Fri., 9am-2:30am Sat., 8am-1:30am Sun.

VEGETARIAN

Chaia $

Who says cheap tacos have to be junk food? Even nonvegetarians will like the fresh appeal of the seasonal, plant-based tacos at this fast-casual eatery, which started as a local farmers market stand and now occupies a small but airy space in Georgetown. The tacos are just $3.75 apiece, or three for $11, and stuffed full of fresh produce; mushrooms, asparagus, kale, and collard greens are all on the menu, topped with fresh cheeses and flavorful sauces.

MAP 7: 3207 Grace St. NW, 202/333-5222, www.chaiadc.com; 11am-9pm Mon.-Fri., 10am-9pm Sat.-Sun.

CAFÉS AND LIGHT BITES

Ladurée $$

For breakfast, lunch, tea, and cocktails, Ladurée serves French favorites like omelets, salads, foie gras, champagne, and, of course, its famous, candy-colored macarons. It's tiny and, just as at the original Ladurée tearooms in Paris, service can be hit or miss, but you go for the Instagramworthy atmosphere, an explosion of pastel and pastries like a scene from Sofia Coppola's *Marie Antoinette*. It's one of a growing global chain popular with tourists, but the Georgetown location serves exclusive cherry blossom macarons, as well as items like avocado toast with a poached egg and a pink, rose-flavored croissant.

MAP 7: 3060 M St. W, 202/737-0492, www.laduree.com; 9am-7pm Mon.-Thurs., 8am-8pm Fri.-Sat., 8am-7pm Sun.

BAKERIES
Baked & Wired $

A hip hideaway in an otherwise stodgy neighborhood, Baked & Wired has the best cupcakes (better than those by the famous cupcake shop up the street that's featured in the TLC reality show *DC Cupcake*). If it's in season, get the cherry blossom cupcake, a pink cake with chunks of fruit and frothy frosting. The small shop sells yummy baked goods (including excellent brownies) as well as coffee and tea; the iced teas on tap are especially refreshing.

MAP 7: 1052 Thomas Jefferson St. NW, 703/663-8727, www.bakedandwired. com; 7am-8pm Mon.-Thurs., 7am-9pm Fri., 8am-9pm Sat., 8am-8pm Sun.

Dog Tag Bakery $

Enjoy one of the famous fudgy brownies at Dog Tag Bakery and support men and women who have fought for our freedom. It's staffed by wounded military vets who take business classes at Georgetown University and put their education into practice by working in all areas of the shop, from the front of the house and the kitchen to the management office. The bakery has plenty of seating and serves breakfast and lunch, with coffee by Compass Coffee, a local roastery founded by two former Marines.

MAP 7: 3206 Grace St. NW, 202/407-9609, www.dogtagbakery.com; 7am-6pm Mon.-Fri., 8am-6pm Sat.-Sun.

COFFEE AND TEA
Grace Street Coffee $

A hangout of Georgetown University students and post-yoga moms, Grace Street Coffee serves small-batch coffee roasted on-site, including pour-over coffee, espresso drinks, and concoctions like a coffee "shrub," which is coffee, sweet balsamic vinegar, and sparkling water, with a similar flavor to *kombucha* (fermented tea). In the spacious, industrial market-style space, you'll also find outposts of **Sundevich** (202/868-6932, www.sundevich.com), making sandwiches inspired by cities from around the world, and **South Block Juice Co.** (202/747-0172, www. southblockjuice.com), offering cold-pressed juices and smoothies as well as a delicious avocado toast with crushed red pepper flakes.

MAP 7: 3210 Grace St. NW, 202/470-1331, www.gracestcoffee.com; 7am-5pm Mon.-Thurs., 7am-6pm Fri.-Sun.

Navy Yard and Anacostia   Map 8

SEAFOOD
Whaley's $$

Whaley's is an attractive restaurant: a light and airy space with an aquatic mural near the rafters; floor-to-ceiling windows provide a view of the Anacostia River and Yards Park. The seafood is attractive, too, all local and sustainable, with the origin printed on the menu. Enjoy Virginia oysters—they're just $1 each 5pm-7pm daily—as well as excellent fish and pasta entrées.

Virginia oysters at Whaley's

In the summer, grab a table outside and pair a shellfish tower with a selection of rosés.

MAP 8: 301 Water St. SE, 202/484-8800, www.whaleysdc.com; 5pm-9pm Mon.-Thurs., 5pm-10pm Fri., 11am-10pm Sat., 11am-9pm Sun.

Capitol Hill Crab Cakes $

It's not actually on Capitol Hill, but this friendly, family-owned storefront in Anacostia does serve crab cakes—which are large, made with jumbo lump meat and golden fried, served with slaw and a side, on a sandwich, or caprese-style, with tomato and mozzarella. Other delicious items include a shrimp po' boy and crab fries, which are seasoned and smothered in crab meat and special sauce. Most patrons take their orders to go, but your made-to-order meal is best enjoyed hot at one of the tables in the sparse but cheerful dining room before touring the Frederick Douglass National Historic Site nearby.

MAP 8: 1243 Good Hope Rd. SE, 202/678-5000, www.capitolhillcrabcakes. net; 11am-9:30pm Mon.-Sat., 11am-7:30pm Sun.

SOUTHERN AND SOUL FOOD
Due South $$

Whether you think DC is in the South depends a lot on where you're from; it's below the Mason-Dixon line, but visitors from farther south may find the weather and the people a bit chilly. Nonetheless, North Carolina transplant Rusty Holman's cooking is the real deal. Due South offers elevated Southern classics—shrimp and grits with heirloom tomatoes and kale, barbecue meats smoked in-house—in a bright space in Navy Yard.

135

MAP 8: 301 Water St. SE, 202/479-4616, www.duesouthdc.com; 11am-10pm Mon.-Thurs., 11am-11pm Fri.-Sat.

ITALIAN

Osteria Morini $$$

This New York import helmed by James Beard winner Michael White has been praised by local food critics for its menu featuring the best of Northern Italy's Emilia-Romagna region: homemade pasta, wood-fired meats, and lots of mortadella and parmigiano. During the popular weekend brunch, choose two or three courses ($30 or $35, respectively) from a selection of breakfast favorites, pastas, and paninis, which can be enjoyed in the bright restaurant with big windows overlooking the Anacostia River or on the patio.

MAP 8: 301 Water St. SE, 202/484-0660, www.osteriamorini.com; 11:30am-9:30pm

Mon.-Thurs., 11:30am-10pm Fri., 11am-10pm Sat., 11am-9pm Sun.

DESSERT

Ice Cream Jubilee $

Close to Nationals Park, Ice Cream Jubilee scoops small-batch ice cream and sorbet made with local, natural ingredients. Try MarionBerry, a nod to DC's infamous former mayor, made with marionberry blackberries from Oregon and graham cracker crumbs; the seasonal menu may have flavors like Nats Red Velvet Cake during baseball season or maple rye pecan ice cream and cranberry sorbet in the winter. You can also get your fix in the U Street Corridor (1407 T St. NW, 202/299-9042).

MAP 8: 301 Water St. SE, 202/863-0727, www.icecreamjubilee.com; 11am-10pm Sun.-Thurs., 11am-11pm Fri.-Sat. summer, noon-9pm daily winter

Greater Washington DC Map 9

CLASSIC AMERICAN

Open City $$

This Woodley Park diner and coffee house is worth the Metro or Uber fare for a hair-of-the-dog brunch, especially if you'd like to visit the pandas at the Smithsonian's National Zoo after. Steps from the Woodley Park-Zoo/Adams Morgan Metro and about a 10-minute walk from the zoo's main entrance, the family-friendly spot serves affordable breakfast all day, every day, plus a large menu of sandwiches, salads, pizza, and cocktails early until late.

MAP 9: 2331 Calvert St. NW, 202/332-2331, www.opencitydc.com; 7am-midnight Sun.-Thurs., 7am-1am Fri.-Sat.

Buffalo & Bergen $

When you need a shopping pit stop, grab a stool at the old-fashioned soda counter located inside Union Market. The sodas, egg creams, and floats made with homemade syrups (booze optional) aren't the only throwback; the prices are very affordable for a trendy brunch spot, with the "New York water" bagels with cream cheese starting at $4 and most of the heaping breakfast and lunch sandwiches under $10.

MAP 9: 1309 5th St. NE, 202/543-2549, www.buffalobergendc.com; 9am-8pm Tues.-Fri., 8am-8pm Sat.-Sun.

ITALIAN
✪ Masseria $$$

Hidden among the warehouses around Union Market, Masseria is a destination. Nicholas Stefanelli's Michelin-starred cuisine is inspired by his childhood in Puglia, Italy's sunny, fertile heel, known for *burrata* cheese, orecchiette pasta, and farm-fresh ingredients. Neither the ingredients nor the pricey bill compare to the *masserias*, or country houses, in Bari or Brindisi, but Stefanelli does a fine job of making you forget you're in DC by the end of one of the rich four-, five-, or six-course meals ($92-135 pp). Go when the weather is nice for a romantic evening on the patio, with dreamy lighting and landscaping plus cozy couches for a nightcap. Make your reservation at least a few days in advance, a week or more for weekends or if you want to dine outside in the summer, though last-minute tables are typically available if you're willing to dine early or late; lounge seating on the patio is first-come, first-served.

MAP 9: 1340 4th St. NE, 202/608-1330, www.masseria-dc.com; 5:30pm-9:30pm Tues.-Thurs., 5pm-10pm Fri.-Sat.

MEXICAN
La Puerta Verde $$

Inside the namesake green door in the Hecht Warehouse in Ivy City, you'll find the most addictive guacamole in the District. The secret? The avocados are grilled. And the tacos, stuffed full of meat and fresh cilantro, are a steal at three for $9. Grab a stool at the festive tiled bar, and enjoy the food with a cold margarita or beer. The bar is surrounded by vibrant murals by Cita Sadeli, who has been creating street art in DC since the 1990s.

MAP 9: 2001 Fenwick St. NE, 202/290-1875, www.lapuertaverdedc.com; 5pm-10pm Tues.-Thurs., 5pm-11pm Fri., 11am-11pm Sat., 11am-10pm Sun.

Masseria in Union Market

La Puerta Verde

PIZZA
2 Amys $

Head to Cathedral Heights, the quiet neighborhood near the Washington National Cathedral, for Washington's first, and very best, D.O.C.-certified pizzeria, meaning it follows the Italian regulations for Neapolitan-style pizza, guaranteed to be made in a wood-burning oven with San Marzano tomatoes and Fior di Latte or Bufala mozzarella, among other ingredients. This casual, subway-tiled restaurant with an open-air deck doesn't take reservations, but these pies are worth any wait. And, best of all, it's cheap—the D.O.C. Margherita is $13 and fills one, or it can easily satisfy two when combined with salad and homemade ice cream (or delicious cinnamon doughnuts during weekend brunch).

MAP 9: 3715 Macomb St. NW, 202/885-5700, www.2amysdc.com; 5pm-10pm Mon., 11am-10pm Tues.-Thurs., 11am-11pm Fri.-Sat., noon-10pm Sun.

DESSERT
Dolcezza Gelato Factory & Coffee Lab $

With more than half a dozen locations throughout the area, Dolcezza Gelato is the king of the cone, serving gelato and sorbet made with local, seasonal ingredients. Flavors range from standbys like Indonesian Vanilla Bean and Coffee & Cookies to more exotic ones like Virginia Peanut Butter, Black Sesame, and White Peach Prosecco. Visit the factory near Union Market, where you can try just-made treats as well as Stumptown coffee drinks in the roomy, industrial space with counter seating and communal tables. The gelato and sorbet are also sold at local grocery stores and restaurants.

MAP 9: 550 Penn St. NE, 202/333-4646, www.dolcezzagelato.com; 11am-7pm Fri.-Sun.

NIGHTLIFE

Downtown and Penn Quarter 141
Capitol Hill and Atlas District 144
Dupont Circle 146
U Street, Shaw, and Logan Circle 148
Adams Morgan.. 153
Georgetown and Foggy Bottom 155
Navy Yard and Anacostia 157
Greater Washington DC 158

In Washington DC, presidential debates, snow days, and news events (like former FBI director James Comey's sensational Senate Intelligence Committee hearing) call for booze, and lots of it.

DC residents guzzle more alcohol per capita than residents of every state except New Hampshire. Washingtonians work hard but party harder. As a result, the city's nightlife centers around bars: cocktail bars, wine bars, beer gardens, posh hotel lounges, and, of course, historic bars, where lobbyists and staffers grease the wheels among the ghosts of presidents and policymakers past.

Jack Rose Dining Saloon

You'll find a few noteworthy dance clubs and late-night music venues, especially in youthful neighborhoods like U Street, Shaw, and the Atlas District, which are humming on weekend nights. But for the most part, DC is an early town, with the nightlife scene most vibrant around 5pm-8pm on weekdays (happy hour!) and relatively quiet on weekends. After all, Washingtonians need time to sleep off the hangover before the 10am hearing. Happy hour is especially bustling downtown.

HIGHLIGHTS

✪ **BEST ROOFTOP BAR:** It's a tie between **POV,** where a chic crowd enjoys cocktails with a view of the White House, and **Top of the Gate,** the sprawling rooftop of The Watergate Hotel, with 360-degree views of the city (pages 141 and 155).

✪ **MOST HISTORIC VENUE:** Senator Henry Clay mixed DC's first mint julep with Kentucky bourbon at **Round Robin Bar,** which has served drinks to many U.S. presidents (page 141).

✪ **QUINTESSENTIAL DC DIVE:** **Tune Inn** is a pub serving cheap beer and fried food in a funky space (page 145).

✪ **MOST INFLUENTIAL VENUE:** Since opening in a hidden spot above a mattress store in 1995, Dupont Circle's **Eighteenth Street Lounge** changed the city's nightlife scene and remains a great place for music and cocktails (page 146).

✪ **BEST PLACE TO PARTY DURING PRIDE:** Located on the parade route, the patio at **JR's Bar** is the place to celebrate during Capital Pride in June (page 147).

✪ **UNIQUE COCKTAIL EXPERIENCE:** Try the three- or five-course cocktail tasting menu at **Columbia Room** (page 148).

✪ **BEST CHANCE TO DANCE ALL NIGHT:** **Black Cat** hosts international DJs as well as theme dance parties like Eighties Mayhem and The Cure vs. The Smiths (page 151).

✪ **BEST LIVE MUSIC VENUE:** Even *Rolling Stone* agrees that the **9:30 Club** is an institution (page 151).

✪ **SUNDAY FUNDAY:** The all-you-can-eat drag brunch is one of the draws at **Nellie's Sports Bar,** as is the expansive rooftop (page 152).

✪ **BEST FOR WHISKY LOVERS:** Jack Rose Dining Saloon has more than 2,500 bottles of whiskey and Scotch from around the world (page 153).

✪ **BEST PEOPLE-WATCHING:** You never know who you'll meet at **The Lounge at Bourbon Steak,** a favorite of celebrities and socialites (page 155).

✪ **BEST NEWCOMER:** Since opening in October 2017, **The Anthem** has brought major musical acts to the high-tech venue for music lovers (page 157).

COCKTAIL BARS AND LOUNGES
✪ POV

At this swanky, colorful bar and lounge on the covered roof of the **W Washington, D.C.**, a chic crowd enjoys cocktails, bar bites, and bottle service year-round with a perfect view of the White House and monuments. Reservations are recommended to guarantee access on Fridays and Saturdays; book your preferred table online, with a minimum spend of $250 for prime views.

MAP 2: 515 15th St. NW, 202/661-2419, www.povrooftop.com; 11am-midnight Sun.-Wed., 11am-1am Thurs., 11am-2am Fri.-Sat.

✪ Round Robin Bar

The bar at the Willard InterContinental has witnessed a lot of history since it was established in 1850. It's where Senator Henry Clay of Kentucky introduced the mint julep to DC in 1851—it remains the bar's signature cocktail—and famous customers have included Walt Whitman, Mark Twain, Buffalo Bill Cody, and many presidents, including Lincoln, Coolidge, Wilson, and Taft. Politicos, lobbyists, and tourists enjoy classic cocktails and bar bites day and night in the mahogany and leather bar with windows looking out to the city.

MAP 2: 1401 Pennsylvania Ave. NW, 202/628-9100, www.washington.

the Round Robin Bar at the Willard InterContinental

intercontinental.com; noon-1am Mon.-Sat., noon-midnight Sun.

Denson Liquor Bar

This hidden speakeasy is across the street from the fire station and down a discreet staircase near a chain pizza parlor. The art deco space is cozy, but there are plenty of stools and booths for enjoying creative riffs on classic cocktails and sophisticated small bites like oysters, caviar, and cheese.

MAP 2: 600 F St. NW 202/499-5018, www.densondc.com; 4:30pm-1am Mon.-Thurs., 4:30pm-2am Fri.-Sat., 3pm-11pm Sun.

Off the Record

Many off-the-record conversations between Washington reporters and their sources have taken place in the basement lounge of The Hay-Adams, a small, dimly lit space where friendly bartenders who have seen everything serve DC-inspired versions of classic cocktails—like the Fill A Buster, a champagne cocktail with gin, or Trumpy Sour, a take on the whiskey sour. It's across the street from the White House, so it can be tough to get a seat during happy hour, but if you do, be careful, because the cocktails are very strong.

MAP 2: 800 16th St. NW, 202/638-6600, www.hayadams.com/washington-dc-bars; 11:30am-midnight Sun.-Thurs., 11:30am-12:30am Fri.-Sat.

LIVE MUSIC

The Hamilton

Before Alexander Hamilton made pop-culture history, Washingtonians long enjoyed late-night entertainment in his namesake concert venue and restaurant. The main stage holds about 600 people in a mix of seated and standing-room areas for blues, country, rock, and cover bands. Performers have included Carbon Leaf; the Old 97's; Beatles, Bruce Springsteen, and Led Zeppelin cover bands; and many local bands. Tickets for main stage performances average $30, but the intimate loft bar has free shows on weekends. After the show, grab a bite in the huge on-site restaurant, which serves everything from burgers to decent sushi.

MAP 2: 600 14th St. NW, 202/787-1000, www.thehamiltondc.com; 11am-2am Mon.-Thurs., 11am-3am Fri.-Sat., 10am-2am Sun.

SPORTS BARS AND DIVES

Rocket Bar

This basement dive in the heart of Chinatown is a favorite spot for 20-somethings to have group outings and birthday parties, because there's plenty of space to invite all your friends for a few games of pool, shuffleboard, and darts. You probably don't want to see what it looks like when the lights are turned on, but that's okay—you can't beat $3 Pabst Blue Ribbon.

MAP 2: 714 7th St. NW, 202/628-7665, www.rocketbardc.com; 4pm-2am Sun.-Thurs., 4pm-3am Fri., 3pm-2am Sat.

COMEDY CLUBS

DC Improv

One of the few dedicated comedy clubs in Washington DC, the DC Improv hosts major standup stars—Dave Chapelle, Ellen DeGeneres, and Jim Gaffigan have performed here—as well as local comedians in the intimate, basement space. The club has a full dinner menu and bar with a two-item minimum per ticket. Seats are allocated first-come, first-served, so arrive early if you want to be close to the front.

MAP 2: 1140 Connecticut Ave. NW, 202/296-7008, www.dcimprov.com; box office 10am-5pm Tues.-Fri., 10am-9pm Tues.-Fri. on days with shows, noon-9pm Sat.-Sun.

HAPPY HOUR

Washington DC is all about who you know and—if you really want business to get done—how often you have a few drinks with them. When visiting the nation's capital, you can take the pulse of the city and the political climate by going to happy hour at one of the many restaurants offering after-work food and drink specials, like bites hearty enough to make dinner plus discounted (sometimes by half) cocktails, beer, and wine. And if you're lucky, you'll overhear well-oiled staffers exchanging snippets of political gossip, especially if you choose a location near the White House or House and Senate office buildings.

If you don't mind saddling up to the bar, happy hour is the best way to try some of the city's best restaurants at a fraction of the price, too.

Joe's Seafood, Prime Steak & Stone Crab

- Enjoy discounted appetizers and American wines while you try to spot Members of Congress at **Charlie Palmer Steak** (page 115).

- Lobbyists from the K Street firms indulge in food and drink specials and gossip from 5pm-7pm on weekdays at **BLT Steak** (page 109).

- Near the White House, **Old Ebbitt Grill** serves 1/2-price oysters to a boisterous crowd from 3-6pm and 11pm-close daily (page 110).

- If you can get a seat at the busy bar, **Joe's Seafood, Prime Steak & Stone Crab** is a glamorous spot for food and drink specials with high-rollers from 2:30pm-6:30pm on weekdays (page 109).

- Night owls should head to **Hank's Oyster Bar,** where the raw bar items are 1/2 off from 10pm-midnight daily (page 119).

- The supper-club-style cocktail hour at **The Riggsby** is one of the best, with $5 classic cocktails (including a champagne cocktail) and bites from 4pm-7pm daily (page 119).

- The Michelin-starred **Sushi Taro** offers an incredible deal from 5:30pm-7pm weekdays at the bar only: 1/2 price sushi and alcoholic drinks. Yes, it gets crowded (page 120).

- The **Fiola Mare** bar is the spot for an Italian-style happy hour from 4pm-5:30pm Monday through Thursday, like $9 Negronis and spritzes and $8 pizza (page 133).

Capitol Hill and Atlas District

Map 3

COCKTAIL BARS AND LOUNGES

Copycat Co.

Tired of bartenders getting too creative with your cocktail? Go to Copycat Co. for a long drinks list that draws from the canon of classic cocktail recipe books, as well as for Chinese street food dishes like pot stickers, skewers, and pork *bao* (stuffed buns), which are served until late. Thanks to its industrial, ground floor kitchen and counter, along with a moody upstairs bar with jade accents and dark lighting, you'll feel like you've been transported to a hip, hidden spot in Hong Kong. Owner Devin Gong is a former bartender at José Andrés's Barmini.

MAP 3: 1110 H St. NE, 202/241-1952, www.copycatcompany.com; 5pm-2am Sun.-Thurs., 5pm-3am Fri.-Sat.

Harold Black

Harold Black is a sleek, intimate speakeasy with a few rules—like no flash photography if you want to Instagram your drink, and a note on the menu encouraging you to keep your voice down. But don't worry, you don't need a secret password to enter; just make a reservation online via OpenTable. Located above Acqua Al 2, this slightly hidden lounge features cocktails inspired by the classics, plus snacks like cheese, charcuterie, and sandwiches.

Harold Black

MAP 3: 212 7th St. SE, no phone, www.
haroldblackdc.com; 5:30pm-12:30am
Tues.-Thurs., 5:30pm-1:30am Fri.-Sat.,
5pm-midnight Sun.

Hill Prince

Named for the winner of the 1950
Preakness Stakes, Hill Prince is just
a bar—in the best way. You won't
find expensive, gimmicky drinks or
a complicated reservation system;
rather, the brick-walled row house
and courtyard with a hint of equestrian decor has a perfectly simple
menu of classic cocktails and an interesting selection of beer, wine, and
snacks, with everything priced $10
or less.

MAP 3: 1337 H St. NE, 202/399-1337, www.
hillprince.com; 5pm-midnight Tues.-Thurs.,
5pm-late Fri., 3pm-late Sat., 3pm-10pm Sun.

LIVE MUSIC
Rock and Roll Hotel

You can't stay overnight at the Rock
and Roll Hotel, but you can catch
live music until late almost every
night of the week in this funeral
parlor turned cool concert venue
and club. The three-level venue features a ground floor concert hall for
400, providing an intimate experience for live indie rock, synth-pop,
punk, and funk acts, like Clap Your
Hands Say Yeah, St. Vincent, and
Modern English, as well as more
obscure and local bands. The second-floor lounge and covered roof
deck often showcase DJs and special
events, but they never have a cover
charge.

MAP 3: 1353 H St. NE, 202/388-7625,
www.rockandrollhoteldc.com; show
dates and times vary, generally 6pm-late
Wed.-Thurs., 5pm-3am Fri.-Sat.; shows
$15-35, no cover for lounge and roof
deck

SPORTS BARS AND DIVES
✪ Tune Inn

It's one of DC's remaining true dive
bars, and an institution: Tune Inn has
been serving beer and beloved pub
grub to Capitol Hill's bigwigs and
residents since 1947. While prices
have increased since the bar opened,
the skinny space with walls full of
memorabilia and taxidermy remains
many locals' favorite spot for cheap
pitchers of beer and fried food, including fried pickles, fried mushrooms, and a beer-battered burger.

MAP 3: 331 Pennsylvania Ave. SE,
202/543-2725; 8am-2am Sun.-Thurs.,
8am-3am Fri.-Sat.

Bullfeathers

Hill staffers and lobbyists are known
for making deals and getting involved
in scandals at Bullfeathers, named for
President Teddy Roosevelt's favorite
expression of frustration. Located
close to the House of Representatives
offices on Capitol Hill, this modern
pub is a good place to stop for a cold
beer ($4-12) after visiting the Capitol
or Library of Congress. While you're
unlikely to see members of Congress
downing martinis at lunch these days,
you are likely to hear political gossip
from House staffers.

MAP 3: 410 1st St. SE, 202/484-0228,
www.bullfeathersdc.net; 11am-11pm
Mon.-Fri., noon-8pm Sat.

H Street Country Club

If you'd like to burn off the beers
as you're drinking them, H Street
Country Club has an indoor, nine-hole
mini golf course ($9 pp per round) as
well as shuffleboard and Skee-Ball.
This spot draws a young crowd for its
specials, like $5 margaritas and two
tacos for $3. While the DC-themed

golf course provides the atmosphere in this grubby hangout, it also boasts the largest roof deck in the neighborhood, a good spot for those tequila specials in nice weather.

MAP 3: 1335 H St. NE, 202/399-4722, www.hstreetcountryclub.com; 4pm-1am Mon.-Thurs., 4pm-3am Fri., 11:30am-3am Sat., 11:30am-1am Sun.

GAY AND LESBIAN BARS
Mr. Henry's

Since 1966, Mr. Henry's has been a Capitol Hill institution, a pub where everyone is welcome—including, and especially, the gay community. Founded by Henry Yaffe, Mr. Henry's has operated continuously with few changes to the decor or menu, until new management added healthier options in 2014. The pub launched the career of Roberta Flack, a local teacher who sang in the upstairs lounge. In addition to reliable pub fare and happy hour specials, enjoy jazz, bluegrass, and soul upstairs several nights a week.

MAP 3: 601 Pennsylvania Ave. SE, 202/546-8412, www.mrhenrysdc. com; 11:15am-midnight Mon.-Fri., 10am-midnight Sat.-Sun.

Mr. Henry's

Dupont Circle   Map 4

COCKTAIL BARS AND LOUNGES
✪ Eighteenth Street Lounge

Eighteenth Street Lounge changed DC nightlife, full stop. When DJ Eric Hilton cofounded the hidden lounge above a mattress store in 1995—even today, just a small plaque marks the spot—it quickly became the most happening venue for a luxe but relaxed night out, with groundbreaking electronic music, and a new scene for the city. It was also the birthplace of Grammy-nominated DJ collective Thievery Corporation, led by Hilton and Rob Garza, who got their start in ESL's maze of rooms. While much has changed about DC nightlife—thanks to Eric and his brother Ian, who have gone on to open several successful restaurants and bars in abandoned buildings in the U Street Corridor—ESL remains the place to drink cocktails on vintage velvet banquettes in what feels more like a cool house party than a bar. Choose from several dimly lit rooms or the roof deck, each with their own bar, and groove to house, hip-hop, reggae, funk, and Latin jazz, depending on the night.

MAP 4: 1212 18th St. NW, www.18thstlounge.com; 5pm-2am Tues.-Thurs., 5pm-3am Fri., 9pm-3am Sat., 9pm-2am Sun.; cover $5-15 after 11pm

McClellan's Retreat

The Civil War is an unusual theme for a bar, but this casual neighborhood lounge named for Union commander George B. McClellan works. Why? The drinks and atmosphere are simply good. Order one of the thoughtful house cocktails, which are prepared by lantern light at the wooden bar, or indulge in the extensive selection of whiskey, rye, and bourbon.

MAP 4: 2031 Florida Ave. NW, 202/265-6270, www.mcclellansretreat.com; 4pm-2am Mon.-Fri., 5pm-2am Sat.-Sun.

Quill at The Jefferson

Quill

If you want to impress your date, you could do worse than the sexy lounge at The Jefferson. You'll find older, well-heeled business and media types sipping seasonal cocktails at the golden-hued bar or gathered around the piano. To seal the deal, ask for a booth in one of the private rooms located just outside the bar.

MAP 4: 1200 16th St. NW, 202/448-2300, www.jeffersondc.com; 10am-midnight Mon.-Fri., 11am-midnight Sat.-Sun.

CRAFT BEER

Bier Baron Tavern

This is the bar for beer connoisseurs. With over 50 drafts on tap, including limited release and seasonal selections, as well as more than 500 bottles, even well-traveled drinkers will find something new, especially on the lengthy "cellar" menu with vintage beers from around the world. It's an ideal spot to while away the hours on a rainy day—it is a dark basement, after all—and try a few pints paired with simple bar snacks and sandwiches.

MAP 4: 1523 22nd St. NW, 202/293-1887, www.thebierbaron.com; 4pm-midnight Sun.-Thurs., 4pm-2am Fri., 3pm-2am-Sat.

GAY AND LESBIAN BARS

✪ JR's Bar

Located in the heart of DC's historic gay neighborhood, JR's Bar attracts a mix of local gay men of all ages, who pack this casual corner bar for happy hour specials like all-you-can-drink for $15. The bar has something for everyone, whether you prefer the popular showtunes night with live cabaret or mingling with the young professional kickball teams. The large covered patio is packed during Capital Pride in June, when rainbow flags cover the street.

JR's Bar in Dupont Circle

MAP 4: 1519 17th St. NW, 202/328-0090, www.jrsbar-dc.com; 4pm-2am Mon.-Thurs., 4pm-3am Fri., 1pm-3am Sat., 1pm-2am Sun.

Cobalt

This three-story restaurant, lounge, and dance club is a Dupont Circle institution with a prime corner location in the center of the neighborhood's gay scene. Cobalt has something fun happening every night of the week—from drag shows and karaoke nights to dance parties on the top floor with unbeatable drink specials (like free Grey Goose cocktails) and a mix of partiers.

MAP 4: 1639 R St. NW, 202/232-4416, www.cobaltdc.com; 4pm-2am Mon.-Thurs.,

4pm-3am Fri.-Sat., 4pm-midnight Sun.; cover $0-10

Larry's Lounge

Follow the neon rainbow sign to Larry's Lounge, which has remained one of the neighborhood's essential dive bars, gay or straight, since before the area was covered in nightlife options. You won't find Edison bulbs or a fancy cocktail menu here, but you will enjoy reasonably priced beer, wine, and mixed drinks, on either a red vinyl bar stool or the dog-friendly patio.

MAP 4: 1840 18th St. NW, 202/483-1483, http://larryslounge-hub.com; 4pm-2am Mon.-Thurs., 4pm-3am Fri.-Sat., 2pm-2am Sun.

U Street, Shaw, and Logan Circle   Map 5

COCKTAIL BARS AND LOUNGES
✪ Columbia Room

For a new spin on the cocktail experience, Columbia Room offers a three-course ($79 per person) or five-course ($108 per person) creative cocktail tasting paired with substantial snacks. Advance tickets are almost always required and can be reserved one month in advance; mixology classes are also available. If you prefer to drink à la carte, the bar's inviting Spirits Library, with leather chairs, serves riffs on the classics, while the outdoor Punch Garden has punches and bottled cocktails; seating for both is first-come, first-served.

MAP 5: 124 Blagden Alley NW, 202/316-9396, www.columbiaroomdc.com;

5pm-12:30am Tues.-Thurs., 5pm-1:30am Fri.-Sat.

Café Saint-Ex

During 14th Street's revival in the early 2000s, Café Saint-Ex was a trailblazer, giving the neighborhood a hip bar and bistro. Today, it remains an essential place to hang at the bar with a classic cocktail or one of a great selection of beers, as well as unpretentious American food. Named for Antoine de Saint-Exupéry, the aviator famous for writing *The Little Prince,* the bar has aviation-themed decor and a vintage wooden bar.

MAP 5: 1847 14th St. NW, 202/265-7839, www.saint-ex.com; 4pm-2am Mon.-Wed., 11am-2am Thurs., 11am-3am Fri., 10am-3am Sat., 10am-10pm Sun.

The Gibson

It's not so secret anymore now that you can make a reservation on OpenTable, but this speakeasy is worth visiting for cleverly named cocktails in a dark, moody space. Look for the unmarked black door to the left of Marvin. If there's space, you'll be shown to a bar stool or candlelit booth, but you won't be allowed to stand at the bar, so make a reservation a few days in advance to guarantee a seat.

MAP 5: 2009 14th St. NW, 202/232-2156, www.thegibsondc.com; 6pm-2am Mon.-Thurs., 6pm-3am Fri.-Sat., 6pm-midnight Sun.

Marvin

It's been around since 2007, but the roof deck at Marvin remains one of the best. The spacious deck and the snug indoor lounge adjacent attract a young, attractive crowd all weekend long, though it's a slightly older and more chill crowd on Sundays. Open year-round, it's known for Belgian beers but has a full bar and snacks, too. The ground floor restaurant serves food inspired by Marvin Gaye's time spent in Washington DC and Ostend, Belgium—think fried chicken and waffles as well as *moules frites* (mussels and fries).

MAP 5: 2007 14th St. NW, 202/797-7171, www.marvindc.com; 5pm-2am Mon.-Thurs., 5pm-3am Fri.-Sat., 4pm-2am Sun.

2 Birds 1 Stone

This slightly hidden basement lounge has excellent cocktails and big booths for groups of friends—no cover charge or pricey bottle service required. And with brick walls and white decor, this basement is chic, not dank. The bartenders offer a changing seasonal menu, as well as the classics; most range $10-15.

2 Birds 1 Stone

Dacha Beer Garden in Shaw

MAP 5: 1800 14th St. NW, no phone, www.2birds1stonedc.com; 6pm-12:15am Tues.-Thurs., 6pm-1:15am Fri.-Sat.

CRAFT BEER
Dacha Beer Garden

When you find Liz Taylor, you've reached Dacha Beer Garden. A huge mural of the actress overlooks this outdoor beer garden located in a corner lot in Shaw, serving American, Belgian, and German craft beers as well as a few cocktails, wine, and seasonal bites. It's best on lazy summer afternoons, but it is open year-round, weather permitting; check the Facebook page to confirm the hours.

MAP 5: 1600 7th St. NW, 202/350-9888, www.dachadc.com; 4pm-10:30pm Mon.-Thurs., noon-midnight Fri., 11am-midnight Sat., 11am-10:30pm Sun., hours may vary seasonally

Right Proper Brewing Co.

One of the best places to try a new beer is at this no-reservations brewpub near The Howard Theatre, where there's almost always something new that's been made on-site. Right Proper has a constantly changing selection of their own beers and other craft varieties, plus a full bar and classic American food, like burgers, ribs, and wood-grilled fish and meats, as well as bar snacks. Enjoy in the industrial-chic pub (think Edison bulbs and exposed brick) or on the front patio.

MAP 5: 624 T St. NW, 202/607-2337, www.rightproperbrewing.com; 5pm-midnight Mon.-Thurs., 11:30am-1am Fri.-Sat., 11:30am-11pm Sun., kitchen closes one hour prior to closing

WINE BARS
Maxwell Park

Brent Kroll spent nearly a decade as sommelier at some of DC's best restaurants before opening this un-stuffy wine bar in 2017. It might take you some time to decide what you want to order, because the menu changes monthly, with about 50 wines by the glass to fit a theme (like "anything but pinot grigio" or "unique bubbles from around the world")—but the helpful staff knows the wines inside and out and can guide you if needed. And while wine rules here, don't ignore the original cocktails.

MAP 5: 1336 9th St. NW, www.maxwelldcwine.com; 5pm-late daily

Vinoteca

This casually elegant wine bar in a row house in the U Street Corridor is always a good idea. When it's cold, hole up in the cozy restaurant for cheese, charcuterie, and a glass of wine or sherry cocktail; in the summer, the outdoor bar with its bocce court is the ideal place to frolic with sparkling rosé and grilled specials. The wine list features dozens available in two- or five-ounce pours, with a heavy focus on French and Italian varietals.

MAP 5: 1940 11th St. NW, 202/332-9463, www.vinotecadc.com; 5pm-close Mon.-Fri., 11am-close Sat.-Sun.

LIVE MUSIC
✪ Black Cat

Since 1993, Black Cat has been one of the best places to dance the night away. The 7,000-square-foot main stage has hosted Arcade Fire, Death Cab for Cutie, The Killers, Moby, and Rancid, among others, while a smaller stage and bar is open most nights for smaller, local bands and DJs. Don't miss theme parties like Eighties Mayhem and The Cure vs. The Smiths, which bring mixed crowds to dance the night away. And bring cash, because the venue doesn't take credit cards for cover at the door or drinks.

MAP 5: 1811 14th St. NW, 202/667-4490, www.blackcatdc.com; box office 6:30pm-midnight Mon.-Fri., 7pm-midnight Sat.-Sun.; tickets $0-25

✪ 9:30 Club

Named one of the top nightclubs in the world by *Rolling Stone* and *Billboard*, 9:30 Club is, simply put, an institution. The club opened in a tiny building in Chinatown in 1980; despite having a capacity of 200, it welcomed Nirvana, R.E.M., and the Red Hot Chili Peppers to the stage. Facing competition from larger venues, the owners moved the club to the much larger current venue, a 1,200-capacity club, which feels much more intimate when local bands like Thievery Corporation return for much-awaited, sold-out shows.

MAP 5: 815 V St. NW, 202/265-0930, www.930.com; box office noon-7pm Mon.-Fri., noon-11pm Mon.-Fri. on show nights, 6pm-11pm Sat. on show nights, 6pm-10:30pm Sun. on show nights; tickets $10-40

New Vegas Lounge

New Vegas Lounge

Open since 1971, New Vegas Lounge is the home of the Out of Town Band, a local, seven-piece rhythm and blues band that performs the best of Motown plus party hits on weekend nights. The small venue can get hot and crowded with 20- and 30-somethings; arrive early to grab one of the few tables, but be prepared to stand up and dance after midnight.

MAP 5: 1415 P St. NW, 202/483-3971, www.newvegasloungedc.com; 9pm-late Fri.-Sat.; cover $10

DANCE CLUBS
Flash

Feel the music in this intimate, two-level dance club that brings chart-topping international electronic DJs to Washington, including house and techno stars who spend their summers in music hubs like Ibiza. Flash is open every Friday and Saturday night until late; check the schedule for other events during the week, including Sunday afternoon sessions.

MAP 5: 645 Florida Ave. NW, 202/827-8791, www.flashdc.com; 8pm-4am Fri.-Sat., other days and times vary; cover $10-20

Tropicalia

Named for the avant-garde Brazilian arts movement of the 1960s, Tropicalia is a spacious, colorful, basement-level club that showcases Afro house and funk, with some electronica, '80s, and live music in the mix, too. The club bills itself as a "dance club for grown-ups," though the crowd is young and ready to party on weekends.

MAP 5: 2001 14th St. NW, 202/629-4535, www.tropicaliadc.com; days and times vary; cover $0-10

U Street Music Hall

Founded by one of the top local DJs, Will Eastman, U Street Music Hall is the club for music lovers, with a state-of-the-art sound system and plenty of space to dance on the cushioned dance floor. The come-as-you-are club hosts top electronic DJs and artists, as well as local performers.

MAP 5: 1115 U St. NW, 202/588-1889, www.ustreetmusichall.com; hours vary based on calendar; tickets $10-30

GAY AND LESBIAN BARS
✪ Nellie's Sports Bar

Named for the owner's great grandmother and great-great grandmother, this U Street institution is the ideal place to pop into for a bucket of beers and the big game, or plan your week around trivia night or the all-you-can-eat brunch with drag performers, which usually sells out in advance. After, soak up the sun on the expansive rooftop into the evening. The crowd varies depending on the day of the week, but everyone is always welcome.

MAP 5: 900 U St. NW, 202/332-6355, www.nelliessportsbar.com; 5pm-1am Mon.-Thurs., 3pm-3am Fri., 10:30am-3am Sat., 10:30am-1am Sun.

COCKTAIL BARS AND LOUNGES

✪ Jack Rose Dining Saloon

It's all about the whiskey at Jack Rose Dining Saloon, a multi-level bar and restaurant known for its 2,500-bottle collection of whiskey and Scotch from around the world. Saddle up to the wooden main bar in the dining saloon, where you can have simple and hearty American fare, cocktails, and whiskey flights, or decamp to the speakeasy-style whiskey cellar (7pm-2am Wed.-Thurs., reservations only at 6:30pm and 9:30pm Fri.-Sat.), which serves whiskey on tap and rare bottles. When the weather's nice, the open-air terrace and separate tiki bar have their own menus of seasonally appropriate libations; enjoy half-price drinks at the tiki bar 5pm-9pm on Thursdays.

MAP 6: 2007 18th St. NW, 202/588-7388, www.jackrosediningsaloon.com; 5pm-2am Sun.-Thurs., 5pm-3am Fri.-Sat.

CRAFT BEER

Meridian Pint

This unfussy pub has more than 20 draft and 50 bottled American craft beers, including many local varieties, which the owner stocks in order to promote sustainable business practices (wherein the beer travels shorter distances from the brewery to the bar, and so reduces vehicle emissions during the transportation process). Pair your beer with American bar food and comforting entrées, like *steak frites* (steak and fries) and roast chicken made with

Jack Rose Dining Saloon

DC'S OFFICIAL COCKTAIL

If you're visiting DC in the dead of summer, a refreshing **rickey** will cool you off better than any beer or rosé. Colonel Joe Rickey, a Confederate Army veteran turned well-connected Democratic lobbyist, was a frequent patron of Shoomaker's, a bar once located near the National Theatre, where he schmoozed and drank rye and water on ice. One summer day in 1883, according to legend, bartender George Williamson added half a lime to the mix, and the rickey was born, though today it's more commonly made with gin rather than rye or bourbon. (Some historians say Rickey asked for the lime, while others say he drank the cocktail with lemon, but either way, he's better known for his contribution to the American cocktail canon than anything he did in politics.)

In July 2011, the city council declared the rickey DC's official drink and the month of July "Rickey Month." While any decent bartender will be able to craft the simple highball, you'll find the drink on menus at bars across the city in July, when the DC Craft Bartenders Guild organizes an annual competition in which bartenders create their own takes. Rickey Month culminates in an all-you-can-drink championship event at one of the participating bars. For details on the competition and other cocktail events, visit the guild's Facebook page.

To make your own, simply combine half a lime, 2 ounces bourbon, rye, or gin, and sparkling water on ice.

local ingredients—and if you're with a group, you can reserve a table with your own tap to serve yourself.

MAP 6: 3400 11th St. NW, 202/588-1075, www.meridianpint.com; 5pm-midnight Mon.-Thurs., 5pm-3am Fri., 10am-3am Sat., 10am-midnight Sun.

LIVE MUSIC
Madam's Organ

Look for the mural of the well-endowed burlesque dancer to find live blues, bluegrass, country, and soul seven nights a week. (In fact, *The Madam* is a bit controversial; the city government fined the owner because they claim the mural violates sign regulations.) The four-level establishment with five bars gets packed and sweaty on the weekends; if you need some fresh air, keep heading up to find space to lounge and a roof deck.

MAP 6: 2461 18th St. NW, 202/667-5370, www.madamsorgan.com; 5pm-2am Sun.-Thurs., 5pm-3am Fri.-Sat.; cover $5

Songbyrd Music House & Record Café

In the 1960s and 1970s, Charlie Byrd played his famous bossa nova guitar in the Showboat Lounge in Adams Morgan; today, the same space is one of the city's most chill live music venues. The intimate basement stage, known as The Byrd Cage, has all-ages shows featuring up-and-coming rock, electronic, soul, and hip-hop musicians as well as classic album listening parties, while upstairs, there's a restaurant, bar and café with vintage-inspired decor, and a record shop. For live music, purchase tickets in advance to guarantee entry, because the basement stage only accommodates about 200.

MAP 6: 2477 18th St. NW, 202/450-2917, www.songbyrddc.com; 5pm-2am Mon., noon-2am Tues.-Thurs., noon-3am Fri., 11am-3am Sat., 11am-2am Sun.; cover $0-20 for live music

SPORTS BARS AND DIVES

Dan's Café

You won't find any frou-frou cocktails, hip DJs, or posh decor at Dan's Café—and that's why locals love it. Consistently named one of the top dive bars in the area, the family-owned establishment has been serving cheap beer and mix-your-own cocktails out of squeeze bottles to neighborhood regulars and rowdy 20-somethings since the 1940s. It's cash only, so come prepared—but you don't need more than $20 for the night.

MAP 6: 2315 18th St. NW, 202/265-9241; 7pm-2am Tues.-Thurs., 7pm-3am Fri.-Sat.

Raven Grill

This neighborhood dive has been serving cheap beer—really cheap, like $3 Natty Bohs—to Mount Pleasant residents since 1935. Its age shows, but that's what makes it unique in a city full of shiny establishments serving $15 cocktails and small plates. Come here for simple drinks (cash only), a full jukebox, and a diverse, relaxed crowd of regulars every night of the week.

MAP 6: 3125 Mt. Pleasant St. NW, 202/387-8411, no website; 4pm-2am Mon.-Tues., 2pm-2am Wed.-Thurs., 2pm-3am Fri.-Sat., 2pm-2am Sun.

The Wonderland Ballroom

Close your Tinder app and head to The Wonderland Ballroom in Columbia Heights, because this millennial paradise boasts that it's hosted nine weddings for couples who met here. During happy hour and until the wee hours on the weekends, 20- and 30-somethings crowd the bar filled with kitschy signs, the sweaty basement dance floor, and the beer garden for $3 Pabst Blue Ribbon and dance music.

MAP 6: 1101 Kenyon St. NW, 202/232-5263, www.thewonderlandballroom.com; 5pm-2am Mon.-Thurs., 4pm-3am Fri., 11am-3am Sat., 10am-2am Sun.

Georgetown and Foggy Bottom
Map 7

COCKTAIL BARS AND LOUNGES

✪ The Lounge at Bourbon Steak

Come for the extensive cocktail menu, stay for the people-watching. You may find celebrities, socialites, dealmakers, lonely hearts, and pretty young things looking to make connections at the long, dimly lit bar at the Four Seasons. If you get hungry, the burgers are good, or you can make your way to a table in the namesake restaurant, a pricey steakhouse by Michael Mina.

MAP 7: 2800 Pennsylvania Ave. NW, 202/944-2026, www.bourbonsteakdc.com; 11:30am-midnight Mon.-Thurs., 11:30am-1am Fri., 2:30pm-1am Sat., 2:30pm-midnight Sun.

✪ Top of the Gate

With a 360-degree view of downtown, Georgetown, and Virginia, including several monuments, the sprawling,

Top of the Gate at The Watergate Hotel

open-air rooftop bar at **The Watergate Hotel** is the best perch in the city—especially for happy hour, when the sun sets over the Potomac River. There's plenty of space to stand at the bar to enjoy refreshing cocktails and champagne, or you can get a table and order a superb pizza, served in a pizza box. Reservations are recommended on weekends, especially when the weather's nice; minimums for seats start at $25-40 per person or $300 for private groups. MAP 7: 2650 Virginia Ave. NW, 202/322-6455, www.thewatergatehotel. com; 5pm-11pm Mon.-Thurs., 5pm-1am Fri., 1pm-1am Sat., 1pm-11pm Sun., weather permitting

The Next Whisky Bar

"Show me the way to the next whisky bar," sang Jim Morrison of The Doors in 1967, the inspiration of the showstopper lounge on the main level of **The Watergate Hotel.** Take a seat in one of the red retro-style chairs, surrounded by 2,500 glittering whiskey bottles, and enjoy whiskey and bourbon cocktails and tastings with a psychedelic rock soundtrack. MAP 7: 2650 Virginia Ave. NW, 202/827-1600, www.thewatergatehotel. com; 4pm-midnight Sun.-Thurs., 4pm-1am Fri.-Sat.

The Observatory

Posh locals play on the roof deck of **The Graham Georgetown** when the weather is nice, where you can enjoy cocktails and bubbles with a view of the city skyline. Wear your new purchases from the nearby boutiques—when it's busy, the door staff may enforce the bar's "Georgetown Chic" dress code, meaning you'll want to be dressed to impress. Reservations are recommended. MAP 7: 1075 Thomas Jefferson St. NW, 202/337-0900, www. thegrahamgeorgetown.com; 4pm-midnight Mon.-Thurs., 4pm-2am Fri., 3pm-2am Sat., 3pm-midnight Sun., weather permitting

WINE BARS
Bar à Vin

There's no better retreat on a chilly evening than Bar à Vin, the dimly lit row house known for a broad list of French wines by the glass, as well as cocktails and noshes like house-made charcuterie and French cheese. No reservations are necessary; grab a plush velvet chair by the wood-burning fire and stay awhile.

MAP 7: 1035 31st St. NW, 202/965-2606, www.chezbillysud.com; 5pm-11pm Sun.-Thurs., 5pm-midnight Fri.-Sat.

LIVE MUSIC
Blues Alley

Hidden in an alley off Wisconsin Avenue, this jazz club has been hosting some of the genre's greatest musicians since 1965, including Dizzy Gillespie, Ella Fitzgerald, Wynton Marsalis, and Sarah Vaughan, among many others, in the intimate space for about 125 guests. You can see live jazz performances—and sometimes, visiting celebrities in the audience—every night of the week.

MAP 7: 1073 Wisconsin Ave. NW, 202/347-4141, www.bluesalley.com; 6pm-12:30am daily; tickets $20-50, plus $12 food or beverage minimum pp

Navy Yard and Anacostia Map 8

CRAFT BEER
Bluejacket

With seating for 200 and beers for every palate, this three-story microbrewery and restaurant inside a former Navy Yard factory is a good bet before or after a baseball game. On any given day, you'll find at least 20 of their own brews on tap, which are all made on site, ranging from IPAs and sour ales to authentic cask ales. Try a few four-ounce pours at the long, lofty bar, or reserve a spot on the brewery tour and tasting (7pm Fri., 3pm Sat.). The on-site restaurant, The Arsenal, serves traditional pub fare, seafood, and steak, as well as a late-night menu for post-game hunger pangs.

MAP 8: 300 Tingey St. SE, 202/524-4862, www.bluejacketdc.com; 11am-1am Sun.-Thurs., 11am-2am Fri.-Sat.

LIVE MUSIC
✪ The Anthem

This sleek District Wharf music venue opened in October 2017 with a sold-out show headlined by the Foo Fighters. With capacity for 6,000, it's bringing the big names—in addition to the Foo Fighters, Bob Dylan, Lorde, and The Killers performed in its first few months. The owners, who also run the iconic 9:30 Club (815 V St. NW, 202/265-0930, www.930.com),

The Anthem

PIZZA, BEER, AND FAKE NEWS

In December 2016, Washington was shaken when a man entered Upper Northwest pizza parlor Comet Ping Pong and fired several shots from an assault rifle before surrendering to police. He traveled from North Carolina to DC to "self-investigate" the conspiracy theory that Hillary Clinton and her campaign manager John Podesta were running a child sex trafficking ring in the establishment, a claim "reported" by right-wing fake news websites and anonymous message boards in the lead-up to the 2016 presidential election. Luckily, nobody was injured, but "Pizzagate" showed how fake news is not just a punchline, but a trend with potential to do real damage.

In the aftermath of Pizzagate, **Comet Ping Pong** (5307 Connecticut Ave. NW, 202/364-0404, www.cometpingpong.com; 5pm-9:30pm Mon.-Thurs., 11:30am-10:45pm Fri.-Sat., 11:30am-9:30pm Sun., bar open late) was flooded with community support. It's a terrific local business to support if you're against the proliferation of fake news—and the wood-fired pizza is good, too. Take the family for a casual weekend lunch or dinner and enjoy free ping pong games while you wait for your pie, or join DC hipsters for beer (most between $5-8) and live music until late. Whatever you do, leave the conspiracy theories at home. It's only 15 minutes by car or taxi from Dupont Circle.

---

know how to put on a show. Despite the venue's large size, every show feels intimate due to a movable stage. Other features include premium, scalper-proof, reserved seat options at every show (including general admission shows), seven bars, and concessions from local businesses.

MAP 8: 901 Wharf St. SW, 202/888-0020, tickets 877/435-9849, www.theanthemdc.com; box office noon-7pm daily or until 9pm on show days

Greater Washington DC   Map 9

TASTING ROOMS AND DISTILLERIES
Cotton & Reed

You'll never want Captain Morgan again after trying the dry-spiced rum made with 17 botanicals at Cotton & Reed. Founded by former NASA employees Reed Walker and Jordan Cotton, DC's first rum distillery also produces a carefully crafted white rum and allspice dram. Try them all in the industrial tiki tasting room and bar near Union Market, which serves until late and regularly hosts public parties to celebrate new blends, or take a 30-minute tour, available at 1pm, 2pm, and 3pm on Saturday and Sunday, which costs $22 and concludes with a flight.

MAP 9: 1330 5th St. NE, 202/544-2805, www.cottonandreed.com; 4pm-midnight Wed.-Fri., noon-midnight Sat.-Sun.

Republic Restoratives

This growing, woman-owned distillery produced a limited-edition rye for November 2016: Rodham Rye, celebrating what they thought would be the election of the first female POTUS. Things didn't quite go as planned, but Pia Carusone and Rachel Gardner released it anyway. Visit their tasting room bar, which is built in a warehouse in the former B&O Railroad Yard in Ivy City and has lots of natural light and sleek wood finishes, where you can try refined cocktails made with their clean Civic Vodka or Borough Bourbon (made with Kentucky whiskey). Check their calendar of events for special tasting events, like yoga classes and brunch parties with local food vendors.

MAP 9: 1369 New York Ave. NE, 202/733-3996, www.republicrestoratives. com; 5pm-11pm Thurs.-Fri., noon-11pm Sat., noon-5pm Sun., tours available Sat.-Sun.

ARTS AND CULTURE

National Mall 162
Downtown and Penn Quarter 164
Capitol Hill and Atlas District 168
Dupont Circle 170
U Street, Shaw, and Logan Circle 172
Adams Morgan 175
Georgetown and Foggy Bottom 175
Navy Yard and Anacostia 177
Greater Washington DC 180
Festivals and Events 181

The first American city to have a black majority, Washington DC was a vibrant hub for African American arts and culture even before Harlem and Motown—

United States Botanic Garden

and as the home of Duke Ellington, Marvin Gaye, and Chuck Brown, DC's most important contribution to American arts is the music. From the early 20th century until the 1960s, U Street and Shaw were known as "Black Broadway," with jazz clubs and iconic theaters like The Howard Theatre and The Lincoln Theatre, which remain the best spots to experience DC's jazz, soul, and go-go sounds.

This history set the stage for DC's rich cultural scene today, with world-class performing arts, eye-popping historical homes and gardens, and of course, dozens of museums and galleries—many of which are free and open to the public almost every day of the year. You could spend weeks exploring the National Mall's museums, but you'll find hubs of niche history and art museums downtown and in Dupont Circle, as well.

DC likewise has a theater and performing arts scene on par with the world capitals, with theaters citywide showcasing Broadway-quality productions of classic and contemporary dramas and musicals as well as premieres of quirky new plays and fringe theater. And in Foggy Bottom, The John F. Kennedy Center for the Performing Arts is one of the country's premier venues, home to the National Symphony Orchestra as well as jazz, opera, and dance programs.

HIGHLIGHTS

✪ **COOLEST CONTEMPORARY ART:** The **Hirshhorn Museum and Sculpture Garden** boasts more than 12,000 modern and contemporary works, housed in a circular building designed by Gordon Bunshaft (page 162).

✪ **BEST FOR ART LOVERS OF ALL KINDS:** The **National Gallery of Art** has something for every fan of art—Da Vinci, Dutch masters, and French impressionists in the West Building, and cool modern art in the East Building (page 162).

✪ **MOST SOBERING REMINDER OF THE PAST:** The **United States Holocaust Memorial Museum** tells the story of the Holocaust in moving detail (page 162).

✪ **MOST NEWSWORTHY MUSEUM:** The interactive **Newseum** explores the First Amendment and the role of the press (page 164).

✪ **MOST INNOVATIVE THEATER:** Any production by the **Woolly Mammoth Theatre Company** is sure to be groundbreaking—and maybe even shocking (page 166).

✪ **OLDEST MODERN ART MUSEUM:** The **Phillips Collection** was founded in 1921 and is considered America's first modern art museum (page 170).

✪ **BEST VENUE TO EXPERIENCE GO-GO:** The historic **Howard Theatre** regularly hosts go-go bands, a uniquely DC style of music (page 173).

✪ **WIDEST-RANGING ARTS VENUE:** The **John F. Kennedy Center for the Performing Arts** showcases world-class music, theater, opera, dance, and comedy for all tastes, with a free performance daily (page 177).

✪ **BEST ALTERNATIVE TO BROADWAY:** Since 1950, Southwest's **Arena Stage** has been premiering award-winning plays and reviving classic American dramas and musicals (page 179).

✪ **MOST OPULENT HISTORIC HOME:** The former estate of Marjorie Merriweather Post, **Hillwood Estate, Museum & Gardens** is the closest thing to Versailles in DC, thanks to the extravagant gardens and art collection (page 180).

✪ **BUCKET-LIST FESTIVAL:** During the **National Cherry Blossom Festival,** you'll get the chance to see thousands of the pink and white flowering trees in bloom (page 181).

✪ **MOST PATRIOTIC EXPERIENCE:** Celebrate **Independence Day** in the nation's capital with a parade, outdoor concert, and a jaw-dropping fireworks display (page 183).

National Mall

Map 1

MUSEUMS

✪ Hirshhorn Museum and Sculpture Garden

This Smithsonian museum dedicated to modern and contemporary art has some of the coolest art in town, with temporary exhibitions by of-the-moment artists like Yayoi Kusama and Ai Wei Wei. In addition to ground-breaking temporary exhibitions, the Hirshhorn is home to more than 12,000 paintings, sculptures, mobiles, and video installations by the likes of Hopper, Bacon, Miró, and Calder, as well as lesser-known artists. Don't miss the four-acre Sculpture Garden, which feels like a scene out of *Alice in Wonderland,* and take a walk around the circular building, a work of art itself by modern architect Gordon Bunshaft.

MAP 1: 7th St. SW and Independence Ave. SW, 202/633-4674, http://hirshhorn. si.edu; museum 10am-5:30pm daily, garden 7:30am-dusk daily; free

✪ National Gallery of Art

The National Gallery of Art has two distinct personalities and always something new on display. The resplendent original building, the **West Building,** is home to classic beauty: *Ginevra de' Benci,* Da Vinci's only painting on view in the Americas, plus Dutch masters, French impressionists, and more from the 15th to 19th centuries in a setting that transports you to Europe. The **East Building,** designed by I. M. Pei, is home to the cool crowd: Matisse, Picasso, Warhol, and Lichtenstein, plus Katharina Fritsch's bright blue *Hahn/Cock* on the roof terrace. The **Sculpture Garden** has 17 major sculptures, and it hosts free jazz concerts on summer Friday evenings.

MAP 1: Constitution Ave. NW between 3rd St. NW and 9th St. NW, 202/737-4215, www. nga.gov; 10am-5pm Mon.-Sat., 11am-6pm Sun. daily; free

✪ United States Holocaust Memorial Museum

The United States Holocaust Memorial Museum must be experienced. The permanent exhibition, "The Holocaust," spans three floors; plan to take several hours to travel through the chronological timeline, from the rise of the Nazi Party to the horrifying treatment and murder of the Jews and, finally, to the liberation of the concentration camps and the end of World War II. You'll be amazed by the level of detail, the personal artifacts and first-hand accounts, and multimedia, although be prepared—it's challenging. The permanent exhibition is recommended for ages 11 and up. "Remember the Children: Daniel's Story," a lighter exhibit about one family's experience during the Holocaust, told through the eyes of a young boy, is a better choice with young children or if you don't have time to explore the permanent exhibition, which requires 2-3 hours. Rotating exhibits cover other Holocaust topics or anti-Semitism and genocide in history and present day.

MAP 1: 100 Raoul Wallenberg Pl. SW between 14th St. SW and 15th St. SW, 202/488-0400, www.ushmm.org; 10am-5:20pm daily; free tickets for the permanent exhibition required Mar.-Aug.

the Tile Wall at the United States Holocaust Memorial Museum

Freer Gallery of Art and Arthur M. Sackler Gallery

Connected on the inside, the Freer and Sackler Galleries showcase one of the most diverse collections of Asian art in the world—from Chinese jade and fine Persian books to contemporary Japanese prints and porcelain, as well as works from Egypt, Korea, India, Iran, Iraq, Pakistan, Syria, and Turkey. The highlight is James McNeill Whistler's Peacock Room, an extravagant dining room he designed for a British shipping tycoon, which Charles Lang Freer purchased, shipped to the United States, and installed in his home in its entirety to showcase his impressive collection of Asian ceramics. The galleries are known for innovative cultural programming, like the annual Iranian Film Festival.

MAP 1: 12th St. SW at Independence Ave. SW, 202/633-4880, http://asia.si.edu; 10am-5:30pm daily; free

National Archives Museum

What exactly does it mean to have the right to life, liberty, and the pursuit of happiness? How did the Founding Fathers come up with this idea, anyway? Explore these questions in the National Archives Museum, home of the Declaration of Independence, the U.S. Constitution, and the Bill of Rights, as well as one of four remaining original Magna Cartas from 1297. The Public Vaults have more than 1,000 items from the National Archives on display at any time.

MAP 1: Constitution Ave. NW between 7th St. NW and 9th St. NW, 202/357-5000, www.archives.gov/museum; 10am-5:30pm daily; free

National Museum of African Art

The only museum in the United States dedicated exclusively to African art, this smaller Smithsonian museum is an excellent choice when

163

the others on the National Mall are packed. The collection spans the African continent, featuring traditional works, like rare ceramics from the Disney-Tishman Collection, one of the most important collections of West and Central African art, as well as contemporary paintings and video installations. Don't rush through the entryway; some of the works hanging there are believed to have spiritual powers, while others address the impact of social problems like the HIV/AIDS crisis on African communities.

MAP 1: 950 Independence Ave. SW, 202/633-4600, http://africa.si.edu; 10am-5:30pm daily; free

National Museum of the American Indian

It's not as thrilling as spacecraft or dinosaurs, but this Smithsonian museum explores a critically important piece of American history. In the five-story limestone building, learn about native culture and spirituality across the Western Hemisphere, as well as treaties between the United States and the American Indian Nations, told through the voices of American Indians, not occupiers. Plan to visit this quieter museum before or after lunch at **Mitsitam Native Foods Café,** the best museum café in the city.
MAP 1: 4th St. SW and Independence Ave. SW, 202/633-6644, http://nmai.si.edu; 10am-5:30pm daily; free

Downtown and Penn Quarter

Map 2

MUSEUMS
✪ Newseum

There's no fake news at the Newseum, which explores the meaning of the First Amendment and the role of the press, a mission that remains critically important today. And in a city full of free museums, this seven-story, interactive treasure trove is well worth the admission fee. Get an in-depth look at headline-making events like the 9/11 terrorist attacks and the fall of the Berlin Wall—and see the largest display of parts of the wall outside of Germany—or try to hack it as a television reporter in the NBC News Interactive Newsroom.

MAP 2: 555 Pennsylvania Ave. NW, 202/292-6100, www.newseum.org;

9am-5pm Mon.-Sat., 10am-5pm Sun.; $25 adults, $20 seniors, $15 children ages 7-18, free for children 6 and under

International Spy Museum

Bring out your inner James Bond at the International Spy Museum, which has the largest collection of spy artifacts like encryption machines, glasses that conceal cyanide pills, and even lipstick and tobacco pipe guns. The interactive, kid-friendly museum gives you an understanding of what motivates spies through historical documents, photographs, and real stories. For an extra fee, Operation Spy allows visitors 12 and over to participate in an immersive mission.
MAP 2: 800 F St. NW, 202/393-7798, www.spymuseum.org; open daily, hours vary;

$22 adults, $16 seniors, military, and law enforcement, $15 children 7-11, free for children 6 and under

National Building Museum

This favorite museum among locals contains stimulating exhibits about architecture, construction, and urban planning, as well as a cool interactive gallery for kids ages 2-6. Located inside a breathtaking Italian Renaissance Revival structure, which was the headquarters of the U.S. Pension Bureau after the Civil War, the galleries—formerly offices for 1,000-plus pension employees—surround a soaring atrium with 75-foot Corinthian columns.

MAP 2: 401 F St. NW, 202/272-2448, www.nbm.org; 10am-5pm Mon.-Sat., 11am-5pm Sun.; $10 adults, $7 students, seniors, and children 3-18, free for children 2 and under

National Museum of Women in the Arts

Shockingly, Washington's National Museum of Women in the Arts is the only major museum in the world dedicated exclusively to women artists. It was founded by Wilhelmina Cole Holladay, a diplomat and art collector who was appalled by the lack of information about women artists in American art textbooks, and she made it her mission to support women artists. Rotating exhibitions draw from the collection of nearly 5,000 pieces by more than 1,000 female artists, including Mary Cassatt, Clara Peeters, and Frida Kahlo, as well as hundreds of lesser-known artists.

MAP 2: 1250 New York Ave. NW, 202/783-5000, www.nmwa.org; 10am-5pm Mon.-Sat., noon-5pm Sun.; $10 adults, $8 students and seniors, free for children 18 and under

Newseum

National Portrait Gallery

Get up close and personal with Robert F. Kennedy, Michael Jackson, Alexander Hamilton, Harriet Beecher Stowe, and Pocahontas, just a few of the prominent Americans whose likenesses are on display at the Smithsonian's National Portrait Gallery. The 17 galleries are arranged chronologically so you can explore American history through the people who made it—including a portrait of every U.S. president, the only such collection outside of the White House. The gallery is collocated with the Smithsonian American Art Museum.

MAP 2: 8th St. NW and F St. NW, 202/633-8300, http://npg.si.edu; 11:30am-7pm daily; free

Renwick Gallery

Designed by architect James Renwick Jr., who was inspired by the Louvre, the Renwick Gallery was the first building in the United States constructed for the purpose of showcasing art. The Smithsonian's contemporary American craft and decorative art collection is housed in the state-of-the-art building. The permanent collection highlights craft as an art form, including furniture and home decor, sculptures and ceramics, and textiles and jewelry. Pieces include glass works by Dale Chihuly, jewelry by Alexander Calder, and Larry Fuente's *Game Fish,* a large 3-D fish sculpture made with tiny toys and game pieces.

MAP 2: Pennsylvania Ave. NW at 17th St. NW, 202/633-7970, http://renwick. americanart.si.edu; 10am-5:30pm daily; free

Smithsonian American Art Museum

With Jonathan Borofsky's 27-foot *Man with Briefcase* looming in front, the Smithsonian American Art Museum shows modern folk and self-taught art you can't see anywhere else, including one of the largest collections of art commissioned by the U.S. government during the New Deal in the 1930s. The gallery shares space with the National Portrait Gallery in one of the oldest buildings in DC.

MAP 2: 8th St. NW and F St. NW, 202/633-7970, http://americanart.si.edu; 11:30am-7pm daily; free

THEATER, MUSIC, AND DANCE

✪ Woolly Mammoth Theatre Company

The Woolly Mammoth Theatre Company produces, hands down, the most innovative theater in DC. It's been making audiences laugh, think, and squirm since 1980. Especially memorable productions include the colorful *Marie Antoinette* for the Kardashian era, as well as *Arguendo,* which explained how the U.S. Supreme Court works, using the exact language of the oral arguments of *Barnes v. Glen Theatre Inc.,* in which exotic dancers in Indiana argued that a state law requiring them to wear g-strings and pasties violated the First Amendment. (Indiana won.) Woolly Mammoth is dedicated to premiering groundbreaking American works but also welcomes performers like Mike Daisey, best known for his controversial *The Agony and the Ecstasy of Steve Jobs.* All performances take place at the company's 256-seat courtyard-style theater, where there's not a bad seat in the house; check the website for post-show panel discussions and pay-what-you-can nights.

MAP 2: 641 D St. NW, 202/393-3939, www. woollymammoth.net; box office noon-6pm Wed.-Sun.; tickets $59-79 hether you want to see a Broadway-quality musical or the premiere of a quirky new ay, DC's theater scene offers something for every taste. Whatever you see, it will be both eative and smart—like the city itself.

Experience world-class music, dance, and opera at **The John F. Kennedy Center for the Performing Arts** (page 177) in Foggy Bottom.

The avant-garde dramas and comedies produced by the **Woolly Mammoth Theatre Company** (page 166) in Penn Quarter will make you think and squirm.

Shakespeare fans will appreciate opportunities to see both popular and obscure works from the **Shakespeare Theatre Company** (page 167) or **Folger Theatre** (page 169).

History buffs might enjoy a play and a tour at **Ford's Theatre** (page 83), where President Lincoln was shot during a performance of *Our American Cousin*.

National Theatre

John Wilkes Booth wasn't a stranger to President Abraham Lincoln when he shot him at Ford's Theatre on April 14, 1865. Lincoln saw his assassin perform the lead in Shakespeare's *Richard III* at the National Theatre two years prior. Today, the theater, which has operated continuously since 1835, hosts national tours as well as world premieres of shows before they head to Broadway, including *Show Boat* in 1927, *West Side Story* in 1957, and *Mean Girls*, based on the cult film of the same name, in 2017.

MAP 2: 1321 Pennsylvania Ave. NW, 202/628-6161, www.thenationaldc.org; box office noon-6pm daily and two hours prior to showtime until 30 min. after showtime; tickets from $45

Shakespeare Theatre Company

The play's the thing at the Tony Award-winning Shakespeare Theatre Company, which has performed Shakespearean works as well as classic dramas and comedies since 1986. The beautifully staged productions are true to Shakespeare's text, with inspiration drawn from contemporary politics. Their 2017 production of *Macbeth* was set in an occupied third-world country

in the present day. The company has two downtown theaters: the 775-seat Sidney Harman Hall (610 F St. NW) and the smaller Lansburgh Theatre (450 7th St. NW).

MAP 2: Sidney Harman Hall, 610 F St. NW, 202/547-1122 or 877/487-8849, www. shakespearetheatre.org; tickets $25-120

Warner Theatre

This downtown theater opened in 1924 as a venue for vaudeville and silent films, and in the 1930s and 1940s it welcomed major stars like Bob Hope, Duke Ellington, and Jerry Lewis. The dazzling red-and-gold, 1,847-seat theater hosts major music and comedy acts, national tours of Broadway musicals, and the Washington Ballet's beloved annual production of *The Nutcracker,* which is set in Georgetown and stars George Washington as the lead. (The George Washington nutcracker doll makes an excellent gift, too.) Founded by Mary Day in 1944, the Washington Ballet is a renowned company and school, performing beloved classics and innovative premieres at theaters around the city, including The John F. Kennedy Center for the Performing Arts and Warner Theatre.

MAP 2: 513 13th St. NW, 202/783-4000, www.warnertheatredc.com; box office 10am-4pm Mon.-Fri. and three hours prior to showtime until 30 min. after showtime; tickets from $39

LIBRARIES

Martin Luther King Jr. Memorial Library

DC's flagship library, the Martin Luther King Jr. Memorial Library in Chinatown, was the last building designed by modernist architect Mies van der Rohe. It was completed in 1972. The library closed in March 2017 for a $208 million renovation. When the library reopens in 2020, it will house a new reading room, art and conference spaces, a café, and more.

MAP 2: 901 G St. NW, 202/727-0321, www.dclibrary.org/mlk

Capitol Hill and Atlas District

Map 3

MUSEUMS

National Postal Museum

If you think postage stamps are boring, you've never visited the Smithsonian Institution's National Postal Museum, which has one of the largest collections of postal paraphernalia in the world, featuring more than six million stamps and artifacts like the world's first postage stamp. The exhibitions examine the history of mail and the impact of the U.S. Postal Service on American communities—much more influential than you might think. The William H. Gross Stamp Gallery is visually stunning. The building originally housed Washington DC's main post office for nearly a decade, and now it contains several vintage mail planes, coaches, and trucks.

MAP 3: 2 Massachusetts Ave. NE, 202/633-5555, http://postalmuseum.si/edu; 10am-5:30pm daily; free

United States Botanic Garden

Located on the grounds of the U.S. Capitol, the United States Botanic Garden is an oasis loved by locals looking for an escape from a rough work day on Capitol Hill. The living museum is one of the oldest botanical gardens in North America, established by Congress in 1820, and one of the largest, with 65,000 plants for study and display. Inside, plants are organized by climate (Tropics, Mediterranean, Southern Exposure) as well as type; the walkway between Medicinal Plants and World Deserts is home to fascinating poisonous specimens. Outside, the National Garden highlights regional plants, while idyllic Bartholdi Park (dawn-dusk daily) features a fountain designed by Frédéric Auguste Bartholdi, who designed the Statue of Liberty.

MAP 3: 100 Maryland Ave. SW, 202/225-8333, www.usbg.gov; 10am-5pm daily; free

THEATER, MUSIC, AND DANCE

Atlas Performing Arts Center

H Street NE between 2nd Street NE and 15th Street NE has been nicknamed the Atlas District due to the

Atlas Performing Arts Center

The 250-seat Elizabethan-style theater regularly hosts music performances, poetry readings, and lectures as well. The theater is also home to the **Folger Shakespeare Library** (10am-5pm Mon.-Sat., noon-5pm Sun.; free), which boasts the world's largest collection of the Bard's works. Serious fans will want to explore the library's exhibits, which include one of the first editions of Shakespeare's plays on display with a digital touch-screen to allow you to look inside the precious 15th-century manuscript, as well as books, playbills, and Renaissance art, costumes, and instruments.

MAP 3: 202 E. Capitol St. SE, 202/544-4600, box office 202/544-7077, www.folger.edu; box office noon-5pm Mon.-Sat. and one hour before events; tickets $35-80

Atlas Performing Arts Center. The art deco movie theater was built in 1938, although the theater and the neighborhood were devastated during the 1968 riots. Following a complete restoration, the theater reopened in 2006 with 59,000 square feet of performance, rehearsal, and office space; the neighborhood has since experienced significant growth. Today, the center showcases theater, music, dance, and film, with a focus on cross-cultural performances as well as fringe works.

MAP 3: 1333 H St. NE, 202/399-7993, www.atlasarts.org; tickets from $30

Folger Theatre

Since 1991, the Folger Theatre has performed the Bard's beloved plays as well as lesser-known works. Recent productions have included *Antony and Cleopatra* and *The Winter's Tale*.

Logan Fringe Arts Space

After taking over venues throughout the city for nearly a decade, DC's annual Fringe Festival got a permanent home in the H Street Corridor in 2015. The Logan Fringe Arts Space is one of the city's most innovative arts venues, with a modern, 200-seat theater, art gallery, indoor bar, outdoor beer garden, and more. The **Capital Fringe Festival** (admission $7, tickets $17) takes place every July, but you can see encores of popular shows as well as other cutting-edge theater, music, and dance performances throughout the year.

MAP 3: 1358 Florida Ave. NE, 866/811-4111, www.capitalfringe.org

ARTS AND CULTURE

DUPONT CIRCLE

MUSEUMS
⊕ The Phillips Collection

In a city full of free museums, The Phillips Collection is worth the admission fee. The nation's first modern art museum was founded in 1921 by banker and arts patron Duncan Phillips to showcase his collection of now-well-known works by Cézanne, Diebenkorn, O'Keeffe, and Van Gogh, to name a few. The showcase piece is Renoir's *Luncheon of the Boating Party* (1880-1881), depicting the artist's chic Parisian friends, but the arresting Rothko Room is a wonderful spot to get lost in thought. On the first Thursday of every month, a stylish crowd packs the intimate museum for Phillips After 5, featuring tours, entertainment, and a cash bar.

MAP 4: 1600 21st St. NW, 202/387-2151, www.phillipscollection.org; 10am-5pm Tues.-Wed. and Fri.-Sat., 10am-8:30pm Thurs., noon-6:30pm Sun.; $12 adults, $10 students and seniors, free for members and children under 18

National Museum of American Jewish Military History

This small museum has an important mission: to document and preserve the stories of Jewish Americans who have served in the U.S. military, particularly the 550,000 who served during World War II. The displays draw from the museum's collection of more than 5,000 artifacts, as well as extensive archival materials. Hours are rather limited; it's worth checking the website for the calendar of guided

The Phillips Collection

tours and discussions with authors and historians.

MAP 4: 1811 R St. NW, 202/265-6280, www.nmajmh.org; 9am-5pm Mon.-Fri., by appointment Sun.; free

The Society of the Cincinnati Anderson House

In 1783, Continental Army officers formed the Society of the Cincinnati, dedicated to remembering the American Revolution. Named for Cincinnatus, the Roman statesman known for his civic virtue, the group supported soldiers and their families, and today it collects artifacts from the period. It's is headquartered in Anderson House, the former home of American diplomat Larz Anderson and his wife, Isabel. This is your chance to explore an Embassy Row mansion and see how wealthy Washingtonians lived back in the day, as much of their original decor is on display, along with swords and firearms and an extensive collection of Revolutionary art.

MAP 4: 2118 Massachusetts Ave. NW, 202/785-2040, www.societyofthecincinnati. org; 10am-4pm Tues.-Sat., noon-4pm Sun.; free

GALLERIES

Hillyer Art Space

Tucked in an alley off Florida Avenue, Hillyer Art Space might introduce you to your new favorite artist; this contemporary gallery showcases fascinating works by emerging local and international artists who deserve a big break. Expect to see something new each time you visit, because the gallery debuts exhibitions on the first Friday of every month to coincide with First Friday Dupont (www.firstfridaydupont.org, 6pm-8pm first Fri. of the month), in which artsy young things

pack about a dozen neighborhood galleries for happy hour receptions and special events.

MAP 4: 9 Hillyer Ct., 202/338-0325, www. hillyerartspace.org; noon-5pm Mon., noon-6pm Tues.-Fri., noon-5pm Sat.-Mon.; free, donations suggested

Studio Gallery

Located on a leafy residential street, Studio Gallery is the gallery for artists. Founded in 1956 by sculptor Jennie Lea Knight, whose work can be seen at the Smithsonian American Art Museum (8th St. and F St. NW, 202/633-7979, http://americanart. si.edu), the two-story gallery and outdoor sculpture garden showcase contemporary works with a focus on DC-based artists. The gallery debuts several exhibitions every month during First Friday Dupont (www.firstfridaydupont.org, 6pm-8pm first Fri. of the month), with receptions that will make you feel like a local art scene insider.

MAP 4: 2108 R St. NW, 202/232-8734, www.studiogallerydc.com; 1pm-6pm Wed.-Fri., 11am-6pm Sat.; free

CULTURAL CENTERS

Dupont Underground

Before cars, buses, and the Metro, Washingtonians got around by a network of underground streetcars, which were powered for decades by horses, then electric cables. The streetcars were shut down in 1962, and the stations and tunnels, like the one under Dupont Circle, were for the most part closed. In 2016, however, the Dupont Circle station was unsealed and given a new life as a contemporary arts space. The 75,000-square-foot space has been cleaned up—although it's still a bit creepy—and now hosts exhibits and events. You can schedule a private tour of the tunnels, or check the website for public events; recent Underground happenings have included contemporary art and graffiti exhibits, music performances, and a fashion show. Tickets are required to enter the space.

MAP 4: 1527 New Hampshire Ave. NW, no phone, www.dupontunderground.org; hours for tours, exhibitions, and special events vary; $15

U Street, Shaw, and Logan Circle

Map 5

GALLERIES
Long View Gallery

At 9,000 square feet, Long View Gallery in Shaw is the largest contemporary gallery in DC, showcasing about 10 exhibitions per year from a roster of more than two dozen local and international artists. Examples include Chris Stephens, a James Madison University professor who paints Shenandoah Valley landscapes, and Sondra N. Arkin, curator of the **D.C. City Hall Art Collection,** whose recent abstract works are made with ink, wax, and wire. Each exhibition opens with an evening party, a fun way to meet artsy locals. With exposed brick walls and lofty ceilings, the gallery is frequently rented for weddings and

The Howard Theatre

While Washington DC in the 1970s was a time of turmoil in the aftermath of the 1968 riots and the subsequent flight of white and middle-class black families to the suburbs, one thing did flourish: go-go. The upbeat, uniquely DC musical genre is classified as funk, with strong soul, salsa, and Latin and African percussion influences, a precursor to the hip-hop sound of the 1980s. The typical show relies heavily on audience participation, with call-and-response elements and danceable music, which would "go and go and go" without stopping for 40 minutes to an hour, giving the genre its name.

The style was popularized by **Chuck Brown,** known as "The Father of Go-Go," a DC icon who performed his signature sound until shortly before his death in 2012, though in the '70s and '80s, there were many popular go-go bands drawing crowds at dance clubs in DC and nearby Maryland suburbs. Of course, most go-go attendees went to dance—it's impossible not to—but as violent crime increased in the 1980s in DC, so too did violent incidents at go-go clubs, and city officials and police worked to shut down the scene. "If you have a black-tie event, you don't have any problem. But if you bring go-go in, you're going to have problems," said a police commander during a 2005 hearing to shut down one of the remaining go-go venues.

The fate of the go-go parallels the story of gentrification, and today, the go-go of Chuck Brown's heyday can only be found at clubs outside the District. However, it's possible to hear some of the legendary go-go bands from the '70s and '80s for special events at theaters, concert halls, and museums citywide, including The Howard Theatre. For a throwback go-go experience, look for shows by the Chuck Brown Band, as well as Rare Essence, founded in 1976; Trouble Funk, founded in 1978; and Experience Unlimited (E.U.), founded in 1975 and one of the few to achieve mainstream fame outside DC, with their song "Da Butt," featured in Spike Lee's 1988 film *School Daze*. Don't be surprised if you recognize some of the songs—notably Brown's "Bustin' Loose," which topped the Billboard R&B chart in 1979 and was sampled in Nelly's 2002 "Hot in Herre."

private events; call ahead to confirm it's open before you go.

MAP 5: 1234 9th St. NW, 202/232-4788, www.longviewgallerydc.com; 11am-6pm Wed.-Sat., noon-5pm Sun.; free

Transformer

This tiny, storefront gallery in Logan Circle has championed emerging artists since 2002, with half a dozen or so exhibitions of contemporary works per year. Recent shows have featured Iranian-American women artists and local artists exploring what it means to live a hyper-local, sustainable lifestyle. This is a good place to find new works to add to your collection from the gallery's FlatFile, which contains more than 200 small photos, paintings, drawings, and prints by DC artists priced $500 or less.

MAP 5: 1404 P St. NW, 202/483-1102, www.transformerdc.org; noon-6pm

Wed.-Sat. during exhibitions or by appointment; free

THEATER, MUSIC, AND DANCE
✪ The Howard Theatre

The Howard Theatre opened in 1910 and quickly became an important part of "Black Broadway," Washington's center of African American arts, culture, and business. For the first half of the 20th century, it was one of the nation's largest venues for black performers including Duke Ellington, Ella Fitzgerald, Marvin Gaye, and The Supremes. After the 1968 riots, the theater and many businesses around it shuttered. In 2012, it reopened after a $29 million renovation, adding modern club-style lighting, sound, and decor as well as a flexible space for 600-capacity seated shows or 1,000-capacity standing shows. Recent performers range from Wale and Lil' Kim, to gospel and jazz, to DC's top go-go bands.

JAZZ CAPITAL

Washington-born Edward "Duke" Ellington spent much of his youth in Shaw, the center of African American arts and culture from the turn of the 20th century through the early 1960s, where jazz legends like Ellington, Billie Holiday, John Coltrane, Ella Fitzgerald, Louis Armstrong, and Miles Davis, to name a few, performed in theaters along U Street NW, known as "Black Broadway." While many of the jazz clubs of yore have closed—most recently, one of Ellington's haunts, Bohemian Caverns at 11th and U—DC's jazz tradition continues in theaters and venues citywide.

In the U Street Corridor and Shaw, **The Howard Theatre** (page 173), which opened in 1910, and **The Lincoln Theatre** (page 174), in 1922, both welcomed some of these jazz greats and remain good spots to see local and national jazz musicians as well other genres (including DC's other music tradition, go-go).

The John F. Kennedy Center for the Performing Arts (page 177) in Foggy Bottom has a robust jazz calendar exploring the diversity of the genre, including the jazz greats as well as modern collaborations, like a 2017 concert featuring jazz pianist and composer Jason Moran with rapper Q-Tip. Nearby in Georgetown, enjoy jazz nightly in **Blues Alley** (page 157), a nightclub were Dizzy Gillespie and Wynton Marsalis have performed.

In the summer, enjoy jazz outdoors during **Jazz in the Garden** (page 182), weekly free jazz concerts on Friday evenings in the National Gallery of Art's Sculpture Garden, and citywide during the **DC Jazz Festival** (page 182) in July.

MAP 5: 620 T St. NW, 202/803-2899, www.thehowardtheatre.com; box office 9:45am-close on show days; tickets from $25

The Lincoln Theatre

After opening in 1922, The Lincoln Theatre was an important cultural center on "Black Broadway" as a place for African Americans to enjoy theater and socializing during segregation. In its heyday, it showcased everything from vaudeville to jazz greats to televised boxing matches. It fell into disrepair after the riots but was fully restored to its former glory in 1993, with seats for more than 1,000 for concert tours ranging from Lauryn Hill to Natalie Merchant, as well as comedy and film screenings.

MAP 5: 1215 U St. NW, 202/888-0050, www.thelincolndc.com; box office 1pm-7pm or until headliner begins Mon.-Fri., 1pm until headliner begins Sat.-Sun. on show days; tickets $25-65

Source Theatre

This theater is the home of the **Source Festival**, which debuts 24 new plays over three weeks every June, launching the careers of local and national actors, directors, and playwrights. The 150-seat, black box theater is likewise where you can see the award-winning **Constellation Theatre Company** (202/204-7741, www.constellationtheatre.org; tickets from $25), which produces fantasy and adventure plays and musicals like *The Arabian Nights* and *Urinetown*, as well as the **Washington Improv Theater** (202/204-7770, www.witdc.org; tickets from $10).

MAP 5: 1835 14th St. NW, www.sourcefestival.org; box office times vary

Studio Theatre

You can truly connect with the actors at Logan Circle's Studio Theatre, which produces memorable, thought-provoking contemporary theater, including U.S. and world premieres, on four stages, each with 225 or fewer seats. See productions that address hot-button cultural and political issues, like *The Apple Family Plays*, Richard Nelson's series following a liberal American family in New York during significant political events.

MAP 5: 1501 14th St. NW, 202/332-3300, www.studiotheatre.org; box office noon-6pm or curtain time Tues.-Sun.; tickets from $52

Adams Morgan

Map 6

THEATER, MUSIC, AND DANCE

GALA Hispanic Theatre

Located in the circa-1920s Tivoli Theatre in Columbia Heights, this company has been showcasing Hispanic performing arts since the 1970s. Short for Grupo de Artistas LatinoAmericanos, GALA produces several classic and contemporary plays and musicals each year by writers from Spain, Latin America, and the United States, including many world premieres, in Spanish with English supertitles. The 265-seat theater also hosts an annual flamenco festival in November.

MAP 6: 3333 14th St. NW, 202/234-7174, www.galatheatre.org; box office 6:30pm-9pm Thurs.-Fri., 2pm-9pm Sat., noon-4pm Sun. during performance weeks; tickets from $30

GALA Hispanic Theatre in Columbia Heights

CULTURAL CENTERS

Mexican Cultural Institute

The former embassy of Mexico is now home to a public educational institute showcasing Mexican arts and culture. The historical mansion is filled with spectacular murals painted by Roberto Cueva del Río in the 1930s and 1940s, depicting events like the Festival of the Flowers in Tehuantepec and Christopher Columbus's landing. The institute frequently hosts exhibits and events about Mexican art, cinema, music, and food; check the schedule on the website before visiting.

MAP 6: 2829 16th St. NW, 202/728-1628, www.instituteofmexicodc.org; 10am-6pm Mon.-Fri., noon-4pm Sat. during exhibitions; free

Georgetown and Foggy Bottom

Map 7

MUSEUMS

George Washington University Museum and the Textile Museum

For an academic look at the history of Washington DC, visit the largest university museum in the city. It features the Albert H. Small Washingtoniana Collection, which consists of 1,000 artifacts, including hand-drawn maps and a letter from George Washington to Congress describing the plans for the new capital. The museum is also home to more than 19,000 textiles from five continents, including carpets from Spain, Turkey, Egypt, and Iran, as well as ancient textiles from as early as 2500-3000 BC.

MAP 7: 701 21st St. NW, 202/994-5200, www.museum.gwu.edu; 11am-5pm Mon. and Fri., 11am-7pm Wed.-Thurs., 10am-5pm Sat., 1pm-5pm Sun.; suggested donation $8 adults, free for members, children, and GWU students, faculty, and staff

Tudor Place

The early days of the nation's capital come to life at Tudor Place, the estate where six generations of Martha Washington's descendants lived from 1816 to 1983. Tour the restored neoclassical mansion, which is home to more than 15,000 decorative art pieces and artifacts from the Federal period—including the largest collection of objects from George Washington's life outside of Mount Vernon—as well as the 5.5 acres of lush gardens, which contain much of the original landscaping. Check the calendar for special holiday-themed events and garden tours.

MAP 7: 1644 31st St. NW, 202/965-0400, www.tudorplace.org; 10am-4pm Tues.-Sat., noon-4pm Sun.; $10 adults, $8 seniors, military, and students, $3 children 5-17, free for members and children under 5, $3 garden tour only

GALLERIES
Book Hill Galleries

High on Wisconsin Avenue NW near Tudor Place, you'll find eight fine art galleries for all tastes, ranging from contemporary painting and photography at Cross MacKenzie Gallery (1675 Wisconsin Ave. NW, 202/337-7970, www.crossmackenzie.com; noon-5pm Tues.-Sat.) to locally made prints at the Washington Printmakers Gallery (1641 Wisconsin Ave. NW, 202/669-1497, www.washingtonprintmakers.com; 11am-6pm

The John F. Kennedy Center for the Performing Arts

Thurs.-Sat., noon-5pm Sun. summer). Even if you're not in the market for fine art, the galleries welcome casual browsing; check the website for opening receptions and special events, including the annual evening spring art walk.

MAP 7: Wisconsin Ave. NW between O St. NW and Reservoir Rd., www. georgetowngalleries.com; hours vary by gallery

THEATER, MUSIC, AND DANCE
❂ The John F. Kennedy Center for the Performing Arts

Named for one of the nation's greatest advocates for the arts, the Kennedy Center showcases world-class music, theater, opera, dance, and comedy for all tastes and ages. One of the premier performing arts venues in the city, if not the country, it's home to the dazzling National Symphony Orchestra, which performs classical and contemporary works, as well as the Washington National Opera and Suzanne Farrell Ballet. The Kennedy Center holds a free performance every day of the year at 6pm in the Grand Foyer. Whatever you're there to see, arrive early to enjoy a pre-show drink at the Roof Terrace Restaurant (5pm-8pm before Concert Hall and Opera House evening performances, 11am-2pm most Sun.).

MAP 7: 2700 F St. NW, 202/467-4600, www.kennedy-center.org; box office 10am-9pm Mon.-Sat., noon-9pm Sun.; tickets $25-175

Navy Yard and Anacostia   Map 8

MUSEUMS
Anacostia Community Museum

This is a museum about communities. Founded in 1967 as part of the Smithsonian Institution's effort to bring the arts to the Anacostia neighborhood, the collection includes art, photographs, documents, and other materials documenting life in Anacostia and surrounding neighborhoods. It's small, with three or four exhibits at any time, but the exhibits are thought-provoking; recent ones have examined the experiences of Latino immigrants in major U.S. cities and the impact of the recent growth and development in Washington DC on various neighborhoods and populations. The museum has a robust schedule of free cultural events, including author talks, music performances, and film screenings. A bit off the beaten path, the museum offers free shuttle service from the Smithsonian's National Air and Space Museum and the Anacostia Metro station.

MAP 8: 1901 Fort Pl. SE, 202/633-4820, http://anacostia.si.edu; 10am-5pm daily; free

GALLERIES
Honfleur Gallery

Built in 2007, Honfleur Gallery was the first gallery developed by Action to Rehabilitate Community Housing (ARCH) Development Corporation, a nonprofit dedicated to providing access to arts, culture, and business services in Anacostia. (The Anacostia Arts Center, another ARCH Development Corporation project, opened a year later.) Ever since, the gallery and neighborhood have become a burgeoning destination for diverse, contemporary art from around the world, with many of the gallery's artists hailing from DC. The gallery opens exhibits every few months, ranging from traditional mediums to photography to more experimental installations.

MAP 8: 1241 Good Hope Rd. SE, 202/365-8392, www.honfleurgallery.com; noon-7pm Wed.-Sat.; free

Vivid Solutions Gallery

This gallery, founded by Action to Rehabilitate Community Housing (ARCH) Development Corporation to bring the arts to Anacostia, is dedicated to showcasing groundbreaking works by contemporary artists, including many local artists. The gallery moved out of the Anacostia Arts Center in October 2017 into its own space, with an opening exhibition featuring works by local multimedia artist Billy Colbert exploring how the media represents African Americans.

MAP 8: 2208 Martin Luther King Jr. Ave. SE, 202/631-6291; 10am-7pm Tues.-Sat., 10am-3pm Sun.

CULTURAL CENTERS

America's Islamic Heritage Museum & Cultural Center

The mission of this cultural center is more important than ever: to foster greater understanding of Islam in the United States. The text- and photo-heavy exhibits tell the story of the significant role of Islam in America from the 1500s—about 30 percent of slaves brought from Africa were Muslim—to modern day, including a look at Muslim American artists, musicians, and athletes, as well as Muslims who served in the military.

If you're visiting during Ramadan, you can go to an *iftar*, the dinner to break the fast. These meals are often attended by Muslim government officials and embassy representatives. Check the website for the schedule and suggested donation.

MAP 8: 2315 Martin Luther King Jr. Ave. SE, 202/610-0586, www.aihmuseum. org; noon-5pm Tues.-Sun., $7 adults, $5 students and seniors

Anacostia Arts Center

While off the beaten path, the Anacostia Arts Center is worth visiting to experience local art and support development in this historic and culturally rich neighborhood. The 9,300-square-foot building has five gallery and boutique spaces rented by local creatives, as well as a black box theater. Check the website for exhibit opening receptions, music and dance performances, and jazz brunches at **Art-drenaline Café** (202/306-5545, www.artdrenalinecafe.com), which serves café fare, coffee, and smoothies inside the center.

MAP 8: 1231 Good Hope Rd. SE, 202/631-6291, www.anacostiaartscenter. com; 10am-7pm Tues.-Sat, 10am-3pm Sun., hours and prices vary for special events

Blind Whino SW Arts Club

How far will you travel for an Instagram shot? This arts center is a little out of the way, but worth the journey to find the abandoned and desanctified Baptist church transformed by HENSE, a public artist from Atlanta who completely covered the facade of the 1886 building in vibrant neon paint. With an interior also covered in murals, the community arts space is frequently rented for private events, but also hosts public art exhibitions and programs, like the 2017

Superfierce, which showcased works by women artists with proceeds from the ticket sales benefiting women with cancer.

MAP 8: 700 Delaware Ave. SW, 202/554-0103, www.swartsclub.org; 5pm-8pm Wed., noon-5pm Sat.-Sun.; free

THEATER, MUSIC, AND DANCE

✪ Arena Stage

Since opening in 1950, Arena Stage has had many "firsts" in theater history: It was one of the first nonprofit theaters in the United States, the first regional theater to send a production to Broadway (*The Great White Hope,* about African American boxing champ Jack Johnson), and the first regional theater to win the Regional Theater Tony Award. With three performance spaces holding 200-680 people, Arena continues to debut American plays and revive classic American dramas and musicals—think *Oklahoma!* and *The Pajama Game.* Recent premieres include *Dear Evan Hansen,* which received nine Tony Award nominations after moving to Broadway in 2016, and *Sweat,* winner of the 2017 Pulitzer Prize for Drama.

MAP 8: 1101 6th St. SW, 202/554-9066, www.arenastage.org

Arena Stage

MUSEUMS AND GARDENS

✪ Hillwood Estate, Museum & Gardens

During the last two decades of her life, General Foods heiress and socialite Marjorie Merriweather Post lived on an estate near Rock Creek Park, where she hosted dinner parties for Washington's A-list and showed off her extravagant art collection, including 18th- and 19th-century French art, pre-revolutionary Russian art and porcelain she purchased while living in the Soviet Union in the 1930s, and decorative objects like a gold chalice commissioned by Catherine the Great and nearly 100 Fabergé pieces. You can see these items and others on display in the home, lavishly decorated in 18th-century French style and the closest thing to Versailles in Washington DC. Wander through the home on your own, or take a guided tour with a docent who will tell you about Post's life and the objects on display, which, if you're lucky, will include some of her enviable designer wardrobe or jewels.

The home is set on 25 acres, including 13 acres of lush, formal gardens with carefully planned landscaping and private nooks; as with the house, you can stroll the gardens on your own (picnics are encouraged) or take one of the popular one-hour guided garden tours in the spring and fall.

MAP 9: 4155 Linnean Ave. NW, 202/686-5807, www.hillwoodmuseum.org;

Hillwood Estate, Museum & Gardens

10am-5pm Tues.-Sun.; suggested donation $18 adults, $15 seniors, $10 students, $5 children 6-18, free for children under 6 and members

Dumbarton Oaks

In 1944, delegates from China, the Soviet Union, the United Kingdom, and the United States met at Dumbarton Oaks to create the United Nations Charter. Today, this tranquil estate high above the Georgetown shopping streets is home to former owners Mildred and Robert Woods Bliss's unparalleled collection of pre-Columbian and Byzantine art, as well as 16 acres of exquisite gardens and orchards designed by the country's first female landscape architect, Beatrix Jones Farrand. Take a guided tour, or simply enjoy some peace.

MAP 9: 1703 32nd St. NW, 202/339-6400, www.doaks.org; museum 11:30am-5pm Tues.-Sun. year-round, garden 2pm-6pm Tues.-Sun. Mar. 15-Oct. and 2pm-5pm

Tues.-Sun. Nov.-Mar. 14; museum free, gardens free in winter and $10 adults, $8 seniors, and $5 children 12 and under Mar. 15-Oct.

The President Woodrow Wilson House

When President Woodrow Wilson left the White House in 1921, he moved to posh Kalorama, where wealthy families and diplomats lived. He died a few years later, but his wife kept the house intact and eventually donated it to the National Trust for Historic Preservation. Get a look at life in the neighborhood's grand mansions during the early 20th century, and see artifacts from his historic presidency, when he led the nation through World War I.

MAP 9: 2340 S St. NW, 202/387-4062, www.woodrowwilsonhouse.org; $10 adults, $8 seniors, $5 students and members of the National Trust for Historic Preservation, free for children 12 and under

Festivals and Events

SPRING

TOP EXPERIENCE

✪ National Cherry Blossom Festival

In March and April, the city celebrates the bloom of the cherry trees, a gift from Japan in 1912. The festival includes many free events: the parade, kite festival, Japanese street festival, fireworks, museum events, and, of course, the showcase of the magnificent pink and white blossoms around the Tidal Basin and National Mall. This is one of the busiest, most

expensive times to visit DC, and it's tough to predict peak bloom, but if you catch it, you'll be glad you braved the crowds.

Citywide: 877/442-5666, www.nationalcherryblossomfestival.org; mid-Mar.-mid-Apr.; most headline events free and open to the public (some require tickets)

Smithsonian Craft Show

The Smithsonian Craft Show brings together over 100 American craftsmen and -women (from over 1,000 applicants) to Washington DC for a public, juried show and sale, with ticket proceeds benefitting the Smithsonian Institution's museums and programs. From housewares and baskets to jewelry and wearable art, there's something for every taste.

Downtown: National Building Museum, 401 F St. NW, 888/832-9554, www. smithsoniancraftshow.org; late Apr.; $15-30 general admission, $250 preview night

Passport DC

Learn some diplomatic secrets when the Embassy Row mansions open to the public for a month of open houses and cultural events. Highlights include the Around the World Embassy Tour, when more than 40 embassies from Afghanistan to Zimbabwe open their doors for one day, and the EU Open House, when the European Union members invite you to experience their arts, culture, and food.

Dupont Circle: Embassy Row, www. culturaltourism.org; May 1-31; free

SUMMER
Jazz in the Garden

It's a summer rite of passage for locals: Skip out of work early on Friday afternoons with a blanket and picnic for Jazz in the Garden, a series of free jazz concerts in the National Gallery's Sculpture Garden featuring American and international jazz musicians. Join them and relax among the gallery's modern and contemporary sculpture collection, enjoying snacks and beverages (including beer, wine, and sangria) from the Pavilion Café.

National Mall: Pavilion Café at the National Gallery of Art Sculpture Garden, 7th St. NW and Constitution Ave. NW, 202/289-3360, www.nga.gov/jazz; Fri. mid-May-mid-Aug., weather permitting; free

Dupont-Kalorama Museum Walk

While they usually charge admission fees, the independent museums, historic homes, and galleries in Dupont Circle and Kalorama welcome the public free of charge for one weekend in June. In addition to the exhibits, enjoy family-friendly activities, arts and crafts, and entertainment all weekend long.

Dupont Circle: www. dupontkaloramamc.com; early June; free

Capital Pride

The highlight of one of the largest pride events in the United States is the celebratory Saturday afternoon parade through Dupont Circle, featuring more than 180 floats, entertainers, and supporting groups; after, the historic gay neighborhood is a massive party as paradegoers continue the celebration into the evening. Recently, the event has expanded to include a week of special events as well as a post-parade concert near the U.S. Capitol, with headliners Miley Cyrus and The Pointer Sisters in 2017.

Dupont Circle: www.capitalpride.org; early-mid-June; free

DC Jazz Festival

Originally named the Duke Ellington Jazz Festival in honor of perhaps the most influential musician from DC, the event showcases DC's jazz tradition, with performances at theaters, clubs, parks, and museums across the city by Grammy Award-winning headliners and local musicians. The major performances take place at The John F. Kennedy Center for the Performing Arts, The Yards in Navy Yard, and The Howard Theatre.

Citywide: www.dcjazzfest.org; June; ticket prices vary

Smithsonian Folklife Festival

At the end of June, the Smithsonian Institution brings the museums outdoors. The part-fair, part-exposition, part-party is a celebration of unique world cultures, with musicians, artists, artisans, athletes, storytellers, and more showcasing specific countries, regions, or cultural identities on the National Mall morning until evening. The 2018 festival will feature food, fashion, and more from Africa, Armenia, and Catalonia, and the 2019 festival will highlight the social power of music.

National Mall: Between 7th St. and 12th St., 202/633-6440, http://festival.si.edu; late June-first week of July; free

TOP EXPERIENCE

✪ Independence Day

Celebrating Independence Day in the nation's capital will give you all the patriotic feels. The holiday begins with a mile-long parade (Constitution Ave. NW between 7th St. NW and 17th St. NW, www.july4thparade.com; 11:45am July 4; free) down Constitution Avenue, featuring bands from across the country as well as military units. In the evening, PBS hosts A Capitol Fourth (U.S. Capitol West Lawn, www.pbs.org/a-capitol-fourth; gates 3pm, concert 8pm-9:30pm July 4; free, no tickets required), the free concert on the West Lawn of the U.S. Capitol featuring celebrity musicians and military bands playing patriotic tunes. The concert builds anticipation for the spectacular fireworks display (National Mall, www.pbs.org/a-capitol-fourth; show begins at dark, approx. 9:15pm July 4; free, no tickets required), which can be viewed from the U.S. Capitol, National Mall, and anywhere you can see the Washington

Monument. Crowds begin forming very early in the day on the National Mall; plan to arrive at the concert shortly after the gates open at 3pm to stake out a spot closer to the stage, and stick around to enjoy the fireworks with the soundtrack of Tchaikovsky's "1812 Overture" and live canon fire at the conclusion of the concert.

Various locations: July 4; free

Capital Fringe

For more than a decade, DC's Fringe Festival has enticed audiences to all corners of the city for more than 100 performances, often news-driven and thought-provoking, with many by local artists. The festival is headquartered at Capital Fringe's new Atlas District venue, Logan Fringe Arts Space, which has a black box theater and bar.

Atlas District/Citywide: 1358 Florida Ave. NE, 866/811-4111, www.capitalfringe.org; July; festival button $7, tickets $17/show, multi-show passes $30-320

AUTUMN

National Book Festival

The Library of Congress celebrates reading at this annual one-day event, featuring more than 100 authors and illustrators across genres who read, sell, and sign their books and participate in panel discussions.

Downtown: Walter E. Washington Convention Center, 801 Mt. Vernon Pl. NW, 202/707-5000, www.loc.gov/bookfest; early Sept.; free

Adams Morgan Day

DC's longest-running neighborhood festival, Adams Morgan Day showcases the diversity of the Northwest neighborhood, known for ethnic restaurants, iconic dives and music venues, and a progressive vibe. The one-day festival features live music and DJs, kids' games and crafts, and arts vendors, plus special deals at neighborhood restaurants, bars, and shops.

Adams Morgan: mid-Sept.; free

H Street Festival

Get to know the vibrant Atlas District during the H Street Festival, covering 11 blocks of H Street NE northeast of Union Station. The festival features several stages showcasing local musicians, fashion, and family-friendly entertainment, as well as the neighborhood's diverse flavors.

Atlas District: www.hstreetfestival.org; mid-Sept.; free

Walkingtown DC

During one week in September, Events DC hosts more than 50 free walking tours around the District, allowing you to explore DC's culturally diverse neighborhoods with in-the-know volunteers. Whether you're interested in exploring presidential history, universities, street art, or areas of new development, there's a walking tour available.

Citywide: www.culturaltourismdc. org; mid-Sept.; free but registration recommended

Taste of DC

There are so many restaurants in DC, and so little time. At the city's largest culinary festival, you can try more than 65 area restaurants and food trucks, plus local beer and wine. The event features local artisans as well as live entertainment and cooking and mixology demos at the Robert F. Kennedy Memorial Stadium in Southeast.

Greater Washington: www. thetasteofdc.org; early Oct.; free admission to festival, tasting packages $10-50

Army Ten-Miler

The second-largest 10-mile race in the country, the Army Ten-Miler starts and finishes at the Pentagon, with several major monuments and memorials on the route. The race takes place in early October, but registration opens in May and typically sells out in a couple days.

Citywide: www.armytenmiler.com; early Oct.; $75 fee

Marine Corps Marathon

Called "The People's Marathon," the Marine Corps Marathon draws runners from around the world in mid-October. It's the largest marathon in the world that does not offer prize money, opting instead to recognize the "honor, courage, and commitment" of runners. Registration is by lottery beginning in March.

Citywide: www.marinemarathon.com; mid-Oct.; $160 fee

High Heel Drag Queen Race

There's only one place to be the Tuesday before Halloween: 17th Street in Dupont Circle, where more than 100 costumed drag queens race—in high heels, no less—by the neighborhood's popular gay bars. JR's Bar started the event in 1986, and it's grown to be a must-attend event, with hundreds of thousands of spectators gathering for happy hour several hours before the 9pm race.

Dupont Circle: 17th St. between P St. NW and S St. NW; Tues. before Halloween; free

Boo at the Zoo

Celebrate Halloween with creepy crawlies and terrifying beasts at the National Zoo's popular Halloween event for families. For three evenings, visitors can trick-or-treat at more than 40 stations throughout the zoo, meet zookeepers and their charges, and enjoy family-friendly entertainment.

Greater Washington: Smithsonian's National Zoo, 3001 Connecticut Ave. NW, 202/633-4888, http://nationalzoo.si.edu; mid-Oct.; $20 members, $30 nonmembers, free for children 2 and under

Fotoweek DC

This citywide photography festival features more than 150 exhibits and photo events, showcasing DC and international talent as well as stirring press photos. Every year, the festival opens with a cool, artsy celebration at the festival headquarters (the Mexican Cultural Institute in 2017).

Citywide: www.fotoweekdc.org; mid-Nov.; most exhibits free (some special events require tickets)

WINTER

National Christmas Tree and Pathway of Peace

Since 1923, the POTUS has lit the National Christmas Tree on the Ellipse near the White House, and no holiday season in DC is complete without a nighttime visit to see the display. Surrounding the main tree, the Pathway of Peace features 56 trees decorated for each U.S. state and territory, as well as live entertainment, refreshments, and cheer.

Downtown: 202/796-2500, www.thenationaltree.org; early Dec.-Jan. 1; free

Zoolights

From Thanksgiving weekend through the New Year, the National Zoo is illuminated with more than 500,000 environmentally friendly holiday lights. From 5pm to 9pm, enjoy festive light shows set to music as well as holiday treats like hot chocolate, egg nog,

and cookies while you shop for zoo-themed holiday gifts.

Greater Washington: Smithsonian's National Zoo, 3001 Connecticut Ave. NW, 202/633-4888, http://nationalzoo.si.edu; mid-Nov.-Jan.; free

Downtown Holiday Market

Skip the big box stores on Black Friday and head to the Downtown Holiday Market, several blocks of regional vendors selling items for everyone on your list, from jewelry and accessories to art and housewares to local food gifts. The market also features live music across many genres, along with bites and beverages.

Downtown: 8th St. NW and F St. NW, www.downtownholidaymarket.com; Black Friday-Dec. 23; free

A Christmas Carol

For 35 years, Ford's Theatre has presented Charles Dickens's *A Christmas Carol* during the holiday season, making a trip to the historic theater a holiday tradition for Washington region families. The festive production tells the story of Ebenezer Scrooge and the Ghosts of Christmas Past, Present, and Future with colorful sets, joyful music, and a diverse cast.

Downtown: Ford's Theatre, 511 10th St. NW, 202/347-4833, www.fords.org; mid-Nov.-late Dec.; $32-105

The Washington Ballet's *The Nutcracker*

Tchaikovsky's beloved holiday ballet gets a Washington DC twist, set in a Georgetown mansion in 1882 and starring General George Washington in the title role as he fights the Rat King, King George III. From late November through Christmas Eve, there are performances in several area theaters, including The Warner Theatre.

Citywide: 202/362-3606, www.
washingtonballet.org; late Nov.-late Dec.;
$30-130

Martin Luther King Jr. Day

Dr. King had an enormous impact on Washington, which celebrates his birthday with several special events. Martin Luther King Jr. Day kicks off with the Memorial Peace Walk, where you can join government officials, media personalities, and community activists on a two-mile walk along Martin Luther King, Jr. Avenue in Southeast DC, one of the first streets in the country bearing his name. After, a parade follows the same route.

Anacostia: 2500 Martin Luther King Jr. Ave. SE, www.mlkholidaydc.org; third Mon. of Jan.; free

Presidential Inauguration

Every four years, Washington DC puts political differences aside and comes together for the Presidential Inauguration. The bipartisan event includes the swearing-in ceremony at the U.S. Capitol and the parade on Pennsylvania Avenue, which are both open to the general public. Both events have free, public viewing areas, but you'll need tickets for the prime seats, which can be obtained through the Presidential Inaugural Committee (PIC) or your senator/representative. The PIC organizes the official inaugural balls, which may be attended by the First Family; information about the official balls as well as dozens of unofficial inaugural balls, concerts, and other special events is usually available several weeks after the November election.

Citywide: Jan. 20 after a presidential election; costs vary by event

Washington Auto Show

The biggest show in DC, and one of the top auto shows in the world, the Washington Auto Show is a local post-holiday favorite, with more than 600 new models and special events at the Walter E. Washington Convention Center from late January to early February.

Downtown: Walter E. Washington Convention Center, 801 Mt. Vernon Pl. NW, www.washingtonautoshow.com; late Jan.-early Feb.; $5-12

SPORTS AND ACTIVITIES

National Mall 189
Downtown and Penn Quarter 190
Capitol Hill and Atlas District 192
Adams Morgan 193
Georgetown and Foggy Bottom 193
Navy Yard and Anacostia 196
Greater Washington DC 199

When Washingtonians aren't relieving their stress at happy hour, they're exercising and taking advantage of the wide variety of outdoor activities and more than 8,000 acres of parks in the District, which ranks fourth among all cities in the United States for park accessibility.

There's no better way to work out in DC than by jogging around the National Mall and U.S. Capitol on a pleasant day, a favorite fitness activity among locals and visitors alike, but you'll also find trails and water sports citywide. In addition to the National Mall, Georgetown and the Southwest Waterfront/Navy Yard are hubs for spacious parks, trails (which connect to other regional trails for longer excursions), and boathouses to allow you to explore the Potomac River and Anacostia River by kayak, canoe, or paddleboard, or take a tour of the monuments by water. If you'd like to spend a nice spring or fall day outdoors, take a walk through the Mall's monuments and memorials, then walk to East Potomac Park and Hains Point, an expansive man-made island with panoramic views and athletic facilities, or head to Rock Creek Park in Upper Northwest.

East Potomac Park

If you prefer to watch sports rather than play them, Washington DC has professional basketball, ice hockey, soccer, baseball, and football teams with intensely loyal fans, as well as several major tennis events. Even casual sports fans will enjoy a ballgame at Nationals Park, where larger-than-life bobblehead U.S. presidents race and rally the crowd.

HIGHLIGHTS

⚙ **BEST WAY TO SEE THE CHERRY BLOSSOMS:** There's no better way to spend a sunny day than by renting one of the **Tidal Basin paddleboats,** especially during cherry blossom season (page 190).

⚙ **BEST TOUR FOR FIRST-TIMERS:** If you want to see the monuments and get out on the water, **DC Ducks** allows you to do both during a 90-minute land and water tour (page 192).

⚙ **COOLEST CITY PARK: Meridian Hill Park** is a 12-acre urban oasis with a storied history and a must-see drum circle on Sundays (page 193).

⚙ **BEST CITY HIKE:** Located in the Potomac River at the DC-Virginia border, **Theodore Roosevelt Island** is a memorial to the 26th POTUS with 2.5 miles of easy trails through forests and swampland (page 193).

⚙ **BEST MULTIUSE TRAIL:** The 20-mile paved **Anacostia Riverwalk Trail** connects Anacostia, Capitol Hill, and Navy Yard to 40 more miles of trails in Maryland (page 196).

⚙ **BEST WAY TO ENJOY AMERICA'S FAVORITE PASTIME:** Cheer on the **Washington Nationals** at one of the top baseball stadiums in the country (page 197).

⚙ **MOST METRO-ACCESSIBLE OUTDOOR EXCURSION:** You can run, bike, fish, picnic, golf, or just relax at **East Potomac Park and Hains Point** (page 199).

⚙ **BEST PLACE TO CONNECT WITH NATURE:** The massive **U.S. National Arboretum** has something new in bloom every month (page 199).

Hains Point

TOURS
Smithsonian National Mall Tours

The Smithsonian Institution partners with professional tour operator **Bike and Roll** to offer two unique tours, which depart from the National Museum of American History. The two-hour Monumental Experience (offered daily at 10am and 2pm) shows you the mall via Segway. If you'd rather walk than roll, the Myths and Misconceptions Walking Tour (2:30pm Fri.-Sun.) is a 1.5-hour exploration of highlights and hidden gems in the museum. Reservations are recommended for both tours.

MAP 1: National Museum of American History, 1300 Constitution Ave. NW between 12th St. NW and 14th St. NW, 202/384-8516, www.nationalmalltours. com; $10-49

PARKS AND TRAILS
West Potomac Park

Stretching from the Washington Monument west to Lincoln Memorial and southeast to the Thomas Jefferson Memorial, West Potomac Park includes many of the major national memorials in its grassy fields. In addition to getting a history lesson, you can kick around in the JFK Hockey Fields south of the Reflecting Pool, which are perfect for a game of Frisbee or soccer. The park includes the **Tidal Basin**, adjacent to the Franklin Delano Roosevelt Memorial and Martin Luther King Jr. Memorial, an artificial inlet of the Potomac River surrounded

Tidal Basin paddleboats

by the cherry trees gifted to the United States by Japan in 1912. The trail around it is approximately two miles; it's a gorgeous, albeit slow, walk during cherry blossom season. You can rent **paddleboats** from March to October.

MAP 1: National Mall from about 17th St NW west to the Lincoln Memorial and south to the Tidal Basin; 24 hours daily

BOATING

✪ Tidal Basin Paddleboats

There's no better way to spend a sunny day than paddleboating around the Tidal Basin, where you'll have an unobstructed view of several monuments. From March through October, rent one of the bright blue paddleboats for two ($18/hour) or four ($30); if you can pedal your feet, you're good to go. During cherry blossom season (Mar.-Apr.), reserve your boat in advance online. This boat dock also offers adorable swan boats for two ($34/hour), which are equipped with motors so everyone can glide even if you aren't able to pedal. The dock is accessible via Maine Avenue SW, on the eastern shore of the Tidal Basin.

MAP 1: 1501 Maine Ave. SW, 202/337-9642, www.tidalbasinpaddleboats.com; 10am-6pm daily (last boat at 5pm) Mar.-Oct., weather permitting; $18-34/hour

Downtown and Penn Quarter
Map 2

TOURS

Old Town Trolley Tours

Catch an open-air, motorized trolley for a breezy way to see the White House, the National Mall, and Capitol Hill. The tours are narrated by entertaining drivers and cover more than 100 major sights at 25 stops in 90 minutes. You can hop off to explore and hop back on another trolley, which run approximately every half hour. Purchase tickets and start the tour at the **Washington Welcome Center** (1000 E St. NW, 202/347-6609; 8:30am-9pm daily), a tourist information center and souvenir shop across from Ford's Theatre. If you already have tickets, pick up the trolley at any stop along the route. It's also possible to transfer trolleys for a tour of Arlington National Cemetery.

MAP 2: 1000 E St. NW, 844/356-2603, www.trolleytours.com; 9am-5pm daily; $40-80 adults, $30-60 children 4-12, free for children 4 and under, advance purchase discounts available online

Segs in the City

This tour operator offers several options for seeing the sights on Segways, including two-hour guided tours around downtown or the monuments and a sunset tour with time for reflection in the Franklin Delano Roosevelt Memorial and Lincoln Memorial. If you don't mind stares from locals, this is the quickest way to tour the monuments and memorials up-close with an engaging, knowledgeable guide. Or, rent your own Segway ($35/hour, $150/five hours) to tour at your own pace. Tours depart outside the Ronald Reagan Building and International

Trade Center and include a training session, helmet, and map.

MAP 2: 1300 Pennsylvania Ave. NW, 800/734-7393, www.segsinthecity.com; 9am-9:30pm daily weather permitting; $40-80 pp, ages 16 and up

SPORTS ARENAS
Capital One Arena

Since 1997, the Capital One Arena has welcomed more than 47 million people to its 20,000 seats for sporting events and major concerts. It's the home of several professional sports teams, including the NBA's **Washington Wizards,** the WNBA's **Washington Mystics,** and the NHL's **Washington Capitals,** as well as the Arena Football League's **Washington Valor** (202/661-5005, www.washingtonvalor.com), which plays from April to August. The **Georgetown University Hoyas** (202/687-4692, www.guhoyas.com) men's basketball team plays here, too. Tickets for all events are available at Ticketmaster outlets, including the arena box office.

MAP 2: 601 F St. NW, 202/628-3200, tickets 800/745-3000, http://capitalonearena. monumentalsportsnetwork.com; box office 10am-5pm Mon.-Fri., 10am to event start time Sat.-Sun.

SPECTATOR SPORTS
BASKETBALL
Washington Mystics

One of the first Women's National Basketball Association (WNBA) franchises, the Washington Mystics had a rough first season in 1998, finishing 3-27. But the ladies made it to the playoffs in 2015 and made some stellar picks in the 2017 WNBA draft. The Mystics play home games from May through September at the **Capital One Arena** (601 F St. NW); single game tickets are readily available via Ticketmaster and the arena box office.

MAP 2: 601 F St. NW, 877/324-6671, http://mystics.wnba.com; tickets from $19

Washington Wizards

National Basketball Association (NBA) followers may remember when DC's franchise was called the Washington Bullets, a controversial choice considering the city's high crime rate in the 1980s and 1990s. The franchise rebranded to the Washington Wizards in 1997, though there's been a movement among long-time fans to change it back. The team hasn't won a final since the Bullets days, but they did win a division title in 2017. The Wizards play home games from October to April at the **Capital One Arena** (601 F St. NW); single game tickets are readily available via Ticketmaster and the arena box office.

MAP 2: 601 F St. NW, 202/661-5050, www.nba.com/wizards; tickets from $19

ICE HOCKEY
Washington Capitals

Founded in 1974, DC's National Hockey League (NHL) team has won one championship and 10 divisional titles, as well as the Presidents' Trophy for the most points at the end of the regular season in 2016 and 2017, thanks in part to star player Alex Ovechkin, who scored his 1,000th point in January 2017. Caps fans are loud and loyal; catch a match from October to April at the **Capital One Arena** (601 F St. NW). Tickets are available via Ticketmaster and the arena box office, but plan ahead—the team sold out every home game in the 2016-2017 season.

MAP 2: 601 F St. NW, 202/266-2277, www.nhl.com/capitals; tickets from $39

Capitol Hill and Atlas District

Map 3

TOURS
✪ DC Ducks

Climb aboard a DC Duck, part tour bus and part boat, for a unique tour of the city by land and water with an entertaining captain to guide you. Departing from Union Station, the tour covers the major sights in 90 minutes, including the U.S. Capitol and the monuments and museums on the National Mall, before plunging into the Potomac River. The vehicles are restored amphibious military carriers, which were once used to carry supplies to ships at Pearl Harbor during World War II. Tours operate daily from mid-March through October, except Memorial Day, Independence Day, and the Marine Corps Marathon in October.

MAP 3: 50 Massachusetts Ave. NE, 866/754-5039, www.dcducks.com; $42 adults, $32 children 12 and under, discounts available online

The DC Ducks tours depart from Union Station.

Adams Morgan

Map 6

PARKS AND TRAILS
✪ Meridian Hill Park

This 12-acre urban oasis has a storied history—and the longest cascading fountain in North America. Located on the United States' original prime meridian, 1.5 miles due north of the White House, the park was the home of powerful Washingtonians, including John Quincy Adams, in the early capital days. The park has played important roles in the city's history, from serving as a camp for the Union Army to being a meeting place for civil rights rallies; when the surrounding neighborhoods burned in the 1968 riots after Martin Luther King Jr.'s assassination, Angela Davis called for the park to be named Malcolm X Park, which some longtime residents call it today. On weekends, locals lounge under statues of Dante, James Buchanan, and Joan of Arc, but the real party is at the top of the hill, where a drum circle has played every Sunday since the 1970s.

MAP 6: Between 15th St. NW and 16th St. NW, running from W St. NW north to Euclid St. NW; dawn-dusk daily; free

Georgetown and Foggy Bottom

Map 7

PARKS AND TRAILS
✪ Theodore Roosevelt Island

Located in the Potomac River at the DC-Virginia border, Theodore Roosevelt Island is a memorial to the 26th POTUS, a dedicated conservationist, and an idyllic spot to experience nature in the heart of the city. The island—which is indeed a real island, though it was cleaned up and landscaped by FDR's Civilian Conservation Corps—contains just over 2.5 miles of easy trails through forests and swampland; you can also pick up the Mount Vernon Trail here. The island is located in DC but accessible only from Virginia. It's a 15-minute walk from the Rosslyn Metro station or a 20-minute walk from Georgetown over the Francis Scott

Theodore Roosevelt Island

Key Bridge; cross the footbridge at the parking lot to access the island.

MAP 7: Enter via the parking lot off the George Washington Memorial Parkway near the Francis Scott Key Bridge and Mount Vernon Trail, 703/289-2500, www. nps.gov/this; accessible 6am-10pm daily weather permitting; free

Capital Crescent Trail

The 11-mile, mostly paved Capital Crescent Trail is popular with joggers, cyclists, and even commuters who travel from the suburbs of Bethesda and Silver Spring to work in DC. The leafy but well-maintained trail is one of the most-traveled in the country, but it's rarely too crowded to enjoy. Take a seven-mile bike ride to Bethesda, where you can break for lunch and still get back to DC in time to rest before dinner. Alternatively, stop at Fletcher's Boathouse (4940 Canal Rd. NW, 202/244-0461) to switch to the water, or pick up the Chesapeake & Ohio Towpath, which runs parallel with the Capital Crescent Trail through Georgetown for about 3.5 miles.

MAP 7: Access via Water St. NW under Whitehurst Freeway, 202/610-7500, www. cctrail.org; 24 hours daily; free

Chesapeake & Ohio Towpath

The Chesapeake & Ohio Towpath follows the C&O Canal for 184.5 miles from Georgetown to Cumberland, Maryland. Mile 0 is located at the canal's "watergate" near the famous hotel, but you can start your journey in Georgetown's shopping district. Look for the redbrick path at 29th Street south of M Street, and head east. If you're up for a long ride, follow the Capital Crescent Trail through Georgetown, which runs parallel for about 3.5 miles, to Fletcher's Boathouse (4940 Canal Rd. NW, 202/244-0461), where you can pick up the towpath to go to Great Falls (14 miles) or Harpers Ferry (60 miles).

MAP 7: Access from Thompson Boat Center or 29th St. NW at M St. NW, 301/739-4200, www.nps.gov/choh; 24 hours daily; free

Georgetown Waterfront Park

This 10-acre urban oasis is the perfect spot for a city picnic with a view of the Potomac River and major sights. The park has wide paved paths for cycling, skating, or jogging, and connects to several regional trails; there's ample green space as well as seating right on the riverbank. Children of all ages will enjoy features like the labyrinth and the fountain, which you're welcome to splash around in on a hot day.

MAP 7: 30th St. NW to 34th St. NW along the Potomac River, www. georgetownwaterfrontpark.org; 24 hours daily; free

BOATING

Key Bridge Boathouse

Rent a canoe, kayak, or paddleboard at the Key Bridge Boathouse and explore the Potomac River via the Georgetown Waterfront; prices range from $16 per hour for singles and $22-25 per hour for doubles. Just under the Francis Scott Key Bridge near the start of the Capital Crescent Trail, the boathouse offers 90-minute guided kayak tours of the monuments and major sights ($45) as well as stand-up paddleboarding ($40 pp), fitness and yoga classes ($10-40), and more.

MAP 7: 3500 Water St. NW, 202/337-9642, www.boatingindc.com; daily Apr. 15-Oct., hours vary

BICYCLE RENTALS

Capital Bikeshare station in Adams Morgan

For short-term or point-to-point rentals, **Capital Bikeshare** (877/430-2453, www.capitalbikeshare.com) makes it easy to find and acquire a bicycle. The program has more than 3,700 bikes at 440-plus stations in DC, Maryland, and Virginia. Look for the stations with their rows of shiny, cherry red bikes, use your credit card at the kiosk to get a code to unlock a bike, and pedal away. You can purchase a single trip up to 30 minutes for $2, a 24-hour pass for $8, or a 72-hour pass for $17; passes allow you to take unlimited 30-minute rides. Download the mobile app to see nearby stations and real-time availability.

DC has several dockless bicycle companies, too, including **LimeBike** (888/546-3345, www.limebike.com) and **Jump** (http://dc.jumpmobility.com), which has bikes powered by an electric motor. Download the company's mobile app to find the nearest bike, scan the bike's code with your phone to unlock it, and park it (almost) anywhere when you get to your destination.

For a longer ride, such as a day trip to Mount Vernon, or multiday rentals, **Bike and Roll** (202/842-2453, www.bikeandrolldc.com) has bicycles and equipment available at several locations; they'll also deliver bikes to your hotel.

The District of Columbia requires riders ages 16 and under to wear a helmet when riding a bike, scooter, or skateboard. For more information on bicycle rentals and trails, visit www.bikewashington.org.

Thompson Boat Center

The slightly hidden boathouse by the Washington Harbor has everything you need for a day outdoors: kayaks ($16-22/hour), canoes ($25/hour), paddleboards ($22/hour), so you can explore the Potomac River and Rock Creek, as well as bike rentals ($11/hour or $35/day). For a workout on the water, try sculling, which is rowing with two oars; certification is required.

MAP 7: 2900 Virginia Ave. NW, 202/333-9543, www.boatingindc.com; daily Apr. 15-Oct., hours vary

SPECTATOR SPORTS

TENNIS

Washington Kastles

The Washington Kastles team, DC's World TeamTennis franchise, has counted major stars like Venus and Serena Williams, Martina Hingis, and Sam Querrey on the team roster. And the team has lived up to the hype, becoming the first team in the league to play a perfect season (2009) and winning five subsequent championships. The Kastles play in July and August at the Charles E. Smith Center at George Washington University; single game tickets are readily available via Ticketmaster, though expect games with big tennis stars to sell out a week in advance.

MAP 7: 600 22nd St. NW, 202/483-6647, www.washingtonkastles.com; tickets from $15

Navy Yard and Anacostia   Map 8

PARKS AND TRAILS

✪ Anacostia Riverwalk Trail

The Anacostia Riverwalk Trail provides 20 miles of safe, paved paths for walking, running, or biking along the Anacostia River, connecting neighborhoods including Anacostia, Capitol Hill, and Navy Yard to Bladensburg, Maryland, and 40 more miles of trails. In addition to wildlife, you'll find conveniently located maps, benches, Capital Bikeshare stations, boating facilities, playgrounds, and more in the parks and communities along the trail, which will cover 28 miles when it's complete in 2019.

MAP 8: Access via Diamond Teague Park, 99 Potomac Ave. SE, or via Anacostia Park, 1900 Anacostia Dr. SE; 24 hours daily

The Yards Park

Set on the Anacostia River, The Yards Park is 5.4 acres of green space and

Anacostia Riverwalk Trail

The Yards Park

relaxing, waterfront views. The park frequently hosts events and festivals, including free concerts every Friday night in the summer. It's also an ideal stop during a bike ride along the Anacostia Riverwalk Trail; nap on a chaise lounge on the boardwalk, or grab a cone at nearby **Ice Cream Jubilee.**

MAP 8: 355 Water St. SE, www. capitolriverfront.org/the-yards-park; sunrise-2 hours after sunset daily

BOATING
Ballpark Boathouse

Head to Ballpark Boathouse, located directly behind Nationals Park, to rent a kayak ($16/hour single, $22/hour double) or canoe ($25/hour) and catch a glimpse of the U.S. Capitol from the Anacostia River. Warning: The river isn't known for being the cleanest body of water in the city, so make sure you don't tip over.

MAP 8: 100 Potomac Ave. SE, 202/337-9642, www.boatingindc.com; Thurs.-Sun. and holidays May-Sept., hours vary

SPORTS ARENAS
Nationals Park

Completed in March 2008, the 41,546-seat Nationals Park is the first Leadership in Energy and Environmental Design (LEED) certified major stadium in the United States. With views of the U.S. Capitol and Washington Monument from some of the upper decks, the stadium's design was inspired by I. M. Pei's East Wing of the National Gallery of Art. In addition to seeing the **Washington Nationals** play home games here, you can see the modern stadium on a **tour** ($15-25 adults, $10-20 seniors, military, and children 12 and under) from April through November. The stadium also hosts major outdoor concerts like Paul McCartney and James Taylor.

MAP 8: 1500 S. Capitol St. SE, 202/675-6287, www.washington.nationals. mlb.com; box office 10am-30 minutes after the end of the game on Mon.-Sat. game days, 9am-30 minutes after on Sun. game days, 10am-5pm Mon.-Fri, 10am-3pm Sat. on non-game days

SPECTATOR SPORTS
BASEBALL
✪ Washington Nationals

Since 2005, many Washingtonians have adopted the Washington Nationals. The team has won four Major League Baseball (MLB) East Division titles since 2012. Even if you don't root for the home team, seeing a Nats game during the April-October season is considered an essential activity for sports fans. Watch for the Presidents Race during the fourth inning, when bobblehead-style mascots George Washington, "Tom" Jefferson, "Abe" Lincoln, and Teddy Roosevelt race on the field (poor Teddy almost always loses, even when he's given a head start). In addition to the usual hot dogs and peanuts, concession stands also sell popular local favorites like half smokes from Ben's Chili Bowl and beer by DC Brau. Single game tickets are readily available at the box office or online, though big weekend games

WASHINGTON REDSKINS

The Washington Redskins have invited controversy several times since the National Football League (NFL) franchise moved from Boston to DC in 1937. During the civil rights era, the owner came under fire for unabashedly refusing to hire black players. In 1962, it became the last team in the league to integrate, when the Kennedy Administration threatened to bar them from playing in their DC stadium, which was owned by the federal government. (Incidentally, the first black player drafted by the Redskins, Ernie Davis, was the first black player to win the Heisman Trophy.)

And, of course, the name is divisive. The current owner, and many fans, argue the name is important to the team's 80-year-plus history; the founding Washington Redskins team's head coach and four players were American Indian. And according to some national polls, a majority of self-identified American Indians aren't bothered by the name, though the National Congress of American Indians says otherwise. In 2017, the U.S. Supreme Court struck down a law banning offensive trademarks on the grounds of the law being a violation of the First Amendment—meaning the name can remain, at least legally.

Since 1997, the Redskins have played home games at **FedEx Field** in Landover, Maryland, about 40 minutes outside DC. This move possibly cost them the "home team advantage," as their only Super Bowl wins occurred when they played at Robert F. Kennedy Memorial Stadium in Southeast DC. The team is currently exploring new stadium options in DC, Maryland, and Virginia.

For information and tickets, visit www.redskins.com.

may sell out in advance. Starting 2.5 hours before the first pitch, you can purchase $5 grandstand seats for most games (one per person at the main box office only). These go quickly on weekends.

MAP 8: 1500 S. Capitol St. SE, 202/675-6287, www.mlb.com/nationals; tickets $5-150, discounts available for seniors, students, government employees, and active-duty military

SOCCER
DC United

Audi Field opened in 2018, finally giving DC United, Washington's Major League Soccer team (and the winningest in the country), the home they deserve. Blocks from Nationals Park, the 20,000-seat stadium is located at Buzzard Point, a new area of development where the Potomac River meets the Anacostia River. The team's fans are some of the most dedicated; expect a loud, raucous, but friendly experience. The regular season runs March to October; single game tickets are readily available via Ticketmaster, though popular matches toward the end of the season commonly sell out.

MAP 8: 100 Potomac Ave. SE, 202/337-9642, www.dcunited.com; tickets $20-200

Greater Washington DC   Map 9

PARKS AND TRAILS
✪ East Potomac Park and Hains Point

If you want to get away and enjoy some time outdoors and still get back to your hotel with plenty of time to rest before dinner, head to this large manmade island in the Potomac River, a popular spot to run, bike, fish, picnic, or just toss a ball around in the wide open space within walking distance of the National Mall. At the tip of the island, **Hains Point** has playgrounds and picnic facilities with panoramic views of the water as well as Southwest DC and Ronald Reagan National Airport. In the middle, play at the **East Potomac Golf Course and Driving Range** and **East Potomac Tennis Center.** It's just over four miles from the Jefferson Memorial around the entire perimeter and back; the golf and tennis clubs are the only places to get water or snacks on the island.

MAP 9: Ohio Dr. SW between E. Basin Dr. SW and Hains Pt., 202/426-6841; dawn-dusk daily; free

✪ U.S. National Arboretum

It's a park, it's a garden, it's a museum—it's the U.S. National Arboretum, the 446-acre living museum and horticultural research center in Northeast, where there's something new blooming every month. It's a bit of a hike from the city center through industrial, up-and-coming parts of the city (and two miles from the closest Metro station, Stadium-Armory) but well worth the

East Potomac Park

Hains Point is a popular spot for picnics.

visit to explore these off-the-beaten-path gardens, groves, monuments, and trails. While it's possible to take a taxi/ride-share and reach some of the must-see sights by foot, a car or bike will allow you to more easily explore the vast grounds. (There are several free parking lots inside the arboretum.) Either way, start your visit at the administration building and visitor center, where you can pick up a map, get advice on what's blooming, and see the magical Aquatic Garden as well as the National Herb Garden and the **National Bonsai and Penjing Museum** (10am-4pm daily). Other highlights include Mount Hamilton in the southwest corner of the arboretum, covered in brilliant azaleas in April and May, and fall foliage in October and November, as well as the National Capitol Columns, 22 Corinthian columns taken the Capitol's East Portico in 1958, which feel almost alien in the vast meadow not far from the visitor center.

MAP 9: Entrance at 24th St. and R St. NE off Bladensburg Rd., 202/245-2726, www.usna.usda.gov; 8am-5pm daily; free

Dumbarton Oaks Park

Escape to the country without leaving the city. The 27-acre Dumbarton Oaks Park was originally part of the lovely estate and gardens at **Dumbarton Oaks** (1703 32nd St. NW, 202/339-6400, www.doaks.org), but it opened to the public as a national park in 1940. Beatrix Jones Farrand, a pioneering female landscape architect, designed the park to feel like the countryside, with dirt paths through naturalistic woodlands and wildflowers, worlds away from the hustle and bustle of DC. It's an idyllic place for a nature walk after exploring the nearby estate; while the two share a name, a fence blocks off the estate, which requires an admission fee, from the park, which is now managed by the National Park Service.

MAP 9: Entrance at Lovers' Lane at R St. NW and 31st St. NW, 202/333-3547, www.dopark.org; daily during daylight hours; free

Rock Creek Park

Covering more than 2,000 acres of parkland and historic sites around Rock Creek in Northwest DC, Rock Creek Park is an oasis for outdoors enthusiasts. Created by Congress in 1890, it's one of the oldest national parks and includes **Meridian Hill Park** in Columbia Heights, the **Old Stone House** and **Thompson Boat Center** in Georgetown, and the **Smithsonian's National Zoo.**

To access trails and athletic facilities, head to the swath of parkland north of the zoo, roughly between Oregon Avenue NW/Broad Branch Drive NW and 16th Street NW. The park has two main hiking trails, which run from the DC-Maryland border at Beach Drive south toward the zoo. The **Western Ridge Trail** is 5.5 miles one way, and the **Valley Trail** on the eastern border is 7 miles one-way; east-west trails connect them. The park has several picnic spots with grills, most of which are first-come, first-served.

The **nature center** (5200 Glover Rd. NW, 9am-5pm Wed.-Sun.; free) has a visitor center with kid-friendly exhibits (including live animals, beehives, and gardens) and the National Park Service's only operating **planetarium,** with free, regularly scheduled shows. The **horse center** (5100 Glover Rd. NW, 202/362-0117, www.rockcreekhorsecenter.com; 10am-6pm Mon.-Fri., 9am-5pm Sat.-Sun.) offers trail and pony rides, while the **tennis center** (16th St. and Kennedy St. NW, 202/722-5949, www.rockcreektennis.com; open daily, hours vary seasonally) has hard and clay courts available year-round, and hosts the **Citi Open** in July. The wooded **golf center** (6100 16th St. NW, 202/882-7332, www.golfdc.com/rock-creek-gc; open daily Mar.-Dec. including most holidays, hours vary seasonally) has a challenging 18-hole course and putting green.

The park is free and open daily during daylight hours; the nature center and horse center are closed Thanksgiving Day, Christmas Day, and New Year's Day. Parking is available at the nature center and at picnic areas near Beach Drive.

Gravelly Point

This flat, grassy stretch adjacent to Ronald Reagan National Airport is the perfect place to while away the hours with a shockingly up-close view of planes landing a few hundred feet away. The open park is a favorite with families, who take picnics on weekend afternoons. Parking is limited; bike there from Theodore Roosevelt Island via the Mount Vernon Trail, which you can take south to Alexandria, Virginia, and Mount Vernon.

MAP 9: Entrance at George Washington Memorial Parkway North, north of the Ronald Reagan National Airport, 703/289-2500, www.nps.gov/gwmp; daily 4am-10pm; free

BOATING
Fletcher's Boathouse

On the Potomac River at the meeting point of the Capital Crescent Trail and mile marker 3.1 of the C&O Towpath, this historical boathouse is where you can start an epic outdoor adventure. Choose a kayak ($16-22/hour), canoe ($25/hour), or rowboat ($16/hour or $30/day) and pick up some fishing tackle at the shop; stand-up paddleboards ($22/hour) are available, too. Or, rent bikes ($11/hour or $35/day) to take one of the trails onward.

MAP 9: 4940 Canal Rd. NW, 202/244-0461, www.boatingindc.com; daily Apr.-Oct., hours vary

East Potomac Golf Course and Driving Range

GOLF
East Potomac Golf Course and Driving Range

Play a round with a view of Southwest DC and the Washington Monument. Located in the middle of East Potomac Park, this public golf club has one 18-hole course and two 9-hole courses, plus putting greens, a heated and covered driving range, and a mini golf course for the whole family to enjoy. The snack bar has cheap breakfast, lunch, and snacks, and the pro shop has you covered if you didn't bring your clubs.

MAP 9: 972 Ohio Dr. SW, 202/554-7660, www.golfdc.com; open daily, hours vary; greens fees $12-30 Mon.-Fri., $13-34 Sat.-Sun.

TENNIS
East Potomac Tennis Center

With five indoor courts plus 19 outdoor clay and hard courts, the East Potomac Tennis Center on the north end of East Potomac Park offers opportunities to play tennis year-round. Reservations are recommended, but walk-in courts and lessons are available; call the center or check the website for the schedule. Facilities include showers and lockers, and a pro shop sells gear and snacks.

MAP 9: 1090 Ohio Dr. SW, 202/554-5962, www.eastpotomactennis.com; 7am-10pm daily

SHOPS

Downtown and Penn Quarter 207
Capitol Hill and Atlas District 210
Dupont Circle 212
U Street, Shaw, and Logan Circle 215
Adams Morgan. 218
Georgetown and Foggy Bottom 220
Navy Yard and Anacostia 222
Greater Washington DC 223

No, Washington DC isn't a shopping capital like New York City or London, but it does have everything you might need or want to buy, from only-in-Washington souvenirs to high-end fashion.

Nike Community Store

While DC isn't known for one specific item, there are plenty of worthy souvenirs, especially at the official gift shops at the White House, U.S. Capitol, and museums, where your purchases of official memorabilia will support the preservation of these important sites. For distinctive DC flag barware, neighborhood art prints, or political gag gifts, as well as local products, home and gift shops citywide stock stylish items.

Until recently, Washingtonians had to go to the suburbs to buy most of their clothes, but today, DC has the world's top luxury brands and mass-market retailers, as well as a growing number of independent boutiques. You'll find the most stores downtown—names like Dior, Gucci, and Louis Vuitton as well as Banana Republic, Macy's, H&M, and several off-price department stores. For something unique, browse Georgetown, home to high-end designers and trendy boutiques for men and women who want to look preppy and polished, or Logan Circle and Shaw, which are more fashion-forward.

Of course, Washington's wonks buy many books, and almost every neighborhood has an independent bookstore. You can find national bestsellers at bigger ones like Politics and Prose and Kramerbooks, but at many, the stock veers toward books about politics, social issues, and DC history.

HIGHLIGHTS

✪ **MOST SPECIAL GIFTS: Tiny Jewel Box** sells beautiful baubles and one-of-a-kind pieces by top designers to DC's elite (page 207).

✪ **BEST OFFICIAL SOUVENIR:** Purchase the annual White House Christmas ornament at the **White House Visitor Center Shop** (page 208).

✪ **BEST GIFTS FOR CHEFS: Hill's Kitchen** stocks local, edible products, plus cookie cutters in the shapes of the monuments and DC-themed kitchen linens (page 212).

✪ **BEST BOOKSTORE: Kramerbooks** is a favorite spot for locals to pick up the latest books (page 213).

✪ **BEST FOR FASHIONISTAS ON A BUDGET:** Many of the pieces at **Violet** are under $100, so shop away (page 215).

✪ **MOST LIKELY TO MAKE YOU WISH YOU'D BROUGHT A TRUCK: Miss Pixie's** offers a highly curated selection of vintage furniture, art, and housewares (page 216).

✪ **BEST EDIBLE PURCHASES: Union Kitchen Grocery** stocks more than 200 local food, beverage, and condiment brands (page 217).

✪ **BEST VINTAGE SHOP: Mercedes Bien Vintage** offers a selection of flawless treasures for men and women (page 218).

✪ **MOST FASHIONABLE: Curio Concept** is like entering the closet of your well-traveled fashionista friend, stocking of-the-minute designers (page 220).

✪ **COOLEST LOCAL LIQUOR: New Columbia Distillers** produces Green Hat Gin, named for one of DC's famous alcohol purveyors during Prohibition (page 223).

Tiny Jewel Box

SHOPPING DISTRICTS

Gallery Place and CityCenterDC

Close to the Capital One Arena, Gallery Place has the world's favorite chains, from Macy's and Banana Republic to H&M and Urban Outfitters. Within Gallery Place, CityCenterDC is the city's shiniest shopping development, with more than two dozen luxury brands like Burberry, Dior, Gucci, and Louis Vuitton, plus buzzy restaurants and cafés.

MAP 2: 7th St. NW to 13th St. NW between F St. NW and I St. NW; CityCenterDC from 9th St. NW to 11th St. NW between H St. NW and I St. NW

Eastern Market

In addition to the outdoor flea market on weekends, Eastern Market is home to cozy, independent shops selling books, housewares, and games, plus several coffee shops. Most are located near the market building on 7th Street SE, as well as the side streets around the Eastern Market Metro station.

MAP 3: 7th St. SE between North Carolina Ave. SE and Pennsylvania Ave. SE and around the Eastern Market Metro station

North End Shaw

A few blocks from the African American Civil War Memorial and 9:30 Club, North End Shaw is a growing hub for niche, high-end fashion and beauty, as well as restaurants, beer gardens, and an outpost of Glen's Garden Market if you need a healthy snack.

MAP 5: 8th St. NW and 9th St. NW between T St. NW and U St. NW

14th Street NW

One of the fastest-growing districts for shopping (and dining and nightlife) is along 14th Street NW, from U Street NW to Logan Circle. You'll find everything from men's and women's apparel and accessories, to cool housewares and reclaimed furniture, to curated wine shops—plus, a ton of boutique fitness studios.

MAP 5: 14th St. NW from P St. NW to U St. NW

Adams Morgan

If you're in the market for smoking paraphernalia, books about social justice issues, or something to wear to a march, head to Adams Morgan, where shops are concentrated around 18th Street NW and Columbia Road NW.

MAP 6: 18th St. NW from California St. NW to Columbia Rd. NW

Georgetown

You can shop till you drop in Georgetown, a dense shopping district with stores lining M Street NW and Wisconsin Avenue NW. It's known for preppy mainstays like Ralph Lauren and Lilly Pulitzer but has a growing number of youthful, fashion-forward boutiques, too. Head north on Wisconsin Avenue for housewares and linens, bridal boutiques, and fine art and antiques.

MAP 7: M Street NW and side streets from 29th St. NW to 34th St. NW, Wisconsin Ave. NW from M St. NW to Reservoir Rd. NW

EXIT THROUGH THE GIFT SHOP

Navajo pottery for sale at the National Museum of the American Indian

When you're visiting one of the Smithsonian Institution's museums or the National Gallery of Art, make a beeline for the gift shop to find some of the best souvenir shopping in DC. Every museum has at least one shop with apparel, accessories, toys, home and office decor, and replicas of the treasures inside the exhibitions, as well as books for all ages. The National Gallery of Art has two shops as well as pop-up boutiques with official prints and catalogues for temporary exhibits. While museum gift shops are more expensive than souvenir shops elsewhere in the city, your purchases will benefit the preservation of these free museums and their treasures for generations to come.

Generally, gift shops keep the same hours as their parent museum. The shops are not accessible from the outside, but Smithsonian Institution museums and the National Gallery of Art are free to enter every day of the year; the National Museum of African American History and Culture requires a timed ticket to enter the museum and the shop.

FASHION

- Fashionistas will want to look at the hats inspired by Mae Reeves, milliner to Marian Anderson and Ella Fitzgerald, at the **National Museum of African American History and Culture** (page 72), eco-friendly jewelry by local Peruvian-American designer Evelyn Brooks at the **National Museum of the American Indian** (page 164), and official replicas of Jackie Kennedy's jewels at the **National Museum of American History** (page 71).

ART AND DECOR

- You can also take home your favorite work from the **National Gallery of Art** (page 162) or the **Hirshhorn Museum and Sculpture Garden** (page 162) in the form of an art print or coffee-table book. The **National Museum of the American Indian** (page 164) and the **Freer Gallery of Art and Arthur M. Sackler Gallery** (page 163) have some of the most interesting home decor.

FOOD

- The tastiest souvenir is the freeze-dried ice cream from the **National Air and Space Museum** (page 72), which will travel well no matter how far you're flying. Kids love this gift shop, which is filled with the coolest gadgets, toys, and child-size astronaut suits.

Downtown and Penn Quarter

Map 2

SHOPS

DOWNTOWN AND PENN QUARTER

CLOTHING, SHOES, AND ACCESSORIES

✪ Tiny Jewel Box

Since 1930, Tiny Jewel Box has been the choice of U.S. presidents and first ladies for fine jewelry and diplomatic gifts. Secretary of State Madeleine Albright purchased many of her colorful pins here, and First Lady Michelle Obama gave a gift to her predecessor that was designed by Tiny Jewel Box. Occupying the corner of Connecticut Avenue NW and M Street NW, it stocks international brands like Cartier and Rolex, as well as designers like David Yurman, who was discovered by owner Jim Rosenheim in 1977. You'll also find one-of-a-kind and vintage pieces, or you can work with the welcoming staff to create a custom design.

MAP 2: 1155 Connecticut Ave. NW, 202/393-2747, www.tinyjewelbox.com; 10am-5:30pm Mon.-Sat.

Charles Tyrwhitt

Washington's well-traveled lobbyists have been wearing shirts from London's Charles Tyrwhitt for years, but since the Jermyn Street men's tailor opened their first DC location just few blocks from the White House, the brand has gotten even more popular among the K Street crowd. The small shop stocks row upon row of the brand's expertly tailored shirts in a variety of fits and colors, as well as suits, ties, and accessories.

MAP 2: 1000 Connecticut Ave. NW, 202/594-3529, www.ctshirts.com; 9am-7pm Mon.-Fri., 10am-6pm Sat., noon-5pm Sun.

Coup de Foudre Lingerie

This pretty boutique in Penn Quarter stocks the finest lingerie from Paris, including Chantelle, Lise Charmel, and Simone Pérèle, as well as hip, lower-priced brands like Commando and Hanky Panky. Meaning "bolt of lightning," a phrase used to describe love at first sight in French, Coup de Foudre has warm staff who will make you feel comfortable during your bra fitting and offer personalized suggestions if you're shopping for a special gift.

MAP 2: 1001 Pennsylvania Ave. NW, 202/393-0878, www.coupdefoudrelingerie. com; 11am-6pm Mon.-Sat.

Tiny Jewel Box

MM.LaFleur

Founded in 2013 by Sarah LaFleur, who struggled to find chic but appropriate office attire when she worked in finance in New York, MM.LaFleur employs Zac Posen's former head designer to create sleek, machine-washable, wrinkle-resistant dresses and separates in sizes 0P to 22W. The Internet startup is best known for sending customers a hand-picked box of 4-6 pieces based on style preferences, but it's possible to visit the minimalist K Street showroom to try on the collection in person. The company prefers you to make an appointment so your stylist can pull looks before you arrive and work with you one-on-one.

MAP 2: 1424 K St. NW, 202/869-4500, www.mmlafleur.com; 11am-8pm Mon.-Fri., 11am-6pm Sat.-Sun.

GIFTS AND HOME
✪ White House Visitor Center Shop

The 16,000-square-foot flagship gift shop inside the White House Visitor Center stocks a large selection of official White House merchandise: cuff links and jewelry (including flag lapel pins), home and office decor like calendars and presidential busts, fine art, books, and the annual White House Christmas ornament and Easter Egg Roll commemorative eggs. Another, smaller shop, the **White House History Shop** (1610 H St. NW, 202/218-4337), has a similar inventory and frequently hosts signings with authors of books about White House history.

MAP 2: 1450 Pennsylvania Ave. NW, 202/208-7031, www.whitehousehistory.org; 7:30am-4pm daily

the official White House Christmas ornament from the White House History Shop

BEST SOUVENIRS

Don't bother with the FBI sweatshirts and caps hawked by street vendors around the National Mall, and take home one of these only-in-Washington souvenirs or local products instead.

Embittermint cocktail bitters are made in Washington DC.

WHITE HOUSE MEMORABILIA
The official **White House Christmas ornament** is a bipartisan piece of Americana that the White House Historical Association has designed every year since 1981 to benefit the preservation of White House art and artifacts. Every year, a new design honors a president or significant anniversary, like the bicentennial of the presidency or the laying of the White House cornerstone. You can purchase it at the **White House Visitor Center Shop** (page 208) and the **White House History Shop** (page 208). The shops also sell other memorabilia, like **cuff links and flag lapel pins** and reproductions of **presidential busts,** too.

FOOD AND DRINK
Noteworthy artisan food and beverage companies have made their mark on the city. For cocktail enthusiasts, a bottle of **Green Hat Gin,** made by **New Columbia Distillers** (page 223) and available at liquor stores around town including **Batch 13** (page 218), will remind you of evenings in DC's historic bars. With its newsprint-style label, it looks cool on your bar cart, too.

While many stores stock DC-themed barware, the **Lincoln Memorial-themed growler jugs** available at brewery **DC Brau** (3178 Bladensburg Rd. NE, 202/621-8890, http://dcbrau.com) stand out. Pair them with a six-pack of the brewery's **The Public Pale Ale** for a great gift.

For a wide selection of "Made in DC" products, ranging from **Gordy's Pickle Jar pickles** to **Embitterment cocktail bitters** to kitchen items featuring the DC flag, be sure to stop by **Salt & Sundry** (page 217), **Union Kitchen Grocery** (page 217), **Hill's Kitchen** (page 212), and Dupont Circle's **Shop Made in D.C.** (page 214).

BOOKS
For readers, there's no better souvenir than a **signed book by a DC author.** Check the lineup of author events at stores like **Politics and Prose** (page 222) or **Kramerbooks** (page 213). And don't forget to get your **Reader Identification Card** from the **Library of Congress** (page 87).

Chocolate Moose

Since 1979, Washingtonians have visited Chocolate Moose for gag gifts for friends and coworkers. The quirky boutique stocks a seemingly random assortment of home decor and barware, jewelry and accessories, games and toys for all ages, Leonidas Belgian chocolates, and funny greeting cards (don't expect to find anything too sentimental). If the weather gets stormy, pop in for an umbrella emblazoned with the Washington Metro map or cherry blossoms.

MAP 2: 1743 L St. NW, 202/463-0992, www.chocolatemoosedc.com; 10am-6pm Mon.-Fri., 10am-5pm Sat.

The Great Republic

Did visiting the museums inspire you to add some Americana to your home or office? In CityCenterDC,

The Great Republic sells authentic American antiques like rare maps and flags from the country's early days, books (including signed copies), and hand-carved eagles meant for hanging over your desk. Yes, they're expensive, but you're welcome to browse, or shop lower-priced, new items like made-in-America leather goods and cuff links.

MAP 2: 973 Palmer Alley NW, 202/682-1812, www.great-republic.com; 10am-8pm Mon.-Sat., 11am-6pm Sun.

GOURMET FOOD AND DRINKS
Chocolate Chocolate

This tiny, friendly shop sells a tasty souvenir: White Houses, Capitol domes, and monuments made from milk, dark, and white chocolate. The walls are packed with artisanal American, Belgian, and Swiss chocolate brands and self-serve gummies and chocolates, while small-batch house truffles and nostalgic candies, like vanilla buttercreams and mint meltaways, twinkle in the glass case.

MAP 2: 1130 Connecticut Ave. NW, 202/466-2190, www.chocolatedc.com; 10am-6pm Mon.-Fri., 11am-4pm Sat.

Capitol Hill and Atlas District
Map 3

BOOKS
Capitol Hill Books

This two-story Eastern Market bookstore is crammed floor to ceiling with used and rare books of all kinds—but don't expect to get lost in the stacks browsing alone, because it's impossible to avoid contact with other people in the shop, especially on Sundays when the market is busy. The fiction books are mostly alphabetical by author; others are organized by category, with a Mystery Room, Business Closet, and foreign language books in the bathroom.

MAP 3: 657 C St. SE, 202/544-1621, www.capitolhillbooks-dc.com; 11:30am-6pm Mon.-Fri., 9am-6pm Sat.-Sun.

East City Bookshop

The service is excellent at this independent bookstore, where the chatty staff can make suggestions or place special orders. Throughout the store, many books have notes scribbled by staff members so you can find a recommended new read. The selection spans politics and history to bestsellers and children's books, with many already-signed copies by authors who have visited the store for readings and book signings.

MAP 3: 645 Pennsylvania Ave. SE, 202/290-1636, www.eastcitybookshop.com; 10am-8pm Mon.-Sat., 11am-6pm Sun.

OUTDOOR GEAR
REI Washington DC Flagship

The Beatles played their first concert in the United States in DC's Uline Arena, which was the site of inaugural balls and major speeches and athletic events throughout history. Now, the building is the DC flagship location of REI. Even without the history, the 51,000-square-foot store is

Politics and Prose in Upper Northwest

Everyone in Washington DC is shopping around a book. And when the author gets a publisher, there's one place in the city where they want to be: **Politics and Prose** (5015 Connecticut Ave. NW, 202/364-1919, www.politics-prose.com), the Upper Northwest independent bookstore known for its robust program of author talks and signings, including many by local newsmakers and newsbreakers. Almost every day, the store hosts well-attended events with U.S. senators, star reporters, and bestselling novelists. Events at the store are almost always free and open to the public, though events with high-profile authors (Dan Rather, Patti Smith, Amy Tan) at other city venues often require advance tickets. For a uniquely DC experience, go to one of the store's evening book signings, then head to Comet Ping Pong, the "Pizzagate" restaurant just a few doors down, for pizza and beer.

The flagship is 15 minutes by taxi or car from Dupont Circle, and one mile from the Van Ness-UDC Metro station. Other locations include **The Wharf** (70 District Sq. SW, 202/488-3867) and **Union Market** (1270 5th St. NE).

If you're looking for a book closer to the city center, locals' top picks include Capitol Hill's **East City Bookshop** (page 210), Dupont Circle's **Kramerbooks** (page 213), and Adams Morgan's **The Potter's House** (page 131), which also functions as a café. And don't miss the bookstores inside **Busboys and Poets** restaurants (page 127) for a curated selection focusing on social justice issues.

a destination, where you can learn skills like bike maintenance and adjustment or knot tying, plan an excursion to one of the national parks with help from the National Park Service experts in the **Adventure Station** (noon-7pm daily), or meet fellow runners. The store has a 1,052-square-foot **La Colombe** (7am-7pm daily), the Philadelphia-based coffee roastery known for draft lattes.

MAP 3: 201 M St. NE, 202/543-2040, www.rei.com; 10am-9pm Mon.-Sat., 11am-7pm Sun.

Summit to Soul

This small Barracks Row shop stocks an impressive selection of high-end athletic apparel and accessories for women. In addition to apparel by Beyond Yoga, Coeur, and Onzie, browse water bottles, yoga mats, sunscreen—everything you might need for an impromptu bike ride or yoga class.

MAP 3: 727 8th St. SE, 202/450-1832, www.summittosoul.com; 11am-7pm Tues.-Fri., 10am-6pm Sat., 11am-5pm Sun.

GIFTS AND HOME
❂ Hill's Kitchen

Hill's Kitchen is a destination for edible goodies either made in the District or inspired by DC's flavors: Embitterment cocktail bitters, True grenadine and tonic syrup, Gordy's Pickle Jar pickles and brine, and Uncle Brutha hot sauce, which was originally sold at Eastern Market before going national. This row house near Eastern Market is the place to pick up U.S. state and monument cookie cutters and dish towels, and anything else you might need for your kitchen.

Hill's Kitchen

MAP 3: 713 D St. SE, 202/543-1997, www. hillskitchen.com; 10am-6pm Tues.-Sat., 10am-5pm Sun.

Labyrinth Games & Puzzles

This quirky store sells classic and unique games, puzzles, and mazes for every interest under the sun. (I was intrigued by Marrying Mr. Darcy, a *Pride and Prejudice* card game in which you must attend events and improve your character to find a suitor.) The exceptionally friendly staff is happy to tell you about any game in stock, as well as the store's weekly game nights and tournaments.

MAP 3: 645 Pennsylvania Ave. SE, 202/544-1059, www.labyrinthgameshop. com; 10am-10pm Tues., 10am-9pm Wed., 10am-10pm Thurs.-Fri., 9am-7pm Sat., 11am-6pm Sun.

Dupont Circle   Map 4

CLOTHING, SHOES, AND ACCESSORIES
Betsy Fisher

Busy Washington women who don't want to sacrifice style for professionalism shop at Betsy Fisher for designer ready-to-wear for all occasions. You'll find dresses, separates, and shoes to take you from work to cocktails to the PTA meeting, from labels like Elie Tahari, Max Mara, and Nicole Miller, as well as lesser-known designers, with regular trunk shows of new wares.

MAP 4: 1224 Connecticut Ave. NW, 202/785-1975, www.betsyfisher.com; 10am-7pm Mon.-Fri., 10am-6pm Sat., 1pm-5pm Sun.

Brooks Brothers

Sure, you can shop at this American retailer online, but if you're in the market for a new suit, get style inspiration from the lobbyists and lawyers who pop in between meetings to browse the sales. After all, Brooks Brothers has real DC street cred—the company has dressed 40 U.S. presidents, including President Lincoln, who was assassinated in his Brooks Brothers coat embroidered with the phrase "One Country, One Destiny."

MAP 4: 1201 Connecticut Ave. NW, 202/659-4650, www.brooksbrothers. com; 10am-7pm Mon.-Fri., 10am-6pm Sat., noon-6pm Sun.

Proper Topper

If you need an outfit for a horserace in the Virginia countryside, Proper Topper has you covered, literally. The tiny store has a selection of hats and fascinators at a variety of price points, as well as pretty dresses from labels like Tracy Reese. And the store always has something new—from mugs and cookbooks to candles and coasters to dainty DC flag jewelry.

MAP 4: 1350 Connecticut Ave. NW, 202/842-3055, www.propertopper.com; 10am-7pm Mon.-Fri., 10am-6pm Sat.

BOOKS

✪ Kramerbooks

Even an e-reader devotee will walk out of Kramerbooks with a shopping bag, because management seems to know exactly which books you didn't know you needed. This is DC, so politics, history, biography, and Washington life and culture dominate the shelves, but you'll also find fiction and nonfiction bestsellers. It's one of locals' favorite spots to pick up new books by their friends, or their political foes; even President Obama dropped by with his daughters for Small Business Saturday in 2011.

MAP 4: 1517 Connecticut Ave. NW, 202/387-1400, www.kramers.com/

Kramerbooks

bookstore; 7:30am-1am Sun.-Thurs., 7:30am-3am Fri.-Sat.

Second Story Books

Since 1973, Second Story Books has been providing Washington area readers with used books, boasting one of the largest collections of rare and collectible books, manuscripts, maps, and prints in the world. On most days, carts outside the store have an eclectic mix of sale books selling for as little as $2 each.

MAP 4: 2000 P St. NW, 202/659-8884, www.secondstorybooks.com; 10am-10pm daily

HOME AND GIFTS
Jenni Bick Custom Journals

Jenni Bick has been selling her gorgeous journals out of her home in Martha's Vineyard since 1990, but her flagship store is located in this city full of writers and dreamers. The store is a treasure trove for lovers of the written word, offering Jenni Bick's own leather journals, which can be embossed with initials or a phrase, as well as rainbows of notebooks by Moleskine and Leuchtturm1917, fine pens and pencils, and letterpress cards.

MAP 4: 1300 Connecticut Ave. NW, 202/721-0246, www.jennibickdc.com; 10am-7pm Mon.-Sat., noon-6pm Sun.

Shop Made in D.C.

Located right off Dupont Circle, this store and café opened in 2017 to celebrate the growing number of artisans in Washington DC. It's small, but stocks a tightly curated selection of excellent gifts and souvenirs, all, of course, made in the District. Merchandise includes "I'm Woke" baby onesies, DC-themed tees by District of Clothing, accessories made from upcycled bicycle parts by BicycleTrash, and DC flag waxed canvas totes by Stitch & Rivet. The café inside the shop features Bullfrog Bagels, ANXO cider, and local brews.

MAP 4: 1330 19th St. NW, no phone, www.shopmadeindc.com; 7am-8pm Mon.-Fri., 11am-6pm Sat.-Sun.

Tabletop

Specializing in quirky but stylish home accessories and gifts, Tabletop is the place to shop for your hard-to-buy-for friend, or to pick up a souvenir for yourself. The DC dish towels, baby onesies, and neighborhood map prints are worth the visit, but the shop also stocks Jonathan Adler and Marimekko home decor, kitchen supplies, jewelry, kids' toys and books, plus unique wrapping paper and greeting cards in case you're en route to a party.

MAP 4: 1608 20th St. NW, 202/387-7117, www.tabletopdc.com; noon-8pm Mon.-Sat., 10am-6pm Sun.

GOURMET FOOD AND DRINKS
Glen's Garden Market

Part grocery store, part café, Glen's Garden Market sells local flavor; almost every item in the store is from a local business. You can get everything you need for an easy meal in your Airbnb, including hormone-free meat, fresh pasta, and organic produce, or pick up a raw Gouter tonic if you need to detox and balance your pH. There's another location in Shaw (1924 8th St. NW, 202/939-2839; 11am-10pm Mon.-Fri., 9am-9pm Sat.-Sun.). Both locations sell soup and sandwiches in the deli, along with growlers of—you guessed it—local beer.

MAP 4: 2001 S St. NW, 202/588-5698, www.glensgardenmarket.com; 8am-10pm Mon.-Fri., 9am-9pm Sat.-Sun.

The Mediterranean Way

Hankering for some manchego and crackers, or perhaps a bottle of Greek wine to take back to your hotel room? This small Mediterranean grocery is chock-full of authentic goodies, stacked on crates like you'd find in a corner store in Europe. You'll find items to take home, such as special olive oils and organic Greek honey, as well as picnic-basket filler, like homemade empanadas. **MAP 4:** 1717 Connecticut Ave. NW, 202/560-5715, www.themediway.com; 10am-9pm Mon.-Sat., 10am-8pm Sun.

U Street, Shaw, and Logan Circle
Map 5

CLOTHING, SHOES, AND ACCESSORIES
✪ Violet

This trendy boutique is a must-visit before a last-minute party; the super-friendly staff will be more than happy to help you pick out an outfit from the selection of young, casual separates and flirty dresses. And best of all, many of the pieces are under $100. It's no wonder so many local fashion bloggers give Violet a stamp of approval. **MAP 5:** 1924 8th St. NW, 202/621-9225, www.violetdc.com; 10am-8pm Mon.-Sat., 10am-7pm Sun.

Current Boutique

This consignment shop sells cast-offs from the neighborhood's pretty young things, who pack the dressing rooms on weekends to try on gently used pieces for work or a night at the nearby bars. It's not uncommon to find new-with-tags items on the racks, where stock tends toward youthful, feminine labels (Kate Spade, Milly). At the front, find a selection of new, trendy dresses, blouses, and rompers from lesser-known labels, mostly under $200. **MAP 5:** 1809 14th St. NW, 202/588-7311, www.currentboutique.com; noon-8pm Mon.-Fri., 11am-8pm Sat., 11am-6pm Sun.

Lettie Gooch

A longtime favorite of neighborhood fashionistas, this boutique is a must-stop shop for trendy but affordable fashion from emerging womenswear brands you won't find elsewhere in DC. The personable staff will help you pick out easy, colorful dresses, tops, and funky fashion jewelry to help you stand out at your casual office job or brunch at the beer gardens in Shaw. **MAP 5:** 1921 8th St. NW, 202/332-4242, www.lettiegooch.com; noon-7pm Mon.-Fri., 11am-8pm Sat., noon-6pm Sun.

Ministry of Supply

Most professional men in DC are still required to wear suits even in the swampy summer. Enter Ministry of Supply, which combines technology from the brains at MIT and NASA with design by former creatives at Theory and Brooks Brothers to create functional, office-appropriate clothing—think wrinkle-resisting, sweat-stopping, machine-washable shirts, pants, jackets, and polos in neutral, wearable hues, plus a few separates for women. Even the shopping part is easy in this uncluttered store, which has Wi-Fi, a desk and couch if you want to relax, and employees who will offer you a beverage when it's hot.

MAP 5: 1924 8th St. NW, 202/851-4942, www.ministryofsupply.com; 11am-7pm Mon.-Sat., 11am-6pm Sun.

Redeem

If you're after the je ne sais quoi of the minimalist fashionistas in Berlin or Paris, head to Reedem for drapey dresses and jumpsuits, cutting-edge denim, and lots of black. Founded in 2006, the austere boutique is staffed by sales associates who look the part for selling edgy, up-and-coming labels for men and women like Assembly, Oak, and Religion, as well as insta-cool accessories and fragrances.

MAP 5: 1810 14th St. NW, 202/332-7447, www.reedemus.com; noon-8pm Mon.-Sat., noon-6pm Sun.

Shinola

In 2013, Central Union Mission, DC's oldest homeless shelter for men, sold its grand building at the corner of 14th and R for $7 million and moved to a new facility by Union Station. And Shinola, which sells watches assembled in Detroit with top-of-the-line watch parts from Switzerland, moved in. In the polished store, studio lights shine from the lofty ceilings to highlight the watch collection for men and women as well as luxe leather goods, journals made with sustainable paper, and sleek, hand-assembled bicycles.

MAP 5: 1631 14th St. NW, 202/470-0200, www.shinola.com; 11am-8pm Mon.-Sat., 11am-7pm Sun.

OUTDOOR GEAR

Filson

Founded by C. C. Filson as a loggers' outfitter during the Klondike Gold Rush, Filson specializes in clothing, luggage, and accessories for outdoor activities like fly fishing, camping, and hiking. This small shop is the brand's only East Coast store outside of New York City. The ruggedly attractive duffels and briefcases are popular on the DC gym-to-office-to-bar commute.

MAP 5: 1631 14th St. NW, 202/759-9570, www.filson.com; 11am-7pm Mon.-Sat., noon-5pm Sun.

HOME AND GIFTS

✪ Miss Pixie's

Inside Miss Pixie's pink doorway is a treasure trove of vintage and repurposed furniture, art, and home accessories in superb condition, crammed into every corner of the store. They'll arrange delivery if you find the perfect piece; in between desks and dining sets, lighter travelers will find easier-to-pack souvenirs, including flawless vintage glassware, books and comic books, and piles of DC postcards.

MAP 5: 1626 14th St. NW, 202/232-8171, www.misspixies.com; 11am-7pm daily

Cherry Blossom Creative

Many shops around town specializing in local products sell the gorgeous, full-color map illustrations of DC neighborhoods made by Cherry Blossom Creative, the design studio that has created logos and collateral for many local businesses. The boutique stocks maps of dozens of neighborhoods, including the ones in this guide, printed on 100-pound Ecosilk paper, as well as elegant notebooks by local brand Appointed and stationery.

MAP 5: 2128 8th St. NW, 202/319-2979, www.cherryblossomworkshop.com; noon-8pm Wed.-Sun.

GoodWood

Fans of Anthropologie will appreciate GoodWood, which has been selling exquisitely curated vintage and

Miss Pixie's

antique home furnishings in the U Street Corridor since 1994. The dimly lit store has a free-spirited but still sophisticated vibe, filled with boho-chic womenswear and accessories from international labels like Almatrichi of Spain and Beautiful Stories of Iceland. On wooden tables and shelves, find candles, fragrances, and beauty products you'll want to keep on your counter.

MAP 5: 1428 U St. NW, 202/986-3640, www.goodwooddc.com; noon-7pm Mon.-Sat., noon-5pm Sun.

Salt & Sundry

It's impossible to leave Salt & Sundry without buying something, because the small shop is jam-packed with the most lovely things: stunning cookbooks and linens, funky jewelry by local designer Rachel Pfeffer, an adorable selection of DC-themed baby books and bibs, and local food and beverage fixings like Embitterment cocktail bitters. Another store is

located inside Union Market (1309 5th St. NE, 202/556-1866).

MAP 5: 1625 14th St. NW, 202/621-6647, www.shopsaltandsundry.com; 11am-7pm Mon.-Fri., 10am-7pm Sat., 10am-6pm Sun.

GOURMET FOOD AND DRINKS

✪ Union Kitchen Grocery

Many local chefs and food companies partially owe their success to Union Kitchen, an incubator of sorts to mentor more than 50 food businesses and connect them with resources, including commercial kitchen space and storage. Union Kitchen Grocery is like a gourmet bodega, stocking more than 200 local brands, such as Capital Candy Jar, Capital Kombucha, and Vigilante Coffee, as well as grocery and pantry items. There's another location near Union Station (538 3rd St. NE; 7:30am-9pm daily).

MAP 5: 1251 9th St. NW, no phone, www.unionkitchendc.com; 7am-10pm Mon.-Fri., 8am-10pm Sat.-Sun.

Union Kitchen Grocery

for something entirely unique. On weekends, the store offers free tastings, with discounts on the products in the tasting.

MAP 5: 1724 14th St. NW, 202/483-0214; 2pm-10pm Mon.-Tues., noon-10pm Wed.-Thurs., noon-11pm Fri.-Sat., noon-6pm Sun.

Grand Cata

Specializing in Latino wines, this well-organized shop sells wine and liquor from the Caribbean, Central America, and South America, including the usual suspects (Chile) and less-familiar regions (Uruguay), as well as heritage regions like Spain and Portugal. The charming owners and employees know wine extremely well; don't hesitate to ask for recommendations for something unique and in your price range, because they have a large selection of wines under $20.

MAP 5: 1550 7th St. NW, 202/525-5702, www.grandcata.com; noon-8pm Sun.-Mon., 11am-9pm Tues.-Sat.

Batch 13

This two-level spirits shop stocks more than 1,000 types of small-batch and craft beers and wine as well as small-batch, even obscure, liquors, including local varieties like Green Hat Gin and Republic Restoratives. In other words, don't go here for rail liquor—or rail-liquor prices—but

Adams Morgan   Map 6

BOOKS

Idle Time Books

This three-story used bookshop is packed full of gems for bookworms, including a large selection of rare and out-of-print books. Rare first editions are locked in a glass case, and there's a section of first editions under $50; browse the shelves full of books about local history for a unique souvenir.

MAP 6: 2467 18th St. NW, 202/232-4774, www.idletimebooks.com; 11am-10pm daily

CLOTHING, SHOES, AND ACCESSORIES

✪ Mercedes Bien Vintage

Flawless treasures await at Mercedes Bien Vintage, on the second floor of an Adams Morgan row house. It's named after the owner, who will help you select items that suit your size and style; she carefully checks each piece before putting it on her well-organized racks, and prices are excellent considering the superb quality and fit. Most of the items are womenswear, though you'll also find pieces for men as well as shoes, jewelry, and accessories,

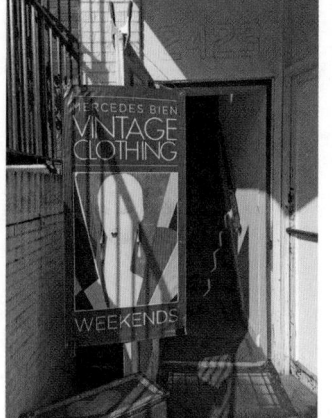

Mercedes Bien Vintage in Adams Morgan

designs celebrating gay pride. The proceeds from every item sold benefit organizations like Planned Parenthood, the American Civil Liberties Union, and The Malala Fund.

MAP 6: 2439 18th St. NW, 202/265-6546, www.the-outrage.com; 10am-8pm daily

mostly from the 1960s to 1990s. The shop is only open on weekends.

MAP 6: 2423 18th St. NW, 202/360-8481; noon-6pm Sat., noon-5pm Sun.

Meeps

This Adams Morgan mainstay feels more like a contemporary boutique than a vintage store, with edited and organized racks of on-trend, in-season clothing for men and women from the 1960s to 1990s. The items are labeled with the decade—and most are under $100. In the back, a costume room stocks more elaborate period pieces as well as new costume accessories.

MAP 6: 2104 18th St. NW, 202/265-6546, www.meepsdc.com; noon-7pm Sun.-Mon., noon-8pm Tues.-Sat.

The Outrage

March over to The Outrage to get your resistance-themed gear, including tees, tanks, totes, leggings, baby onesies, jewelry, art, and much more with feminist and equality slogans— think "Nevertheless, She Persisted" and "Nasty Women Unite" as well as

HOME AND GIFTS

Capitol Hemp

The owners of Capitol Hemp have fought the nation's draconian cannabis laws and played a key role in decriminalizing possession of marijuana and cannabis plants for personal use in the District. Their accessible, brightly colored Adams Morgan shop sells pipes, vaporizers, cultivation equipment, and similar products, as well as ordinary household items made with industrial hemp, including nutritious food products as well as clothing and accessories.

MAP 6: 1770 Columbia Rd. NW, 202/846-1934, www.capitolhemp.com; 11am-6pm Sun.-Mon., noon-9pm Tues.-Sat.

Hudson & Crane

This hip furniture and home decor store, located where Dupont Circle meets Adams Morgan, is a must-stop for design inspiration. The store's nooks and shelves are filled with local gifts that are easier to pack than a couch, like city map glassware, Shrub District seasonal cocktail vinegars made in Northeast, and Ella B. candles, which have a scent for almost every major neighborhood in DC. There's another location at District Wharf (33 District Sq. SW, 202/322-7155).

MAP 6: 1781 Florida Ave. NW, 202/436-1223, www.hudsonandcrane.com; 11am-7pm Mon.-Sat., noon-6pm Sun.

Urban Dwell

If you can't find a cool souvenir or gift at Urban Dwell, it probably doesn't exist. The warm staff members will welcome you as you shop a vast assortment of whimsical DC and political-themed souvenirs and kitsch, ranging from lovely DC prints to Trump-themed toilet paper. The shop stocks luxury beauty products, ethical jewelry, fun office supplies, and baby gear and books, too.

MAP 6: 1837 Columbia Rd. NW, 202/558-9087, www.urbandwelldc.com; 11am-8pm Mon.-Tues., 11am-9pm Wed.-Fri., 10am-9pm Sat., 11am-6pm Sun.

Georgetown and Foggy Bottom
Map 7

CLOTHING, SHOES, AND ACCESSORIES

✪ Curio Concept

Visiting this bright boutique is like entering the closet of your well-traveled fashionista friend. Stocked with of-the-minute darlings of the fashion world, like Isa Arfen, Charlotte Olympia, and Sandra Mansour, Curio Concept specializes in cocktail dresses and party-worthy separates, shoes, and accessories you're unlikely to find elsewhere in DC—plus, a friendly bulldog.

MAP 7: 1071 Thomas Jefferson St. NW, 202/851-4946, www.curioconcept.com; 10am-7pm Tues.-Fri., 11am-6pm Sat.-Sun.

Ella-Rue

The stylish ladies of Georgetown take their (gently loved) cast-offs to luxury consignment boutique Ella-Rue, where you may find Chanel jackets, Tory Burch sheath dresses, and Manolo Blahnik pumps on the tightly packed racks, curated by the owner, who will help you find your desired look. The selections include party, professional, and casual clothing, but they're all high-end labels; many pieces have the original tags, and prices are fair for designer goods.

MAP 7: 3231 P St. NW, 202/333-1598, www.ella-rue.com; 10am-6pm Tues.-Sat., noon-5pm Sun.

Hugh & Crye

Founded by two locals who were tired of the ill-fitting dress shirts available for men, Hugh & Crye offers a better option without the price tag of a custom tailor. Offering 12 sizes based on the height and shape

Curio Concept in Georgetown

of the torso, the brand sells professional and casual dress shirts, as well as blazers, tees, and accessories. Find your perfect fit at the Georgetown showroom, but be sure to make an appointment first.

MAP 7: 3212 O St. NW, 202/250-3807, www.hughandcrye.com; 10am-7pm Mon.-Fri., noon-6pm Sat.-Sun.

Hu's Shoes

For the most luxurious, most covetable, most eat-ramen-for-a-month-to-own-them shoes in the city, run to Hu's Shoes, which has been adorning the feet of DC's most fashionable since 2005. In the luxe, minimalist shop, find brands you already love—Jimmy Choo, Manolo Blahnik, Fendi—plus new ones straight from New York, Paris, and Milan.

MAP 7: 3005 M St. NW, 202/342-0488, www.husonline.com; 10am-7pm Mon.-Sat., noon-5pm Sun.

Hu's Wear

Owned by a former graphic designer who decided to follow her passion for fashion, Hu's Wear, the sibling of Hu's Shoes across the street, is known for a tightly edited selection of staples fresh from the runways, from Altuzarra to Yigal Azrouel. The stock tends to be on the pricier side, though you'll find contemporary labels and denim, too.

MAP 7: 2906 M St. NW, 202/342-2020, www.husonline.com; 10am-7pm Mon.-Sat., noon-5pm Sun.

Lynn Louisa

Shop the most of-the-minute silhouettes at Lynn Louisa, a womenswear boutique specializing in casual, mid-priced finds from up-and-coming labels from the United States and Europe—think easy dresses and tops plus on-trend denim and accessories that will take you from the

Lynn Louisa

Georgetown shops to the U Street Corridor's coolest bars. Feel free to browse the fashionable finds in the bright, airy space, where chic but approachable employees will welcome you and fill you in on the sales.

MAP 7: 1631 Wisconsin Ave. NW, 202/350-0406, www.lynnlouisa.com; 11am-6pm Wed.-Sat., noon-5pm Sun., by appointment Mon.-Tues.

Relish

This Georgetown mainstay has been dressing well-dressed Washingtonians since 1996, with a fashion-forward selection that's current without being overly trendy. Here, you'll find clothing, shoes, and accessories from labels in the vein of Dries van Noten, Marni, and Simone Rocha, as well as emerging designers.

MAP 7: 3312 Cady's Alley NW, 202/333-5343, www.relishdc.com; 10am-6pm Mon.-Sat.

Tuckernuck

Get the fresh, all-American look, or a new wardrobe for your Nantucket vacation, at Tuckernuck, which started as an online boutique and opened a flagship in 2016 in Georgetown, the founder's hometown. In a space that looks like an upscale beach house, you'll find the prettiest, preppiest fashion of the season from labels like Rebecca Taylor, Shoshanna, and Jack Rogers—plus stuff for guys, too.

MAP 7: 1053 Wisconsin Ave. NW, 202/856-7260, www.tnuck.com; 10am-7pm Tues.-Sat., 11am-5pm Sun.

Navy Yard and Anacostia   Map 8

BOOKS
Politics and Prose

Since opening in 1984, Upper Northwest's Politics and Prose has long been a favorite local shop to purchase books and meet authors, including many local political, media, and entertainment celebrities at the store's readings and signings that take place almost daily. (See *Where the Wonks*

Read on page 211 for more about the original location.) Opened in 2017, this Metro-accessible, 2,300-square-foot location at the District Wharf is where you can find a large selection of fiction, non-fiction, and children's books as well as cards, gifts, and other items; check the website for author events.

MAP 8: 70 District Sq. SW, 202/488-3867, www.pollitics-prose.com; 10am-10pm daily

Greater Washington DC Map 9

CLOTHING, SHOES, AND ACCESSORIES

Nike Community Store

Located in the historic art deco Hecht Warehouse in up-and-coming Ivy City, the Nike Community Store does more than sell sneakers and workout pants. The brand's first community store on the East Coast has a mission to employ people who live within a five-mile radius and support athletic programs for local kids. This factory store has merchandise you might find at an outlet mall, with some good deals on apparel and gear for men and women; you can purchase merchandise from the store and Nike's website in a single transaction, and get your online order shipped to you for free.

MAP 9: 1403 New York Ave. NE, 202/529-1868, www.nike.com; 10am-8pm Mon.-Sat., noon-6pm Sun.

GOURMET FOOD AND DRINKS

✪ New Columbia Distillers

DC's first distillery opened in 2011 and sells Green Hat Gin, inspired by George Cassiday, "The Man in the Green Hat" who provided bootleg liquor to Washington's elite during Prohibition. This distilled gin is perfect in the rickey, DC's official cocktail, and the rectangular bottles with a vintage-style label are made for Instagram. At the Ivy City distillery in a nondescript brick warehouse, you can purchase the classic gin and seasonal blends as well as take a free tour of the factory.

MAP 9: 1832 Fenwick St. NE, 202/733-1710, www.greenhatgin.com; 1pm-4pm Sat.

SHOPS

GREATER WASHINGTON DC

WHERE TO STAY

National Mall 228
Downtown and Penn Quarter 229
Capitol Hill and Atlas District 232
Dupont Circle 234
U Street, Shaw, and Logan Circle 237
Adams Morgan. 238
Georgetown and Foggy Bottom 239
Navy Yard and Anacostia 242
Greater Washington DC 243

Hotels in Washington DC are notoriously expensive, especially around major events like the National Cherry Blossom Festival, Independence Day, and major conferences.

The Mayflower

Nonetheless, the District has more than 31,000 rooms and dozens of international hotel chains from high-end to budget brands, so while prices may increase astronomically during busy seasons, you can almost always find a room if you're willing to pay. Alas, the most historic and unique properties tend to be luxury properties, with rates to match. If you can swing it, they're worth the price, offering the chance to walk in the footsteps of policymakers of the past while enjoying views of the monuments. For those who can't afford the high-end digs, there are plenty of midpriced boutique hotels and a few pod-style properties offering lower-priced, tiny rooms in convenient locations.

Most properties are downtown, home to many of the historic hotels. While prices tend to be higher, you have many choices—and, you can walk or take public transportation almost everywhere. Dupont Circle and Georgetown/Foggy Bottom are hubs, as well, with many stately, quiet properties close to dining, nightlife, and shopping. Capitol Hill and Logan Circle have noteworthy, midpriced properties, but again, expect prices to rise to five-star levels during major events. If you're willing to venture away from the tourist centers to Woodley Park or even the suburbs, you can often find deals at Metro-accessible properties.

HIGHLIGHTS

✪ **BEST VIEW: The Hay-Adams** boasts views of the White House from many of its rooms (page 229).

✪ **MOST FASHIONABLE: Sofitel Washington DC Lafayette Square** is très chic, with French style and luxurious beds (page 229).

✪ **COOLEST ROOMS:** The guest rooms at the **Kimpton Hotel Monaco Washington DC** used to be offices; they have soaring ceilings and trendy decor (page 231).

✪ **MOST SCANDALOUS:** Famous for its role in more than one DC scandal, **The Mayflower** is a sophisticated hotel that embraces its long, storied history with photos and memorabilia of the infamous events (page 232).

✪ **BEST BASE FOR SEEING THE SIGHTS:** The **Liaison Capitol Hill** is a short walk from the U.S. Capitol and National Mall, and it has a resort-style rooftop pool for relaxing after a long day of sightseeing (page 232).

✪ **BEST FOR ROMANCE: The Jefferson** has everything you need for a romantic getaway: beautifully restored rooms with soaking tubs, a Michelin-starred restaurant, and a sexy lounge with discreet nooks for canoodling over cocktails (page 234).

✪ **BEST HOME AWAY FROM HOME: The Carlyle** offers art deco style with modern conveniences for business or pleasure travelers, who will appreciate up-to-date rooms and top-notch amenities on a quiet, residential street (page 235).

✪ **BEST PLACE TO MEET LOCALS:** The stylish **Kimpton Mason & Rook Hotel** is steps away from the action on 14th Street (page 237).

✪ **BEST POOL:** Designed by Morris Lapidus, **Washington Plaza Hotel** is an affordable option with a large, resort-style outdoor pool (page 238).

✪ **BEST PRESIDENTIAL SUITE: The Watergate Hotel** has two posh presidential suites with breathtaking view of the water and monuments (page 239).

✪ **BEST WITH KIDS:** Steps from the zoo, the **Omni Shoreham Hotel** is affordable luxury with a large, heated, outdoor pool (page 243).

PRICE KEY

$	Less than $150 per night
$ $	$150-300 per night
$ $ $	More than $300 per night

CHOOSING WHERE TO STAY

National Mall

While many must-see sights are located on the National Mall, hotels (as well as dining and nightlife) are limited. The Mandarin Oriental Washington, D.C. and several budget-friendly chains are directly south of the Mall. They are good options if the sole purpose of your trip is to explore the monuments and museums. However, other neighborhoods, including Downtown and Capitol Hill, are equally convenient while providing more choices in restaurants, bars, and accommodations.

Downtown and Penn Quarter

Whether you're visiting DC to party or to protest, you'll find convenient hotels downtown and in Penn Quarter at all price points, within walking distance to the National Mall and U.S. Capitol and accessible by several Metro lines and DC Circulator routes. It's the city's central business district and busiest on weekdays, but restaurants, bars, theaters, and shops keep the area lively on evenings and weekends, too.

Capitol Hill and Atlas District

With the Capitol dome in sight, Capitol Hill provides both proximity to power and quiet residential streets lined with casual pubs. Most of the neighborhood's hotels are within blocks of Union Station but walking distance to dining hot spots like Eastern Market and Barracks Row. It's a quick taxi or streetcar ride to the Atlas District, known for hip nightlife.

Dupont Circle

If you don't require a monument view, Dupont Circle's many hotels provide easy access to public transportation and the buzziest dining and nightlife, as well as the chance to get to know the quieter side of DC while exploring neighborhood restaurants, galleries, and boutiques on tree-lined streets. (Bonus: The major sights are not far, and you can even walk to them if you're feeling ambitious.)

U Street, Shaw, and Logan Circle

This part of town is where the city's young and fashionable spend their weekends brunching, shopping, and imbibing in the many cocktail bars, beer gardens, and nightclubs. The area is quiet on weekdays, and many restaurants don't open until the evening, but it's no matter; take the Metro or use a ride-sharing app to get to the sights, then return to explore the humming nightlife scene, stumbling distance from a few noteworthy hotels.

Adams Morgan

This ethnically diverse, residential neighborhood is a hub for good food and laid-back bars, but not hotels. You will find the new luxury boutique hotel The LINE as well as a solid hostel; otherwise, you can utilize Airbnb—or stay elsewhere, like Dupont Circle, a quick walk or taxi ride away. Nearby, Columbia Heights and Mount Pleasant offer similar attractions.

Georgetown and Foggy Bottom

Home to college students and socialites, Georgetown has chic boutique hotels and a charming, historical atmosphere, with good restaurants and shopping on the brick-lined sidewalks as well as outdoor activities. However, it's not Metro accessible, so prepare to use taxis/ride-sharing apps or take the DC Circulator to Dupont

YOU ONLY HAVE ONE WEEKEND:
Downtown, because you're walking distance to both the major sights and the best dining and nightlife.

YOU'RE ON A BUDGET:
Penn Quarter or **Dupont Circle.** While hotels are expensive citywide, these neighborhoods have a few wallet-friendly deals if you plan ahead, plus lots of choices for dining and the ability to walk or take public transportation to the major sights.

YOU'RE SEEKING QUIET:
Woodley Park in **Greater Washington DC,** with several family-friendly hotels nestled near Rock Creek Park.

YOU WANT TO EAT, DRINK, AND PARTY:
U Street or **Logan Circle,** where you're a stone's throw from the hippest restaurants, cafés, bars, and nightclubs.

YOUR MUST-SEES ARE ARLINGTON NATIONAL CEMETERY OR THE NATIONAL 9/11 PENTAGON MEMORIAL:
Georgetown, which is a quick taxi ride across the Potomac River.

YOU WANT TO FEEL LIKE YOU'RE IN THE WASHINGTON DC OF MOVIES AND TELEVISION:
Capitol Hill, where hotels with DC-inspired details are steps from the top monuments and museums and offer scenic views of the halls of power.

Circle or downtown. Foggy Bottom is more convenient, with a few of the city's most luxurious (albeit expensive) hotels.

Navy Yard and Anacostia

These neighborhoods are experiencing some of the most rapid growth in DC—most notably, District Wharf, which opened in October 2017 with dozens of restaurants and a few chain hotels at various price points. You'll find budget-friendly options around Nationals Park, a quick Metro ride to the business and tourism centers. There are no hotels east of the Anacostia River; stay elsewhere and take the Metro or a taxi to explore the Anacostia Historic District.

Greater Washington DC

Woodley Park is a mini hub for family-friendly hotels, steps from the Metro's Red Line as well as good dining and the zoo. And north of Georgetown up Wisconsin Avenue, Glover Park is a laid-back residential neighborhood minutes from shopping and dining, if you don't mind using ride-hailing apps heavily.

ALTERNATIVE LODGING OPTIONS

Washington DC is a transient town, with residents coming and going as their jobs change with the political winds, or to work on campaigns or U.S. State Department assignments, for example. As a result, short-term rentals are plentiful, with thousands of listings on sites like AirBnB (www.airbnb.com) and VRBO (www.vrbo.com) to allow you to experience the city like a local. More than two-thirds of these listings are private residences offering privacy at a lower price, especially in residential neighborhoods in Northwest and Capitol Hill.

When hotel prices are exceptionally high during major events or conferences, hotels near Ronald Reagan Washington National Airport are sometimes cheaper while still being Metro accessible and convenient to the city center; there are more than a dozen international chain hotels ranging from The Ritz-Carlton and Hilton to budget options in Crystal City and Pentagon City, Virginia. Similarly, there are chain hotels near Washington Dulles International Airport in Dulles and Herndon, Virginia, but these are 45-60 minutes from the city center in normal traffic, requiring a taxi ride or several changes on public transportation. Instead, consider staying in Alexandria, Virginia (see the *Day Trips* chapter), an easy Metro journey from DC, or Metro-accessible Maryland suburbs, like Bethesda, which is 15-20 minutes from Dupont Circle or Farragut North station, or downtown Silver Spring, 30 minutes from Gallery Pl-Chinatown station.

You can't pitch a tent on the National Mall—unless it's part of a public protest or demonstration and you get a permit from the National Park Service—but there are a few camping facilities in the region. Cherry Hill Park (800/801-6449, www.cherryhillpark.com) is the closest campsite, located in College Park, Maryland, approximately 30-40 minutes from DC by car and offering amenities including tent sites, RV hookups, laundry facilities, outdoor pools, and miniature golf. Between DC and Dulles, Lake Fairfax Park (703/471-5414, www.fairfaxcounty.gov) has tent and RV sites near the 18-acre lake, and next to Manassas National Battlefield Park, Bull Run Regional Park (703/631-0550, www.novaparks.com) has cabins as well as campsites close to hiking trails, golf, and outdoor activities. Alternatively, you're within two hours from several national parks with camping facilities in Virginia and Maryland, including Shenandoah National Park; visit www.recreation.gov for information and reservations.

National Mall

Map 1

Mandarin Oriental Washington, D.C. $$$

This luxurious but family-friendly hideaway is convenient to the major sights, boasting 373 well-appointed blue and silver rooms with city or water views. Empress Lounge in the lobby serves light meals, cocktails, and elegant high tea, opening to a grassy lawn with space for the kids to run around.

The tranquil, resort-style spa houses a 1,400-square-foot fitness center and indoor pool (complimentary for hotel guests) and offers transformative massages and other treatments. You will probably want to take a cab to dining, nightlife, and shopping, but CVS and Starbucks are outside the front door. MAP 1: 1330 Maryland Ave. SW, 202/554-8588, www.mandarinoriental.com

Downtown and Penn Quarter

Map 2

WHERE TO STAY

DOWNTOWN AND PENN QUARTER

✪ The Hay-Adams $$$

The next best option to staying at the White House is getting a room at The Hay-Adams—ideally, one of the suites with an unobstructed view of the White House. The 145-room historic hotel has been impeccably preserved, offering understated luxury that recalls a more civilized time in the capital. Enjoy impeccable service as well as a discreet basement bar, **Off the Record.** The roof terrace, often booked for Washington's most exclusive events, boasts the best view in town.

MAP 2: 800 16th St. NW, 202/638-6600, www.hayadams.com

✪ Sofitel Washington DC Lafayette Square $$$

The Sofitel Washington DC Lafayette Square is très, très chic, with Parisian style fitting for its proximity to the park named for French general Lafayette, a key player in the Revolutionary War. The 237 guest rooms have black and white decor and luxurious, float-on-a-cloud beds, as well as white marble bathrooms with Lanvin toiletries. The cocktail lounge, **Le Bar** (202/730-8701, www.iciurbanbistro.com), isn't the hot spot it used to be, but nonetheless it's a lovely choice for a glass of champagne.

MAP 2: 806 15th St. NW, 202/730-8800, www.sofitel.com

Sofitel Washington DC Lafayette Square

HOTEL BARS

The Next Whisky Bar at The Watergate Hotel

Whether they're meeting a friend, a date, or a source, Washingtonians frequent the city's many hotel bars, known for strong cocktails, inviting ambience, and discreet bartenders. These are the top six.

- For the history: Round Robin Bar at the **Willard InterContinental Washington, D.C.**
- For schmoozing a source: Off the Record at **The Hay-Adams**
- For only-in-Washington views: POV at **W Washington, D.C.**
- For people-watching: Lounge at Bourbon Steak at the **Four Seasons Hotel Washington, D.C.**
- For romance: Quill at **The Jefferson**
- For cool music and decor: The Next Whisky Bar at **The Watergate Hotel**

The St. Regis Washington, D.C. $$$

Two blocks from the White House, the St. Regis Washington, D.C. exudes classic luxury, with 172 elegant guest rooms in warm hues and five-star service (personal butler optional). The presidential suite was refreshed to celebrate the hotel's 90th anniversary in 2016, and the grand lobby with its red and gold bar is a popular spot for afternoon tea, nightly champagne sabering, and the hotel's signature bloody Mary with Old Bay.

www.stregiswashingtondc.com

MAP 2: 923 16th St. NW, 202/638-2626,

Willard InterContinental Washington, D.C. $$$

The term "lobbying" was coined at the Willard InterContinental by President Ulysses S. Grant, who was annoyed by the "lobbyists" bothering him in the lobby while he was trying to enjoy a drink. Dr. Martin Luther King Jr. finalized his "I Have A Dream" speech in the same lobby in 1963. These are just two of the countless significant events that have taken place at the stately, 335-room property. Even if you don't stay here, have a drink at the Round Robin Bar (202/628-9100)

and peruse the History Gallery on the ornate ground floor.

W Washington, D.C. $$$

The W Washington, D.C. is best known for the rooftop lounge, POV (202/661-2419, www.povrooftop. com), where locals wait in line or reserve pricey tables for cocktails overlooking the monuments. It's located in the former Hotel Washington, which opened in 1918; today, many of the 317 rooms are small but modern. The tiny basement hideaway, Bliss Spa (202/661-2416, www.blissspa. com), offers a full menu of luxurious treatments.

MAP 2: 515 15th St. NW, 202/661-2400, www.wwashingtondc.com

MAP 2: 1401 Pennsylvania Ave. NW, 202/628-9100, www.wwashington. intercontinental.com

☆ Kimpton Hotel Monaco Washington DC $$

The Hotel Monaco, in a neoclassical former post office, has some of the coolest architecture of any Washington hotel. Get swept away in the long hallways, swirling staircases, and marble surfaces throughout the property, which covers an entire city block. The 183 guest rooms used to be offices, so they have soaring ceilings; following the top-to-bottom renovation in 2015-2016, they're decorated with bold blue and purple decor and a five-foot lion's head mounted above the bed. Enjoy amenities like daily complimentary wine in the colorful lobby lounge. Dirty Habit (202/449-7095, www. dirtyhabitdc.com) serves global small plates and cocktails in an edgy, industrial space with a year-round patio.

MAP 2: 700 F St. NW, 202/628-7177, www. monaco-dc.com

✪ The Mayflower $$

Get involved in a scandal at The Mayflower, where President Bill Clinton was photographed hugging Monica Lewinsky during a campaign event in 1996, and, infamously, where New York governor Eliot Spitzer (client no. 9) met Ashley Dupré. For those not looking for trouble, it's still a good choice to rest your head for business or pleasure, boasting 581 comfortable rooms with spacious bathrooms, plus a surprisingly large, state-of-the-art fitness facility. Explore the public spaces and the guest room floors, which have artifacts and plaques explaining the history of the hotel in a particular decade.

MAP 2: 1127 Connecticut Ave. NW, 202/347-3000, www.themayflowerhotel. com

Morrison-Clark Historic Inn and Restaurant $

This 19th-century mansion was the home of a wealthy flour and feed merchant before being converted into an affordable boarding house for soldiers in 1923. It's still a great value; the $14 million renovation completed in 2016 kept many historical details, including chandeliers from 1864, while giving the 144 guest rooms a sophisticated refresh, to rave reviews. The restaurant and bar serve American breakfast, lunch, and dinner 7am-11pm daily.

MAP 2: 1011 L St. NW, 202/898-1200, www.morrisonclark.com

Pod DC $

The Pod DC opened in Chinatown in 2017 with a new concept for the city: affordable "micro" rooms plus amenities you actually want, like free Wi-Fi, access to a fitness center, a whiskey lounge and rooftop bar, and a hip diner that stays open late. The 245 rooms measure about 150 square feet, but they're clean and well designed with private baths.

MAP 2: 627 H St. NW, 202/847-4444, www.thepodhotel.com

Capitol Hill and Atlas District   Map 3

✪ Liaison Capitol Hill $$

Literally steps away from the U.S. Capitol and a short walk from the monuments and museums on the National Mall, the Liaison Capitol Hill is the ideal base for sightseeing— especially during the summer, when you can enjoy the rooftop pool with resort-style cabanas and a bar featuring tropical cocktails, sangria, and snacks. The 343 modern guest rooms have super-comfortable beds, plus plenty of space to work or relax. Art & Soul

(202/393-7777) serves Southern and comfort-food favorites for breakfast, lunch, dinner, and weekend brunch.

MAP 3: 415 New Jersey Ave. NW, 202/638-1616, www.jdvhotels.com

Capitol Hill Hotel $$

Nestled between the Library of Congress and the neighborhood's best restaurants and bars, the Capitol Hill Hotel is your home away from home. The 152 suites are chic and spacious, and the amenities are thoughtful, like

the rooftop pool at the Liaison Capitol Hill

self-service laundry, on-site bikes, and, for extended-stay guests, grocery service and discounts on meeting space. There's no restaurant or bar on-site, but every suite has a full kitchen or kitchenette, and the hotel provides free continental breakfast daily.

MAP 3: 200 C St. SE, 202/543-6000, www.capitolhillhotel-dc.com

The George $$

This posh boutique hotel, in sight of the U.S. Capitol, will make you feel patriotic; you'll find silhouettes of George and Martha Washington and other, clever details inspired by the first U.S. president throughout the hotel. The 139 smart guest rooms provide a zen-like environment with beige and blue decor as well as marble bathrooms; expect the usual amenities from Kimpton, including on-site bikes, yoga mats, and the daily wine hour in the recently renovated lobby.

Bistro Bis (202/661-2700, www.bistrobis.com), a longtime favorite of U.S. Senate staffers and lobbyists, serves excellent French fare and cocktails.

MAP 3: 15 E St. NW, 202/347-4200, www.hotelgeorge.com

Phoenix Park Hotel $$

Do you have an early train home? Check in to Phoenix Park Hotel, directly across the street from Union Station. In November 2016, the hotel completed an $8 million renovation, revamping the public spaces and 149 guest rooms and suites, which have glam furniture and finishes. Many offer views of the U.S. Capitol. The Dubliner serves classic pub fare, including Irish favorites like fish-and-chips and beef stew, from early morning until late.

MAP 3: 520 N. Capitol St. NW, 202/639-6900, www.phoenixparkhotel.com

Dupont Circle

Map 4

✪ The Jefferson $$$

The Jefferson is pure, discreet luxury. The beaux arts structure, built in 1923 as a premier residential building, was meticulously renovated in 2009. The result mixes the best of old and new: 99 beautiful guest rooms with patterns Thomas Jefferson brought to the United States from Paris, a tiny, practically private spa specializing in treatments using herbs grown at Monticello, and antique furniture, art, and books throughout the property. For a romantic weekend, dine at Michelin-starred **Plume** (202/448-3227, www.plumedc. com), the only Forbes five-star restaurant in DC, and canoodle over cocktails in the sexy lounge **Quill** before retiring to your suite's soaking tub.

MAP 4: 1200 16th St. NW, 202/448-2300, www.jeffersondc.com

The Dupont Circle Hotel $$$

Located steps from the Dupont Circle Metro station, The Dupont Circle Hotel is the ideal base for shopping, dining, and gallery-hopping. The 327 guest rooms are posh; expect muted but stylish decor and marble baths, plus hardwood floors in the suites. If you can swing it, book one of those suites with a balcony and enjoy sweeping city views. Locals frequent **Bar Dupont** for happy hour on the patio or a nightcap in one of the comfy leather chairs in the lounge.

MAP 4: 1500 New Hampshire Ave. NW, 202/483-6000, www.doylecollection.com

the Thomas Jefferson Suite at The Jefferson

✪ The Carlyle $$

This recently renovated Kimpton property is perfect for travelers who don't want to sacrifice style for convenience. The designer, Miami Beach artist Michele Oka Doner, kept many of the original art deco details—like the stunning marble floor in the entry—while adding modern touches, including her own art. The 198 refreshed rooms in blues and grays have sparkling marble and subway tile bathrooms; 56 have kitchenettes. The fitness center is spacious, though every guest room has a yoga mat and 24-hour yoga and Pilates channel on the giant television if you prefer to zen out in private; bikes are also available for guest use. Like all Kimptons, the hotel hosts a wine hour 5pm-6pm every evening in the Living Room, which displays contemporary art installations that rotate quarterly. Don't miss The Riggsby (202/787-1500, www.theriggsby.com), serving supper club-style food and classic cocktails day and night.

MAP 4: 1731 New Hampshire Ave. NW, 202/234-3200, www.carlylehoteldc.com

The Embassy Row Hotel $$

Despite the prime location, walking distance from Georgetown, Adams Morgan, and the U Street Corridor,

standard king room with desk at the Hotel Madera

you may never want to leave The Embassy Row Hotel. The property is infused with a fresh dose of cool: a bright interior with eye-popping furniture; Station Kitchen & Cocktails, featuring a 24-hour snack pantry for guests; and the neighborhood's only rooftop pool, offering tropical drinks and spa treatments in the summer. The large hotel is also full of local flavor, like cherry blossom wallpaper and Compass Coffee in the lobby.

MAP 4: 2015 Massachusetts Ave. NW, 202/265-1600, www.destinationhotels.com

The Fairfax at Embassy Row $$

Where Dupont Circle meets the foreign embassies stands a stately hotel that's been hosting politicians and diplomats since 1927. President Eisenhower had his first inaugural breakfast here, and Vice President Gore spent his childhood on the top floor while his father served as the U.S. senator from Tennessee. The hotel maintains historical character with modern updates, like cherry-wood furniture and original crown molding in the 259 beige and green rooms with Frette linens. The Jockey Club, the hotel's former restaurant and bar, frequented by JFK and Jackie in its heyday, has been replaced with a breakfast room, but The Fairfax Grill & Lounge serves American fare and cocktails.

MAP 4: 2100 Massachusetts Ave. NW, 202/293-2100, www.fairfaxwashingtondc.com

Hotel Madera $$

Hotel Madera offers a true boutique experience with the amenities of the Kimpton brand. The friendly staff will greet you in the cozy lobby—and offer you coffee in the morning and wine 5pm-6pm daily—and give you personalized suggestions for a perfect stay one block from Dupont Circle. The 82 guest rooms have neutral decor with bright pops of color (and a yoga mat); families can book one of four bunk bed rooms, which comfortably sleep six. **Firefly** (202/861-1310) is often busy with locals who enjoy the well-priced comfort food brunch and lunch (and truffle fries), especially when the windows are open on a nice day.

MAP 4: 1310 New Hampshire Ave. NW, 202/296-7600, www.hotelmadera.com

Washington Hilton $$

The Washington Hilton has welcomed every U.S. president since it opened in 1965—perhaps most infamously President Reagan, who was shot by John Hinckley Jr. while leaving the 1981 AFL-CIO luncheon. The massive brutalist structure is prepared for VIPs with amenities like a bulletproof carport and hidden passageway to DC's second-largest ballroom. Even if you didn't bring your Secret Service detail, the hotel has everything you need for any kind of trip: a large gym with fitness classes, 11,000-square-foot sundeck and outdoor pool (with a view of the fireworks on July 4), and many business services. The **Big Bus Tour** (www.bigbustours.com) stops at the hotel's doorstep, and the staff can provide curated itineraries to help you personalize your trip.

MAP 4: 1919 Connecticut Ave. NW, 202/483-3000, www.hilton.com

Dupont Place Boutique Inn $

For longer stays or family vacations without the element of surprise when booking an apartment through Airbnb, Dupont Place is a good bet. You'll be able to relax in one of nine homey but updated studio suites with amenities like kitchenettes and on-site laundry facilities. While there's no restaurant, bar, or fitness center on the property, there is a Zipcar parked on-site (Zipcar account required to use).

MAP 4: 1905 19th St. NW, 202/525-7368, www.dupontplacedc.com

Washington Hilton

Tabard Inn $

Each of the 35 guest rooms at the Tabard Inn has a unique personality, just like the hotel itself, with lovely vintage furniture and decor. You don't stay here for high-tech conveniences; there are creaky staircases instead of an elevator, no televisions, and some rooms with shared baths. But you do stay here for a charming retreat in the heart of the city and for the unbeatable rates in this neighborhood. Have brunch at the restaurant and a cocktail in the cozy bar, a local favorite to hole up by the fire on winter nights.

MAP 4: 1739 N St. NW, 202/785-1277, www.tabardinn.com

U Street, Shaw, and Logan Circle

Map 5

WHERE TO STAY

U STREET, SHAW, AND LOGAN CIRCLE

✪ Kimpton Mason & Rook Hotel $$

Steps from the bustling nightlife of 14th Street, Kimpton's Mason & Rook Hotel is the best place to enjoy DC like the locals—and maybe meet a few cute ones, too. The 178 rooms are huge, with modern decor and lots of space to work at the large desk or relax. There are several cool public spaces to enjoy, too, including Radiator (202/742-3150, www.radiatordc.com), with creative cocktails and outdoor fire pits, and a rooftop bar.

MAP 5: 1430 Rhode Island Ave. NW, 202/742-3100, www.masonandrookhotel.com

The Darcy $$

Part of the Curio Collection by Hilton, this boutique hotel feels much more luxurious than the typical chain hotel, with 226 sophisticated rooms and suites with oak and chrome finishes as well as original artwork and high-tech amenities. It's equally convenient to downtown and the major sights as well as the Logan Circle nightlife. Siren by RW (202/521-7171, www.sirenbyrw.com) is a swish spot for seafood.

MAP 5: 1515 Rhode Island Ave. NW, 202/232-7000, www.thedarcyhotel.com

guestroom at Kimpton Mason & Rook Hotel

pool at the Washington Plaza Hotel

✪ Washington Plaza Hotel $

Did you really want to go to Miami instead? Book the Washington Plaza Hotel, designed by Morris Lapidus, the architect of the Fontainebleau in South Beach. It's a good compromise—walking distance to the White House, plus a large, resort-style outdoor pool with plenty of sun loungers and a bar. And the 340 clean, comfortable rooms, many with balconies overlooking the pool, are perfect for resting your head after a late night on U Street.

MAP 5: 10 Thomas Cir. NW, 202/842-1300, www.washingtonplazahotel.com

Adams Morgan   Map 6

The LINE $$$

Any chain property could have been a welcome addition to Adams Morgan, with its shortage of accommodations. But The LINE, which opened in 2017 in a renovated circa-1912 church, brings a lot of panache (if a little pretension). In the soaring lobby, a grand chandelier made from the church's organ pipes welcomes guests. The 220 guest rooms, which range from well-appointed king and queen rooms with custom furniture to apartment-style suites, boast works by local female artists and photographers as well as a small library in each. The restaurants and bars led by two James Beard Award-winning chefs elevate the neighborhood's options, too. From Spike Gjerde of Baltimore's Woodberry Kitchen, A Rake's Progress features local ingredients, including in the cocktails. Erik Bruner-Yang's Brothers and Sisters serves American fare with Asian influences. The 12-person

Spoken English is a standing-room-only restaurant specializing in Asian street food and sake, and Gjerde's The Cup We All Race 4 serves Counter Culture Coffee, sandwiches, and pastries. In addition to standard 24-hour room service from Bruner-Yang's kitchen, guests can avail themselves of a roaming cocktail cart from 4pm to 7pm.

MAP 6: 1770 Euclid St. NW, 202/588-0525, www.thelinehotel.com/dc

Highroad Hostel DC $

This recently renovated hostel has amenities worthy of a boutique hotel—sleek decor, memory-foam mattresses, Netflix—at a fraction of the price. On a residential street off the bustling Adams Morgan business district, it has space for 92 guests, including cheap beds in shared dorm rooms, plus private rooms (all with shared baths), though the private room rates can run as high as hotel rooms during busy times. It's an easy walk, bike ride, or Uber anywhere you want to go, though the hostel encourages mingling on-site with dinners and social events.

MAP 6: 1804 Belmont Rd. NW, 202/735-3622, www.highroadhostels.com

Georgetown and Foggy Bottom

Map 7

✪ The Watergate Hotel $$$

The Watergate Hotel—yes, the one in the same complex as President Nixon's 1972 crime—reopened in June 2016 following a complete renovation, with design that nods to the hotel's heyday in the '60s and '70s while still being thoroughly modern. Almost every one of the 336 sophisticated guest rooms and suites has views of the Potomac River, but the two 2,400-square-foot presidential suites are the best in the city, more like posh apartments than hotel rooms, with dark wood floors, a working fireplace, and a private kitchen in case you invite guests to experience your breathtaking view of the water and monuments. If you want to leave your room—which would be surprising—unwind at three restaurants and bars, or the Argentta Spa, which has custom treatments, a state-of-the-art fitness center, and the original indoor pool.

MAP 7: 2650 Virginia Ave. NW, 844/617-1972, www.thewatergatehotel.com

The Avery $$$

You'll feel like you live in Georgetown at this luxe inn, a few blocks back from the main shopping drags. The 15 cheery guest rooms and suites are just a couple of years old; some have private patios, fireplaces, or soaking tubs. There's no on-site restaurant or fitness center, but the inn has complimentary breakfast and evening drinks—and there are plenty of options for dining and exercising in the neighborhood.

MAP 7: 2616 P St. NW, 202/827-4390, www.averygeorgetown.com

the Presidential Suite at The Watergate Hotel

Fairmont Washington, D.C., Georgetown $$$

With 413 spacious, elegant rooms—and exceptionally comfortable beds—plus countless amenities, this Fairmont outpost offers five-star service at a four-star price point. Everything sparkles—including the large courtyard, where you can enjoy dinner or drinks under the cherry trees. Keep your eyes peeled—former president Barack Obama has offices in the World Wildlife Fund next door, and Michelle frequents the SoulCycle across the street.

MAP 7: 2401 M St. NW, 202/429-2400, www.fairmont.com

Four Seasons Hotel Washington, D.C. $$$

The contemporary brick Four Seasons Hotel is not the most attractive on the outside, but inside, it's five-star, five-diamond luxury. The 222 neutral rooms and suites—including the only bullet-resistant suite in DC—draw power players and celebrities, as does the spa and salon, known for primping first ladies and Hollywood stars. Michael Mina's Bourbon Steak (202/944-2026, www.bourbonsteakdc.com) has good food and even better people-watching.

MAP 7: 2800 Pennsylvania Ave. NW, 202/342-0444, www.fourseasons.com

Park Hyatt Washington $$$

In town for a big meeting? Unwind at the modern Park Hyatt Washington, conveniently located between

Fairmont Washington, D.C., Georgetown

Georgetown and downtown. There's plenty of room to work and relax in the 220 guest rooms and suites; you'll appreciate the clean, contemporary lines and spa-like bathrooms. The Michelin-starred Blue Duck Tavern (202/419-6755, www.blueducktavern. com) is excellent for breakfast, lunch, or dinner; the intimate bar is nice for a nightcap, but the tea cellar (202/419-6755) with more than 50 global varieties is especially soothing.

MAP 7: 1201 24th St. NW, 202/789-1234, www.washingtondc.parkhyatt.com

Rosewood Washington, D.C. $$$

On a quiet street along the C&O Canal, Rosewood Washington, D.C. feels like a sumptuous Georgetown mansion; the 61 well-appointed guest rooms and suites have wood and leather details, including parquet flooring from a real European chateau.

The Rye Bar (202/617-2425), specializing in seasonal rye cocktails, feels like a private club; the rooftop bar (202/617-2400) offers cocktails and snacks with a sweeping view, plus an indoor-outdoor pool.

MAP 7: 1051 31st St. NW, 202/617-2400, www.rosewoodhotels.com

The Georgetown Inn $$

Visitors rave about the cozy Georgetown Inn, which provides historical charm reminiscent of when it first opened in 1962, along with modern amenities. Located in the center of the action near the neighborhood's best restaurants and attractions, the hotel's 96 rooms have classic decor with updated finishes; the affordable suites are perfect for families.

MAP 7: 1310 Wisconsin Ave NW, 866/971-6618, www.georgetowninn.com

rooftop of the Rosewood Washington, D.C.

The Graham Georgetown $$

Named for Alexander Graham Bell, who lived in the neighborhood and taught at Georgetown University, The Graham Georgetown is a boutique hotel with 57 stylish guest rooms and suites. Meet young, fashionable locals at the hotel's two bars: The Alex, the basement speakeasy—ask for the passcode at the front desk—and The Observatory, the popular rooftop bar.

MAP 7: 1075 Thomas Jefferson St. NW, 855/341-1292, www. thegrahamgeorgetown.com

Hotel Hive $

The 83 rooms at DC's first micro-hotel may be small—they measure 125-250 square feet each, with a maximum occupancy of two people—but they're well designed and perfect for minimalist travelers on a budget. The hotel has the essentials—private bathrooms, Wi-Fi, charging stations, in-room amenities on request—as well as a popular pizza joint and rooftop bar serving local spirits and beers.

MAP 7: 2224 F St. NW, 202/849-8499, www.hotelhive.com

Navy Yard and Anacostia Map 8

InterContinental Washington D.C. The Wharf $$

Located at the District Wharf, this hotel is sleek and luxurious, with amenities like a 5,000-square-foot spa and a rooftop infinity pool and bar overlooking the city. The 278 guest rooms have high-tech amenities, like smart TVs and touch-panel room controls; high rollers can book the two-level penthouse suite, featuring a wrap-around balcony and offering panoramic views. District Wharf, one of DC's newest developments, is home to more than 20 restaurants, plus entertainment venues and retail.

MAP 8: 801 Wharf St. SW, 202/800-0844, www.wharfintercontinentaldc.com

Capitol Skyline Hotel $

Designed by Morris Lapidus, Capitol Skyline Hotel offers modern design at affordable rates. The hotel boasts a small but stylish outdoor pool and bar, open Memorial Day to Labor Day with DJs on weekends. The 203 guest rooms and public spaces were designed by Scott Sanders, former in-house interior designer for Ralph Lauren; some rooms offer pool or U.S. Capitol views. It's at least a mile from most of the sights, but the hotel offers free daily shuttle service to major attractions; it's a couple blocks to Nationals Park.

MAP 8: 10 I St. SW, 202/488-7500, www. capitolskyline.com

✪ Omni Shoreham Hotel $$

A quick walk from Smithsonian's National Zoo, the Omni Shoreham Hotel provides affordable, family-friendly luxury, plus games and amenities for the kids when you arrive. When you need a break from sightseeing, relax by the large, heated, outdoor pool set on 11 acres of gardens. Many of the 834 classically decorated rooms have views of nearby Rock Creek Park, and several on-site dining options mean you don't need to leave the property if the giant pandas wore you out.

MAP 9: 2500 Calvert St. NW, 202/234-0700, www.omnihotels.com

Glover Park Hotel $$

This quietly elegant hotel has 154 up-to-date guest rooms, some with kitchenettes, in calming white with black accents. You're not close to the Metro, but you are a leisurely walk from Embassy Row and Georgetown. On the property, Casolare (202-625-5400, www.casolaredc.com; 7am-9:30pm Mon., 7am-10pm Tues.-Thurs., 7am-10:30pm Fri., 11am-10:30pm Sat., 11am-9:30pm Sun.), led by James Beard winner Michael Schlow, serves noteworthy Italian, while the Glover Park Cocktail Garden (202/904-0040, www.gloverparkcocktailgarden.com; 5pm-11pm Mon.-Thurs., 4pm-1am Fri., 1pm-1am Sat., 1pm-10pm Sun.) is a charming spot for a nightcap.

MAP 9: 2505 Wisconsin Ave. NW, 202/337-9700, www.gloverparkhotel.com

Omni Shoreham Hotel

Washington Marriott Wardman Park $$

When the Wardman Park Hotel opened in 1918, it was the largest in the city. Langston Hughes was a busboy there before he became a famous poet. Now managed by Marriott, the hotel is massive, with more than 1,000 guest rooms and suites and frequent conferences, but it offers good value (and an outdoor pool) in a convenient location steps from the Metro and close to Rock Creek Park and the international flavor of Adams Morgan.

MAP 9: 2660 Woodley Rd. NW, 202/328-2000, www.marriott.com

DAY TRIPS

Alexandria. 248
Annapolis and Maryland's Eastern Shore 258
Shenandoah National Park and Vicinity. 271

While you could spend weeks exploring Washington's museums and parks, you'll find worthwhile excursions nearby, from bustling cities to quiet country towns—both with an abundance of history tracing back to the country's founding—to battlefields, spacecraft, innovative wineries, and destination dining. And outdoor enthusiasts will find much to love in the Mid-Atlantic, including some of the best spots for sailing and hiking in the country, less than two hours from DC's city center.

With a car, the region is your oyster—from the idyllic Chesapeake Bay (and famous blue crabs) in Maryland, to the bucolic Virginia countryside, to Shenandoah National Park, covering nearly 198,000 acres in the shadow of the Blue Ridge Mountains. Do you like the water? Cross the Chesapeake Bay Bridge to explore the Eastern Shore's humble small towns, and walk in the footsteps of Frederick Douglass and generations of shipbuilders, sailors, crabbers, and oyster canners. Do you prefer scrambling rocky peaks to find views of expansive valleys you'll only find in America? Head to Shenandoah National Park and Skyline Drive, where you can hike miles upon miles of trails and stay in rustic lodges—or, spend the night in luxe country inns, known for farm-to-

The George Washington Masonic National Memorial

table dining and local wine. (And foodies won't want to miss the spectacular Inn at Little Washington, which redefined farm-to-table dining and earned two Michelin stars in 2016.)

Even without a car, you can find history and adventure. After a quick journey on the Metro, Civil War history and water views await in Old Town Alexandria; venture a little farther to explore George Washington's Mount Vernon, perhaps the region's best historic site outside of DC.

245

HIGHLIGHTS

✪ **BEST HISTORIC SIGHT: Mount Vernon,** George Washington's immaculately preserved Virginia estate and plantation, is reachable by car, boat, or bike from Washington DC (page 255).

✪ **BEST SPOT TO GET ON THE WATER:** Head to America's Sailing Capital to catch a boat tour or rent your own sailboat from **Annapolis Harbor and City Dock** (page 258).

✪ **BEST PLACE TO HAVE CRABS ON THE WATER:** Cross the Chesapeake Bay Bridge to **St. Michaels,** where you can crack Maryland's famous steamed blue crabs with an Old Bay Bloody Mary (page 269).

✪ **BEST EXCURSION WITH KIDS:** The National Air and Space Museum's **Steven F. Udvar-Hazy Center** has massive hangars with eye-popping airplanes and spacecraft, 45 minutes from DC near Dulles Airport (page 271).

✪ **BEST SCENIC DRIVE: Skyline Drive** is the destination, not the journey, especially when the leaves in Shenandoah National Park are changing in the fall (page 273).

✪ **BEST ROMANTIC GETAWAY:** Dinner at **The Inn at Little Washington** will be one of the most memorable (and probably most expensive) meals of your life (page 276).

✪ **BEST PLACE TO HIDE FROM A SCANDAL:** In America's Horse and Hunt Capital, **Historic Middleburg** has been a favorite hideaway for wealthy Washingtonians for decades (page 277).

The Inn at Little Washington is a must-visit for foodies.

Day Trips

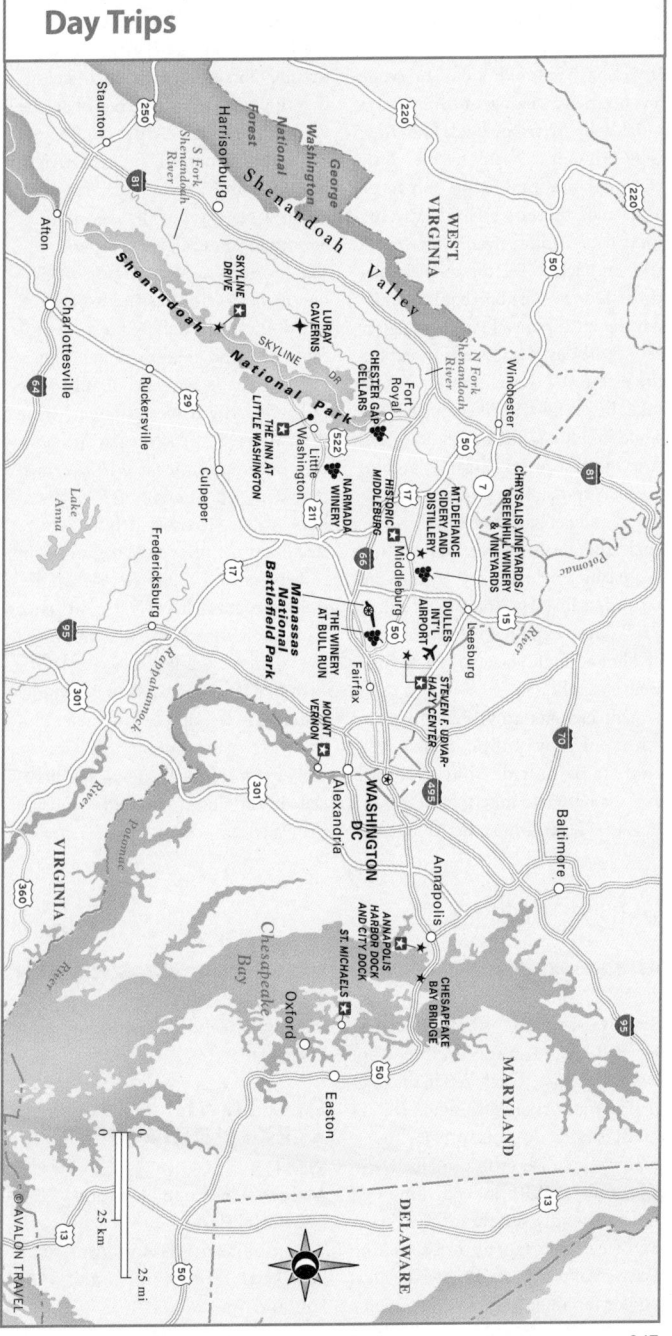

PLANNING YOUR TIME

If you have just half a day, or even a few hours, you can get to Alexandria quickly by Metro or boat; Old Town is 30 minutes by water taxi from the National Mall, allowing you to get a taste of the city's Civil War history, have dinner by the water, and still get back to DC for an early bedtime. Mount Vernon requires half a day, including travel time; give yourself a full day if you want to explore the estate at a more leisurely pace or take the round-trip bike journey from Theodore Roosevelt Island. Similarly, Annapolis requires half a day at minimum; it's possible to go for a crab cake lunch and get back to DC for evening cocktails, but why not spend a little more time exploring the sailing capital and its history? You'll need at least a full day to explore the Eastern Shore or Shenandoah National Park, but a weekend is better.

You can get to Alexandria and Annapolis by public transportation, taxi, or ride-sharing app—and it's better to take the Metro or a taxi to Alexandria rather than drive

yourself—but you'll need a car to see the Eastern Shore or Virginia countryside. In some cases, such as taking the frightening drive over the Chesapeake Bay Bridge or, better yet, traveling part of Skyline Drive in Shenandoah National Park, the journey is a key part of the destination. Serious foodies can take car service to The Inn at Little Washington for dinner, or on a wine-tasting excursion, but doing both makes for a memorable weekend getaway. The Virginia countryside is most beautiful in the fall when the leaves change, while the Eastern Shore shines in the summer, but these times will be the most crowded, too. Shenandoah National Park is open year-round, but be aware that many facilities close beginning in November, and winter weather conditions can make hikes more difficult. Parts of Skyline Drive may be closed in inclement weather.

While DC, Maryland, and Virginia share borders, don't try to see all of these excursions in one trip. Choose one or two towns or sights, and luxuriate in the slower pace of life outside the District.

Alexandria

Southwest of DC on the Potomac River, Alexandria was an important colonial port city, included in the original boundaries of Washington DC but given back to Virginia in 1846. Today, many people who work in DC live in Alexandria. With its charming Old Town, friendly restaurants and bars, and a few important historic sites from the capital's earliest days, it's the ideal choice for an easy getaway, or even a

relaxing place to stay when you want to visit DC.

OLD TOWN ALEXANDRIA
SIGHTS
African American Heritage Memorial Park

The nine-acre African American Heritage Memorial Park (500 Holland Ln., 703/838-4356, www.

Old Town Alexandria

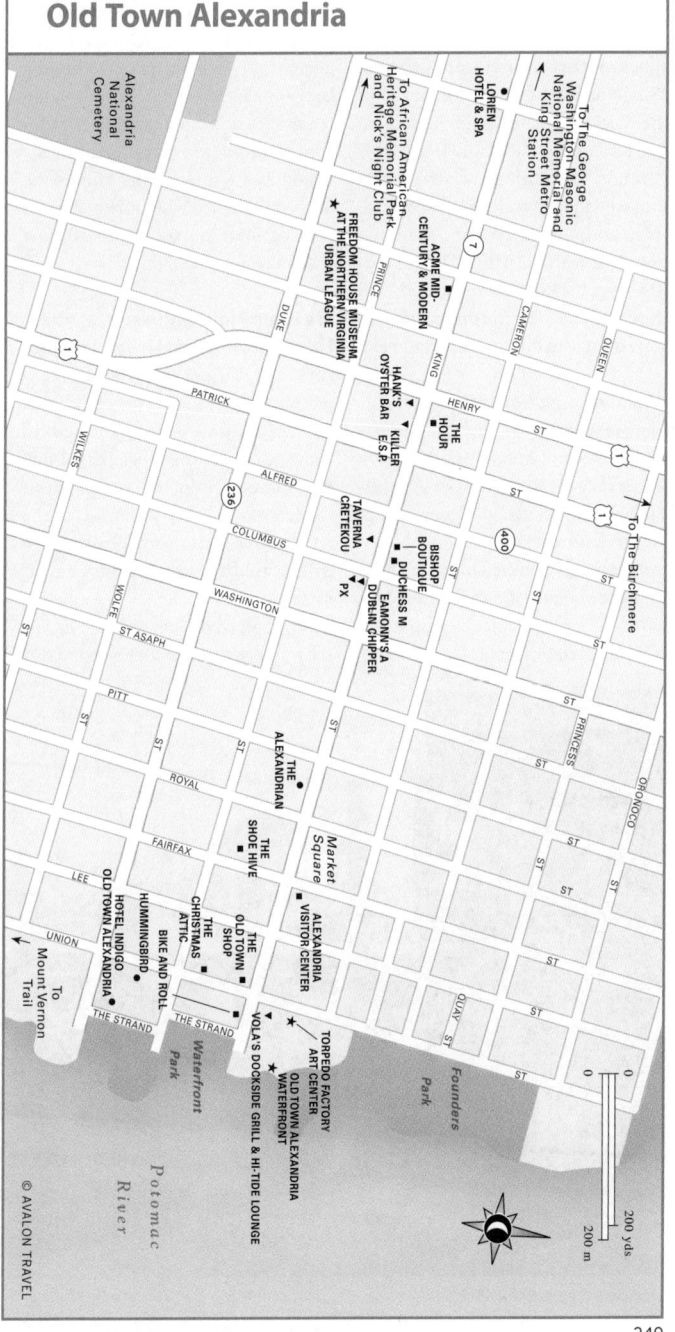

LORIEN HOTEL & SPA

To The George Washington Masonic National Memorial and King Street Metro Station

To African American Heritage Memorial Park and Nick's Night Club

Alexandria National Cemetery

★ FREEDOM HOUSE MUSEUM AT THE NORTHERN VIRGINIA URBAN LEAGUE

ACME MID-CENTURY & MODERN

PRINCE

DUKE

CAMERON

QUEEN

KING

7

1

PATRICK

HANK'S OYSTER BAR

HENRY

THE HOUR

WILKES

ALFRED

KILLER E.S.P.

236

TAVERNA CRETEKOU

COLUMBUS

BISHOP BOUTIQUE

DUCHESS M

400

1

1

WASHINGTON

PX

EAMONN'S A DUBLIN CHIPPER

To The Birchmere

WOLFE

ST ASAPH

PITT

PRINCESS

THE ALEXANDRIAN

ONOROCO

ROYAL

THE SHOE HIVE

Market Square

FAIRFAX

THE CHRISTMAS ATTIC

THE OLD TOWN SHOP

ALEXANDRIA VISITOR CENTER

LEE

HUMMINGBIRD

QUAY ST

HOTEL INDIGO OLD TOWN ALEXANDRIA

UNION

BIKE AND ROLL

Founders Park

To Mount Vernon Trail

THE STRAND

THE STRAND

VOLA'S DOCKSIDE GRILL & HI-TIDE LOUNGE

TORPEDO FACTORY ART CENTER

★

★ OLD TOWN ALEXANDRIA WATERFRONT

Waterfront Park

Potomac River

0   200 yds
0   200 m

© AVALON TRAVEL

249

alexandriava.gov/blackhistory; dawn-dusk daily; free) opened in 1995, after archaeologists uncovered the graves of 26 Alexandrians who were buried in the Black Baptist Cemetery, founded in 1885 and located on the park's grounds. The park incorporates natural wetlands as well as three bronze trees sculpted by Jerome Meadows, inscribed with the words "Truths that Rise from the Roots Remembered" and the names of African Americans who played a role in the city's development.

Alexandria National Cemetery

Explore Alexandria's Civil War history at the five-acre Alexandria National Cemetery (1450 Wilkes St., 703/221-2183, www.cem.va.gov/cems/nchp/alexandriava.asp; dawn-dusk daily; free). It was established in 1862 to bury soldiers who died around Alexandria, which was a strategically important camp and supply center for the Union

Army. In just two years, however, the cemetery was full, and the government began to make plans to build a larger one in Arlington. In addition to the graves of more than 229 African American soldiers who fought in the Union Army, a memorial honors the four civilian men who drowned while chasing John Wilkes Booth after he killed President Lincoln.

Freedom House Museum at the Northern Virginia Urban League

One of the largest slave trading companies in the country, Franklin & Armfield, was headquartered in Alexandria, selling more than 1,000 slaves annually during its most profitable years. After arriving at the Alexandria port, people were kept in the holding pens at the company's row house on Duke Street before being shipped farther south. The last slave trader to work for the company

Old Town Alexandria waterfront

NATIONAL HARBOR

While technically located in Maryland, **National Harbor** (www.nationalharbor.com) is most easily accessed from the Old Town Alexandria waterfront via water taxi across the Potomac River. The journey takes 30 minutes, and round-trip tickets cost $16 for adults and $10 for children. Truthfully, the National Harbor is not worth visiting over the sights and parks in DC or Alexandria, but if you want to take a boat ride anyway, or you're attending a conference at the gigantic convention center, the complex has dozens of restaurants and several affordable hotels—plus, views from the **Capital Wheel** (116 Waterfront St., Oxon Hill, 301/842-8650, www.thecapitalwheel.com; 10am-midnight daily; $15 adults, $13.50 seniors, $11.25 children ages 3-11).

The real reason to make the journey is the **MGM National Harbor** (101 MGM National Ave., Oxon Hill, 877/646-6847, www.mgmnationalharbor.com), which opened in December 2016. The legalization of gambling in Maryland is one of the reasons why Atlantic City is on the decline, and the property's 125,000-square-foot, Vegas-style casino is the largest, shiniest in the state, and the closest to DC. The property has a 308-room luxury hotel and spa as well as a 3,000-seat theater and concert venue, which has hosted Cher, The Who, and Journey. There are several restaurants on-site; **Fish by José Andrés** (301/971-6050; 5pm-10pm Sun.-Thurs., 5pm-11pm Fri.-Sat.), highlighting Mid-Atlantic seafood, is the best in the entire development. From National Harbor Marina, catch the circulator shuttle, which runs 11am-7pm Sunday-Thursday and 11am-1am on weekends; an all-day pass costs $5 per person. The MGM is 20-30 minutes by taxi from DC.

was James Birch, who was behind the kidnapping and sale of free black man Solomon Northup, as depicted in *12 Years a Slave*. In 1996, the Northern Virginia chapter of the National Urban League, the African American advocacy and educational organization, purchased the building. Today it operates **Freedom House Museum** (1315 Duke St., 703/836-2858, www.nvulypn.wildapricot.org; 10am-4pm Mon.-Fri., weekends and holidays by appointment; free), where you can learn about the slave trade that infested Washington DC and Virginia, which is not discussed enough.

Old Town Alexandria Waterfront

The main draw of a trip to Alexandria, the Old Town Alexandria waterfront has sparkling views of the Potomac River as well as dining, entertainment, and leisure activities, accessible via Strand Street at King Street or Prince Street. In addition to enjoying dockside dining at several restaurants and bars, you can catch a river cruise to see the National Mall from the water, as well as water taxis to Nationals Park,

District Wharf, Georgetown, or the National Harbor. The waterfront has several parks, including Founders Park (N. Union St., between Oronoco St. and Queen St.), a grassy stretch a quick walk from the marina.

The George Washington Masonic National Memorial

George Washington was a member of the Masons, one of the world's oldest and largest fraternal societies. Masons are committed to the ideals of brotherly love, truth, and relief, or charity—ideals that undoubtedly influenced the Founding Fathers, many of whom were Masons, too, in their quest for liberty and justice for all. (In fact, 9 of the 56 signers of the Declaration of Independence, and 13 of the 39 signers of the U.S. Constitution, were Masons.) The George Washington Masonic National Memorial (101 Callahan Dr., 703/683-2007, www.gwmemorial.org; 9am-5pm daily; $15 adults, free children 12 and under) honors the nation's first president, who served as Master of the Masons' Alexandria Lodge later in life. Tour the grandiose temple, inspired by the ancient lighthouse in Alexandria, Egypt, and get a peek inside the secret society at the center of many conspiracy theories.

Torpedo Factory Art Center

Founded in 1974, Torpedo Factory Art Center (105 N. Union St., 703/746-4570, www.torpedofactory. org; 10am-6pm Fri.-Wed., 10am-9pm Thurs.) is home to 160 resident artists, who open their studios to the public daily. Housed in a former torpedo plant right on the waterfront, the center has seven galleries to showcase contemporary and community art, as well as the Alexandria Archaeology Museum (10am-3pm Tues.-Fri., 10am-5pm Sat., 1pm-5pm Sun.; free), which displays artifacts unearthed from Alexandria's history during excavations of the city.

RESTAURANTS

If the view is what you're after, try Vola's Dockside Grill (101 N. Union St., 703/935-8890, www.volasdockside. com; 11am-11pm Mon.-Thurs., 11am-midnight Fri., 10am-midnight Sat., 10am-11pm Sun.; $15-27), named for Alexandria's first female city manager, Vola Lawson, and enjoy casual seafood outdoors right on the Potomac River. The beachy, boozy brunch beverages (with $4 refills) paired with oysters or fish tacos will complete your vacation. For the very best seafood, however, locals will tell you to go to Hank's Oyster Bar (1026 King St., 703/739-4265, www.hanksoysterbar.com; 11:30am-midnight Mon.-Fri., 11am-midnight Sat.-Sun.; $18-32), an outpost of the Dupont Circle restaurant, serving fresh catches for lunch, dinner, and weekend brunch—plus, oyster specials during happy hour (3pm-7pm

daily) and a half-price raw bar from 10pm until closing.

In the heart of the King Street shopping district, Taverna Cretekou (818 King St., 703/548-8688, www.taverna-cretekou; 11:30am-2:30pm and 5pm-10pm Tues.-Fri., noon-10:30pm Sat., 11am-3pm and 5pm-9:30pm Sun.; $18-36) has been a local favorite for more than 40 years. Enjoy authentic, regional Greek food, wine, and atmosphere, with live music and dancing on Thursday evenings; the brick-patio garden is open seasonally.

Eamonn's A Dublin Chipper (728 King St., 703/299-8384, www. eamonnsdublinchipper.com; 11:30am-10pm Mon.-Wed., 11:30am-11pm Thurs., 11:30am-midnight Fri., noon-midnight Sat., noon-9pm Sun.; $6-10) has, without a doubt, the best fish-and-chips in the region, ordered at the counter and served in brown paper with the shop's secret sauces and a selection of Irish beers. Skip if you're on a diet; the fried desserts are hard to pass up.

The cozy Killer E.S.P. (1012 King St., 703/200-3200, www.killeresp. com; 9am-9:30pm Sun.-Thurs., 9am-11:30pm Fri.-Sat.) does indeed serve killer coffee, including espresso drinks made with Stumptown Coffee. Pop in for a shopping break and pair your coffee or tea with homemade gelato and sorbet, or a slice of sweet or savory pie, warmed on request by the friendly staff.

NIGHTLIFE

There are cocktail bars aplenty in Old Town, but the best is PX (728 King St., no phone, www.barpx.com; 6pm-midnight Wed.-Thurs., 6pm-1:30am Fri.-Sat.), a speakeasy identifiable only by the blue light next door to Eamonn's A Dublin Chipper. Before the cocktail boom in DC, Washingtonians flocked here, and still do, for superb drinks in the intimate space that seats only 25 people. Reservations are strongly recommended. For a more spur-of-the-moment drink, the Hi-Tide Lounge at Vola's Dockside Grill (101 N. Union St., 703/935-8890, www.volasdockside. com; 3pm-11pm Mon.-Thurs., 3pm-1am Fri., noon-1am Sat., noon-11pm Sun.) is a casual, indoor tiki bar with 1960s decor and frozen drinks.

Two nightclubs are worth the Uber fare outside of Old Town, or outside of the District, for that matter. Just 15 minutes from Old Town, The Birchmere (3701 Mt. Vernon Ave., 703/549-7500, www.birchmere. com; box office open 5pm-9pm on show nights) has hosted major rock, country, folk, and jazz performers since 1966, including Mary Chapin Carpenter, Emmylou Harris, and the Dave Matthews Band, among others. The 500-seat music hall has first-come, first-served seating and a full dinner menu; Flex Stage shows are standing-room only. And, about 20 minutes west of Old Town close to Red Lobster and a few self-storage centers, Nick's Night Club (642 S. Pickett St., 703/751-8900, www.nicksnight-club.com; 4pm-midnight Tues., 4pm-11:30pm Wed., 4pm-10:30pm Thurs., 4pm-1:30am Fri., 6pm-1:30am Sat.) is an authentic country bar, where a wide mix of folks from Virginia and DC go for live country music and cheap beer. This crowd knows their line dances; put on your cowboy boots and arrive by 7:45pm on Fridays and Saturdays for $10 lessons.

SHOPS

Old Town is one of the region's best shopping districts, with dozens of independent boutiques lining King Street and the side streets, from Henry Street west to the waterfront.

The Old Town Boutique District (www.oldtownboutiquedistrict.com) is heavy on women's apparel and accessories with colorful, contemporary styling, where the area's self-proclaimed fashionistas go for pretty dresses and shoes. Bishop Boutique (815-B King St., 571/312-0042, www. bishopboutique.com; 10am-7pm Mon.-Sat., 11am-6pm Sun.) is a tiny shop with big trends, carrying labels like Loeffler Randall, Joie, and L.K. Bennett, with shoe boxes stacked floor to ceiling. Duchess M (805 King St, 571/982-3118, www.duchessm.com; 10am-7pm Mon.-Sat., noon-5pm Sun.) is the place to go for cocktail dresses, while The Shoe Hive (127 S. Fairfax St., 703/548-7105, www.theshoehive. com; 10am-7pm Mon.-Sat., noon-5pm Sun.) has been selling delicious designer shoes by brands like Butter, Rag & Bone, and Stuart Weitzman since 2003.

No shopping spree is complete without a stop at The Hour (1015 King St., 703/224-4687, www.the-hourshop.com; 11am-6pm Wed.-Sat., 12:30pm-5:30pm Sun.), selling authenticated, mint-condition vintage barware, glassware, and dining accessories, from the Prohibition era to the middle of the 20th century. Take home a set of like-new martini glasses and feel like Don Draper during cocktail hour. And if you need a cocktail table for your new set, Acme Mid-Century & Modern (1218 King St., no phone, www.acmemidcentury.com, 3pm-7pm Fri., 11am-6pm Sat., 11am-5pm Sun.) sells, as the name suggests, furniture and home decor from the midcentury and modern eras, including designers like Eames.

For souvenirs and gifts, The

BIKING TO ALEXANDRIA

Old Town Alexandria is accessible by bicycle via the 18-mile **Mount Vernon Trail,** which starts near **Theodore Roosevelt Island** and ends at **George Washington's Mount Vernon.** From DC, you can get on the trail near the entrance of the island, just under the George Washington Memorial Parkway in Rosslyn, and follow the parkway and the Potomac River south for approximately 7.5 miles to Old Town. Stop for lunch and get back to DC in time for dinner, or continue onward another 10 miles to Mount Vernon. The trail gets a little lost in the busy streets of Old Town; just keep riding south to the end of Union Street or Royal Street to pick the trail back up. The trail is paved or wooden boardwalks the entire ride, and mostly flat until right before you reach Mount Vernon; the trail can get very crowded on weekends, so prepare to dodge other bikers as well as hikers and joggers.

It's easy to bike from DC to Alexandria and Mount Vernon.

If you're already in Alexandria and want to bike to Mount Vernon or DC and back, there are several **Capital Bikeshare** (www.capitalbikeshare.com) stations in the city. **Bike and Roll** (1 Wales Alley between Union St. and Strand St., 202/842-2453, www.bike-androlldc.com; 10am-6pm Tues.-Sun.) offers bike rentals (first two hours $16-30 adults, $10 children) and a package that includes a boat ride from Mount Vernon back to the Old Town waterfront; reservations are recommended.

Old Town Shop (105 S. Union St., 703/684-4682, www.theoldtownshop.com; 10am-9pm Mon.-Sat., 11am-8pm Sun.) stocks Alexandria and DC souvenirs, including apparel, housewares, tchotchkes, and locally made products, such as gourmet food and Virginia peanuts. **The Christmas Attic** (125 S. Union St., 703/548-2829, www.christmasattic.com; 10am-5pm daily) has been selling high-end, collectible holiday decorations as well as everything you need to deck your halls since 1971; it's festive year-round, worth a visit anytime you need some holiday cheer.

WHERE TO STAY

It's not necessary to stay overnight in Alexandria—in fact, many people live in Alexandria and commute to DC daily—but there are several noteworthy hotels, ranging from boutique hotels with every amenity to budget-friendly chains. And, when rates are exorbitant in DC, such as during major events like an inauguration or large convention, hotels in Alexandria are sometimes slightly more affordable while still being a short Metro ride away from the capital.

For a luxurious stay blocks from the King Street Metro Station, check in to the **Lorien Hotel & Spa** (1600 King St., 703/894-3434, www.lorienhotelandspa.com; $169-270), a Kimpton property that was completely renovated in January 2017. The 107 guest rooms are decorated in calming light blue and white decor, providing respite following a day of sightseeing or a massage at the spa, the only hotel spa in Alexandria. **Brabo** (703/894-3440, www.braborestaurant.com;

5pm-10pm Mon.-Thurs., 5pm-11pm Fri.-Sat., 11am-2:30pm and 5pm-9pm Sun.; $85) serves excellent Belgian-American fare.

Just four blocks from the waterfront and across the street from city hall, The Alexandrian (480 King St., 703/549-6080, www.thealexandrian. com; $125-250) is an excellent choice for exploring Old Town with the family; it's about a 20-minute walk from the Metro. Part of Marriott's Autograph Collection, the hotel has 241 colorful guest rooms, including 11 recently renovated suites, as well as four-star amenities in a historic, Civil War-era building.

You can't get much closer to the water than the Hotel Indigo Old Town Alexandria (220 S. Union St., 703/721-3800, www.hotelindigooldtownalexandria.com; $150-250), which opened in May 2017. The 120 guest rooms are simple but cheerful and modern, with hardwood floors and city or water views. Hummingbird (703/566-1355, www. hummingbirdva.net; 6:30am-10pm Mon.-Thurs., 6:30am-11pm Fri., 7am-11pm Sat., 7am-9pm Sun.; $18-32) is already getting attention from DC food critics for the seafood and view.

INFORMATION AND SERVICES

For directions and tickets for sights, tours, and transportation, visit the Alexandria Visitor Center (221 King St., 703/746-3301, www.visitalexandriava.com; 10am-6pm Sun.-Wed., 10am-8pm Thurs.-Sat. Apr.-Sept.; 10am-5pm daily Oct.-Mar.), located in a historical former home near the city hall. Visit Alexandria (www.visitalexandria.com) has a wealth of information about little-known sights, recreational activities, and the city's history.

TRANSPORTATION

It's easy to reach Alexandria from Washington DC. Many Alexandrians commute to DC daily, so you have several transportation options. Old Town is very walkable.

The King St-Old Town Metro station (1900 King St., www.wmata. com) serves the Blue and Yellow Lines of the Metro. From the station, walk or catch the free King Street Trolley (www.dashbus.com; every 10-15 minutes, 10:30am-10:30pm Sun.-Wed., 10:30am-midnight Thurs.-Sat.; free) to reach Alexandria's sights, restaurants, shops, and hotels.

Old Town is approximately 20-25 minutes by car from DC. Unless you're staying at a hotel with parking, take a taxi or ride-hailing service because parking can be limited.

Alternatively, you can take a water taxi (Ohio Dr. SW and West Basin Dr. SW, west side of the Tidal Basin, 877/511-2628, www.potomacriverboatco.com) from the National Mall to the Old Town Alexandria waterfront; the trip takes about 30 minutes. Round-trip tickets cost $28 for adults and $16 for children under 12. It's also possible to take a water taxi from District Wharf (round-trip tickets from $20 adults, from $14 children) to reach Alexandria.

✪ MOUNT VERNON

You'll step back in time when you arrive at George Washington's Mount Vernon (3200 Mount Vernon Memorial Hwy., 703/780-2000, www. mountvernon.org; 9am-5pm daily Apr.-Oct., 9am-4pm daily Nov.-Mar., $20 adults, $19 seniors, $9 children ages 6-11, and free for children under 6), George and Martha Washington's Virginia estate and plantation, which has been immaculately preserved and

George Washington's Mount Vernon

restored—the farm even has some of the same breeds from Washington's time.

It's possible to power through your visit in a few hours, but you could easily spend a day or two exploring. Admission includes access to the mansion and museum, as well as the outside buildings and six acres of gardens and farm, including the tombs of George and Martha. For a more in-depth look at life on the estate, add one of a dozen specialty tours to your ticket, in which you'll meet Washington family members and employees (portrayed by actors).

If you have time, **George Washington's Distillery and Gristmill** (5513 Mount Vernon Memorial Hwy., www.mountvernon.org/the-estate-gardens/distillery; 10am-5pm daily Apr.-Oct.), where he produced flour, cornmeal, and whiskey, is worth a visit; shuttles are available from the estate. When he died, it was the largest distillery in America, and it continues to produce his whiskey today. **Mount Vernon Inn Restaurant** (703/799-6800, www.mountvernon.org/inn; 11am-2pm Mon., 11am-10pm Tues.-Sat., 11am-3:30pm Sun.; $14-26) serves lunch, dinner, and weekend brunch, while a food court serves quick meals and snacks; nearby, the shops sell souvenirs including reproductions of estate items and the distillery's whiskey.

Open 365 days a year, including Christmas and New Year's Day, Mount Vernon is magical when decorated during the holiday season; special holiday events include candlelight tours and festivals.

INFORMATION AND SERVICES

George Washington's Mount Vernon (www.mountvernon.org) is the definitive resource for planning your visit to the estate, with history, virtual tours, and details on tours and special events. Purchase tickets online in advance for discounts; note that boat cruises from DC and Alexandria to Mount Vernon include admission.

TRANSPORTATION

There are several ways to get to Mount Vernon from DC and Alexandria.

By car, take the George Washington Memorial Parkway south toward Reagan National Airport/Mount Vernon, approximately 20 miles (30-35 minutes) from DC and approximately 8 miles (18-20 minutes) from Old Town Alexandria. There is ample free parking at the estate.

By Metro, take the Yellow Line to Huntington station (2501 Huntington Ave., www.wmata.com) and catch the southbound Fairfax Connector bus 101 (703/339-7200, www.fairfaxconnector.com), running about every 5-10 minutes daily; the bus ride is approximately 20 minutes from the station to the Mount Vernon entrance. This route is the least efficient, but it's the cheapest if you don't have a car.

Alternatively, you can take a boat from DC or Alexandria; choose this option if you'd like a scenic, albeit longer, journey. From DC, *Spirit of Washington* river cruises (866/302-2469, www.spiritcruises.com, round-trip tickets $48 adults, $43 children 6-11, free for children 5 and under) travel from the Southwest Waterfront directly to Mount Vernon from March to October; the journey takes approximately 90 minutes, departing DC at 8am and leaving Mount Vernon at 1:30pm. From Alexandria, Potomac Riverboat Company (877/511-2628, www.potomacriverboatco.com, round-trip tickets $42 adults, $22 children) offers 90-minute cruises with two stops at the National Harbor, departing Old Town at 10:30am and leaving Mount Vernon at 4pm. Mount Vernon admission is included with both river cruises; reservations are strongly recommended.

You can bike to the estate via the Mount Vernon Trail, which links DC, Alexandria, and Mount Vernon. It's 18 miles from DC to Mount Vernon, but the trip will not be too difficult for experienced riders. From Alexandria, it's just 8 miles to the estate's entrance. (See *Biking to Alexandria* on page 254 for more information.)

Annapolis and Maryland's Eastern Shore

Annapolis is the state capital of Maryland, and the sailing capital of the country, a good choice to spend a day on the water and explore colonial history before you try Maryland's famous blue crab cake. Or, continue over the Chesapeake Bay Bridge to explore some of the Eastern Shore's most charming small towns; Easton, Oxford, and St. Michaels are close enough to one another to visit in one day, or you can make a relaxing weekend.

ANNAPOLIS
SIGHTS
✪ Annapolis Harbor and City Dock

Getting out on the water is a must when visiting "America's Sailing Capital," and **City Dock** (1 Dock St., Main St. at Compromise St.) is the place to do it. Head southeast on Main Street until you see the sailboats—you'll see a lot of them in the busy harbor.

After perusing the restaurants, pubs, and boutiques around the dock, take a boat cruise to see the Annapolis shoreline from the water. Enjoy a 40-minute, narrated tour on the circa 1973 river boat *Harbor Queen* (410/268-7601, http://cruisesonthe-bay.com; daily cruises Mar.-Oct.; $17 adults, $6 children 3-11, free for children 2 and under), or board one of the elegant **Woodwind schooners** (80 Compromise St., 410/263-7837, www.schoonerwoodwind.com; daily cruises

Annapolis skyline

Annapolis

Apr.-Oct.; $43-46 adults, $41-44 seniors, $29 children under 12), which offer daytime and sunset cruises as well as private charters.

To sail yourself, go to the **Annapolis Sailing School** (7001 Bembe Beach Rd., 410/267-7205, www.annapolis-sailing.com), where you can rent one of their Rainbows or take a class. Prefer to stay on dry land? Catch one of the races on Wednesday evenings at 6pm in July and August, or visit for one of biggest sailboat shows in the world, the **Annapolis Spring Sailboat Show** in April and the **United States Sailboat Show** (www.annapolis-boatshows.com) in October.

Where Main Street meets Compromise Street at the traffic circle by the dock, the **Kunta Kinte-Alex Haley Memorial** pays tribute to Alex Haley, author of *Roots: The Saga of an American Family.* Haley's novel is based on his ancestor Kunta Kinte, who was captured in Gambia and brought to Annapolis in 1767, where he was sold as a slave.

Historic Annapolis

Founded by Puritans seeking religious freedom in 1649 and chartered as the capital of the colony of Maryland in 1708, Annapolis was a thriving center of politics, culture, and the tobacco

259

and slave trade for the young nation. With more than 100 18th-century buildings still standing today, the city is a time capsule of colonial architecture, with important historic sites situated around State Circle near the harbor.

The centerpiece is the Maryland State House (100 State House Cir., www.msa.maryland.gov; 9am-5pm daily except Christmas Day and New Year's Day; free), the oldest state house in the country still in use. Here, the United States and Great Britain signed the Treaty of Paris in 1783, ending the Revolutionary War, and the Continental Congress met shortly after.

East of the State House, William Paca House & Garden (186 Prince George St., 410/990-4543, www. annapolis.org; 10am-5pm Mon.- Sat., noon-5pm Sun. Mar.-Dec.; $10 guided house/self-guided garden tour, $8 guided first floor/self-guided garden tour, $5 self-guided garden tour) is the home of the third governor of Maryland and one of the state's four signers of the Declaration of Independence, fully restored to its 18th-century glory. Nearby, Hammond-Harwood House (19 Maryland Ave., 410/263-4683, www. hammondharwoodhouse.org; noon-5pm Tues.-Sun. Apr.-Dec.; $10 adults, $8 seniors/students, $5 children) is another beautifully restored 18th-century mansion with an extensive collection of colonial furniture and fine art.

Founded in 1696 as the King William's School, St. John's College (60 College Ave., 410/263-2371, www. sjc.edu; admissions office 8:30am-5pm Mon.-Fri.) is one of the oldest educational institutions in the country. And while the current structure west of the State House on Church Circle was built

United States Naval Academy

in 1858-1859, St. Anne's Parish (199 Duke of Gloucester St., 410/267-9333, www.stannes-annapolis.org; free tours at 10am on the first and third Mon. of the month, 12:30pm every Wed.) was founded in 1692 and named for Queen Anne, who signed the Establishment Act allowing Annapolis to build a state house, church, and school.

Finally, named for Maryland natives Benjamin Banneker and Frederick Douglass, the small Banneker-Douglass Museum (84 Franklin St., 410/216-6180, www.bd-museum.maryland.gov; 10am-4pm Tues.-Sat.; free) highlights Maryland's African American history in the former Mount Moriah African Methodist Episcopal Church, built in 1875.

United States Naval Academy

Since 1845, the United States Naval Academy has trained generations of America's brightest sailors. Located on the Severn River at the site of former naval base, the campus provides an in-depth look at U.S. naval history. Start at the Armel-Leftwich Visitor Center (52 King George St., entrance at Prince George St. or Randall St., 410/293-8687, www.usnabsd.com; 9am-5pm daily Mar.-Dec., 9am-4pm Mon.-Fri. Jan.-Feb.; free, government identification required) to embark on a free guided tour, available daily though times vary depending on the season. Key sights include the chapel, with the iconic dome and crypt of Revolutionary War commander John Paul Jones, and Tecumseh, the rescued figurehead from the USS *Delaware*, which was sunk during the Civil War so it could not be taken over by Confederates. The U.S. Naval Academy Museum (118 Maryland Ave., 410/293-2108, www.usna.edu; 9am-5pm Mon.-Sat., 11am-5pm Sun;

free, government identification required) showcases the history of the U.S. Navy and the academy.

RESTAURANTS

When dining in Annapolis, you must have Chesapeake Bay seafood—particularly the famous Maryland crab cakes. You'll find them, as well as other crab dishes, at any seafood restaurant in the Annapolis vicinity. The best ones boast lump crab meat with very little filler, and a lot of Old Bay seasoning—and while you'll find upscale entrées as well as casual sandwiches, they're best enjoyed on a dock with coleslaw and a cold beer.

Two blocks from the harbor, Chick & Ruth's Delly (165 Main St., 410/269-6737, www.chickandruths.com; 6:30am-11:30pm Sun.-Thurs., 6:30am-12:30am Fri.-Sat.; $6-15) is something out of a Norman Rockwell painting, known for affordable breakfasts, sandwiches, and homemade pies as well as a daily recitation of the Pledge of Allegiance, at 8:30am on weekdays, 9:30am on weekends. While prices have increased since the deli opened in 1965, you'd be hard-pressed to find better than the half-pound jumbo lump crab cake for $14.95.

Or, have your crab with politicos at Harry Browne's (66 State Cir., 410/263-4332, www.harrybrownes.com; 11am-10pm Mon.-Sat., 10am-9pm Sun., lounge until 2am daily; $24-36). Directly across from the Maryland State House, the old-school restaurant is where legislators and lobbyists dine on crab cakes, cream of crab soup, and cocktails; the well-priced happy hour includes $6 soup and $5 martinis and manhattans.

For dinner, head across the harbor to Eastport for a view of the Annapolis skyline and several restaurants and bars. **Carrol's Creek Café** (410 Severn Ave., 410/263-8102, www.carrolscreek.com; 11:30am-9pm Mon.-Thurs., 11:30am-10pm Fri.-Sat., 10am-8:30pm Sun.; $22-34) is a white-tablecloth restaurant on the water serving lunch, dinner, and Sunday brunch with views of Spa Creek, formerly Carrol's Creek, named for Charles Carroll, one of Maryland's signers of the Declaration of Independence. **Boatyard Bar & Grill** (400 4th St., 410/216-6206, www.boatyardbarandgrill.com; 7:30am-midnight Mon.-Fri., 8am-midnight Sat.-Sun.; $10-22) is a family-friendly restaurant with a yachty interior whose famous "no-filler" crab cake ranks among the best in the Annapolis area. (First Lady Michelle Obama supposedly said it was the best crab cake she'd ever had.)

If you want to try the Maryland tradition of cracking crabs, locals urge you to drive 15 minutes (4.2 miles) across the Severn River to **Cantler's Riverside Inn** (458 Forest Beach Rd., 410/757-1311, www.cantlers.com; 11am-midnight daily; $10-32) on Mill Creek. The steamed, hard-shell crabs are served by the dozen, half dozen, or per piece at market prices; other menu items include fresh fish and peel-and-eat shrimp, crab cake sandwiches, and burgers.

End your night with ice cream. **Storm Bros. Ice Cream Factory** (130 Dock St., 410/263-3376, www.stormbros.com; 11am-11pm Sun.-Thurs., 11am-midnight Fri.-Sat.) on the dock has been around since 1976; the cash-only shop has over 40 flavors, plus yogurt, sorbet, and sherbet, starting at just $2.95 for a single scoop. On Main Street, **Annapolis Ice Cream Company** (196 Main St., 443/482-3895, www.annapolisicecream.com; 11am-10pm Sun.-Thurs., 11am-11pm Fri.-Sat.) is frequently named best in Annapolis for their more than 17 percent butterfat ice cream made in-house.

NIGHTLIFE

Leave the expensive cocktails and rooftops to Washington DC; nightlife in Annapolis is all about laid-back taverns and pubs. Established in 1750, **Middleton Tavern** (2 Market Space, 410/263-3323, www.middletontavern.com; 11:30am-1:30am Mon.-Sat., 10am-1:30am Sun.) served ale to several Founding Fathers; today, it's known for beer specials, bar snacks, and seafood, as well as live music on weekends.

Rams Head (33 West St., 410/268-4545, www.ramsheadtavern.com; 11am-2am Mon.-Sat., 10am-2am Sun.) is a casual spot to dine and drink until late, with a **live music venue** (www.ramsheadonstage.com; box office 9am-9pm daily) that seats 500 for folk, rock, country, and tribute bands. For drinks on the dock, **Pusser's Caribbean Grille** (80 Compromise St., 410/626-0004, www.pussersusa.com; 6:30am-midnight Mon.-Thurs., 6:30am-2am Fri., 7am-2am Sat., 7am-midnight Sun.) serves boat drinks made with Pusser's Rum from the British Virgin Islands.

SHOPS

The downtown Annapolis shops are full of colorful, preppy, yacht-worthy clothing and accessories, Navy sweatshirts, and only-in-Maryland souvenirs—a crab mallet is the perfect gift for the cook. You'll find dozens of independent boutiques lining Main Street, between Church Circle and City Dock, and Maryland Avenue, between Prince George Street and State

CROSSING THE BAY BRIDGE

Chesapeake Bay Bridge

Crossing the Chesapeake Bay Bridge, which connects Washington DC and Annapolis to the small towns and beaches of Maryland's Eastern Shore, is a rite of summer for many Washington locals. But, be warned—the bridge's soaring heights and seasonal traffic are not for nervous drivers. The dual-span, five-lane bridge is 4.3 miles (6.9 kilometers) long and 190 feet above the windy bay at its highest, providing enough clearance for ocean-going ships to pass underneath. Part of US-50 and the most efficient route over the bay, the bridge is one giant traffic jam on Friday afternoons and Saturday mornings during peak beach season.

To reach the bridge from Washington DC, just stay on US-50 E for about 40 miles, or just under an hour. The bridge has a one-way toll eastbound; currently, it's $4 per car, or $2.50 per car with E-ZPass. During the summer, traffic is heaviest eastbound on Friday through Saturday evening, and westbound on Sunday. For more information, including traffic advisories and lane closures, call 877/229-7726 or visit www.baybridge.maryland. gov.

Can't handle the heights? **Kent Island Express** (410/604-0486, www.kentislandexpress.com) will drive your car over the bridge for you, 24 hours per day, seven days per week. Call one hour before you're ready to cross the bridge to arrange a meeting point; the service costs $30 one-way 7am-8pm daily; additional fees may apply outside of those hours.

Circle. For fine art galleries, head to the **Annapolis Arts District** (www.annapolisartsdistrict.org), located on West Street between Westgate Circle east to Church Circle; from May through December, the Arts District comes alive for **First Sundays** (www.firstsundayarts.com), a street festival with dozens of artists and artisans, live music, and food. For the most up-to-date information on Annapolis shops, hours, and special events, check www.visitannapolis.org.

WHERE TO STAY

Stay right on the water at the **Annapolis Waterfront Hotel** (80 Compromise St., 888/773-0786, www.annapoliswaterfront.com; $250-400), the city's only hotel directly on the **Annapolis Harbor.** The Autograph Collection property has 150 guest rooms—some with waterfront balconies—and the entire hotel is decorated in a jaunty blue and white nautical style. **Pusser's Caribbean Grille** (410/626-0004, www.pussersusa.

com; 6:30am-midnight Mon.-Thurs., 6:30am-2am Fri., 7am-2am Sat., 7am-midnight Sun.; $20-30) is on the property.

Historic Inns of Annapolis (58 State Cir., 410/263-2641, www.historicinnsofannapolis.com; $120-250) manages three charming properties in 17th- and 18th-century homes, updated with 21st-century amenities and elegant decor in the combined 124 rooms and suites. Governor Calvert House, where you check in, and Robert Johnson House are located on State Circle, while Maryland Inn is nearby on Church Circle; all three have access to a restaurant serving daily breakfast, an English-style pub, and 24-hour fitness center. These well-priced rooms book up in advance, especially during major events and busy wedding weekends in the spring and fall.

INFORMATION AND SERVICES

In the center of Historic Annapolis near Church Circle, Visit Annapolis & Anne Arundel County (26 West St., 410/280-0445, www.visitannapolis.org; 9am-5pm daily) can help you plan your trip to Annapolis and the surrounding area as well as provide brochures, maps, and event calendars. A satellite Visitor Information Booth is located at City Dock. The website has a wealth of information as well as mobile apps with up-to-date information and driving tours.

TRANSPORTATION

The best way to get from Washington DC to Annapolis is by car; the 30-mile trip will take approximately 45-60 minutes depending on traffic. From downtown DC, head east on New York Avenue NW to US-50 E to Maryland.

Take exit 24/MD-70 S to get to the harbor and historic downtown area. There are several convenient parking garages, lots, and metered spaces; www.visitannapolis.org has maps and pricing details.

While renting a car is recommended to explore Annapolis and the Chesapeake Bay, you can use ride-hailing apps like Uber and Lyft to get from DC to Annapolis and back; expect to pay $50-60 for a standard car and $160-180 for a black car each way during non-surge periods.

It's possible to take public transportation to Annapolis, as well, but it's rather inconvenient. Take Amtrak or Metro Orange Line to New Carrollton station (4700 Garden City Dr., www.wmata.com), then catch the Young Transportation Services bus 921 (www.ytsonline.net); bus hours are limited, so check the schedule online, and plan to use a ride-hailing service or take a taxi back to DC if you're having dinner in Annapolis.

It's very easy to walk around Annapolis and see the harbor, historic sights, and United States Naval Academy by foot. The free Annapolis Circulator trolley (every 20 minutes, 7:30am-11pm Mon.-Sat., 8am-8pm Sun.; free) runs from four of the parking garages around the city, hitting City Dock, Church Circle, and other key points of interest.

To get to the restaurants in Eastport, you can catch a water taxi from City Dock; taxis and ride-hailing services are readily available, as well.

EASTON
SIGHTS
Historic Easton

Once the capital of Maryland's Eastern Shore, Easton is the Talbot County seat, founded in 1661 and named for

Easton

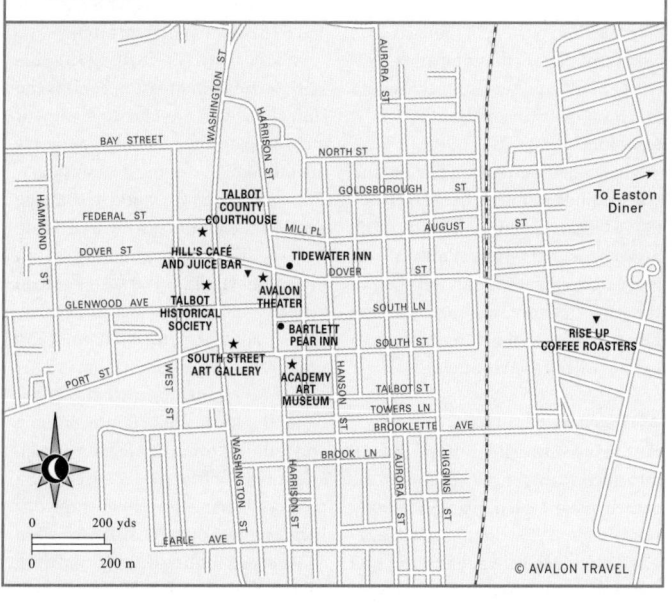

© AVALON TRAVEL

Lady Grace Talbot, sister of the second Lord Baltimore. Today, Easton is considered one of the "top small towns in America," with a population of about 16,000 and a historic district with quaint streets filled with 18th- and 19th-century architecture. **Talbot Historical Society** (30 S. Washington St., 410/822-0773, www. hstc.org; 10am-4pm Thurs.-Sat.; free) manages a small museum in one of the oldest buildings with exhibits about the history and residents of Easton and Talbot County, as well as idyllic gardens, free to the public daily during daylight hours.

Speaking of Talbot County's former residents, Frederick Douglass is perhaps the most famous. The abolitionist's autobiography, *Narrative of the Life of Frederick Douglass,* begins, "I was born in Tuckahoe, near Hillsborough, and about 12 miles from Easton, in Talbot County, Maryland."

In 2004, the Talbot County Council voted to place a statue of Douglass in front of the **Talbot County Courthouse**—directly adjacent to *Talbot Boys,* the controversial 1916 memorial to 84 Confederate veterans from the county. In September, the town celebrates **Frederick Douglass Day** (www.frederickdouglassday.com) with lectures by historians, concerts, and family activities.

RESTAURANTS

Hill's Café and Juice Bar (32 E. Dover St., 410/822-9751, www.hillscafeand-juice.com; 8am-3pm daily; $6-10), serves simple, healthy breakfasts, sandwiches, salads, and juice, in the historic Hill's Drug Store, founded in 1928. Need caffeine after navigating the traffic jam on the Bay Bridge? **Rise Up Coffee Roasters** (618 Dover Rd., 410/822-1353, www.riseupcoffee.com; 6am-7pm daily) has been waking up the Eastern Shore with certified organic and fair-trade coffee since 2005. The Easton roastery is housed in a 1920s gas station; the company's food truck, Mad Eggs, serves breakfast and lunch sandwiches and healthy bowls, 6am-3pm.

On US-50 near Dunkin Donuts and several budget hotels, Easton Diner (8451 Ocean Gateway, 410/819-0535, no website; 6am-10pm daily; $7-15) is a good stop on your way out of the Eastern Shore, serving cheap but hearty breakfast, lunch, and dinner in a colorful, retro-style diner.

ARTS AND CULTURE

Easton is a surprising cultural hub. In a former 19th-century schoolhouse turned historical landmark, Academy Art Museum (106 South St., 410/822-2787, www.academyartmuseum.org; 10am-8pm Tues.-Thurs., 10am-4pm Fri.-Mon., 10am-7pm first Friday Apr.-Dec.; $3 nonmembers, free children under 12, free on Wed.) is one of the Eastern Shore's premier arts venues, with more than 1,400 works from 1850 to present day by the likes of Chuck Close, Gene Davis, Robert Rauschenberg, and Picasso as well as regional artists. In addition to rotating exhibits featuring works from the impressive permanent collection, the museum frequently shows works from the National Gallery of Art. Visit during First Friday, when Easton's galleries and shops open their doors until 7pm or 8pm on the first Friday of the month from April to December.

Built in 1922 as a movie theater, Avalon Theatre (40 E. Dover St., 410/822-0345, www.avalonfoundation.org; box office 11am-5pm Wed.-Fri. and two hours prior to every show) brings live blues, folk, jazz, and rock musicians to the Eastern Shore, with performances several nights a week in the renovated 380-seat art deco theater and 60-seat cabaret-style room.

In July, Plein Air Easton (410/822-7297, www.pleinaireaston.com) is the United States' largest juried festival of plein air painting, or landscape painting outdoors, bringing dozens of artists from around the world to compete and sell their works. And coinciding with the start of goose hunting season in November, the Waterfowl Festival (410/822-4567, www.waterfowlfestival. org; $15 adults, free for children 10 and under) showcases Talbot County's art and sportsmanship in what has become the most important economic and cultural event for Easton as well as a fundraiser for local conservation projects. During the festive, three-day event, see works by local artists, learn about goose hunting, fishing, and duck calling, and enjoy local food and beverage tastings.

WHERE TO STAY

Tidewater Inn (101 E. Dover St., 410/822-1300, www.tidewaterinn. com; $160-280) is an excellent base for a weekend exploring the Eastern Shore, with 92 clean and modern guest rooms, a fitness center, and recently renovated public spaces. It's walking distance to Easton's attractions and a quick drive to neighboring towns, but you may want to stick around and enjoy a relaxed dinner and drinks at Hunter's Tavern (410/822-4034, www. tidewaterinn.com; 7am-9pm Sun.-Thurs., 7am-10pm Fri.-Sat.; $28-38), the on-site restaurant with an expansive American menu.

One of the Chesapeake Bay's top-rated bed-and-breakfasts, Bartlett Pear Inn (28 S. Harrison St., 410/770-3300, www.bartlettpearinn.com; $139-289) is ideal for a romantic getaway.

Located in an 18th-century home, the inn has seven charming rooms with private baths, and it serves a superb breakfast.

INFORMATION AND SERVICES

The **Talbot County Office of Tourism** (11 S. Harrison St., 410/770-8000, www.tourtalbot.org; 8:30am-5pm Mon.-Fri., 10am-2pm Sat.) has all the information you need to plan your trip to Easton and the surrounding area, in-person in Easton or online. For the calendar of events and more information about dining, shopping, and accommodations, visit www.eastonmd.org or www.discovereaston.com.

TRANSPORTATION

By car, Easton is approximately one hour (42 miles) from Annapolis and 1.5-2 hours (70 miles) from Washington DC, depending on traffic.

From either city, take US-50 East to the Chesapeake Bay Bridge. After crossing, continue on US-50 E/Ocean Gateway about 25 miles, approximately 25 minutes. Veer right on MD-322. Turn left on Glebe Road, then continue on North Harrison Street into Easton's historic center. You should have no problem finding street parking or space in a lot near the Talbot Historical Society or Avalon Theatre; during events like the Waterfowl Festival, signs will direct you to parking lots.

While driving is the most convenient way to get to Easton, **Greyhound** (www.greyhound.com) buses run daily from Union Station in Washington DC to Easton and back; the bus stops at a gas station on US-50, about one mile from Easton's historic district.

Easton is just 10 miles from both Oxford and St. Michaels, so you can easily explore all three towns in one day by car or bike.

OXFORD
SIGHTS
Historic Oxford

Founded in 1683, Oxford is the oldest town in Maryland, and one of the oldest in the country. Once an international shipping hub for tobacco trade on par with Annapolis, Oxford now has a population of just over 600. This sleepy boat town played an important role in the American Revolution as a vital port and home of several Founding Fathers and war heroes, including Robert Morris Jr., the first and only superintendent of finance (precursor to the treasury secretary), and Colonel Tench Tilghman, George Washington's aide de camp, who carried the message that the British Army had surrendered at Yorktown to the Continental Congress. Explore the history at the **Oxford Museum** (100 S. Morris St., 410/226-0191, www.oxford-museum.org; 10am-4pm Mon., Wed., and Fri.-Sat., 1pm-4pm Sun.; free); it's tiny, but colonial history buffs may enjoy the artifacts and family heirlooms on display.

Then, take a ride on the **Oxford-Bellevue Ferry** (101 East Strand, 410/745-9023, www.oxfordbellevueferry.com; 9am-sunset daily Apr.-Oct., 9am-sunset Sat.-Sun. in Nov.), the oldest private ferry operating in the United States, which has connected Oxford to Bellevue across the Tred Avon River since 1683. There's not much on the other side; the attraction is the 10-minute, three-quarter-mile ride, a chance to get on the water without renting a boat. The ferry runs every 15-20 minutes daily from April to November; rates range from

Oxford-Bellevue Ferry

$5 round-trip for pedestrians to $20 round-trip for cars.

RESTAURANTS AND WHERE TO STAY

Oxford has several lovely inns with well-regarded restaurants. Founded in 1710, Robert Morris Inn (314 N. Morris St., 410/226-5111, www. robertmorrisinn.com; $145-240) claims to be the oldest in America, in the yellow house one block from the ferry. And while the age does show, the 35 rooms are lovingly maintained, and many have water views. The restaurant, Salter's Tavern (8am-10:30am, noon-2:30pm, 5pm-9pm Mon.-Sat., 8am-2:30pm and 5pm-9pm Sun., hours vary seasonally so call ahead to confirm; $19-32), is one of the best in the area, led by chef Mark Salter, who combines local seafood and produce with his experience cooking at some of the finest hotels in Europe.

Built in 1880, Oxford Inn (504 S. Morris St., 410/226-5220, www.

oxfordinn.net; $110-195) has seven cozy rooms with old-fashioned floral decor but good prices year-round, as well as the highly rated Pope's Tavern (5:30pm-9pm Sun.-Mon., 5:30pm-9pm Thurs., 5:30pm-10pm Fri.-Sat.; $15-36), serving New American cuisine with local, seasonal ingredients.

For something more casual, Doc's Sunset Grille (104 W. Pier St., 410/226-5550; 11am-10pm Tues.-Sun., hours may vary seasonally; $10-30) is a beachy dockside restaurant and bar on the Tred Avon River with steamed crabs and live music on weekends; check the Facebook page for the daily specials and lineup.

For dessert, don't miss Scottish Highland Creamery (314 Tilghman St., 410/924-6298, www.scottish-highlandcreamery.com; noon-8pm daily in May, noon-9pm Sun.-Thurs., noon-10pm Fri.-Sat. June-Labor Day, weekends only Sept.-Apr., weather permitting), consistently ranked one of the top ice cream shops in the country.

INFORMATION AND SERVICES

For information on attractions, accommodations, and events in Oxford, visit www.portofoxford.com, www.oxfordmd.net, or the Talbot County Office of Tourism in Easton (11 S. Harrison St., 410/770-8000, www.tourtalbot.org; 8:30am-5pm Mon.-Fri., 10am-2pm Sat.).

TRANSPORTATION

By car, Oxford is approximately one hour (52 miles) from Annapolis and 1.5-2 hours (80 miles) from Washington DC, depending on traffic.

From either city, take US-50 East to the Chesapeake Bay Bridge. After crossing, continue on US-50 E/Ocean Gateway about 30 minutes to MD-322/Easton Parkway. Turn right on MD-322 and drive about three miles to MD-333 S/Oxford Road/Peachblossom Road. Continue about nine miles over a few creeks to the center of Oxford. There is a public parking lot near the ferry dock, and the entire town is easily walkable.

Oxford is 10 miles from Easton, and it's just under 20 miles to St. Michaels—nine miles if you take the Oxford-Bellevue Ferry.

☢ ST. MICHAELS

SIGHTS

Boat Cruises on the Miles River

Get to know Maryland's historic hub of shipbuilding and oyster harvesting during a boat cruise on the Miles River. Patriot Cruises (213 N. Talbot St., 410/745-3100, www.patriotcruises.com; daily in summer, weekends in off-season; $24.50-29.50 adults, $22 seniors, $12.50 children 12-17, $5 children 3-11, free for children under 3) offers 60- to 75-minute tours as well as cocktail cruises on summer Saturday evenings.

Or, board the historic H.M. *Krentz* (213 N. Talbot St., 410/745-6080, www.oystercatcher.com; daily Apr.-Oct.; $47.50 adults, $39 seniors, $33 military ID, $28 ages 7-20, $20 for children ages 2-6, free for children under 2), one of the few remaining skipjacks, the oyster dredge boats built specifically for use on the Chesapeake Bay in the late 19th and early 20th centuries. The Chesapeake Bay Maritime Museum (213 N. Talbot St., 410/745-2916, www.cbmm.org) offers cruises and summer boat rentals as well.

Chesapeake Bay Maritime Museum

Covering 18 acres on the banks of the Miles River, the Chesapeake Bay Maritime Museum (213 N. Talbot St., 410/745-2916, www.cbmm.org; 9am-5pm daily May-Oct., 10am-4pm daily Nov.-Apr.; $15 adults, $12 seniors/students/retired military, $6 children ages 6-17, free for children 5 and under and active military) catalogues the region's history, from the American Indian residents and settlement by English explorers to an in-depth look at the region's more modern industries of shipbuilding, oyster harvesting and canning, and crabbing. On campus, explore the working boatyard, where the museum preserves and restores dozens of Chesapeake Bay watercraft, as well as the circa 1879 lighthouse.

St. Michaels Museum and Walking Tours

Located in three restored historical buildings, St. Michaels Museum (201 E. Chestnut St., 410/745-9561, www.stmichaelsmuseum.org; 1pm-4pm Fri., 10am-4pm Sat., 1pm-4pm Sun. May-Oct.; $3 adults, $1 children ages 6-17, free for children under 6) chronicles the history of the town. The buildings have small exhibits on everyday life and commerce in 19th-century St. Michaels; one, the Chaney House, was built by three free African American brothers who eventually bought their father's freedom. On Saturdays, the museum offers several guided walking tours, including one tracing Frederick Douglass's teenage years in the town before he escaped slavery.

RESTAURANTS

For a small town, St. Michaels has substantial dining options, ranging from elegant bistros to classic crab houses to quick-serve coffee shops and bakeries.

For a sophisticated dinner date, make a reservation at **208 Talbot** (208 N. Talbot St., 410/745-3838, www.208talbot.com; 5pm-9pm Wed.-Thurs., 5pm-10pm Fri.-Sat., 5pm-9pm Sun.; $13-36), where Eastern Shore native David Clark prepares top-rated local seafood in the white-tablecloth, brick-walled space. **Bistro St. Michaels** (403 S. Talbot St., 410/745-9001, www.bistrostmichaels.com; 5pm-9pm Mon.-Thurs., 5pm-10pm Fri., 10am-1:30pm, 5pm-10pm Sat., 10am-1:30pm Sun.; $20-39) serves French favorites inspired by the Chesapeake Bay and made with local, sustainable ingredients.

Marylanders recount childhood memories of taking boats to **The Crab Claw** (304 Burns St., 410/745-2900, www.thecrabclaw.com; from 11am daily Mar.-Oct.; $15-30) for Maryland's famous steamed crabs, which opened in 1965 in a former clam- and oyster-shucking shed on the water. Order steamed crabs by the dozen or the piece, which are best enjoyed on the covered deck as you watch fishing boats bring in fresh catches for the restaurant.

Had enough seafood? **Ava's Pizzeria & Wine Bar** (409 S. Talbot St., 410/745-3081, www.avaspizzeria.com; 11:30am-9pm Sun.-Thurs., 11:30am-10pm Fri.-Sat.; $10-20) is frequently rated the best pizza on Maryland's Eastern Shore, with brick-oven pizza, pasta, and subs made with seasonal produce.

WHERE TO STAY

The most polished of the Eastern Shore's small towns, St. Michaels is home to the luxurious **Inn at Perry Cabin** (308 Watkins Ln., 410/745-2200, www.belmond.com/inn-at-perry-cabin-st-michaels; $515-860), the Belmond property on the banks of the Miles River. (Yes, the main reception in *Wedding Crashers* was filmed here.) The colonial mansion has 78 plush rooms and suites, an outdoor pool and acclaimed spa, and lots of resort activities. From the inn's dock, you can catch a boat cruise or embark on crabbing, fishing, or kayaking excursions.

St. Michaels has at least a dozen bed-and-breakfasts of various sizes and price points. The adults-only **Five Gables Inn & Spa** (209 N. Talbot St., 410/745-0100, www.fivegables.com; $140-195) has 20 rooms in three 19th-century homes, plus an Aveda spa, indoor pool, and thoughtful touches like bicycles and in-room fireplaces. One of the oldest homes in the town, **Snuggery Bed & Breakfast** (203 Cherry St., 410/745-2800, www.snuggery1665.com; $200-250) has just two suites but plenty of charm, with antique decor and an old-fashioned porch; enjoy a farmers market breakfast daily before exploring the town.

INFORMATION AND SERVICES

For information on attractions, accommodations, and events in St.

Michaels, visit www.stmichaelsmd.org or www.townofstmichaels.com, or the **Talbot County Office of Tourism in Easton** (11 S. Harrison St., 410/770-8000, www.tourtalbot.org; 8:30am-5pm Mon.-Fri., 10am-2pm Sat.). In addition to guided tours, the **St. Michaels Museum** (201 E. Chestnut St., 410/745-9561, www.stmichaelsmuseum.org; 1pm-4pm Fri., 10am-4pm Sat., 1pm-4pm Sun. May-Oct.) has information and self-guided walking tour maps.

TRANSPORTATION

By car, St. Michaels is approximately one hour (50 miles) from Annapolis

and 1.5-2 hours (80 miles) from Washington DC, depending on traffic.

From either city, take US-50 East to the Chesapeake Bay Bridge. After crossing, continue on US-50 E/Ocean Gateway about 30 minutes to MD-322/Easton Parkway. Turn right on MD-322 and drive about two miles to MD-33 W/St. Michaels Road. Take St. Michaels Road for about nine miles to the town center. There's ample public parking near the marina, and the entire town is easily walkable.

St. Michaels is 10 miles from Easton, and it's just under 20 miles to Oxford—nine miles if you take the Oxford-Bellevue Ferry.

Shenandoah National Park and Vicinity

Skyline Drive is the 105-mile scenic drive through Shenandoah National Park, which offers abundant hiking. Shenandoah makes a choice getaway from Washington DC.

I-66 is your gateway to Skyline Drive and Shenandoah National Park, which is especially glorious in the fall, and hundreds of miles of hiking trails and wilderness to explore. But don't miss the attractions along the way, including the lovely small towns of Middleburg and Little Washington—home to the famous, two-Michelin-star Inn at Little Washington, the ideal destination for a milestone birthday or anniversary—as well as wineries, horse racing, and even Civil War battlefields along the way. You can reach the Virginia countryside in one day, but you won't want to head back to the hustle and bustle of DC after

experiencing life in the shadow of the Blue Ridge Mountains.

WASHINGTON DC TO SHENANDOAH NATIONAL PARK
✪ STEVEN F. UDVAR-HAZY CENTER

Near Washington Dulles International Airport in Chantilly, Virginia, this outpost of the Smithsonian's National Air and Space Museum is the best excursion with kids, whether you go for the afternoon or make it your first stop on an adventure in the Virginia countryside. The **Steven F. Udvar-Hazy Center** (14390 Air and Space Museum Pkwy., 703/572-4118, http://airandspace.si.edu; 10am-5:30pm daily except Christmas Day; free admission, $15 parking) might be even more impressive than the museum in

Shenandoah National Park

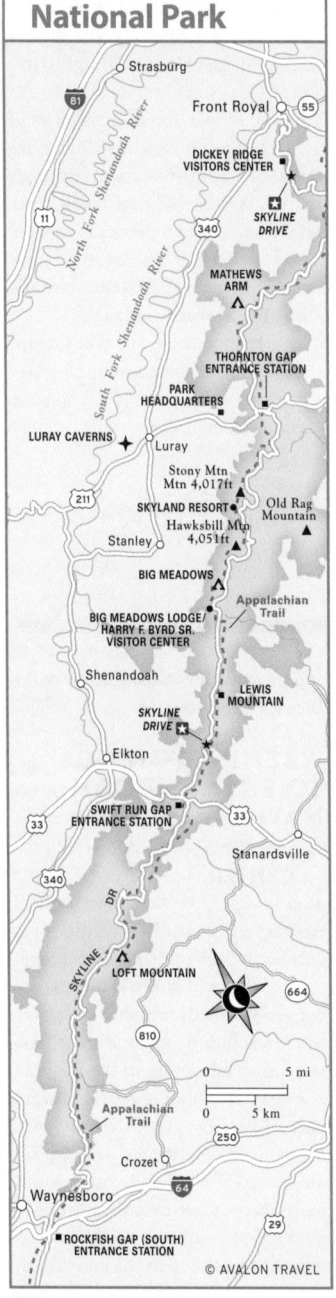

DC, with two massive hangars full of airplanes and spacecraft, including the space shuttle *Discovery*, a Concorde, and even American and German World War II planes. See a film at the IMAX theater, or check out the view from the observation tower. Visit the restoration hangar to see Smithsonian employees preserving aircraft for generations to come.

The center is approximately 45-60 minutes from DC by car and 90 minutes by public transportation. If driving, take I-66 W to exit 53B for Route 28 N and follow the signs to the center, or take I-495 W/Capital Beltway to Dulles Toll Road West/Route 26 and exit via Route 28 S/exit 9A. By Metro, take the Silver Line to Wiehle-Reston East and catch the Fairfax Connector bus 983 (703/339-7200, www.fairfax-connector.com) directly to the center.

MANASSAS NATIONAL BATTLEFIELD PARK

On July 21, 1861, the Union and Confederacy met in Manassas, about 30 miles from Washington DC, to fight the first major battle of the Civil War. The Union was expected to win handily, but the Confederates scraped by, giving Confederate general Thomas Jonathan "Stonewall" Jackson his nickname; 4,700 men died, an omen of things to come in America's bloodiest war. About one year later, the Second Battle of Bull Run left nearly 3,000 dead and countless wounded or missing.

Manassas National Battlefield Park (6511 Sudley Rd., 703/361-1339, www.nps.gov/mana; daily dawn-dusk; free) is a must-visit for history buffs and a good pit stop on the way to Shenandoah National Park. At the entrance, Henry Hill Visitor Center (8:30am-5pm daily except

© AVALON TRAVEL

Manassas National Battlefield Park

Thanksgiving Day and Christmas Day) has interactive maps and exhibits as well as park information; guided tours of both battles are available daily, or you can take a self-guided tour across 40 miles of trails. Throughout the year, interpreters reenact both battles at Chinn Ridge (check the website for the schedule).

From Washington DC, take I-66 W to exit 47B, Route 234 N/Sudley Road. The visitor center is on the right.

EXPLORING THE PARK
✪ SKYLINE DRIVE

Whether it's your access point to an outdoor adventure in Shenandoah National Park or simply a leisurely drive to see the Blue Ridge Mountains and Virginia's storybook landscape, Skyline Drive (www.visitskylinedrive.org) is the most beautiful byway in the region. The Civilian Conservation Corps broke ground on the Depression-era infrastructure project in 1931; the full, 105-mile route was completed in 1939. Today, the drive will take you to 500 miles of hiking trails, horseback riding, and otherworldly caverns—or, you can just enjoy the drive. If you're going for the drive, you can't beat autumn, when the foliage changes to red and yellow and gold, but the views over the Shenandoah Valley from one of the 75

scenic overlooks are beautiful any time of year.

There are four entrances to Skyline Drive; the Front Royal entrance is the closest to Washington DC and the best option if the drive itself or outdoor activities are your goal, though you can easily reach the Thornton Gap entrance and Luray Caverns via Little Washington.

The Shenandoah National Park entrance fee ranges from $25 per vehicle to $10 per individual, and the pass is good for seven days beginning the day of purchase; check www.nps.gov for free-fee days, though expect crowds.

LURAY CAVERNS

Luray Caverns (101 Cave Hill Rd., 540/743-6551, www.luraycaverns.com; tours from 9am daily, hours vary seasonally; from $28 adults, $25 seniors, $15 children ages 6-12, free children 5 and under) is a bit of a tourist trap, but for good reason. The caverns were discovered in 1878 but formed much earlier, when acid and water eroded layers of limestone and clay, creating huge rooms with golden-hued stalactites, stalagmites, and other amazing formations. Descend through a nondescript building for the one-hour, 1.25-mile guided tour via lighted, paved path, in which you'll see the 47-foot column in Giant's Hall, the Great Stalacpipe Organ "playing" the formations, and even a lake. These are the largest caverns on the East Coast, and while it can get crowded, it's an impressive geology lesson and unique diversion when bad weather cancels outdoor plans.

Included with caverns admission, Luray Valley Museum tells the story of the Shenandoah Valley's history from the earliest inhabitants to the 19th century, and the Car and

Carriage Caravan Museum has one of the oldest working cars in the country, a Mercedes-Benz from 1892.

Luray is to the west of the park. To get there, head to the Thornton Gap entrance, approximately 80 miles from DC via I-66 West to US-211 West, through Little Washington.

SPORTS AND ACTIVITIES

Shenandoah National Park offers outdoor activities year-round, for all levels, whether you're an advanced, adventuresome hiker or just looking for a fun day exploring the great outdoors.

There are more than 500 miles of hiking trails inside the park, with options suitable for families with children as well as the most advanced hikers, including 101 miles of the Appalachian Trail. **Old Rag Mountain** is the park's most famous—as well as the most difficult and dangerous, as you must trek 9 miles and complete a rock scramble to get to the summit. Considered the must-do hike in the Mid-Atlantic, it gets very crowded, especially on weekends. Before attempting the hike, you're advised to read about the trail conditions and tips on the National Park Service website.

From the **Dickey Ridge Visitor Center** near the Front Royal entrance, which is the closest to DC, you'll find the **Fox Hollow Trail Hike,** an easy, 1.2-mile nature walk, as well as the **Sneed Farm Loop Hike,** a moderately challenging but still family-friendly 3.7-mile loop. If the Appalachian Trail is on your bucket list, summit **Mary's Rock,** a moderate, 3.7-mile round-trip hike that crosses part of the trail; you can access the trailhead from Thornton Gap close to Little Washington and Luray. For more information on Shenandoah hiking

trails, including maps and directions, visit www.nps.gov/shen or either of the visitor centers.

The park is a popular spot for horseback riding, as well. **Skyland Stables** (Skyline Dr. mile 42.5, 877/847-1919) offers one-hour and 2.5-hour guided trail rides on horseback or pony, daily April through November, weather permitting.

While you're in the park, keep your eyes peeled for the animals—if you're lucky, you'll see one of the famous black bears.

RESTAURANTS AND WHERE TO STAY

If you're looking for luxury, stay in **Middleburg,** closest to the Front Royal entrance, or **Little Washington,** near to the Thornton Gap entrance. If you're looking for a rustic experience with hiking trails outside your doorstep, Shenandoah National Park operates two family-friendly lodges, which are rated relatively high for rustic accommodations inside a park. **Skyland Resort** (Skyline Dr. mile 41.7-42.5; $120-210), built in 1888, has 178 motel-style rooms and cabins. It's close to **Skyland Stables** and several hikes, including **Mary's Rock.** On the National Register of Historic Places, **Big Meadows Lodge** (Skyline Dr. mile 51.2; $120-185) has 25 rooms in the main lodge plus 75 cabins, some with valley views. Both have dining rooms serving breakfast, lunch, and dinner daily, as well as taprooms with a full bar and a quick-serve counter selling coffee and sandwiches; considering the lack of options inside the park, the restaurants have substantial variety and reasonable prices.

The National Park Service operates four campgrounds on Skyline Drive with space for tents, campers, and

Virginia is the fifth-largest wine-producing region in the United States, and there are dozens of wineries 45-90 minutes from DC on the country roads to Shenandoah National Park. About 45 minutes from DC on the edge of Manassas National Battlefield Park, **The Winery at Bull Run** (15950 Lee Hwy./Rte. 29, Centreville, 703/815-2233, www.winery-atbullrun.com; 11am-7pm Sat.-Wed., 11am-8pm Thurs., 11am-10pm Fri.; $14 tasting) is a good introduction to the Virginia terroir with several award-winning wines, including fruit wines. As you head toward Shenandoah, **Chester Gap Cellars** (4615 Remount Rd., Front Royal, 540/636-8086, www.chestergapcellars; 11am-6pm Fri.-Sat., 11am-5pm Sun.) has some of the best views, 10 minutes from the Front Royal entrance of the park.

In Middleburg, **Chrysalis Vineyards** (39025 John Mosby Hwy., Middleburg, 540/687-8222, www.chrysaliswine.com; 10am-6pm Mon.-Thurs., 10am-7pm Fri.-Sun. Apr.-Oct., 10am-5pm daily Nov.-Mar.; $15 tasting) is known for the Norton grape, the country's oldest native wine grape, which was bred in Richmond. **Greenhill Winery & Vineyards** (23595 Winery Ln., Middleburg, 540/687-6968, www.greenhillvineyards.com; noon-sunset daily; $14 tasting) has 100 percent Virginia wines and a tasting room set on 128 rolling acres of gorgeous countryside.

Little Washington Winery (72 Christmas Tree Ln., Washington, 540/987-8330, www.littlewashingtonwinery.com, 11am-6pm Fri.-Sun., 11am-5pm holiday Mon.) produces some of the top-rated wines in Virginia, while **Narmada Winery** (43 Narmada Ln., Amissville, 540/937-8215, www.narmadawinery.com; 11am-5pm Mon., 11am-5pm Thurs.-Fri., 11am-7pm Sat., 11am-6pm Sun., hours may vary seasonally) is known for some of the best food in the area, offering classic Indian dishes paired with their award-winning wines.

For something different, don't miss **Mt. Defiance Cidery & Distillery** (207 W. Washington St., Middleburg, 540/687-8100, www.mtdefiance.com; noon-6pm Tues.-Sun.; tasting prices vary), where you can try ciders and unique, apple-based liquors; a bottle of the surprisingly smooth apple brandy, one of the original American spirits, is a good souvenir.

To plan your Virginia wine tour, visit www.virginiawine.org or www.discovershenandoah.com/wineries.

RVs; some are first-come, first-served while others accept reservations, and fees range $15-20 per night depending on the season. In addition, most of the park is open for camping if you prefer to rough it; a few areas around some of the more popular hiking trails, including Old Rag Mountain, are limited, so check with the National Park Service for details.

There are a few food stops along Skyline Drive, some with grocery and camping supplies, gift shops, gasoline, and shower facilities. For details on the resorts and other Skyline Drive facilities, visit www.goshenandoah.com.

INFORMATION AND SERVICES

There are two major visitor centers along Skyline Drive, with maps and information on hikes, activities, accommodations, and the history of the park. **Dickey Ridge Visitor Center** (Skyline Dr. mile 4.6, 9am-5pm daily early Apr. to late Nov.) is near the beginning of Skyline Drive near the Front Royal entrance. **Harry F. Byrd, Sr. Visitor Center** (Skyline Dr. mile 51, 9am-5pm daily late Mar. to late Nov., 9am-5p, Fri-.Sun. late Nov. to late Mar.) is farther along, just past Big Meadows Lodge. For more information, visit www.nps.gov/shen, www.skylinedrive.org, and www.goshenandoah.com.

TRANSPORTATION

Skyline Drive and Shenandoah National Park are approximately 1.5-2 hours (70 miles) from Washington DC. The Front Royal entrance is the start of Skyline Drive, and the closest entrance to DC, via I-66 W to VA-79/VA-55 W (this road has tolls). You can detour through Middleburg on your way to or from the entrance. You'll need a car to get to Skyline Drive, though, of course, you can hike or bike through the park.

Middleburg is approximately 45 minutes (30 miles) to Skyline Drive, and Little Washington is very close, about 20 minutes (12 miles) to Skyline Drive via the Thornton Gap entrance.

LITTLE WASHINGTON
SIGHTS
✪ The Inn at Little Washington

The Inn at Little Washington (Middle St. and Main St., 540/675-3800, www.theinnatlittlewashington. com), the sublime destination restaurant and inn, is perhaps the best reason to leave the District for the weekend. When visionary chef Patrick O'Connell opened the restaurant in a former garage in tiny Washington, Virginia, in the 1970s, entrées started at $4.95. Today, Washingtonians happily spend close to $1,000 for two for the two-star, four-course menus featuring produce and dairy from the inn's farm and orchard, plus dessert or cheese from the charming mooing,

clanging cow cart, just one of the many whimsical details.

If you can swing the pricey meal and one of the 24 refined rooms, it's worth it to stay the night, because they think of everything—from the keepsake menu and journal to help you remember your stay (as if you could ever forget), to the tasting of freshly pressed juices at breakfast, to a hand-written card from O'Connell if you're there for a special occasion. A decadent afternoon tea is included with the price of the room—though you may want to skip it so you don't spoil your appetite for the main event, and instead take the three-quarter-mile leisurely walk around the fields and gardens, where chickens, sheep, and a llama named Francesca live in splendor. And you can leave your phone in your room, because cell service is, blissfully, limited.

Historic Little Washington

There's not much to do in "Little" Washington, population just under 200—but that's entirely the point. In 1749, the young surveyor George Washington dropped by the town, which later became the first in the nation bearing his name. Today, The Inn at Little Washington houses gift shops (www.theinnatlittlewashington.com/tavern-shops; 10am-6pm Mon., 10am-noon Tues., 1pm-6pm Wed., 10am-6pm Thurs.-Fri., 10am-7pm Sat., 10am-6pm Sun.) and a farmers market. Little Washington Theatre (291 Gay St., 540/675-1253, www.littlewashingtontheatre.com) has community theater, jazz, and even Smithsonian-sponsored concerts, and Little Washington Wellness & Spa (261 Main St., 540/675-1031, www. littlewashingtonspa.com; 10am-6pm Mon. and Thurs.-Sat., 10am-4:30pm

view from the balcony at The Inn at Little Washington

Sun., by appointment Wed.) has a full menu of spa services and hair and beauty treatments. And the town has a smattering of shops and galleries, such as R. H. Ballard Shop & Gallery (307 Main St., 540/675-1411, www.rhballard.com; 10am-6pm Wed.-Mon.), a housewares shop and fine art gallery worth a stop.

WHERE TO STAY

The Inn at Little Washington (Middle St. and Main St., 540/675-3800, www.theinnatlittlewashington.com; $520-900) is simply the best, conveniently located to explore Shenandoah National Park. But if you can't get a room or want something a little more budget friendly, you aren't entirely out of luck, as there are several inns and bed-and-breakfasts within stumbling distance from dinner. The six modern rooms at The White Moose Inn (291 Main St., 540/675-3207, www.whitemooseinn.com; $425-625) are decorated in white with high-tech amenities and Molton Brown toiletries, while Gay Street Inn (160 Gay St., 540/316-9220, www.gaystreetinn.com; $279-329) has five homey guest rooms in a restored 1850s farmhouse.

INFORMATION AND SERVICES

Staff at The Inn at Little Washington (Middle St. and Main St., 540/675-3800, www.theinnatlittlewashington.com) are experts on the region and can provide directions to key sights and Shenandoah Valley hikes, wineries, and other activities; the website has lots of information and links.

For more information on the surrounding area, visit the Rappahannock Historical Society (328 Gay St., 540/675-1163, www.rappahannockhistsoc.org; 11am-5pm Mon., Tues., and Thurs.) a block from the inn, or the Rappahannock County Visitors Center (3 Library Rd., 540/675-3153, www.rappahannock.com; 9am-5pm Fri.-Sat. and Mon. holidays, noon-5pm Sun., hours may vary seasonally), less than one mile east.

GETTING THERE

Little Washington is approximately 1.5-2 hours (about 70 miles) west of Washington DC, and a good base to explore Shenandoah National Park and nearby wineries. Take I-66 W to US-29 S (exit 43A toward Gainesville/Warrenton). Continue on Route 29 S for 12 miles to Warrenton, then turn right on US-211 W. Stay on US-211 W for 23 miles to the town. While you don't need a car within Little Washington, you'll need one to get there and explore the surrounding area; if you want to go for dinner and back, the Inn at Little Washington can arrange car service for you, or contact Reston Limousine (703/478-0500, www.restonlimo.com).

Little Washington is about 20 minutes (12 miles) from the closest Skyline Drive entrance at Thornton Gap, via US-211 W/US-522 S, which will also take you to Luray Caverns in 35 minutes. It's one hour (36 miles) from Middleburg, a great scenic route/detour on the way back to Washington DC.

MIDDLEBURG
SIGHTS
✪ Historic Middleburg

Founded in 1787 by Revolutionary War lieutenant colonel and politician John Leven Powell on a busy trading route from Alexandria, Middleburg is the "Nation's Horse and Hunt Capital," a retreat for wealthy Washingtonians for decades (including JFK and Jackie), and an ideal place to spend the night while exploring **Virginia wine country.** The quiet, one-mile **Middleburg Historic District** has several historic inns, antiques and fine art, and equestrian shops to help you play the part of moneyed socialite spending a casual weekend in the country. It also holds **The Christmas Sleigh** (5A E. Washington St., 540/687-3665, www. thechristmassleigh.com; 11am-5pm daily, holiday hours may vary), the German-style Christmas shop owned by Linda Tripp (yes, that Linda Tripp) and her husband. The **National Sporting Library & Museum** (102 The Plains Rd., 540/687-6542, www. nationalsporting.org; 10am-5pm Wed.-Sun.; $10 adults, $8 seniors/youth ages 13-18, free for children 12 and under) showcases fine art related to equestrian sports and country activities from the 17th century to present day.

Virginia Horse Racing

While Middleburg gets significantly more crowded, the best time to visit is during one of the famed steeplechase races. Since 1911, the **Middleburg Spring Races** (540/687-6545, www. middleburgspringraces.com) have drawn, as one local newspaper wrote in 1936, "turf folk representing high society of New York, Philadelphia, Baltimore, Washington, and Virginia." The event takes place annually on the third Saturday in April. Similarly, the **Virginia Fall Races** (540/687-9797, www.vafallraces.com) on the second Saturday in October have attracted top equestrians and fox hunters from across the country since 1955. Both happen at the 112-acre **Glenwood Park** (Rte. 626/Foxcroft Rd.,), the oldest continually operating racecourse

The Red Fox Inn & Tavern in Historic Middleburg

in Virginia, where you can reserve a tent for a crowd or tailgate with your family.

RESTAURANTS AND WHERE TO STAY

Rooms in Middleburg book up months in advance for the horse races, so plan ahead. It may be cheaper to rent a car or get car service from DC to Middleburg for these events and make it a day trip.

Established in 1728, **The Red Fox Inn & Tavern** (2 E. Washington St., 540/687-6301, www.redfox.com; $285-355) is the top place to dine and dream in Middleburg. First Lady Jackie Kennedy was a frequent guest, as was, some believe, young George Washington. The inn has 17 historical but luxe rooms—think four-poster beds and luxury toiletries—plus one two-story, two-bedroom house with a full kitchen. And the cozy **tavern** (8am-10am and 5pm-9pm Mon.-Fri., 11:30am-2:30pm and 5pm-9pm Sat., 11:30am-2:30pm and 5pm-8pm Sun.; $28-46) showcases local ingredients and wine.

In the heart of wine and hunt country, the five-star **Goodstone Inn & Restaurant** (36205 Snake Hill Rd., 540/687-3333, www.goodstone.com; $395-545) is an idyllic haven perfect for a romantic getaway, with 18 rooms and suites with their own personalities set on 265 acres. In addition to an outdoor pool, hiking trails, and spa, the estate has a working farm and gardens, which supply the stately **restaurant.**

Salamander Resort & Spa (500 N. Pendleton St., 844/303-2723, www.salamanderresort.com; $385-515) is a getaway itself, as you'll never want to (or need to) leave the 350-acre estate, with 168 contemporary rooms and suites and dozens of amenities and resort activities. Spend the day lounging at the 23,000-square-foot spa and outdoor pool, play tennis or lawn games, or even go horseback riding at the on-site stable. The hotel has several restaurants and bars, as well as kids' activities.

For a quick meal in the village between shopping or wine tasting, **Market Salamander** (200 W. Washington St., 540/687-8011, www.marketsalamander.com; 8am-6pm Mon.-Sat., 8am-4pm Sun.; $5-10) has excellent made-to-order sandwiches and picnic-ready food, with several outdoor tables. Or, grab a coffee, tea, or breakfast or lunch sandwich at **Middleburg Common Grounds** (114 W. Washington St., 540/687-7065, www.middleburgcommongrounds.com; 6am-6pm Mon.-Fri., 7am-6pm Sat.-Sun.; $5-10), with a cozy space to sit and plan your next adventure.

INFORMATION AND SERVICES

The **Middleburg Visitor Center** (12 N. Madison St., 540/687-8888, www.visitmiddleburgva.com; 11am-3pm daily) is in the village, or you can visit www.visitmiddleburgva.com to plan your trip and obtain more information on wineries, shopping, and special events.

TRANSPORTATION

Middleburg is approximately one hour (45 miles/72 kilometers) west of Washington DC. Take I-66 W to US-50 W (exit 57B toward Fair Oaks/Winchester) and continue on US-50 W about 25 miles directly to the historic center. Glenwood Park is just under two miles north of the historic district via Foxcroft Road, and the wineries and inns are spread around Middleburg. If you don't have a car, or want to explore the wineries worry-free, car service is recommended; **Reston Limousine** (703/478-0500, www.restonlimo.com) is popular for point-to-point service to and from the District as well as wine tours. The center of Middleburg is easily walkable, though you'll need transportation to the countryside sights.

Middleburg is approximately 45 minutes (30 miles) from the closest Skyline Drive entrance at Front Royal. Or, head about one hour (36 miles) west to Little Washington, where you can reach Skyline Drive and Luray Caverns via the Thornton Gap entrance.

BACKGROUND

The Landscape...280
History...282
Government and Economy..284
Local Culture...286

The Landscape

GEOGRAPHY

dome of the U.S. Capitol

Washington DC gets a bad reputation for being a swamp, both literally and figuratively. This may be an exaggeration, though it's easy to see why the nickname sticks if you visit during July and August, when the humidity can be overbearing. Built on the banks of the Potomac River, an important waterway for trade and transportation during most of the city's history, the nation's capital is on sturdy land, and while you don't need to worry about sinking into the marsh while exploring the monuments, DC is nonetheless a water town, selected for the prime location nestled between the Potomac and Anacostia Rivers, which connect to the Chesapeake Bay. While part of the National Mall is, indeed, built on marshland, George Washington certainly did not choose swampland for his great experiment.

But, he did choose the site for the strategic location in the middle of the 13 original colonies, easily accessible from the most important ports and the earlier capitals New York and Philadelphia. Today, it comprises 68 square miles between Maryland, Virginia, and the Potomac River. By design, Washington, District of Columbia, is not a state but a territory under federal jurisdiction, created in 1790 from land from the surrounding states specifically to serve as the independent capital of the young nation.

CLIMATE

DC has four distinct seasons—though the temperate and frankly glorious spring and fall are far too short, giving way rather quickly to high heat and humidity for most of the summer and cold, dark winters. The occasional snow or ice storm debilitates the city, which is mocked by northern states for being unable to handle a winter storm and thus shutting down. (But, cut us some slack, because we're the southernmost northern city—or, the northernmost southern city, depending how you want to look at it.) In recent years, the climate has gotten extremely unpredictable, so unless you're traveling in the dead of winter or summer, pack layers and be prepared for sunshine or rain.

ENVIRONMENTAL ISSUES

The unpredictable climate has led to environmental issues, which have an impact on one of DC's top industries after governing: tourism and hospitality. Specifically, the erratic temperatures make predicting the peak bloom of the cherry blossom trees, which draw 1.5 million visitors to DC annually, nearly impossible. In 2017, for example, the blossoms started to bloom early after an exceptionally warm winter, but they were quickly damaged by a cold spell just before reaching their peak. DC had a beautiful display nonetheless, but not to the extent of past years. Not to mention, environmentalists warn that the sheer magnitude of visitors traipsing around the trees at the Tidal Basin each year could lead to the trees' demise.

Another environmental concern is the notorious pollution of the city's rivers. Why can't the home of the Environmental Protection Agency keep its own waterways sewage-free and thriving? Thanks to extensive cleanup efforts, the Potomac River has improved in recent years, but the Anacostia River, DC's "forgotten river," still has a long way to go to address the sediment, chemicals, and sewage as well as, sadly, the garbage floating in the rivers and Tidal Basin. While the rapid growth and development around the District has led to runoff, it's also led to residents waking up to the need to clean up and preserve the natural habitat. If you're interested in learning more about the history of the Anacostia River and present-day environmental challenges, Anacostia Riverkeeper (www.anacostiariverkeeper.org) runs free boat tours. These tours, and more importantly, the cleanup efforts, are funded by 5-cent fee charged for every disposable paper or plastic bag at any business that sells food or alcohol (with a few exceptions for things like restaurant leftovers in a paper bag).

Given the focus on the famous Maryland blue crabs and crab cakes served at many local restaurants, it's important to know that, while the species was overfished about a decade ago, the population has since rebounded, with an estimated 254 million female adult crabs in the Chesapeake Bay at the start of the 2017 crabbing season, comfortably above the recommended 215 million. Still, the overall crab population declined the same year, leading scientists to shorten the crab season by 16 days. You should feel free to enjoy the regional specialty, knowing you're contributing to an important aspect of the economy, and knowing the Bay region is actively addressing this environmental issue.

ANIMALS

You may notice a somewhat unusual animal while walking around the city, particularly the Northwest quadrant: the black squirrel, which will have no qualms sprinting across your path even in heavily trafficked areas. These melanistic squirrels first arrived in DC from Rondeau Provincial Park in Ontario, Canada, which sent eight of them to the National Zoo in 1902, then eight more a few years later, in exchange for some of America's gray squirrels. Rather than put them in a cage, the zoo simply released them into the park. The squirrels thrived in their new habitat, and today, they make up about 25 percent of the District's squirrel population.

History

BIRTH OF THE CAPITAL

Needless to say, George Washington and his contemporaries were not the first people to inhabit the land around the Potomac River. When European settlers first arrived, several Algonquin-speaking tribes lived in the Chesapeake Bay region, including the Piscataway. While colonization forced these tribes to new settlements, or tragic demise, they left their mark in the names of major geographic features; "Potomac" (or "Patowmack," as it was spelled on early maps) is their name for the river that played such an important role in the choice of this region as the capital city, while "Anacostia" is the evolution of "Nacotchtank," as the area tribe was named by Captain John Smith in 1612.

George Washington, however, knew the area perhaps better than anyone in colonial America, having worked as a land surveyor in the region from the age of 17 and having inherited Mount Vernon (on the banks of the Potomac) in his 20s. Washington, Virginia, near Shenandoah National Park, was the first town of many to bear his name. So it's no surprise that, when he led the team to select the site of the new capital city, he chose this area.

After the American Revolution, the United States Constitution called for the creation of "a District (not exceeding ten miles square) as may, by cession of particular states, and the acceptance of Congress, become the seat of the government of the United States." For the Founding Fathers, it was important that the capital remain independent, under federal control and not a state, though this has caused contention in more recent years. Pulling land from Georgetown, which was part of Maryland and remains part of DC today, as well as Alexandria, Virginia (given back in 1846), the location was a compromise between Alexander Hamilton and northern states, who wanted the new federal government to pay the debts of the war, and James Madison and the southern states, who agreed to the plan in exchange for placing the capital in the south.

To build his vision, Washington hired Major Pierre Charles L'Enfant, the French engineer who served with Americans in the war, to design the new capital. He was inspired by the baroque architecture and grand landscapes of Paris and Versailles, with their wide, tree-lined boulevards and major buildings in prominent positions in the city (such as the Capitol and presidential mansion). While his plan was never fully realized, any visitor to both DC and Paris will recognize the similarities.

In August 1814, during the War of 1812, British troops invaded the young capital and burned many of the buildings, including the Capitol, Library of Congress (with 3,000 books), Treasury, and White House, which First Lady Dolley Madison fled in the nick of time. Less than a day after the invasion, thunderstorms put out the fires, and the resourceful government quickly began reconstruction, with the new White House ready for President James Monroe's inauguration in 1817.

THE CIVIL WAR TO THE NEW DEAL

The government and capital continued to thrive—though as northern states began to abolish slavery one by one, tensions heightened between the north and south. Alexandria, a major hub of the slave trade, petitioned the federal government to return the land to Virginia in 1846; just a few years later, the federal government ended slave trading (though, notably, not slavery) in the capital, while newly returned Alexandria continued to sell slaves through the busy port to the more southern plantation states. For a detailed look at the slave trade in Washington DC, visit the corner of 7th Street NW and Independence Avenue NW, near the Federal Aviation Administration. Signs describe the horror of the Williams Slave Pen, where Solomon Northup, whose story was told in *12 Years A Slave,* was held

after being kidnapped. Nearly one-third of the slaves brought to the United States were brought through the ports of DC, Maryland, and Virginia, and many built the new capital city, including structures like the Capitol and White House.

Shortly after Abraham Lincoln was elected the 16th president (in 1860) on an anti-slavery platform, tensions broke. The Confederates seceded, hoping to make Washington DC their capital. Lincoln, who freed the slaves of the District of Columbia eight months prior to the Emancipation Proclamation, built the Union military, bringing troops from all over the country to defend the capital, including many freed blacks.

The Civil War had a huge impact on everyday life in Washington DC—namely, creating massive growth of the federal government, to manage the war effort and then the reconstruction of the nation, and the population, which continued well after the war. Thousands who had moved to the capital to serve in the military or provide service to the war stuck around, and slowly but surely, this swampy backwater with limited infrastructure would grow to become a cosmopolitan city on par with New York and Philadelphia. As the federal government grew in size and scope, so, too, did the District of Columbia, with monuments, museums, and government buildings sprouting up amid the District's creeping borders. This growth and development continued into the 20th century.

CIVIL RIGHTS ERA TO PRESENT DAY

The civil rights era brought turmoil to this racially diverse, growing city, once on the rise but destroyed by the racial divisions continuing to divide America, 100 years after the end of the Civil War and Lincoln's assassination in Ford's Theatre. Nearly 250,000 people gathered on the National Mall to watch Martin Luther King Jr. deliver his "I Have A Dream" speech from the steps of the Lincoln Memorial on August 28, 1963. And less than five years later, when he was assassinated, the District of Columbia was torn to shreds by five days of violent riots, which burned many of the vibrant African American neighborhoods, once centers of jazz and culture, to the ground. As in so many cities in America, the white and middle class populations fled to the nearby suburbs, leaving burned-out, and increasingly crime-ridden, DC to deal with the remains. Through the 1980s and early 1990s, Mayor Marion Barry, one of the most iconic and controversial figures of late 20th century DC, brought more attention to DC, first in his work as a civil rights leader and popular city official who brought social programs and growth projects to the city. His waning years as mayor were notorious because of scandal, when he claimed "bitch set me up" during a crack cocaine sting at a downtown hotel.

The 1990s brought reinvestment in the city, and interest once again in moving to the federal metropolis, and slowly but surely, the city rebuilt after the turmoil of the 1970s and 1980s. With Presidents Clinton and Bush II, the federal government, and the city it calls home, began growing once again. As tanks rolled into the streets on September 11, 2001, the future of the city was briefly uncertain, but again, more federal growth in the aftermath of the terrorist attack and the wars in Afghanistan and Iraq led to more growth, period.

When President Barack Obama was inaugurated on January 20, 2009, in the largest inauguration to date with some 1.8 million people crowding the National Mall and the city's hotels and businesses, Washington DC finally seemed to have overcome the turbulence of the 20th century, embarking on a renaissance of growth and innovation that continues today.

Government and Economy

TAXATION WITHOUT REPRESENTATION

"Taxation without representation" is the way of life for Washingtonians, because, as the Founding Fathers intended, Washington DC remains a territory of the federal government rather than a state. Until 1961, Washington residents had no voice in the government, but the 23rd Amendment gave them three electoral votes in the presidential election—the same as the least populous state—and these votes have gone to the Democratic Party candidate ever since. Since 1970, the District has, theoretically, had representation in the House of Representatives, as well, but while the at-large delegate has an office on Capitol Hill, she cannot vote. Of course, like the residents of the 13 original colonies, who were required to pay taxes to the King of England without having representation in the British Parliament, residents of Washington DC are still required to pay federal taxes, despite the fact that their legally elected Representative cannot voice their concerns on federal tax policy, or any other policy, for that matter.

The District of Columbia Home Rule Act of 1973 allowed DC a mayor and 13-member city council to make laws and manage services, schools, and social and cultural programs for the increasingly growing population. But, Congress still has the final say—like when DC voted to legalize medical marijuana in 1998, for example, and Congress prohibited the city from using funds to start the program. In 2014, voters legalized possession by nearly 65 percent, but Congress continues to try to limit DC's ability to regulate the sale of the substance even today.

A COMPANY TOWN

If you aren't comfortable talking about, or hearing about, politics and policy differences—well, you'd better get comfortable, because Washington DC is a company town, and policy is the product. Nearly one in three jobs in the District is a federal government job, with many DC residents working in these roles; the rest are filled by residents of neighboring suburbs in Maryland and Virginia, who, while they may not have a DC zip code, spend their workdays, and many evening and weekend hours, contributing to the economy.

As for the rest of jobs in the District? It's hard to get a totally accurate count, but it's safe to say that most of them are related to the government in some way: lobbyists and lawyers and communications experts employed by the famous firms on K Street, or representing companies, trade associations, and constituencies large and small; a massive media presence, who report on the minutiae of politics and life in DC, and hold elected officials accountable; private consultants who are hired at large salaries to manage government projects when federal employees can't, or won't; nonprofits and charities, who either try to influence or fight the government at any given time; think tanks that, well, think about the issues (and sometimes provide recommendations); international bodies, like the World Bank, and international embassies, because this is the most important city in the world, if you ask a Washingtonian; even hospitality employees, who have undoubtedly heard many state secrets as those government employees meet with reporters or friends across the aisle for clandestine cocktails in restaurants and hotel bars across the city. And everyone, from the head of the public relations firm to the bartender to the reporter, has an opinion, even if the report claims they're neutral.

In other words, you can't escape politics in DC—but really, why would you want to? And the key, whatever your politics, is that there's someone here who's working for your candidate or your cause—even if they voted the other way.

Washington DC does have other important industries. Related to hospitality and tourism, DC has a booming dining and nightlife scene, and more and more critically acclaimed chefs are setting up shop in this city where there's always disposable income. Increasingly, there are niche industries, too—food manufacturers and distilleries, boutiques and designers, and small businesses of all shapes and sizes—though, of course, they'll all be glad for the gossip column blurb when the VIP patronizes their business.

Local Culture

DIVERSITY

Washington DC is a racially and culturally diverse city where all races, ethnicities, sexual orientations, and backgrounds are welcome and represented. And we mean diverse: Of the nearly 700,000 residents, 47.7 percent are black or African American, 36.4 percent are white, 10.9 percent are Hispanic or Latino, and 4.1 percent are Asian. The demographics have shifted rather rapidly; until 2011, the population was 50.7 percent black or African American, the first city in the nation to have a black majority, but this is no longer the case. As DC grows and neighborhoods once in turmoil in parts of Northeast and Southeast are now experiencing growth—and getting very expensive—white people, especially young white people, are moving to the city in droves, while black and immigrant families who have historically occupied these neighborhoods since the mid-20th century are moving to the more affordable suburbs in Maryland and Virginia.

LITTLE ETHIOPIA

Washington DC has a large Ethiopian population, and the Washington metro region has the largest Ethiopian population in the country. While Ethiopian immigrants are increasingly priced out of the District and now live and open businesses in suburbs like Silver Spring, Maryland, and Alexandria, Virginia, parts of the U Street Corridor and Shaw around 9th Street NW are still known as "Little Ethiopia," as evidenced by the many Ethiopian restaurants. It's more likely these days, however, that you'll encounter a young Ethiopian immigrant driving your Uber or Lyft, rather than opening a restaurant.

LGBTQ LIFE AND CULTURE

In 2017, Gallup found 8.6 percent of DC residents self-identify as gay, lesbian, bisexual, or transgender; Vermont came in second, with 5.3 percent. According to the U.S. Census, 4 percent of DC households are same-sex couples, compared to the national average of about 1 percent—and DC legalized same-sex marriage in 2009, well before many states. Dupont Circle has historically been the center of LGBTQ life and culture in DC since the 1970s, and while 17th Street has several of the most popular gay bars and annual events like Capital Pride and the High-Heel Drag Race, the neighborhood isn't really seen as the gay community hub anymore, as gay bars are everywhere throughout the city—and the LGBTQ community is wholly embraced.

MUSIC AND THE ARTS

Believe it or not, Washington, DC is an artsy town, home to world-class theaters and performing arts venues, outside-the-box troupes, and concert halls and music clubs even the professionals love. If you're lucky, you'll see street musicians performing around Metro stations or busy, downtown intersections, some of them large bands, or you can always go to Meridian Hill Park to see the famous drum circle on Sunday afternoons.

Historically, DC was one of the nation's hubs for African American performing arts (even before Harlem), especially jazz. Duke Ellington was born in Washington DC and spent much of his life here, starting his career playing in the city's jazz clubs around "Black Broadway," along with stars like Ella Fitzgerald, Marvin Gaye, and The Supremes, until the riots of 1968 decimated the area, which didn't bounce back until the 1990s. Today, you can walk by the ghosts of some of these clubs, including Bohemian Caverns on U Street, or listen at Blues Alley in Georgetown and even The John F. Kennedy Center for the Performing Arts, which has a robust jazz program.

In the 1960s and 1970s, DC gave birth to an important musical tradition: go-go, made famous by Chuck Brown, "Godfather of Go-Go," who lived in DC most of his life, though there were dozens of go-go groups in the Washington area. At go-go shows, the music continues seemingly non-stop for hours. Today, you can see some of the remaining top go-go bands, like Rare Essence and Experience Unlimited (EU), at The Howard Theatre and The Lincoln Theatre.

In the 1980s and 1990s, DC had an influential hardcore punk movement, as well, with bands like Minor Threat and Bad Brains creating socially conscious music.

ESSENTIALS

Transportation 288
Health and Safety 293
Travel Tips 295

Transportation

Ronald Reagan Washington
National Airport

GETTING THERE

AIR

The Washington metropolitan region is served by three airports.

Ronald Reagan Washington National Airport (DCA, 2401 S. Smith Blvd, Arlington, Virginia, www.flyreagan.com) is just over the DC line in Arlington, Virginia. It's 10-20 minutes from the city center by car via the George Washington Memorial Parkway, and 20 minutes from Metro Center via the Metro Blue and Yellow Lines (National Airport station). This small, easy-to-navigate airport provides service on 10 domestic carriers, and while it's the most convenient, flights can be a little more expensive.

Washington Dulles International Airport (IAD, 1 Saarinen Cir., Dulles, Virginia, www.fly-dulles.com) is in Dulles, Virginia, about 45-60 minutes (26 miles) by car via I-66 West or the George Washington Memorial Parkway/VA-267 West and the Dulles Access Road; follow signs for airport traffic to avoid the toll. This is the largest airport in the region, serving national and international destinations via many major carriers. Leave yourself plenty of time to get to the airport, especially during weekday rush hour (3pm-7pm). Taxis cost $70-100 with tip each way, though ride-hailing app services cost as little as $35-40. From the airport, you can get an airport-approved Washington Flyer taxi to your destination, or have your Uber or Lyft driver pick you up at the arrivals level.

Dulles is accessible by public transportation, too. Take the Metro Silver Line to Wiehle-Reston East station, about 40 minutes from Metro Center. From there, catch the Silver Line Express Bus to the terminal, which costs $5 for the 15-minute trip. This route may feel inefficient, but it can be faster than driving during rush hour. Eventually, the Metro Silver Line will go directly to the airport; construction is expected to be completed in 2019.

Baltimore/Washington International Thurgood Marshall Airport (BWI, 7035 Elm Rd., Baltimore, Maryland, www.bwiairport.com) is another option for domestic budget carriers and a few international carriers, including Air Canada, British Airways, and Wow Air. It's about an hour from DC via the Baltimore-Washington Parkway, but only 30 minutes from Union Station via Amtrak or 50 minutes via MARC (Maryland Area Regional Commuter) train; take your train to BWI Marshall Airport and catch a free shuttle every six minutes. (If you time it correctly, it's possible to get from Union Station to your gate in one hour.)

CAR

"Inside the Beltway" is the phrase used to describe the political baseball in DC, played by career politicians and lobbyists and media and Washington insiders, and often has a negative connotation to anyone who doesn't live here. Where does it come from? These Beltway insiders live and work within the Capital Beltway, or I-495, the 64-mile highway that encircles Washington DC and a few close suburbs of Maryland and Virginia (like Chevy Chase and McLean, where many lobbyists live), and a road you'll probably have to travel if you're arriving by car. The Beltway connects to I-95, the longest north-south interstate in America, and it's notorious for heavy traffic, especially during rush hours (6am-9:30am weekday mornings and roughly 3pm-7pm on weekday evenings). Other major routes through DC include US-50, which crosses the National Mall, and I-66, which ends at the road's easternmost point in DC.

If you're driving to DC, your best bet is to ditch your car at your hotel and utilize public transportation, taxis and ride-sharing apps, and walking. In addition to heavy traffic in and around the immediate vicinity of DC and unexpected road closures due to motorcades and security concerns, parking can be difficult; parking garages are typically expensive, and street parking is challenging to find and maneuver, especially with so many one-way streets in the city.

TRAIN

Amtrak (800/872-7245, www.amtrak.com) serves **Union Station** (50 Massachusetts Ave. NE, 202/289-1908, www.unionstationdc.com) on Capitol Hill. Amtrak Acela Express service runs hourly to major East Coast cities including Baltimore, Philadelphia, New York, and Boston, getting to New York's Penn Station in less than three hours, though tickets for the higher-speed service are often more expensive unless you plan far in advance. (Don't be surprised if you see DC celebrities, or even real celebrities, traveling this route.) The Northeast Regional is the other major East Coast route, serving dozens of stations between Boston and Newport News, Virginia. Other services passing through DC include Silver Service/Palmetto from New York to Miami, Florida; the Capitol

Limited and Cardinal, which head west to Chicago; and the Vermonter, which starts in Washington DC and travels to cities in Connecticut and Vermont.

Union Station is easy to navigate and generally efficient, with quick-service dining and shops on the same level as the tracks, as well as table-service restaurants and a food court. Amtrak announces the track early, sometimes more than one hour in advance, so travelers line up at the tracks, but you can arrive 10-15 minutes before the train and have plenty of time to spare if you're not checking luggage; there's plenty of space to bring normal-sized luggage on board. If you're traveling first class or have ClubAcela or United Club membership, you can enter the lounge and board the train through the lounge about 10 minutes earlier than other passengers, allowing you time to choose your seat and get comfortable before the rush.

From Union Station, you can catch the MARC train (866/743-3682, http://mta.maryland.gov/marc-train), Maryland's commuter rail service, a cheap and relatively efficient route to Baltimore and Baltimore Washington International Airport, as well as the Virginia Railway Express (703/684-1001, www.vre.org), Virginia's commuter rail service to suburbs of Northern Virginia. Union Station connects to the Metro Red Line and Metrobus service, as well as DC Circulator and tour buses.

BUS

Greyhound (202/789-4318, www.greyhound.com) arrives at and departs from Union Station (50 Massachusetts Ave. NE, 202/289-1908, www.unionstationdc.com) on Capitol Hill; the bus terminal is connected to the main station terminal, so just follow the signs for buses. The bus terminal does not have any amenities, so grab food or coffee from the shops in the train terminal before heading to your bus.

There are several relatively inexpensive bus services between DC and New York City, which are especially popular among 20-something travelers. From Union Station, BoltBus (877/265-8287, www.boltbus.com) and the double-decker Megabus (online reservations only at www.megabus.com) have daily, nonstop departures to New York as low as $15-20 each way, if you're willing to book a few weeks in advance; both offer service to a few other cities, as well. Washington Deluxe (866/287-6932, www.washny.com) has departures from Union Station and Dupont Circle Metro station to several stops in New York, with prices ranging $20-30 each way in advance.

GETTING AROUND
NAVIGATING THE CITY
Washington DC is a walkable city, with broad, well-maintained streets and sidewalks. And it's relatively easy to navigate, especially around the central tourist areas like the National Mall and Capitol Hill, once you understand the layout. True to L'Enfant's original plan, DC has four "quadrants" around the U.S. Capitol: Northeast, Southeast, Northwest, and Southwest. When traveling to a new address, check for the quadrant signifier (NE, SE, NW, SW), because some streets will cross two quadrants. Most, but not all, of the streets are arranged in a grid around the U.S. Capitol. The numbered streets run north to south, the lettered streets run east to west, and the diagonal streets are named

after states (Pennsylvania Avenue and Massachusetts Avenue are two you'll likely encounter). There's no J Street, so don't be alarmed when you walk from H Street to I Street, which is sometimes written out as "Eye Street." And "B Street" is now Constitution Avenue and Independence Avenue. The letters stop at W Street, which is near the boundary of the original capital city; now, as you pass W Street and head north into Columbia Heights and Upper Northwest, east-west street names will continue in alphabetical order (Belmont, Clifton, Euclid, Fairmont, etc.) and start over again until you reach Maryland, always skipping X, Y, and Z.

PUBLIC TRANSPORTATION

Washington Metropolitan Area Transit Authority (202/637-7000, www.wmata.com) operates **Metrorail** (more commonly referred to simply as "Metro"), DC's network of underground and above-ground subway service, and **Metrobus.** Together, the services reach every neighborhood in DC as well as nearby Maryland and Virginia suburbs. While locals love to joke about the inefficiency of Metro and frequent delays during rush hour, the rail system is simple to navigate, cheap, and efficient, most of the time, especially if you're traveling across quadrants to destinations close to a station. While Georgetown and some farther-flung destinations, like Union Market and the U.S. National Arboretum, don't have stations nearby, most everywhere else you'll visit does, especially downtown and around the National Mall and Capitol Hill. Metrorail operates 5am-11:30pm Monday through Thursday, 5am-1am Friday, 7am-1am Saturday, and 8am-11pm Sunday; trains run anywhere from every four minutes during rush hour to every 10-20 minutes in the evening, but you'll want to check the trip planner for the last train from your particular station.

Metrobus, on the other hand, is a little more difficult to navigate, with 325 routes hitting more than 11,000 stops; don't hop on a bus unless you know where you're going. **DC Circulator** (www.dccirculator) is more straightforward, with six routes in prime tourism areas; this is a good option to get to Georgetown or to travel around the National Mall. For both bus options, schedules vary by route.

Metrorail, Metrobus, and DC Circulator accept the reloadable SmarTrip card, which you can purchase at blue fare vending machines in every Metro station. Each person must have their own card to travel on these services, though up to two children under age 5 may travel for free with each paying adult. Metrorail fares vary depending on how far you're traveling and the time of day, with peak fares ($2.25-6 per ride) from opening to 9:30am and 3pm-7pm weekdays; Metrorail accepts only SmarTrip cards. Metrobus fares are $2 for regular routes, $4.25 for express routes ($1 for regular routes and $2.10 for express routes for seniors or those with disabilities), but can be paid with SmarTrip or cash with exact change on the bus. If you're planning to use public transportation a lot, a SmarTrip card provides free bus-to-bus transfers and discounted rail-bus transfers.

The **DC Streetcar** (www.dcstreetcar.com, 6am-midnight Mon.-Thurs., 6am-2am Fri., 8am-2am Sat., 8am-10pm Sun. and holidays) operates every 10-15 minutes between Union Station and the Atlas District/H Street Corridor. The streetcar is currently free, though it's not especially efficient; it's a little easier to take a taxi or ride-sharing service to your destination on H Street NE, or even walk from Union Station if you're a fast walker. From Union Station, follow the signs for the streetcar through the bus station and look for yellow DC Streetcar signs to lead you to the stop outside the station.

As in any major city, be aware of your surroundings at transportation stations, and you'll want to use common sense with regards to your valuables and traveling late at night, but generally, you can feel safe using all of these services.

TAXIS AND RIDE-HAILING APPS

You can hail taxis throughout the city, though there's no one, main taxi company, so service and car quality can vary greatly. Taxis are required to accept credit cards, and most have touch-screen payment machines in the back seat, but it's honestly not uncommon to encounter a taxi driver whose machine doesn't work. Rates are $3.50 for the first one-eighth mile and $2.16 for each additional mile. The DC Department of For-Hire Vehicles has an authorized mobile app, www.dc-taxi.com, to allow you to hail and pay for a vetted taxi. Virginia-based taxi companies, including Washington Flyer (888/927-4359, www.flydulles.com/iad/washington-flyer) and Red Top Cab of Arlington (703/522-3333, www.redtopcab.com) can pick you up to take you to the Virginia airports, and both accept reservations.

Ride-hailing apps are just one of the reasons why there has been such a boom in more far-flung parts of Northeast and Southeast Washington, and these apps, including Uber (www.uber.com), Lyft (www.lyft.com), and Via (http://ridewithvia.com), are strongly recommended for travel around the District and to/from nearby suburbs in Maryland and Virginia. You can save a substantial amount of money—as much as 50 percent—using lower-cost services like UberX to get to and from the airports versus a taxi. Uber and Lyft can pick you up at all three airports; check in the app for your meeting point.

DRIVING

Unless you like the adventure of confusing traffic circles, surprising one-way streets, road blockades and motorcades, and of course, crazy traffic, it's best to leave driving to the pros, and utilize public transportation, taxis/ride-sharing apps, and walking to get around the city. If you decide you want a car—say, to explore the U.S. National Arboretum, or drive to Mount Vernon—there are major car rental agencies convenient to downtown, and car-sharing services like Car2go (877/488-4224, www.car2go.com) and ZipCar (866/494-7227, www.zipcar.com) have pickup points around the city and rentals by the minute, hour, or day.

BICYCLE

DC is a great city for cycling, with a growing number of on-street bike lanes and marked routes as well as parks and trails to explore. If you want to explore DC by two wheels, you'll be in good company—about 4 percent of Washingtonians citywide bike to work, with as many as 20 percent from neighborhoods in Upper Northwest. For traveling from point to point around the city, Capital Bikeshare (www.capitalbikeshare.com) has 440 stations and nearly 4,000 bikes available 24/7 daily in DC, Maryland, and Virginia. You can rent a bike for $2 per ride, up to 30 minutes, or purchase a day pass for $8 or three-day pass for $17. When you're finished, just drop the bike at any station with space. If you want to rent a bike for a longer journey, such as to ride the Mount Vernon Trail to Virginia, you can rent bikes, helmets, and locks from **Bike and Roll** (202/842-2453, www.bike-androlldc.com), which has locations at the National Mall, Union Station, and Old Town Alexandria. Increasingly, many hotels offer bikes for guest use, as well.

Health and Safety

HOSPITALS AND EMERGENCY SERVICES

DC has several major emergency rooms. The closest to downtown tourist areas is **George Washington University Hospital** (900 23rd St. NW, 202/715-4000, www.gwhospital.com) in Foggy Bottom, which treated President Ronald Reagan when he was shot in 1981. Other emergency rooms close to the city center include **Howard University Hospital** (2041 Georgia Ave. NW, 202/865-6100, www.huhealthcare.com) in Shaw, **MedStar Washington Hospital Center** (110 Irving St. NW, 202/877-7000, www.medstarwashington.org) near Columbia Heights, and **MedStar Georgetown University Hospital** (3800 Reservoir Rd. NW, 202/444-2000, www.medstargeorgetown.org). If you're having an emergency, don't try to figure out which emergency room is closest to you—just dial 911.

For urgent but not emergency situations, **MedStar PromptCare** (www.medstarhealth.org) offers walk-in services in **Capitol Hill** (228 7th St. SE, 855/546-1970; 8am-8pm daily) and **Adams Morgan** (1805 Columbia Rd., 855/546-1973; 8am-8pm daily). In addition, several **CVS Pharmacy** (www.cvspharmacy.com/minuteclinic) stores operate walk-in clinics; hours and locations vary.

PHARMACIES

CVS Pharmacy (www.cvspharmacy.com) has dozens of stores in the Washington metropolitan area, with prescription pharmacy services as well as over-the-counter medicines and personal care products; several locations are open 24 hours daily, including the store and pharmacy one block from the Metro on **Dupont Circle** (6 Dupont Cir., 202/785-1466, www.cvspharmacy.com). Walgreens, Rite Aid, and local pharmacies are available, as well.

CRIME

In the latter half of the 20th century, DC got a bad reputation for violent, often drug-related crime, which peaked in the 1980s and early 1990s as the nation's capital earned its "murder capital" nickname and got caught up in the crack epidemic. This has changed, and tourists do not need to fear visiting any major sight, or any neighborhood in this guide, for that matter, especially during daylight hours.

As in any major city, however,

tourists are advised to use common sense, in any neighborhood: Take care with your valuables, don't talk on the phone while pulling out your money to buy a Metro fare card, use public transportation and stick to well-lit and busy streets at night, and avoid walking alone on deserted streets or empty parks in the middle of the night, especially if you're not familiar with the neighborhood. And be wary of locals' advice. We never fear our city and will venture to the most desolate corner for interesting food or off-the-beaten-path sightseeing or art, but it doesn't mean visitors should necessarily walk there.

Thanks especially to the ease of ride-sharing apps, many neighborhoods once considered dangerous are experiencing a boom of growth and development. While neighborhoods like the Atlas District/H Street Corridor, Anacostia, and Union Market/Ivy City, best accessed by taxis/ride-sharing apps, have important tourist sights, growing dining and nightlife scenes, and friendly residents, keep your wits about you at night, when parts of these neighborhoods can become more deserted. However, it's important to note that no neighborhood, including the National Mall or Dupont Circle or Georgetown, for example, is immune to crime, and you're advised to take care anywhere you go. When in doubt, use public transportation or taxis/ride-sharing apps.

HOMELESS POPULATION

More than 7,000 people in Washington DC are homeless, and while walking in almost any part of town, especially downtown and near popular tourist sights, parks, and major Metro stations, you're likely to encounter friendly (but persistent) panhandlers. It's kind to give them your change if you desire, but you will not encounter any problems if you choose to keep walking. If you'd like to help the homeless while you're exploring the city, look for people selling copies of Street Sense (www.streetsense. org), a biweekly newspaper written and sold primarily by the DC homeless population.

REGULATED SUBSTANCES

The drinking age in the United States is 21 years old, and this is strictly enforced in Washington DC; don't be surprised if you're asked for identification at restaurants and bars, even if you're in your 20s or 30s, and expect to show identification to enter live music venues and dance clubs. While some venues, including the 9:30 Club and Black Cat, have some "all-ages" or "18 and over" shows, most nightlife venues are 21-plus. Bars in DC may serve alcohol until 2am on weekdays, 3am Friday and Saturday, though a lot of bars will shut down around 1:30am or 2am on weekends and much earlier on weekdays—DC is generally an early town.

Smoking is prohibited in all enclosed public spaces in DC, including restaurants, bars, and clubs, though there are a few cigar bars.

In 2015, possession of small amounts of marijuana for personal use became legal in Washington DC (though Congress wasn't happy about it). Adults 21 and older may possess two ounces or less of marijuana and transfer one ounce or less to another adult, as long as no money is exchanged. A growing number of local businesses legally sell marijuana paraphernalia or other items like T-shirts and provide a "free gift" of marijuana with purchase. You may use marijuana on private property, but it's prohibited on public property, and this law is enforced especially on federal property—so don't try to smoke around the monuments, because you can be arrested. (It's not uncommon to catch a whiff around populous nightlife areas like the U Street Corridor on a weekend night, but we can't recommend you take the risk in public, because arrest is a possibility.) If you do acquire marijuana in DC, don't cross the border: It's illegal for all purposes in Virginia and illegal for recreational use in Maryland, though possession of 10 grams or less has been decriminalized and the state is working toward establishing a medical marijuana program.

Travel Tips

ACCESS FOR TRAVELERS WITH DISABILITIES

DC is relatively flat and easy to get around, including in the main tourist areas, and even sights like the Lincoln Memorial and Thomas Jefferson Memorial have elevators. Most attractions, museums, and performance venues offer accessible tours, seating, and other accommodations, and many offer frequent ASL-interpreted tours and performances. One exception may be Georgetown, which has hilly, uneven sidewalks. All Metro stations, rail cars, and buses are accessible, and there's an elevator at every station; if the elevator is not working, Washington Metropolitan Area Transit Authority will provide free transportation to the next station. Visit the Metro Transit Accessibility Center (600 5th St. NW) for the Metro Disability ID card, which provides fare discounts for up to one month.

TRAVELING WITH CHILDREN

Washington DC is an excellent city for a family vacation, with a wealth of free, fun, and educational sights, museums, and activities. No matter how long you're visiting, you can spend your entire trip taking advantage of free activities, though attractions with admission fees typically offer discounts for children and free tickets for very young children with paying adults. Most of DC's hotels and popular, bustling restaurants welcome families with children, with the exception of a few of the finest restaurants specializing in tasting menus—your kid is unlikely to enjoy Komi or The Inn at Little Washington, and nor will anyone else around you. For quick meals when kids are restless, diners, fast-casual restaurants, and food trucks are plentiful.

SENIOR TRAVELERS

While most of the major sights and museums are free for everyone, those with an entrance fee typically offer discounts for seniors, though age requirements may vary. The Senior SmarTrip card allows adults age 65 and older to get reduced fares on Metrorail and Metrobus, which can be purchased at the Metro sales office

(600 5th St. NW) by showing government identification.

LGBTQ TRAVELERS

Headquarters of the Human Rights Campaign and home to annual pride events, Washington DC is extremely friendly to LGBTQ travelers. The city celebrated the Supreme Court's 2015 gay marriage ruling near the White House, which was illuminated in rainbow colors, and DC's status as one of the most gay-friendly cities in America has not changed with the new administration taking office. (If anything, it's become even more gay friendly as locals resist the administration's rhetoric about social issues.) Two local LGBTQ publications, *Washington Blade* (www.washingtonblade.com), which has been around since 1969, and *Metro Weekly* (www.metroweekly.com), provide news and information on DC's LGBTQ community and events.

INTERNATIONAL TRAVELERS

All international visitors are required to have a valid passport to enter the United States. Canadian citizens traveling by air need a passport or NEXUS card, but those arriving by land may show an enhanced driver's license/identification card instead. Depending on your country of origin, a visa may be required, or you may be eligible for the Visa Waiver Program (VWP), allowing travel to the United States for business or leisure for 90 days or less without a visa. All visitors and their baggage may be subject to an interview or inspection by U.S. Customs and Border Protection; be prepared to provide details about the purpose of your visit, where you are staying, and when you plan to leave. For more information on entry requirements and restrictions, including prohibited items, visit www.cbp.gov.

MONEY
DC ON A BUDGET

Washington DC has the third-highest cost of living in the United States, after San Francisco and New York City, and expensive prices extend to tourism. Luckily, the best sights are free, and it's possible to spend your entire trip exploring the national parks and monuments and Smithsonian Institution museums, which offer free guided tours and other special programs. In addition, the Kennedy Center has a free performance at 6pm, every day of the year, including Christmas Day and New Year's Day, while other theaters and performance venues will offer last-minute or under-30 discounts on tickets for many shows.

Generally, hotels are expensive year-round, and rates are exorbitant during major events like the National Cherry Blossom Festival and presidential inaugurations, though conferences can cause rates to spike regularly, too. Book in advance, or look at some of the new, lower-cost pod-style hotels; conference hotels that gear to business travelers (like the Washington Hilton) often have good deals on weekends. Many Washingtonians put their homes on Airbnb, and you can find private apartments in prime neighborhoods like Dupont Circle and the U Street Corridor for much cheaper than hotels.

Restaurants and bars have gotten more expensive; extravagant tasting menus are the trend, and it's not uncommon to spend $15 (or more) on a cocktail. At the same time, foodies on a budget will find good diners, delicious fast-casual dining, food trucks, and markets with inexpensive vendors serving the city's innovative cuisine without the restaurant markup. If you're willing to dine 3pm-7pm, even some of the finest restaurants have happy hour drink and appetizer specials, which you can make into a meal. The Riggsby has one of the best, but almost every nice restaurant with a bar has happy hour. And many restaurants offer late-night happy hours, like Hank's Oyster Bar's late-night oyster deals, or half-price bottles of wine on slower weekdays. If you're a big eater, weekend brunch is extremely popular—almost every restaurant serves it—and can provide bigger bang for your buck with an abundance of food and bottomless beverages.

Save money getting around by buying a SmarTrip card and taking advantage of public transportation.

Note that some restaurants, including some fast-casual chains and coffee shops, are moving to cash-free payment, though most still take cash.

SALES TAX AND TIPPING

The DC sales tax is 5.75 percent (groceries and prescription and nonprescription drugs are exempt). Tourists need to account for the much higher tax on dining and accommodations; DC charges 10 percent on restaurant meals, alcohol (both in restaurants/bars and liquor stores), and rental cars, and 14.8 percent on hotel accommodations.

Standard tipping guidelines in the United States apply in DC, although 20 percent is the minimum for good service in restaurants, bars, and lounges. In many quick-service restaurants and independent coffee shops, you'll have the option to add tip via the touch-screen payment terminal; if you're grabbing a bottle of water, for example, a tip is not necessary, but if you're ordering made-to-order food or beverages, add $1-5, depending on the cost of your order. The same rules apply for tip jars; it's much appreciated if you drop the change in the jar at a food truck. In bars, $1 per drink is acceptable, but tip more generously if you're ordering complicated cocktails, getting advice from the bartender on wines or beers, or sitting at the bar for a long time.

TOURIST INFORMATION
VISITOR CENTERS AND INFORMATION

Destination DC (901 7th St. NW, 202/789-7000, www.washington. org) is the official tourism office for Washington DC. Explore their comprehensive website before your trip, and download their free, interactive guide, or place an order for a paper copy, in advance.

Around the **National Mall** (www. nps.gov/nama), you'll find **National Park Service kiosks** providing information, maps, and souvenirs; the National Park Service website is the best resource for up-to-date information on closures and special events.

Located in the Smithsonian Castle, the **Smithsonian Visitor Center** (1000 Jefferson Dr., 202/633-1000, www.si.edu/visit; 8:30am-5:30pm daily) has information about every museum and volunteers who can help you decide which museum to tackle first. The Smithsonian website has downloadable maps and brochures, as well as a mobile app to help you access information while you're on the go.

The **White House Visitor Center** (1450 Pennsylvania Ave. NW, 202/208-1631, www.nps.gov/whho; 7:30am-4pm daily) and **U.S. Capitol Visitor**

Center (1st St. & E. Capitol St. SE, 202/226-8000, www.visitthecapitol. gov; 8:30am-4:30pm Mon.-Sat.) have exhibits, information on tours, and gift shops.

COMMUNICATIONS AND MEDIA
TELEPHONE

In the United States, dial 1 followed by the area code (202 in DC) and the seven-digit phone number. There are several area codes in Virginia and Maryland. Calls to area codes 800, 866, 887, and 888 are toll-free from any U.S. phone.

In case of an emergency, dial 911 from any U.S. phone to reach emergency services.

POSTAL SERVICES

The **United States Postal Service** (www.usps.com) has several branches throughout the city; check the USPS website for locations and hours. There is no central post office in DC, as the historic post offices have since been turned into the Trump International Hotel Washington, D.C. and the Smithsonian's National Postal Museum.

WEIGHTS AND MEASURES

Washington DC is in the eastern time zone and observes daylight saving time between the second Sunday of March and the first Sunday of November. International travelers may need an adapter and a converter for appliances to fit the outlets; in the United States, electricity is set at 110 volts. Most hotels will provide hair dryers, and inexpensive personal appliances and device chargers are available at most pharmacies.

RESOURCES

Suggested Reading

HISTORY

Lewis, Tom. *Washington: A History of Our National City.* New York: Basic Books, 2015. This is a comprehensive but readable introduction to the history of the nation's capital, describing in captivating detail everything from how George Washington chose the site to the impact of the 20th century's wars and riots on the city and its residents.

Savage, Kirk. *Monument Wars: Washington, D.C., the National Mall, and the Transformation of the Memorial Landscape.* Berkeley: University of California Press, 2009. Discover American history and key players through the dramatic story of the development of the National Mall and the capital's iconic monuments and memorials.

POLITICS AND MEDIA

Bernstein, Carl, and Woodward, Bob. *All the President's Men.* New York: Simon & Schuster, 1974. Before you visit The Watergate Hotel, read the *Washington Post* investigative reporters' telling of how they uncovered the political scandal of the 20th century.

Brower, Kate Anderson. *The Residence: Inside the Private World of the White House.* New York: HarperCollins, 2015. Fans of *Downton Abbey* will devour this White House correspondent's look at life inside the presidential mansion, based on her interviews with the household staff for first families from the Kennedys to the Obamas.

Caro, Robert A. *Master of the Senate.* New York: Vintage Books/Random House, 2002. At over 1,000 pages, this biography of Lyndon Johnson's 12 years in the U.S. Senate provides in-depth insight into power in Washington, and how Congress really works.

Leibovich, Mark. *This Town: Two Parties and a Funeral—plus plenty of valet parking!—in America's Gilded Capital.* New York: Penguin Group, 2013. In his juicy tell-all, a *New York Times* correspondent introduces you to the city's power players and wannabes, and how things get done in "this town," as the locals call Washington DC.

Wolff, Michael. *Fire and Fury: Inside the Trump White House.* New York: Henry Holt and Company, 2018. Washington gleefully ate up this exposé of the new political landscape, a tome that blurs the line between fact and fiction.

ARTS, CULTURE, AND SOCIETY

Davis, Margaret Leslie. *Mona Lisa in Camelot: How Jacqueline Kennedy and Da Vinci's Masterpiece Charmed and Captivated a Nation*. New York: Da Capo Press/Perseus Books Group, 2008. Art lovers will enjoy this delightful read about first lady Jackie Kennedy's mission to bring the Mona Lisa to the National Gallery.

Hopkinson, Natalie. *Go-Go Live: The Musical Life and Death of a Chocolate City*. Durham: Duke University Press, 2012. A former *Washington Post* reporter explores black life and culture and racial divisions in DC through the lens of the city's homegrown music genre.

FICTION

Buckley, Christopher. *Thank You for Smoking*. New York: Random House, 1994. There's a lot of truth in this satire about lobbying, in which cigarette company spokesman Nick Naylor promotes the benefits of smoking.

Cutler, Jessica. *The Washingtonienne*. New York: Hachette Book Group, 2005. Long before the days when adult film stars and the Steele Dossier were part of the Washington news cycle, a Hill-staffer-turned-sex-blogger lit up the local gossip columns with her salacious novel inspired by her real-life exploits with DC power players.

Kafka-Gibbons, Paul. *Dupont Circle*. New York: Houghton-Mifflin, 2001. In this charming romantic comedy, meet the diverse residents of Dupont Circle as the DC Court of Appeals prepares to hear a groundbreaking case about same-sex marriage.

Mengestu, Dinaw. *The Beautiful Things That Heaven Bears*. New York: Penguin Group, 2007. Both joyful and heartbreaking, this novel tells the story of an Ethiopian immigrant who owns a bodega near Logan Circle, and his budding romance with a white woman who moves into the neighborhood during a time of racial divisions in the city.

Internet Resources

GENERAL INFORMATION

DC.gov
www.dc.gov
The official website of the Washington, DC city government has information about parking and transportation, recreation facilities, and citywide events.

Destination DC
www.washington.org
The official website of DC's tourism authority, Destination DC is the most thorough guide to the city's neighborhoods and happenings.

POLITICS AND MEDIA

Congress.gov
www.congress.gov
Find your Senator or Representative, see the congressional calendar, and learn about the history of the legislative branch on the official website of the U.S. Congress.

POLITICO
www.politico.com
This print and digital publication dives into the nitty gritty of national politics and policymaking, and publishes the early morning newsletter Playbook, the morning must-read for those inside the beltway.

The Hill
www.thehill.com
In addition to comprehensive coverage of Capitol Hill, this rag is known for the annual 50 Most Beautiful list of hot and high-profile Washingtonians.

The Washington Post
www.washingtonpost.com
In addition to publishing some of the best national, international, and local reporting, DC's major newspaper has excellent dining, arts and culture, and nightlife content; food critic Tom Sietsema can make or break a restaurant with one review.

Washington City Paper
www.washingtoncitypaper.com
For everything other than national politics, from coverage of the city council and public transportation to concert reviews, locals turn to this print and digital publication; the annual crowd-sourced Best of D.C. list will help you find everything from the best cupcake or dive bar, to the best drycleaner, bike shop, or dance company.

Washingtonian
www.washingtonian.com
This magazine combines original reporting about life in the Washington metropolitan area with some of the best coverage of dining, shopping, real estate, and day trips; foodies will want to check out the annual 100 Very Best Restaurants and Cheap Eats lists.

ARTS, CULTURE, AND SOCIETY

Brightest Young Things
www.brightestyoungthings.com
This colorful lifestyle website has the most complete list of concerts, happy hours, and comedy events geared toward young partiers.

Cultural Tourism DC
www.culturaltourismdc.org
In addition to organizing free walking

tours and embassy open houses and maintaining a comprehensive list of cultural events, Cultural Tourism DC manages more than a dozen Neighborhood Heritage Trails throughout the city; find the trails, and download interactive mobile apps, here.

DC Theatre Scene
www.dctheatrescene.com
What's on stage? This website covers everything from Kennedy Center productions and national tours to local troupes and fringe festivals in detail.

Metro Weekly
www.metroweekly.com
This publication is one of the most comprehensive guides to LGBTQ events and nightlife, with excellent arts and entertainment coverage.

Smithsonian Institution
www.si.edu
The Smithsonian's website is a one-stop shop for planning your museum hopping, with information on opening hours, exhibits, and special events at every Smithsonian museum and cultural center.

Washington Blade
www.washingtonblade.com
This publication has been covering LGBTQ news, life, and culture since 1969.

Washington Life
www.washingtonlife.com
This local glossy covers the city's power players and the events they frequent; check out the "My Washington" feature for locals' dining and nightlife picks.

PARKS AND RECREATION

National Park Service
www.nps.gov
Whether you're planning a tour of the National Mall's monuments and memorials, or an excursion to Rock Creek Park or Shenandoah, the National Park Service's website details operating hours, tours, travel tips, and more.

Index

A

Academy Art Museum: 266
A Capitol Fourth: 183
accessibility: 295
accommodations: 224-244; *see also Hotels Index*
A Christmas Carol: 185
Adams Morgan: arts and culture 175; hotels 226, 238-239; map 328-329; neighborhood overview 52-53; nightlife 153-155; restaurants 128-131; shops 205, 218-220; sports and activities 193
Adams Morgan Day: 183-184
Admissions Welcome Center: 93
African American Civil War Memorial and Museum: 49, 50, 91
African American culture/history: African American Civil War Memorial and Museum 91; African American Heritage Memorial Park 248; Douglass, Frederick 95, 265; Frederick Douglass National Historic Site 95-96; Howard University 91-92; Kunta Kinte-Alex Haley Memorial 259; Martin Luther King Jr. Memorial 76; National Museum of African American History and Culture 72, 73
African American Heritage Memorial Park 248
AirBnB: 227
Air Force memorial: 103
air museum: 72
airports: 228, 288-289
Alexandria Archaeology Museum: 252
Alexandria National Cemetery: 250
Alexandria, Virginia: 228, 248-257
American University: 100
American University Museum at the Katzen Arts Center: 100
America's Islamic Heritage Museum & Cultural Center: 61, 178
Anacostia: *see* Navy Yard and Anacostia
Anacostia Arts Center: 62, 178
Anacostia Community Museum: 56, 71, 177
Anacostia Riverwalk Trail: 56, 59, 188, 196
Anderson House: 171
animals: 282
Annapolis and Maryland's Eastern Shore: 258-271

Annapolis Harbor and City Dock: 246, 258-259
Annapolis Spring Sailboat Show: 259
architecture: Basilica of the National Shrine of the Immaculate Conception 100; Department of State 92-93; Easton 265; Embassy Row 91; Healy Hall 93; highlights 17; historic Annapolis 260; J. Edgar Hoover Building 82; Library of Congress 87-88; Lincoln Memorial 69; National Building Museum 165; Renwick Gallery 166; Spanish Steps 91; Thomas Jefferson Memorial 77; Union Station 89; U.S. Capitol 84; Vietnam Veterans Memorial 77; Washington Monument 68; Washington National Cathedral 103-104; White House 79; World War II Memorial 78
Arena Stage: 161, 179
Arlington House: 98
Arlington National Cemetery: 11, 64, 67, 97
Armel-Leftwich Visitor Center: 261
Army Ten-Miler: 184
art galleries/museums: American University Museum at the Katzen Arts Center 100; Annapolis 263; Diplomatic Reception Rooms of the Department of State 92-93; Downtown and Penn Quarter 164-166; Dupont Circle 171; Easton 266; Georgetown and Foggy Bottom 176-177; Little Washington 277; National Gallery of Art 77, 162; National Mall 162-164; Navy Yard and Anacostia 177-178; U Street, Shaw, and Logan Circle 172-173
Arthur M. Sackler Gallery: 163
arts and culture: 160-186; Easton 266; resources 300, 301
Atlas District: *see* Capitol Hill and Atlas District
Atlas Performing Arts Center: 168-169
Audi Field: 198
auto shows: 186
Avalon Theatre: 266

B

Ballpark Boathouse: 24, 59, 197
Banneker-Douglass Museum: 261
baseball: 59, 197

Basilica of the National Shrine of the Immaculate Conception: 100
basketball: 191
Bay Bridge: 263
best-of itinerary: 12-15
Big Meadows Lodge: 274
Bike and Roll: 28, 195, 254, 293
bike rentals: 195
biking: Alexandria 254; transportation 292-293; see also trails
Blind Whino SW Arts Club: 178
Boat Cruises on the Miles River: 269
boating: Annapolis 258-259; Chesapeake Bay Maritime Museum 269; Georgetown and Foggy Bottom 194; Greater Washington DC 202; Mount Vernon 257; National Mall 190; Navy Yard and Anacostia 197; St. Michaels 269
Boo at the Zoo: 184
book festivals: 31, 183
Book Hill Galleries: 176
books: 209; see also bookstores
bookstores: Adams Morgan 218; Capitol Hill and Atlas District 210; Dupont Circle 213; Navy Yard and Anacostia 222; Politics & Prose 211
Brown, Chuck: 173
budget tips: 117, 296
Bull Run Regional Park: 228
Bureau of Engraving and Printing: 74
bus travel: 290

C
Café Saint-Ex: 51
camping: 228
Capital Bikeshare: 195
Capital Crescent Trail: 194
Capital Fringe Festival: 169, 183
Capital One Arena: 94, 191
Capital Pride: 25, 182
Capital Wheel: 251
Capitol Hill and Atlas District: arts and culture 168-169; hotels 226, 232-233; itinerary 12-14; map 322-323; neighborhood overview 40-41; nightlife 144-146; restaurants 114-118; shops 210-212; sights 84-89; sports and activities 192
Car and Carriage Caravan Museum: 273-274
Catholic University of America: 102
cherry blossoms: 11; National Cherry Blossom Festival 181; paddleboat on the Tidal Basin 190
Cherry Hill Park: 228

Chesapeake & Ohio Towpath: 194
Chesapeake Bay Bridge: 263
Chesapeake Bay Maritime Museum: 269
Chester Gap Cellars: 275
children's activities: Boo at the Zoo 184; H Street Festival 184; International Spy Museum 164; itinerary of 16-19; National Air and Space Museum 73, 206; Rock Creek Park 201; Smithsonian National Zoo 99; Steven F. Udvar-Hazy Center 271; travel tips for families 295
Chinatown: 38, 83
Chinn Ridge: 273
Christmas: 25, 31, 185, 278
Christmas Sleigh: 278
Chrysalis Vineyards: 275
churches: Basilica of the National Shrine of the Immaculate Conception 100; Washington National Cathedral 103-104
Citi Open: 30, 201
CityCenterDC: 29, 205
City Dock: 258-259
civil rights era: 283-284
Civil War history: 283
Civil War sights: 91, 272-273
climate: 281
clothing and accessories: Adams Morgan 218; Downtown and Penn Quarter 207-208; Dupont Circle 212; Georgetown and Foggy Bottom 220-222; Greater Washington DC 223; U Street, Shaw, and Logan Circle 215-216
cocktail bars: Adams Morgan 153; Capitol Hill and Atlas District 144; Downtown and Penn Quarter 141; Dupont Circle 146; Georgetown and Foggy Bottom 155-156; U Street, Shaw, and Logan Circle 148
cocktails: happy hour 143; rickeys 154
Columbia Heights: 52
comedy clubs: 142
Comet Ping Pong: 158
communications: 298
Constellation Theatre Company: 174
craft beer: Adams Morgan 153; Dupont Circle 147; Navy Yard and Anacostia 157; U Street, Shaw, and Logan Circle 150
Craft Show, Smithsonian: 181-182
crime: 293-294
Cross MacKenzie Gallery: 176-177
culinary festivals: 184
cultural centers: Adams Morgan 175; Dupont Circle 171; Navy Yard and

Anacostia 178; Passport DC 182; Smithsonian Folklife Festival: 183
cultural diversity: 286
currency museum: 74

D

dance: see performing arts
dance clubs: 152
day trips: 245-279; Alexandria, Virginia 248-257; Annapolis and Maryland's Eastern Shore 258-271; highlights 246; map 247; planning tips 248; Shenandoah National Park 271-279
D.C. City Hall Art Collection: 172-173
DC Ducks: 16, 188, 192
DC Jazz Festival: 174, 182
DC Sail: 95
DC United: 198
Del Mar: 95
Department of State: 92-93
Dickey Ridge Visitor Center: 274
Le Diplomate: 51
Diplomatic Reception Rooms of the Department of State: 92-93
discounts: 27
distilleries: 158
District Wharf: 29, 56, 95
dive bars: Capitol Hill and Atlas District 145; Downtown and Penn Quarter 142
diversity, cultural: 286
Douglass, Frederick: 265
Downtown and Penn Quarter: arts and culture 164-167; hotels 226, 229-232; itinerary 12-14; map 320-321; neighborhood overview 38-39; nightlife 141-142; restaurants 109-114; shops 207-210; sights 79-84; sports and activities 190-191
Downtown Holiday Market: 185
driving: 289, 292
Dumbarton Oaks: 181, 200
Dupont Circle: 14, 15, 44, 90; arts and culture 170-172; hotels 226, 234-236; map 324-325; neighborhood overview 42-45; nightlife 146-148; restaurants 119-121; shops 212-215; sights 90-91; walking tour 44-45
Dupont-Kalorama Museum Walk: 182
Dupont Underground: 171-172

E

Eastern Market: 13, 86-87, 205
Easton: 264-267
East Potomac Golf Course and Driving Range: 37, 199, 202

East Potomac Park and Hains Point: 37, 188, 199
East Potomac Tennis Center: 202
Embassy Row: 101
emergency services: 293
environmental issues: 281
Ethiopian culture: 124, 286
events: 28-31, 181-186
Exorcist stairs: 94

F

farmers markets: Freshfarm Dupont Circle Market 90; Maine Avenue Fish Market 95; Union Market 102
Federal Bureau of Investigation (FBI): 82
FedEx Field: 198
festivals: see events
fireworks: 30, 183
First Friday Dupont: 171
First Friday Easton: 266
Fletcher's Boathouse: 194, 202
Foggy Bottom: see Georgetown and Foggy Bottom
Folger Shakespeare Library: 169
Folger Theatre: 86, 167, 169
folk art: 166
food: see food shops, gourmet; Restaurants Index
food shops, gourmet: Downtown and Penn Quarter 210; Dupont Circle 214-215; Greater Washington DC 223; U Street, Shaw, and Logan Circle 217-218
food souvenirs: 209
food trucks: 117, 138
Ford's Theatre: 18, 83, 167
Fotoweek DC: 185
Founders Park: 251
Fox Hollow Trail Hike: 274
Franklin Delano Roosevelt Memorial: 14, 17, 36, 74-75
Frederick Douglass Day: 265
Frederick Douglass National Historic Site: 13, 56, 63, 67, 95-96
Freedom House Museum at the Northern Virginia Urban League: 250
Freer Gallery of Art and Arthur M. Sackler Gallery: 23, 71, 163, 206
Freshfarm Dupont Circle Market: 90
Friendship Archway: 84
Fringe Festival: 169, 183

G

GALA Hispanic Theatre: 175
Gallery Place: 205
gardens: Dumbarton Oaks 181; Hillwood

Estate, Museum & Gardens 180; United States Botanic Garden 168; U.S. National Arboretum 199; William Paca House & Garden 260
geography: 280
George Mason Memorial: 36
Georgetown and Foggy Bottom: 15; arts and culture 175-177; hotels 226, 239-242; map 330-331; neighborhood overview 54-55; nightlife 155-157; restaurants 132-134; shops 205, 220-222; sights 92-94; sports and activities 193-196
Georgetown University: 93
Georgetown University Hoyas: 191
Georgetown Waterfront Park: 194
George Washington Masonic National Memorial: 251
George Washington's Distillery and Gristmill: 256
George Washington's Mount Vernon: 255-256
George Washington University: 93
George Washington University Hospital: 93
George Washington University Museum: 93, 175-176
go-go music: 173
golf: 199, 201, 202
government: 284-285
Graham Georgetown: 15, 156
gratuities: 297
Gravelly Point: 201
Greater Washington DC: arts and culture 180-181; hotels 227, 243-244; map 334-335; neighborhood overview 64-65; nightlife 158-159; restaurants 136-138; shops 223; sights 97-104; sports and activities 199-202
Greenhill Winery & Vineyards: 275

H

Hains Point: 37, 199
Haley, Alex: 259
Hammond-Harwood House: 260
happy hour: 11, 143
Harbor Queen: 258-259
Healy Hall: 93
Henry Hill Visitor Center: 272-273
High Heel Drag Queen Race: 184
hiking: 274
Hillwood Estate, Museum & Gardens: 161, 180
Hillyer Art Space: 171
Hirshhorn Museum and Sculpture Garden: 17, 70, 161, 162, 206

Hispanic Theatre, GALA: 175
Historic Middleburg: 246, 277
historic sights: African American Heritage Memorial Park 248-250; Annapolis 259-260; Arlington National Cemetery 97; Capitol Hill 84-89; Easton 264-265; Ford's Theatre 83; Frederick Douglass National Historic Site 95-96; George Washington Masonic National Memorial 251; Manassas National Battlefield Park 272-273; Middleburg 277-278; Mount Vernon 255-257; National 9/11 Pentagon Memorial 98; National Mall 68-78; Old Stone House 94; Oxford, Maryland 267; President Lincoln's Cottage 101-102; President Woodrow Wilson House 181; Society of the Cincinnati Anderson House 171; Tudor Place 176; White House 79-80
history: 71, 282-284, 299
H.M. *Krentz:* 269
Holocaust Memorial Museum: 162
home decor/gifts: Adams Morgan 219-220; Capitol Hill and Atlas District 212; Downtown and Penn Quarter 208-210; Dupont Circle 214; U Street, Shaw, and Logan Circle 216-217
homeless population: 294
Honfleur Gallery: 62, 177-178
horseback riding: 201, 274
horse racing: 278
hospitals: 293
hotel bars: 230
hotels: 224-244; Adams Morgan 226; Alexandria, Virginia 254-255; alternative lodging 227-228; Annapolis 263-264; Capitol Hill and Atlas District 226; Downtown and Penn Quarter 226; Dupont Circle 226; Easton 266; Georgetown and Foggy Bottom 226; Greater Washington DC 227; highlights 225; Inn at Little Washington, The 276; National Mall 226; Navy Yard and Anacostia 227; St. Michaels 270; U Street, Shaw, and Logan Circle 226; *see also* Hotels Index
House of Representatives: 20, 84
Howard Theatre: 46, 50, 161, 173, 174
Howard University: 91
H Street Festival: 184

I

ice hockey: 191
improv comedy: 174
Independence Day: 10, 25, 29, 30, 183

Inn at Little Washington, The: 246, 276
International Spy Museum: 18, 164
international travelers: 296
Iranian embassy, former: 101
Islamic cultural center: 178
itineraries: 12-24
Ivy City: 29, 137, 158, 223
Iwo Jima memorial: 103

JK

James Madison Memorial Building: 88
Japanese Pagoda: 36
jazz: 174, 182
Jazz in the Garden: 24, 174, 182
J. Edgar Hoover Building: 82
Jefferson, Thomas: 37, 77
Jewish Military History Museum: 170
John Adams Building: 88
John F. Kennedy Center for the
    Performing Arts: 15, 54, 161, 167, 174,
    177
Kennedy, John F.: 97
Kent Island Express: 263
Key Bridge Boathouse: 194
King Jr., Martin Luther: Martin Luther
    King Jr. Day 186; Martin Luther King
    Jr. Memorial 36, 76-77; Martin Luther
    King Jr. Memorial Library 168
Korean War Veterans Memorial: 35, 75-76
Kunta Kinte-Alex Haley Memorial: 259

L

Lafayette Square: 13, 14, 18, 80
Lake Fairfax Park: 228
LGBTQ+ events/travel tips: general
    discussion 296; Capital Pride 30, 182;
    Capitol Hill and Atlas District bars
    146; cultural life 286; Dupont Circle
    42; Dupont Circle bars 147; High Heel
    Drag Queen Race 184; U Street, Shaw,
    and Logan Circle 152
Library of Congress: 13, 86, 87
Library of Congress Reader Identification
    Card: 87
Lincoln, Abraham: Ford's Theatre 83;
    Lincoln Memorial 69; President
    Lincoln's Cottage 101-102
Lincoln Memorial: 9, 14, 24, 35, 67, 69, 98
Lincoln Theatre: 46, 174
Lisner Auditorium: 93
Little Ethiopia: 286
Little Washington Theatre: 276
Little Washington Winery: 275
Logan Circle: see U Street, Shaw, and
    Logan Circle

Logan Fringe Arts Space: 169
Long View Gallery: 172-173
Luray Caverns: 273
Luray Valley Museum: 273

M

Maine Avenue Fish Market: 95
Manassas National Battlefield Park:
    272-273
marathons: 184
Marine Corps Marathon: 184
Martin Luther King Jr.: holiday 29, 186;
    library 17, 168; memorial 14, 36, 71,
    76-77
Maryland's Eastern Shore: 258-271
Maryland State House: 260
Mary's Rock: 274
Masonic Memorial: 251
Maxwell Park: 24, 150
media: 298, 299, 301
Memorial Peace Walk: 186
Memorial Wall (Vietnam Veterans
    Memorial): 77
Meridian Hill Park: 14, 52, 188, 193, 201
Metro (transportation): 26, 29, 291
Metropolitan Washington Restaurant
    Week: 29, 31
Mexican Cultural Institute: 175
MGM National Harbor: 251
Michelin Guide: 29
Middleburg: 274, 277-279
Middleburg Historic District: 278
Middleburg Spring Races: 278
Mt. Defiance Cidery & Distillery: 275
Mount Pleasant: 52
Mount Vernon: 19, 246, 254, 255-257
Mount Vernon Inn Restaurant: 256
Mount Vernon Trail: 193, 254
museum gift shops: 206
museums: Alexandria, Virginia 250,
    252; Annapolis 261; Capitol Hill and
    Atlas District 168; DC Jazz Festival
    182; Dupont Circle 170; Dupont-
    Kalorama Museum Walk 182; Easton
    266; Georgetown and Foggy Bottom
    175-176; Greater Washington DC 180;
    Middleburg 278; National Mall 162-
    164; Navy Yard and Anacostia 177;
    President Woodrow Wilson House 181;
    Steven F. Udvar-Hazy Center 271; St.
    Michaels 269
music: general discussion 286; Adams
    Morgan 154; Capitol Hill and Atlas
    District 145; Downtown and Penn
    Quarter 142; Georgetown and Foggy

Bottom 157; go-go 173; jazz 174; Jazz in the Garden 182; Navy Yard and Anacostia 157-158; U Street, Shaw, and Logan Circle 151; see also performing arts

N

Narmada Winery: 275
National Air and Space Museum: 14, 17, 21, 67, 70, 72, 206
National Arboretum: 188
National Archives: 21, 77, 163
National Bonsai and Penjing Museum: 200
National Book Festival: 31, 183
National Building Museum: 165
National Cherry Blossom Festival: 25, 29, 181
National Christmas Tree and Pathway of Peace: 185
National Gallery of Art: 14, 77, 161, 162, 206
National Gallery of Art East Building: 17, 162
National Harbor: 251
National Independence Day Parade: 30, 183
National Mall: 16, 22, 29; arts and culture 162-164; hotels 226, 228; itinerary 14-15; map 318-319; neighborhood overview 32-37; restaurants 107-108; sights 66-78; sports and activities 189-190; tours 69; walking tour 34-37
National Mall and Memorials Walk: 10, 34
National Museum of African American History and Culture: 13, 27, 67, 70, 72, 73, 206
National Museum of African Art: 23, 71, 163
National Museum of American History: 14, 21, 67, 70, 71, 206
National Museum of American Jewish Military History: 170
National Museum of Natural History: 17, 67, 70, 73
National Museum of the American Indian: 14, 17, 70, 164, 206
National Museum of Women in the Arts: 165
National 9/11 Pentagon Memorial: 21, 64, 67, 98
National Portrait Gallery: 71, 166
National Postal Museum: 71, 168
Nationals Park: 24, 56, 59, 197
National Sporting Library & Museum: 278

National Theatre: 167
Native American culture: 206
natural history museum: 73
Navy, U.S.: 261
Navy Yard and Anacostia: arts and culture 179-181; hotels 227, 242; map 332-333; neighborhood overview 56-63; nightlife 157-158; restaurants 134-136; shops 222; sights 95-96; sports and activities 196-198; walking tours 58-63
neighborhoods: 32-65; Adams Morgan 52-53; Capitol Hill and Atlas District 40-41; Downtown and Penn Quarter 38-39; Dupont Circle 42-45; Georgetown and Foggy Bottom 54-55; Greater Washington DC 64-65; maps 318-335; National Mall 32-37; Navy Yard and Anacostia 56-63; U Street, Shaw, and Logan Circle 46-51
New Deal: 283
Newseum: 15, 18, 161, 164
nightlife: 139-159; Adams Morgan 153-155; Annapolis 262; Capitol Hill and Atlas District 144-146; Downtown and Penn Quarter 141-142; Dupont Circle 146-148; Georgetown and Foggy Bottom 155-157; Greater Washington DC 158-159; highlights 140; Navy Yard and Anacostia 157-158; U Street, Shaw, and Logan Circle 148-152; see also Nightlife Index
North End Shaw shopping district: 51, 205
Northern Virginia Urban League: 250

O

Observatory at Graham Georgetown: 15, 156
Old Post Office: 298
Old Rag Mountain: 274
Old Stone House: 94, 201
Old Town Alexandria Waterfront: 19, 251
Old Town Trolley Tours: 190
outdoor gear: 210, 216
Oxford: 267-269
Oxford-Bellevue Ferry: 267
Oxford Museum: 267

P

parks: Dumbarton Oaks 200; Dupont Circle 90; Greater Washington DC 199-202; Lafayette Square 166; Meridian Hill Park 193; National Mall 189-190; Navy Yard and Anacostia 196-197; President's Park and the Ellipse 81-82;

resources 302; Shenandoah National Park 271-279; Theodore Roosevelt Island 193

Passport DC: 101, 182

passports: 26

Pathway of Peace: 185

Patriot Cruises: 269

Penn Quarter: see Downtown and Penn Quarter

Pentagon Memorial: 21, 98

performing arts: general discussion 286-287; Adams Morgan 175; Capital Fringe Festival 169, 183; Capitol Hill and Atlas District 168-169; Downtown and Penn Quarter 166-168; Easton 266; GALA Hispanic Theatre 175; John F. Kennedy Center for the Performing Arts 177; Little Washington 276; Navy Yard and Anacostia 179; theater scene 167

pharmacies: 293

Phillips Collection: 15, 45, 161, 170

photography festivals: 185

Pizzagate: 158

planetariums: 201

Plein Air Easton: 266

politics: 20-22, 284-285, 299, 301

Pool of Remembrance: 76

postal museum: 168

postal services: 298

Potomac River: 15, 187, 189

Presidential Inauguration: 26, 28, 186

President John F. Kennedy's gravesite: 97

President Lincoln's Cottage: 101-102

President's Park and the Ellipse: 81-82

President William Howard Taft gravesite: 98

President Woodrow Wilson House: 181

public transit: 291-292

QR

Rappahannock Oyster Co.: 103

reading, suggested: 299-300

Reflecting Pool: 16, 69

Renwick Gallery: 71, 80, 166

reservations: 27

resources, internet: 301-302

restaurants: 105-138; Adams Morgan 128-131; Annapolis 261; budget tips 117; Capitol Hill and Atlas District 114-118; District Wharf 95; Downtown and Penn Quarter 109-114; Dupont Circle 119-121; Easton 265; Georgetown and Foggy Bottom 132-134; Greater Washington DC 136-138; highlights 106; Inn at Little Washington 276; Metropolitan Washington Restaurant Week 29; National Mall 107-108; Navy Yard and Anacostia 134-136; reservations 27; St. Michaels 270; U Street, Shaw, and Logan Circle 122-128; see also Restaurants Index

rickeys: 154

ride-hailing apps: 292

Rock Creek Park: 201

romantic sights: 24

Ronald Reagan Washington National Airport: 228, 288

Roof Terrace Restaurant: 177

Roosevelt, Franklin Delano: 74-75

S

sailing: 259

sales tax: 297

Salt & Sundry: 51, 102

Sculpture Garden (National Gallery of Art): 14, 24, 162

Section 27: 98

security screenings: 26

Segs in the City: 190

Senate buildings: 20, 84, 87

senior travelers: 295

Shakespeare Theatre Company: 167

Shaw: see U Street, Shaw, and Logan Circle

Shenandoah National Park: 271-279

shops: 203-223; Adams Morgan 218-220; Alexandria, Virginia 253; Annapolis 262-263; Capitol Hill and Atlas District 210-212; Downtown and Penn Quarter 207-210; Dupont Circle 212-215; Georgetown and Foggy Bottom 220-222; Greater Washington DC 223; highlights 204; museum gift shops 206; Navy Yard and Anacostia 222; shopping districts 205; souvenirs 209; U Street, Shaw, and Logan Circle 215-218; see also Shops Index

sights: 66-104; Capitol Hill and Atlas District 84-89; Downtown and Penn Quarter 79-84; Dupont Circle 90-91; Georgetown and Foggy Bottom 92-94; Greater Washington DC 97-104; highlights 67; National Mall 66-78; Navy Yard and Anacostia 95-96; U Street, Shaw, and Logan Circle 91-92

Skyland Stables: 274

Skyline Drive: 246, 271, 273

slavery, history of: 250

Smithsonian American Art Museum: 71, 166, 171

Smithsonian Craft Show: 181-182
Smithsonian Folklife Festival: 25, 183
Smithsonian Institution: 10, 32, 70-71; *see also individual museums*
Smithsonian National Mall Tours: 189
Smithsonian National Zoo: 99, 201
Smithsonian's National Zoo: 19, 67
Sneed Farm Loop Hike: 274
soccer: 198
Society of the Cincinnati Anderson House: 171
Source Theatre: 174
souvenirs: 206, 209
space museum: 72
Spanish Steps: 45, 91
spas: 276
spectator sports: Downtown and Penn Quarter 191; Georgetown and Foggy Bottom 195; Navy Yard and Anacostia 197
Spirit of Washington river cruise: 19, 257
sports and activities: 187-202; Adams Morgan 155, 193; Capitol Hill and Atlas District 192; Downtown and Penn Quarter 190-191; Georgetown and Foggy Bottom 193-196; Greater Washington DC 199-202; highlights 188; National Mall 189-190; Navy Yard and Anacostia: 196-198; resources 302; Shenandoah National Park 274
sports bars: Capitol Hill and Atlas District 145; Downtown and Penn Quarter 142
spy museum: 164
St. Anne's Parish: 261
Star-Spangled Banner: 21, 71
steeplechase races: 278
Steven F. Udvar-Hazy Center: 246, 271
St. John's College: 260
St. Michaels: 246, 269-271
St. Michaels Museum and Walking Tours: 269
Studio Gallery: 171
Studio Theatre: 15, 174
summer itinerary: 23-24, 25
Supreme Court of the United States: 13, 86, 88-89

T

Talbot County Courthouse: 265
Talbot Historical Society: 264-265
Taste of DC: 184
taxis: 292
tennis: 30, 195, 201, 202
Textile Museum: 93, 175-176
The Nutcracker: 185

Theodore Roosevelt Island: 188, 254
Thomas Jefferson Building: 87
Thomas Jefferson Memorial: 14, 16, 37, 77
Thompson Boat Center: 195, 201
The Three Soldiers: 77
Tidal Basin paddleboats: 14, 188, 190
tipping: 297
Tomb of the Unknown Soldier: 97
top experiences: 7-11; Arlington National Cemetery 97; cherry blossoms 181, 190; happy hour 143; Independence Day 183; Lincoln Memorial 69; National Cherry Blossom Festival 181; National Mall walking tour 34-37; Smithsonian Institution museums and galleries 70-71; U.S. Capitol 84; Washington Monument 68-69; White House 79-80
Torpedo Factory Art Center: 252
tourist information/tips: 26, 297
tours: general discussion 27-28; Arlington National Cemetery 97; Capitol Hill and Atlas District 192; DC Ducks 188, 192; Downtown and Penn Quarter 190; National Mall 189; St. Michaels 269; U.S. Capitol 87; White House 81
trails: Adams Morgan 193; Georgetown and Foggy Bottom 193-194; Greater Washington DC 199-202; National Mall 189-190; Navy Yard and Anacostia 196-197
train travel: 289-290
Transformer: 173
transportation: 26-27, 33, 39, 41, 43, 47, 53, 55, 57, 288-293
Trump Hotel: 298
Tudor Place: 176

U

Union Market: 29, 64, 102
Union Station: 16, 17, 89
United States Air Force Memorial: 103
United States Botanic Garden: 13, 168
United States Holocaust Memorial Museum: 69, 161, 162
United States Marine Corps War Memorial: 103
United States Naval Academy: 261
United States Sailboat Show: 259
U.S. Capitol: 8, 12, 16, 18, 67, 84; dome 13, 84; reservations 27; tours 20, 84; visitors center 13, 88
U.S. National Arboretum: 199
U.S. Naval Academy Museum: 261
U Street, Shaw, and Logan Circle: 15;

arts and culture 172-174; hotels 226, 237-238; map 326-327; neighborhood overview 46-51; nightlife 148-152; restaurants 122-128; shops 215-218; sights 91-92; walking tour 48-51

VWXYZ

Valley Trail: 201
Vietnam Veterans Memorial: 36, 71, 77
Vietnam Women's Memorial: 77
Virginia Fall Races: 278
visitor centers: 297
Vivid Solutions Gallery: 178
VRBO: 227
walking tours: Anacostia 60-63; Dupont Circle 44-45; National Mall and Memorials 34-37; Navy Yard 58-59; U Street and Shaw 48-51
Walkingtown DC: 184
Warner Theatre: 167
Washington Auto Show: 186
Washington Ballet: 185
Washington Capitals: 191
Washington Dulles International Airport: 228, 288
Washington Improv Theater: 174
Washington Kastles: 195
Washington Monument: 8, 14, 16, 67, 68-69
Washington Mystics: 191

Washington National Cathedral: 17, 19, 76, 103
Washington Nationals: 24, 188, 197
Washington Printmakers Gallery: 176-177
Washington Redskins: 198
Washington Wizards: 191
Waterfowl Festival: 266
weather: 281
Western Ridge Trail: 201
West Potomac: 35, 71
West Potomac Park: 189
White House: 7, 13, 16, 18, 21, 67, 79; reservations 27; shop 204, 208; souvenirs 209; tours 81; visitors center 18, 80, 82
William Paca House & Garden: 260
Wilson, Woodrow: 181
wine bars: Georgetown and Foggy Bottom 157; Greater Washington DC 158; U Street, Shaw, and Logan Circle 150
wine country: 275, 278
Winery at Bull Run: 275
Women in the Arts Museum: 165
Woodwind schooners: 258-259
Woolly Mammoth Theatre Company: 15, 161, 166, 167
World War II Memorial: 35, 78
Yards Park: 196
Zoolights: 185
zoos: 99

Restaurants Index

Acqua Al 2: 13, 116
Afterwords Café: 119
Ambar: 115
Amsterdam Falafelshop: 130
ANXO Cidery & Pintxos Bar: 126
Astro Doughnuts and Fried Chicken: 18, 113
Bad Saint: 129
Bagels Etc.: 44, 106, 121
Baked & Wired: 134
Beefsteak: 117, 121
Ben's Chili Bowl: 15, 49, 106, 117, 122
Bistrot du Coin: 120
BLT Steak: 109, 143
Blue Duck Tavern: 132
Bombay Club: 111
Buffalo & Bergen: 102, 136
Bullfrog Bagels: 118
Busboys and Poets: 51, 106, 117, 127

Buttercream Bakeshop: 127
Cafe Milano: 22, 106, 133
Calabash Tea & Café: 127
Capitol Hill Crab Cakes: 135
Cascade Café: 108
Centrolina: 111
Chaia: 133
Charlie Palmer Steak: 106, 115, 143
Compass Coffee: 14, 128
Crimson: 110
The Dabney: 123
DAS Ethiopian Cuisine: 132
DBGB Kitchen & Bar: 15, 110
Diner, The: 106, 128
Dog Tag Bakery: 134
Dolcezza Gelato Factory & Coffee Lab: 138
Due South: 135
Dukem Ethiopian Restaurant: 15, 106, 124, 125

Duplex Diner: 129
Elizabeth's Gone Raw: 113
Etete: 15, 124, 125
Ethiopic: 116
Federalist Pig: 128
Fiola Mare: 15, 24, 106, 133, 143
Florida Avenue Grill: 51, 124
Fruitive: 15, 113
Garden Café: 108
Garrison: 106, 114
Good Stuff Eatery: 17, 86, 115, 117
Grace Street Coffee: 134
Granville Moore's: 116
Hank's Oyster Bar: 95, 106, 119, 143, 252
Harry's: 110
Hazel: 122
Henry's Soul Café: 120
Ice Cream Jubilee: 59, 136, 197
Jaleo: 14, 18, 106, 112
Joe's Seafood, Prime Steak & Stone Crab:
    80, 109, 143
Johnny's Half Shell: 106, 128
JRINK Juicery: 131
Komi: 27, 120
Kyirisan: 125
Ladurée: 133
Lapis: 130
La Puerta Verde: 137
Le Diplomate: 125
Little Serow: 121
Maketto: 117
Market Lunch: 13, 86, 117, 118
Martin's Tavern: 123, 133
Masseria: 103, 106, 137
minibar by José Andrés: 27, 109
Mirabelle: 22, 80, 106, 110

Mitsitam Native Foods Café: 14, 17, 106, 107
Old Ebbitt Grill: 13, 18, 80, 110, 123, 143
Open City: 19, 136
Osteria Morini: 23, 59, 136
Oyamel Cocina Mexicana: 112
Palm, The: 14, 21, 119, 123
Pavilion Café: 14, 24, 108
Pearl Dive Oyster Palace: 51, 122
Pete's Diner: 12, 118
Pineapple and Pearls: 114
Potter's House: 131
Pupuseria San Miguel: 117, 130
Purple Patch: 129
RareSweets: 114
Rasika West End: 132, 133
Riggsby: 119, 143
Rose's Luxury: 114–115
1789: 132
Siren by RW: 122
Slipstream: 127
Source by Wolfgang Puck: 112
Sticky Fingers Sweets & Eats: 131
Sushi Capitol: 116
Sushi Taro: 120, 143
Sweet Home Café: 14, 69, 107
Tabard Inn: 119
Tail Up Goat: 130
Taqueria Nacional: 126
Thip Khao: 129–130
Tryst: 131
2 Amys: 19, 117, 138
We, the Pizza: 17, 118
Whaley's: 23, 59, 134
Woodward Table: 109
The Wydown: 127
Zaytinya: 112

Nightlife Index

Anthem, The: 95, 140, 157
Bar à Vin: 157
Bier Baron Tavern: 147
Black Cat: 140, 151
Bluejacket: 59, 157
Blues Alley: 157, 174
Bullfeathers: 13, 86, 145
Café Saint-Ex: 148
Cobalt: 148
Columbia Room: 140, 148
Copycat Co.: 144
Cotton & Reed: 158
Dacha Beer Garden: 24, 150

Dan's Café: 155
DC Improv: 142
Denson Liquor Bar: 142
Eighteenth Street Lounge: 140, 146
Flash: 152
The Gibson: 149
The Hamilton: 142
Harold Black: 144
Hill Prince: 145
H Street Country Club: 145–146
Jack Rose Dining Saloon: 140, 153
JR's Bar: 140, 147
Larry's Lounge: 148

Lounge at Bourbon Steak: 15, 140, 155
Madam's Organ: 154
Marvin: 149
Maxwell Park: 150
McClellan's Retreat: 147
Meridian Pint: 153
Mr. Henry's: 146
Nellie's Sports Bar: 24, 50, 140, 152
New Vegas Lounge: 151
Next Whiskey Bar, The: 156
9:30 Club: 15, 51, 140, 151
Observatory, The: 156
Off the Record: 80, 142
POV: 13, 140, 141
Quill: 147

Raven Grill: 155
Republic Restoratives: 158
Right Proper Brewing Co.: 150
Rock and Roll Hotel: 145
Rocket Bar: 142
Round Robin Bar: 13, 140, 141
Songbyrd Music House & Record Café: 154
Top of the Gate: 13, 140, 155
Tropicalia: 152
Tune Inn: 86, 140, 145
2 Birds 1 Stone: 149
U Street Music Hall: 152
Vinoteca: 151
Wonderland Ballroom: 155

Shops Index

Batch 13: 218
Betsy Fisher: 212
Brooks Brothers: 212
Capitol Hemp: 219
Capitol Hill Books: 210
Charles Tyrwhitt: 207
Cherry Blossom Creative: 216
Chocolate Chocolate: 210
Chocolate Moose: 209
Coup de Foudre Lingerie: 207
Curio Concept: 204, 220
Current Boutique: 215
East City Bookshop: 210
Ella-Rue: 220
Filson: 216
Glen's Garden Market: 214
GoodWood: 216
Grand Cata: 218
Great Republic: 209
Green Hat Gin: 223
Hill's Kitchen: 204, 212
Hudson & Crane: 219
Hugh & Crye: 220
Hu's Shoes: 221
Hu's Wear: 221
Idle Time Books: 218
Jenni Bick Custom Journals: 214
Kramerbooks: 15, 45, 204, 213
Labyrinth Games & Puzzles: 212

Lettie Gooch: 215
Lynn Louisa: 221
Mediterranean Way: 215
Meeps: 219
Mercedes Bien Vintage: 204, 218
Ministry of Supply: 215
Miss Pixie's: 51, 204, 216
MM.LaFleur: 208
New Columbia Distillers: 204, 223
Nike Community Store: 223
The Outrage: 219
Politics and Prose: 211, 222
Proper Topper: 213
Redeem: 216
REI Washington DC Flagship: 210
Relish: 222
Salt & Sundry: 217
Second Story Books: 214
Shinola: 216
Shop Made in D.C.: 214
Summit to Soul: 211
Tabletop: 214
Tiny Jewel Box: 24, 204, 207
Tuckernuck: 222
Union Kitchen Grocery: 204, 217
Urban Dwell: 220
Violet: 204, 215
White House Visitor Center Shop: 204, 208

Hotels Index

The Avery: 239
Capitol Hill Hotel: 232
Capitol Skyline Hotel: 242
The Carlyle: 225, 235
The Darcy: 237
Dupont Circle Hotel: 234
Dupont Place Boutique Inn: 236
Embassy Row Hotel: 235
Fairfax at Embassy Row: 235
Fairmont Washington, D.C., Georgetown: 240
Four Seasons Hotel Washington, D.C.: 15, 155, 240
The George: 233
Georgetown Inn: 241
Glover Park Hotel: 243
Graham Georgetown: 242
Hay-Adams: 225, 229
Highroad Hostel DC: 239
Hotel Hive: 242
Hotel Madera: 235
Jefferson, The: 24, 225, 234
Kimpton Hotel Monaco Washington DC: 225, 231
Kimpton Mason & Rook Hotel: 225, 237
Liaison Capitol Hill: 225, 232
The LINE: 238
Mandarin Oriental Washington, D.C.: 228
Mayflower: 225, 232
Morrison-Clark Historic Inn and Restaurant: 232
Omni Shoreham Hotel: 225, 243
Park Hyatt Washington: 240
Phoenix Park Hotel: 233
Pod DC: 232
Rosewood Washington, D.C.: 241
Sofitel Washington DC Lafayette Square: 225, 229
St. Regis Washington, D.C.: 230
Tabard Inn: 236
Washington Hilton: 45, 236
Washington Marriott Wardman Park: 243
Washington Plaza Hotel: 225, 238
Watergate Hotel: 22, 54, 156, 239
Willard InterContinental: 13, 141, 230
W Washington, D.C.: 141, 231

Photo Credits

Acknowledgments

This book could not have been possible without the savvy, supportive team at Avalon Travel. Thanks especially to my editor Leah Gordon, for your guidance, your encouragement, and skillfully shaping and polishing this book into something better than I could have imagined, and Nikki Ioakimedes, for your enthusiastic support of my proposal and giving me this opportunity. Thanks also to Holly Birchfield, Kat Bennett, Elizabeth Jang (whose thoughtful but fast responses eased my anxiety about the photos), and Darren Alessi. It was truly a joy to work with all of you.

I'm indebted to Kevin Fisher, a most assiduous lawyer. Thank you for being in my corner.

There are so very many people in the DC tourism and hospitality community who provided assistance with my research and helped me obtain photos, tours, and insight into the evolution of our city. You are making DC more cosmopolitan, and more fun, one opening at a time, and I'm honored to shine a light on you and your clients' creativity and vision and showcase the best of the best to visitors.

I can never thank my parents enough for your unconditional love, and for the hours upon hours you spent reading to me and encouraging me to pursue my dreams.

And last, but certainly not least, *merci* to Matt, for your love, for always believing in me, for your brilliant eye and willingness to talk through ideas and challenges with me, for your coffee (and martini) making skills, and for putting up with me, especially when you would come home in the evening and find me in the same gray sweats in the same place you left me, hammering away before a deadline. I love you, and I'm so lucky to call you my partner, and my friend. In all things, you make me better.

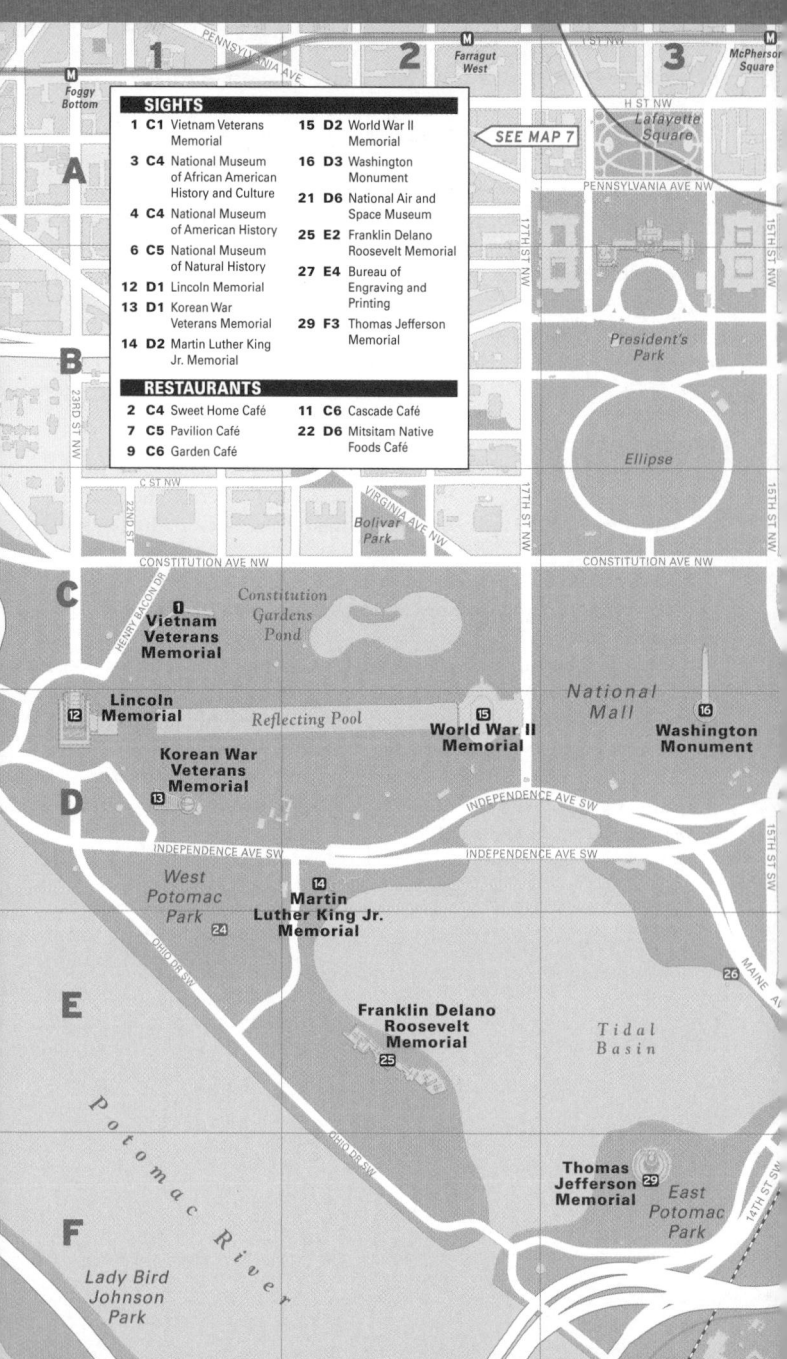

SEE MAP 7

SIGHTS

1	C1	Vietnam Veterans Memorial
3	C4	National Museum of African American History and Culture
4	C4	National Museum of American History
6	C5	National Museum of Natural History
12	D1	Lincoln Memorial
13	D1	Korean War Veterans Memorial
14	D2	Martin Luther King Jr. Memorial
15	D2	World War II Memorial
16	D3	Washington Monument
21	D6	National Air and Space Museum
25	E2	Franklin Delano Roosevelt Memorial
27	E4	Bureau of Engraving and Printing
29	F3	Thomas Jefferson Memorial

RESTAURANTS

2	C4	Sweet Home Café
7	C5	Pavilion Café
9	C6	Garden Café
11	C6	Cascade Café
22	D6	Mitsitam Native Foods Café

SEE MAP 2

4

5

CHINATOWN

6

ARTS AND CULTURE

8	**C5**	National Archives Museum
10	**C6**	National Gallery of Art
17	**D4**	United States Holocaust Memorial Museum
18	**D4**	Freer Gallery of Art and Arthur M. Sackler Gallery
19	**D5**	National Museum of African Art
20	**D5**	Hirshhorn Museum and Sculpture Garden
23	**D6**	National Museum of the American Indian

SPORTS AND ACTIVITIES

5	**C4**	Smithsonian National Mall Tours
24	**E1**	West Potomac Park
26	**E3**	Tidal Basin Paddleboats

HOTELS

| 28 | **E4** | Mandarin Oriental Washington, D.C. |

Metro Center

Freedom Plaza

PENNSYLVANIA AVE NW

FEDERAL TRIANGLE

Federal Triangle

CONSTITUTION AVE NW

Archives-Navy Memorial-Penn Quarter

John Marshall Place Park

PENNSYLVANIA AVE NW

National Museum of American History

National Museum of Natural History

National Museum of African American History and Culture

THE MALL

MADISON DRIVE NW

National Mall

SEE MAP 3

Smithsonian

INDEPENDENCE AVE SW

JEFFERSON DRIVE SW

National Air and Space Museum

Bureau of Engraving and Printing

L'Enfant Plaza

Federal Center SW

395

Benjamin Banneker Park

Jefferson Field

SEE MAP 8

CASE BRIDGE

Washington Channel

395

SOUTHWEST WATERFRONT

Town Center Park

| 0 | 300 yds |
| 0 | 300 m |

DISTANCE ACROSS MAP
Approximate: 2.2 mi or 3.6 km

© AVALON TRAVEL

SIGHTS

23	**D2**	Lafayette Square
24	**D2**	The White House
36	**D5**	Friendship Archway
46	**E2**	President's Park and the Ellipse
57	**E4**	Ford's Theatre
58	**E5**	Federal Bureau of Investigation (FBI)

RESTAURANTS

6	**B3**	Elizabeth's Gone Raw
9	**C2**	BLT Steak
10	**C2**	Mirabelle
12	**C2**	The Bombay Club
18	**C4**	Fruitive
20	**C4**	Centrolina
21	**C5**	RareSweets
25	**D3**	Joe's Seafood, Prime Steak & Stone Crab
26	**D3**	Woodward Table
27	**D3**	Old Ebbitt Grill
29	**D3**	Astro Doughnuts and Fried Chicken
30	**D5**	DBGB Kitchen & Bar
32	**D5**	Zaytinya
37	**D5**	Crimson
54	**E4**	Harry's
60	**E5**	minibar by José Andrés
62	**E5**	Jaleo
63	**E5**	Oyamel Cocina Mexicana
66	**F6**	The Source by Wolfgang Puck

SEE MAP 4

Q ST NW

M ST NW

18TH ST NW

CONNECTICUT AVE NW

17TH ST NW

Farragut North Ⓜ

L ST NW

16TH ST NW

VERMONT AVE NW

14TH ST NW

DOWNTOWN

K ST NW

Farragut West Ⓜ

Farragut Square

McPherson Square

Franklin Square

I ST NW

17TH ST NW

McPherson Square Ⓜ

H ST NW

PENNSYLVANIA AVE NW

Lafayette Square

Lafayette Square

18TH ST NW

NEW YORK AVE NW

15TH ST NW

14TH ST NW

SEE MAP 7

G ST NW

17TH ST NW

PENNSYLVANIA AVE NW

F ST NW

The White House

President's Park

President's Park and the Ellipse

Pershing Park

Freedom Plaza

E ST NW

18TH ST NW

Ellipse

15TH ST NW

14TH ST NW

FEDERAL TRIANGLE

0	200 yds
0	200 m

DISTANCE ACROSS MAP
Approximate: 1.6 mi or 2.6 km

SEE MAP 1

CONSTITUTION AVE NW

National Mall

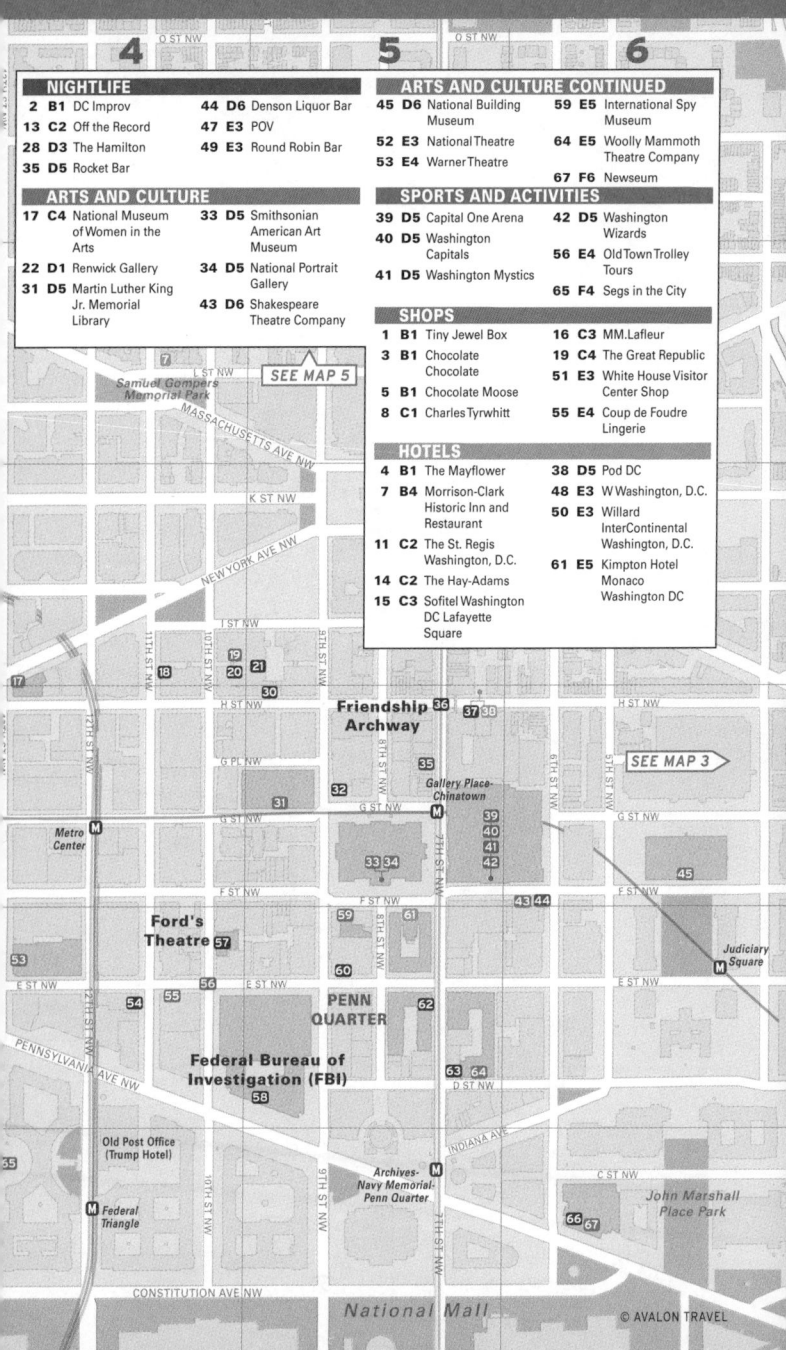

NIGHTLIFE
- 2 **B1** DC Improv
- 13 **C2** Off the Record
- 28 **D3** The Hamilton
- 35 **D5** Rocket Bar
- 44 **D6** Denson Liquor Bar
- 47 **E3** POV
- 49 **E3** Round Robin Bar

ARTS AND CULTURE
- 17 **C4** National Museum of Women in the Arts
- 22 **D1** Renwick Gallery
- 31 **D5** Martin Luther King Jr. Memorial Library
- 33 **D5** Smithsonian American Art Museum
- 34 **D5** National Portrait Gallery
- 43 **D6** Shakespeare Theatre Company

ARTS AND CULTURE CONTINUED
- 45 **D6** National Building Museum
- 52 **E3** National Theatre
- 53 **E4** Warner Theatre
- 59 **E5** International Spy Museum
- 64 **E5** Woolly Mammoth Theatre Company
- 67 **F6** Newseum

SPORTS AND ACTIVITIES
- 39 **D5** Capital One Arena
- 40 **D5** Washington Capitals
- 41 **D5** Washington Mystics
- 42 **D5** Washington Wizards
- 56 **E4** Old Town Trolley Tours
- 65 **F4** Segs in the City

SHOPS
- 1 **B1** Tiny Jewel Box
- 3 **B1** Chocolate Chocolate
- 5 **B1** Chocolate Moose
- 8 **C1** Charles Tyrwhitt
- 16 **C3** MM.Lafleur
- 19 **C4** The Great Republic
- 51 **E3** White House Visitor Center Shop
- 55 **E4** Coup de Foudre Lingerie

HOTELS
- 4 **B1** The Mayflower
- 7 **B4** Morrison-Clark Historic Inn and Restaurant
- 11 **C2** The St. Regis Washington, D.C.
- 14 **C2** The Hay-Adams
- 15 **C3** Sofitel Washington DC Lafayette Square
- 38 **D5** Pod DC
- 48 **E3** W Washington, D.C.
- 50 **E3** Willard InterContinental Washington, D.C.
- 61 **E5** Kimpton Hotel Monaco Washington DC

Samuel Gompers Memorial Park

SEE MAP 5

Friendship Archway

Gallery Place-Chinatown

SEE MAP 3

Metro Center

Ford's Theatre

PENN QUARTER

Federal Bureau of Investigation (FBI)

Old Post Office (Trump Hotel)

Federal Triangle

Archives-Navy Memorial-Penn Quarter

Judiciary Square

John Marshall Place Park

CONSTITUTION AVE NW

National Mall

© AVALON TRAVEL

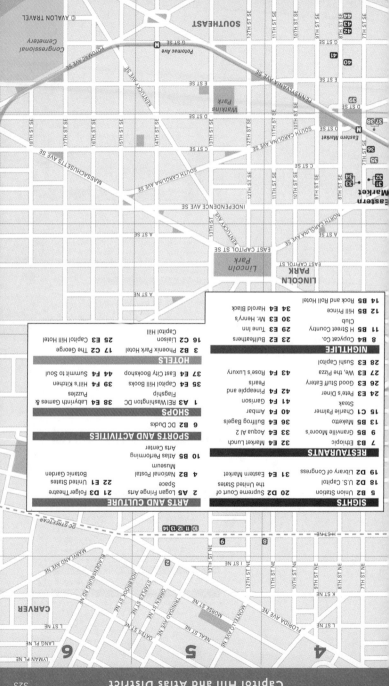

© AVALON TRAVEL

SIGHTS

5	B2	Union Station
18	D2	U.S. Capitol
20	D2	Supreme Court of the United States
19	D2	Library of Congress

RESTAURANTS

7	B3	Ethiopic
9	B5	Granville Moore's
13	B5	Maketto
15	C1	Charlie Palmer Steak
40	F4	Ambar
41	F4	Garrison
42	F4	Pineapple and Pearls
43	F4	Rose's Luxury
24	E3	Pete's Diner
26	E3	Good Stuff Eatery
27	E3	We, the Pizza
28	E3	Sushi Capitol
31	E4	Eastern Market
32	E4	Market Lunch
33	E4	Acqua Al 2
36	E4	Bullfrog Bagels
23	E2	Bullfeathers

NIGHTLIFE

8	B4	Copycat Co.
11	B5	H Street Country Club
12	B5	Hill Prince
30	E3	Mr. Henry's
34	E4	Harold Black
14	B5	Rock and Roll Hotel

ARTS AND CULTURE

21	D3	Folger Theatre
2	A5	Logan Fringe Arts Space
4	B2	National Postal Museum
22	E1	United States Botanic Garden
10	B5	Atlas Performing Arts Center

SPORTS AND ACTIVITIES

| 6 | B2 | DC Ducks |

SHOPS

1	A3	REI Washington DC Flagship
35	E4	Capitol Hill Books
37	E4	East City Bookshop
38	E4	Labyrinth Games & Puzzles
39	F4	Hill's Kitchen
44	F4	Summit to Soul

HOTELS

3	B2	Phoenix Park Hotel
16	C2	Liaison Capitol Hill
17	C2	The George
25	E3	Capitol Hill Hotel

WYOMING AVE NW   WYOMING AVE

KALORAMA HEIGHTS

24TH ST NW   23RD ST NW

TRACY PL NW

CALIFORNIA ST NW

COLUMBIA RD NW

PHELPS PL

LEROY PL NW

BANCROFT PL NW

Spanish Steps 5

PHELPS PL

SIGHTS
5	B2	Spanish Steps
27	D4	Dupont Circle

RESTAURANTS
4	A6	Henry's Soul Café
7	B3	Bistrot du Coin
9	B5	The Riggsby
19	D3	Bagels Etc.
24	D4	Beefsteak
25	D4	Afterwords Café
30	D6	Hank's Oyster Bar
32	D6	Little Serow
33	D6	Komi
34	D6	Sushi Taro
39	E5	Tabard Inn
41	F4	The Palm

NIGHTLIFE
3	A5	Larry's Lounge
6	B3	McClellan's Retreat
17	C6	Cobalt
18	D2	Bier Baron Tavern
31	D6	JR's Bar
43	F5	Eighteenth Street Lounge
45	F6	Quill

ARTS AND CULTURE
11	C3	Hillyer Art Space
12	C3	Studio Gallery
13	C3	The Phillips Collection
16	C5	National Museum of American Jewish Military History
20	D3	The Society of the Cincinnati Anderson House
29	D4	Dupont Underground

SHOPS
8	B4	Glen's Garden Market
14	C4	The Mediterranean Way
15	C4	Tabletop
23	D4	Second Story Books
26	D4	Kramerbooks
36	E4	Shop Made in D.C.
37	E4	Proper Topper
38	E4	Jenni Bick Custom Journals
42	F5	Betsy Fisher
44	F5	Brooks Brothers

HOTELS
1	A3	Washington Hilton
2	A4	Dupont Place Boutique Inn
10	B5	The Carlyle
21	D3	The Fairfax at Embassy Row
22	D3	The Embassy Row Hotel
28	D4	The Dupont Circle Hotel
35	E3	Hotel Madera
40	E5	Tabard Inn
46	F6	The Jefferson

0   150 yds
0   150 m

DISTANCE ACROSS MAP
Approximate: 1.1 mi or 1.8 km

22ND ST NW

FLORIDA AVE NW

21ST ST NW

HILLYER PL NW

MASSACHUSETTS AVE NW

P ST NW

HOPKINS ST NW

O ST NW

NEWPORT PL NW

N ST NW

Rock Creek

SEE MAP 7

25TH ST NW   24TH ST NW   23RD ST NW

WEST END

22ND ST NW

21ST ST NW

NEW HAMPSHIRE AVE NW

WARD PL NW

Duke Ellington Park

© AVALON TRAVEL

SIGHTS

1 **A5** Howard University

19 **C4** African American Civil War Museum

RESTAURANTS

2 **B3** Maydan
3 **B4** Florida Avenue Grill
5 **C3** Busboys and Poets
10 **C3** The Wydown
11 **C3** Taqueria Nacional
15 **C4** Ben's Chili Bowl
17 **C4** Dukem Ethiopian Restaurant
21 **C4** Etete
23 **C4** Hazel
24 **C4** Kyirisan

29 **C5** Calabash Tea & Café
38 **D3** Pearl Dive Oyster Palace
42 **D6** ANXO Cidery & Pintxos Bar
43 **E3** Le Diplomate
48 **E3** Slipstream
51 **E5** Compass Coffee
53 **F2** Siren by RW
57 **F4** Buttercream Bakeshop
60 **F4** The Dabney

NIGHTLIFE

6 **C3** The Gibson
7 **C3** Marvin
8 **C3** Tropicalia
12 **C3** Café Saint-Ex
16 **C4** U Street Music Hall
18 **C4** Vinoteca
20 **C4** Nellie's Sports Bar
22 **C4** 9:30 Club
28 **C5** Flash

30 **C5** Right Proper Brewing Co.
33 **D3** 2 Birds 1 Stone
34 **D3** Black Cat
45 **E3** New Vegas Lounge
49 **E4** Maxwell Park
50 **E5** Dacha Beer Garden
59 **F4** Columbia Room

ARTS AND CULTURE

13 **C3** Source Theatre
14 **C3** The Lincoln Theatre
31 **C5** The Howard Theatre

44 **E3** Studio Theatre
46 **E3** Transformer
58 **F4** Long View Gallery

SHOPS

4 **B4** Cherry Blossom Creative
9 **C3** GoodWood
25 **C4** Violet
26 **C4** Ministry of Supply
27 **C5** Lettie Gooch
32 **D3** Redeem
35 **D3** Current Boutique

36 **D3** Batch 13
37 **D3** Miss Pixie's
39 **D3** Shinola
40 **D3** Filson
41 **D3** Salt & Sundry
52 **E5** Grand Cata
56 **F4** Union Kitchen Grocery

HOTELS

47 **E3** Kimpton Mason & Rook Hotel
54 **F2** The Darcy Washington DC

55 **F3** Washington Plaza Hotel

0   300 yds
0   300 m

DISTANCE ACROSS MAP
Approximate: 1.7 mi or 2.7 km

SEE MAP 4

© AVALON TRAVEL

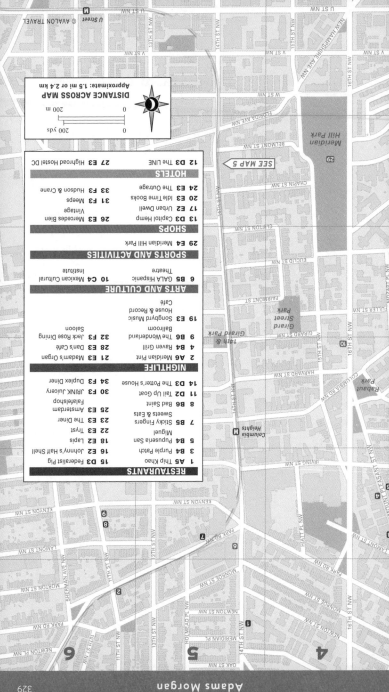

DISTANCE ACROSS MAP
Approximate: 1.5 mi or 2.4 km

0 — 200 yds
0 — 200 m

© AVALON TRAVEL

RESTAURANTS
- 1 A5 Thip Khao
- 15 D3 Federalist Pig
- 3 B4 Purple Patch
- 5 B4 Pupuseria San Miguel
- 16 E2 Johnny's Half Shell
- 18 E2 Lapis
- 7 B5 Sticky Fingers Sweets & Eats
- 22 E3 Tryst
- 23 E3 The Diner
- 8 B6 Bad Saint
- 25 E3 Amsterdam Falafelshop
- 11 D2 Tail Up Goat
- 30 F3 JRINK Juicery
- 14 D3 The Potter's House
- 34 F3 Duplex Diner

NIGHTLIFE
- 2 A6 Meridian Pint
- 21 E3 Madam's Organ
- 4 B4 Raven Grill
- 28 E3 Dan's Café
- 9 B6 The Wonderland Ballroom
- 32 F3 Jack Rose Dining Saloon
- 19 E3 Songbyrd Music House & Record Café

ARTS AND CULTURE
- 6 B5 GALA Hispanic Theatre
- 10 C4 Mexican Cultural Institute

SPORTS AND ACTIVITIES
- 29 E4 Meridian Hill Park

SHOPS
- 13 D3 Capitol Hemp
- 26 E3 Mercedes Bien Vintage
- 17 E2 Urban Dwell
- 31 F3 Meeps
- 20 E3 Idle Time Books
- 33 F3 Hudson & Crane

HOTELS
- 12 D3 The LINE
- 27 E3 Highroad Hostel DC
- 24 E3 The Outrage

SEE MAP 5

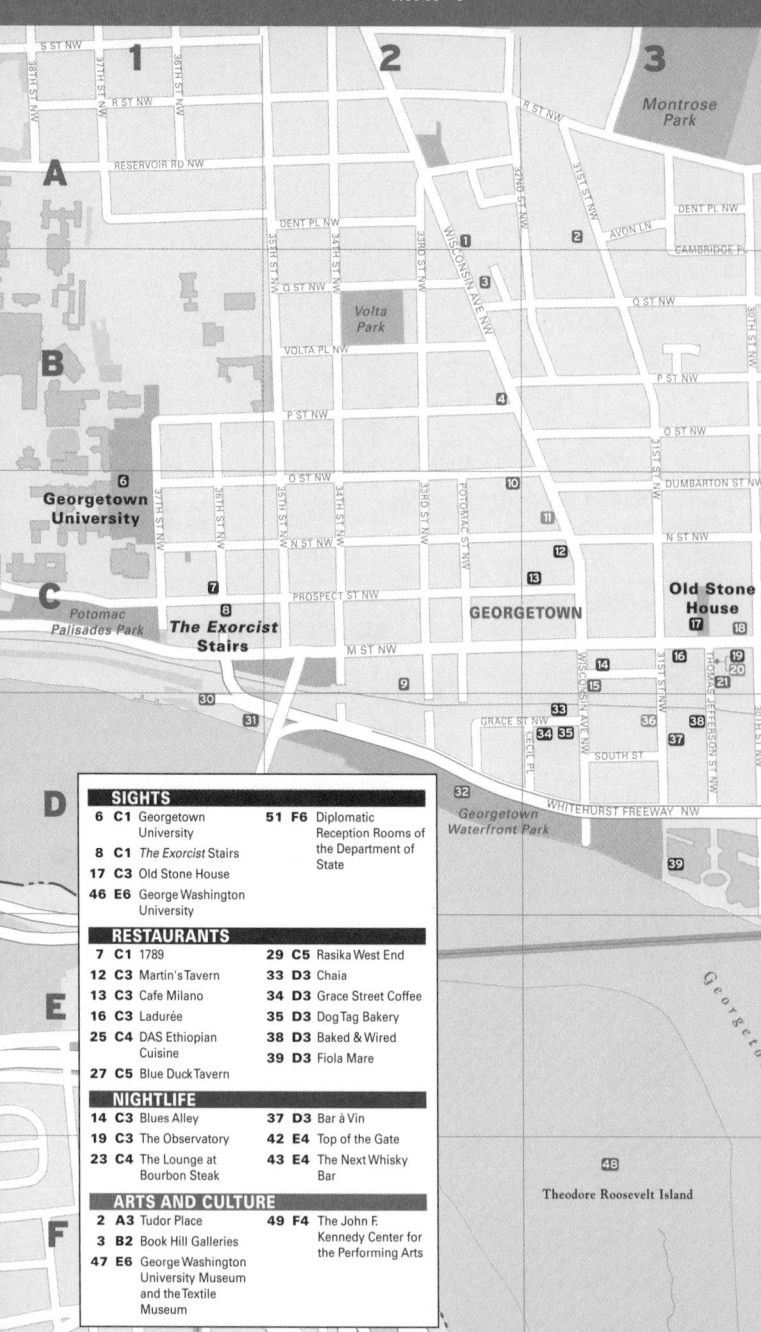

SIGHTS

6	C1	Georgetown University
8	C1	*The Exorcist* Stairs
17	C3	Old Stone House
46	E6	George Washington University
51	F6	Diplomatic Reception Rooms of the Department of State

RESTAURANTS

7	C1	1789
12	C3	Martin's Tavern
13	C3	Cafe Milano
16	C3	Ladurée
25	C4	DAS Ethiopian Cuisine
27	C5	Blue Duck Tavern
29	C5	Rasika West End
33	D3	Chaia
34	D3	Grace Street Coffee
35	D3	Dog Tag Bakery
38	D3	Baked & Wired
39	D3	Fiola Mare

NIGHTLIFE

14	C3	Blues Alley
19	C3	The Observatory
23	C4	The Lounge at Bourbon Steak
37	D3	Bar à Vin
42	E4	Top of the Gate
43	E4	The Next Whisky Bar

ARTS AND CULTURE

2	A3	Tudor Place
3	B2	Book Hill Galleries
47	E6	George Washington University Museum and the Textile Museum
49	F4	The John F. Kennedy Center for the Performing Arts

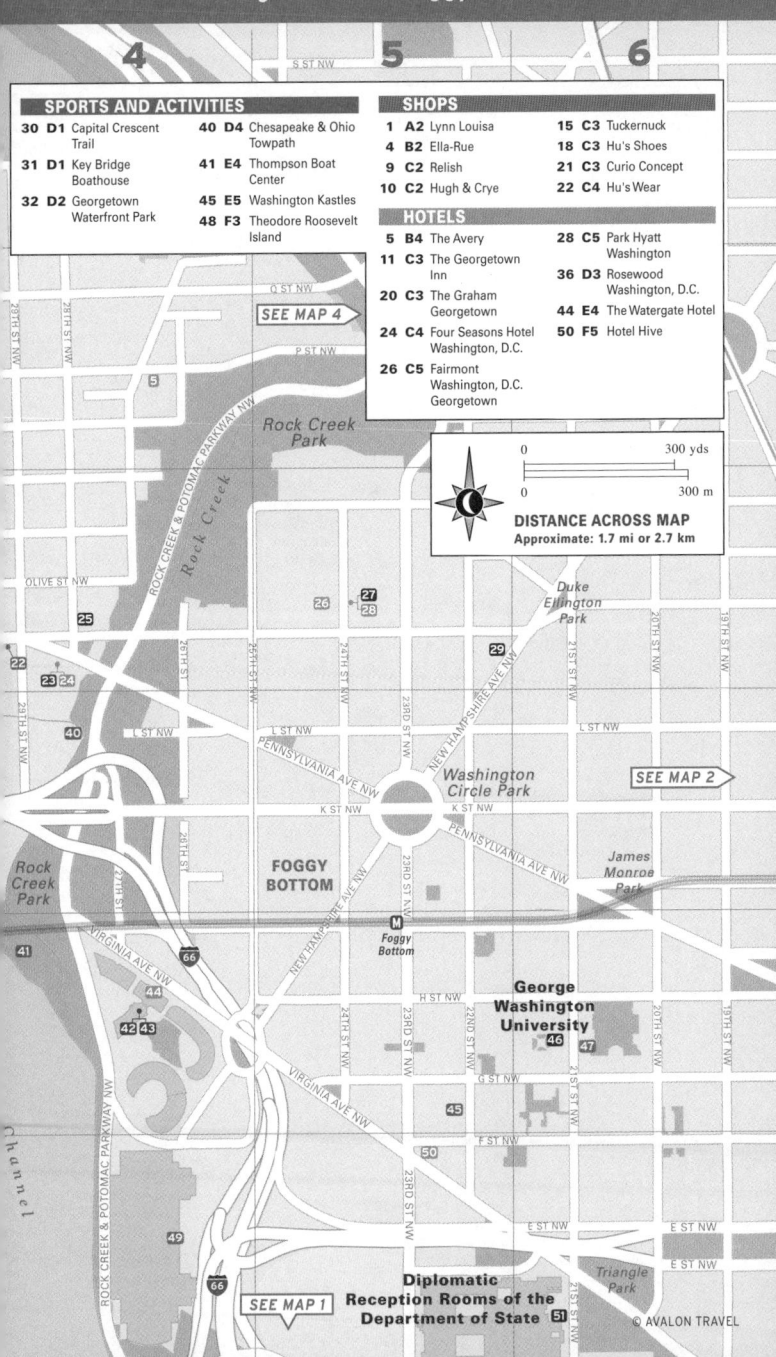

SPORTS AND ACTIVITIES

- **30 D1** Capital Crescent Trail
- **31 D1** Key Bridge Boathouse
- **32 D2** Georgetown Waterfront Park
- **40 D4** Chesapeake & Ohio Towpath
- **41 E4** Thompson Boat Center
- **45 E5** Washington Kastles
- **48 F3** Theodore Roosevelt Island

SHOPS

- **1 A2** Lynn Louisa
- **4 B2** Ella-Rue
- **9 C2** Relish
- **10 C2** Hugh & Crye
- **15 C3** Tuckernuck
- **18 C3** Hu's Shoes
- **21 C3** Curio Concept
- **22 C4** Hu's Wear

HOTELS

- **5 B4** The Avery
- **11 C3** The Georgetown Inn
- **20 C3** The Graham Georgetown
- **24 C4** Four Seasons Hotel Washington, D.C.
- **26 C5** Fairmont Washington, D.C. Georgetown
- **28 C5** Park Hyatt Washington
- **36 D3** Rosewood Washington, D.C.
- **44 E4** The Watergate Hotel
- **50 F5** Hotel Hive

0   300 yds

0   300 m

DISTANCE ACROSS MAP
Approximate: 1.7 mi or 2.7 km

© AVALON TRAVEL

SIGHTS

4 **C1** District Wharf

24 **F6** Frederick Douglass National Historic Site

RESTAURANTS

13 **D4** Ice Cream Jubilee
14 **D4** Whaley's
15 **D4** Osteria Morini

16 **D4** Due South
20 **E6** Capitol Hill Crab Cakes

NIGHTLIFE

2 **C1** The Anthem

11 **D4** Bluejacket

ARTS AND CULTURE

1 **B2** Blind Whino SW Arts Club
5 **C1** Arena Stage
18 **E6** Anacostia Arts Center
19 **E6** Honfleur Gallery

21 **F5** America's Islamic Heritage Museum & Cultural Center
22 **F6** Vivid Solutions Gallery
23 **F6** Anacostia Comminuty Museum

SPORTS AND ACTIVITIES

7 **D3** Washington Nationals
8 **D3** Nationals Park
9 **D3** Ballpark Boathouse

10 **D3** Anacostia Riverwalk Trail
12 **D4** The Yards Park
17 **E2** DC United

HOTELS

3 **C1** InterContinental Washington D.C.-The Wharf

6 **C3** Capitol Skyline Hotel

DISTANCE ACROSS MAP
Approximate: 2.3 mi or 3.7 km

0 ——— 300 yds
0 ——— 300 m

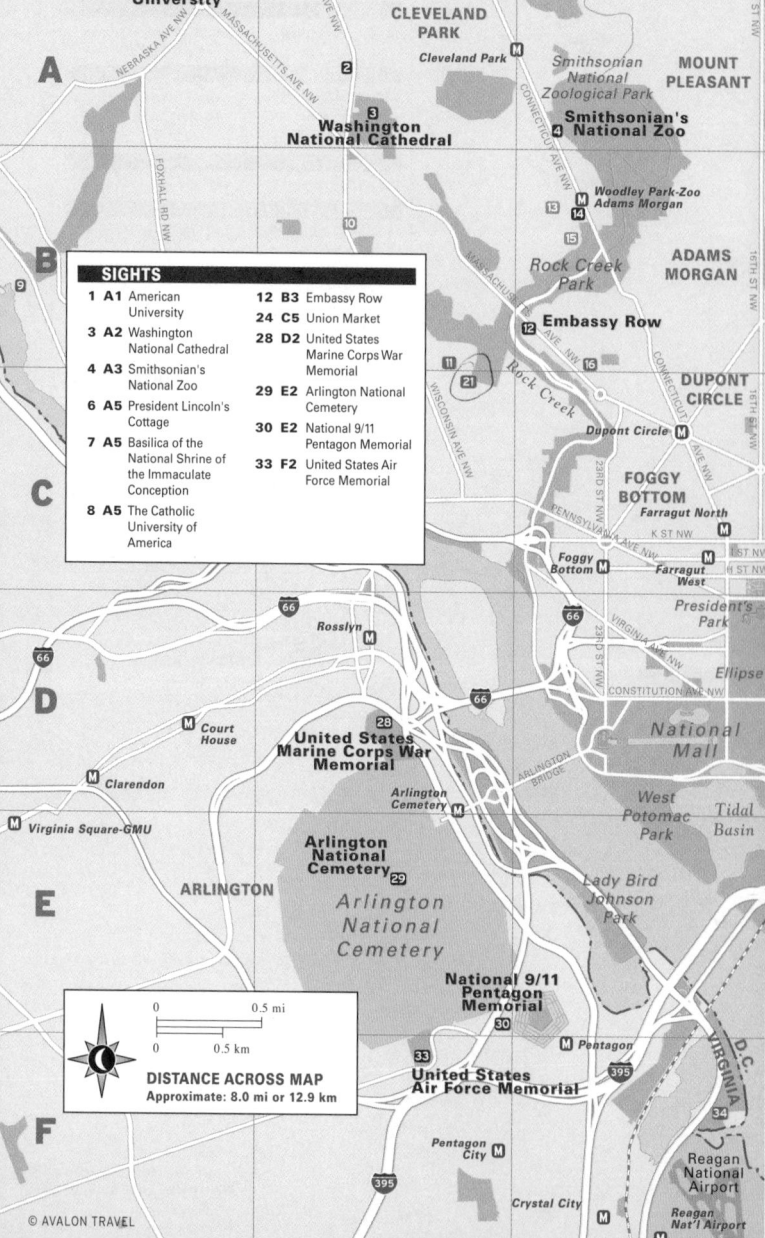

SIGHTS

1 **A1** American University
3 **A2** Washington National Cathedral
4 **A3** Smithsonian's National Zoo
6 **A5** President Lincoln's Cottage
7 **A5** Basilica of the National Shrine of the Immaculate Conception
8 **A5** The Catholic University of America
12 **B3** Embassy Row
24 **C5** Union Market
28 **D2** United States Marine Corps War Memorial
29 **E2** Arlington National Cemetery
30 **E2** National 9/11 Pentagon Memorial
33 **F2** United States Air Force Memorial

American University

CLEVELAND PARK

Cleveland Park

Smithsonian National Zoological Park

MOUNT PLEASANT

Washington National Cathedral

Smithsonian's National Zoo

Woodley Park-Zoo Adams Morgan

ADAMS MORGAN

Rock Creek Park

Embassy Row

DUPONT CIRCLE

Dupont Circle

FOGGY BOTTOM

Farragut North

Farragut West

Rosslyn

President's Park

Ellipse

Court House

United States Marine Corps War Memorial

Arlington Cemetery

National Mall

Clarendon

Virginia Square-GMU

Arlington National Cemetery

West Potomac Park

Tidal Basin

ARLINGTON

Arlington National Cemetery

Lady Bird Johnson Park

National 9/11 Pentagon Memorial

0 0.5 mi
0 0.5 km

DISTANCE ACROSS MAP
Approximate: 8.0 mi or 12.9 km

United States Air Force Memorial

Pentagon

Pentagon City

VIRGINIA

D.C.

Reagan National Airport

Crystal City

Reagan Nat'l Airport

© AVALON TRAVEL

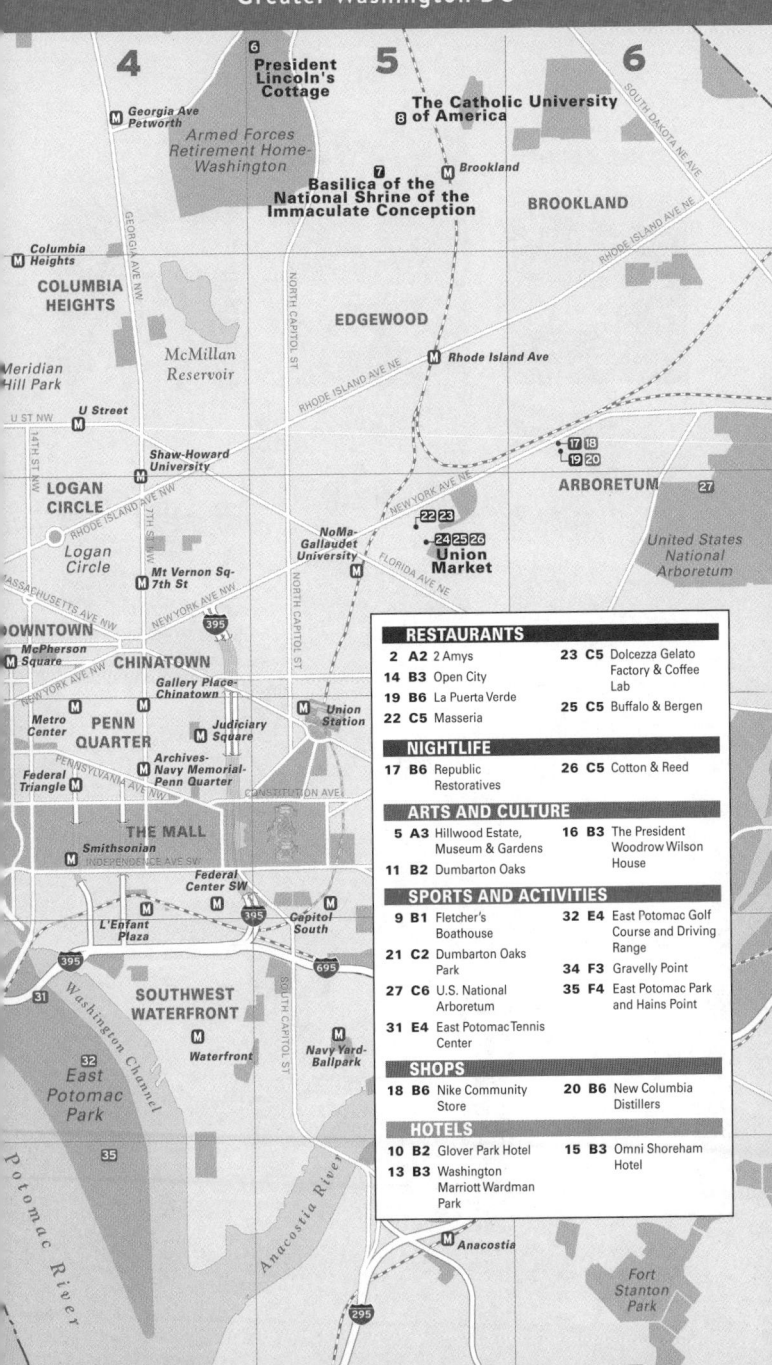

RESTAURANTS

2	**A2**	2 Amys
14	**B3**	Open City
19	**B6**	La Puerta Verde
22	**C5**	Masseria
23	**C5**	Dolcezza Gelato Factory & Coffee Lab
25	**C5**	Buffalo & Bergen

NIGHTLIFE

17	**B6**	Republic Restoratives
26	**C5**	Cotton & Reed

ARTS AND CULTURE

5	**A3**	Hillwood Estate, Museum & Gardens
11	**B2**	Dumbarton Oaks
16	**B3**	The President Woodrow Wilson House

SPORTS AND ACTIVITIES

9	**B1**	Fletcher's Boathouse
21	**C2**	Dumbarton Oaks Park
27	**C6**	U.S. National Arboretum
31	**E4**	East Potomac Tennis Center
32	**E4**	East Potomac Golf Course and Driving Range
34	**F3**	Gravelly Point
35	**F4**	East Potomac Park and Hains Point

SHOPS

18	**B6**	Nike Community Store
20	**B6**	New Columbia Distillers

HOTELS

10	**B2**	Glover Park Hotel
13	**B3**	Washington Marriott Wardman Park
15	**B3**	Omni Shoreham Hotel

Road Trip Guides

BLUE RIDGE PARKWAY
Road Trip

INCLUDING SHENANDOAH & GREAT SMOKY MOUNTAINS NATIONAL PARKS

JASON FRYE

NASHVILLE TO NEW ORLEANS
Road Trip

NATCHEZ TRACE PARKWAY · MEMPHIS · TUPELO · MISSISSIPPI BLUES TRAIL

MARGARET LITTMAN

NEW ENGLAND
Road Trip

BOSTON, ACADIA NATIONAL PARK, WHITE MOUNTAINS, BERKSHIRES, NEWPORT, AND CAPE COD

JEN ROSE SMITH

City Guides

ASHEVILLE
& THE GREAT SMOKY MOUNTAINS

JASON FRYE

ATLANTA

TRAY BUTLER

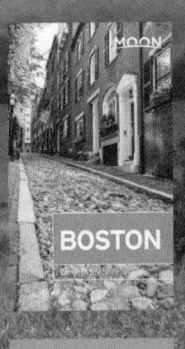

BOSTON

CHICAGO

REBECCA HOLLAND

NASHVILLE

MARGARET LITTMAN

PITTSBURGH

EMILY KING

MOON NATIONAL PARKS

In these books:

- Full coverage of gateway cities and towns
- Itineraries from one day to multiple weeks
- Advice on where to stay (or camp) in and around the parks

MAP SYMBOLS

■	Sights	◉	National Capital	▲	Mountain	══════	Major Hwy
■	Restaurants	◉	State Capital	✦	Natural Feature	┈┈┈┈┈	Road/Hwy
■	Nightlife	○	City/Town	🏞	Waterfall	┄┄┄┄┄	Pedestrian Friendly
■	Arts and Culture	★	Point of Interest	⬧	Park	------	Trail
■	Sports and Activities	•	Accommodation	⬟	Archaeological Site	▪▪▪▪▪▪▪	Stairs
■	Shops	▼	Restaurant/Bar	◨	Trailhead	··········	Ferry
■	Hotels	■	Other Location	◪	Parking Area	─ ─ ─ ─	Railroad

CONVERSION TABLES

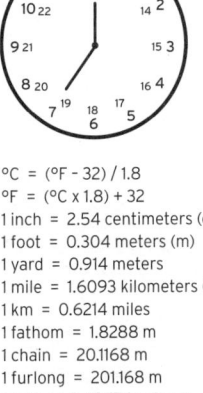

°C = (°F - 32) / 1.8
°F = (°C x 1.8) + 32
1 inch = 2.54 centimeters (cm)
1 foot = 0.304 meters (m)
1 yard = 0.914 meters
1 mile = 1.6093 kilometers (km)
1 km = 0.6214 miles
1 fathom = 1.8288 m
1 chain = 20.1168 m
1 furlong = 201.168 m
1 acre = 0.4047 hectares
1 sq km = 100 hectares
1 sq mile = 2.59 square km
1 ounce = 28.35 grams
1 pound = 0.4536 kilograms
1 short ton = 0.90718 metric ton
1 short ton = 2,000 pounds
1 long ton = 1.016 metric tons
1 long ton = 2,240 pounds
1 metric ton = 1,000 kilograms
1 quart = 0.94635 liters
1 US gallon = 3.7854 liters
1 Imperial gallon = 4.5459 liters
1 nautical mile = 1.852 km

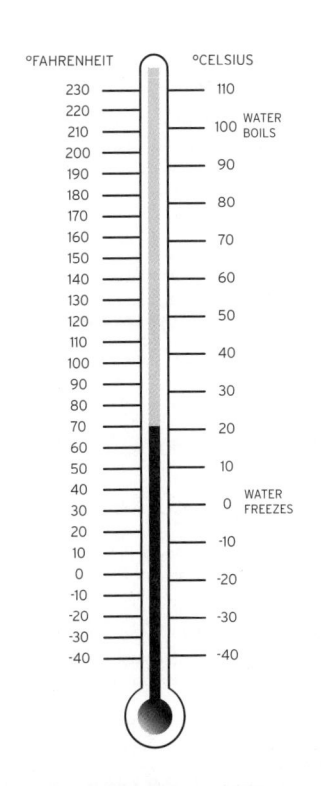

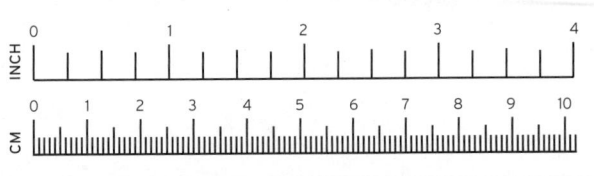

MOON WASHINGTON DC
Avalon Travel
Hachette Book Group
1700 Fourth Street
Berkeley, CA 94710, USA
www.moon.com

Editor and Series Manager: Leah Gordon
Copy Editor: Deana Shields
Graphics and Production Coordinators: Elizabeth Jang, Darren Alessi
Cover Design: Faceout Studios, Charles Brock
Interior Design: Megan Jones Design
Moon Logo: Tim McGrath
Map Editor: Kat Bennett
Cartographers: Moon Street Cartography (Durango CO), Brian Shotwell, Kat Bennett
Proofreader: Rosemarie Leenerts
Indexer: Rachel Kuhn

ISBN-13: 9781631219962

Printing History
1st Edition — August 2018
5 4 3 2 1

Text © 2018 by Samantha Sault.
Maps © 2018 by Avalon Travel.

D0051896

Also available from
DIANA PALMER

Magnolia
Renegade
Lone Star Winter
Dangerous
Desperado
Merciless
Heartless
Fearless
Her Kind of Hero
Lacy
Nora
Big Sky Winter
Man of the Hour
Trilby
Lawman
Hard to Handle
The Savage Heart
Courageous
Lawless
Diamond Spur
The Texas Ranger
Lord of the Desert
The Cowboy and the Lady
Most Wanted

Fit for a King
Paper Rose
Rage of Passion
Once in Paris
After the Music
Roomful of Roses
Champagne Girl
Passion Flower
Diamond Girl
Friends and Lovers
Cattleman's Choice
Lady Love
The Rawhide Man
Outsider
Night Fever
Before Sunrise
Protector
Midnight Rider
Wyoming Tough
Wyoming Fierce
Wyoming Bold
Wyoming Strong
The Morcai Battalion:
The Recruit

Coming Summer 2015

Untamed

DIANA
PALMER

INVINCIBLE

HQN™

HQN™

ISBN-13: 978-0-373-77949-9

Invincible

Copyright © 2014 by Diana Palmer

In Memoriam

For my friend Verna Jane Clayton; wife of Danny,
sister of Nancy, mother of Christina and Daniel,
grandmother of Selena Marie and Donovan Kyle

Your smile burns bright in our memories

Where you will live on, forever young, forever loved.

Never forgotten.

Dear Reader,

Carson, the hero of *Invincible*, is one of the Oglala Lakota people. For many years, the Lakota have had a special place in my heart. During World War II our mother dated a Lakota man and spoke of marrying him. Our father came along before that could happen. But my sister and I grew up hearing stories about the Plains tribes, especially the Lakota (whom most people outside the tribe refer to as Sioux).

I wrote a book once called *Paper Rose*, whose hero had Lakota blood. I thought at the time how nice it would be to do something useful for the nation I held in such esteem. I contacted the Oglala Lakota College in Kyle, South Dakota, and asked about founding a nursing scholarship there in the name of our mother, who was a nurse. So the Eloise Cliatt Spaeth Nursing Scholarship was born.

Over the years, the scholarship has helped a great many people with families afford to go back to school. My friend Marilyn sends me letters from them, which I keep and treasure. I can't tell you how proud I am to be contributing, even in a small way, to such a grand cause. I grew up poor. I can tell you that education makes all the difference in the world.

One other thing about this book that is special is the dedication. Last year, I lost a friend. She was my daughter-in-law's mother, Jane Clayton. Since Christina was seventeen years old, she and her mother, Jane, her father, Danny, and her brother, Daniel, have been part of my family. Of all my memories of Jane, there is this special one: at the kids' wedding rehearsal in Atlanta, she sat with my sister, Dannis, and my son, Blayne, her husband, Danny, and son, Daniel, and daughter, Christina, and my niece Maggie and me, shooting down enemy aircraft in an arcade game. I remember her laughing as if she were a kid. She did have the most beautiful laugh.

Oh, what fun that was! Jane, laughing, with stars in her eyes.

This book is for you, Jane, so that your name will be remembered as long as the book stays in print anywhere in the world. Good night, my friend.

Thank you for reading *Invincible*. As always, I am your fan.

Love,

Diana Palmer

INVINCIBLE

CHAPTER ONE

IT WAS A rainy Friday morning.

Carlie Blair, who was running late for her job as secretary to Jacobsville, Texas police chief Cash Grier, only had time for a piece of toast and a sip of coffee before she rushed out the door to persuade her ten-year-old red pickup truck to start. It had gone on grinding seemingly forever before it finally caught up and started.

Her father, a Methodist minister, was out of town on business for the day. So there was nobody to help her get it running. Luck was with her. It did, at least, start.

She envied her friend Michelle Godfrey, whose guardian and his sister had given her a Jaguar for Christmas. Michelle was away at college now, and she and Carlie still spoke on the phone, but they no longer shared rides to town and the cost of gas on a daily basis.

The old clunker ate gas like candy and Carlie's salary only stretched so far. She wished she had more than a couple pairs of jeans, a few T-shirts, a coat and one good pair of shoes. It must be nice, she thought, not to have to count pennies. But her father was always optimistic about their status. *God loved the*

poor, because they gave away so much, he was fond
of saying. He was probably right.

Right now, though, her rain-wet jeans were uncomfortable, and she'd stepped in a mud puddle with her
only pair of good shoes while she was knocking cor-
rosion off the battery terminals with the hammer she
kept under the front seat for that purpose. All this in
January weather, which was wet and cold and miserable, even in South Texas.

Consequently, when she parked her car in the small
lot next to the chief's office, she looked like a be-
draggled rat. Her dark, short, wavy hair was curling
like crazy, as it always did in a rainstorm. Her coat
was soaked. Her green eyes, full of silent resignation,
didn't smile as she opened the office door.

Her worst nightmare was standing just inside.

Carson.

He glared at her. He was so much taller than she
that she had to look up at him. There was a lot to look
at, although she tried not to show her interest.

He was all muscle, but it wasn't overly obvious.
He had a rodeo rider's physique, lean and powerful.
Like her, he wore jeans, but his were obviously designer ones, like those hand-tooled leather boots on
his big feet and the elaborately scrolled leather holster
in which he kept his .45 automatic. He was wearing
a jacket that partially concealed the gun, but he was
intimidating enough without it.

He was Lakota Sioux. He had jet-black hair that
fell to his waist in back, although he wore it in a ponytail usually. He had large black eyes that seemed to
see everything with one sweep of his head. He had
high cheekbones and a light olive complexion. There

were faint scars on the knuckles of his big hands. She noticed because he was holding a file in one of them.

Her file.

Well, really, the chief's file, that had been lying on her desk, waiting to be typed up. It referenced an attack on her father a few weeks earlier that had resulted in Carlie being stabbed. Involuntarily, her hand went to the scar that ran from her shoulder down to the beginning of her small breasts. She flushed when she saw where he was looking.

"Those are confidential files," she said shortly.

He looked around. "There was nobody here to tell me that," he said, his deep voice clear as a bell in the silent room.

She flushed at the implied criticism. "Damned truck wouldn't start and I got soaked trying to start it," she muttered. She slid her weather-beaten old purse under her desk, ran a hand through her wet hair, took off her ratty coat and hung it up before she sat down at her desk. "Did you need something?" she asked with crushing politeness. She even managed a smile. Sort of.

"I need to see the chief," he replied.

She frowned. "There's this thing called a door. He's got one," she said patiently. "You knock on it, and he comes out."

He gave her a look that could have stopped traffic. "There's somebody in there with him," he said with equal patience. "I didn't want to interrupt."

"I see." She moved things around on her desk, muttering to herself.

"Bad sign."

She looked up. "Huh?"

"Talking to yourself."

She glared at him. It had been a bad morning altogether and he wasn't helping. "Don't listen, if it bothers you."

He gave her a long look and laughed hollowly. "Listen, kid, nothing about you bothers me. Or ever will."

There were the sounds of chairs scraping wood, as if the men in Cash's office had stood up and pushed back their seats. She figured it was safe to interrupt him.

Well, safer than listening to Mr. Original American here run her down.

She pushed the intercom button. "You have a visitor, sir," she announced.

There was a murmur. "Who is it?"

She looked at Carson. "The gentleman who starts fires with hand grenades," she said sweetly.

Carson stared at her with icy black eyes.

Cash's door opened, and there was Carlie's father, a man in a very expensive suit and Cash.

That explained why her father had left home so early. He was out of town, as he'd said he would be; out of Comanche Wells, where they lived, anyway. Not that Jacobsville was more than a five-minute drive from home.

"Carson," Cash said, nodding. "I think you know Reverend Blair and my brother, Garon?"

"Yes." Carson shook hands with them.

Carlie was doing mental shorthand. Garon Grier was senior special agent in charge of the Jacobsville branch of the FBI. He'd moved to Jacobsville some time ago, but the FBI branch office hadn't been here quite as long. Garon had been with the bureau for a number of years.

Carlie wondered what was going on that involved both the FBI and her father. But she knew that question would go unanswered. Her father was remarkably silent on issues that concerned law enforcement, although he knew quite a few people in that profession.

She recalled with a chill the telephone conversation she'd had recently with someone who called and said, "Tell your father he's next." She couldn't get anybody to tell her what they thought it meant. It was disturbing, like the news she'd overheard that the man who'd put a knife in her, trying to kill her father, had been poisoned and died.

Something big was going on, linked to that Wyoming murder and involving some politician who had ties to a drug cartel. But nobody told Carlie anything.

"Well, I'll be off. I have a meeting in San Antonio," Reverend Blair said, taking his leave. He paused at Carlie's desk. "Don't do anything fancy for supper, okay?" he asked, smiling. "I may be very late."

"Okay, Dad." She grinned up at him.

He ruffled her hair and walked out.

Carson was watching the interplay with cynical eyes.

"Doesn't your dad ruffle your hair?" she asked sarcastically.

"No. He did lay a chair across it once." He averted his eyes at once, as if the comment had slipped out against his will and embarrassed him.

Carlie tried not to stare. What in the world sort of background did he come from? The violence struck a chord in her. She had secrets of her own from years past.

"Carson," Garon Grier said, pausing at the door. "We may need you at some point."

Carson nodded. "I'll be around."

"Thanks."

Garon waved at his brother, smiled at Carlie and let himself out the door.

"Something perking?" Carson asked Cash.

"Quite a lot, in fact. Carlie, hold my calls until I tell you," he instructed.

"Sure thing, Boss."

"Come on in." Cash went ahead into his office.

Carson paused by Carlie's desk and glared at her.

She glared back. "If you don't stop scowling at me, I'm going to ask the chief to frisk you for hand grenades," she muttered.

"Frisk me yourself," he dared softly.

The flush deepened, darkened.

His black eyes narrowed, because he knew innocence when he saw it; it was that rare in his world. "Clueless, aren't you?" he chided.

She lifted her chin and glared back. "My father is a minister," she said with quiet pride.

"Really?"

She frowned, cocking her head. "Excuse me?"

"Are you coming in or not?" Cash asked suddenly, and there was a bite in his voice.

Carson seemed faintly surprised. He followed Cash into the office. The door closed. There were words spoken in a harsh tone, followed by a pause and a suddenly apologetic voice.

Carlie paid little attention. Carson had upset her

nerves. She wished her boss would find someone else to talk to. Her job had been wonderful and satisfying until Carson started hanging around the office all the time. Something was going on, something big. It involved local and federal law enforcement—she was fairly certain that the chief's brother didn't just happen by to visit—and somehow, it also involved her father.

She wondered if she could dig any information out of her parent if she went about it in the right way. She'd have to work on that.

Then she recalled that phone call that she'd told her father about, just recently. A male voice had said, simply, "Tell your father, he's next." It had been a chilling experience, one she'd forced to the back of her mind. Now she wondered if all the traffic through her boss's office involved her in some way, as well as her father. The man who'd tried to kill him had died, mysteriously poisoned.

She still wondered why anybody would attack a minister. That remark of Carson's made her curious. She'd said her father was a minister and he'd said, "Really?" in that sarcastic, cold tone of voice. Why?

"I'm a mushroom," she said to herself. "They keep me in the dark and feed me manure." She sighed and went back to work.

SHE WAS ON the phone with the sheriff's office when Carson left. He went by her desk with only a cursory glance at her, and it was, of all things, placid. Almost apologetic. She lowered her eyes and refused to even look at him.

Even if she'd found him irresistible—and she was

trying not to—his reputation with women made her wary of him.

Sure, it was a new century, but Carlie was a small-town girl and raised religiously. She didn't share the casual attitude of many of her former classmates about physical passion.

She grimaced. It was hard to be a nice girl when people treated her like a disease on legs. In school, they'd made fun of her, whispered about her. One pretty, popular girl said that she didn't know what she was missing and that she should live it up.

Carlie just stared at her and smiled. She didn't say anything. Apparently the smile wore the other girl down because she shrugged, turned her back and walked off to whisper to the girls in her circle. They all looked at Carlie and laughed.

She was used to it. Her father said that adversity was like grit, it honed metal to a fine edge. She'd have liked to be honed a little less.

They were right about one thing; she really didn't know what she was missing. It seemed appropriate, because she'd read about sensations she was supposed to feel with men around, and she didn't feel any of them.

She chided herself silently. That was a lie. She felt them when she was close to Carson. She knew that he was aware of it, which made it worse. He laughed at her, just the way her classmates had laughed at her in school. She was the odd one out, the misfit. She had a reason for her ironclad morals. Many local people knew them, too. Episodes in her childhood had hardened her.

Well, people tended to be products of their upbringing. That was life. Unless she wanted to throw away her ideals and give up religion, she was pretty much settled in her beliefs. Maybe it wasn't so bad being a misfit. Her late grandfather had said that civilizations rested on the bedrock of faith and law and the arts. Some people had to be conventional to keep the mechanism going.

"What was that?" Sheriff Hayes's receptionist asked.

"Sorry." Carlie cleared her throat. She'd been on hold. "I was just mumbling to myself. What were you saying?"

The woman laughed and gave her the information the chief had asked for, about an upcoming criminal case.

SHE COOKED A light supper, just creamed chicken and rice, with green peas, and made a nice apple pie for dessert.

Her father came in, looking harassed. Then he saw the spread and grinned from ear to ear. "What a nice surprise!"

"I know, something light. But I was hungry," she added.

He made a face. "Shame. Telling lies."

She shrugged. "I went to church Sunday. God won't mind a little lie, in a good cause."

He smiled. "You know, some people have actually asked me how to talk to God."

"I just do it while I'm cooking, or working in the yard," Carlie said. "Just like I'm talking to you."

He laughed. "Me, too. But there are people who make hard work of it."

"Why were you in the chief's office today?" she asked suddenly.

He paused in the act of putting a napkin in his lap. His expression went blank for an instant, then it came back to life. "He wanted me to talk to a prisoner for him," he said finally.

She raised both eyebrows.

"Sorry," he said, smoothing out the napkin. "Some things are confidential."

"Okay."

"Let's say grace," he added.

LATER, HE WATCHED the news while she cleaned up the kitchen. She sat down with him and watched a nature special for a while. Then she excused herself and went upstairs to read. She wasn't really interested in much television programming, except for history specials and anything about mining. She loved rocks.

She sat down on the side of her bed and thumbed through her bookshelf. Most titles were digital as well as physical these days, but she still loved the feel and smell of an actual book in her hands.

She pulled out a well-worn copy of a book on the Little Bighorn fight, one that was written by members of various tribes who'd actually been present. It irritated her that many of the soldiers had said there were no living witnesses to the battle. That was not true. There were plenty of them: Lakota, Cheyenne, Crow and a host of other men from different tribes who were at the battle and saw exactly what happened.

She smiled as she read about how many of them ended up in Buffalo Bill Cody's famous traveling Wild West show. They played before the crowned heads of Europe. They learned high society manners and how to drink tea from fancy china cups. They laughed among themselves at the irony of it. Sitting Bull himself worked for Cody for a time, before he was killed.

She loved most to read about Crazy Horse. Like Carson, he was Lakota, which white people referred to as Sioux. Crazy Horse was Oglala, which was one of the subclasses of the tribe. He was light-skinned and a great tactician. There was only one verified photograph of him, which was disputed by some, accepted by others. It showed a rather handsome man with pigtails, wearing a breastplate. There was also a sketch. He had led a war party against General Crook at the Battle of the Rosebud and won it. He led another party against Custer at the Little Bighorn.

Until his death, by treachery at the hands of a soldier, he was the most famous war leader of the Lakota.

Sitting Bull did not fight; he was not a warrior. He was a holy man who made medicine and had visions of a great battle that was won by the native tribes.

Crazy Horse fascinated Carlie. She bought book after book, looking for all she could find in his history.

She also had books about Alexander the Third, called the Great, who conquered most of the civilized world by the age of thirty. His ability as a strategist was unequaled in the ancient past. Hannibal, who fought the Romans under Scipio Africanus in the Second Punic War at Carthage, was another favorite. Scipio fascinated her, as well.

The ability of some leaders to inspire a small group

of men to conquer much larger armies was what drew
her to military history. It was the generals who led
from the front, who ate and slept and suffered with
their men, who won the greatest battles and the greatest honor.

She knew about battles because her secret vice
was an online video game, "World of Warcraft." A
number of people in Jacobsville and Comanche Wells
played. She knew the gamer tags, the names in-game,
of only a very few. Probably she'd partnered with
some of them in raid groups. But mostly she ran battlegrounds, in player-versus-player matches, but only
on weekends, when she had more free time.

Gaming took the place of dates she never got. Even
if she'd been less moral, she rarely got asked on dates.
She could be attractive when she tried, but she wasn't
really pretty and she was painfully shy around people she didn't know. She'd only gone out a couple of
times in high school, once with a boy who was getting even with his girlfriend by dating her—although
she hadn't known until later—and another with a boy
who'd hurt another girl badly and saw Carlie as an
easy mark. He got a big surprise.

From time to time she thought about how nice
it would be to marry and have children. She loved
spending time in the baby section of department
stores when she went to San Antonio with her father
occasionally. She liked to look at knitted booties and
lacy little dresses. Once a saleswoman had asked if
she had children. She said no, she wasn't married. The
saleswoman had laughed and asked what that had to
do with it. It was a new world, indeed.

She put away her book on the Little Bighorn fight,

and settled in with her new copy of a book on Alexander the Great. The phone rang. She got up, but she was hesitant to answer it. She recalled the threat from the unknown man and wondered if that was him.

She went to the staircase and hesitated. Her father had answered and was on the phone.

"Yes, I know," he said in a tone he'd never used with her. "If you think you can do better, you're welcome to try." He paused and a huge sigh left his chest. "Listen, she's all I've got in the world. I know I don't deserve her, but I will never let anyone harm her. This place may not look secure, but I assure you, it is..."

He leaned against the wall near the phone table, with the phone in his hand. He looked world-weary. "That's what I thought, too, at first," he said quietly. "I still have enemies. But it isn't me he's after. It's Carlie! It has to have something to do with the man she saw in Grier's office. I know that the man who killed Joey and masqueraded as a DEA agent is dead. But if he put out a contract before he died... Yes, that's what I'm telling you." He shook his head. "I know you don't have the funds. It's okay. I have plenty of people who owe me favors. I'll call in a few. Yes. I do appreciate your help. It's just...it's worrying me, that's all. Sure. I'll call you. Thanks." He hung up.

Carlie moved back into the shadows. Her father looked like a stranger, like someone she'd never seen before. She wondered who he'd been speaking to, and if the conversation was about her. It sounded that way; he'd used her name. What was a contract? A contract to kill someone? She bit her lower lip. Something to do with the man she saw in the chief's office, the man she'd tried to describe for the artist, the DEA agent who wasn't an agent.

She frowned. But he was dead, her father had said. Then he'd mentioned that contract, that the man might have put it out before he died. Of course, if some unknown person had been paid in advance to kill her...

She swallowed down the fear. She could be killed by mistake, by a dead man. How ironic. Her father had said the house was safe. She wondered why he'd said that, what he knew. For the first time in her life, she wondered who her father really was.

SHE FIXED HIM a nice breakfast. While they were eating it she said, "Why do you think that man came to kill me?"

His coffee cup paused halfway to his mouth. "What?"

"The man with the knife."

"We agreed that he was after me, didn't we?" he said, avoiding her face.

She lifted her eyes and stared at him. "I work for the police. It's impossible not to learn a little something about law enforcement in the process. That man wasn't after you at all, was he? The man who was poisoned so he couldn't tell what he knew?"

He let out a breath and put the coffee cup down. "Well, Carlie, you're more perceptive than I gave you credit for." He smiled faintly. "Must be my genes. Your mother, God rest her soul, didn't have that gift. She saw everything in black and white."

"Yes, she did." Talk of her mother made her sad. It had just been Carlie and Mary for a long time, until Mary got sick. Then Mary's mother, and her hophead boyfriend, had shown up and ransacked the place. Carlie had tried to stop them… She shivered.

It had been several days later, after the hospital visit and the arrests, when her father had come back to town, wearing khaki pants and shirt, and carrying a pistol.

There had been no money for doctors, but her father had taken charge and got Mary into treatment. Mary's mother and her boyfriend went to jail. Sadly, it had been hopeless from the start. Mary died within weeks. During those weeks, Carlie got to know her absent father. He became protective of her. She liked him very much. He was gone for a day after the funeral. When he came home, he seemed very different.

Carlie's father spoke to someone on the phone then, too, and when he hung up he'd made a decision. He took Carlie with him to Atlanta, where he enrolled in a seminary and became a Methodist minister. He said it was the hardest and the easiest thing he'd ever done, and that it was a good thing that God forgave people for horrible acts. She asked what they were. Her father said some things were best left buried in the past.

"We're still not sure he didn't come after me," her father said, interrupting her reverie.

"I heard you talking on the phone last night," she said.

He grimaced. "Bad timing on my part," he said, sighing.

"Very bad. So now I know. Tell me what's going on."

"That phone call you had came from a San Antonio number. We traced it, but it led to a throwaway phone," he replied. "That's bad news."

"Why?"

"Because a few people who use those phones are connected to the underworld in some fashion or other, to escape detection by the authorities. They use the phone once to connect with people who might be wiretapped, then they dispose of the phone. Drug lords buy them by the cartload," he added.

"Well, I didn't do anybody in over a drug deal, and the guy I gave the artist the description of died in Wyoming. So why is somebody still after me?" she concluded.

He smiled. "Smart. Very smart. The guy died. That's the bottom line. If he hired somebody to go after you, to keep you from recognizing him in a future lineup, and paid in advance, it's too late to call him off. Get the picture?"

"In living color," she said. She felt very adult, having her father give her the truth instead of a sweet lie to calm her.

"I have a couple of friends watching you," he said. "I don't think it's a big threat, but we'd be insane not to take it seriously, especially after what's already happened."

"That was weeks ago," she began.

"Yes, at the beginning of a long chain of growing evidence." He sipped coffee. "I still can't believe how many people's lives have been impacted by this man and whoever he was working for."

"You have some idea who his boss is…was?"

He nodded. "I can't tell you, so don't ask. I will say that several law enforcement agencies are involved."

"I still don't understand why you're having meetings with my boss and that...that man Carson."

He studied her flushed face. "I've heard about Carson's attitude toward you. If he keeps it up, I'll have a talk with him."

"Don't," she asked softly. "With any luck, he won't be around long. He doesn't strike me as a man who likes small towns or staying in one place for any length of time."

"You never know. He likes working for Cy Parks. And he has a few projects going with locals."

She groaned.

"I can talk to him nicely."

"Sure, Dad, and then he'll accuse me of running to Daddy for protection." She lifted her chin. "I can take whatever he can hand out."

He smiled at her stubbornness. "Okay."

She made a face. "He just doesn't like me, that's all. Maybe I remind him of someone he doesn't care for."

"That's possible." He stared into his coffee cup. "Or it could have something to do with asking him for a grenade to start a fire..."

"Aww, now, I wasn't trying to start anything," she protested.

He chuckled. "Sure." He studied her face. "I just want to mention one thing," he added gently. "He's not housebroken. And he never will be. Just so you know."

"I have never wanted to housebreak a wolf, I assure you."

"There's also his attitude about women. He makes

no secret of it." His face hardened. "He likens them to party favors. Disposable. You understand?"

"I understand. But honestly, that's not the sort of man I'd be seriously interested in. You don't have to worry."

"I do worry. You're not street-smart, pumpkin," he added, with the pet name that he almost never used. "You're unworldly. A man like that could be dangerous to you…"

She held up a hand. "I have weapons."

He blinked. "Excuse me?"

"If he starts showing any interest in me, I'll give him my most simpering smile and start talking about how I'd love to move in with him that very day and start having children at once." She wiggled her eyebrows. "Works like a charm. They actually leave skid marks…"

He threw back his head and laughed. "So that's what happened to the visiting police chief…?"

"He was very persistent. The chief offered to punt him through the door, but I had a better idea. It worked very nicely. Now, when he comes to see the chief, he doesn't even look my way."

"Just as well. He has a wife, God help her."

"What a nasty man."

"Exactly." He looked at his watch. "Well, I have a meeting with the church officials. We're working on an outreach program for the poor. Something I really want to do."

She smiled. "You know, you really are the nicest minister I know."

He bent and kissed her forehead before he left.

"Thanks, sweetheart. Be sure to check your truck, okay?"

She laughed. "I always do. Don't worry."

He hesitated. He wanted to tell her that he did worry, and the whole reason why. But it was the wrong time.

She was already halfway in love with Carson. He knew things about the man that he'd been told in confidence. He couldn't repeat them. But if Carlie got too close to that prowling wolf, he'd leave scars that would cripple her for life. He had to prevent that, if he could. The thing was, he didn't know how. It was like seeing a wire break and being too far away to fix it.

He could talk to Carson, of course. But that would only make matters worse. He had to wait and hope that Carlie could hang on to her beliefs and ignore the man's practiced charm if he ever used it on her.

Carson seemed to hate her. But it was an act. He knew it, because it was an act he'd put on himself, with Carlie's late mother. Mary had been a saint. He'd tried to coax her into bed, but she'd refused him at every turn. Finally, in desperation, he'd proposed. She'd refused. She wasn't marrying a man because he couldn't have her any other way.

So he'd gone away. And come back. And tried the soft approach. It had backfired. He'd fallen in love for the first time in his life. Mary had tied him to her with strings of icy steel, and leaving her even for a few weeks at a time had been agonizing. He'd only lived to finish the mission and get home, get back to Mary.

But over the years, the missions had come closer together, taken longer, provoked lengthy absences. He'd tried to make sure Mary had enough money to cover her bills and incidentals, but one job had resulted in no pay and during that time, Mary had gotten sick. By the time he knew and came home, it was too late.

He blamed himself for that, and for a lot more. He'd thought an old enemy had targeted him and got Carlie by mistake. But it wasn't a mistake. Someone wanted Carlie dead, apparently because of a face she remembered. There might be another reason. Something they didn't know, something she didn't remember seeing. Even the death of the man hadn't stopped the threat.

But he was going to. Somehow.

CHAPTER TWO

CARLIE LOVED THE WEEKENDS. At work she was just plain old Carlie, dull and boring and not very pretty at all.

But in this video game, on her game server, she was Cadzminea, an Alliance night elf death knight, invincible and deadly with a two-handed great sword. She had top-level gear and a bad attitude, and she was known even in battlegrounds with players from multiple servers. She was a tank, an offensive player who protected less well-geared comrades. She loved it.

Above the sounds of battle, clashing swords and flashing spells thrown by magic-users, she heard her father's voice.

"Just a minute, Dad! I'm in a battleground!"

"Okay. Never mind."

There were footsteps coming up. She laughed as she heard them behind her. Odd, they sounded lighter than her father's....

"Sorry, we're almost through. We're taking out the enemy commander...."

She stopped while she fought, planting her guild's battle flag to increase her strength and pulling up her Army of the Dead spell. "Gosh, the heals in this battleground are great, I've hardly even needed to use a potion… Okay!" she laughed, as the panel came up displaying an Alliance win, that of her faction.

"Sorry about that…" She turned and looked up into a pair of liquid black eyes in a surprised face.

"A gamer," he said in a tone, for once, without sarcasm. "Put up your stats."

She was too startled not to obey. She left the battle-ground and brought up the character screen.

He shook his head. "Not bad. Why an NE?" he asked, the abbreviation for a night elf.

"They're beautiful," she blurted out.

He laughed deep in his throat. "So they are."

"How do you know about stats?"

He pulled out his iPhone and went to the game's remote app. He pulled up the Armory and showed her a character sheet.

"Level 90 Horde Tauren druid," she read, indicating that the player was from the Alliance's deadly counter faction, the Horde. "Arbiter." She frowned. "Arbiter?" She caught her breath. "He killed me five times in one battleground!" she exclaimed. "He stealthed up to me, hit me from behind, then he just… killed me. I couldn't even fight back."

"Don't you have a medallion that interrupts spells?"

"Yes, but it was on cooldown," she said, glowering. "And you know this guy?" she asked.

He put up the iPhone. "I am this guy."

She was stunned.

"It's a small world, isn't it?" he asked, studying her face.

Too small, she thought, but she didn't say it. She just nodded.

"Your father asked a couple of us to take turns doing a walk-around when he's not here. He had to go out, so I've got first watch."

She frowned. "A what?"

"We're going to patrol around the house."

"Carrying a Horde flag?" she asked, tongue-in-cheek.

He smiled with real amusement. "We'll be concealed. You won't even know we're on the place."

She was disconcerted. "What's going on?"

"Just a tip we got," he replied. "Nothing to worry about."

Her green eyes narrowed. "My father can pull that stunt. You can't. Give it to me straight."

His eyebrows arched.

"If it concerns me, I have the right to know. My father is overprotective. I love him, but it's not fair that I have to be kept in the dark. I'm not a mushroom."

"No. You're Alliance." He seemed really amused.

"Proudly Alliance," she muttered. "Darn the Horde!"

He smiled. "Better rune that two-hander before you fight me again," he advised, referring to a special weapons buff used only by death knights.

"It's brand-new. I haven't had time," she said defensively. "Don't change the subject."

"There may be an attempt. That's all we could find out."

"Why? The guy I recognized is dead!"

"We're pretty sure that he paid the contract out before he died," he replied. "And we don't know who has it. We tried backtracking known associates of the man who made the first attempt, the one who was poisoned awaiting trial. No luck whatsoever. But an informant needed a favor, so he gave up some information. Not much. There's more at stake than just your memory of a counterfeit DEA agent. Much more."

"And that's all I'm getting, right?"

He nodded.

She glared.

"So much frustration," he mused, studying her. "Why don't you go win a few battles for the Alliance? It might help."

"Not unless you're in one of them." Her eyes twinkled. "Better watch your back next time. I'm getting the hang of it."

He shrugged. "I don't want to live forever." He glanced around the room. It was Spartan. No lace anywhere. He eyed the title of a book on the desk next to her computer and frowned. "Hannibal?"

"Learn from the best, I always think."

He looked at her. He didn't look away.

Her eyes met his and she felt her body melting, tingling. There was a sudden ache in the middle of her body, a jolt of pure electricity. She couldn't even manage to look away.

"Wolves bite," he said in a soft, gruff whisper.

She flushed and dragged her eyes back to the computer. Somebody sold her out. She wondered if it was the chief. She'd only called Carson a wolf to two people and her father would never have betrayed her.

He chuckled softly. "Be careful what you say when you think people aren't listening," he added. He turned and left her staring after him.

LATER, SHE ASKED her father if he'd ratted her out.

He chuckled. "No. But the house is bugged like a messy kitchen," he confessed. "Be careful what you say."

"Gee, thanks for telling me after I said all sorts of things about Carson," she murmured.

He laughed. "He's got a thick skin. It won't bother him."

She studied him quietly. "Why are they after me?"

He drew in a long breath. "There are some political maneuvers going on. You have a photographic memory. Maybe you saw someone other than the murder victim, and the man behind the plot is afraid you'll remember who it is."

"Shades of Dalton Kirk," she said, recalling that the Wyoming rancher had been warned by the woman who became his wife about a vision of him being attacked for something he didn't even remember he'd seen.

"Exactly."

She poured them second cups of coffee. "So I guess it's back to checking under the truck every time I drive it."

"Oh, that never stopped," her father said with a chuckle. "I've just been doing it for you."

She smiled at him. "That's my dad, looking out for me," she said with real affection.

His pale blue eyes were sad. "There was a long period of time when I didn't look out for anybody except myself," he said quietly. "Your mother wouldn't even let anybody tell me how sick she was until it was too late." He lowered his gaze to the coffee. "I made a lot of mistakes out of selfishness. I hope that someday I'll be able to make up for a little of it."

She sipped coffee. "You never talk about your life before you went to the seminary," she pointed out.

He smiled sadly. "I'm ashamed to."

"You were overseas a lot."

He nodded. "In a number of dangerous foreign places, where life is dirt cheap."

She pursed her lips and stared at him. "You know, Michelle's guardian, Gabriel Brandon, spent a lot of time overseas also."

He lifted an eyebrow and smiled placidly. "Are you fishing?"

She shrugged. But she didn't look away.

He finished his coffee. "Let's just say that I had connections that aren't obvious ones, and I made my living in a shadow world."

She frowned. "You aren't wanted in some country whose name I can't pronounce?"

He laughed. "Nothing like that."

"Okay."

He stood up. "But I do have enemies who know where I live. In a general sense. So it's smart to take precautions." He smiled gently. "I wasn't always a minister, pumpkin."

She was remembering Carson's sarcastic comment when she'd mentioned that her father was a minister. She hadn't known that he was aware of things about her parent that she wasn't.

"I feel like a mushroom," she muttered.

He bent and kissed her hair. "Believe me, you're better off being one. See you later. I have some phone calls to make."

He LOCKED HIMSELF in his study and she went to watch the news on television. It was mostly boring, the same rehashed subjects over and over again, interspersed with more commercials than she could stomach. She turned it off and went upstairs.

"No wonder people stopped watching television," she grumbled as she wandered back to her bedroom. "Why don't you just stop showing any programs and show wall-to-wall commercials, for heaven's sake!"

She pulled up her game and tried to load it when she noticed that the internet wasn't working.

Muttering, she went downstairs to reset the router, which usually solved the problem. Except the router was in the study, and her father was locked in there.

She started to knock, just as she heard her father's raised voice in a tone she'd rarely ever heard.

"I told you," he gritted, "I am not coming back! You can't say anything, threaten anything, that will make me change my mind. And don't you say one more word about my daughter's safety, or I will report you to the obvious people. I understand that," he continued, less belligerently. "Trust me when I say that nobody short of a ghost could get in here after dark. The line is secure and I've scrambled important conversations, like this one. I appreciate the tip, I really do. But I can handle this. I haven't forgotten anything you taught me." He laughed shortly. "Yes, I remember. They were good times."

There was another pause. "No. But we did find out who his enforcer is, and our local law enforcement people are keeping him under covert surveillance. That's right. No, I didn't realize there were two. When did he hire the other? Wait a minute—blond hair, one eye, South African accent?" He burst out laughing. "He hired Rourke as an enforcer?"

There was another pause. "Yes, please, tell him to come see me. I'd enjoy that. Like old times, yes. Okay. Thanks again. I'll be in touch."

Totally confused, Carlie softly retraced her steps, made a racket coming down the staircase and went directly to the study. She rapped on the door.

"Dad? The internet's out! Can you reset the router?"

There was the sound of a chair scraping the floor, but she never heard his footsteps. The door suddenly opened.

He pursed his lips and studied her flushed face. "Okay. How much did you hear?"

"Nothing, Mr. Gandalf, sir, I swear, except something about the end of the world," she paraphrased Sam from *Lord of the Rings*.

Her father laughed. "Well, it wasn't really anything you didn't already know."

"Who's Rourke?" she wondered.

"A man of many talents. You'll like him." He frowned. "Just don't like him too much, okay? He has a way with women, and you're a little lamb."

She gave him a blithe look. "If I could get around Barry Mathers, I can get around Rourke."

Her father understood the reference. Barry, a classmate, had caused one of Carlie's friends a world of hurt by getting her into bed and bragging about it. The girl had been as innocent as Carlie. He wasn't even punished.

So then he'd bet his friends that he could get Carlie into bed. She heard about it from an acquaintance, led him around by the nose, and when he showed up at her house for the date, she had two girlfriends and their boyfriends all ready to go along. He was stunned. But he couldn't call off the date, or he'd have to face the razzing of his clique.

So he took all of them out to dinner and the movies, dutch treat, and delivered Carlie and the others back to her house where her friends' cars were parked.

She waited until the others left and she was certain that her father was in the living room before she spoke to Barry. She gave him such a tongue-lashing that he literally turned around and walked the other way every time he saw her after that. He never asked her out again. Of course, neither did anybody else, for the rest of her senior year.

Barry, on the other hand, was censured so much that his wealthy parents sent him to a school out of state. He died there soon afterward in a skiing accident.

"You had a hard time in school," her father said gently.

"No harder than most other people with principles do," she replied. "There are more of us than you might think."

"I reset the router," he added. "Go try your game."

"I promised to meet Robin for a quest," she said. "I'd hate to let him down."

Her father just smiled. They knew about Robin's situation. He was in love with a girl whose family hated his family. It was a feud that went back two generations, over a land deal. Even the principals didn't really remember what started it. But when Robin expressed interest in Lucy and tried to date her, the hidden daggers came out.

It was a tragic story in many ways. Two people in love who weren't even allowed to see each other because of their parents. They were grown now, but Lucy still lived at home and was terrified of her father. So even if Robin insisted, Lucy wouldn't go against her kin.

Robin worked in his dad's real estate office, where he wasn't harassed, and he was a whiz with figures. He was going to night classes, studying real estate up in San Antonio, where he hoped to learn enough to eventually become a full-fledged real estate broker. Carlie liked him. So did her father, who respected a parent's rights but also felt sympathy for young people denied the right to love whom they pleased.

CARLIE WENT ONLINE and loaded the game, then looked for Robin, who played a shaman in the virtual world. His was a healing spec, so it went well with Carlie's DK, who couldn't heal.

I have a problem, he whispered to her, a form of typed private communication in-game.

She typed, How can I help?

He made a big smiley face. I need a date for the Valentine's Day dance.

Should I ask why? she typed.

There was a smiley face. Lucy's going to the dance with some rich rancher her father knows from out of town. If you'll go with me, her dad won't suspect anything and I can at least dance with her.

She shook her head. One day the two of them were going to have to decide if the sneaking around was less traumatic than just getting together and daring their parents to say anything. But she just typed, I'll buy a dress.

There was a bigger smiley face. It's so nice to have a friend like you, he replied.

That works both ways.

LATER, SHE TOLD her father she had a date. He asked who, and she explained.

"You're both hiding, Carlie," he said, surprising her. His eyes narrowed. "You need to think about finding someone you can have a good relationship with, someone to marry and have children with. And Robin and Lucy need to stand up and behave like adults."

She smiled sadly. "Chance would be a fine thing," she replied. "You might not have noticed, but men aren't exactly beating a path to my door. And you know why."

"Young men look at what's outside," he said wisely. "When they're more mature, men look for what's inside. You're just at the wrong period of your life. That will change."

She drew in a long breath. "You know, not everybody marries…"

He glared at her.

She held up both hands. "I'm not talking about moving in with somebody," she said hastily. "I mean, not everybody gets married. Look at Old Man Barlow, he never did."

"He never bathed," he pointed out.

She glowered at him. "Beside the point. How about

the Miller brothers? They never married. Their sister was widowed and moved back in with them, and they're all single now. They seem perfectly happy."

He looked down his nose at her. "Who spends half her time in department stores, ogling baby booties and little gowns?"

She flushed and averted her eyes.

"Just what I thought," he added.

"Listen, there really aren't many communities in Texas smaller than Comanche Wells, or even Jacobsville. Most of the men my age are either married or living with somebody."

"I see your point."

"The others are having so much fun partying that they don't want to do either," she continued. "Come on, Dad, I like my life. I really do. I enjoy working for the chief and having lunch at Barbara's Café and playing my game at night and taking care of you." She gave him a close scrutiny. "You know, you might think about marrying somebody."

"Bite your tongue," he said shortly. "There was your mother. I don't want anybody else. Ever."

She stared at him with consternation. "She'd want you to be happy."

"I am happy," he insisted. "I'm married to my church, pumpkin. I love what I do now." He smiled. "You know, in the sixteenth century, all priests were expected to be single. It wasn't until Henry VIII changed the laws that they could even marry, and when his daughter Mary came to the throne, she threw out all the married priests. Then when her half sister Elizabeth became Queen, she permitted them to marry, but she didn't want married ministers preaching before her. She didn't approve of it, either."

"This is the twenty-first century," she pointed out. "And why are you hanging out with McKuen Kilraven?" she added, naming one of the federal agents who sometimes came to Jacobsville.

He laughed. "Does it show?"

"I don't know of anybody else who can hold forth for an hour on sixteenth-century British politics and never tell the same story twice."

"Guilty," he replied. "He was in your boss's office the last time I was there."

"When was that? I didn't see him."

"You were at lunch."

"Oh."

He didn't volunteer any more information.

"I need to go buy a new dress," she said. "I think I'll drive up to San Antonio after work, since it's Saturday and I get off at 1 p.m."

"Okay. I'll let you borrow the Cobra." He laughed at her astonished look. "I'm not sure your truck would make it even halfway to the city, pumpkin."

She just shook her head.

IT WAS A CONCESSION of some magnitude. Her father loved that car. He washed and waxed it by hand, bought things for it. She was only allowed to drive it on very special occasions, and usually only when she went to the big city.

San Antonio wasn't a huge city, but there was a lot to see. Carlie liked to stop by the Alamo and look at it, but El Mercado was her port of call. It had everything, including unique shops and music and restaurants. She usually spent half a day just walking around it. But today she was in a hurry.

She went from store to store, but she couldn't find exactly what she was looking for. She was ready to give up when she pulled, on impulse, into a small strip mall where a sale sign was out in front of a small boutique.

She found a bargain dress, just her size, in green velvet. It was ankle length, with a discreet rounded neckline and long sleeves. It fit like a glove, but it wasn't overly sensual. And it suited her. It was so beautiful that she carried it like a child as she walked to the counter to pay for it.

"That was the only size we got in this particular design," the saleslady told her as she packaged it on its hangar. "I wish it was my size," she added with a sigh. "You really are lucky."

Carlie laughed. "It's for a dance. I don't go out much."

"Me, either," the saleslady said. "My husband sits and watches the Western Channel on satellite when he gets off work and then he goes to bed." She shook her head. "Not what I thought marriage would be like. But he's good to me and he doesn't cheat. I guess I'm lucky."

"I'd say you are."

CARLIE WAS IN the Jacobs County limits on a long, deserted stretch of road. The Cobra growled as if it had been on the leash too long and wanted off. Badly.

With a big grin on her face, Carlie floored the accelerator. "Okay, Big Red," she said, using her father's affectionate nickname for the car, "let's run!"

The engine cycled, seemed to hesitate, and then the car took off with a growl that would have done a hungry mountain lion proud.

"Woo-hoo!" she exclaimed.

She was going eighty, eighty-five, ninety, ninety-six and then one hundred. She felt an exhilaration she couldn't remember ever feeling before. The road was completely open up ahead, no traffic anywhere. Well, except for that car behind her...

Her heart skipped. At first she thought it was a police car, because she was exceeding the speed limit by double the posted signs. But then she realized that it wasn't a law enforcement car. It was a black sedan, and it was keeping pace with her.

She almost panicked. But she was close to Jacobsville, where she could get help if she needed it. Her father's admonition about checking the truck before she drove it made her heart skip. She knew he'd checked the car, but she hadn't counted on being followed. Someone was after her. She knew that her father's friends were watching her, but that was in Jacobsville.

Nobody was watching her now, and she was being chased. Her cell phone was in her purse on the floor by the passenger seat. She'd have to slow down or stop to get to it. She groaned. Lack of foresight. Why didn't she have it in the console?

Her heart was pumping faster as the car behind gained on her. What if it was the shadowy assassin come for a second try? What was she going to do? She couldn't outrun him, that was obvious, and when she slowed down, he'd catch her.

She saw the city-limit sign up ahead. She couldn't

continue at this rate of speed. She'd kill someone at the next crossroads.

Groaning, she slowed down. The black sedan was right on top of her. She turned without a signal into the first side street and headed for the police station. If she was lucky, she just might make it.

Yes! The traffic light stayed green. She shot through it, pulled up in front of the station and jumped out just as the sedan pulled in front of her, braked and cut her off.

"You damned little lunatic, what the hell were you thinking!" Carson raged at her as he slammed out of the black sedan and confronted her. "I clocked you at a hundred miles an hour!"

"Oh, yeah? Well, you were going a hundred, too, because you were right on my bumper. And how was I supposed to know it was you?" she told him, red-faced with embarrassment.

"I called your cell phone half a dozen times, didn't you hear it ring?"

"I had it turned off. And it was on the floor in my purse," she explained.

He put his hands on his slim hips and glared at her. "You shouldn't be allowed out by yourself, and especially not in a car with that sort of horsepower!" he persisted. "I should have the chief arrest you!"

"Go ahead, I'll have him arrest you, too!" she yelled back.

Two patrol officers were standing on the side-lines, spellbound. The chief came out and stopped, just watching the two antagonists, who hadn't noticed their audience.

"What if you'd hit something lying in the middle

of the road? You'd have gone straight off it and into a tree or a power pole, and you'd be dead!"

"Well, I didn't hit anything! I was scared because I saw a car following me. Who wouldn't be paranoid, with people watching you all the time and my father having secret phone calls…!"

"If you'd answered your damned cell phone, you'd have known who was following you!"

"It was in my purse and I was afraid to slow down and try to grab it out of my pocketbook!"

"Of all the stupid assignments I've ever had, this takes the prize," he muttered. "And why you had to go to San Antonio…?"

"I went to buy a dress for the Valentine's Day party!"

He gave her a cold smile. "Going alone, are we?"

"No, I'm not." She shot back. "I have a date!"

He looked oddly surprised. "Do you have to pay him when he takes you home?" he asked in a long, sarcastic drawl.

"I don't have to hire men to take me places!" she raged back. "And this man doesn't notch his bedpost and take in strays to have somebody to sleep with."

He took a quick step forward, and he looked dangerous. "That's enough," he snapped.

Carlie sucked in her breath and her face paled.

"It really is enough," Cash Grier said, interrupting them. He stepped between them and stared at Carson. "The time to tell somebody you're following them is not when you're actually in the car. Especially a nervous young woman whose life has been threatened."

Carson's jaw was set so firmly she wondered if his teeth would break. He was still glaring at Carlie.

"And you need to keep your phone within reach when you're driving," he told Carlie in a gentler tone and with a smile.

"Yes, sir," she said heavily. She let out a long sigh.

"She was doing a hundred miles an hour," Carson said angrily.

"If you could clock her, you had to be doing the same," Cash retorted. "You're both lucky that you weren't in the city limits at the time. Or that Hayes Carson or one of his deputies didn't catch you. Speeding fines are really painful."

"You'd know," Carson mused, relaxing a little as he glanced at the older man.

Cash glowered at him. "Well, I drive a Jaguar," he said defensively. "They don't like slow speeds."

"How many unpaid speeding tickets is it to date? Ten?" Carson persisted. "I hear you can't cross the county border up around Dallas. And you, a chief of police. Shame, shame."

Cash shrugged. "I sent the checks out yesterday," he informed the other man. "All ten."

"Threatening to put you under arrest, were they?"

"Only one of them," Cash chuckled. "And he was in Iraq with me, so he stretched the rules a bit."

"I have to get home," Carlie said. She was still shaking inside over the threat that turned out to be just Carson. And from Carson's sudden move toward her. Very few people knew what nightmares she endured from one very physical confrontation in the past.

"You keep under the speed limit, or I'm telling your father what you did to his car," Carson instructed.

"He wouldn't mind," she lied, glaring at him.

"Let's find out." He jerked out his cell phone and started punching in numbers.

"All right!" she surrendered, holding up both hands. "All right, I'll go under the speed limit." Her eyes narrowed. "I'm taking that sword to a rune forge tonight. So the next time you meet me on a battleground, Hordie, I'm going to wipe the ground with you."

He pursed his lips. "That would be a new experience for me, Alliance elf."

Cash groaned. "Not you, too," he said. "It's bad enough listening to Wofford Patterson brag about his weapons. He even has a dog named Hellscream. And every time Kilraven comes down here, he's got a new game he wants to tell me all about."

"You should play, too, Chief," Carlie said. She glanced at Carson. "It's a great way to work off frustration."

Carson raised an eyebrow. "I know a better one," he said with a mocking smile.

He might not mean what she thought he did. She flushed helplessly and looked away. "I'm leaving."

"Drive carefully. And buckle up," Cash told her.

"Yes, sir, Boss," she said, grinning.

She started the car, pulled it around and eased out of the parking lot.

She really hoped that her father wouldn't find out how she'd been driving his pet car. It would be like Carson to tell him, just for spite.

Odd, though, she thought, how angry he'd been that she'd taken such chances. It was almost as if he was concerned about her. She laughed to herself.

Sure. He was nursing a secret yen for her that he couldn't control.

Not that he ever would ask her out or anything, but she had grave misgivings about him. He was known for his success with women, and she was soft where he was concerned. He could push her into something that he'd just brush off as insignificant, but her life would be shattered. She couldn't let her helpless interest in him grow. Not even a little. She had to remember that he had no real respect for women and he didn't seem capable of settling down with just one.

She pulled into her driveway and cut off the engine. It was a relief to be home. Just as she got out of the car she saw the black sedan drive by. He didn't stop or wave. He just kept going. Her heart jumped up into her throat.

In spite of all the yelling, he'd shepherded her home and she hadn't even noticed. She hated the warm feeling it gave her, knowing that.

CHAPTER THREE

CARLIE HAD HOPED that her father wouldn't hear about her adventure. But when she got inside the house, he was waiting for her, his arms crossed over his chest.

"He lied," she blurted out, blushing, the dress in its plastic bag hanging over one arm.

He blinked. "Excuse me?"

She hesitated. He might not know after all. She cocked her head. "Are you…angry about something?"

"Should I be?"

He made her feel guilty. She drew in a breath and moved toward him. "I was speeding. I'm sorry. Big Red can really run…"

"A hundred miles an hour," he said, nodding. "You need special training to drive at those speeds safely, and you don't have it," he added patiently.

"I didn't know it was Carson behind me," she said heavily. "I thought it might be whoever still has me targeted."

"I understand that. I gave him…well, a talking-to," he amended. "It won't happen again. But you keep your cell phone where you can get to it in a hurry, whatever you're driving. Okay?"

"Okay, Dad," she promised.

"Got the dress, did you?" he asked, and smiled.

"Yes! It's beautiful! Green velvet. I'll wear Mama's

pearls with it, the ones you brought her from Japan when you first started dating."

He nodded. "They're very special. I bought them in Tokyo," he recalled, smiling. "She had the same skin tone that you inherited from her. Off-white pearls are just right for you."

She frowned. "You buy them for a skin color?"

"I always did. Pearls come in many colors, and many prices. Those are Mikimoto pearls. An armed guard stands in the room with them."

She lost a little color. "Maybe I should wear something else…"

"Nonsense. They need to be worn. That would be like getting a special dress and letting it hang in your closet for fear of spilling something on it. Life is what matters, child. Things are expendable."

"Most things," she agreed.

"I made supper, since I knew you were going to be late," he said.

Her eyebrows arched. "That was sweet of you, Dad," she said.

"It's just a macaroni and cheese casserole. Your mother taught me how to do it when we were first married. I never forgot."

"It's one of my favorite dishes. Let me hang up my dress and I'll be right down."

"Sure."

THE MEAL WAS DELICIOUS, even more so because she hadn't had to cook it. She noticed her father's somber expression.

"I'm really sorry about pushing Big Red," she began.

He leaned back in his chair. "It's not the car I was worried about." His pale eyes were narrow and thoughtful. "It might not be a bad idea to send you over to Eb Scott and let one of his guys teach you the finer points of defensive driving. Just in case."

Her heart jumped. "Dad, maybe there isn't a real threat," she said. "I mean, the guy who was afraid of what I remembered about him is dead."

He nodded. "Yes, but there are things going on that you don't know about."

"You were talking to somebody on the phone who wanted you to come back. Come back where?" she asked bluntly.

He grimaced. "I used to work for the feds. Sort of. It was a long time ago."

"Feds?" she repeated, trying to draw him out.

His chest rose and fell. "When you're young, you think you can do anything, be anything. You don't worry about consequences. You take the training and do the job. Nobody tells you that years down the line, you may have regrets." He studied her oval face. "I was away when your mother got sick. What happened to you, because nobody was at home, was my fault. I should have been there."

She glanced down. "They paid for it."

"Not enough," he said coldly, and his face was suddenly hard and merciless. "I don't wish harm to anyone as a rule, but when your grandmother left the world, I didn't shed a tear."

Carlie managed a smile. "Me, neither. I guess he's still around somewhere."

"No. He died in a prison riot last year."

"You didn't say," she faltered.

"I didn't know. My former boss and I were making connections. We looked for anyone dangerous who knew you in the past. I had someone do some checking. I only found out yesterday."

"It's a relief, sort of," she said heavily. She shook her head. "They were both crazy. She was the worst. My poor mother..."

He put his hand over hers and squeezed. "Mary was such a ray of light that nobody blamed her for what her mother did," he reminded her.

"I know, but people have long memories in small towns."

"You have your own spotless reputation," he said gently. "Don't worry about it."

"I guess you're right." She laughed. "Robin hired a limo for us, can you believe it?"

"I like Robin," he said. "I just wish he had more guts."

"Now, now, we can't all be real-life death knights with great swords."

"You and that game. You do need to get out more." He pursed his lips. "Maybe we need to organize some things for the young, single members of our church."

"All four of us?" she mused.

He rolled his eyes.

"I like my life," she declared. "Maybe it lacks excitement, but I'm happy. That should count for something, Dad."

He laughed softly. "Okay. I see your point."

THE CHIEF WAS UNHAPPY. He didn't come out and say so, but he was on a short fuse and it was difficult to get anything out of him past one-syllable words.

"Sir, what about the new patrolman's gear?" she asked gently. "You were supposed to give me a purchase order for it, weren't you?"

"New patrolman?" He frowned. "Oh, yes. Bartley. Okay. I'll do that today."

She bit her tongue so that she didn't remind him that he'd said the same thing the day before.

He caught her expression and laughed hollowly. "I know. I'm preoccupied. Want to know why?" He shoved a newspaper across his desk. "Read the headline."

It said, Matthew Helm to Fill Unexpired Term of U.S. Senator. She stared at Cash without understanding what he was upset about.

"There were three men in the running for the appointment," he said. "One was found by police in San Antonio, on the street, doped up by an apparent drug habit that nobody knew he had. A tip," he added. "The second withdrew from the nomination because his son was arrested for cocaine possession—a kid who'd never even used drugs, but apparently the glove compartment in his car was stuffed with the stuff. Another tip. The third contender, Helm, got the appointment."

"You think the others were set up," she began.

"Big-time," he replied. He glared at the headline. "If he wins the special election in May, we're in for some hard times in law enforcement. I can't prove it, but the prevailing theory is that Mr. Helm is in bed with Charro Mendez. Remember him?"

She nodded. "The enforcer who worked for the late El Ladrón," she said. "He was a cousin to the Fuentes brothers."

"The very same ones who used to run the distribution hub. He's now head of the drug cartel over the border in Cotillo. In fact, he's the mayor of that lovely little drug center."

"Oh, dear."

"I really wish somebody had furnished Carson with more than three hand grenades," he muttered.

"Shame!" she said.

He chuckled. "Okay. I'll get the purchase order filled out." He leaned forward. "Hell of a thing, to have a politician like this in Washington."

"He'll be a junior senator," she pointed out. "He won't have an important role in anything. He won't chair any important committees and he won't have powerful alliances."

"Yet."

"Surely, he won't win the special election," she ventured.

He looked at her. "Carlie, remember what I just told you about his rivals for the appointment?"

She whistled. "Oh, dear," she said again.

"Exactly."

The phone rang. She excused herself and went out to answer it.

CARSON WAS CONSPICUOUS by his absence for the next few days. Nobody said anything about him, but it was rumored that he was away on some job for Eb Scott. In the meantime, Carlie got her first look at the mysterious Rourke.

He stopped by her office during her lunch hour one day. He was wearing khakis with a sheepskin coat. He grinned at her where she sat at her desk eating hot soup out of a foam cup.

"Bad habit," he said, with a trace of a South African accent. "Eating on the job. You should be having that out of fine china in some exotic restaurant."

She was staring at the attractive man wearing an eye patch, with her spoon suspended halfway between the cup and her mouth. "Excuse me?" she faltered.

"An exotic restaurant," he repeated.

"Listen, the only exotic restaurant I know of is the Chinese place over on Madison, and I think their cook is from New York."

He chuckled. "It's the sentiment, you know, that counts."

"I'll take your word for it." She put down the cup. "How can I help you?"

"Is the boss in?" he asked.

She shook her head. "Sorry. He's at the exotic local café having a thick hamburger and fries with a beautiful ex-motion picture star."

"Ah, the lovely Tippy," he chuckled. "Lucky man, to have a wife who's both kind and beautiful. The combination is rare."

"I'll say."

"So, okay if I leave a message?"

She pushed a pad and pen across the desk and smiled. "Be my guest."

He scribbled a few words and signed with a flourish.

She glanced at it. "You're Rourke?"

He nodded. His one pale brown eye twinkled. "I guess my reputation has preceded me?"

"Something like that," she said with a grin.

"I hope you were told it by your boss and not Carson," he said.

She shook her head. "Nobody told me. I overheard my dad talking about you on the telephone."

"Your dad?"

She nodded. "Reverend Jake Blair."

His face softened. "You're his daughter, then." He nodded. "It came as a shock to know he had a child, let me tell you. Not the sort of guy I ever associated with family."

"Why?" she asked, all innocence.

He saw that innocence and his face closed up. "I spoke out of turn, there."

"I know he did other things before he came home," she said. "I don't know what they were."

"I see."

In that instant, his own past seemed to scroll across his hard face, leaving scars that were visible for a few seconds.

"You need to go to one of those exotic restaurants and have something to cheer you up," she pointed out.

He stared at her for a moment and then chuckled. "How about going with me?" he teased.

She shook her head. "Sorry. I've been warned about you."

"How so?" he asked, and seemed really interested in her answer.

She grinned. "I'm not in your league, Mr. Rourke," she said. "Small-town girl, never been anywhere, never dated much…" He looked puzzled. She gave him her best starstruck expression. "I want to get married and have lots of kids," she said enthusiastically. "In fact, I'm free today after five…!"

He glowered at her. "Damn! And I've got a meeting at five." He snapped his fingers. "What a shame!"

"Just my luck. There, there, I'm sure you'll find someone else who can't wait to marry you," she added.

"No plans to marry, I'm afraid," he replied. Then he seemed to get it, all at once. His eyebrows arched. "Are you having me on?"

She blinked. "Am I having you on what?"

He stuffed his hands in his pockets. "I can't marry you," he said. "It's against my religion."

"Which religion would that be?"

"I'm not sure," he said. "I'll have to find one that prohibits marriage..." He burst out laughing.

She grinned.

"I get it. I'm a bit slow today. Must stem from missing breakfast." He shook his head. "Damned weird food you Yanks serve for breakfast, let me tell you. Grits? What the hell is a grit?"

"If you have to ask, you shouldn't eat one," she returned, laughing.

"I reckon." He smiled. "Well, it was nice meeting you, Ms. Blair."

"Miss," she said. "I don't run a company and I'm not planning to start my own business."

He blinked. "Come again?"

She frowned. "How can I come again if I haven't left?"

He moved closer to the desk. "Confound it, woman, I need a dictionary to figure out what you're saying."

"You can pin a rose on that," she agreed. "Are you from England?"

He glared at her. "I'm South African."

"Oh! The Boer Wars. You had a very famous general named Christiaan de Wet. He was a genius at guerilla warfare and was never captured by the British, although his brother, Piet, was."

He gaped at her.

She smiled shyly. "I collect famous generals. Sort of. I have books on famous campaigns. My favorites were American, of course, like General Francis Marion of South Carolina, the soldier they called the 'Swamp Fox' because he was so good at escaping from the British in the swamps during the Revolutionary War," she laughed. "Then there was Colonel John Singleton Mosby, the Gray Ghost of the Confederacy. I also like to read about Crazy Horse," she added shyly. "He was Oglala Lakota, one of the most able of the indigenous leaders. He fought General Crook's troops to a standstill at the Battle of the Rosebud."

He was still gaping.

"But my favorite is Alexander the Great. Of all the great military heroes, he was the most incredible strategist…"

"I don't believe it." He perched himself on the edge of her desk. "I know South Africans who couldn't tell you who de Wet was!"

She shrugged. "I used to spend a lot of time in the library. They had these old newspapers from the turn of the twentieth century. They were full of the Boer Wars and that famous Boer General de Wet," she laughed. "I almost missed class a couple of times because I was so entranced by the microfilm."

He laughed. "Actually, I'm distantly related to one of the de Wets, not really sure if it was Christiaan, though. My people have been in South Africa for three generations. They were originally Dutch, or so my mother said."

"Rourke is not really a Dutch name, is it?" she asked.

He sighed. "No. Her name was Skipper, her maiden name."

"Was your father Irish?"

His face closed up. That one brown eye looked glittery.

"Sorry," she said at once. "That was clumsy. I have things in my past that I don't like to think about, either."

He was surprised at her perception. "I don't speak of my father," he said gently. "Didn't mean to unsettle you."

"No problem," she said, and smiled. "We're sort of the sum total of the tragedies of our lives."

"Well put." He nodded thoughtfully. "I might reconsider about that marriage thing…"

"Sorry. My lunch hour's over."

"Damn."

She laughed.

He studied her with real interest. "There's this do, called a Valentine's Day dance, I think. If you need a partner…?"

"Thanks, but I have a date," she said.

"Just my luck, being at the end of the line, and all," he chuckled.

"If you go, I'll dance with you," she promised.

"Will you, now? In that case, I'll dust off my tux."

"Just one dance, though," she added. "I mean, we wouldn't want to get you gossiped about or anything."

"Got it." He winked and got to his feet. "If you'll

pass that note along to the chief, I'll be grateful. See you around, I expect."

"I expect so," she replied.

WHAT A VERY strange man, she thought. He was charming. But she really didn't want to complicate her life. In his way, he seemed far more risky than even Carson, in a romantic sense.

When she got home, she mentioned his visit to her father.

"So now you know who Rourke is," he chuckled.

"He's very nice," she said. "But he's a sad sort of person."

"Rourke?" he asked, and seemed almost shocked.

"Yes. I mean, it doesn't show so much. But you can tell."

"Pumpkin, you really are perceptive."

"He said he'd take me to the Valentine's dance. That was after he reconsidered the wedding, but I told him my lunch hour was over…"

"What?" he blurted out.

"Nothing to worry about, he said he wasn't free today anyway."

"Listen here, you can't marry Rourke," he said firmly.

"Well, not today, at least," she began.

"Not any day," came an angry voice from the general direction of the front door. Carson came in, scowling. "And what did I tell you about keeping that cell phone with you?" he added, pulling it out of his pocket. "You left it on your desk at work!"

She grimaced. "I didn't notice."

"Too busy flirting with Rourke, were you?" Carson added harshly.

"That is none of your business," she said pertly.

"It really isn't," her father interjected, staring at Carson until he backed down. "What's going on?" he added, changing the subject.

Carson looked worn. "Dead ends. Lots of them."

"Were you at least able to ascertain if it was poison?"

He nodded. "A particularly nasty one that took three days to do its work." He glanced at Carlie, who looked pale. "Should you be listening to this?" he asked.

"I work for the police," she pointed out. She swallowed. "Photos of dead people, killed in various ways, are part of the files I have to keep for court appearances by our men and women."

Carson frowned. He hadn't considered that her job would involve things like that. "I thought you just typed reports."

She drew in a breath. "I type reports, I file investigative material, photos, I keep track of court appearances, call people to remind them of meetings, and from time to time I function as a shoulder for people who have to deal with unthinkable things."

Carson knew what she was talking about. His best friend, years ago, had been a reservation policeman. He'd gone with the man on runs a time or two during college vacation. In the service, overseas, he'd seen worse things. He was surprised that Carlie, the innocent, was able to deal with that aspect of police work.

"It's a good job," she added. "And I have the best boss around."

"I have to agree," her father said with a gentle smile. "For a hard case, he does extremely well as a police chief." He sighed. "I do miss seeing Judd Dunn around."

"Who's Judd Dunn?" Carson asked.

"He was a Texas Ranger who served on the force with Cash," Jake said. "He quit to be assistant chief here when he and Christabel had twins. But he was offered a job as police chief over in Centerville. It's still Jacobs County, just several miles away. He took it for the benefits package. And, maybe, to compete with Cash," he chuckled.

"They tell a lot of stories about the chief," Carlie said.

"Most of them are true," Reverend Blair replied. "The man has had a phenomenal life. I don't think there's much he hasn't done."

Carson put Carlie's phone on the table beside her and glanced at his watch with a grimace. "I have to get going. I'm still checking on the other thing," he added to Reverend Blair. "But I... Sorry."

Carson paused to take a call. "Yes, I know, I'm running late." He paused and smiled, gave Carlie a smug look. "It will be worth the wait. I like you in pink. Okay. See you in about thirty minutes. We'll make the curtain, I promise. Sure." He hung up. "I'm taking Lanette to see *The Firebird* in San Antonio. I have to go."

"Lanette?" Reverend Blair asked.

"She's a stewardess. I met her on the plane coming down with Dalton Kirk a few weeks ago." He paused. "There's still the matter of who sent a driver for him, you know. A man was holding a sign with his name on it. I tried to trace him, but I couldn't get any information."

"I'll mention it to Hayes," Reverend Blair said. "He's still hoping to find Joey's computer." Joey was the computer technician who'd been killed trying to recover files from Hayes's computer. The computer itself had disappeared, leading Hayes to reset all the department's sensitive information files and type most of his documentary evidence all over again.

Carson's expression was cold. "Joey didn't deserve to die like that. He was a sweet kid."

"I didn't know him," Reverend Blair said. "Eb said he was one of the finest techs he'd ever employed."

"One day," Carson said, "we'll find the person who killed him."

"Make sure you take a law enforcement officer with you if it's you who finds him," Reverend Blair said shortly. "You're very young to end up in federal prison on a murder charge."

Carson smiled, but his eyes didn't. "I'm not as young as I look. And age has more to do with experience than years," he said, and for a minute, the sadness Carlie had seen on Rourke's face was duplicated on Carson's.

"True," Reverend Blair said quietly.

Carlie was fiddling with her phone, not looking at Carson. She'd heard about the stewardess from one of the sheriff's deputies, who'd heard it from Dalton Kirk. The woman was blond and beautiful and all over Carson during the flight. It made Carlie sad, and she didn't want to be. She didn't want to care that he was going to a concert with the woman.

"Well, I'll be in touch." He glanced at Carlie. There

was that smug, taunting smile again. And he was
gone.

Her father looked at her with sympathy. "You can't
let it matter," he said after a minute. "You know that."

She hesitated for a second. Then she nodded. "I'm
going up. Need anything?"

He shook his head. He took her by the shoulders
and kissed her forehead. "Life is hard."

"Oh, yes," she said, and tried to smile. "Night,
Dad."

"Sleep well."

"You, too."

SHE PLUGGED IN her game and went looking for Robin
to run some battlegrounds. It would keep her mind
off what Carson was probably doing with that beautiful blond stewardess. She saw her reflection in the
computer screen and wished, not for the first time,
that she had some claim to beauty and charm.

Robin was waiting for her in the Alliance capital
city. They queued for a battleground and practiced
with their weapons on the target dummies while they
waited.

This is my life, she thought silently. A computer
screen in a dark room. I'm almost twenty-three years
old and nobody wants to marry me. Nobody even
wants to date me. But I have bright ideals and I'm
living the way I want to.

She made a face at her reflection. "Good girls
never made history," she told it. Then she hesitated.
Yes, they did. Joan of Arc was considered so holy
that her men never approached her in any physical
way. They followed her, a simple farm girl, into battle

without hesitation. She was armed with nothing except her flag and her faith. She crowned a king and saved a nation. Even today, centuries later, people know who she was. Joan was a good girl.

Carlie smiled to herself. So, she thought. There's my comeback to that!

SHE WAS TYPING up a grisly report the next day. A man had been found on the town's railroad tracks. He was a vagabond, apparently. He was carrying no identification and wearing a nice suit. There wasn't a lot left of him. Carlie tried not to glance at the crime scene photos as she dealt with the report.

Carson came in, looking weary and out of sorts.

She stared at him. "Well, it wasn't you, after all," she said enigmatically.

He blinked. "Excuse me?"

"We found a man in a nice suit, carrying no identification. Just for a few minutes, we wondered if it was you," she said, alluding to his habit of going everywhere without ID.

"Tough luck," he returned. He frowned as he glanced at the crime scene photos. He lifted one and looked at it with no apparent reaction. He put it back down. His black eyes narrowed on her face as he tried to reconcile her apparent sweetness with the ability it took to process that information without throwing up.

"Something you needed?" she asked, still typing.

"I want to speak to Grier," he said.

She buzzed the chief and announced the visitor. She went back to her typing without giving Carson the benefit of even a glance. "You can go in," she said, nodding toward the chief's office door.

Carson stared at her without meaning to. She wasn't pretty. She had nothing going for her. She had ironclad ideals and a smart mouth and a body that wasn't going to send any man running toward her. Still, she had grit. She could do a job like that. It would be hard even on a toughened police officer, which she wasn't.

She looked up, finally, intimidated by the silence. He captured her eyes, held them, probed them. The look was intense, biting, sensual. She felt her heart racing. Her hands on the keyboard were cold as ice. She wanted to look away but she couldn't. It was like holding a live electric wire...

"Carson?" the chief called from his open office door.

Carson dragged his gaze away from Carlie. "Coming."

He didn't look at her again. Not even as he left the office scant minutes later. She didn't know whether to be glad or not. The look had kindled a hunger in her that she'd never known until he walked into her life. She knew the danger. But it was like a moth's attraction to the flames.

She forced her mind back on the job at hand and stuffed Carson, bad attitude and blonde and all, into a locked door in the back of her mind.

CHAPTER FOUR

THINGS WERE HEATING UP. Reverend Blair went to San Antonio with Rourke. They seemed close, which fascinated Carlie.

Her dad didn't really have friends. He was a good minister, visiting the sick, officiating at weddings, leading the congregation on Sundays. But he stuck close to home. With Rourke, he was like another person, someone Carlie didn't know. Even the way they talked, in some sort of odd shorthand, stood out.

THE WEATHER WAS COLD. Carlie grimaced as she hung up the tattered coat, which was the only protection she had against the cold. In fact, she was worried about going to the dance with Robin because of the lack of a nice coat. The shoes she was going to wear with the green velvet dress were old and a little scuffed, but nobody would notice, she was sure. People in Jacobs County were kind.

She wondered if Carson might show up there. It was a hope and a worry because she knew it was going to hurt if she had to see him with that elegant, beautiful woman she'd heard about. The way he'd looked at her when he was talking to the woman on the phone was painful, too; his smug expression taunted her with his success with women. If she could keep that in mind, maybe she could avoid some heartbreak.

But her stubborn mind kept going back to that look she'd shared with Carson in her boss's office. It had seemed to her as if he was as powerless to stop it as she was. He hadn't seemed arrogant about the way she reacted to him, that once. But if she couldn't get a grip on her feelings, she knew tragedy would ensue. He was, as her father had said, not tamed or able to be tamed. It really would be like trying to live with a wolf.

On her lunch hour, she drove to the cemetery. She'd bought a small plastic bouquet of flowers to put on her mother's neat grave. A marble vase was built into the headstone, just above the BLAIR name. Underneath it, on one side, was the headstone they'd put for her mother. It just said Mary Carter Blair, with her birth date and the day of her death.

She squatted down and smoothed the gravel near the headstone. She took out the faded plastic poinsettia she'd decorated the grave with at Christmas and put the new, bright red flowers, in their small base, inside the marble vase and arranged them just so.

She patted her mother's tombstone. "It isn't Valentine's Day yet, Mama, but I thought I'd bring these along while I had time," she said, looking around to make sure nobody was nearby to hear her talking to the grave. "Dad's gone to San Antonio with this wild South African man. He's pretty neat." She patted the tombstone again. "I miss you so much, Mama," she said softly. "I wish I could show you my pretty dress and talk to you. Life is just so hard sometimes," she whispered, fighting tears.

Her mother had suffered for a long time before she finally let go. Carlie had nursed her at home, until that last hospital stay, taken care of her, just as her mother had taken care of her when she was a baby.

"I know you blamed yourself for what happened. It was never your fault. You couldn't help it that your mother was a...well, what she was." She drew in a breath. "Daddy says they're both gone now. I shouldn't be glad, but I am."

She brushed away a leaf that had fallen onto the tombstone. "Things aren't any better with me," she continued quietly. "There's a man I...well, I could care a lot about him. But he isn't like us. He's too different. Besides, he likes beautiful women." She laughed hollowly. "Beautiful women with perfect bodies." Her hand went involuntarily to her coat over her shoulder. "I'm never going to be pretty, and I'm a long way from perfect. One day, though, I might find somebody who'd like me just the way I am. You did. You weren't beautiful or perfect, and you were an angel, and Daddy married you. So there's still hope, right?"

She moved the flowers a little bit so they were more visible, then sat down. "Robin's taking me to the Valentine's Day dance. You remember Robin, I know. He's such a sweet man. I bought this beautiful green velvet dress to wear. And Robin's rented us a limo for the night. Can you imagine, me, riding around in a limousine?" She laughed out loud at the irony. "I don't even have a decent coat to wear over my pretty dress. But I'll be going in style."

She caressed her hand over the smooth marble. "It's hard, not having anybody to talk to," she said after a minute. "I only ever had one real girlfriend, and she moved away years ago. She's married and has kids, and she's happy. I hear from her at Christmas." She sighed. "I know you're around, Mama, even if I can't see you.

"I won't ever forget you," she whispered softly. "And I'll always love you. I'll be back to see you on Mother's Day, with some pretty pink roses, like the ones you used to grow."

She patted the tombstone again, fighting tears. "Well…bye, Mama."

She got to her feet, feeling old and sad. She picked up the faded flowers and carried them back to her truck. As she was putting them on the passenger's side floor, she noticed a note on the seat.

Keep the damned cell phone with you! It does no good sitting in the truck!

It was signed with a big capital *C*.

She glared at it, looking around. She didn't see anybody. But he'd been here, watching her. He'd seen her talking to her mother. Great. Something else for him to hold against her. She started to crumple up the note, but it was the first one he'd ever written her. She liked the way he wrote, very legible, elegant longhand. With a sigh, she folded it and stuck it in the glove compartment.

"Mental illness must be contagious," she muttered to herself. "Maybe I got it from Rourke."

She got in under the wheel and started the engine. It didn't occur to her until much later that it seemed to matter to Carson if something happened to her. Of course, it could have just been pride in his work that she wouldn't get killed on his shift. Still, it felt nice. Unless he'd seen her talking to Mary and thought she needed to be committed.

HER FATHER CAME in with Rourke that night just as she was taking the cornbread out of the oven. She'd made a big pot of homemade chili to go with it.

"What a delightful smell," Rourke said in the kitchen doorway.

She grinned. "Pull up a chair. All you need is some butter for the cornbread. I have real butter. Homemade chili to go with it. There's always plenty."

"By all means," Reverend Blair chuckled. "Carlie always makes extra, in case I bring someone home with me."

"Do you do that often?" Rourke asked.

"Every other day," the reverend confessed. "She never complains."

"He only brings hungry people who like the way I cook," she amended, and laughed. Her face, although she didn't realize it, was very pretty when she smiled.

Rourke studied her with real appreciation. If his heart hadn't been torn, he might have found her fascinating.

He looked around the stove and the cabinets.

"Did I forget something?" she asked.

"I'm looking to see if you cooked a grit."

She and her father both laughed.

"It isn't a grit, it's grits. They're made with corn," she pointed out.

He shook his head. "Foreign fare."

"Yes, well, I expect you know how to cook a

springbok, but I'd have no idea," she said as she put the pot of chili on the table.

"And she knows about springboks!" Rourke groaned. He sat down and put his napkin in his lap. "She also knows the history of the Boer Wars," he said.

Her father shook his head. "She's a student of military history. A big fan of Hannibal," he confided.

"So am I. He was from Carthage. Africa," Rourke added.

There was silence while they ate. Rourke seemed fascinated with the simple meal.

"I've had cornbread before, but it's usually so dry that I can't eat it. My mother used to make it like this," he added quietly. "She was from the States. Maryland, I believe."

"How in the world did she end up in Africa?" Carlie exclaimed. She blushed. "I mean, if you don't mind my asking."

He put down his spoon. "I was very rude about my father. I'm sorry," he said, his brown eyes steady on her face. "You see, my birth certificate lists my mother's husband in that capacity. But a covert DNA profile tells a very different story." His face was hard. "I don't speak of it in company because it's painful, even now."

She was really blushing now. She didn't know what to say.

"But I wouldn't have hurt you deliberately just for asking an innocent question," Rourke continued gently. "You don't even know me."

She bit her lower lip. "Thanks," she said shyly.

"Now, if you'd been a *man*..." her father mused, emphasizing the last word.

Carlie looked at him inquisitively.

He exchanged a look with Rourke. "There was a bar in Nassau," her father said. "And a member of the group we were with made a sarcastic remark. Not to add that he did know Rourke, and he certainly knew better, but he'd had one too many Bahama mamas." He pursed his lips and studied Rourke's hard face. "I believe he made a very poetic dive into the swimming pool outside the bar."

"Deliberately?" Carlie asked.

"Well, if it had been deliberate, I don't think he'd have done it through the glass patio door," her father added.

Carlie sucked in a breath. She looked behind her.

"What are you looking for?" her father asked.

"Glass patio doors..."

Rourke chuckled. "It was a while back," he remarked. "I'm less hotheaded now."

"Lies," her father said. "Terrible lies."

"Watch it," Rourke cautioned, pointing his chili spoon at the reverend, "or I'll tell her about the Russian diplomat."

"Please do!" Carlie pleaded.

Her father glowered at Rourke. "It was a long time ago, in another life. Ministers don't hit people," he said firmly.

"Well, you weren't a minister then," Rourke teased, "and your embassy had to call in a lot of favors to keep you out of jail."

"What in the world did you people do in those days?" Carlie asked, shocked.

"Bad things," Reverend Blair said softly. "And it's time to change the subject."

"The things we don't know about our parents," Carlie mused, staring at her father.

"Some things are better not known," was the reply. "And isn't your chili getting cold, pumpkin?"

"Why do you call her 'pumpkin'?" Rourke wanted to know.

"Now that's a really long story…"

"And we can forget to tell it unless we want burned meat for a week," Carlie interjected.

The reverend just smiled.

HER FATHER WENT to answer a phone call while Carlie was clearing the dishes in the kitchen. Rourke sat at the kitchen table with a second cup of black coffee.

"You really don't know a lot about your dad, do you?" he asked her.

"Apparently not," she laughed, glancing at him with mischievous green eyes. "Do you take bribes? I can make almost any sort of pie or cake—"

"I don't like sweets," he interrupted. "And it's worth my life to tell you," he added with a laugh. "So don't ask."

She made a face and went back to the dishes in the sink.

"Don't you have a dishwasher?" he asked, surprised.

She shook her head. "Money is always tight. We get a little extra and there's a pregnant woman who can't afford a car seat, or an elderly man who needs dentures, or a child who needs glasses…" She smiled. "That's life."

He frowned. "You just give it away?"

She turned toward him, curious. "Well, can you take it with you when you go?" she asked.

He paused, sipping coffee.

"The Plains tribes had this philosophy," she began, "that the richest man in the village was the one who had the least because he gave it all away. It denoted a good character, which was far more important than wealth."

"I would ask why the interest in aboriginal culture," he began.

She turned, her hands around a soapy plate. "Oh, my best friend was briefly engaged to a Lakota man," she said. "We were juniors in high school. Her parents thought she was too young, and they made them wait a year."

"From your tone, I gather things didn't go well?"

She shook her head. She turned back to the sink to rinse the dish, aware of a pang in the region of her heart because the story hit close to home. "His parents talked him into breaking the engagement," she said. "He told her that his religion, his culture, everything was so different from hers that it would be almost impossible to make a life together. She'd have had to live on the reservation with him, and his parents already hated her. Then there was the problem of the children, because they would have been trapped between two cultures, belonging to neither."

"That's very sad," Rouke commented.

She turned to look at him, then lowered her eyes to the sink again. "I didn't realize how much difference there was, until I started reading about it." She smiled sadly. "Crazy Horse, Tashunka Witko in his own tongue—although that's translated different ways in English—was one of my favorite subjects. He was Oglala Lakota. He said that one could not sell the ground upon which the People—what the Lakota called themselves—walked." She glanced at him. "Things never mattered to them. Materialism isn't really compatible with attitudes like that."

"You're one of the least materialistic people I know, Carlie," her father said as he came back into the room. "And I'd still say it even if I wasn't related to you."

"Thanks, Dad," she said with a smile.

"I need to talk to you," he told Rourke. "Bring your coffee into the office. Carlie, that new science fiction movie you wanted to see is playing on the movie channel."

"It's not new, it's four months old," she laughed. "But you're right, I guess, it's new to me. I'll watch it later. I promised Robin I'd help run one of his little toons through a dungeon." She made a face. "I hate dungeons."

"Dungeons?" Rourke asked.

"She plays an online video game," her father explained, naming it.

"Oh, I see. You're Horde, too, huh?" Rourke teased.

She glared at him. "I'm Alliance. Proudly Alliance."

"Sorry," Rourke chuckled. "Everyone I know is in Horde."

She turned away. "It seems like it sometimes, doesn't it?" She sighed. She turned at the staircase and held up her hand as if it contained a sword. "For the Alliance!" she yelled, and took off running up-stairs.

Her father and Rourke just laughed.

IT WAS FRIDAY. And not just any Friday. It was the Friday before the Saturday night when the Valentine's Day dance was being held at the Jacobsville Civic Center.

Carlie was all nerves. She was hoping that it would be warmer, so she could manage to go to the dance without wearing a coat, because she didn't have anything nice to go with her pretty dress. She had to search out a file for the chief, which she'd put in the wrong drawer, and then she hung up on a state senator by pushing the wrong button on her desk phone.

The chief just laughed after he'd returned the call. "Is it Robin that's got you in such a tizzy?" he teased.

She flushed. "Well, actually, it's the…"

Before she could finish the sentence and tell him it was her wardrobe that was the worry, the door opened and Carson came in. But he wasn't alone.

There was a beautiful blond woman with him. She was wearing a black suit with a red silk blouse, a black coat with silver fur on the collar, and her purse was the same shade of deep red as the high-heeled shoes she was wearing. Her platinum-blond hair was pulled back into an elegant chignon. She had a flawless complexion, pale blue eyes, and skin like a peach. Carlie felt like a cactus plant by comparison.

But she managed a smile for the woman just the same.

The blonde looked at her with veiled amusement and abruptly looked toward the chief.

"Chief Grier, this is Lanette Harris," Carson said.

"So charmed to meet you," the blonde gushed in an accent that sounded even more Southern than Carlie's Texas accent. She held out a perfectly manicured hand. "I've heard so much about you!"

Cash shook her hand, but he didn't respond to her flirting tone. He just nodded. His eyes went to Carson, who was giving Carlie a vicious, smug little smile.

"What can I do for you?" he asked Carson.

Carson shrugged. "I was at a loose end. I wondered if you'd heard anything more from your contact?"

Cash shook his head. Just that. He didn't say a thing.

Carson actually looked uncomfortable. "Well, I guess we'll get going. We're having supper in San Antonio."

He was wearing a dark suit with a spotless white shirt and a blue pinstriped tie. His long hair was pulled back into a neat ponytail. He was immaculate. Carlie had to force herself not to look at him too closely.

"That desk is a mess! Don't you know how to file things away?" Lanette asked Carlie with studied humor, moving closer. Her perfume was cloying. "However do you find anything?"

"I know where everything is," Carlie replied pleasantly.

"Sorry," Lanette said when she saw Cash Grier's narrow look. "I can't abide clutter." She smiled flirtatiously.

"Don't let us keep you," Cash replied in a tone that sounded as icy as his expression looked.

"Yes. We'd better go." Carson moved to the door and opened it.

"Nice to have met you, Chief Grier," Lanette purred. "If you ever want a competent secretary, I might be persuaded to come out of retirement. I used to work for a law firm. And I know how to file."

Cash didn't reply.

"Lanette," Carson said shortly.

"I'm coming." She smiled again at Cash. "Bye now." She didn't even look at Carlie.

She went to the door and through it. Carlie didn't look up from her computer screen. She hoped she wasn't going to bite through her tongue. Only when she heard the door close did she lift her eyes again and looked through the window.

Carson was striding along beside the blonde and not with his usual smooth gait. He was almost stomping toward his black sedan.

Carlie started coughing and almost couldn't stop.

"You okay?" Cash asked with concern.

"Got…choked on the air, I guess," she laughed. She could barely stop. "Gosh, do you think she bathes in that perfume?"

"Go outside and take a break. I'll turn the AC on for a few minutes to clear the room," Cash said abruptly. "Go on."

She wasn't about to go out front and risk running into Carson and his beautiful companion. "I'll just step out back," she managed, still coughing.

She got outside and leaned against the door, dragging in deep breaths until she was able to get her breath again. There must be something in that perfume that she was allergic to. Although, come to think of it, she'd almost choked sitting next to a woman in church the week before who'd been wearing a musky sort of perfume. She'd learned long ago that she could only manage the lightest of floral colognes, and not very often. Funny, her lungs giving her so much trouble over scent, and she didn't even smoke.

She went back inside after a couple of minutes. Cash was talking to two patrolmen who'd stopped by with a legal question about a traffic stop.

She went back to her desk and sat down.

"You should see your doctor," Cash said when the patrolmen went out.

She raised both eyebrows. "He's married."

He burst out laughing. "That's not what I meant, Carlie. I think you had a reaction to Ms. Harris's perfume."

"Too much perfume bothers me sometimes, it's just allergies." She shrugged. "I have a problem with pollen, too."

"Okay. If you say so."

"I'll get the files in better order," she offered.

"Don't let some outsider's comment worry you," he said curtly. "Women like that one tear holes in everything they touch."

"She was very beautiful."

"So are some snakes."

He turned and went back into his office. Carlie tried not to mind that Carson's elegant girlfriend had treated her like dirt. She tried to pretend that it didn't bother her, that Carson hadn't brought her into the office deliberately to flaunt her.

If only I was beautiful, she thought to herself. I'd be twice as pretty as his friend there, and I'd have oodles of money and the best clothes and drive an expensive car. And I'd stick my nose up at him!

Fine words. Now, if she could only manage to forget the miserable afternoon. She was going to a dance, with a nice man. There might be an eligible man there who'd want to dance with her when he saw her pretty dress.

She smiled. It was a gorgeous dress, and she was going to look very nice. Even if she wasn't blond.

THE LIMOUSINE WASN'T what she expected. It wasn't one of the long, elegant ones she'd seen in movies. It was just a sedan.

"Sorry," Robin said when they were underway, the glass partition raised between them and the driver. "I did order the stretch, but they only had one and somebody got there before I did. Some local guy, too, darn the luck."

"It's okay," she said, smiling. "I'm just happy I didn't have to bring my truck!"

He laughed. Then he frowned. "Carlie, why aren't you wearing a coat?" he asked. He moved quickly to turn up the heat. "It's freezing out!"

"I don't have a nice coat, Robin," she said, apologizing. "I didn't want to embarrass you by wearing something ratty…"

"Oh, for God's sake, Carlie," he muttered. "We've known each other since first grade. I don't care what the coat looks like, I just don't want you to get sick."

She smiled. "You really are the nicest man I know. Lucky Lucy!"

He laughed. "Well, at least she and I will get to dance together," he said, sighing. "You're so kind to do this for us." He shook his head. "I've tried everything I know to make her folks like me. They just can't get past who my grandfather was. Some grudge, huh?"

"I know." She searched his dark eyes. "You and Lucy should elope."

"Don't I wish." He grimaced. "When I get established in my own business, that's exactly what I have in mind. They're pushing Lucy at the guy who's bringing her tonight. He's old money from up around Fort Worth. She likes him but she doesn't want to marry him."

"They can't make her," she pointed out.

"No, they can't. She's as stubborn as I am."

THEY PULLED UP at the door to the civic center, just behind the stretch limousine that belonged to the same car service Robin had used.

"There's our car. At least, the car I wanted to order for us." He frowned. "Who is that?" he added.

Carlie didn't say, but she knew. It was Carson, resplendent in an immaculate dinner jacket. Getting out of the vehicle beside him was the blond woman, in a saucy black gown that hugged every curve from shoulder to ankle, and left a lot of bare skin in between. Her breasts were almost completely uncovered except for a bit of fabric in strategic places, and her long skirt had a split so far up the thigh that you could almost see her panty line.

"Well, that's going to go over big in conservative Jacobsville," Robin muttered as the driver opened the backseat door for them. "A half-naked woman at a dance benefiting the local church orphanage."

"Maybe she'll get cold and put more clothes on," Carlie mused, only half-jokingly.

"Let's get you inside before you freeze," he added, taking her hand to pull her toward the building.

There was a crowd. Carlie spotted the chief and his beautiful wife, Tippy, over in a corner talking over glasses of punch. Rourke was standing with them. He looked oddly handsome in his formal attire. Tippy was exquisite in a pale green silk gown, decked out in emeralds and diamonds. Her long, red-gold hair was up in a French twist, secured with an emerald and diamond clasp. She looked like the world-class model she'd once been.

Close at hand was Lucy Tims, wearing a long blue gown with a rounded neckline, her black hair hanging down her back like a curtain. She was standing with a tall, lean man who seemed far more interested in talking to two of the local cattlemen than with his date.

She waved to Robin, said something to the tall man, who nodded, and made a beeline for Carlie and Robin.

"You made it!" Lucy enthused. "Oh, Carlie, bless you!" she added, hugging the other woman.

"You may call me Cupid," Carlie whispered into her ear, laughing.

"I certainly will. You don't know how grateful we are."

"Yes, she does because I told her all the way over here," Robin chuckled. "Shall we get some punch?"

"Great idea." Carlie looked down at the spotless green velvet dress. "On second thought, the punch is purple and I'm clumsy. I think I'll just look for a bottle of water!"

They both laughed as she left them.

Well, at least she didn't see Carson and his new appendage, she thought, grateful for small blessings. She walked down the table with a small plate, studying the various delicacies and grateful that food was provided. She'd been too nervous to eat anything.

She was trying to decide between cheese straws and bacon-wrapped sausages when she felt the plate taken from her hand.

She started to protest, but Carson had her by the hand and he was leading her out toward the dance floor.

"You…didn't ask," she blurted out.

He turned her into his arms and slid his fingers into hers. "I didn't have to," he said at her forehead.

Her heart was beating so hard that she knew he had to feel it. He had her wrapped up against him, so close that she could almost taste his skin. He was wearing just a hint of a very masculine cologne. His shirtfront was spotless. His black tie was ruffled. Just above her eyes she could see the smooth tan of his jaw.

He moved with such grace that she felt as if she had two left feet. She was stiff because it disturbed her to be so close to him. Her hand, entwined with his, was cold as ice. She could just barely get enough air to breathe.

"Your boyfriend's dancing with someone else," he observed.

She could have told him that she didn't have a boyfriend, that she was only helping play Cupid, but it wasn't her secret to tell.

"Will you relax?" he said at her ear, shaking her gently. "It's like dancing with a board."

She swallowed. "I was getting something to eat."

"The food will still be there when you go back."

She stopped protesting. But it was impossible to relax. She followed him mechanically, vaguely aware that the song they were playing was from the musical *South Pacific* and that the evening actually did seem enchanted. Now.

"Whose tombstone were you talking to?" he asked after a minute.

She cleared her throat. "Nobody was around."

"I was."

"You weren't supposed to be there."

He shrugged.

She drew in a steadying breath and stared at his shirt. "I took my mother a bouquet," she said after a minute. "I go by the cemetery and talk to her sometimes." She looked up belligerently. "I know it's not normal."

He searched her soft green eyes. "Normal is subjective. I used to talk to my mother, too, after she was gone."

"Oh." She glanced down again because it was like a jolt of lightning to look into those black eyes.

His fingers became caressing in between her own where they rested on top of his dinner jacket. "I was six when she died," he said.

"I was fourteen."

"How did she die?"

"Of cancer," she said on a long breath. "It took months. At least, until she went into hospital. Then it was so fast…" She hesitated. "How did your mother die?"

He didn't answer.

She groaned inside. She'd done it again. She couldn't seem to stop asking stupid questions…!

His hand contracted. "My father was drunk. She'd burned the bread. She tried to get away. I got in front of him with a chair. He took it away and laid it across my head. When I came to, it was all over."

She stopped dancing and looked up at him, her eyes wide and soft.

"She was very beautiful," he said quietly. "She sang to me when I was little."

"I'm so sorry," she said, and meant every word.

He smoothed his fingers over hers. "They took him away. There was a trial. One of her brothers was in prison, serving a life sentence for murder. He had the bad luck to be sent to the same cell block."

She studied his hard, lean face. She didn't say anything. She didn't have to. Her eyes said it for her.

The hand that was holding hers let go. It went to her face and traced the tear down to the corner of her full, soft mouth. It lingered there, the knuckle of his forefinger moving lazily over the pretty line of her lips.

She felt on fire. Her legs were like rubber. She could feel her heart beating. She knew he could, because his eyes suddenly went down to the discreet rounded neckline, and lower, watching the fabric jump with every beat of her heart, with her strained breathing.

Her whole body felt tight, swollen. She shivered just a little from the intensity of a feeling she'd never experienced before. She swallowed. Her mouth was so dry…

"You'd be a pushover, little girl," he whispered in

a deep, gentle tone as he looked at her soft mouth. "It wouldn't even be a challenge."

"I...know," she managed in a broken tone.

His head bent. She felt his breath on her lips. She felt as if she were vibrating from the sensuous touch of his hand at her waist, pulling her close to the sudden, blunt hardness of his body.

He was burning. Hungry. Aching. On fire to touch her under that soft bodice, to feel her breasts under his lips. He wanted to push her down on the floor here, right here, and press himself full length against her and feel her wanting him. Her heartbeat was shaking them both. She was dying for him. He knew it. He could have her. She wouldn't even try to stop him. He could take her outside, into the night. He could feed on her soft mouth in the darkness, bend her to his will, back her up against the wall and...

"Carson!"

CHAPTER FIVE

"CARSON!" THE STRIDENT voice came again.

The second time, Carson heard it. He steeled himself to look away from Carlie's rapt, shocked face and slowly let her move away from him.

He turned to Lanette. She was glaring at them.

"You promised me the first dance," she accused, pouting.

He managed to look unperturbed. "So I did. If you'll excuse me?" he asked Carlie without actually meeting her eyes.

She nodded. "Of course."

He took Lanette's hand and moved to the other side of the room.

Carlie was almost shaking. She went back to the buffet table mechanically and picked up another plate.

"Might better calm down a little before you try to eat," Rourke murmured. He took the plate away from her, just as Carson had, and pulled her onto the dance floor. "Just as well to escape before complications arise," he added with a chuckle. "You seem to be the subject of some heated disagreement."

She tossed a covert glance toward the other side of the room where Carson and his date appeared to be exchanging terse comments.

"I was just trying to get something to eat," she began.

He studied her. "That's a nice young man you came in with. Very polite. Odd, how he's ignoring you."

She looked up at him. "Private matter," she said.

"Ah. So many things are, yes?"

The way he said it amused her. She laughed.

"That's better," he replied, smiling. "You were looking a bit like the hangman's next victim."

She lowered her eyes to his shirt. It had ruffles, and crimson edging. He had a red carnation in the lapel of the jacket. "You're not quite conventional," she blurted out.

"Never," he agreed. "I like to buck the odds. Our friend over there is Mr. Conservative," he added. "He doesn't like the assumption of ownership, so you can figure the beautiful companion will be gone quite soon."

She tried not to look pleased.

He tilted her face up to his and he wasn't smiling. "That being said, let me give you some sound advice. He's living on heartache and looking for temporary relief. Do you get me?"

She bit her lip. She nodded.

"Good. You remember that. I've seen him walk on hearts wearing hobnailed boots, and he enjoys it. He's getting even."

"But I haven't done anything to him," she began.

"Wrong assumption. He's paying back someone else. Don't ask," he said. "I'm not privy to his past. But I know the signs."

There was such bitterness in his voice that she just stared at him.

"Long story," he said finally. "And no, I won't share it. You just watch your step. Carson's big trouble for a little innocent like you."

"I'm the only one of my kind," she said a little sadly. "Everybody says I'm out of step with the world."

"Would you enjoy being used like a cocktail napkin and tossed in the bin after?" he asked bluntly.

She caught her breath at the imagery.

"I thought not." He drew her back into the dance. "That platinum-armored blond tank he's with doesn't care what she's asked to do if the price is right," he said with icy disdain. "She's for sale and she doesn't care who knows it."

"How do you know...?"

He looked down at her with weary cynicism. "This isn't my first walk round the park," he replied. "She's the sort to go on the attack if anything gets between her and something she wants."

"Well, he doesn't want me," she said, "but thanks for the warning."

He chuckled. "Not to worry, I'll be around."

"Thanks, Rourke."

"Stanton."

She pulled back and looked up at him with real interest. "Stanton?"

He smiled. "It's my first name. I only share it with friends."

She smiled back, shyly. "Thanks."

"And *Carlie?* Is it your name or a nickname?"

She looked around to make sure nobody was close enough to hear. "Carlotta," she whispered. "My mother thought it sounded elegant."

"Carlotta." He smiled gently. "It suits you."

"Just don't tell anyone," she pleaded.

"Your secret's safe with me," he promised.

She was remembering Lanette's nasty comment about her desk, right in front of her boss. She imagined the other woman was furious that she'd even danced with Carson. She just hoped there wouldn't be a price to pay.

APPARENTLY CARSON DIDN'T like possessive women, because Carlie had no sooner finished her small plate of canapés than he was back again. He stopped by the bandleader and made a request. Then he went straight to Carlie, took the punch out of her hand and led her to the dance floor.

"That's a tango," she protested. "I can't even do a two-step...!"

"I lead, you follow," he said quietly. He shot a look of pure malice at the blonde, who was standing across the room with an angry expression.

"You're getting even," she accused as the band began to play again.

"Count on it," he snarled.

He pulled her close and began to move with exquisite grace. He stopped abruptly, turned, and in a series of intricate steps, wound his legs around hers.

It shocked her that he was so easy to follow in such a hard dance. She laughed self-consciously. "This doesn't look like tangos in movies," she began.

"That's Hollywood," he mused. "This is how they do it in Argentina. People go to dance halls and do it with strangers. It's considered part of the culture. Strangers passing in the night."

"I see."

He pulled her close again, enjoying the soft feel of her slender young body in his arms. She smelled just faintly of roses. "Have you ever been to South America?"

"You're kidding, right?" She gasped as he pulled her suddenly closer and made a sharp turn, holding her so that she didn't stumble.

"Why would I be kidding?" he asked.

"I've never been any place in my life except San Antonio."

He frowned. "Never?"

"Never." She sighed. "I went up with Tommy Tyler once in his airplane when he bought it. It was one of those little Cessna planes. I threw up. I was so embarrassed that I never wanted to get on an airplane again."

He chuckled deeply. "I imagine he was unsettled, as well."

"He was so nice. That just made it worse. I apologized until we landed. He got somebody to come and clean it up. To his credit, he even offered me another ride. But I wouldn't go."

"Were you serious about him?"

"Oh, not that way. He was in his fifties, with grown children," she chuckled. "His wife and my mother were great friends."

"People around here are clannish."

"Yes. Most of us have been here for several generations. I had a teacher in grammar school who taught my grandfather and my mother."

He looked down at her curiously as he did another series of intricate steps, drawing her along with him.

The close contact was very disturbing. He loved it. He glanced at the blonde, who was steaming. He enjoyed that. He didn't like possessive women.

Carlie followed his glance. "She'll be out for blood soon," she murmured.

"Which is none of your business." He said it gently, but his tone didn't invite comment.

She clenched her teeth and tried not to give away how hungry the contact was making her. She was astonished at how easy a partner he was. The tango was one of the hardest dances to master, she'd heard. She'd always wanted to try it, but she'd never had a date who could actually dance.

Carson could. He was light on his feet for such a big man, and very skilled. She didn't let herself think about how many partners he must have had to be so good on the dance floor. She drew in a quick breath. She was getting winded already. It irritated her that she couldn't run or even walk fast for long without needing to stop and catch her breath.

She'd never have admitted it to Carson. The feel of his body against hers was intoxicating. She felt his hand firm at her waist, his fingers curled around hers, as he led her around the dance floor.

She was vaguely aware that they were being watched by more people than just the angry blonde, and that the police chief and his wife had taken the dance floor with them.

Cash was a master at the tango. He and Tippy moved like one person. He danced closer to them, and winked. "You're outclassed, kid," he told Carson. "But not bad. Not bad at all."

Carson laughed. "Don't rest on your laurels. I'm practicing."

"I noticed," Cash said with a grin at Carlie, and he danced Tippy, who also smiled at them, to the other part of the dance floor.

Several other couples came out, trying to keep up with the two accomplished couples on the floor. Their attempts ranged from amusing to disastrous.

Carson's chest rose and fell with deep, soft laughter. "I think square dancing has a larger following in this vicinity than the tango," he pointed out.

"Well, not many men can dance. Even square-dance," she added shyly.

He slowed his movements, and held her even closer, his head bent to hers so that she could feel his breath, smell its minty tang, on her mouth. "My mother danced," he whispered. "She was like a fairy on her feet. She usually won the women's dances at powwows."

She looked up into liquid black eyes. "The Lakota have powwows?"

He nodded. "It's what we call them. The first in is the drum. Several men sit around it and play, but it's always called the drum. There are men's dances and women's dances. They're very old."

She nodded. "I went to a powwow up near San Antonio once," she recalled. "There were Comanche people there."

His fingers moved sensuously against hers. "I have Comanche cousins."

"Your people are clannish, too," she remarked.

"Very. Both sides."

"Both sides?"

"One of my great-great-grandmothers was blond and blue-eyed," he said. "She married a Lakota man. He was a rather famous detective in Chicago at the turn of the twentieth century. He was at Wounded Knee. She nursed him back to health. Later, he was with Buffalo Bill's Wild West show for a time."

She wouldn't have mentioned it, but his skin was a light olive shade. She'd guessed that his blood was mixed.

"That must have been one interesting courtship," she said.

He chuckled. "So I'm told." He searched over her face. "Your father has Norwegian ancestors somewhere."

"Yes, from someplace with a name I can't even pronounce. I never met any of his people. He didn't come back here until I was thirteen…" Her voice trailed away. She didn't like thinking about that. "Mama had pictures of him, but I only saw him a few times when I was growing up. He'd stay for a day or two and go away again, and Mama would cry for weeks after."

He scowled. "Why didn't he stay with her?"

She stared at his shirtfront as the music began to wind down. "They argued once. I heard. He said that she trapped him into marrying her because I was on the way. I wouldn't speak to him after that when he came home. I never told him why. It wasn't until she was dying that he came home. He's…different now."

"That's what I've heard from other people who knew him. He seems to enjoy the life he has now."

"He says he has to do a lot of good to make up for the bad things he used to do," she replied. "He won't talk about them. At least, he wouldn't. Rourke had supper with us and he and Daddy talked about old times. It was fascinating."

"Rourke?"

She smiled. "He's really nice. He likes my cooking, too."

His hand on her waist contracted as if he were angry. "Rourke's more of a lobo wolf than I am. You'll break your heart on him."

She looked up at him with wide, shocked eyes. "What?"

He pulled her closer, bent her against his body in such a sensual way that she gasped. His head lowered until his mouth was almost touching hers as he twirled her around to the deepening throb of the music. "But better him than me, baby," he whispered at her soft mouth. "I don't do forever. Even a child on the way wouldn't change that."

She was barely hearing him. He'd called her "baby." No man had ever called her that, and certainly not in such a sexy, hungry sort of tone. She felt herself shiver as his hand smoothed up her rib cage, stopping just under her breast on the soft fabric. And she couldn't even protest.

She felt as if her body was going to explode from the tension he raised in it. She bit off a soft moan as she felt him drag her even closer, so that she was pressed against him from breasts to hips.

In all her life, she'd never felt a man become aroused, but he wanted her, and he couldn't hide it. She shivered again, her heart beating so hard that she thought it might break out of her chest.

"You...shouldn't," she choked.

His cheek rasped against hers. "You'd be the sweetest honey I ever had," he breathed at her ear. "I'd go so hard into you that you'd go up like a rocket."

She moaned and hid her face, shocked, embarrassed...excited. Her nails bit into his jacket. Her body moved against his helplessly as his long leg moved in and out between hers as the dance slowly wound down.

He arched her against him as it ended, positioning her so that her head was down and leaning back, his mouth poised just over hers.

She held on for dear life. Her eyes were locked into his, imprisoned, helpless. He pulled her up with exquisite slowness, held her against him while people clapped. Neither of them noticed.

He let her go, his cheeks ruddy, as if he were angry and unsettled by what had happened. He had to recite math problems in his mind to force his body to relax before he let her go. She wouldn't realize what was going on, but that blonde would see it immediately.

"You dance well," he said stiffly. "All you need is practice."

She swallowed. "Thanks. You're...amazing."

His eyes, narrow and wise, searched hers. "You have no idea how amazing, in the right circumstances," he whispered huskily, his eyes falling to her mouth. "And if you're very lucky, you won't find out."

She felt her heart shaking her. She knew he must be able to feel it, too. She could barely get her breath. Funny, it felt as if air could get in but couldn't get back out. She coughed slightly.

He frowned. "What's wrong?"

"Perfume," she faltered. "It bothers me sometimes."

He arched an eyebrow. "I don't wear perfume."

"Not you," she muttered. "Other women."

He sniffed the air and smiled. "Florals, musk,
woodsy tones," he said. His eyes smoothed over her
face. "You smell of roses."

"I love roses," she told him.

"Do you?"

She nodded. "I grow them at home. Antique roses.
My mother used to plant them."

"My mother was an herbalist," he replied. "She
could cure anything."

"The music has stopped," the blonde pointed out
coldly.

Carlie and Carson turned and looked at her blankly.

"And I'd like some punch, if you please?" Lanette
added icily.

Carson let Carlie go. He hadn't realized that the
music had stopped, or that he and Carlie were standing so close together…alone on the dance floor.

"I'll be back in a minute," he told Lanette. He let
go of Carlie's hand and moved toward the restrooms.

Carlie, left alone with the overperfumed blond
wildcat, braced herself for what she knew to expect.

"WELL, THAT WAS an exhibition if I ever saw one!" Her
pale blue eyes were like ice. "Don't you get any ideas
about Carson, you little hick secretary. He's mine.
Hands off. Do you understand me?"

Carlie just stared at her with equally cold green
eyes. She was still shaking inside from Carson's sensual dance and the things he'd said to her. But she

wasn't going to let the other woman cow her. "That's his choice."

"Well, he's not choosing you. I'm not kidding," the other woman persisted. She smiled coldly. "You think you're something, don't you?" She looked Carlie up and down. "Did your dress come from some bargain basement up in San Antonio?" she asked sarcastically. "Marked down 75 percent, perhaps?" she added and laughed when Carlie blushed. "And those shoes. My God, they must be ten years old! I'm surprised he wasn't embarrassed to be seen dancing with you in that dress…!"

"Got yours at a consignment sale, darling?" came a soft, purring voice from beside Carlie.

Tippy Grier moved closer, cradling a cup of punch in her hands. She looked elegant in her green silk gown, dripping diamonds and emeralds. She smiled at the blonde. "That particular dress was in a collection of only five gowns. I recognize it because I know the designer," she added, watching the blonde's eyes widen. "It isn't to my taste," she added, "because I don't sell myself."

"How dare you…I was on the runway!" Lanette almost spat at her, reddening.

"Honey, the only runway you've been on is at the airport," Tippy drawled. She looked down. "Those shoes are two seasons out of date, too, but I suppose you thought nobody would notice." She pursed her bow lips in a mock pout. "Shame."

Lanette's hands were clenched at her sides.

"Run along now, kitty cat," Tippy dismissed her. "Your saucer of cream's waiting outside the door." She smiled. "Do have a lovely evening."

Lanette was almost sputtering. She turned and went storming off toward Carson, who was just returning. She ran into his arms, making a big production of crying, wiping at her eyes, and gesturing toward Tippy and Carlie. The look Carson gave Carlie was livid before he took Lanette's arm and walked her toward the front door.

"Wow," CARLIE SAID to Tippy. She shook her head. "You're just incredible! I didn't even have a comeback."

Tippy laughed. It sounded like silver bells. Her reddish-gold hair burned like fire in the lights from overhead. Her green eyes, lighter than Carlie's, twinkled. "I've seen her kind in modeling. They think they're so superior." Her smile was mischievous. "When I was new to the runway, there was this terrible woman from upstate New York who made fun of everything from my big feet to my accent. I cried a lot. Then I got tough." She pursed her lips. "You know, if you time it just right, you can trip someone on the runway and make it look like a terrible accident!"

"You wicked woman," Carlie gasped, laughing.

"She really did have it coming." She shook her head. "I almost felt sorry for her. She lost her contract with the designer. She didn't work for six months. When she finally got another job, she was a different person." Her green eyes glittered. "I hate people like that woman. I know what it is to be poor."

"Thanks," Carlie said. "I couldn't think of a thing to say. It is a sale dress, and my shoes are really old."

"Carlie, you look lovely," Tippy told her solemnly.

"It doesn't matter how much the dress cost if it flatters you. And it does." She smiled. "I hope she tells Carson what I said to her."

"If she does, he might have something to say to you."

Tippy laughed again. "He can take it up with my husband," she replied, and raised her cup of punch to her lips.

"How was the dance?" Reverend Blair asked when Carlie came in the front door.

"It was very nice," she said.

He moved closer, his eyes probing. "What happened?"

She drew in a breath. "Carson danced with me and his girlfriend got really angry. She said some really unpleasant things to me."

His pale blue eyes took on a glitter. "Perhaps I should speak to her."

She smiled. "Tippy Grier spoke to her."

"Say no more. I've heard about Mrs. Grier's temper."

"She was eloquent," Carlie said. She shook her head. "And she never said a single bad word the whole time."

"Good for her. You don't have to use bad words to express yourself. Well, unless you're trying to start a lawnmower," he amended.

She pursed her lips. "Daddy, you think 'horsefeathers' is a bad word."

He frowned. "It is!"

She laughed. "Well, I did enjoy the dancing. Rourke is really light on his feet."

"Yes." He gave her a concerned look.

She waved a hand at him. "No way I'd take on that South African wildcat," she said. "I have a good head on my shoulders."

He seemed relieved.

"I'm going on up. You sleep well, Daddy."

"You, too, pumpkin," he replied with a smile.

SHE WAS HALF-ASLEEP when her cell phone rang. She picked it up and punched the button. "Hello?" she asked drowsily.

There was a pause. "It will come when you least expect it," came an odd-sounding masculine voice. "And your father won't walk away." The connection was broken.

"Right." She turned off the phone and closed her eyes. She'd remember to tell her father in the morning, but the last threat about her father had never materialized, nor had any threat against herself. She was beginning to think that it was a campaign of terror. If so, it wasn't going to work. She refused to live her life afraid.

But she did say an extra prayer at church the next day. Just to be on the safe side.

HER FATHER WASN'T at the breakfast table Monday morning. She had a cup of coffee and two pieces of toast and paused to check the truck over before she started it. She wasn't afraid, but caution wasn't too high a price to pay for safety.

She got into the office, put her coat away and shoved her purse under the desk. She pushed her hair back. It was a damp morning, so her naturally wavy hair was curling like crazy because of the humidity.

She turned the mail out of its bag onto the desk. She'd stopped by the post office, as she did every morning on her way to work. There was a lot of it to go through before the chief came in. She made coffee and shared it with one of the patrolmen. He went out, leaving the office empty.

She sat down at her desk and picked up a letter opener. She'd just started on the first letter when the door opened and a cold wind came in.

Carson was furious. His black eyes were snapping like flames. He stopped in front of the desk.

"What the hell did you say to Lanette Saturday night?" he demanded.

She blinked. "I didn't—"

"She was so upset she couldn't even talk," he said angrily. "She cried all the way home. Then she phoned me this morning, still in tears, and said she was having to go to the doctor for anxiety meds because of the upset."

"I didn't say anything to her," she repeated.

His eyes narrowed. "Don't get ideas."

"Excuse me?"

"It was only two dances," he said in a mocking tone. "Not a marriage proposal. I've told you before, you're not the sort of woman who appeals to me. In any way."

She stood up. "Thank God."

He just stared at her. He didn't speak.

"Your girlfriend was showing more skin than a bikini model," she pointed out. "Obviously that's the sort of woman you like, one who advertises everything she's got in the front window, right? You know why you like her? Because she's temporary. She's a throwaway. She's not the sort of woman who'd want anything to do with a permanent relationship or children…"

His face went hard. His black eyes glittered. "That's enough."

She bit her lip. "You're right, it's none of my business. But just for the record," she added angrily, "you're the sort of man I'd run from as fast as my legs would carry me. You think you're irresistible? You, with your notched bedpost and years of one-night stands? God only knows what sorts of diseases you've exposed yourself to…!"

The insult put a fire under him. He started toward her with blood in his eye, bent on intimidation. The movement was quick, threatening, dangerous. The shock of it took her stumbling backward toward the wall. On the way, she grabbed a chair and held it, trembling, legs out, toward him while she cursed herself for her stupid runaway tongue.

He stopped suddenly. He realized, belatedly, that she was afraid of him. Her face was chalk-white. The chair she'd suspended in midair was shaking, like her slender young body. She was gasping for breath. Wheezing. Coughing.

He frowned.

"Don't…!" she choked, swallowing, coughing again.

The door opened. "What in the hell…?"

"Stay with her," Carson said curtly, running past Cash. He made a dash to his car, grabbed his medical kit and burst back in the door just as Cash was taking the chair from Carlie and putting her firmly down in it.

"Grab her driver's license," he ordered Cash as he unzipped the kit. He pulled a cell phone out of his slacks. "Who's her doctor?"

"Lou Coltrain," Cash replied.

Carlie couldn't speak. She couldn't even breathe.

She heard Carson talking to someone on the other end of the phone. She heard her boss relaying statistics. Why did they need her weight? She couldn't breathe. It felt as if the air was stuck inside her lungs and couldn't get out. She heard a weird whistling sound. Was that her?

Carson tore open packages. He swabbed the bend of her elbow and pulled up a liquid from a small bottle into a syringe. He squirted out a drop.

"This may hurt. I'm sorry." He drove the needle into her arm. His face was like stone. He was almost as pale as she was.

Her breathing began to ease, just a little. Tears sprung from her eyes and ran, hot, down her cheeks.

"Call the emergency room," Carson told Cash. "Tell them I'm bringing her in. She needs to be checked by a physician."

"All right," Cash said tightly. "Then we'll have a talk."

Carson nodded curtly. He handed Carlie her purse, picked her up in his arms and carried her out the door.

CHAPTER SIX

OUTSIDE, A PATROL car was waiting, its lights flashing like mad.

"Chief said for me to lead you to the emergency room," the patrolman called to Carson.

"Thanks," he said. He put Carlie in the passenger seat, strapped her in and threw himself behind the steering wheel.

He ran two red lights, right behind the police car. It was only a short drive to the hospital, but he wanted to get Carlie there as quickly as he could. Her color was still bad, although she was breathing a little easier.

"Damn...you," she cursed, sobbing.

"Yes," he rasped. He glanced at her as he pulled up at the emergency entrance. "God, I'm sorry!"

He got out, unfastened her seat belt and carried her right past the waiting gurney with its attendant, past the clerk, back into a waiting room, trailing irritated people.

"Dr. Coltrain is ready for her, we called ahead," he said over his shoulder.

"Is that Carlie?" the clerk exclaimed. "Is she all right?"

"Not really," Carson said in a rough tone. He carried her into a treatment room. Seconds later, a blond woman in a white lab coat came in, a stethoscope around her neck.

"Are you the one who called me from her office?" she asked, glancing at Carson. "You said that she was upset and having trouble breathing."

"Yes," Carson said quietly. "I'd bet my left arm on asthma."

"Asthma?" Dr. Lou Coltrain frowned at him.

She turned to Carlie, who was still gasping. "Epinephrine. You said on the phone that you were giving her epinephrine."

"Yes," Carson replied tersely. He reminded her of the dosage. "I checked her weight on her driver's license first."

She nodded. "Fran, bring me an inhaler," she said to a nurse nearby. She gave the name brand and the dosage. "Hurry."

"Yes, Doctor," the woman said, and went to get it.

Lou examined Carlie, aware that she was glaring at the man who'd brought her in. He had his hands shoved deep in his pockets and he looked as if somebody had cut the life out of him. She didn't have to guess what had prompted Carlie's attack. Guilt was written all over him.

"She has no history of asthma," Lou said.

"Allergies to perfume, difficulty breathing after exertion, coughing fits," Carson said.

Lou frowned as she glanced at him. "Sporadic?"

"Very. Difficult to diagnose without proper equipment. I'd recommend an allergist."

"Yes. So would I."

She finished her examination. Fran was back with

the inhaler. Lou instructed her in its use and waited until she'd taken several puffs.

"You're lucky that you had no underlying heart conditions, like a sinus node issue," Lou said as she watched Carlie suck in the meds. "Epinephrine can kill someone with a serious arrhythmia." She glanced at Carson. "You knew that."

He nodded. His face was solemn, still. He didn't add anything to the nod.

"One more puff, and then I want you to lie there and rest. I'll be back to check on you in a minute. Feeling better?" Lou asked Carlie, and smiled as she smoothed the ruffled wavy dark hair.

"Much. Thanks, Lou."

Lou turned to Carson. "Can I speak with you?"

He glanced at Carlie. She averted her eyes. He sighed and followed Lou into an empty treatment room nearby.

Lou turned, pinning him with pale eyes. "You know too much for a layman."

"Field medic in the military," he replied.

She pursed her lips. "Try again."

He drew in a breath. She was quick. Nobody else had ever questioned his skills. "I finished medical school and got my degree. I'd have gone into an internship after, but I quit."

"I thought so. Why did you quit?"

His face closed up. "Personal issues. Serious ones. I went off the deep end for a few years."

"I think you're still there," Lou replied. "Off the deep end, I mean." She jerked her head toward Carlie. "What do you know about her?"

"A hell of a lot more than I thought I did, after the

past few minutes," he said flatly. "We had an argument. My fault. I'm hotheaded and I was…frustrated. I started toward her…" He held up a hand when she looked ready to explode. "I've never hit a woman in my life," he interrupted, his black eyes flashing. "My father beat my mother to death in a drunken fit. He went to prison and he was killed by one of her relatives who was serving life on a murder charge. I know more about violence than you have time to hear."

Her face relaxed, just a little. "I'm sorry."

"I would never have struck her. I just went closer." He drew in a breath and leaned back against the block wall, his arms crossed over his chest, his eyes sad. "She backed away and picked up a chair to hold me at bay. That's when I noticed that she was barely able to breathe. I frightened her. I don't know why. Unless there's some violence in her past that I'm not aware of."

"There is," Lou said quietly. "But I don't discuss patients." She smiled to soften the words.

"I understand."

"You reacted very quickly. You may have saved her life." She studied him from across the cubicle. "You also treated Sheriff Hayes Carson when you rescued him and Minette, across the border. You know, doctors are getting thin on the ground. Except for specialists, there's just me and Copper," she added, referring to her husband, also a physician, "and Micah Steele."

His face tautened. "I'm doing a job I like."

"Really?"

He averted his eyes.

"I'm no psychologist," she said after a minute, "but

even I can see through the anger. You're hiding, inside yourself."

"Don't we all do that?" he asked.

"To some extent, yes." She smiled. "I'll stop. I just hate to see waste. You surely don't want to spend the rest of your life feeding people to crocodiles?" she added.

He groaned. "Does everybody know everything in this town?"

"Pretty much," she agreed. "We don't have secrets from each other. We're family," she explained. "We come from all backgrounds, all cultures, all religions. But there are so few of us in Jacobsville and Comanche Wells that we think of ourselves as just one big family."

"Not what I connected with small towns," he confessed. "And I don't share my secrets."

"You never carry ID with you," she began. "You work for Cy Parks, but Eb Scott sends you on assignments periodically. You have a very bad reputation for being a womanizer. You don't drink or smoke, you keep to yourself, and you and Rourke are friends."

"Damn," he muttered.

"See?" she added smugly. "Family."

He shouldered away from the wall. "Not for long. I'm moving on soon."

"Because of Carlie." She laughed softly.

He glared at her. "Because I don't stay in one place long. Ever."

She crossed her arms with a sigh. "You can't run away from the past," she said gently. "It's portable. No matter how far you go, it travels with you. Until you come to grips with it, face what you're running away from, you'll never be satisfied."

"Well, if it catches up with me, it had better be wearing track shoes," he replied. He stood erect. "I need to get Carlie home."

"She's more fragile than she looks," Lou said surprisingly. "Try not to hurt her too much."

He didn't say a word. He just walked by her.

CARLIE REFUSED TO be carried. She walked out the front door beside him, slowly, although her breathing was easier.

"I have to go to the pharmacy," she began.

"I'll drive you. Don't argue," he said heavily. "It's the least I can do."

She shrugged. "Okay. Thanks."

She got in and fastened her seat belt so that he wouldn't have to do it for her. She didn't want him any closer than necessary. He affected her too much, and her nerves were raw after what had happened.

HE DROVE HER to the pharmacy and went inside with her. Bonnie, at the counter, smiled at Carlie.

"How's it going?" she asked as Carlie handed her the prescription. She read it and grimaced. "Oh. I see how it's going."

"Can you fill it while I wait?" Carlie asked in a subdued tone.

"Sure. Let me see if we have this in stock." She went to talk to the pharmacist Nancy, who waved and smiled. Bonnie gave Carlie a thumbs-up and went to fill the order.

One of the other clerks, a new girl, who was returning from lunch, stopped by Carson and smiled. "Can I help you?" she asked in a very sweet tone.

He didn't even look at her. "I'm with her." He nodded toward Carlie.

"Oh. Okay." She gave him a hopeful look. He didn't even glance her way.

She went on to the pharmacy, smiling at Carlie.

Carlie was breathing much better, but the experience had shaken her badly. She hated showing weakness in front of the enemy. Because that's what Carson was, however much she tried to convince herself otherwise.

Filling the prescription didn't take long. Bonnie motioned her to the counter and smiled as Carlie handed her a debit card.

"Directions are on the box," Bonnie said. "I hope you feel better."

"Me, too." Carlie sighed. "Asthma. Bummer. I never even guessed I had it. Dr. Lou's sending me to an allergist, too."

"It will probably be Dr. Heinrich," Bonnie said. "He comes here every Friday to see patients. He's from San Antonio. It will save you that long drive." She looked at Carlie over her glasses as she finished ringing up the purchase, returned the card and handed Carlie the medicine in its white bag. "Especially after you were doing a hundred on the straightaway in your dad's Cobra," she added with pursed lips.

Carlie flushed. "Don't you start."

"I like you," Bonnie replied. "And I hate funerals."

"Same here!" Nancy called across the counter.

"Okay. I'll drive like an old lady," she muttered.

"Mrs. Allen is an old lady, and she pushes that Jaguar of hers over a hundred and twenty when the sheriff's deputies aren't looking," Nancy reminded her.

"I'll drive like a conventional old lady," Carlie corrected.

"Senior citizen," Bonnie whispered. "It's more politically correct!"

Carlie laughed, for the first time since the ordeal began.

THEY WERE BACK in the car. Carlie glanced at Carson, who still looked like a locked and boarded-up house. "Thanks for taking me to the pharmacy," she began.

He ignored her. He wasn't driving toward her house. He went down the highway until he spotted a roadside park by the Jacobs River. He stopped at a convenience store and parked the car.

"Come on," he said gently, helping her out.

"Where are we going?" she asked.

"Lunch." He led the way inside. She picked out a packaged ham and cheese sandwich, a bag of chips, and a soft drink. He got a roast beef sandwich and a soft drink. He paid for all of it and led her behind the store to a picnic area beside the river, complete with concrete table and benches.

The sound of the river, even in winter, was soothing. It was February, and her ratty old coat felt good, but she could have taken it off. It was warmer in the sun.

They ate in silence for several minutes. She liked being outside. When she was at home, she did all the yard work, planted a garden, tended flowers, raked leaves, did all the things she could to keep her out of the house. She loved the seasons, the rain and the rare snowfall. She was an outdoor girl at heart.

When they finished eating, he took the waste paper and put it in a container. There was a recycling bin for the soft drink cans, and he put them in it.

She started toward the car, but he caught her hand gently in his and led her down to the river. He leaned against a tree, still holding her hand.

"Your Dr. Coltrain said that I'm hiding from the past. She's right." He drew in a long breath. "I was married."

Carlie caught her breath. His hand tightened around her fingers.

"She was younger than me. Pretty, bright, full of fun. She teased me and provoked me. I loved her more than my life. We grew up together on the Wapiti Ridge Sioux Reservation in South Dakota. Our people had known each other for generations. She was several grades behind me, but we were always friends. I was in my final year of…graduate school—" he didn't want to say "medical school" "—when we went to a dance together and fell in love. Her parents thought she was too young, but we wouldn't listen. We were married by the local priest."

He hesitated, then went on. "It was a long commute for me, and expensive because I had to fly there. And I had to stay in the dorm during the week. I had a scholarship, or I could never have managed it. My people were poor." He watched the river, his eyes sad and quiet. "She got tired of staying in the little house all alone. She liked to party. She thought I was a real stick-in-the-mud because I didn't drink or smoke." He laughed hollowly. "I guess she understood the drinking part because my father was a drunkard. Everybody on the rez knew about him."

She swallowed. "They say that alcoholism is a problem in some Native American cultures…"

"My father was white," he said, and his voice was cold as ice. "He sold seed and fertilizer for a living. He met my mother at a feed store when he was restocking there. He flattered her, took her places, bought her flowers. She was crazy about him. They got married and he moved onto the rez to live with her. She didn't know he was an alcoholic until she was pregnant with me. He started beating her then, when he lost his temper." His eyes closed. "When I was six, and he was beating my mother, I tried to block him with a kitchen chair. He picked it up and laid it across my head. When I came to, she was lying on the floor, still and quiet, and he was gone. I ran for help. It was too late."

She held her breath, listening. He'd told her some of this before, but not in such detail. She could only imagine the terror he'd felt.

"He went to prison and I went to live with my mother's uncles, aunts and cousins in a small community on the rez. One of my uncles was a reservation cop. He formally adopted me in a tribal ceremony, so I call him Dad, even though he isn't really. He's great with livestock. He and my other relatives were good to me, but they were poor and we didn't have much. I wanted more. I knew the only way to get out was to get an education. So I studied like crazy. I worked at anything I could get paid for, on ranches, in stores, on the land, and I saved every penny. When I graduated from high school, I was second in my class.

I got scholarships and commuted back and forth. I graduated with honors and went on to grad school. But then, suddenly, there was Jessie. I couldn't really afford to get married, but I was conventional in those days. My people were religious." He let go of Carlie's hand and folded his arms across his broad chest. His eyes had a lost, faraway look. "Things were good the first two years. But we were drifting apart. I still had a long way to go to a profession and I was away a good deal of the time. There was a man on the rez who wanted her. He bought her stuff, took her to dances, while I was at school or working after classes to help pay for the tuition. I came home one weekend, just after finals, and she was gone. She'd moved in with him."

He drew in a breath. "I tried to get her to come home, but she said she loved him and she was carrying his child. She wasn't coming back. I was sick at heart, but I couldn't force her to leave him. I went back to school and gave up the house. No reason to keep renting it just for weekends, anyway.

"I was getting ready for the graduation exercises when one of my cousins came to see me at school. Another relative back home told him that she'd lied. The child she was carrying was mine. The man she was living with couldn't have children. And worse, he was beating her. She'd just come back from the hospital. He'd beaten her so badly that she had a concussion."

His face hardened. "So I went home. I had a beat-up old car parked in Rapid City that would hardly make the trips back and forth from my house to the airport, and there were heavy floods, but I made it home. I went to see her. I told her that I knew about the child and that if she wouldn't come back to me, I'd have her boyfriend put in jail for beating her. She looked ancient," he said, his face twisting. "What she'd endured was written all over her. But she loved him, she told me. She was very sorry, but she loved him. I could see the child when it came, but she wasn't leaving him, even if I refused to give her a divorce."

He swallowed. "He drove up. We exchanged words. He said no way was she leaving him. He grabbed her by the hand and dragged her out to his car. I tried to stop him, but he was a big guy and I had no combat skills at the time. He wiped the floor with me. He threw her into his car and took off. I picked myself up, got in my own car and chased after him."

He shook his head. "I don't know what I thought I could do. She wanted to stay with him and he wasn't going to give her up. But I knew if she stayed he'd kill her one day, just as my father had killed my mother. And my child would die with her.

"He speeded up and so did I. His car was all over the road." His eyes closed. "If I'd had any sense, I'd have stopped, right then, but I didn't. He went onto a bridge that was unsafe. There was even a sign, but he didn't pay it any attention." He looked away, hesitated. "The bridge collapsed. They fell down in the car, into the river below. It was deep and in full flood." His eyes closed. He shuddered. "They found the bodies almost two days later. If they'd been found sooner, the child might have lived." He bit his lower lip. "It was a boy…"

"I'm so sorry," she whispered. Her eyes were wet. "So sorry."

He turned, pulled her to him and held her. Just held her. Rocked her. "I've never spoken of it, except once. Dalton Kirk's wife, in Wyoming, sat at a table with me and told me all about it, and she'd never met me or heard anything about me. It was a shock."

"I heard about her." She savored the feel of his jacket. It was leather, but soft and warm from his body, fringed and beaded. She'd never seen anything so beautiful. She closed her eyes. He'd frightened her earlier. Now she began to understand him, just a little.

He smoothed over her dark, wavy hair. "I would never have hit you," he whispered at her ear. "I know too much about brutality and its result."

"You move so quickly," she faltered.

"And for all the wrong reasons sometimes." He sighed. "Dalton Kirk's wife told me that my wife's boyfriend was drinking at the time. I didn't really notice, but if you drink something like vodka, others may not be able to smell it on your breath. She said that was why he went off the bridge, not because of me. I checked the police report. She was right. But it didn't help much. Nothing does. I still feel like a murderer."

"It isn't fair, to blame yourself for something like that." She drew back and looked up at him. "You aren't a person of faith."

"No," he said stiffly. "I don't believe in anything anymore."

"I believe that things happen the way they're meant to," she said softly. "That sometimes God uses people to say things or do things that hurt us, so that we learn lessons from it. My dad says that we should always remember that events in our lives have a purpose. It's all lessons. We learn from adversity."

He searched her green eyes quietly. "You're such an innocent, Carlie," he said gently, and her heart leaped because it was the first time he'd ever called her by name. "You know nothing about the world, about life."

"And you know everything," she murmured with a flash of laughter.

"I do." He traced a line down her cheek. "We're total opposites."

"What happened," she asked. "After?"

He looked over her head. "I went to my own graduation, alone, and enlisted in the military the same week. I learned how to fight, how to kill. I took the most dangerous assignments I could find. For a long time, I avoided women like the plague. Then it became second nature to take what was offered and walk away." That wasn't quite true, but he'd shared enough secrets for one day. "I never got serious about anyone again. I met Cy Parks overseas. He and his group were doing a stint as private contractors for the military, teaching tactics to locals. I fell in with them and came back here to work for Cy and, occasionally, for Eb Scott. It's an interesting life. Dangerous. Unpredictable."

"Sort of like you," Carlie mused.

He looked down into her eyes. "Sort of like me," he agreed.

She drew in a breath. It was much easier to do that now.

"I am truly sorry for what happened this morning," he said, searching her eyes. "I had no right to frighten you."

"You're scary when you lose your temper," she replied.

"Sheltered little violet, under a stair," he said softly.

"Not so much," she replied. "It just seems that way." Her own eyes were sad and quiet.

"You know my secrets. Tell me yours."

She swallowed. "When I was thirteen, my mother was diagnosed with cancer. She was in and out of hospitals for a year. During one of those times, her mother showed up." Her face hardened. "My grandmother was a pig, and that's putting it mildly. She had a reputation locally for sleeping with anything in pants. She had a boyfriend with her, a man who used drugs and supplied them to her. I had the misfortune to come home while they were ransacking my mother's bedroom, looking for things they could sell. I'd hidden Mama's expensive pearls that Daddy brought her from Japan, just in case, but they were trashing the house. I tried to stop them."

She shivered.

He pulled her closer. "Keep talking," he said over her head.

Her small hand clenched on his jacket. "Her boyfriend picked up a beer bottle and started hitting me with it." She shivered again. "He kept on and on and on until I was on the floor. I fought until I was so numb that I just gave up." She laughed. "You think you can fight back, that you can save yourself in a desperate situation. But that's not how it works. You feel such…despair, such hopelessness. After a while, it seems more sensible to just lie down and die…"

"Go on."

"Our next-door neighbor heard me scream and called the police. They got there just in time to keep him from killing me. As it was, I had a concussion and broken ribs. I spent several days in the hospital. They took my grandmother and her boyfriend to jail. She testified against him and got off, but our police chief—one of the ones before Cash Grier—had a nice talk with her and she left town very quickly. She didn't even apologize or come to see me. I heard later that she died from a drug overdose. He was killed in a prison riot just recently." She shook her head. "I've been terrified of violent behavior ever since."

"I can see why."

"One of our patrolmen brought a man in handcuffs in the office once to ask the chief a question. The man grabbed a nightstick off the counter and came at me with it. I fainted." She sighed. "The chief turned that man upside down, they said, and shook him like a rat until he dropped the nightstick. Then he threw him into the patrol car and told the officer to get him to the county detention center right then. He took me to the emergency room himself. I had to tell him why I fainted." She shrugged. "He isn't what he seems, is he?" she asked, looking up. "I mean, criminals are terrified of him. Even some local men say he's dangerous. But he was like a big brother with me. He still is."

"I respect him more than any other man I know, with the possible exception of Cy Parks."

"Mr. Parks is pretty scary, too," she added.

He smiled. "Not when you get to know him. He's had a hard life. Really hard."

"I know a little about him. It's a sad story. But he and his wife seem to be very happy."

"They are."

She searched his serious eyes. "I didn't say anything to your...date," she said quietly. "She was making fun of my dress and my old shoes." She lowered her eyes. "I didn't have a comeback. It was a bargain dress, and my shoes are really old. I didn't wear a coat because this is the only one I have—" she fingered the frayed collar "—and I didn't want to embarrass Robin by showing up in it."

He was very still. "She said that you insulted her."

"Tippy Grier did," she replied. She tried not to smile at the memory. "She was eloquent. She said that my dress looked nice on me and it didn't matter where it came from."

He let out a long breath. "Damn."

"It's all right. You didn't know."

His hand smoothed over her dark hair as he stared down at the river below. For a minute, there was only the sound of the water running heavily over the rocks. "She didn't mention Tippy."

"I just stood there," she said. "I guess she was mad that I danced with you."

His hand caught her hair at her nape and turned her face up to his. Black eyes captured hers and held them. "She was mad that I wanted you," he said curtly.

"Wa...wanted me?" She hesitated.

He let out a rough breath. "God in heaven, can't you even tell when a man wants you?" he burst out.

"Well, I don't know a lot about men," she stammered.

His hand slid down her back and plastered her hips to his. His smile was smug and worldly as he let her feel the sudden hardness of his body. "Now you do."

She flushed and pulled away from him. "Stop that."

He actually laughed. "My God," he said heavily. "I'm dying and you're running for cover." He shook his head. "Just my luck."

She swallowed. It was embarrassing. She tried to draw away completely but he held her, gently but firmly.

"Doesn't your friend Robin ever touch you?" he asked sarcastically. "Or are you having a cerebral relationship with him?"

She wasn't about to admit the truth to him. Robin felt like protection right now, and she needed some.

"He reads poetry to me," she choked. Actually, he wrote poetry about Lucy and read it to Carlie, but that was beside the point.

"Does he now?" He brushed his nose against hers and began to quote. "When I am dead, and above me bright April shakes out her rain-drenched hair, though you should lean above me broken-hearted, I shall not care. I shall have peace, as leafy trees are peaceful when rain bends down the bough; and I shall be more silent and cold-hearted than you are now," he whispered deeply, reciting lines from a poem called "I Shall Not Care," by Sara Teasdale. "It was written in 1919," he added. "Long before either of us was born."

Her heart jumped, stopped and ran away. His voice was like velvet, deep and sexy and overwhelmingly sensual. Her nails curled against the soft leather of his jacket.

"Yes, I read poetry," he whispered, his mouth hovering just above hers. "That was one of my favorites. I learned it by heart just before Jessie died."

Her mouth felt swollen. Her whole body felt swollen. "D…did you?" she asked in a voice that wasn't quite steady.

His lips brushed like a whisper over hers. "Are you sure you don't know what desire is, Carlie?" he whispered huskily.

She was almost moaning. His mouth teased hers, without coming to rest on it. His body was close, warm, powerful. She felt the heat of it all the way down. She couldn't get her breath, and this time it wasn't because of the asthma. She knew he could feel her heartbeat. She could hear it.

"Your father is going to kill me," he said roughly.

"For…what?"

"For this." And his mouth went down against hers, hard enough to bruise, hard enough to possess.

CHAPTER SEVEN

CARLIE WAS DYING. Her whole body was pressing toward Carson's, pleading for something she didn't quite understand. She shivered as his mouth pressed harder against hers, insistent, parting her lips so that he could possess them.

Her arms reached up, around his neck. He lifted her, riveted her body to his, as the kiss went on and on and on. She moaned under his mouth, shivering, wanting something more, something to end the torment, to ease the tension that seemed bent on pulling her young body apart.

"Carlie," he whispered roughly as his fingers tightened in her hair and he paused to catch his breath. "This is not going to end well," he rasped.

She looked up at him, breathless, wordless, shivering with needs she hadn't even known she could feel.

"Oh, what the hell," he muttered. "I'm damned already!"

He kissed her as if he'd never felt a woman's mouth under his own, as if he'd never felt desire, never known hunger. He kissed her with utter desperation. She was an innocent. He couldn't have her. He wasn't going to marry her, and he couldn't seduce her. It was one hell of a dead end. But he couldn't stop kissing her.

Her mouth was soft and warm and sweetly innocent, accepting his, submitting, but not really responding. It occurred to him somewhere in the middle of it that she didn't even know how to kiss.

He lifted his mouth and searched her wide, soft, dreamy eyes. "You don't even know how," he whispered huskily.

Her lips were as swollen as her body. "Know how to what?" she began dazedly.

The sound of a car horn intruded just as he started to bend his head to her again. She jumped. He caught his breath and moved back from her just as Cash Grier got out of his patrol car and started down to the river where they were standing, now apart from each other.

"Dum dum de dum dum de dum da da de dum," Carson hummed Gounod's "Funeral March of a Marionette" as Cash approached. He smiled wryly, through the piercing agony of his unsatisfied need.

Carlie chuckled.

"Your father was concerned," Cash told Carlie. "He asked me to look for you."

"I'm okay," Carlie said, trying to disguise the signs that she'd been violently kissed. She pushed back her disheveled hair. "He bought me lunch." She nodded at Carson.

"Did you have it tested for various poisons first?" Cash asked blandly.

She laughed again.

"I was apologizing," Carson said heavily. "I jumped on her for something she didn't even do."

"Which was?" Cash asked, and he wasn't smiling.

"Lanette said that Carlie insulted her and made her cry," he returned.

"That wasn't Carlie. That was my wife." Cash smiled coldly. "I understand that she was eloquent."

"Quite," Carlie confirmed.

"Your friend has a rap sheet," he told Carson. He smiled again. This time it was even colder.

Carson scowled. "A rap sheet?"

"It appears that she wasn't always a stewardess. In fact, I don't know how she got to be accepted in that type of job. Probably her lawyer helped her out more than once," he said.

"What was she arrested for?" Carson asked.

"Assault with a deadly weapon. A smart lawyer got her off by pleading temporary insanity, acting in a fit of jealousy." He pursed his lips, enjoying Carson's discomfiture. "She went after another woman with a knife. Accused her of trying to steal her boyfriend."

Carson didn't show it, but he felt uneasy. Lanette had made some threats about Carlie, and he hadn't taken them seriously.

Carlie's face fell at the realization that the blonde might be more dangerous than she'd realized already.

"I'd watch my back if I were you," Carson told Carlie somberly. "The rest of us will help. It seems you've got more trouble than we realized."

"There was another phone call the other night, too," she said, suddenly recalling the cryptic message. "It was a male voice. He said to tell Dad he was coming soon. It didn't make sense."

"A male voice?" Cash asked at once.

"Yes." She frowned. "Odd-sounding voice. If I ever heard it again, I think I'd remember it. Why is somebody after Dad?"

"I don't know," Cash said tersely.

"Rourke and I are trying to dig that out," Carson said abruptly. "We have contacts in, shall we say, unusual places."

"So do I," Cash reminded him. "But mine were a dead end."

"One of my cousins is a U.S. senator," Carson said, surprisingly. "He's using some of his own sources for me."

"A senator." Cash grinned. "Not bad."

"Well, not quite in the same class with having a vice president or a state attorney general for a relative," Carson retorted, smiling back.

Cash shrugged. "We all have our little secrets." He glanced at Carlie, who'd reddened when he said "secrets." His eyes narrowed. "You told him?"

She nodded.

He looked at Carson and the smile was gone. "I'll tell you once. Don't ever do that again."

"I can promise you that I never will."

Cash jerked his head in a nod.

Carson glanced at Carlie. "I tried to take him once, in a fight." He grimaced. "It wasn't pretty."

"I was a master trainer in Tae Kwon Do," Cash explained. "Black belt."

Carson rubbed one arm. "Very black."

Cash laughed.

"I was going to take her home, but we hadn't had lunch," Carson explained.

"Or dessert," Carlie mused.

Carson glanced at her with warm, hungry eyes. "Oh, yes, we had dessert."

She blushed further, and he laughed.

"Come on," Cash told them. "It isn't wise to be out in the woods alone with crazy people on the loose."

"Did somebody escape from jail?"

"Nothing like that," Cash said. "I was remembering Carlie's phone call and your girlfriend's rap sheet."

"Oh." Carson didn't say another word. He helped Carlie into the passenger seat of his car and made sure her seat belt was fastened before he closed the door.

Cash drew him over to the patrol car, and he was somber. "You need to do something about that temper."

"I had anger management classes," Carson said quietly. "They helped, for a while." He shook his head. "It's the past. I can't deal with it. I can't live with what I did. I'm at war with myself and the world."

Cash put a heavy hand on the younger man's shoulder. He knew about Carson's past. The two were close. "I'll tell you again that it was her time. Nothing could have stopped it. Somewhere inside, you know that. You just won't accept it. Until you do, you're a walking time bomb."

"I would never hurt her," he assured Cash, nodding toward the car. "I've never hit a woman."

"The threat of force is as bad as the actual thing," Cash replied. "She hasn't gotten over what happened to her, either. We carry the past around like extra luggage, and it gets heavy from time to time."

"You'd know," Carson said gently.

Cash nodded. "I've killed men. I have to live with it. It's not easy, even now."

"For me, either." He shoved his hands into his pockets. "I didn't realize Lanette had started the trouble. She was so upset that it really got to me. She's just someone to take around. Something pretty to show off." He shrugged. "Maybe a little more than that. But nothing permanent."

"Your past in that respect isn't going to win you points with certain people around here," Cash said.

"I'm just beginning to realize that. When I was in Wyoming, Dalton Kirk's wife told me that my past was going to have a terrible impact on my future, that it was going to stand between me and something I want desperately."

"It wouldn't matter so much if you didn't flaunt it, son," Cash replied.

Carson drew in a breath. "I don't know why I taunt her," he said, and they both knew he meant Carlie. "She's a kind, generous woman. Innocent and sweet."

"Something to keep in mind," Cash added. "You'd walk away and forget about it. She'd throw herself off a cliff. You know what I'm talking about."

Carson seemed to pale. "Nothing so drastic…"

"You don't know anything about people of faith, do you?" he asked. "I didn't, until I came here and had to face living my life with what I'd done hanging over me like a cloud. I came to faith kicking and screaming, but it gave me the first peace I've ever known. Until that happened, I didn't understand the mindset of people like Carlie." His face tautened. "I'm not joking. Her faith teaches her that people get married, then they become intimate, then children come along. It doesn't matter if you agree, if you disagree, if you think she's living in prehistoric times. That's how she thinks."

"It's radical," Carson began. "She's totally out of step with the times. Everybody does it—"

"She doesn't," Cash interrupted. "And everybody around here knows it. It's why she doesn't date. Her grandmother was the town joke. She had sex with a department store manager in a closet and they got caught. He was married with three kids. She thought it was hilarious when his wife left him. In fact, that's why she did it. She was angry at the woman for making a remark about her morals."

"Good grief," Carson exclaimed.

"She was caught with men in back rooms, in parked cars, even once in a long-haul truck in the front seat at a truck stop with people walking by." He shook his head. "It was before I came here, but I heard about it. Carlie's mother was a saint, an absolutely good woman, who had to live with her mother's reputation. Carlie's had to live it down, as well. It's why she won't play around."

"I didn't realize that people knew about it."

"We know everything," Cash said simply. "If you don't care about gossip, it doesn't affect you. But Carlie's always going to care. And if something happens to her, it will show like a neon sign. Everybody will know. She won't be able to hide it or live with it in a small community like this."

"I get your point." He grimaced. "Life is never easy. I don't want to make it even harder for her," he added, glancing toward Carlie, who was watching them curiously.

"No." Cash studied the younger man. "The world is full of women like your pretty blonde, and they work for scale. Don't try to class Carlie with them."

He smiled coldly. "Or you'll have more trouble than you can handle. You do not want to make an enemy of Reverend Blair."

"I do have some idea about her father's past," Carson confessed.

"No, you don't," Cash replied. "Just take my word that you don't ever want to see him lose his temper. And you work on controlling yours."

"I'm reformed." Carson took his hands out of his pockets. "I suppose we all have memories that torment us."

"Count on it. Just try not to make more bad ones for Carlie."

"I'll drive her home." He hesitated. "Is her father there?"

Cash nodded.

Carson sighed. "There are a few unmarked places on me," he commented wryly. "I guess I can handle some more. Time to face the music."

Cash laughed. "Well, you've got guts, I'll give you that."

"Not going to arrest me?" he added.

"Not this time," Cash said.

"Just as well. You can't prove I'm me."

"Why in the hell don't you carry identification?" Cash asked. "Don't you realize that if you were ever injured, nobody would know anything about you, right down to your weight or your medical history?"

Carson smiled wryly. "When I was doing wet work overseas, it would have been fatal to carry any. I just got into the habit of leaving it behind."

"I know, but you're not in the same line of work now," Cash said.

"Certain of that, are you?" he asked with a vague smile.

"Yes."

Carson made a face. "All right," he said after a minute. "I'll think about it."

"Good man."

Carson went around the car and got in under the steering wheel. Cash drove off as Carson was starting up the car.

"Look in the glove compartment and hand me my wallet, will you?" he asked Carlie.

She rummaged around through the papers and produced it. "Do you have a last name?" she wondered aloud.

"Look at the license."

Curious, she opened the wallet. His driver's license read "Carson Allen Farwalker."

She handed it to him. He shoved it into his jacket while they were at a stoplight.

"No comment?" he asked.

"I'd be embarrassed," she replied softly.

He laughed. "On the morning I was born, a man came into our small rural community, walking. It was driving snow, almost a blizzard. He said he'd come from Rapid City, all the way on foot in his mukluks and heavy coat, hitching rides, to see a sick friend who lived near us. It was a far walk. So my mother named me Far Walker." He glanced at her. "Our names don't translate well into English sometimes, but this one did." His face tautened. "I refused to take my father's name, even as a child. So I was known on the rez as Far Walker. When I got my first driver's license, that's what I put on it, Anglicized into one word. It's my legal name now."

"It suits you," she said. "You walk like an outdoorsman."

He smiled.

"I read about how native people get their names. We tend to distort them. Like Crazy Horse. That wasn't his Lakota name, but it was what he was called by Wasichu—by white people," she said, and then flushed. She hadn't meant to give away her interest in his culture.

"Well," he said and chuckled. "Hannibal and Crazy Horse. You have wide interests. Do you know his Lakota name?" he added.

"Yes. It was Tashunka Witko." She laughed. "Although I've seen that spelled about four different ways."

"And do you know what it really means, in my tongue?" he asked.

She grinned. "'His horse is crazy,'" she replied. "I read somewhere that the day he was born, a man on a restless horse rode by and his people named him Crazy Horse."

"Close enough." He smiled gently as he met her eyes. "You're an eternal student, aren't you?"

"Oh, yes. I might have gone to college, but I didn't make high grades and we were always poor. I take free classes on the internet, though, sometimes. When I'm not grinding Horde into the ground," she added without looking at him.

"Runed that sword, did you? We'll find out how well it works on the next battleground we fight."

"I can't wait," she said smugly. "I've been practicing." She glanced at him. "What's a mukluk?"

"Heavy boots that come up to the knee, made of fur. I have some at home. I bought them in Alaska. They're made with beaver fur, with wolf fur trim and beadwork."

"Your jacket is beautiful," she remarked, glancing at it. "I've never even seen one that looks like that before."

"You never will. A cousin made it for me." He smiled. "He makes these from scratch, right down to the elk he hunts for them. He eats the meat and cures the hides. Not the wolves, however. It's illegal to kill them in the States, so he buys the fur from traders in Canada."

"I saw this movie with Steven Seagal, about Alaska. He was on a talk show wearing a jacket a lot like yours. He said the native people he worked with on the movie made it for him."

"Not a bad martial artist. I like Chuck Norris best, however, for that spinning heel kick. The chief does one just like it. Ask him sometime how he learned it," he teased.

"I already know," she laughed. "He says it's his claim to fame locally."

"Feeling better?"

She nodded. "I never dreamed it was asthma," she said heavily. She frowned and glanced at him. "But you knew right away," she said. "You even knew what to give me…"

"I was a field medic in the army," he said easily. "Emergencies were my specialty."

"You must have been very good at it," she said.

"I did what the job called for."

He pulled up in front of her house. Reverend Blair was waiting on the porch, wearing a leather bomber jacket and a black scowl.

He came down the steps and opened Carlie's door. He hugged her close. "You okay?" he asked tersely.

"I'm fine. Honest. I just overreacted."

He didn't reply. He was glaring at Carson, who came around the car to join them.

"It was my fault," Carson said bluntly. "I accused her of something she didn't do and I was overly aggressive."

The reverend seemed to relax, just a little. "You take it on the chin, don't you?" he asked half-admiringly.

"Always." He sighed. "If you want to hit me, I'll just stand here. I deserve it."

The reverend cocked his head. His blue eyes were glittery and dangerous, hinting at the man he might once have been.

"He treated me in the office, took me to the emergency room, then the pharmacy and bought me lunch after," Carlie said.

The reverend lifted an eyebrow and glanced at Carson. "Treated her?"

"I was a field medic in the army," Carson replied. "I recognized the symptoms. But if you're thinking I acted without a doctor's orders, you're wrong. I had her doctor on the phone before I opened my medical kit."

The reverend relaxed even more. "Okay."

"I was more aggressive than I meant to be, but I

would never have raised a hand to her," he added. "Violence is very rarely the answer to any problem."

"Rarely?"

Carson shrugged. "Well, there was this guy over in South America, in Carrera. Rourke and I sort of fed him to a crocodile."

The reverend glowered at him. "You're not helping your case."

"The guy cut up a young woman with his knife and left her scarred for life," Carson added. His black eyes glittered. "He bragged about it."

"I see."

"It was an act of mercy, anyway," Carson added doggedly. "The crocodile was plainly starving."

Reverend Blair couldn't suppress a laugh, although he tried. "I begin to see why you get along so well with Grier."

"Why, does he feed people to reptiles, too?"

"He's done things most men never dream of," the reverend said solemnly. "Lived when he should have died. He took lives, but he saved them, as well. A hard man with a hard past." The man's pale blue eyes pinned Carson's. "Like you."

Carson scowled. "How do you know anything about me?"

"You might be surprised," was the bland reply. He shook a finger at Carson. "You stop upsetting my daughter."

"Yes, sir," he said on a sigh.

"I'd invite you to supper but she might have some poisonous mushrooms concealed in the cupboard."

"I won't poison him," Carlie promised. She smiled.

"You can come to supper if you like. I'll make beef Stroganoff."

Carson looked torn, as if he really wanted to do it. "Sorry," he said. "I promised to take Lanette out to eat. I need to talk to her."

"That's okay," Carlie said, hiding the pain it caused her to hear that. "Rain check."

"Count on it," he said softly, and his eyes said more than his lips did. "You okay?"

She nodded. "I'll be fine."

"I'm really sorry," he said again.

"Stop apologizing, will you? You'll hurt your image," she said, grinning.

"I'll see you."

She nodded. He nodded to the reverend, got in the car and left.

"I HAVE TO see an allergist," Carlie said miserably. "Asthma, can you believe it? I couldn't get my breath, I felt like I was suffocating. Carson knew what it was, and what to do for it. He was amazing."

"He needs to work on his self-control," her father said tersely, sipping coffee while she dished up pound cake for dessert.

For just an instant she thought of Carson out of control at the river, hungry for her, and she flushed. Then she realized that he was talking about another sort of self-control.

The reverend wasn't slow. He had a good idea why she was blushing.

"Carlie," he said gently, "he goes through women like hungry people go through food."

"I know that, Dad."

"He isn't a person of faith. He works in a profession that thrives on the lack of it, in fact, and he's in almost constant danger." He hesitated. "What I'm trying to say is that he isn't going to settle down in a small town and become a family man."

"I know that, too," she replied. She put his cake down in front of him on the table and refilled his coffee cup.

"Knowing and walking away are two different things," he said curtly. "Your mother was like you, sweet and innocent, out of touch with the real world. I hurt her very badly because we married for the wrong reasons. I wasn't ready. Before I knew it, I was a father." He looked down at the uneaten cake. "I felt trapped, hog-tied, and I resented it. I made her pay for it." His lips made a grim line. "I stayed away, out of that resentment. She didn't deserve the life I gave her."

She was shocked to hear him say such things. She knew that they'd had to get married. She'd heard him say it. But even so, she'd thought her parents married for love, that her father was away because he was making a living for them.

He didn't seem to notice Carlie's surprise. He wasn't looking at her. "I didn't know she was sick. One of my friends had a cousin here, who told him, and he told me that she was in the hospital. I got back just after her mother and her drug-crazed boyfriend did a number on you." His teeth ground together. "That was when I realized what a mess I'd made of all our lives. I walked away from the old life that same day and never looked back. I only wish I'd been where

I was supposed to be so that you'd have been spared what happened to you."

"You're the one who's always saying that things happen to test us," she reminded him.

"I guess I am. But for someone who'd never hurt anybody in her life, you paid a high price," he added.

"Mama said that if she'd been a different sort of person, you would have been happy with her," she recalled. "She said her way of thinking ruined your life." She frowned. "I didn't understand what that meant at the time. But I think I'm beginning to." She did, because Carson was the same sort of person her father must have been.

"No. I ruined hers," he said. "I knew I couldn't settle down. I let my heart rule my head." He smiled sadly. "You see, pumpkin, despite how it must sound, I really loved your mother. Loved her desperately. But I loved my way of life, too, loved being on my own, working in a profession that gave me so much freedom. I was greedy and tried to have it all. In the process, I lost your mother. I will never get over what happened to her because of me. If I'd been here, taking care of her…"

"She would still have died," Carlie finished for him. "It was an aggressive cancer. They tried chemo and radiation, but it only made her sicker. Nothing you could have done would have stopped that, or changed a thing."

He studied her soft eyes. "You always make excuses for me." He shook his head. "Now you're making them for the wild man from South Dakota."

"He's wild for a reason," she said quietly.

"And you're not sharing it, right?"

"I'm not," she agreed. "It's his business."

"Nice to know you can keep a secret."

"For all the good it does me. You won't share any of yours," she pointed out.

"Why give you nightmares over a past I can't change?" he asked philosophically. He glanced at his watch and grimaced. "I'm late for a prayer meeting. You'll be okay here, right? Got the inhaler Lou prescribed?"

She pulled it out of her pocket and showed it to him.

"Okay." He shook his head. "I should have recognized the symptoms. My father had it."

"Your father? I never met him."

"He was dead by the time I married your mother," he said. He smiled. "You'd have liked him. He was a career officer in the navy, a chief petty officer."

"Wow."

"I've got photographs of him somewhere. I'll have to look them up."

"What was your mother like?"

"Fire," he chuckled. "She left trails of fire behind her when she lost her temper. She had red hair and an attitude. Tippy Grier reminds me of her, except that my mother wasn't really beautiful. She was a clerk in a hotel until she retired. She died of a stroke." He shook his head. "Dad was never the same after. He only outlived her by about two years."

"I'm sorry."

"Me, too."

"Mama said my grandfather was a kind man. He died when she was very small. He worked for the sheriff's department. His wife was my crazy grand-mother who couldn't control herself."

"I remember Mary speaking of him." He cocked his head. "Your family goes back generations in this community. I envy you that continuity. My folks moved a lot, since Dad was in the service. I've lived everywhere."

"And I've never been anywhere," she mused. "Except to San Antonio."

"Next time you go there, I'm driving," he said flatly.

She made a face at him.

"I'll be home soon."

"Please be careful. Check your car before you start it."

"Cash and Carson told me about the phone call," he replied. "Apparently I'm the target."

"I don't know why," she said. "I was the one who could identify the man who was killed in Wyoming. You never saw him."

"Pumpkin, you're not the only one with enemies," he said softly.

"Would this be connected with that past you won't tell me about?"

"Dead right." He bent and kissed her forehead. "Keep the door locked."

"I will. Drive safely."

He chuckled as he went out the door.

Carlie cleaned up the kitchen, played her video game with Robin for an hour and went to bed. Her dreams were vivid and vaguely embarrassing. And of Carson.

CHAPTER EIGHT

ROURKE WAS SITTING with a worried politician in one of the best restaurants in San Antonio. Unknown to the man, Rourke was working with the feds. Rourke had managed to wiggle himself into the man's employ.

This particular politician, Matthew Helm, had been named the acting U.S. senator, and was hoping to be elected to a full term at the special election in a few months. Rourke was equally determined to find a way to connect him with the murder of a local assistant district attorney. All the evidence had been destroyed. But there were other ways to prove collusion.

Rourke had been in touch with Lieutenant Rick Marquez of the San Antonio Police Department and was keeping him informed through Cash Grier. This politician had also been responsible for the attempt on Dalton Kirk's life, and the one on Carlie Blair's father—or Carlie herself—the intended victim had never been determined—in Jacobsville.

His murdering henchman, Richard Martin, had been killed in Wyoming, but the man's evil deeds persisted. Word was that before he'd died, he'd hired someone to kill Carlie. Nobody knew who had the contract.

Rourke was hoping against hope that this man might provide answers to many questions. But Helm was secretive. So far he hadn't said one incriminating word. Rourke would have known. He was wearing a wire, courtesy of Rick Marquez.

"There are too many loose ends," Matthew Helm said after a minute. He glanced at his other enforcer, Fred Baldwin, and glared at him. "You take care of that problem up in Wyoming?"

"Oh, yes, sir," the big, brawny man assured him. "You can stop worrying."

"I always worry." Helm then glared at Rourke. "What have you found out about my competition for the job?"

"Both men are clean as a whistle," Rourke replied easily. "No past issues we can use against them."

Helm smiled secretly. "So far," he murmured.

"You thinking of planting some?" Rourke asked conversationally.

Helm just stared at him. "What the hell does that mean?"

"Just a comment."

"Well, keep your comments to yourself," Helm said angrily. "I don't fix elections, in case you wondered."

"Sorry. I'm new here," Rourke apologized.

"Too new," Helm said suspiciously. "I can't dig out any information on you. Any at all."

"I'm from South Africa, what do you expect?" he added.

"Well, that last name you gave, Stanton," Helm began, "is a dead end."

"I like to keep my past in the past," Rourke returned. "I'm a wanted man in some places."

"Is that it?" Helm studied him for a long moment.

"Then maybe you're not as suspicious as you seem, huh?" He snickered. "Just don't expect instant trust. I don't trust anybody."

"That's a good way to be," Rourke agreed.

Helm drew in a long breath. "Well, we need to get back to the office and work up some more ads and a few handouts for the campaign office. Not much time to bring this all together."

"Okay, Boss," Rourke said. "I'll see you there." He got up, nodded to both men, paid for his coffee and pie, and left.

Helm studied his other enforcer. "I don't trust him," he told the man. "You keep a close eye on him, hire extra men if you have to. See where he goes, who he associates with. I don't want any complications."

"Yes, Boss."

"And start checking out our sources. We'll need some more drugs planted. I can't afford competition for the job," he added. His face firmed. "You don't share that information with Rourke, got it? You don't tell him anything unless you clear it with me."

"I got it, Boss."

"You destroyed the watch, right?"

The other man nodded vigorously. "Oh, yeah, Boss, I smashed it into bits and tossed it into a trash bin."

"Good. Good."

The other man was hoping his uneasiness didn't show. He couldn't destroy the watch, he just couldn't. It was the most beautiful timepiece he'd ever seen, and it played that song he liked.

Fred Baldwin had envied Richard Martin, wearing that watch that cost as much as a sports car. He'd tried to borrow it once, but Martin had looked at him like he was a worm.

Well, Martin was dead now, and Baldwin had the watch. It was warm against his fingers, warm in his pocket where he kept it. He'd set the alarm so it wouldn't go off accidentally. Nobody was crazy enough to throw away a watch that cost so much money! Who knew, one day he might be desperate enough to pawn it. A man had to live, after all, and what Mr. Helm paid him was barely enough to afford his keep. His criminal record made him vulnerable. He couldn't get another job and Mr. Helm warned him that if he even tried to leave, he'd make sure Fred never worked again. It wasn't a threat. It was a promise. Fred knew better than to try to quit, although he hated the job.

Of course, that watch had a history, and Fred knew it. He might be desperate enough one day to talk to somebody in law enforcement about it. The watch could tie Mr. Helm to a murder. So, no, Fred wasn't about to throw it away. That didn't mean he didn't have to keep it hidden, of course. And he did.

ROURKE STOPPED BY Carlie's house that evening to talk to Reverend Blair. He was amused that Helm's men had tried to follow him. He'd had Carson take his car to San Antonio and park it at a bar. The trackers were sitting out in the parking lot in the freezing cold, waiting for Rourke to come out. He laughed. It was going to be a long night for them.

"Well, you look happy," Carlie remarked when she let him in.

"I've discovered that misdirection is one of my

greater talents," he mused, grinning. "Got any more of that wonderful cornbread?"

She shook her head. "But I just took a nice enchilada casserole out of the oven, and I have sour cream and tortilla chips to top it with," she said.

"Be still my heart," Rourke enthused. "Listen, are you sure you wouldn't like to marry me tomorrow?"

"Sorry," she said, "I'm having my truck waxed."

"Ah, well," he sighed in mock sorrow.

"Stop trying to marry my daughter," Jake Blair muttered, his ice-blue eyes penetrating, as Rourke joined him at the kitchen table. "You are definitely not son-in-law material."

"Spoilsport," Rourke told him. "It's hard to find a nice woman who can also cook and play video games."

"You don't play video games," Jake pointed out.

"A lot you know! The police chief is teaching me."

"Cash Grier?" Carlie exclaimed. "My boss doesn't play."

"Apparently that's why he thinks it's a good idea if he does the teaching. His young brother-in-law has forced him into it," he laughed, "because he can't get any friends to play with him. Cash is always up for anything new and exciting."

Jake shook his head. "I just don't get it. Running around a cartoon world on dragons and fighting people with two-handed swords. It's...medieval."

"Teaches combat skills, strategy, social interaction and how to deal with trolls," Carlie retorted, pouring coffee for all of them.

"Trolls?" Rourke asked. "Those great Norwegian things...?"

"Internet trolls," she clarified with a glower. "People who start fights and stand back and watch. They're really a pain sometimes, especially if somebody new to the game makes the mistake of asking for help on trade chat." She started laughing.

"What's so funny?" her father asked.

"Well, this guy wanted a mage port—that's a portal they can make to the major cities. He didn't know what class could do ports, so he asked if anybody could send him to the capital. This warlock comes on and offers to port him for fifty gold." She was laughing heartily. "Warlocks can't port, you see. They can summon, but that's a whole other thing." She shook her head. "I've spent months wondering how that came out."

"Probably about like the death knight your boss told me about, who offered to heal for a dungeon group," Rourke replied, tongue-in-cheek.

Carlie looked shocked. "DKs can't heal!"

"I'm sure the dungeon group knows that now," he quipped, and he was rakishly handsome when he smiled.

"I guess I'm missing a lot," Jake Blair said.

"You should come and play with us," Carlie said.

He shook his head. "I'm too old to play, pumpkin."

"You're kidding, right? One of the best raid leaders on our server is seventy-three years old."

His eyebrows arched. "Say what?"

"Not only that, there's a whole guild that plays from a nursing home."

"I met them," Rourke said. "Cash and I were in a dungeon with several of them. Along with a ten-year-old Paladin who kicked butt, and a sixty-eight-year-old grandmother who was almost able to kill the big boss single-handed."

"I suppose my whole concept of gaming is wrong," Jake laughed. "I had no idea so many age groups played together."

"That's what makes it so much fun," Carlie replied. "You meet people from all over the world in-game, and you learn that even total strangers can work together with a little patience."

"Maybe I'll get online one of these days and try it," Jake conceded.

"That would be great, Dad!" Carlie exclaimed. "You can be in our guild. Robin and I have one of our own," she explained. "We'll gear you and teach you."

"Maybe in the summer, when things are a little less hectic," Jake suggested.

"Oh. The building committee again," Carlie recalled.

"One group wants brick. The other wants wood. We have a carpenter in our congregation who wants the contract and doesn't understand that it has to be bid. The choir wants a loft, but the organist doesn't like heights. Some people don't want carpet, others think padded benches are a total sellout... Why are you laughing?" he asked, because Rourke was almost rolling on the floor.

"Church," Rourke choked. "It's where people get along and never argue...?"

"Not in my town," Reverend Blair said, sighing. He smiled. "We'll get it together. And we argue nicely." He frowned. "Except for Old Man Barlow. He uses some pretty colorful language."

"I only used one colorful word," Carlie remarked

as she served up the casserole, "and he—" she pointed at her father "—grounded me for a month and took away my library card."

He shrugged. "It was a very bad word." He glowered at her. "And Robin should never have taught it to you without explaining what it meant!"

"Robin got in trouble, too," she told Rourke. "But his parents took away his computer for two weeks." She shook her head. "I thought withdrawal was going to kill him."

"He uses drugs?" Rourke asked curiously.

"No, withdrawal from the video game we play together," she chuckled. She glanced at her father. "So I had to do battlegrounds in pugs for those two weeks. It was awful."

"What's a pug?" Reverend Blair asked.

"A pickup group," Rourke replied. "Cash taught me." He glared. "There was a tank in the last one that had a real attitude problem. Cash had him for lunch."

"Our police chief is awesome when he gets going," Carlie laughed. "We had one guy up for speeding, and when he came in to pay the ticket he was almost shaking. He just wanted to give me the fine and get out before he had to see the chief. He said he'd never speed in our town again!"

"What did Cash do?" Jake asked.

"I asked. He didn't really do anything. He just glared at the man while he wrote out the ticket."

"I know that glare." Rourke shook his head. "Having been on the receiving end of it, I can tell you truly that I'd rather he hit me."

"No, you wouldn't," Carlie mused. "I wasn't working for him then, but I heard about it. He and Judd Dunn were briefly interested in the same woman, Christabel, who eventually married Judd. But it came to blows in the chief's office at lunch one day. They said it was such a close match that both men came out with matching bruises and cuts, and nobody declared victory. You see, the chief taught Judd Dunn to fight Tae Kwon Do–style."

"Wasn't he going to teach you and Michelle Godfrey how to do that?" Jake asked suddenly.

"He was, but it was sort of embarrassing, if you recall, Dad," she replied. She glanced at Rourke, who was watching her curiously. "I tripped over my own feet, slid under another student, knocked him into another student on the mat, and they had to go to the emergency room for pulled tendons." She grimaced. "I was too ashamed to try it again, and Michelle wouldn't go without me. The chief wanted us to try again, but I'm just too clumsy for martial arts."

Rourke's eyes twinkled. "I can sympathize. On my first foray into martial arts, I put my instructor through a window."

"What?" she exclaimed.

"We were standing near it. He threw a kick, I caught his foot and flipped him. The momentum took him right into a backward summersault, right out the window. Fortunately for him it was a low one, raised, and very close to the ground."

"Well!" she laughed.

"I've improved since then." He shared an amused look with Jake.

"Shall we say grace?" Jake replied, bowing his head.

"YOU DIDN'T TELL me that it was the police chief's wife, not Carlie, who insulted you," Carson said as they shared coffee during intermission at the theater in San Antonio.

Lanette looked at him under her long lashes. "I was very upset," she remarked. "Perhaps I was confused. Honestly, that girl is so naïve. And she isn't even pretty! I don't understand why you were dancing with her in the first place!"

He studied her covertly. She was getting more possessive by the day, and she was full of questions about Carlie. It bothered him. He kept thinking of her rap sheet, too.

"Several of us are watching her," he said after a minute. "There was an attempt on her father's life, and she was injured. We think there may be another one."

"On a minister?" she exclaimed, laughing loudly. "Who'd want to kill a preacher?"

His black eyes narrowed. "I don't recall telling you that her father was a man of the cloth," he said.

Her face was blank for just an instant and then she smiled prettily. "I was asking about her at the dance. Someone told me who her father was."

"I see."

"She's just a backward little hick," she muttered irritably. "Let's talk about something else. Are we going to see the symphony Friday night? I bought a new dress, specially!"

He was thoughtful. He didn't like the way Lanette had started to assume that he was always available to take her out. She was beautiful to look at, to show off in public. The poor reservation kid in him enjoyed the envious looks he got from other men when he escorted his striking blond companion in the evenings. But she was shallow and mean-spirited. He forgave a lot because she eased the ache in him that Carlie provoked.

Funny thing, though. Although he enjoyed the physical aspects of their relationship, he couldn't quite manage to go all the way with his gorgeous blonde. It unsettled him, and irritated and insulted her, but expensive presents seemed to pacify her.

He didn't understand his reticence. Lanette was eager and accomplished, but her talents were wasted on him. Deep down, he knew why. It didn't help the situation. Carlie was never going to fall into bed with him. And if she did, her father would kill him and Cash Grier would help.

"I'll be very happy when you're finished with this dumb assignment and you don't have to be around that little hick," Lanette was saying. She brushed back her long, thick, blond hair.

"People in Jacobs County are very protective of her," was all he said.

"She's probably not even in trouble," she muttered. "I expect people are just overreacting because of that attack on her father. For goodness sake, maybe whoever's after her isn't even after her, maybe it's her father!" She glanced at him. "Isn't that what you said about that knife attack, that he was trying to kill her father and she tried to stop him?"

"That's what they said."

She shook her head. "Well, it was a really stupid job," she murmured. "Imagine a man going to the victim's house in the middle of the day, in broad daylight, and attacking a minister in his own house!"

Carson frowned as he listened. "I didn't know it was in broad daylight."

"Everybody knows," she said quickly. "They were even talking about it at that silly dance you took me to."

"Oh."

She glanced away, smiling to herself. "They also said that the man who tried to kill the preacher ended up dead himself."

"Yes, poisoned. A very nasty, slow poison. Something the late Mr. Martin was quite well-known for in intelligence circles."

"I hate poison," she said under her breath. "So unpredictable."

"Have you been poisoning people, then?" he mused.

She laughed. "No. I like to watch true crime shows on television. I know all about poisons and stuff." She moved very close to him. "Not to worry, handsome, I'd never want to hurt you!" she added, and lifted her arms toward his neck.

He raised an eyebrow and stepped back.

"Oh, you and your hang-ups," she muttered. "What's wrong with a hug in public?"

"It would take too long to tell you," he said, not offering the information that in his culture, such public displays were considered taboo by the elders.

"All right," she said with mock despair. "Are we going to the theater Friday?"

"Yes," he said. It would keep his mind off Carlie.

"Wonderful!" She smiled secretly to herself. "I'm

sure we'll have a lovely time." She paused. "That mad South African man you know, he isn't coming to the theater, is he?"

"Rourke?" He laughed to himself. "Not likely on a Friday night."

"Why not on a Friday?" she asked.

He almost bit his tongue. Rourke played poker with Cash Grier. He didn't dare let that slip, just in case Lanette knew anyone who had contact with Matthew Helm. "Rourke drinks on weekends," he lied.

"I see." She thought for a minute. "What about your friend the police chief?" she asked, laughing. "I'll bet he takes that prissy wife of his to the theater."

"Not on a Friday night," he chuckled. "The police chief and several other men get together at the chief's house and play poker after supper."

"Exciting game, poker. Especially the strip kind," she purred.

He sighed. "I don't gamble. Sorry."

"Your loss, sweetie," she said with pursed red lips. "Your loss."

FRIDAY NIGHT, REVEREND BLAIR had a call from a visitor to the community who was staying in a local motel outside town.

"I just want to die," the man wailed. Jake couldn't quite place the accent, but it definitely wasn't local. "I hate my life! They said you were a kind man who would try to help people. They gave me your number, here at this motel—" he named it "—so I said I'd call you. Before I did it, you know. Will God forgive me for killing myself? I got some rat poison…"

"Wait," Jake Blair said softly. "Just wait. I'll come to see you. We'll talk."

"You'd come all this way, just to talk to me?" The man sounded shocked.

"I know the motel you mentioned you were staying at," Jake said. "It's just a few minutes from here. I'll be on my way in a jiffy. What's your room number?"

The man told him. "Thank you. Thank you!" he sobbed. "I just don't want to live no more!" He hung up.

"Pumpkin, I have to go out," he informed his daughter as he shrugged into his bomber jacket. "I've been contacted by a suicidal man in a motel. I'm going to try and talk him down before he does something desperate."

She smiled. "That's my dad, saving the world."

He shrugged. "Trying to, anyway. You stay inside and keep the doors locked," he added. "And keep that cell phone close, you hear me?"

"I'll put it in my pocket, I swear."

"Good girl." He kissed her forehead. "Don't wait up. This may take a while."

"Good luck," she called after him.

He waved at her, left and closed the door behind him.

Carlie finished cleaning up the kitchen and went upstairs to play her game. On the kitchen table, forgotten, was the cell phone she'd promised to keep with her. The only other phone in the house was a fixed one, in her father's office…

"GOODNESS, COFFEE JUST goes right through me," Lanette whispered into Carson's ear. "Be right back."

He just nodded, aware of irritated glances from other theatergoers nearby. He wasn't really thrilled with the play. It was modern and witty, but not his sort of entertainment at all, despite the evident skill of the actors.

His mind went back to Carlie on the riverbank, standing so close that he could feel every soft line of her body, kissing him so hungrily that his mind spun like a top. Carlie, who was as innocent as a newborn, completely clueless about the hungers that drove men.

He wanted her until he couldn't sleep for wanting her. And he knew he could never have her. He wasn't going to settle down, as Cash Grier had, with a wife and child and a job in a small town. He liked adventure, excitement. He wasn't willing to give those up for some sort of middle-class dream life in a cottage or a condo, mowing the grass on weekends. The thought of it turned his stomach.

He brushed away a spec on his immaculate trousers and frowned. He didn't understand why Carlie appealed to his senses so strongly. She wasn't really pretty, although her mouth was soft and beautiful and tasted as sweet as honey. Her body was slender and she was small-breasted. But she had long, elegant legs and her waist was tiny. He could feel her small breasts swelling against his hard chest when he kissed her, feel the tips biting into his flesh even through layers of fabric.

He groaned silently. His adventures with women had always been with beautiful, practiced, elegant women. He'd never been with an innocent. And he wasn't about to break that record now, he assured himself firmly.

He'd been vulnerable with Carlie because he felt guilty about sending her to the hospital when he lost his temper. That was all. It was a physical reaction, prompted only by guilt. He was never going to forgive himself for frightening her like that. Her white face haunted him still. He'd only moved closer to make his point, it hadn't been a true aggression. But it must have seemed that way to a young girl who'd been beaten, and then later stabbed by an assassin.

But he hadn't hurt her at the dance, when they'd moved together like one person, when he'd felt the hunger so deeply that he could have laid her down on the dance floor right then. What the hell was he going to do? It was impossible. Impossible!

While he was brooding, Lanette returned. She slid her hand into his and just smiled at him, without saying a word. He glanced at her. She really was beautiful. He'd never seen a woman who was quite this exquisite. If it hadn't been for her attitude, and her other flaws, she might have seemed the perfect woman. That made it all the more inexplicable that he couldn't force himself to sleep with her; not even to relieve the ache Carlie gave him.

CARLIE WAS FIGHTING two Horde in the battleground. Sadly, neither of them was Carson. She flailed away with her two-handed sword, pulled out her minions, used every trick she could think of to vanquish them, but they killed her. She grimaced. She had the best gear honor points could buy, but there were these things called conquest points that only came from doing arenas. Carlie couldn't do arena. She was too slow and too clumsy.

So there were people far better geared than she was. Which was just an excuse, because the playing field was level in battlegrounds, regardless of how good your armor was.

The painful truth was that there were a lot of players who were much better at it than Carlie was. She comforted herself with the knowledge that there was always somebody better at the game, and eventually everybody got killed once or twice during a battle. She was just glad that she didn't have to do it in real life.

"Ah, well," she said, and sighed.

She resurrected at the battleground cemetery, got on her mount and rode back off to war. Before she got to either her home base or the enemy's, the end screen came up. The Alliance had lost to the Horde. But it had been an epic battle, the sort that you really didn't mind losing so much because it was fought by great players on both sides.

"Next time," she told the screen. "Next time, we'll own you, Hordies!"

She was about to queue for the battleground again when she heard a knock at the door downstairs.

She logged out of her character, although not out of the game, mildly irritated by the interruption, and went down the staircase. She wondered if maybe her father had forgotten to take his house key with him. He was so forgetful sometimes, it was funny. Twice now, he'd had to wake Carlie up when he came back from a committee meeting that lasted longer than expected, or when he returned from visiting and comforting congregation members at hospitals.

She peered through the safety window and

frowned. There was a big man in a suit outside. He looked uneasy.

"Is there something you want?" she asked through the door.

"Yeah," he said after a minute. "I need help."

"What sort of help?" she answered.

He paused for a minute. He looked through the small window at the suspicious young woman who was obviously not about to open that door to a man she didn't know.

He thought for a minute. He was slow when it came to improvisation. Maybe he could fool her if he was smart. Yeah. Smart. Who would she open the door for?

"I, uh, came to tell you about your dad," he called through the door. "There's been an accident. I was passing by and stopped. He asked me to come and get you and drive you to the hospital where they're taking him."

"Dad's been in a wreck?" she exclaimed. "Why didn't the police come?"

What did she mean? Did police notify people about wrecks here? He supposed they did. He'd done that once, long ago. He paused.

"Well, they were coming, but I told them your dad wanted me to bring you, and they said it was okay."

She still hesitated. Perhaps it was one of the new patrolmen, and her father had been impatient about getting word to her. A kind stranger might have been imposed upon to fetch Carlie.

"He's hurt pretty bad, Miss," he called again. "We should go."

She couldn't bear to think of her father injured. She

had to go to him. She grabbed her coat off the rack near the door. Her pocketbook was upstairs, but she couldn't think why she'd need it. Her father would have money in his wallet and a house key.

"Okay, I'm coming," she said, and opened the door.

He smiled. "I'll take you to him," he promised.

She closed and locked the door behind her. Too late, she remembered her cell phone lying on the kitchen table.

"Have you got a cell phone?" she asked abruptly.

"Yeah, I got one," he said, leading the way to his late model sedan. "Why?"

"In case we have to call somebody," she explained.

"You can call anybody you like, Miss," he said. "Just get right in."

She bent down to slide into the open passenger side when she felt a cloth pressed against her mouth and pressure behind it. She took a breath. The whole world went black.

THE BIG MAN cuffed her hands together behind her before he slid her onto the backseat. She was breathing sort of funny, so he didn't gag her. He hoped that would be okay with the boss. After all, where they were going, nobody was likely to hear her.

Before he got into the car, he dropped a piece of paper on the ground deliberately. Then he got in the car, started it and drove away.

CHAPTER NINE

REVEREND JAKE BLAIR knocked at the motel door, but there was no answer. He immediately thought the worst, that the man had actually attempted suicide before his arrival. He might be inside, fatally wounded.

He ran to the motel office, explained the situation, showed his ID and pleaded with the man to open the door.

The manager ran with him to the room, slid home the key and threw open the door.

"Is this some sort of joke?" the manager asked.

Jake shook his head. "He phoned me at home and begged me to come and speak with him. He said that someone locally had recommended that he call me and gave him the number. He said he was suicidal, that he was going to take poison." He turned to the man. "Did you rent this room tonight?"

"Yes. To some big guy with a Northern accent," he replied. "He didn't have any luggage, though, and he didn't look suicidal to me." He glowered. "He just left without paying the bill or handing back the key," he muttered.

"Isn't that the key?" Jake asked, nodding toward the bedside table.

It was. There was a fifty-dollar bill under it.

"Well," the manager chuckled drily. "A man with a sense of honor, at least. Sort of."

"Sort of." Jake shook his head. "I can't imagine why he'd fake something like this." Then he remembered. Carson had a date. Rourke was playing poker with Cash Grier. Jake was here. Carlie was alone. At home.

He bit off a bad word, chided himself for the slip and ran for his car. On the way he dialed Carlie's cell phone, but there was no answer. He was referred to her voice mail. He'd told her to keep that phone with her. She never remembered. He dialed the home phone. The answering machine picked up after four rings. Now, that was unusual. Carlie would hear it, even if she was playing, and she'd pick it up before the message finished playing.

He was very concerned. He wasn't certain that someone was after him because of his past, despite the threatening phone call Carlie had taken. The man with the knife went for Carlie deliberately, it had seemed to Jake. He groaned as he pictured it, recalled her pain and terror. She'd had so much misery in her short life, so much violence. He hated what she'd gone through. Some of it was his fault.

He burned rubber getting home. He ran up the porch steps, put his key in the lock and went in like a storming army. But the house was empty. Carlie's computer was still on. And, although she'd logged out temporarily, her character screen was still up and the game was still running. That meant she'd been interrupted while she was playing. He checked every room. In the kitchen he found her cell phone, lying on the table.

He backtracked out the front door and, with a flashlight in addition to the porch light, searched around. He noticed tire tracks that weren't his. He also noted a piece of paper. It was a rough drawing, a map of sorts. It was a clue that the police would want undisturbed. He had no idea what the map depicted. But he knew what to do at once. He pulled out his cell phone and called Cash Grier.

"I HAD TO call Hayes," Cash apologized when he was on the scene. "You don't live in the city limits."

"That's okay." Jake clapped him on the back. "You're forgiven."

"Don't worry. Hayes has an investigator who dines out on forensics. He even has membership in several professional societies that do nothing else except discuss new techniques. Zack's good at his job."

"Okay." Jake shoved his hands into his pockets. He felt as if it was the end of the world. "I should have realized it was a ruse. Why didn't I think?"

"We'll find her," Cash promised.

"I know that. It's what condition we'll find her in that concerns me," Jake said tautly.

"I don't think they'll harm her," Cash said. "They want something. Maybe it's you."

"They can have me, if they'll let my daughter go," he rasped.

"I phoned my brother," Cash added. "It's a kidnapping. That makes it a federal crime. He'll be over as soon as he gets dressed."

Cash's brother, Garon Grier, was the senior special agent at the Jacobsville FBI office. He was formerly with the FBI's Hostage Rescue Team, and one of the best people to call in on the case. But Jake was concerned that the police presence might cause the kidnapper to panic and kill Carlie in order to get away.

"Where's Rourke?" Jake asked. "Was he playing poker with you?"

"He was, but he had a call from the politician he's supposedly the enforcer for," came the reply. "It seems the other enforcer was indisposed and he needed Rourke to run an errand for him."

"Interesting timing," Jake said.

Cash knew that. He could only imagine how he'd feel if it was his little girl, his Tris, who was missing. He drew in a breath and patted Jake on the back. "Don't worry," he said again. "It's going to be all right."

"Yes," Jake said and managed a smile. "I know that."

JAKE BLAIR EXCUSED himself in the early hours of the morning by saying that he had to visit a sick member of his congregation at the hospital. He left his cell phone number with Cash and asked him to please call if there was any word from the kidnapper.

He went inside and put on jeans and a pair of high-topped moccasins with no soles and his bomber jacket, along with a concealed knife in a scabbard, a .45 magnum in a Velcro holster and a pair of handcuffs.

With his equipment carefully hidden under the roomy bomber jacket, he waved to local law enforcement and spun out of the yard in the Cobra.

Unknown to the others, he'd had time to process the crude drawing on that map. He didn't for a moment think it had been dropped accidentally. No, this was a setup. They wanted Jake to come after Carlie. Which meant that, in his opinion, Jake was the real target.

He assumed that someone in his past was out to get him. He didn't know why. But there were plenty of reasons. His former life had been one of violence. He'd never expected that he would ever revisit it. Until now. His old skills were still sharp. Nobody was hurting Carlie. And as the Good Book said, God helps those who help themselves.

Probably, he amended, God didn't mean with guns. But then, he rationalized, they hadn't had guns in Biblical days, either. He was winging it. He wouldn't kill anybody. Unless it came to a choice between that and watching Carlie die. He couldn't do that. He couldn't live with it.

He followed the highway to a dirt road leading off to a deserted area with just the beginnings of scrubland, with cactus and sand. He parked the car, got out, checked his weapon, stuck it back in the holster and belted it around his waist. He strapped the bottom of the holster to his thigh with the Velcro tabs. He pulled out his knife in its sheath from under the jacket and fixed it on the other side of the belt buckle. Then he started off, with uncanny stealth, down the road.

CARLIE REGAINED CONSCIOUSNESS slowly. Her mind felt as if it was encased in molasses. She couldn't imagine why she was so sluggish, or why it was so hard to breathe.

She tried to move and realized, quite suddenly, that it was because her hands were tied behind her. She was lying on her side on a makeshift pallet. A big, worried man was standing nearby, wearing a business suit and a big gun. He wasn't holding it on her. It was on his belt, inside his open jacket.

"You okay?" he asked. "You was breathing awful jerkylike."

"I'm okay." She tried to take small breaths. She was scared to death, but she was trying not to let it show. "What am I doing here?" She swallowed. "Are you going to kill me?"

"No!" he said, and looked shocked. "Look, I don't do women. Ever." He blinked. "Well, there was one, once, but she shot me first." He flushed a little.

He was the oddest sort of kidnapper she'd ever seen. He was as big as a house and he seemed oddly sympathetic for a man who meant her harm.

"Then why did you bring me here? You said my father was hurt...!" she remembered, almost hysterical.

"Not yet," he said. "We had to get him out of the house so we could get to you," he explained. "It takes time to do these things right, you know. First we get you. Then he comes out here, all alone, and we get him. Real easy."

"Why do you want my father?" she asked, relieved that her dad was all right, but nervous because the man was making threats.

"Not me," he said with a shrug. "Somebody else."

"Why?"

"Lady, I don't know," he muttered. "Nobody tells me nothing. They just say go do something and I go do it. I don't get paid to ask questions."

"Please don't hurt my dad," she said plaintively.

He made a face. "Look, I'm not going to do anything to him," he promised. "Honest. I don't kill people for money. I just had to get him out here. There's two guys outside…they'll do it."

Her heart jumped up into her throat. Her father would be lured here because she was under threat. He'd walk right up to the door and they'd kill him. She felt sick all over. "Couldn't you stop them?" she asked. "Don't you have a father? Would you like to see that done to him?"

His face closed up. "Yeah, I had a father. He put me in the hospital twice. I wouldn't care if somebody did it to him. No way."

Her eyes were soft with sadness. "I'm so sorry," she said gently.

He looked uncomfortable. "Maybe you should try to sleep, huh?"

"My wrists hurt."

"I can do something about that." He went around behind her and fiddled with the handcuffs. They were less tight. "So funny, I got kicked off the force five years ago, and here I am using cuffs again," he mused.

"The force?"

"I was a cop. I knocked this guy down a staircase. Big guy, like me. He was trying to kill his kid. They said I used excessive force. There was a review and all, but I got canned anyway." He didn't add that it was really because he'd ruffled his partner's feathers when he wouldn't take bribes or kickbacks. That was sort of blowing his own horn. He'd been set up, but that was ancient history now. The bad thing was that it had given Mr. Helm a stick to hit him with, because he'd been honest about losing his job. He hadn't known at the time that Mr. Helm was even more crooked than his old partner.

"I work for the police chief, here," she said. "He'd use excessive force with a guy who was trying to kill his kid, too, but nobody would fire him for it."

He moved back around in front of her. He smiled faintly. He had dark eyes and a broad face with scars all over it. He had thick black wavy hair. He was an odd sort of gangster, she thought.

"Maybe he knows the right people," he told her. "I didn't."

She studied him curiously. "You aren't from Texas," she said.

He shrugged. "From Italy, way back," he said.

Her eyes widened. "Are you in the Mafia?" she asked.

He burst out laughing. He had perfect white teeth. "If I was, they'd kill me for telling people about it."

"Oh. I get it."

"Your wrists okay now? That feel better?"

"Yes. Thanks." She made a face. "What did you do to me?"

"Chloroform," he said. "Put it on a handkerchief, see, and it works quick."

She drew in another breath. Her chest felt tight.

"You ain't breathing good," he remarked, frowning.

"I have asthma."

"You got something to use for it?"

"Sure. It's back at my house. Want to take me there to pick it up?" she asked. She wasn't really afraid of him. Odd, because he looked frightening.

He smiled back. "Not really, no. I'd get fired."

"Not a bad idea, you could do something honest for a living before your bosses get you locked up for life," she returned.

He seemed disturbed by that. He checked his watch. It was an oddly expensive-looking one, she thought. He'd said they didn't pay well, but if he could afford a timepiece like that, perhaps he'd just been joking about his salary.

He drew in a long breath. "I have to make a phone call," he said. "You just stay there and be quiet so I don't have to gag you, okay?"

"I can't let them kill my father," she said. "If I hear him coming, I'm going to warn him."

"You're an honest kid, ain't you?" he asked admiringly. "Okay. I'll try not to make it too tight, so you can breathe."

He took out a clean handkerchief and rolled it up, tied it around her mouth. "That okay?" he asked.

She groaned.

"Come on, don't make me feel no worse than I do. You're just a kid. I wouldn't hurt you. Not even if they told me to."

She made a face under the gag. Reluctantly, she nodded.

"Okay. I won't be long."

She heard him go to the door. Just as he started to open it, she thought she must be hallucinating, because she heard a chiming rock song. It went away almost at once, followed by a mild curse. The door opened and closed. She heard voices outside.

What could she possibly do that would save her father? She squirmed her way to the edge of the bed and wiggled so that her feet made it to the floor. She was still a little dizzy, but she managed to get to her feet.

She moved to the door and listened. She heard distant voices. She looked around. The room had no windows. There was a pallet on the floor, nothing else. There wasn't even a table, much less anything she could try to use to untie herself.

Well, she could at least listen and try to hear her father's voice. She might be able to warn him before they shot him. She groaned inwardly. It was going to be on her conscience forever if he died because she'd opened the door to a stranger. When she recalled what the big man had told her, it was so obviously a ruse that she couldn't imagine why she hadn't questioned his story. He'd said her father was hurt. After that, her brain had gone into panic mode. That was why she'd agreed to leave with him.

But it was going to make a really lousy epitaph for her father. If she was lucky, the FBI would involve itself because it was a kidnapping. There was also her boss, who'd come looking for her. Maybe Carson would, too. Her heart jumped. Sure he would. He was probably up in San Antonio with that gorgeous blonde, out on a date. He wouldn't even know she was missing and probably wouldn't mind unless somebody asked him to help find her. That made her even more depressed.

But how would they ever find her in time to save her father? She hoped he had no idea where to find her, that they hadn't left some sort of clue that would lead him here. But there were armed guards at the door, and they were waiting for him, her kidnapper had said. That meant they had to have left some clue to help him find this place.

She closed her eyes and began to pray silently, the last hope of the doomed...

CARSON HAD JUST walked back into his apartment, after insistently leaving Lanette at hers, when his cell phone went off.

He locked himself in and answered it, tired and out of sorts. "Carson," he said shortly.

"It's Cash. I thought you might want to know that we've had some developments down here."

He grimaced as he went into the kitchen to make coffee. "Somebody confessed to trying to off the preacher?"

There was a pause. "Someone's kidnapped Carlie..."

"What the hell! Who? When?"

Cash wanted to tell him to calm down, but he had some idea about Carson's feelings for the woman, so he bit his tongue. "We don't know who. Her father was hoaxed into going to a motel to counsel a suicidal man, who conveniently disappeared before he showed up. Rourke and I were playing poker. We had no idea Carlie was going to be home alone. Somehow she was lured out. Her father said that he found her telephone on the kitchen table and her purse upstairs."

"That damned phone..."

"I know, she's always forgetting it," Cash replied heavily. "It seems that Carlie was the target all along. There was one clue, a crude drawing of a building in the area, but nobody knows where it is. The map isn't very helpful."

"Where's her father?"

"Funny thing," Cash mused. "He says he has to visit a sick member of his congregation at the hospital. The timing strikes me as a bit odd."

"I'll be there in fifteen minutes."

"You won't help her if you die on the way."

"Thanks for the tip." He hung up.

"JAKE BLAIR'S ONLY been gone a few minutes," Cash told Carson when he arrived.

Carson glanced past him. "Crime scene guys at work already, I gather."

"Yes."

Carson went inside and looked at the map lying on the table in a protective cover. It had already been dusted for prints—none found—and cataloged in position. He also saw Carlie's cell phone.

"May I?" he asked.

"It's been dusted. Only prints are hers," Zack, Sheriff Hayes Carson's chief investigator, told him with a smile. "We checked her calls, too. Nothing." He went back to work.

Carson's fingers smoothed over the phone absently. It might have been one of the last things she touched. It was comforting, in some odd way. He thought of her being held, terrified, maybe smothering because the asthma would be worsened by the fear and confusion. His face mirrored his own fear.

He stuck the phone in his pocket absentmindedly as he studied the map once more. His black eyes narrowed. The drawing was amateurish, but he recognized two features on that map because they were on the way to Cy Parks's ranch. He drove the road almost every day. There was a ranch house that had burned down some time back, leaving only a ramshackle barn standing. It had to be where they had Carlie.

He was careful not to let his recognition show, because if the gangbusters here went shoving in, they'd probably shock the kidnappers into killing her quickly so they could escape. He couldn't risk that.

"Any idea where this place is?" he asked Cash with a convincing frown.

"Not a clue," Cash said tautly, "and I've been here for years."

"It's a pretty bad map," Carson replied.

"Yes."

"You said her father just left?" Carson asked in a low voice, incredulous. "His daughter's been kidnapped, and he's visiting the sick?"

Cash motioned him aside, away from his brother and the sheriff's department. "He was carrying a .45 magnum in his belt. Nicely hidden, but I got a glimpse of it." He pursed his lips. "Can you still track?"

"Not on pavement," he returned.

"He drives a red Cobra," he pointed out. "Not the easiest ride to conceal. And this is a small community."

"I'll have a look around."

"I'd go with you, but I can't leave." He hesitated. "Don't try to sneak up on him," he advised tersely, lowering his voice. "He's a minister now, but you don't ever lose survival instincts."

"What do you know that I don't?" Carson asked.

"Things I can't tell. Go find him."

"I'll do my best." He glanced past Cash at the other law enforcement people. "Why aren't they looking?"

"Forensics first, then action," Cash explained. His face hardened. "I know. I never really got the hang of it, either." His dark eyes met Carson's. "Her father knows where she is, I'm sure of it. Find him, you find her. Try to keep them both alive."

Carson nodded. He turned and went out the door.

JAKE SLOWED AS he neared the turnoff that led, eventually, to Cy Parks's ranch. Carlie, if the map was accurate, was being held at an old cattle ranch. The ranch house was long since burned down and deserted, but there was a barn still standing. He got around to the back of the building without being detected and observed two men standing guard in front of the door.

They were obviously armed, judging from the bulges under their cheap jackets. Apparently whoever hired them didn't pay much.

Jake had spent years perfecting his craft as a mercenary. He could move in shadow, in light, in snow or sleet, without leaving a trace of himself. He was going to have to take down two men at once. He would also have to do it with exquisite care, so as not to alert what might be a third man inside the structure holding Carlie.

It would seem impossible to survive a frontal assault against armed men. He only smiled.

He was able to get very close before he moved out into the open with both arms up. He approached the men who belatedly drew their weapons and pointed them at him. The element of surprise had confused them just enough, he hoped.

"Stop there," one of them said.

He kept walking until he was close to them.

"I said stop!" the other threatened.

"Here?" Jake asked, looking down at his feet. "Next to this snake?"

They looked down at his feet immediately. Big mistake. He ducked under them, hit one in the diaphragm to momentarily paralyze him while he put pressure to the carotid artery of the other man and watched him go down, unconscious. The second one, with his gun drawn, bent over, was easy to knock out with the .45.

Very quiet. Very precise. Not a sound came after. And he hadn't had to kill them. He drew out two lengths of rawhide from his bomber jacket and got busy trussing up the gunmen.

He knew he'd have to work fast. If someone had Carlie at gunpoint inside, they might have heard the men ordering him to stop. It was a long shot, though. He wasn't that close to the barn.

He secured them by their thumbs, on their bellies with their hands behind them, and moved quickly toward the shed.

On the way, he had company, quite suddenly, but not from ambush. The man, moving quickly, seemed to deliberately make a sound. He'd been warned, Jake thought and smiled. He turned to the newcomer with the knife still in his hand. When he recognized the man, he slid it quickly into its sheath.

The action wasn't lost on Carson, who was remembering what Cash had told him about this enigmatic man.

"Good thing you came with a little noise," the minister said softly. His glittering blue eyes were those of a different person altogether. "I wouldn't have hesitated, under the circumstances."

Carson stared at him with open curiosity. "I've never seen an action carried out more efficiently."

"Son, you haven't seen anything yet," Jake told him. "You get behind me. And you don't move unless I tell you to. Got it?"

Carson just nodded.

They got to the door. Jake pulled a device out of his pocket and pressed it to the old wood. His jaw tautened.

He drew back and kicked the door in, an action that is much easier in movies with balsa wood props than in real life with real wood. It flung back on its hinges. Jake had the automatic leveled before it even moved, and he walked in professionally, checking corners and dark places on his way to an inner room.

Carlie was, fortunately, on her feet about a yard away from the door her father had just broken down. She cried out through the gag as she saw him.

"Dear God," Jake whispered, holstering the gun as he ran to her. "Honey, are you okay?"

"Dad!" she managed through the gag. She hugged him with her cuffed hands around his neck, sobbing. She was breathing roughly.

Carson dug an inhaler out of his pocket and handed it to her while he took off the gag. "Two puffs, separated," he instructed. He touched her hair. "What did they do to you?" he asked angrily.

"Nothing," she choked. "I mean, he brought me in here and tied me up, but he promised he wouldn't hurt me and he didn't. Except for keeping me tied up all night, I mean," she stammered between puffs of the inhaler. "Thanks," she told Carson. "I forgot mine."

"And your damned phone," Carson muttered, digging it out of his jacket pocket. He handed it to her.

"They had armed men at the door," she exclaimed, gaping at her father. "He said the idea of taking me was to lure you here. He wasn't going to hurt you. But he said the two men, they were going to do it! They were supposed to kill you…!"

He shrugged. "They're not a threat anymore, pumpkin." He pulled a tool from his pocket and very efficiently unlocked her cuffs, touching only the chain. He turned to Carson. "You wouldn't happen to have an evidence bag on you?" he mused.

Carson pursed his lips, produced one from his jacket pocket and handed it to Jake. "I had a feeling," he replied.

Carlie watched her father slide the cuffs, gently and still without touching the parts that had locked her wrists, into the evidence bag. He laid them on the table and took a quick shot with his smartphone's camera. "Just in case," he told them.

"Someday, you have to tell me about your past," Carlie said.

"I don't, pumpkin. There are things that should never be spoken of." He smoothed over her hair. "Let's get out of here."

"I couldn't agree more," she said.

Carson took her arm. "Can you walk?" he asked softly, his eyes darker with concern.

"Sure," she said, moving a little stiffly. "I'm fine. Honest." It delighted her that he'd come with her father to rescue her. She hadn't expected it. She imagined his girlfriend was livid.

Her father led the way out. He had the automatic in his hand and he didn't apologize or explain why.

Carson let him lead, Carlie moving stiffly at his side.

The two previously armed men were still lying on the ground where Jake had left them. "Did one of these guys kidnap you?" her father asked.

She was staring almost openmouthed at them. Two automatic weapons lay in the dirt near them. They weren't moving. But they were certainly vocal.

"No," she said. "I didn't see these ones. Just the man who tied me up."

"You'll pay for this!" one of the captives raged.

"Damned straight!" the other one agreed. "The boss will get you!"

"Well, not if he's as efficient as you two," Jake replied blithely. "And I expect you're going to have a little trouble with the feds. Kidnapping is a felony."

"Hey, we didn't kidnap nobody! We was just guarding her!" the small man protested.

"Yeah. Just guarding her. So she didn't get hurt or nothing," the other man agreed.

As he spoke, several cars came into view along the road. Two of them had flashing blue lights.

Jake turned to Carson with a sigh. They'd figured out the map and now he was going to be in the soup for jumping the gun and leaving them out of the loop. He just shook his head. "You can bring Carlie to visit me in the local jail tonight. I hope they have somebody who can cook."

For the first time, Carson grinned.

BUT JAKE WASN'T ARRESTED. Cash Grier had already briefed his brother, who was in charge of the operation. A man with Jake's background couldn't convincingly be excluded from a mission that involved saving his child from kidnappers. So no charges were pressed. It would have been unlikely anyway, since Jake knew one of the top men at the agency and several government cabinet members, as well. Carlie hadn't known that, until she overheard her dad talking to Garon Grier.

"How did you get past the men with guns?" Carlie asked Carson while she was being checked out at the emergency room. Her father had insisted that Carson take her there, just in case, while he tried to explain his part in her liberation.

"I didn't," he mused. "Your father took them down." He shook his head. "I never saw it coming, and I was watching."

She signed herself out, smiled at the clerk and followed Carson out the front door. "My father is a mystery."

"He's very accomplished," he remarked.

"I noticed."

He stopped at his car and turned to her on the passenger side. "Are you sure you're all right?" he asked.

"Don't you start," she muttered. "I'm fine. Just a little bruised."

He caught her face in his big, warm hands and tilted it up to his eyes. "I thought they might kill you," he said with involuntary concern.

"And you'd miss killing me in battlegrounds online?" she asked, trying to lighten the tension, which was growing exponentially.

"Yes. I'd miss that. And other…things," he whispered as he bent and kissed her with a tenderness that was overwhelming. Then, just as suddenly, he whipped her body completely against his and kissed her with almost bruising intensity. He jerked his mouth away before she could even respond. "Next time, if there is a next time, don't open the door to anybody you don't know!"

"He said Daddy was in a wreck," she faltered. The kiss had shaken her.

"Next time, call Daddy and see if he answers," he retorted.

She searched his angry eyes. "Okay," she whispered softly.

"And for the last time, keep that damned cell phone with you!"

She nodded. "Okay," she said again, without an argument.

The tenderness in her face, the soft, involuntary hunger, the unexpected obedience almost brought him to his knees.

He'd been out of his mind when he'd heard she'd been taken; he couldn't rest until he'd got to her. After Cash had called him, he'd gone crazy on the way down from San Antonio as his mind haunted him with all the things that could have happened to her. The thought of a world without Carlie was frightening to him. He was only just beginning to realize what an impact she had on him. He didn't like it, either.

He fought for self-control. People were walking around nearby, going to and from cars. He let her go and moved away. He felt as if he were vibrating with feeling. "I need to get you home," he said stiffly.

"Okay," she said.

He helped her inside the car, started it and drove her home. He didn't say a word the whole way.

When he let her out at the front door, she ran to her father and hugged him tightly.

"I'm okay," she promised.

He smoothed her hair, looking over her head at Carson. "Thanks."

Carson shrugged. "No problem. Lock her in a closet and lose the key, will you?" he added, not completely facetiously.

Jake chuckled. "She'd just bang on the door until I let her out," he said, giving her an affectionate smile.

"Where's local law enforcement?" Carson asked.

"Packed up all the vital clues and left. They were just a little late backtracking the kidnapper to a lonely barn over near your boss's house," Jake said with biting criticism.

"You did that quite neatly yourself," Carson replied. "I'm reliably informed that local law enforcement followed you there after being tipped off."

"Did you tip them off?" Jake asked with a knowing smile.

Carson sighed. "Yes. I didn't want to have to bury both of you."

Jake became less hostile. "Carson," he said softly, "I wasn't always a minister. I can handle myself."

"And now I know that." Carson managed a smile, glanced at Carlie with painfully mixed feelings and left.

LATER, IN THE corner table at the local café, Carson cornered Rourke. "Okay, let's have it," he demanded.

"Have what?" Rourke asked with a smile.

"That mild-mannered minister—" he meant Jake Blair "—took down two armed men with a speed I've never seen in my life. I didn't even hear him walk toward them, and I was out of my car and heading that way at the time."

"Oh, Jake was always something special," Rourke replied with a smile of remembrance. "He could move so silently that the enemy never knew he was around. They called him 'Snake,' because he could get in and out of places that an army couldn't. He had a rare talent with a knife. Sort of like you," he added, indicating the big bowie knife that Carson was never without. "He'd go in, do every fourth man in a camp, get out without even being heard. The next morning, when the enemy awoke, there would be pandemonium." He hesitated. "Don't you ever tell her," he added coldly, "or you'll find out a few more things about the reverend Blair."

"I never would," Carson assured. "There are things in my past just as unsavory."

Rourke nodded. "His specialty was covert assassination, but he didn't work with a spotter or use a sniper kit. He went in alone, with just a knife, at night." He shook his head. "We tried one night to hear him leave. None of us, not even those with sensitive hearing, could ever spot him. The government begged him to come back when he left for the seminary. He told them he was through with the old life and he was never doing it again. Carlie's his life, now. Her, and his church." He glanced at Carson. "He says she's the only reason he didn't commit suicide after her mother died. You know, I don't really understand religion, but I guess it has its place."

"I guess it does," Carson replied thoughtfully.

"How was your date?" Rourke asked.

Carson made a face. "Tedious."

"She's a looker."

Carson stared at him with cool, cynical eyes. "They all look alike, smell alike, sound alike," he said. "And they don't last long. I don't like possession."

Rourke toyed with his coffee cup. "I don't, either," he said slowly, thinking of Tat. The last he'd heard, she went into a small, war-torn African nation, named Ngawa in Swahili, for a species of civet cat found there, to cover the agony of the survivors. She wouldn't answer his phone calls. She wouldn't return his messages. She might as well have vanished off the face of the earth. He had…feelings for her, that he could never, ever express. He, like Carson, had placated the ache with other women. Nothing did much good.

Carson finished his coffee. "I have to get back up to San Antonio. I may have an offer soon."

Rourke studied him. "Tired of working for Cy?"

Carson's lips made a thin line. "Tired of aching for something I can never have."

"Boy, do I understand that feeling," Rourke said tersely.

Carson laughed, but it had a hollow sound.

He was supposed to take Lanette dancing tonight. He wasn't looking forward to it, but he'd given his word, so he'd go. The job offer would involve travel to some South American nation for a covert op with some ex-military people, on the QT. They needed a field medic, and Carson's reputation had gotten around.

It was a good job, paid well, and it would get him away from Carlie. Suddenly that had become of earth-shaking importance. He didn't want to pursue that line of thought, so he called Lanette before he left Jacobsville and told her he'd pick her up at six.

CHAPTER TEN

CARLIE DESCRIBED THE kidnapper to Zack the next day, with her boss and the FBI special agent in charge, Garon Grier, listening in Cash's office.

"He sounded just like one of those gangsters in the old black-and-white movies," she said. "He was big as a house and a little clumsy. He was kind to me. He didn't say a thing out of the way or even threaten me."

"Except by kidnapping you," Garon Grier mused.

"Well, yes, there was that," she agreed. "But he didn't hurt me. He said he was supposed to take me out there to lure my dad to come get me. I suppose that meant they wanted to get him out of town to someplace deserted. I was so scared," she recalled. "I managed to get to my feet, to the door. I listened really hard, so if I heard Dad's voice, I might have time to warn him."

"You weren't afraid for yourself?" Cash asked.

"Not really. He didn't want to hurt me. I was just afraid for Dad. He's absentminded and he forgets things, like his house keys," she said with a smile. Then the smile faded. "But he took down these two huge guys. They had guns, too." She frowned worriedly. "I don't know how he did it. He even kicked in the door! I only just managed to get out of the way in time! And Dad had a gun…"

"He didn't use it," Cash reminded her.

"No. Of course not." She rubbed her wrists. "The kidnapper apologized for the handcuffs. He knew how to loosen them. He said he was a cop once. He knocked a man down a staircase for roughing up a child and they fired him." She looked up. They were all staring at her.

"What else did he say?" Garon asked. He was taking notes on his cell phone.

"I asked why he wanted my dad hurt and he said his bosses didn't pay him to ask questions," she recalled. She was going to add that he was wearing an expensive watch, and about that funny chiming sound she thought she'd heard, but she wasn't certain that she hadn't been confused by the chloroform the kidnapper had used on her. No use making wild statements. She needed to stick to the facts.

"That's not much to go on, but it's more than we had," Garon said a few minutes later. "Thanks, Carlie."

"You're very welcome." She got up. "I'll just get the mail caught up," she told her boss, rolling her eyes. "I expect that will last me a few hours."

Cash chuckled. "No doubt. Hey," he added when she reached the door. She turned. "I'm glad you're okay, kid," he said gently.

She grinned. "Me, too, Chief. Where would you ever get another secretary who didn't hide in the closet every time you lost your temper?"

She went out before he could come back with a reply.

"Isn't this lovely?" Lanette asked Carson as they did a lazy two-step on the dance floor.

"Lovely," he said without feeling it.

"You're very distracted tonight," she said. She moved a little away so that he could see how nicely her red sequined cocktail dress suited her, exposing most of her breasts and a lot of her thigh in a side split. Her exquisite hair was put up in a nice French twist with a jeweled clasp that matched the dress and her shoes. She looked beautiful and very expensive. He wondered vaguely how she managed to afford clothes like that on a stewardess salary. And she never seemed to go on any trips.

"Do you work?" he asked, curious.

"I work very hard," she said. She smiled secretively. "I was a stewardess, but I have a new job now. I work in…personnel," she concluded. "For a big corporation."

"I see."

"What do you do?" she asked.

He smiled enigmatically. "I work for a rancher in Jacobsville mostly, but I'm also a field medic."

"A medic? Really?" she exclaimed. "That's such a…well, I know it's noble and all that, but it sounds just really boring."

Boring. He was recalling several incidents, trying to treat men under fire and get them evacuated by helicopter or ambulance in trouble spots all over the world. Saving lives. "Maybe not as boring as it sounds," he concluded.

She shrugged. "If you say so." She looked up at him as they danced. "I heard on the news that there was a kidnapping in that town where your rancher boss lives. Was anybody hurt?"

"Carlie was frightened, but they didn't hurt her."

"Shame."

He stopped dancing. "Excuse me?"

"Well, she's a little prude, isn't she?" she said cattily. "Doesn't know how to dance properly, wears cheap clothes. My God, I'll bet she's still a virgin." She laughed heartily at the other woman's stupidity. This woman was annoying. He was beginning, just beginning, to understand how Carlie saw the world. She was blunt and unassuming, never coy, never shallow like this beautiful hothouse flower. Carlie was like a sunflower, open and honest and pretty. The fact that she didn't sleep around was suddenly appealing to him. He hated the implication of that thought. He wasn't going to get trapped. Not by some small-town girl with hang-ups.

"They say her father rescued her," Lanette purred.

"Yes. That's what I heard, too," he said, without adding that he'd been in on the rescue. Not that he'd had much work to do. Jake Blair had done it all.

"One guy against two armed men," she said, almost to herself. "It sounds…incredible. I mean, they were really tough guys. That's what I heard, anyway."

"Not so tough," Carson corrected her. "Blair had them trussed up like holiday turkeys."

She let out a rough breath. "Idiots," she murmured. She saw Carson's sudden scrutiny and laughed. "I mean, whoever planned that kidnapping was obviously not intended for a life of crime. Wouldn't you say?"

"I'd say they'd better be on a plane out of the country pretty soon," he replied. "The FBI got called in."

She stopped dancing. "The FBI? That's no threat. Those people are always in the news for doing dumb things—"

"The local FBI," he interrupted. "Garon Grier. He was formerly with the Hostage Rescue Team. His brother is Jacobsville's police chief Cash Grier. You met him at the dance."

She nodded slowly. "I see."

"So the kidnapper will not be sleeping well anytime soon," he concluded.

"Maybe he'll just have to step up his plans while the local FBI get their marbles together," she laughed.

"That's what bothers me," he replied. "What nobody understands is why someone would try to kill a minister."

"Loads of reasons," she said. "Maybe he's one of those radicals who wants everybody to take vows of chastity or something."

"A political opinion shouldn't result in murder," he pointed out.

"Well, no, but maybe the people who want him dead aren't interested in his opinions. Maybe it's just a job to them. Somebody big calling the shots, you know?"

Somebody big. Big. Like the politician who was finishing out the Texas U.S. senator's term and was campaigning for the May special election to earn his own term.

"What are you thinking so hard about?" Lanette asked.

"Work," he said.

"Oh, work." She threw a hand up. "We're here to have fun. We could dance some more," she said, sliding close to him. "Or we could go back to my apartment…?"

He felt like a stone wall. The thought of sleeping with her had once appealed, but now he felt uncomfortable even discussing it. He thought of all the men Lanette had bragged to him about, the men she'd had. Of course men bragged about their conquests. It was just…when she did that, he thought of Carlie. Carlie!

"Ow," Lanette complained softly. "That's my hand you're crushing, honey."

He loosened his hold. "Sorry," he snapped.

"You are really tense. Please. Let me soothe that ache," she whispered sensually.

"I want to dance." He pulled her back onto the dance floor.

THE NEXT MORNING, just before daylight, he drove back down to Cy Parks's place. He couldn't sleep. He and Lanette had argued, again, about his coldness to her and about Carlie. She was venomous about the small-town girl.

Carson was angry and couldn't hide it. He didn't like hearing her bad-mouth Carlie. He was tired of the city anyway. He just wanted to get back to work.

Cy was working on a broken hoof on one of the big Santa Gertrudis bulls. He filed the broken part down while a tall African-American cowboy gently held the animal in place, soothing it with an uncanny gift.

"That's good, Diamond," the other cowboy murmured softly, using part of the pedigree bull's full name, which was Parks's Red Diamond. "Good old fellow."

Cy grinned. "I don't know what I'd do without you, Eddie," he chuckled. "That bull's just like a dog when you talk to him. He follows you around like one, anyway. Nice of Luke to let me borrow you." He glanced up at Carson. "You've been AWOL," he accused. "Couldn't find anybody to hold Diamond while I filed the hoof down, so I had to call Luke Craig and ask him to lend a hand. He sent Eddie Kells here. Eddie, this is Carson."

Carson nodded politely.

Kells just grinned.

"Kells came down here to a summer camp some years ago that Luke Craig's wife, Belinda, started for city kids in trouble with the law. Didn't know one end of a horse from another. Now he's bossing cowboys over at Luke's place," Cy chuckled.

"Yeah, Mr. Parks here saved my life," Kells replied. "I was in trouble with the law in Houston when I was younger," he said honestly. "I was on Mr. Parks's place trying to learn roping with his cattle, trespassing, and he caught me." He let out a whistle. "Thought I was a goner. But when he saw how crazy I was about cattle, he didn't press charges and Mr. Craig hired me on as a cowboy when I graduated from high school." He smiled. "I got no plans to ever leave, either. This is a good place to live. Fine people."

Carson studied the tall young man. He'd have thought that a place like this would have a lot of prejudice. It didn't seem to be the case at all, not if Kells wanted to stay here.

"You Indian?" Kells asked, and held up a hand

when Carson bristled. "No, man, it's cool, I got this friend, Juanito, he's Apache. Some of his ancestors ran with Geronimo. He's hired on at Mr. Scott's place. He's been trying to teach me to speak his language. Man, it's hard!"

Carson relaxed a little. "I'm Oglala Lakota."

"I guess you couldn't speak to Juanito and have him understand you, huh?"

Carson smiled. "No. The languages are completely different."

"Only thing I can manage is enough Spanish to talk to some of the new cowboys. But I guess that's what I need to be studying, anyway."

"You do very well, too," Cy told the young man, clapping him on the shoulder. "That's it, then. You go down to the hardware and get yourself a new pocket-knife, and put it on my account," he told Kells. "I'll call and okay it before you get there. Don't argue. I know Luke sent you, but you should have something. That knife's pretty old, you know," he added. Kells was using it to clean under his fingernails.

"Only one I had," Kells said, smiling. "Okay, then, I'll do it. Thanks, Mr. Parks."

They shook hands.

"Nice to meet you," Kells told Carson before he left.

"I had a different concept of life here," Carson told Cy quietly.

Cy chuckled. "So did I. Blew all my notions of it when I moved here. You will never find a place with kinder, more tolerant people, anywhere in the world."

Carson was thinking of some of the places he had been which were far less than that.

"Sorry I didn't get back in time to help," he told Cy. "There's a new complication. I need to talk to Jake Blair. I think I've made a connection, of sorts. I just want to sound him out on it."

"If you dig anything out, tell Garon Grier," Cy replied.

"Certainly." He hesitated. "I'm going to be moving on, soon," he said. "I've enjoyed my time here."

"I've enjoyed having you around." Cy gave him a cynical smile. "I was like you, you know," he said. "Same fire for action, same distaste for marriage, kids. I went all over the world with a gun. Killed a lot of people. But in the end, it was the loneliness that got me. It will eat you up like acid."

"I like my own company."

Cy put a hand on his shoulder. His green eyes narrowed. "Son," he said gently, "there's a difference between being alone and being lonely."

"I'm not lonely," Carson said doggedly.

Cy just chuckled. "Go see Jake. He'll be up. He never was a late sleeper."

"You knew him before?" he asked slowly.

Cy nodded. "He was on special duty, assigned to support troops. We ended up in the same black ops group." He shook his head. "The only person I've ever known who comes close to him is Cash Grier. Jake was…gifted. And not in a way you'd ever share with civilians."

"I heard that from Rourke."

Cy pursed his lips. "Make sure you never share that information with Carlie," he cautioned. "You do not want to see Jake Blair lose his temper. Ever."

"I'm getting that impression," Carson said with a mild chuckle.

It was barely daylight. Carson knew it was early to be visiting, but he was certain Jake would be up, and he needed to tell him what he thought might be going on. Lanette had, without realizing it, pointed him in a new direction on the attempted kidnapping.

When he got to Reverend Blair's house, he was surprised to find Carlie there alone. She seemed equally surprised to find him at her door.

She was wearing a T-shirt and jeans. It was late February and still cold outside. In fact, it was cold in the house. Heat was expensive, and Carlie was always trying to save money. The cold had become familiar, so that she hardly noticed it now.

"What can I do for you?" she asked quietly.

He shrugged. "I came to see your father," he told her.

Her eyebrows arched over wide green eyes. "He didn't mention anything…"

"He doesn't know." He smiled slowly, liking the way her face flushed when he did that. "Is he here?"

"No, but he'll be back…soon," she faltered. She bit her lower lip. "You can come in and wait for him, if you like."

The invitation was reluctant, but at least she made one.

"Okay. Thanks."

She opened the door and let him in. Why did she feel as if she were walking into quicksand?

He closed the door behind him and followed her into the living room. On the sofa was a mass of yarn.

Apparently she was making some sort of afghan in soft shades of blue and purple.

"You crochet?" he asked, surprised.

"Yes," she replied. She sat down beside the skeins of yarn and moved them aside. Carson dropped into the armchair just to her left.

"My mother used to do handwork," he murmured. He could remember her sewing quilts when he was very small. She did it to keep her hands busy. Maybe she did it to stop thinking about how violent and angry his father was when he drank. And he never seemed to stop drinking...

Carlie toyed with the yarn, but her hands were nervous. The silence grew more tense by the minute. He didn't speak. He just looked at her.

"Would you mind...not doing that, please?" she asked in a haunted tone.

"Doing what exactly?" he asked with a slow, sensuous smile.

"Staring at me," she blurted out. "I know you think I'm ugly. Couldn't you stare at the— Oh!"

He was sitting beside her the next minute, his hands on her face, cupping it while he looked straight into her eyes. "I don't think you're ugly," he said huskily. He looked at her mouth.

She was confused and nervous. "You said once that you liked your women more...physically perfect," she accused in a throaty voice.

He drew in a breath. "Yes. But I didn't mean it."

His thumb rubbed gently over her bow mouth, liking the way it felt. It was swollen and very soft. She caught his wrist, but not to pull his hand away.

She hadn't felt such sensations. It was new and exciting. He was exciting. She wanted to hide her reaction from him, but he knew too much about women. She felt like a rabbit walking into a snare.

She should get up right now and go into the kitchen. She should…

His mouth lowered to her lips. He touched them softly, tenderly, smoothing her lips apart so that he could feel the softness underneath the top one. He traced it delicately with his tongue. His hands on her face were big and warm. His thumbs stroked her cheekbones while he toyed with her lips in a silence that accentuated her quick breathing.

He hadn't expected his own reaction to her. This was explosive. Sweet. Dangerous. He opened his mouth and pushed her lips apart. He let go of her face and lifted her across his lap while he kissed her as if her mouth was the source of such sweetness that he couldn't bear to let it go.

Helplessly, her arms went around his neck and she kissed him back, with more enthusiasm than expertise.

He could feel that lack of experience. It made him feel taller, stronger. She had nothing to compare this with, he could tell. He nibbled her lower lip while one big hand shifted down to her T-shirt and teased under the sleeve.

She caught his wrist and stayed it. "No," she protested weakly.

But it was too late. His long fingers were under the sleeve, and he could feel the scars.

She bit her lip. "Don't," she pleaded, turning her face away.

He drew in a harsh breath. "Do you think a scar

matters?" he asked roughly. He turned her face up to his. "It doesn't."

Her eyes were eloquent, stinging with tears.

"Trust me," he whispered as his mouth lowered to hers again. "I won't hurt you. I promise."

His mouth became slowly insistent, so hungry and demanding that she forgot to protest, and let go of his wrist. He slid it under the hem of her T-shirt while he kissed her and lifted it, sliding his hand possessively over her small breast and up to the scar.

"You mustn't!" she whispered frantically.

He nibbled her upper lip. "Shh," he whispered back, and quickly lifted the shirt over her head and tossed it aside.

She was wearing a delicate little white lacy bra that fastened in front. Just above the lacy cup was a scar, a long one running from her collarbone down just to the beginning of the swell of her breast.

Tears stung her eyes. She hadn't shown the wound to anyone except the doctor and a woman police officer. She tried to cover it with her hand, but he lifted it gently away and unfastened the bra.

"Beautiful," he whispered when he saw the delicate pink and mauve mound that he'd uncovered.

"Wh...what?" she stammered.

His hand smoothed boldly over her delicate flesh, teasing the nipple so that it became immediately hard. "Your breasts are beautiful," he said softly, bending. "I wonder if I can fit one into my mouth...?"

As he spoke, he did it. His tongue rubbed abrasively over the sensitive nipple while his mouth covered and possessed the pert little mound.

Her reaction was unexpected and violent. She shivered and cried out, and then suddenly arched up toward his lips as he made a slow suction that caused unspeakable responses in her untried body.

"No...nooooo!" she groaned as she felt the tension grow to almost painful depths and then, suddenly, snap. The pleasure was unlike anything she'd ever known in her life. She shivered and shivered, her short nails digging into his shoulders as she held on and convulsed with ecstasy.

He felt her body contort, felt the shudders run through her as he satisfied her with nothing more than his mouth on her breast. His hand went to her hip and ground it into his while he continued the warm pressure of his mouth on her damp flesh. He wanted her. He'd never wanted anything so much!

She was lost. She couldn't even protest. The pleasure swept over her in waves, like breakers on the ocean, on the beach. She arched her back and shuddered as her body gave in to him, hungered for him, ached to have more than this, something more, anything....

Finally, he lifted his head and looked down at her. She lay shivering in the aftermath, tears running down her cheeks. She wept silently, her eyes wide and wet and accusing.

"It's all right," he whispered. He kissed away the tears. "There's no reason to be embarrassed."

She sobbed. She felt as if she'd betrayed everything she believed in. If he hadn't stopped, she wouldn't have been able to. She was embarrassed and humiliated by her own easy acceptance of his ardor. He was a womanizer. God only knew how many women he'd had. And she was so easy...

She pushed gently at his chest.

He let her go, very slowly, his eyes riveted to her taut breasts, to the red marks on the one he'd suckled so hard.

She tried to pull the bra over them, but he prevented her with a gentle movement of his hand. He wasn't looking at her breasts. He was looking at the scar. He traced it, noting the ridge that was forming.

She drew in a sharp breath.

"It was deep, wasn't it?" he asked softly.

She swallowed. He didn't seem repulsed. "Yes."

He traced it tenderly. His finger moved down over her breast to the hard nipple and caressed it. He loved touching her. It was surprising.

"I've never had a virgin," he whispered. "I didn't realize how exciting it would be."

She flushed. "I'm…not perfect physically," she choked, remembering the hurtful things he'd said in her boss's office.

He looked into her eyes with regret darkening his own. "Here," he said quietly. "Show-and-tell."

He unbuttoned his shirt and pulled it away from his broad, muscular chest. He pulled her up into a sitting position on his lap and drew her fingers to the worst scar, where a long, deep wound went just below his rib cage on the side near his heart.

"This was deep, too," she said softly, tracing it.

He nodded. "He came at me with a sword, of all things. I drew him in and guided the blade where it would do the least damage, before I killed him." His eyes were narrow and cold.

She shivered. She could never kill anyone.

"He'd just raped a young woman. A pregnant woman," he said quietly.

Her expression changed. Her eyes went back to the scars. "These are...strange," she said, tracing several small round scars below his collarbone.

"Cigarette burns," he said with a faint smile. "I was captured once. They tortured me for information." He chuckled. "They got my name, rank and serial number. Eventually they got tired of listening to it, but my squad came and rescued me before they killed me."

"Wow," she whispered.

He cocked his head and studied her. "You are... unexpected."

Her eyebrows lifted. "I am?"

His eyes went down to her bare breasts. He drew her against him, very gently, and moved her breasts against his bare chest. She moaned. He bent and kissed her, hungrily, urgently.

"I want you," he murmured.

His hands were on her breasts again, and she was dying for him. She wanted that pleasure again, that he'd given her so easily, so sensually, with just his mouth. But with a harsh moan, she dragged herself away from him and pulled her T-shirt across her bare breasts like a shield.

"Please," she whispered when he started to draw her back into his arms. "Please. I'm sorry. I can't. I just...can't!"

She looked as if he'd asked her to go through the entire catalog of sins at once. Probably she felt that way. She was a person of faith. She didn't believe in quick rolls in the hay. She was innocent.

He felt oddly ashamed. He buttoned his shirt while

she fumbled her bra closed and put her shirt back on with tattered pride. As cold reality set in, she was horrified by what she'd let him do. All her principles had flown out the window the minute he touched her.

"I see," he said quietly. "You believe it's the road to hell. And I don't believe in anything," he added coldly.

She met his eyes. "You don't really even like women, do you?" she asked perceptively.

His smile was icy. "She said she loved me," he replied. "We were married for all of a year when she became pregnant. But by then there was another man." His eyes closed, and his brows drew together in pain at the memory while Carlie listened.

"It was almost two days after the wreck before they found the bodies. They thought they could have saved the child, a boy, if they'd found them just a little sooner." His face contorted. "I killed them all..."

"No, you didn't," she said. "You couldn't hurt a woman if you tried."

He looked at her with narrow, intent eyes. "Really? I scared you to death in your boss's office," he reminded her tautly.

"Yes, but you wouldn't have hurt me. It was the association with the past that frightened me, not you," she repeated softly. She touched his cheek, drew her soft fingers down it. "Some things are meant to be. We don't make those decisions. We can't. God takes people away sometimes for reasons we can't understand. But there's a reason, even if we don't know what it was."

His face hardened. "God," he scoffed.

She smiled gently. "You don't believe in anything."

"I used to. Before she destroyed my life." His eyes were dark with confusion and pain.

"You have to accept the fact that you can't control the world, or the people in it," she continued quietly. "Control is just an illusion."

"Like love?" he laughed coldly.

"Love is everywhere," she countered. "You aren't looking. You're living inside yourself, in the past, locked up in pain and loss and guilt. You can't forgive anything until you can forgive yourself."

He glared at her.

"The key to it all is faith," she said gently.

"Faith." He nodded. His eyes were hostile. "Yours took a hike when I started kissing your breasts, didn't it? All those shiny ideals, that proud innocence, would have been gone in a flash if I'd insisted."

She blushed. Her hand left his face. "Yes. That's true. I never realized how easy it would be to fall from grace." Her wide, soft eyes, wounded and wet, met his. "Is that why you did it? To show me how vulnerable I am?"

He wanted to say yes, to hurt her again. But suddenly it gave him no pleasure. No woman had ever reacted to him that way, been so tender with him, so patient, so willing to listen.

"No," he confessed curtly.

That one word took the pain away. She just looked at him.

He drew her hand to his mouth and kissed the palm hungrily. "I've never told anyone about my wife, except Grier and you, and one other person."

"I never tell anything I know," she replied huskily. She searched his dark eyes. "Ever."

He managed a smile. "You have a gift for listening."

"I learned it from my father. He's very patient."

He touched her soft mouth. "The angle of that wound is odd," he said after a minute, staring at the T-shirt. "Was the attacker very tall?"

"Not really," she confessed. "He reached around my father to do it." She shivered. She could still feel the pain of the knife.

"He'll never do it to anyone else," he assured her.

"I know. He died. They said it took a long time." She touched the scar involuntarily. "I'm sorry that his life took such a turn that he felt he was justified in killing people."

"He was an addict and they offered him product," Carson said coldly. "It works, most of the time."

"I'm sorry for him, for the way it happened. But I'm not sorry he's gone." She grimaced. "My dad wouldn't like hearing me say that."

"I won't tell him," he said gently. He looked down at her with faint possession. "Don't beat your conscience to death over what happened," he said quietly. "Any experienced man can overcome an innocent woman's scruples if he tries hard enough. And if she's attracted to him," he added gently.

She colored even more. "Yes, well, I…I didn't mean…I don't…"

He put a finger across her mouth. "It's an intimate memory. For the two of us. No one else will ever know. All right?"

She nodded. "All right."

He brought her hand to his mouth and kissed the

palm. "Keep your doors locked when your father isn't here," he said.

The tone of his voice was disturbing. "Why?"

"I can't tell you."

She just sighed. As she started to speak, there was a terrible rapping sound against the side of the house.

Carson was on his feet at once, his hand on the hilt of the big bowie knife.

"That's just George."

He scowled. "Who?"

"George. He's my red-bellied woodpecker." She grimaced. "I put nuts out for him at daylight every day. He's telling me he's hungry and I'm late." She laughed. "Listen." There was another sound, like something small bounding across the roof. "That's one of the squirrels. They let George do the reminding, and then they queue for the nuts." She listened again. There was a loud cacophony of bird calls. "And those are the blue jays. They fight George for the nuts..."

"You know them by sound?" he asked, surprised.

"Of course." She got up, frowning slightly. "Can't everybody identify them from the songs they sing?"

He shook his head. "I don't believe this."

"You can help me feed them if you want to. I mean, if you don't have something else to do," she added quickly, not wanting him to feel pressured.

But he wasn't looking for a way out. He just smiled. "Put on a coat," he said.

She pulled her ratty one out of the closet and grimaced. "This is what it's best for," she sighed. "Feeding birds."

"You should buy a new one."

She gave him a world-weary glance. "With what?" she asked. "We just had to fill up the propane tank again because winter doesn't appear to be leaving anytime soon. New things are a luxury around here."

He was estimating the age of her shoes and jeans. The T-shirt appeared new. He cocked his head. It was black with writing—it had a picture of a big black bird on it. Underneath it read, "Hey, you in the house, bring more birdseed!"

He chuckled. "Cool shirt."

"You like it? I designed it. There's this website. It has nice T-shirts for a reasonable price and you can design your own. This is one of the grackles that come every spring. I haven't seen one just yet."

She led the way, picking up a container of birdseed and one of shelled nuts on the way.

"The pecans came from our own trees," she said. "The farm produce store that sells them has a sheller you can run them through. I did enough to last several weeks."

"Back home, we have ravens," he told her, his hands in his jeans as he followed her out to the big backyard. Towering trees gave way to a small pasture beyond. "And crows." He pursed his lips and grinned. "Did you know that crows used to be white?"

"White?"

He nodded. "It's a Brulé Lakota legend. The crow was white, and he was brother to the buffalo. So he would warn the buffalo when the people came to hunt it. The warriors grew angry that they couldn't get close to the buffalo, so one of them put on a buffalo skin and waited for the crow to come and give its warning. When it did, he caught it by the feet.

Another warrior, very angry, took it from him and dashed it into the fire in revenge. The crow escaped, but its feathers were burned. So now the crow is black."

She laughed with pure delight. "I love stories."

"Our legends fill books," he mused. "That's one of my favorites."

That he'd shared something from his culture with her made her feel warm, welcome. She turned to look for the woodpecker. He was clinging to a nearby tree trunk making his usual lilting cry. "Okay, George, I'm here," she called. She went to a ledge on the fence and spread the nuts along it. She filled the bird feeder. Then she motioned to Carson and they moved away from the feeder.

A flash of striped feathers later, George was carting off the first pecan. He was followed by blue jays and cardinals, a tufted titmouse and a wren.

She identified them to Carson as they came in. Then she laughed suddenly as a new birdcall was heard, and started looking around. "That's a red-winged blackbird," she said. "I don't see him."

"I do know that call," he replied. He shook his head, smiling. "I've never known anyone who could listen to a birdsong and identify the bird without seeing it first."

"Oh, I can't do them all," she assured him. "Just a few. Listen. That one's a grackle!" she exclaimed. "Hear it? It sounds like a rusty hinge being moved... There he is!"

She indicated a point high in the bare limbs above. "They're so beautiful. They're so black that they have a faint purple tinge, sort of like your hair," she added, looking at it in its neat ponytail. Her eyes lingered there. He was so handsome that she thought she'd never tire of watching him.

He smiled knowingly and she flushed and averted her eyes. He was wearing that incredible fringed jacket that suited him so. Its paleness brought out the smooth olive tan of his complexion, made him look wild and free. She thought back to what her father had said, that Carson was a lobo wolf who could never be domesticated. The better she got to know him, the more certain she was of that. He'd never be able to stop picking up beautiful women, or looking for the next fight. Her heart felt sick.

She tossed seed onto the ground while the last of the nuts vanished from the fence. Carson reached into the bucket and pulled out a handful of his own and tossed it.

They stood very close, in the cold light of the morning, feeding the birds. Carlie thought it was a time she'd never forget, whatever came after. Just her and Carson, all alone in the world, without a word being spoken.

It felt…like coming home.

Carson was feeling something similar. He didn't want to think about it too much. His life was what it was. He wasn't going to get married again, settle down and have children. It was too tame for him, for his spirit. He'd lived wild for too long.

He knew she must have hopes. Her physical response to him was purely headlong. She would probably give in to him if he pushed her. He thought about doing that. He wanted her very badly. But no form of birth control was surefire. Carlie was an innocent, and she had strong beliefs. She'd never give up a child she conceived, especially his. It would lead to terrible complications…

He scowled. He was remembering some tidbit of gossip he'd heard. He glanced down at Carlie. She looked up, her eyes full of soft memory.

"Your father married your mother because you were on the way," he said gently. "True?"

She swallowed. "Well, yes. She was like me," she said, lowering her eyes to his chest. "She'd never put a foot out of line, never been…with a man. My father was dashing and exciting, well-traveled and smart. She just went in headfirst. She told me once," she recalled sadly, "that she'd ruined both their lives because she couldn't say no, the one time it really counted. She loved me," she added quickly. "She said I made everything worthwhile. But her love for my father, and his for her, never made up for the fact that he'd been pressured into marrying her."

"This isn't Victorian times," he pointed out.

"This is Jacobsville, Texas," she returned. "Or, in my case, Comanche Wells. I live among people who have known my people since the Civil War, when my family first came here from Georgia and settled on this land." She swept a hand toward it. "Generations of us know each other like family. And like family, there are some social pressures on people in terms of behavior."

"Prehistoric ones," he scoffed.

She looked up at him. "Is the world really a better place now that nothing is considered bad? People just do what they want, with anyone. How is that different from what animals do in the wild?"

He was lost for words.

"Everything goes. But the one thing that separates human beings from animals is a nobility of spirit, a sense of self-worth. I have ideals. I think they're what holds civilization together, and that if you cheapen yourself with careless encounters, you lose sight of the things that truly matter."

"Which would be…?" he prompted, stung by her reply.

"Family," she said simply. "Continuity. People get married, have children, raise children to be good people, give them a happy home life so that they grow up to be responsible and independent. Then the next generation comes along and does the same thing."

"Permissive people still have kids," he said drolly.

"They have them out of wedlock a lot, though," she pointed out. "So it's a one-parent family trying to raise the kids. I saw the result in school, with boys who had no fathers around to discipline them and teach them the things men need to know to get along in the world."

He averted his eyes. "Maybe my life would have been happier in a single-parent family."

She recalled what he'd told her, about his father's drinking problem, that he'd beat Carson's mother to death, and she grimaced. "I am so sorry for what happened to you," she said softly. "Except for my grandmother's evil boyfriend, nobody ever hurt me in my life, least of all my parents."

He drew in a long breath. His eyes were solemn as he stared off into the distance. "We attach the same importance to family that you do," he said quietly. "We live in small communities, people know each other for generations. Children are brought up not only by their parents, but by other parents, as well. It's a good way."

"But it isn't your style," she said without looking at him. "You have to be free."

He scowled and looked down at her, but she wouldn't meet his eyes.

"Here, spread the seeds over there, would you?" she asked, indicating another feeder. "I forgot to put up a seed cake for them." She pulled it out of her pocket and took the wrapper off.

In the house, unseen, Jake Blair was watching them with wide, shocked eyes. He turned. "Come here," he told Rourke. "You're not going to believe this."

Rourke followed his gaze out the window and let out a hoot of laughter. "You're having me on," he chuckled. "That can't be Carson, feeding the birds!"

"Oh, yes, it can." He pursed his lips. "I wonder…"

"I wouldn't even think it. Not yet. He's got a lot to work through before he's fit for any young woman, especially your daughter."

"Men can change. I did," Jake said quietly. "And in my day, I was a harder case than he is."

"You did change," Rourke agreed. "But you don't have the scars he's carrying."

"Tell me," Jake said.

Rourke shook his head and smiled sadly. "I won't do that. It's his story, his pain. He'll have to be the one to tell it."

Jake just nodded. He watched his daughter lead Carson around the yard, saw them laughing together as the birds came very close and they paused, very still, so that they came right up almost to their feet.

That jacket Carson wore was really gorgeous, he thought. Then he compared it to Carlie's old coat and he winced. He'd tried to give her all the necessities. He hadn't realized how difficult it was going to be, living on a minister's small salary in an equally small community. The days of big money were long gone. His conscience wouldn't let him go back to it. He did love his work, anyway.

He turned away from the window, leading Rourke back into his office.

CHAPTER ELEVEN

CARLIE WENT AHEAD of Carson into the house through the back door. Rourke and her father were just having coffee.

Jake held up the pot and raised his eyebrows.

"Please," Carson said. "I haven't had a cup this morning. Withdrawal symptoms are setting in," he added, deliberately making his hand shake.

The other men laughed.

"Breakfast?" Carlie asked, but she was looking at Carson. "I can make biscuits with scrambled eggs and sausage. Fresh sausage. One of our congregation brought it over yesterday."

"Sounds good to me, pumpkin," Jake said easily. "Make enough for everybody."

"You bet." She could almost float. It was one of the best days of her life so far. She had to make sure she didn't linger over Carson when she looked his way. She didn't want to embarrass him.

"Did you come over to help feed the local wildlife?" Rourke asked with a grin.

Carson chuckled. "No. I made a connection. Actually, I made it from something Lanette said. That whoever planned the kidnapping was sloppy, but that it must be somebody big. So I thought of the politician who's connected to the Cotillo drug cartel across the border."

"Why would he be after you, though?" Rourke asked Jake, frowning. "Have you had any contact with people who know things about the cartel?"

"None," Jake said. He sipped coffee and shook his head. "I have no idea at all why I've been targeted, or by whom." He smiled faintly. "Someone from the old life, possibly, after revenge. But if that's the case, they've waited a long time for it."

"I don't think it's that," Carson said quietly. "It just feels…I don't know, jagged."

The other two men stared at him.

"Jagged?" Rourke prompted.

"A man with a drug habit comes after Carlie, but tries to make it look like he was after you," Carson told Jake. "Now, a kidnapping attempt on Carlie to bring you into the line of fire so they could take you out. Why?"

"Jagged," Jake agreed. "Like someone jumped from one victim to another."

"It's just a thought," Carson continued, "but the man who hired the first assassin was on drugs."

"The man who died in the fire up in Wyoming, who was trying to kill Dalton Kirk for something he remembered," Rourke told Jake. "I mentioned it to you. The man, Richard Martin by name, was a former DEA agent, a mole who fed information to the drug cartel over in Cotillo. I'm pretty sure he hired the man who came after Carlie, to stop her from remembering what he looked like. With her photographic memory, she was giving out exact information about him. He didn't want that."

"Because he worked for Matthew Helm, a crooked politician who's just been named to the unexpired U.S. Senate seat in Texas," Carson concluded. "We know now why our computer expert Joey was killed and the computer was trashed, and why Carlie was targeted. You see, the killer had murdered an assistant D.A. in San Antonio who was investigating Helm for embezzlement and drug trafficking. He had files that mysteriously disappeared. Every bit of the evidence that could have been used against him is gone, and Lieutenant Rick Marquez of San Antonio PD told Cash Grier that two witnesses in the case have refused to testify. One just left the country, in fact."

"How convenient for Helm," Rourke commented.

"This is pretty big," Jake said, listening intently. "He didn't want his link to Helm to get out, obviously, but why kill a computer tech and try to kill Carlie?"

"Because of the watch and the shirt," Rourke said.

"Excuse me?" Jake asked, wide-eyed.

"The assistant D.A.'s wife was loaded," Carson said. "She'd just bought her husband a very expensive watch that played a song and chimed on the hour. She also bought him an exclusive, equally expensive, designer paisley shirt. Martin took a shine to both, so he stole them. He didn't want anyone to remember what he was wearing, because it linked his boss to the assistant D.A.'s murder."

Jake exchanged glances with his daughter. "You told me about this."

"Yes," Carlie said. She was deep in thought.

"What happened to the watch and the shirt?" Jake asked Carson.

"I assume whoever ransacked the room Richard

Martin was occupying at the local motel took both and destroyed them." Rourke sighed. "It would be insane to keep something so dangerous."

"The watch played a song, but nobody ever told me which song," Carlie said. She looked at Rourke.

He sang it, "I Love Rock 'n' Roll," and grinned because he was totally off-key. "It was a Joan Jett song from—"

"That's it," Carly cried. "I thought I was just react-ing to the stuff he knocked me out with, so I didn't say anything. The kidnapper was wearing a cheap suit, but he had this expensive watch on his wrist. It was sort of like the one Calhoun Ballenger wears. You know, that Rolex."

"I know," Jake mused. "I told him once that he could feed a whole third-world country on the pro-ceeds if he sold that thing. He just laughed and said it was two generations old and a family heirloom. He wouldn't sell it for the world." He glanced at Rourke. "He's going to run for that U.S. Senate seat against Helm. He told me yesterday. I ran into him in town."

"He'd be a wonderful senator," Carlie mused. "His brother Justin is dealing with the feedlot and the ranch anyway, since Calhoun's been a state senator for the past few years. He's done so much for our state…"

"He'll be a target, too," Jake said heavily.

"Yes," Carson said. "The other candidates for the temporary appointment ended up arrested on various drug charges. They swore the drugs were planted. I believe them."

"That politician needs to be taken down," Jake said shortly. "Once he has real power, he'll cause untold misery."

"I'm game," Rourke volunteered. "And since I'm officially his gofer, I have the inside track on what he's up to."

"You be careful," Jake told him.

"You know me," Rourke chuckled.

"I do. That's why I made the remark."

Carson was quiet. He was just remembering something. He didn't want to share it with the others. Lanette had excused herself at the theater the night Carlie had been kidnapped. It was a small, insignificant thing in itself and might be quite innocent. But Lanette hated Carlie. She wore expensive clothes, not the sort she could pay for on a meager salary working personnel for a company. A lot of things about her didn't quite add up.

"You're very quiet," Rourke prompted him.

"Sorry." He smiled faintly. "I was thinking about patterns." He glanced at Carlie. "The man who used the chloroform on you, he was wearing the watch?"

She nodded. "I thought I was hallucinating when it chimed. I mean, I've heard musical watches, but that was totally different."

"I'm reliably informed that the price of a new Jaguar convertible is in the same price range," Rourke commented wryly.

"The kidnapper is the connection," Carson said, frowning thoughtfully. "He can link Helm to the assistant D.A.'s murder."

"The watch by itself won't help a lot," Jake commented.

"Yes, but don't you see, the kidnapper has to be working for Matthew Helm. The fact that he has the watch connects him to Helm, through Helm's man,

Richard Martin, who killed the assistant D.A.," Carson emphasized. "It's a pattern, a chain of evidence."

"You're right!" Rourke said, drawing in a breath. "I didn't make the connection."

Carson gazed at Carlie quietly, his eyes dark and concerned. "You don't leave the house without the phone in the console of the truck, and not until it's been checked for devices," he told her.

She just nodded.

Jake hid a smile.

"Promise me," Carson added, staring her down.

She grimaced. "Okay. I promise."

Carson's gaze turned to Jake and became amused. "I've learned already that if she gives her word, she'll keep it. You just have to make sure she gives it."

Jake ruffled Carlie's hair. "That's my girl, all right." Carlie grinned.

"One of us needs to go up to San Antonio and talk to Rick Marquez," Rourke said, getting out of his chair. "This is a development he'll enjoy pursuing."

"If he needs to talk to me, I'll go up there, too," Carlie said.

"Not in the Cobra, you won't."

Jake and Carson stared at each other. They'd both said exactly the same thing at the same time, and they burst out laughing.

"Okay, okay," Carlie muttered. "If you're ganging up on me, I'll take the truck if I have to go. Just expect a call for help halfway there because my truck barely makes it to work every day. It won't make it to San Antonio without major engine failure!"

"I'll drive you," Jake told his daughter with a smile. "How's that?"

She grinned. "That's great, Dad."

"Carson, you're the best person to talk to Marquez," Rourke told the other man. "I can't be seen near anyone in law enforcement right now. You can ask if he needs a statement from Carlie," Rourke added. "But he lives in Jacobsville, you know. He could probably take a statement down here."

"I forgot. His mother is Barbara, who runs Barbara's Café," she told Carson, who looked puzzled.

"And his father-in-law runs the CIA," Jake added with a chuckle.

"Nice connections," Rourke said. He glanced at his watch. "I have to get back before Helm misses me. I'll be off, then."

"See you," Jake replied.

Rourke punched Carson on the shoulder and grinned as he walked out.

CARSON FINISHED HIS coffee. Carlie was clearing away breakfast. She glanced at Carson with her heart in her eyes. He looked at her as if she were a juicy steak and he was a starving man.

Jake turned his attention suddenly to Carson and jerked his head toward the office. Carson nodded.

"Breakfast was very good," Carson told her. "You have a way with food."

She smiled brightly. "Thanks!"

Carson followed her father into his study. "No calls for a few minutes, Carlie," Jake called before he shut the door. As an afterthought, he locked it.

Carson drew in a long breath as he studied the man across from him. Jake had been personable over breakfast, but at the moment he'd never looked less like a minister. His long, fit body was almost coiled. His pale blue eyes glittered with some inner fire.

"You're me, twenty-two years ago," Jake said without preamble. "And that child in there is my whole life. I'm seeing connections of my own," he added in a low tone. "I destroyed her mother. I'm not going to stand by and let you destroy her. She deserves better than a womanizing mercenary."

Carson sighed. He slid into a chair beside the desk where Jake sat down, and crossed his legs. "People are not what they seem to be," he began heavily. "You're thinking about the reputation I have with women. Carlie's already thrown it at me. It's why we argued the day I had to take her to the emergency room with the asthma attack."

"I thought as much," Jake replied.

"Six years ago," Carson began, "I was in the last two years of graduate school when I fell in love with a brash, outgoing, beautiful girl at a powwow on the reservation in South Dakota where I grew up. Her name was Jessica and I'd known her for years. I loved her insanely, so she married me. The first year was perfect. I thought it would never end. But my last year in college, she got tired of having me away so much at school. She took a lover. He was one of the most militant men on the reservation," he continued, his eyes cold and haunted. "He had a rap sheet, and the rez police knew him on sight. I tried to get her to come home, but she said she loved him, she wasn't coming back to a boring life as the wife of a college student. She didn't think much of higher education in the first place. So I let her go."

He shifted in the chair. "But I wouldn't give her

a divorce. I knew he was beating her. I heard it from my cousins. I talked to her on the phone, and tried to get her to press charges. She said he didn't mean it, he loved her, he'd never do it again." He met Jake's world-weary eyes. "My father gave my mother the same spiel after he beat her up, over and over again," he said coldly. "I was six years old when he hit her too hard and ran. He was prosecuted for murder and ended up in the same prison with one of my mother's brothers. He died not long after that. My uncle had nothing to lose, you see, and he loved my mother."

Jake's face was relaxing, just a little. He didn't interrupt.

"I went to live with cousins. One of my uncles, a rez cop, adopted me as his son since he had no children of his own. I was given all the necessities, but there's no substitute for loving, real parents. I missed my mother." He paused, took a breath and plowed ahead. "Jessie was pregnant and near her due date. She was living with her lover and she swore the child was his. But I had a visitor who knew one of my cousins. He said it was my child, that Jessie lied about it because she didn't want me to drag her into court for paternity tests."

He leaned forward, his eyes downcast. "I finished my last final and flew back to the rez to see her. She was alone at her house. She was afraid of me." He laughed coldly. "She said okay, it was my child, and I could see it when it was born, but she was staying with Jeff no matter what I did. I was about to tell her I'd let her get the divorce, when Jeff drove up. He stormed into the house and accused her of two-timing him. I tried to restrain him, but he blindsided me. While I was getting back up, he dragged Jessie out the door with him. I managed to get outside in time to watch him throw her into the passenger seat. She was screaming. She thought he was going to kill her. So did I."

Jake's pale eyes were riveted to him.

"So I got in my car and went after them. He saw me in the rearview mirror, I guess, because he sped up and started weaving all over the road. I didn't have a cell phone with me or I'd have called the police on the rez and had them pick him up. I followed them around the dirt roads. He started across a bridge that had been condemned. There were spring floods, huge ones, water coming right up over the wooden bridge."

He closed his eyes. "He went through the rotten boards on the side and right into the river. The car, with both of them inside, washed away." He lifted his head. His eyes were cold, dead. "They found the bodies almost two days later. The child was almost full-term, but they couldn't save him." He closed his eyes. "I graduated, joined the military, asked for combat because I wanted to die. That was almost eight years ago."

He felt a hand on his shoulder. He opened his eyes and looked into pale blue ones. "Listen, son," Jake said quietly, "you were trying to save her. In the process, a madman miscalculated his driving skills and wrecked his car. If it hadn't been that, he might have shot her and then shot himself. He might have died in a fight. She might have died from complications of childbirth. But, it would still have happened. When a life is meant to be over, it's over. That's God's business. You can't control life, Carson," he concluded.

"It's a fool's game to think you can even try. You're tormenting yourself over something that nobody could have prevented."

Carson averted his eyes. "Thanks," he said huskily.

"How did you end up with Cy?"

His eyes had a faraway look as he recalled that meeting. "I was doing black ops overseas," Carson said. "Political assassination, like Grier used to do." He drew in a long breath. "Cy and Eb Scott and Micah Steele were attached to the unit I was with as independent contractors. We went on missions together, discovered that we worked very well as a group. So I mustered out and signed on with them. It's been... interesting," he concluded with a mild laugh.

"I worked with mercs a time or two," Jake replied. He hesitated. "I also worked in covert assassination."

"I heard some gossip about that," Carson replied, without blowing the whistle on Rourke.

"She can't ever know," he said, nodding toward the other part of the house where Carlie was. "I gave it up for her. I had a crisis of conscience when her mother died. It took me to a bad place. A minister gave me the strength I needed to turn my life around, to do something productive with it." He leaned back with a sigh and a smile. "Of course, I'll starve doing it," he chuckled. "We're always broke, and there's always somebody who wants me fired because I say something offensive in a sermon. But I belong here now. Odd feeling, belonging. I never wanted it in the old days."

"Your wife," Carson said hesitantly. "Was she like Carlie?"

Jake's eyes narrowed with sorrow. "Exactly like

Carlie. I didn't believe in a damned thing. I had no
faith, no understanding of how people lived in small
towns. I wanted her. I took her. She got pregnant." His
face was like stone. "I married her to stop gossip. Her
mother was a slut. I mean, a real slut. She even tried
to seduce me! So everybody locally would have said,
'like mother like daughter,' you know?" He leaned
forward on his forearms. "I refused to stay here and
be a tamed animal. I provided for her and the child
when Carlie was born. I gave them everything except
love. It wasn't until Mary was dying that I realized
how much I had loved her, how much I had cost her
with my indifference. You think you killed your wife?
I know I killed mine. I've been trying ever since to
find a way to live with it, to make up for some of the
terrible things I've done. I'm still trying."

Carson was speechless. He just stared at the older
man, with honest compassion.

"If you're wondering," Jake added softly, "this is
a moral tale. I'm telling you about what happened
to me so that you won't repeat it with my daughter.
I think you have some idea of her feelings already."

Carson nodded solemnly. "I don't want to hurt
her."

"That makes two of us. You've lived the way I
used to. Women were like party favors to me, and I
had my share…"

Carson held up a hand. "Slight misconception."

"About…?"

Carson let out a breath and laughed softly. "I pick
up women. Beautiful women. I take them to the theater, the opera, out dancing, sailing on the lake, that
sort of thing." He hesitated. "Then I take them home

and leave them at the door," he said with a rueful smile.

Jake's confusion was evident.

"My wife was my first woman," Carson said with blunt honesty. "After she died, every woman I took out had her face, her body. I...couldn't," he choked out.

Jake put a firm hand on his shoulder, the only comfort he could offer.

"So other guys think I score every night, that I'm Don Juan." Carson laughed coolly. "I'm a counterfeit one. It makes me look heartless, so that honest women won't waste their time on me. But it backfired." He jerked his head toward the kitchen. "She thinks I'm dirty, because of my reputation. Funny thing, a visionary woman up in Wyoming told me that my past would threaten my future. She was very wise."

"Some obstacles can be overcome," Jake commented.

"So, you want me to go out and involve myself intimately with women...?"

"Shut up, or I'll put you down," Jake said in a mock growl. He laughed. "I could do it, too."

"I believe you," Carson said, with true admiration. "You haven't lost your edge."

"Where do you go from here?" Jake continued.

"When we wrap up this mess with Carlie's kidnapper, I don't know," Carson said honestly. "If I stay here, things will happen that will destroy her life, and maybe mine, too. I have to leave."

"For now, or for good?" Jake asked.

Carson drew in a breath. "I...don't know."

"If you graduated, then you got a degree, I take it?" Jake asked.

Carson pursed his lips. "Yes."

"You couldn't go into a normal profession?"

"It would mean a commitment I'm not sure I can make. I need time."

"Most life-changing decisions require it," Jake agreed. "What degree program were you pursuing?"

Carson smiled. "Medicine. I have my medical degree and I keep up my license. I just can't practice without doing the internship." He sighed. "I was going to specialize in internal medicine. I see so many heart patients with no resources, no money."

"On the reservation, you mean?"

"No. Here, in Jacobs County. I was talking to Lou Coltrain. She said they're short on physicians, not to mention physicians who specialize."

Jake searched the other man's face. He jerked his head toward the kitchen. "Going to tell her?"

Carson shook his head. "Not until I'm sure."

Jake smiled. "I knew I liked you."

Carson just laughed.

CARLIE WALKED HIM to the door. "Was Dad intimidating you?" she asked when they were outside on the front porch, with the door closed.

"No. He was listening. That's such a rare gift. Most people want to talk about themselves."

She nodded. "He's talked several people out of suicide over the years."

"He's a good man."

"He wasn't always," she replied. "I've heard a little

about his old life, although he won't tell me a thing himself." She looked up at him with raised eyebrows.

"It would be the end of my life to say a single word about it," he said firmly.

"Okay," she said, sighing.

He tilted her chin up and searched her green eyes. "What color were your mother's eyes?" he asked.

"They were brown," she said. "Like the center of a sunflower."

He traced her mouth with a long forefinger. "You're very like a sunflower yourself," he said softly. "Bright and cheerful, shining through storms."

Her lips parted on a surprised breath.

"I'm leaving, Carlie," he said softly.

She started to speak, but he put his fingers across her lips.

"You know how it is between us," he said bluntly. "I want you. If I stay here, I'll take you. And you'll let me," he said huskily.

She couldn't deny it.

"We'll be like your parents, one brokenhearted, one running away until tragedy strikes. I don't want to be the cause of that."

Her hand went up to his hard cheek. She stroked it gently, fighting tears. "You can't live a tame life. I understand."

It sounded harsh. Selfish. He scowled at the look on her face, dignity and courage mixed with heartbreak. It hurt him.

He drew her into his arms and held her, rocked her, in a tight embrace. "It wouldn't work. You know that."

She nodded against his chest.

He drew back finally and tilted her face up to his. It was streaked with hot tears that she couldn't help. He bent and kissed them away.

"I'll be around for a while," he promised. "Until we make sure we have the kidnapper in custody."

"Can they catch him, you think?"

"I believe so," he replied. "Just be careful."

She smiled. "I usually am."

"And if someone shows up and says your dad's been in a wreck…" he began.

She pulled her cell phone out of her jeans. "I'll call him up first."

He grinned. "That's my girl." He bent and brushed his mouth softly over hers, savoring the smile she couldn't help.

He left her on the porch and drove away. She stood there until she couldn't see the car anymore.

ROURKE HAD FINALLY convinced Matthew Helm that it was safe to trust him. He did a few discreet jobs—mostly by warning the people he was supposed to muscle first, and having them cooperate—and was finally handed something useful. Useful for the case against Helm, at least.

"I want you to go talk to Charro," Helm told Rourke. He pursed his lips, deep in thought. "That Ballenger man who's running against me has a following. He's local. People know him and like him. He's got three sons. One of them, Terry, is still in high school. I want you two to find a way to plant some cocaine on him. Put it in his locker at school, in his car and tip off the cops, whatever. I don't care what you do, just make sure you do it. I'll handle the press. I'll have one of my campaign workers release the collar, to make sure it doesn't come directly from me and seem like I'm slinging mud. Got it?"

"Oh, yeah, Boss, I got it," Rourke said with a nod.

"Get going, then."

"You bet."

Rourke was too old a hand to go straight to Calhoun Ballenger or even to Cash Grier's office, much less up to San Antonio to see Rick Marquez. He wasn't trusting his cell phone, either, because Helm could very easily find out who he'd talked to recently.

So he went to Cotillo.

Charro Mendez gave him a careful scrutiny. "So Helm trusts you, does he?" he asked.

"He doesn't really trust anybody," Rourke replied. "Neither do I," he added, hands in his jeans pockets. "It doesn't pay, in this line of work. But he trusts me enough to relay messages, I believe."

"And what message does he wish you to bring me?" Mendez asked, propping his booted feet on his own desk in the mayor's office.

"He wants some product planted in a particular place," he replied, leaning back against the wall.

"Ah. Something to do with a rival in the political arena, *si?*"

"Exactly."

"This is not a problem. Who does he expect to perform this task, *señor,* you or me?"

"He didn't say," Rourke replied. "He told me you'd supply the product. I assume that means I'll have to plant it."

"I see." The man grinned, displaying gold-filled teeth. "I would assume that he would not expect a man in my position to perform such a menial chore, however."

"Exactly," Rourke said, nodding.

"Excellent! I will have the…product," he said, "delivered to you across the border. When?"

"He didn't tell me that, either. But it would be convenient to do two Saturdays from now," Rourke continued. "There's going to be a dance at the high school. I can sneak it into the glove compartment of the boy's vehicle while he's inside the building."

"I could almost feel sorry for his father. I also have sons." His face darkened. "I would kill someone who did that to me. But these rich men in Texas—" he waved a hand "—they can buy justice. I have no doubt the politician can have the charges dropped. The publicity, however, will be very damaging I think."

"I agree."

"Give me a cell phone number where my man can reach you," Charro said.

Rourke handed him a slip of paper. "It's a throwaway phone," he told the other man. "I'll answer it this once and then toss it in a trash bin somewhere. It will never be found or traced to me."

"A wise precaution."

"I try to be wise, always," Rourke replied.

"Then we agree. I will have my man contact you within the week."

"I'm certain my boss will express his appreciation for your help."

"Indeed he will," Charro returned thoughtfully. "Many, many times, whenever I ask." He smiled coldly. "I will have him, how do you say? Over a barrel."

"A big one," Rourke chuckled.

"Very big. Yes."

CHAPTER TWELVE

ROURKE COULDN'T RISK being seen with any law enforcement official, or overheard talking to one, not with things at this critical juncture. He called Carson.

"Have you been to see Marquez yet?" he asked quickly.

"Well, no," Carson replied. "Something came up over at Cy's ranch…"

"This is urgent. I want you to go see Marquez right now. I've got some news."

So Carson drove up to San Antonio to relay the information Rourke had transferred over to another throwaway phone, a pair he and Carson had arranged at an earlier time.

Rick Marquez did a double take when he saw Carson. The other man was almost his age, with the same olive complexion and long, black hair in a ponytail.

"Lieutenant Marquez?" Carson greeted the other man when the clerk showed him in.

"That would be me. Amazing," Rick mused. "We could almost be twins."

Carson smiled faintly. "Only if you turned out to be from South Dakota."

He shrugged. "Sorry. Mexico. Well, that's where my father was born. He's now president of a small

Latin American nation. Sit down." He offered his visitor a chair.

"I assume you have regular checks for bugs in here?" Carson asked, glancing around.

"My father-in-law runs the CIA," Rick told him as he dropped into his aging desk chair. "He might bug us, but nobody else would dare. What can I do for you?"

"There have been some new developments that you might not have heard about," Carson began.

"Jake Blair's daughter was kidnapped, you and her father freed her and took out two guards, the kidnapper got away," Rick rattled off. "I know everything."

"Not quite," Carson replied. He pursed his lips. "How about coffee?"

"We've got a pot right over there…"

Carson shook his head. "Real coffee. Come on."

Rick was puzzled, but he caught on pretty quickly that Carson didn't trust telling him in the office.

They drove to a specialty coffee shop and moved to a corner table.

"Sorry, I know you think it's secure in your office, but this information could get Rourke killed if it slips out somehow. He's working for Matthew Helm and there's a plot underway. But let me tell you this first. Carlie Blair's kidnapper was wearing a watch. An expensive watch that chimed an old Joan Jett rock tune—"

"You're kidding!" Rick exploded. "We thought the watch burned up with the man who was wearing it, in Wyoming!"

"No," Carson replied. "I was there when he died. There was no watch on him. The local police were trying to backtrack him to any motels he'd stayed at. I assume his boss's men got to the room first."

"What a stroke of luck," Rick said with a short laugh. "That watch, if we can get our hands on it, is the key to a murder and perhaps the end of a truly evil political career."

"The problem is that we don't know where the watch is. The kidnapper has vanished into thin air."

"We have to find him."

"I agree. Rourke's working on it. He's wormed his way into the political process. That's why I'm here."

"Okay. Shoot."

"Helm sent Rourke over the border today to arrange for the delivery of some cocaine. Enough to charge someone with intent to distribute. The idea is for Rourke to plant it in the glove compartment of Calhoun Ballenger's youngest son, Terry, at a school dance in two weeks."

Rick's face hardened. "What a low-down, dirty, mean…"

"All of the above," Carson agreed grimly. "But we know it's going down, and when, and where. Believe me, this is going to send Helm up the river. All we have to do is set a trap and spring it."

"Why isn't Rourke here?" Rick asked.

"Because he's being watched, and probably listened to, as well. We used throwaway phones to communicate, just to exchange this much information."

"And you think my own office isn't secure?" Rick sounded a little belligerent.

"This man has ex-cops working for him," Carson explained. "They'll know all the tricks. It isn't far-fetched to assume he has a pipeline into your office. The missing evidence the assistant D.A. had on Helm, for example, that was destroyed right here in impound?"

Rick let out a heavy sigh. "I get your point. I've been careless."

"Don't sell yourself short. Helm has some pros on his team. His main enforcer is gone, but he's got others. One is an ex-cop who got fired for using excessive violence. Carlie's kidnapper. He knocked a perp down the stairs when he caught him beating a child."

"Know where?" Rick asked suddenly.

"Carlie said the kidnapper had an accent, like you hear in those old gangster movies of the '30s and '40s."

"Chicago, maybe, New Jersey, New York…" Rick's eyes were thoughtful. "I can send out some feelers to people I know in departments there, ask around. Some of the veterans might remember something."

"Good idea. Meanwhile, Rourke's on the job."

"Should we warn Calhoun Ballenger?" Rick wondered aloud.

"If he knows, he'll warn his son, and his son might mention it to a classmate," Carson replied. "It's better to keep him in the dark. We'll make sure his son is watched and protected."

"Don't toss any hand grenades around," Rick warned.

Carson sighed as he stood up. "My past will haunt me."

"Actually, if it was up to me, you'd get a medal," Rick said. "So many dead kids because rich men want to make a profit off illegal drugs." He shook his head. "Crazy world."

"Getting crazier all the time."

"Thanks for the heads-up," Rick said, shaking hands with the other man. "By the way," he added, "nice hairstyle." He grinned. Carson grinned back.

FRED BALDWIN WAS WORRIED. Mr. Helm had promised that he was going to protect him, that he was in no danger of getting arrested for kidnapping Carlie Blair. But he knew from painful experience that Mr. Helm didn't keep many of the promises he made. That was, unless he promised to get you for crossing him. He kept all those promises.

He fingered the expensive watch that he still had, that Mr. Helm didn't know about. He knew why the watch was important. It had belonged to Richard Martin, who burned up in Wyoming after trying to kill two women. He'd killed an assistant prosecutor for that watch. But Martin was dead. And Fred had the watch.

Mr. Helm didn't know that he hadn't destroyed it. He liked the watch. That chime it sounded wasn't a song he knew, but it was okay. It was the two-tone gold on the timepiece, very expensive, and that made him feel good. His father had been a low-level worker at an automobile plant in Detroit. His mother had kept a day care in their home. There were four kids and never enough money. His father drank it up as fast as he got paid.

Two of his brothers were in jail. His oldest brother had died last year. His mother had finally left his father, and went to live with a sister in California. He hadn't heard from her in a long time. She'd loved her oldest child best, the one who died. She hadn't wanted the others. She thought they were too stupid to be her kids. She said so, often.

The only time she'd liked Fred was when he became a policeman. Finally, one of her kids besides her favorite might actually amount to something.

Then he got arrested and fired and she turned her back on him. Well, it was no surprise.

Fred didn't like women much. His mother was cold as ice, heartless. Maybe his father had made her that way. Maybe she was that way to begin with.

He liked that little woman he'd kidnapped, though. She should have hated him. He'd terrified her. But she'd been sorry for him when he told her about his father beating him up. He felt bad that he'd scared her. He was glad to know she'd escaped, that her father hadn't been killed.

Luckily for him, the two would-be assassins got blamed for the screwup. Mr. Helm hadn't hired them in person, so he wouldn't be connected with them.

On the other hand, Fred had hired them for the person who was contracted by Richard Martin to kill Reverend Blair, on Mr. Helm's orders. If they talked, Fred was going to be the one who'd go to prison.

Well, that little woman knew what he looked like, and he had no reason to believe she wouldn't have told the law about him. He knew from something Mr. Helm had let slip once that Carlie Blair had a photographic memory. Mr. Helm said not to worry about it, that he'd make sure Fred was okay. But Fred had seen what had happened to the man Richard Martin had hired to kill Carlie Blair, the same woman he'd kidnapped. Martin had poisoned the would-be killer, right under the cops' noses, and apparently on Mr. Helm's orders.

Funny, that he'd been ordered to kidnap Carlie, when Richard Martin had been ordered to hire somebody to kill her. Not only that, when the first killer failed, Martin had hired someone else to finish the job. But the person he was taking orders from had sent him to kidnap Carlie to draw the reverend out to be killed.

Why did Mr. Helm want the preacher dead? As far as Fred knew, the preacher didn't have anything on Mr. Helm at all. And what Carlie knew didn't matter before, because she remembered Richard Martin and he was dead.

She'd remember Fred now, though. That would be a motive. But they were trying to kill her father!

Well, his opinion was that Richard Martin had been so high on drugs that he hadn't made it clear who was supposed to be the victim. And his hire, to put it politely, was as crazy a person as Fred had ever met. He'd been sent to kidnap Carlie on that person's orders, to strike at a time when she was unprotected at her home. He shook his head. It was nuts. Worse, he was the one who was being set up to take the fall.

He looked at the watch again. He'd never been tempted to talk about it. But after what he'd just overheard Mr. Helm say to his new enforcer, that South African guy, he had to do something. The South African man was going to plant drugs on the son of a politician who was the only serious contender for the U.S. Senate seat. If the man had been a stranger, he might not have cared. But Fred knew Calhoun Ballenger.

He'd seen the cattleman a few months ago, coming out of a downtown hotel where some cattlemen's conference was being held. Two men were waiting in the shadows. One of them was armed. When Mr. Ballenger started down the street, they jumped him.

He was a big man, and he handled himself well, but the man with the gun struck him in the head.

Fred didn't like bullies. He'd never been one, for all his size, and he hated seeing anybody pick on an unarmed man. It was why he'd become a cop in the first place years ago. So without really thinking about it, he jumped in, subdued the man with the pistol and knocked out his accomplice.

He'd left them in the alley and dropped a dime on them while he took Mr. Ballenger down the street to the emergency room of a local hospital.

He didn't dare tell the cattleman who he was, but Mr. Ballenger had wanted to do something for him, to pay him back for the kindness. He'd looked at Fred with admiration, with respect. Those were things sadly lacking in his life. It had made him feel good about himself for the first time in years. He'd waved away the older man's thanks and left the hospital without identifying himself.

Mr. Ballenger's son was going to be targeted by Matthew Helm, and Fred didn't want to be any part of it. But how was he going to warn the man without incriminating himself and his boss? Mr. Helm would turn on him, make sure he went to prison for the kidnapping if he lifted a finger.

He couldn't go to the law, as much as he'd have liked to. But there was one other possibility. This watch was important. The right people could do good things with it. And suddenly, right in front of him, was the very girl he'd kidnapped...

CARLIE WAS PUTTING her groceries into the back of the pickup truck when she came face-to-face with the man who'd kidnapped her.

"Don't scream," Fred said gruffly, but he didn't threaten her. He was wearing a raincoat and a hat, looking around cautiously. "You got to help me."

"Help you? You kidnapped me!" she blurted out.

"Yeah, I'm sorry," he said heavily. "I got in over my head and I can't get out. I can't go to the law. They're always watching. Mr. Helm is going to plant drugs on Mr. Ballenger's youngest son," he said hastily, peering over the truck bed to make sure nobody was nearby. "He's going to try to get him out of that Senate race."

"Terry?" she exclaimed. "He's going to try to set Terry Ballenger up?"

"Yeah. That South African guy who works for him, he's going to plant the evidence," he said quickly. "You got to tell your boss."

She was absolutely dumbfounded. She couldn't even find words. He didn't know that Rourke was working with the authorities and she didn't dare tell him. But he was risking his very life to try and save Calhoun's son from prosecution. It really touched her.

His dark eyes narrowed. "I'm so sorry for what I done," he said, grimacing. "You're a nice girl."

Her face softened. "Why do you work for that rat?" she wondered.

"He's got stuff on me," he explained. "I can't ever get another job. But I can help you." He took off the watch, looked at it admiringly for just a few seconds and grimaced. "Never had nothing so fancy in my whole life," he said, putting it in her hands. "He told me to bust it up and throw it away. I couldn't. It was so special. Anyway, that watch belonged to some prosecutor that had evidence on Mr. Helm. Richard Martin killed him. It was his watch. Martin took the watch and then killed people who remembered he had it."

"He tried to have me killed," she told him.

"Yeah, and then he hired somebody to kill your dad." He shook his head. "See, Martin was high on drugs, out of his mind. I think he got confused, gave the contract out on the wrong person. I think it was supposed to be you, again, but we got sent after your dad."

"You know who's behind it," she said, surprised.

He nodded solemnly. "Mr. Helm's behind it. But the contract was given out by Martin."

"Who's got it?" Carlie asked. "Please?"

He searched her eyes. "Some pretty blond woman up in San Antonio. I didn't know until a day ago. Funny, she didn't even know about my connection to Mr. Helm. She asked around for some muscle to help with a hit, and the other guys got hired. One of them was a man I knew, he said I could do it on the side and Mr. Helm would never have to know." He laughed coldly. "Well, Mr. Helm knew already. He just didn't tell us."

"Blond woman…?"

"Yeah. She used to work for Mr. Helm, years ago, when he started out in the local rackets."

Blond woman. Hit woman. Contract killer. Somebody who knew that Carlie would be home alone on that Friday night. Somebody with ties to Jacobsville.

"Do you know her name?" Carlie asked.

He frowned. "Funny name. La…La…something."

Carlie's blood froze. "Lanette?"

"Yeah. That's it. How'd you know?"

Now wasn't the time to fill him in on personal information. But it meant that Carson could be in real danger if Lanette suspected that he might blow her cover. She'd be in jeopardy if her link to the kidnapper here was ever found out.

She slid the watch into her pocket, gnawed her lower lip. She looked up into his broad, swarthy face. "They'll kill you if they find out you gave me the watch."

His dark eyes were quiet and sad. "I don't care," he said. "I never done anything good in my whole life except for being a cop, and I even fouled that up. You were nice to me." He forced a smile. "Nobody ever liked me."

She put a small hand on his arm. "How do you feel about small towns?"

He frowned. "What do you mean?"

"You have to trust me," she said quickly.

"Why?"

"Because I'm going to do something that will seem crazy."

"Really? What?"

She threw back her head and screamed.

"JUST RELAX," CASH GRIER told his prisoner under his breath. "This isn't what it seems. You may think she sold you out, but we're trying to save you. Your boss will think you're being arrested for assault."

Fred Baldwin went along, stunned but willing to cooperate on the off chance that he might not have to spend his whole life in federal prison. "Okay, Boss," he said. "It's your play."

Cash marched him out to the police car, put Carlie in front beside him, and left a patrolman to take her truck home and explain things to her father.

ONCE THEY WERE in the police station, Cash took Fred into his office and removed the handcuffs. He put Fred's automatic in his desk drawer and locked it. Carlie produced the watch out of her pocket.

"And I've got you filing," Cash said, shaking his head at her. "You should be wearing a badge, kid."

"No, no," she protested. "He—" she pointed at Fred "—just turned state's evidence. So to speak. He can make the connections. But we have to get word to Carson," she added quickly. "His girlfriend is the woman who hired Fred and the other two guys to kidnap me and kill my dad."

"Why did you give Carlie the watch?" Cash asked Fred. "You had everything to lose!"

"She was nice to me," he murmured, glancing at Carlie. "They tried to kill her dad, with my help. And now they're trying to frame Mr. Ballenger's son. I took down two hoods who jumped him in San Antonio. Never seen a rich man so grateful for just a little help. I liked him. It's not right, to punish a man's son because the father's just doing something good for the community. I got tired of being on the wrong side of the law, I guess. I thought if I gave her the watch, she'd give it to you and maybe you could stop Mr. Helm before he hurts somebody else."

"I'll stop it, all right," Cash said. He frowned. "But it's suicide on your part. You think Helm wouldn't know who gave us the watch?"

Fred smiled sadly. "I ain't got no place to go, nobody who cares about me. I thought, maybe I could do one good thing before he took me out."

"You're not going anywhere," Cash told him firmly.

"And you do have somebody who cares about you," Carlie said firmly. She took the big man's hand in her own and held it. "Right here."

Incredibly, tears ran down his wide cheeks.

"Now, don't do that, you'll have me doing it, too," Carlie muttered. She pulled a tissue out of her pocket and wiped his eyes and then wiped her own.

"I'm Italian," Fred muttered, embarrassed. "We don't hide what we feel."

"You'd better let me get this on paper," Cash said, smiling. "Coffee?"

"Thanks."

"I'll make a pot," Carlie said. She glanced at Cash. "Carson…" she began.

"I'm two steps ahead of you," Cash promised, picking up the telephone.

CARSON HAD HIS phone turned off, which was a pity. Lanette had already heard from an informant that Fred Baldwin was in custody down in Jacobsville, Texas, for apparently confronting that pitiful little secretary that Carson was so crazy about.

She was livid. Fred was stupid. It was why she'd

hired him, because he was expendable and too dumb to realize she was setting him up to take the fall for her when she killed Jake Blair.

But somewhere along the line, he'd had a flash of genius. He was probably spilling his guts. They'd be after her in a heartbeat. That little secretary would be gloating, laughing, feeling so superior to the beautiful woman who was obviously her superior in every single department.

Fred had flubbed his assignment. His cohorts were in jail. Now he'd been arrested, too. She'd been paid for a job that she hadn't completed. Word would get around that she was incompetent. She'd never get another contract. Worse, Fred would implicate her to save himself. She'd be running from the law for the rest of her life. The perks of her profession, all that nice money, her spectacular wardrobe, everything would be lost because her own plan had backfired on her.

Even Matthew Helm had refused to help her. Oh, he made promises, but his back was to the wall right now, and he was trying to save his own skin. He had to know that Fred would rat on him.

Well, she reasoned, at least she was going to have one bit of satisfaction on the run. That stupid little hick in Jacobsville wasn't going to get to gloat. Her feelings for Carson were so apparent that a blind woman could see them. Carlie loved Carson. So Lanette would go to prison for kidnapping and assault and conspiracy, and little Carlie would end up with Carson.

No way. If she lost Carson, for whom she had a

real unrequited passion, Carlie wasn't going to have
him. She'd make sure of it.

She reached into the purse she carried to make
sure the automatic was where it was supposed to be.

"I can't stay long," she told Carson, who was impatient to be gone and seemed surprised and irritated to
have found her at his apartment door when he arrived.

"Just as well," he said curtly, "because I have
someplace to go and I'm already late."

"Couldn't we have just one cup of coffee first?" she
asked, smiling softly. "I found out something about
that attempt on the preacher."

"You did? How?" he asked, instantly suspicious.

"Well, let's just sit down and talk, and I'll tell you
what I know," she purred.

CASH PHONED ROURKE, using the number Rourke had
sent him. "Carson's in danger," he told the other man.
"His blond girlfriend is the contract killer Richard
Martin hired to take out Reverend Blair."

"What!" Rourke exploded.

"I don't have time to go into the particulars," Cash
said. "Suffice it to say I have a witness," he glanced
at Fred, who was smiling as Carlie handed him a mug
of black coffee, "and no time to discuss it. Do you
know where he is?"

"At the apartment he rented," Rourke said, shell-
shocked. "In San Antonio."

"Can you get in touch with him?"

Rourke let out a breath. "No. Not unless I do it in
the open."

"Rourke will have to blow his cover to call Carson, they're monitoring his phone," Cash said aloud.

"I'll do it," Carlie said urgently. "Give me the number."

"Rourke, give me the number," Cash said.

He did. Cash scribbled it down and handed it to Carlie.

"What's this written in, Sanskrit?" she exclaimed.

Cash glared at her, took it back and made modifications. "It's just numbers, for God's sake," he said irritably

"Sir, your handwriting is hands-down, without a doubt, the worst I ever saw in my life," she muttered as she pushed numbers into her cell phone.

"Hear, hear!" Rourke said over the phone. "I have to go. I'll let you know about Ballenger's son as soon as I have word." He hung up.

Carlie held her breath as the phone rang once, twice, three times...

"Hello?"

Carlie recognized the voice. It wasn't Carson's. It was hers. Lanette's.

She swallowed, hard. "I want to speak to Carson," she said.

"Oh, do you? I'm sorry," Lanette said in a silky sweet tone. "I'm afraid he's indisposed at the moment. Really indisposed." She laughed out loud. "I can't have him. But, now, neither can you, you little backward country hick! And you can spend hours, days, just watching him die!" She cut off the connection.

"She's with him," Carlie said with an economy of words. "You have to get someone to him, quick!"

Cash was already punching in numbers.

While her boss worked to get a medical team

to Carson, Carlie hovered, tears running down her cheeks.

"You sit down," Fred said softly. "They'll get there in time. It will be all right. Everything will be all right."

She just looked at him, her face that of a terrified child. It hit him in the heart so hard that he let out a breath, as if it had been a blow to his stomach.

He put down his coffee, got up, picked her up and sat down with her in his lap, wrapped up in his big arms, sobbing her heart out on his broad shoulder. He patted her back as if she were five years old, smiling. "It's okay, honey," he said softly. "It's okay."

Cash watched them and mentally shook his head. What a waste. That man had a heart as big as the world, and he was going to take the fall for that crooked politician unless Cash could find him a way out. That might just be possible. But first he had to save Carson. And that mission had a less hopeful outcome.

THE PARAMEDICS HAD to wait while San Antonio PD broke down a door to get inside, on Lieutenant Marquez's orders. Once the way was clear, they rushed in with a gurney. They found Carson in the kitchen, facedown on the floor. He was unconscious and bleeding from a wound in his chest. There was a lump on his head, as well.

One paramedic looked at the other and winced. This was not going to be an easy run. He keyed his mike and started relaying medical information. It was complicated by the fact that the victim apparently had no ID on him.

BECAUSE FRED BALDWIN could make all the right connections to Matthew Helm, and because they knew about the fate of the former failed hit man, Cash Grier refused to turn him over to the authorities in San Antonio, where Helm would have to be arrested and tried.

"You'll get him over my dead body," Cash assured Rick Marquez on the telephone. "I'm not risking his life. He's too valuable. You come down here and take a deposition, bring all the suits you need and add your district attorney to the list. I'll give you free access. But he is not, under any circumstances, leaving Jacobsville!"

Rick drew in a breath. "Cash, you're putting me in a tough spot."

"No, I'm not. My cousin is still the state attorney general. He'll pull some strings for me if I ask him," Cash added. "Besides that," he said with a whimsical smile, "I have a few important connections that I don't talk about."

"You and my father-in-law would get along," Marquez chuckled. "All right. I'll get the process started. But I'm going to need that watch."

"No way in hell," Cash said pleasantly.

"It's state's evidence!"

"Yes, it is. And evidence doesn't walk out of *my* property room," he added, emphasizing the "my."

"Rub it in," Rick muttered. "Carson already did, in fact." He sobered. "They have him in intensive care."

"I know. My secretary is up there with him. Or as close as she can get," Cash said heavily.

"So I heard. She's parked in the corridor next to the emergency room surgical suite and won't move."

"Stubborn."

"Yes, and very much in love, apparently," Rick replied solemnly. "It won't end well. I know the type, and so do you. Even if he makes it out of the hospital, he'll never settle down."

"Are you a betting man?" Cash mused.

"Why?"

"Because several years ago, you'd have laid better odds that I'd never marry and live in a small Texas town. Wouldn't you?"

Rick laughed. "Point taken." He hesitated. "Well, can we at least see the watch and photograph it?"

"Mi casa es su casa," Cash said smugly. "My house is your house."

"I'll bring an SUV full of people down. May I assume that the state crime lab has already dusted the watch for prints?"

"Our own Alice Jones Fowler did the job herself. She does still work as an investigator for state crime," Cash reminded him, "although she lives here with her husband, Harley, on their ranch. She's not only good, she's unforgettable."

"Nobody who ever met Alice would forget her," Rick agreed. "She even makes autopsies bearable."

"No argument there. Anyway, the watch is adequately documented, even for a rabid prosecutor. And you're going to need the best you've got for Helm," he added quietly. "The man is a maniac, and I don't mean that kindly. He'll sacrifice anybody to save himself. Even assistant district attorneys."

"You don't know how much I'd love to tie him to

that murder," Rick said. "The watch is the key to it all. Good luck for us that it wasn't destroyed."

"Even better luck that the man wearing it decided to also turn state's evidence. He can put Helm away for life."

"You've got him in the county jail, I hope?"

Cash hesitated. "Someplace a little safer."

"Safer than the lockup?" Rick burst out laughing. "What, is he living with you and Tippy and Tris?"

"Let's just say that he's got unique company. I'll give you access with the D.A. when you get down here."

"This is going to be an interesting trip," Rick predicted. "See you soon."

"Copy that."

THE HOSPITAL WAS very clean. Carlie noted that the floors must be mopped frequently, because when she got up to use the ladies' room, the back of her jeans didn't even have dust. She knew she was irritating the staff. Security had talked to her once. But she refused to move. They could throw her out, but that was the only way she was leaving. Her heart was in that intensive care emergency surgery unit, strapped to machines and tubes, fighting for his life. They could put her in jail, after, she didn't care. But she wasn't moving until they could assure her that Carson would live. And she told them so.

CHAPTER THIRTEEN

THE NEUROLOGIST ON Carson's case, Dr. Howard Deneth, paused at the nurses' station in ICU, where they'd taken Carson an hour ago, and glanced toward the cubicle where Carson was placed.

"She's still there?" he mused.

The nurse nodded. "She won't leave. The nurses called security, but she said they'd have to drag her out. She wasn't belligerent. She just stared them down, with tears rolling down her cheeks the whole time."

"Unusual in these days, devotion like that," the doctor remarked. "Are they married?"

"Not that we know. Of course, we don't know much, except what she was able to tell us. He doesn't carry identification."

"I noticed. Some sort of covert work, I imagine, classified stuff."

"That's what we thought."

Dr. Deneth looked down at the nurse over his glasses. "He's deteriorating," he said heavily. "The wound was superficial. There was minor head trauma, but really not enough to account for his condition. However, head injuries are tricky. Sometimes even minor ones can end fatally." He pursed his lips. "Let her in the room."

"Sir?"

"On my authority," he added. "I'll write it on the chart, in case you have any flak from upper echelons. They can talk to me if they don't like it."

The nurse didn't speak. She just smiled.

CARLIE HELD HIS HAND. She'd been shocked when the nurse came to tell her that she could have a comfortable chair beside Carson's bed. One of the other nurses had been curt to the point of rudeness when she tried to make Carlie leave the hall.

She guessed that nurses were like policemen. Some were kindhearted and personable, and some were rigorously by-the-book. She worked for a policeman who'd thrown the book away when he took the job. He believed in the rule of law, but he wasn't a fanatic for the letter of it. Case in point was big Fred Baldwin, who was now living in a safe but undisclosed location, so that he didn't end up dead before he could testify against his former boss.

No arrests had been made yet, that she was aware of. She did know that they had an all points bulletin out for the blond woman who'd left Carson in this condition. She really hoped the woman resisted arrest, and then she bit her tongue and said a silent apology. That wasn't really a wish that a religious person should make.

Her father had come to see Carson a few minutes ago. The nurses had at least let him into the room. But when he came out he was somber and although he tried to get Carlie to come home, he understood why she wouldn't. He'd done the same when her mother was in the hospital dying. He'd refused to leave, too.

Carlie supposed he'd seen cases like Carson's many times. Judging by the look on his face, the results had been fatal. He reminded Carlie that God's will had precedence over man's desires. He wanted to stay with his daughter, but she reminded him that having two people in the corridor to trip over would probably be the straw that broke the camel's back for the nursing staff. He went home, leaving Carlie's cell phone—which she'd forgotten—with her so that she could keep him posted.

Unknown to her, one of Rourke's buddies was nearby, posing as a family member in the intensive care waiting room. Just in case Helm had any ideas about hurting Carlie. It was a long shot, but nobody wanted to leave anything to chance.

Meanwhile, the forces of good were coalescing against Matthew Helm. He knew they had Baldwin in custody, and the man was probably spilling his guts. But his attorney could take Baldwin apart on the stand. The man had a criminal record, which is how he was pressured into taking Helm's jobs in the first place. He had a conviction for assault when he was a cop in Chicago. That could be used against his testimony.

After all, Helm's hands were clean. He'd never broken the law. They might have Baldwin and a lot of hearsay evidence, but there was nothing that could connect him to the murder of the assistant D.A. He'd made sure of it.

So now he was free of that worry, and he could concentrate on the Senate race. He was in Washington, D.C., of course, learning his way around, making contacts, making use of all the connections that

Charro Mendez had in the country's capital. He liked
the power. He liked the privilege. He liked bumping
elbows at cocktail parties with famous people. Yes,
he was going to enjoy this job, and nobody was taking it away from him in that special election in May!

What he didn't know was that Fred, like Carlie,
had an excellent memory for dates and places. With
it, the authorities could check telephone records,
check stubs, gas receipts, restaurant tickets, even
motel logs to see where Helm was at particular times
and with particular people. They could now connect
him directly to the assistant district attorney's murder through Richard Martin because of the theft of
the watch. It went from the assistant D.A.'s body to
Richard Martin, who worked for Helm, to Fred Baldwin whom Helm had sent to retrieve it, right back to
Helm himself.

The San Antonio D.A.'s office put together a network, a framework, that they were going to use to
hang Matthew Helm from. The watch was going to
put Helm away for a very long time. Added to Baldwin's testimony, it would be the trial of the century.
It had all the elements: intrigue, murder, politics,
kidnapping—it was almost a catalog of the deadly
sins. And now, with Rourke ordered to set up Calhoun Ballenger's youngest son—with cocaine provided by Charro Mendez—a concrete link between
the two men had been formed. The trap was about
to spring shut.

Fred had been kept in the dark about Rourke's true
allegiance. What he didn't know, he couldn't accidentally let slip.

"TONIGHT'S THE NIGHT," Rourke told Cash Grier on a secure line. "Seven o'clock. Helm himself ordered the plant and I have it on tape."

"Sheer genius," Cash announced. "We're going to catch you in the act." He groaned. "Calhoun Ballenger is going to use me for a mop when he finds out that his son was the bait."

"I'll save you," Rourke promised. "But it's what we need to make the case."

"Good thing we spoke to Blake Kemp about this before you agreed to do it," Cash added.

"Yes, the Jacobs County D.A. should be in on such matters. Just to keep yours truly out of the slammer," Rourke chuckled. "Don't be late, okay? I'm not absolutely sure that Helm won't assign backup in case I get cold feet or he suspects I'm not reliable."

"No worries. We've got one of Eb Scott's men watching you, and one with Carlie up in San Antonio."

"How is he?" Rourke asked.

"No change," Cash said heavily. "Well, one change. They finally let Carlie into the room with him."

"Probably because they got tired of tripping over her in the hall," Rourke remarked. "Stubborn girl."

"Very." Cash's voice lowered. "It doesn't look good. Head injuries…well, you know."

"Any luck turning up that deadly blonde?" Rourke added coldly.

"Not yet, but I'm told they have a lead. She ordered the kidnapping. That's a federal offense. It means my brother gets involved." There was real pride in his tone. "Nobody gets away from Garon."

"Maybe they'll hit her over the head and shoot her while she's lying helpless," Rourke said icily.

"In real life, it doesn't go down like that." Cash sighed. "Pity."

"Yeah. Okay, I'll see you later."

"Be careful," Cash cautioned.

"Always."

CARLIE HELD CARSON'S hand tightly in both of her small ones. He had beautiful hands, the skin smooth and firm, the nails immaculately clean and neatly trimmed. No jewelry. No marks where jewelry might ever have been. She remembered the feel of his hands on her skin, the tenderness, the strength of them. It seemed like an age ago.

The neurosurgeon had come in to check Carson's eyes, and how his pupils reacted to light. He was kind to Carlie, telling her that sometimes it took a little time for a patient to regain consciousness after a blow like the one Carson had sustained. If they were lucky, there wouldn't be too much impairment afterward. He didn't add that the head trauma didn't seem damaging enough to account for the continued unconsciousness. That bothered him.

The head trauma being the predominant condition, Carson was in the ICU on the neurological ward. The gunshot injury, by comparison, was far less dangerous and had a better prognosis. That damage had been quickly repaired by the trauma surgeon.

She only half heard him. She wanted him to tell her that Carson would wake up and get up and be all right. The doctor couldn't do that. Even he, with his

long experience, had no guarantees. At the moment,
they weren't certain why he was still unconscious.

Carson had been in shock when they transported
him, but now he was still breathing well on his own,
his levels were good, BP was satisfactory. In fact, he
should be awake and aware. But he wasn't. They'd
done a CT scan in the emergency room. It did not
show extensive brain injury. There was some minor
bruising, but nothing that should account for the continued unconsciousness.

Blood had been sent to the lab for analysis, but it
was a busy day and a few patients in far worse shape
were in the queue ahead of him.

The doctor asked, again, if Carson had any next
of kin in the area. She shook her head. Carson was
from the Wapiti Ridge Sioux Reservation in South
Dakota, but she didn't know anything about that part
of his life. Neither did anybody else locally.

He suggested that it might be wise to contact the
authorities there and inquire about relatives who
might know more about his health history. So Carlie
phoned Cash Grier and asked him to do it. She was
too upset to talk to anyone. His medical history would
certainly be useful, but he was fighting for his life
from a set of circumstances other than illness. She
prayed and prayed. Please let him live, she asked rev-
erently, even if he married some pretty sweet young
woman from his hometown and Carlie never saw him
again.

She whispered it while she was holding Carson's
hand. Whispered it over and over again while tears
ran hot and salty down her pale cheeks.

"You just can't die," she choked, squeezing his

hand very hard. "Not like this. Not because of that sick, stupid, beautiful blond female pit viper!" She swallowed, wiping tears away with the tips of her fingers. "Listen, you can go home and marry some nice, experienced girl who'll be everything you want, and it will be all right. I want you to be happy. I want you to live!" She sniffed. "I know I'm not what you need. I've always known it. I'm not asking for anything at all. I just want you to live until you're old and grayheaded and have a houseful of kids and grandkids." She managed a smile. "You can tell them stories about now, about all the exotic places you went, the things you saw and did. You'll be a local legend."

He shifted. Her heart jumped. For an instant she thought he might be regaining consciousness. But he made a soft sound and began to breathe more deeply. Her hands tightened around his. "You just have to live," she whispered. "You have to."

While she was whispering to him, the door opened and a woman with jet-black hair and black eyes came into the room. She was wearing a white jacket and had a stethoscope around her neck. She glanced at Carlie and smiled gently.

"No change, huh?" she asked softly.

Carlie swallowed. Her eyes were bloodshot. She shook her head.

The newcomer took something out of her pocket and removed Carlie's hand, just for a few seconds, long enough to press a small braided circle with a cross inside into Carson's palm.

"What is it?" Carlie asked in a whisper. "It looks like a prayer wheel…and those are Lakota colors…"

"You know that?" the visitor asked, and the smile

grew bigger. "It is a prayer wheel. Those are our colors," she added. "Red and yellow, black and white,
the colors of the four directions."

"It may be just what he needs," Carlie replied, fold-
ing his hand back inside both of hers, with the prayer
circle inside it. "Are you a *wicasa wakan?*" she added,
her eyes wide with curiosity as she referenced a holy
person in the tribe who could heal the sick.

"A *wasichu,* and you know that?" she laughed,
using the Lakota word that referred to anyone outside the tribe. She grinned from ear to ear. "No. I'm
not. But my grandfather is. He still lives on the rez in
Wapiti Ridge Sioux Reservation. It's where I'm from.
Somebody called the rez to find a relative who knew
him, so my cousin answered their questions and then
he called me. We've got family all over," she added
with a twinkle in her eyes. "Even in South Texas."

Carlie smiled. "Nice to know. It's like where I live,
in Comanche Wells. I know everybody, and everybody knows my family for generations."

She nodded. "It's that way back home, too." She
looked at Carson. "Cousin Bob Tail is praying for
him. Now he is a *wicasa wakan,*" she added.

"I believe in prayer," Carlie replied, looking back
at Carson. "I think God comes in all colors and races
and belief systems."

The visitor laid a hand on her shoulder and leaned
down. "Cousin Bob Tail says he's going to wake up
soon." She stood up and chuckled. "Don't you tell
a soul I said that. They'll take back my medical degree!"

"You're a doctor," Carlie guessed, smiling.

"Neurologist," she said. "And I believe in modern

medicine. I just think no technology is so perfect that it won't be helped by a few prayers." She winked, glanced at Carson again, smiled, and went out.

"You hear that?" she asked Carson. "Now you have to get better so people won't think Cousin Bob Tail is a fraud."

EVEN SHE, WITH no medical training, could tell that Carson was getting worse. She got up and bent over him, brushing back the unruly long black hair that had escaped the neat ponytail he usually wore it in.

She leaned close to brush her mouth over his. She stopped. Frowned. There was a fleeting wisp of memory. Garlic. He smelled of garlic. She knew he hated it because he'd once told Rourke he couldn't abide it in Italian dishes and Rourke had told her, just in passing conversation.

Another flash of memory. Wyoming. Merissa Kirk. She'd been poisoned with the pesticide malathion disguised in capsules by Richard Martin, who'd substituted it in her migraine headache capsules. A cohort of Martin's, a woman, had tried again to poison Merissa when she was in the hospital. The woman, on Martin's orders, had put malathion in a beef dish that Merissa had for supper. It had smelled of overpowering garlic! Cash Grier had told her all about it. She let go of Carson's hand and rushed out the door. The doctor, the Lakota neurologist, was standing at the desk.

"Please, may I speak with you?" she asked hurriedly.

"Yes…"

Carlie pulled her into Carson's cubicle. While she

was walking, she was relaying the memories that had gone through her head. "Smell his breath," she asked softly.

Dr. Beaulieu caught her breath. "Poison?" She was thinking out loud. "It would account for the deterioration better than the slight head injury…"

"The woman who did it, she answered the phone when I called Carson. She said I'd get to watch him die slowly, over days!"

"Poison," the doctor agreed, black eyes narrowed. "That could explain it."

SHE WENT OUT. They came and took Carson out of the cubicle and wheeled him quickly back to the emergency surgical suite.

"It will be all right," Dr. Beaulieu assured her as she went by. "We're running a blood screen for poison right now, and I have a phone call in to the doctor whose name you gave me in Wyoming." She pressed Carlie's arm with her hand. "I think you may have saved his life."

"Cousin Bob Tail will be happy," Carlie said with just a hint of a smile.

"Oh, yes."

It seemed to take forever. Carlie sat in the waiting room this time, as close to the door as she could get, her legs pressed tightly together, her hands clenched in her lap, praying. She didn't have the presence of mind to call anyone. She was too involved in the moment.

She remembered Carson being so hostile to her in the beginning, antagonizing her with every breath, flaunting Lanette in front of her, insulting her. Then he'd frightened her, and with incredible skill, he'd treated her, taken her to the emergency room and then to have lunch by a flowing stream in the woods.

Afterward, in his arms, she'd felt things she'd never known in her young life. They'd fed the birds together and he'd told her the Brulé legend of the crow and how it became black. At the end, he'd told her it would never work out for the two of them and he was going to have to leave.

Now, there was the danger. She knew he wasn't tame. He would never be tame. He wouldn't marry her and settle down in Comanche Wells, Texas, and have children with her. He was like her father. Jake Blair had overcome his own past to change and transform himself into a man of God, into a minister. But Carson was different.

She looked at her hands, tightly clenched in her lap. Ringless. They'd be that way forever. She was never going to get married. She would have married Carson, if he'd asked. But nobody else. She'd be an old maid and fuss in her garden. She smiled sadly. Maybe one day Carson would marry someone and bring his children to visit her. Maybe they could at least remain friends. She hoped so.

The door to the surgical suite opened and Dr. Beaulieu came out. She sat beside Carlie and held her cold hands.

"We were in time," she said. "They've just finished washing out his stomach. They're giving him drugs to neutralize the effects of the poison. Your quick thinking saved his life."

Tears, hot and wet, rolled down Carlie's pale face. "Thank you."

"Oh, it wasn't me, honey," she laughed. "I just re-layed the message to the right people. I only do head injuries, although I've put in my time in emergency rooms." She smiled sadly. "Back home, there are so many sick people with no money, no way to afford decent health care. I tried to go back and work there, but I was just overwhelmed by the sheer volume of people. I decided I needed more training, so I special-ized and came here to do my residency. This is where my life is now. But one day, I'll go back to the rez and open a free clinic." She smiled, showing white teeth. "That's my dream."

"You're a nice person."

"You really love that man, don't you?" she asked with a piercing gaze.

Carlie smiled sadly. "It doesn't help much. He's a wolf. He isn't tameable."

"You know, that's what I said about my husband." She chuckled. "But he was. I have three kids."

"Lucky you."

"I am, truly." She cocked her head. "You know, Carson's great-great-grandfather rode with Crazy Horse. His family dates back far beyond the Little Big Horn."

The knowledge was surprising. Delightful. "Like mine in Comanche Wells," Carlie said softly.

"Yes. You both come from villages where families grow together. We aren't so very different, you know."

"He doesn't…love me," Carlie replied sadly. "If he did, I'd follow him around the world on my knees through broken glass."

"How do you know he doesn't?"

"He was leaving when this happened. He said it would never work out."

"I see." The other woman's face was sad. "I am truly sorry."

"I'm happy that he'll live," Carlie replied. "Even if he marries someone else and has ten kids and grows old, I'll still be happy."

Dr. Beaulieu nodded slowly. "And that is how love should be. To wish only the best for those we love, even if they choose someone else."

"When can I see him?"

"They'll take him out to a room very soon," she said, smiling. "We had him in ICU because he wasn't improving. But while they still had the tube down his throat he woke up and began cursing the technician." She chuckled. "I think they'll be very happy to release him to the poor nurses on the ward."

Carlie grinned. "He's conscious?"

"Oh, yes." She stood up. "Now will you relax?"

"I'll try." She stood up, too. *"Pilamaya ye,"* she said softly in Lakota. The feminine form of *thank you.*

Dr. Beaulieu's eyes widened. "You speak Lakota?"

"Only a few words. Those are my best ones, and I imagine my accent is atrocious."

"I've been here for two years and not one person has ever spoken even one word of Lakota to me," the other woman said with pursed lips. "However few, I appreciate the effort it took to learn them." She nodded toward the emergency suite. "Does he know you speak them?"

Carlie hesitated and then shook her head. "I was afraid he'd think I was, well, doing it just to impress him. I learned it when I was still in school. I loved reading about Crazy Horse. Of course, his mother was Miniconjou Lakota and his father was part Miniconjou, but he was raised Oglala Lakota…"

Dr. Beaulieu put her hand on Carlie's shoulder. "Okay, now you have to marry him," she said firmly. "Even on the rez, there are some people who don't know all that about Crazy Horse." And she laughed.

CARSON WAS MOVED into a room. Carlie had phoned her father and her boss to tell them Carson was out of danger.

She was allowed in when they got him settled in the bed and hooked up to a saline drip. He was sitting up, glaring, like a wolf in a trap.

"You look better," she said, hesitating in the doorway.

"Better," he scoffed. He was hoarse, from the tube. "If you agree that having your stomach pumped with a tube down your throat is better!"

"At least you're alive," she pointed out.

He glared at her. "What are you doing here?"

She froze in place. Flushed. She wasn't certain what to say. "I phoned you for Rourke and Lanette answered…"

"Lanette." He blinked. "We were having coffee. I was about to tell her that I'd never tasted worse coffee when she came up behind me and hit me in the head. A gun went off." He shifted uncomfortably. "She shot me!" He glanced at Carlie. "Where is she?"

"They have a BOLO for her," she replied, using the abbreviation for a "Be on the lookout." "She hasn't surfaced yet. Fred Baldwin, who kidnapped me, is in custody in Jacobsville, along with the watch that

Richard Martin stole from the assistant prosecutor he killed. He's turned state's evidence against Matthew Helm. They should be at his door pretty soon."

Carson was staring at her. "That doesn't answer the question. Why are you here?"

"Nobody else could be spared," she lied. "My father came by earlier. The others will be along soon, I'm sure."

His black eyes narrowed. He didn't speak. He didn't offer her a chair or ask her to sit down.

"There's a neurosurgeon here. A Dr. Beaulieu. She's Lakota. She said your cousin Bob Tail was praying for you, and that he said you'd live."

"Cousin Bob Tail usually can't even predict the weather," he scoffed.

"Well, he was right this time," she said, feeling uncomfortable. She twisted her small purse in her hands.

"Was there anything else?" he asked, his eyes unblinking and steady on her face.

She shook her head.

"Then I imagine visiting hours are over and you should go home before it gets dark."

"It's already dark," she murmured.

"All the more reason."

She nodded.

"They'll have someone watching you," he said.

"I guess."

"Don't go down any back roads and keep your phone with you."

"It's in my purse."

"Put it in your coat pocket so that you can get to it in a hurry if you have to," he continued curtly.

She grimaced, but she took it out and slid it into her coat pocket.

"Good night," he said.

She managed a faint smile. "Good night. I'm glad you're okay."

He didn't answer her.

She walked out, hesitated at the door. But she didn't look back when she left. She didn't want him to see the tears.

THEY'D GIVEN HIM something for pain. The gunshot wound, while nonfatal, was painful. So was his throat, where the tube had gone down. He was irritated that Carlie had come to see him out of some sort of obligation. Nobody else was available, she'd said. It was a chore. She hadn't come because she was terrified that he was going to die, because she cared. She'd come because nobody else was available.

Yet he was still concerned that she was driving home alone in the dark, when there had been attempts on her life. He'd wanted to phone Cash and ask him to watch out for her. Then he laughed inwardly at his own folly. Of course Cash would have her watched. He probably had somebody in the hospital the whole time, somebody who would keep her under surveillance even when she drove home.

He fell asleep, only to wake much later, feeling as if he had concrete in his side where the bullet had hit.

"Hurts, huh?"

He looked up into a face he knew. "Sunflower," he said, chuckling as he used the nickname he'd hung on her years ago. Dr. Beaulieu had been a childhood playmate. He knew her very well, knew her family for generations.

She grinned. "You're looking better."

"I feel as if a truck ran through my side," he said, grimacing. "They pumped my stomach."

"Yes. Apparently the woman who shot you also hit you on the head to show us an obvious head injury. But she poisoned you first. The poison was killing you. If it hadn't been for your friend from Comanche Wells, you'd be dead. We were treating the obvious injuries. None of us looked for poison because we didn't expect to see it." She hesitated. "We did blood work, but it was routine stuff."

"My friend?" He still felt foggy.

"Yes. The dark-headed girl who speaks Lakota," she replied. "She smelled garlic on your breath and recalled that you hated it and would never ingest it willingly. Then she remembered a poisoning case in Wyoming in a hospital there, a woman who was given malathion in a beef dish..."

"Merissa Kirk," Carson said heavily. "Yes."

"So we checked with the attending physician there for verification. I was involved only peripherally, of course, since my specialty is neurology. We thought you were unconscious because of the head wound."

"The coffee," Carson recalled. "The coffee tasted funny."

She nodded. "She told the dark-haired girl that she would get to watch you die slowly. When she smelled your breath, she remembered what the woman told her."

"Lanette." His face tautened. "I hope they hang

her. If they'll let me out, I'll track her down, wherever she goes."

Dr. Beaulieu was smiling. "She said you were like a wolf, that you could never be tame. She said it didn't matter, that she only wanted you to be happy, even if it was with some other woman." She shook her head. "She thanked me in Lakota. It was a shock. Most *wasicus* can't speak a word of our language."

"I know."

"She even knew that Crazy Horse's mother was Miniconjou," she said.

"Where's my cell phone?" he asked.

She raised both eyebrows. "Cell phone?"

"Yes. Wasn't it brought in with me?" he asked.

"Let me check." She phoned the clerk at the emergency room where he was brought in. They checked the records. She thanked them and hung up. "There was no cell phone with you when you were admitted," she said.

He grimaced. All his private numbers were there, including Carlie's, her father's and Rourke's. If Lanette had taken it...

"Will you hand me the phone, please? And tell me how to get an outside line..."

CARLIE WAS NO sooner back home than her phone rang while she was opening the front door. She answered it.

There was nobody there. Only silence.

"Hello?" she persisted. "Look, tell me who you are or I'm calling the police."

There was a dial tone.

It worried her. She went inside to talk to her father.

But he wasn't there. A note on the hall table said that he'd been called to a meeting of the finance committee at the church. He wouldn't be long.

Carlie hung up her old coat. She started upstairs when she remembered that she'd left her cell phone in her coat. She went to get it just as there was a knock on the door.

CHAPTER FOURTEEN

"WHAT DO YOU MEAN, you can't get her on the phone?" Carson raged at Cash Grier. "Get somebody over there, for God's sake! Lanette has my cell phone. It has Carlie's number and Rourke's real number on it!"

"Will you slow down and calm down?" Cash asked softly. "I've got people watching Carlie's house. Believe me, nobody's touching her."

"Okay. How about her father?"

"At a church meeting. We have someone outside."

"Rourke?"

Cash laughed. "I arrested Rourke two hours ago in the act of placing cocaine in the glove compartment of Calhoun Ballenger's son's truck."

"Arrested?"

"You've been out of the loop," Cash told him. "Blake Kemp, our district attorney, was on the scene, along with agents from the DEA, ICE and several other agencies. We had to make it look good, in case Helm slips through our fingers and Rourke has to go undercover again."

"All right." Carson's head was throbbing. His wound hurt. "Carlie said she came because nobody else was available to sit with me—"

"Really? You should talk to the staff. She sat in

the corridor outside the E.R. and refused to budge. When they got you to ICU, she did the same thing. They even called security. She sat where she was and cried. Finally, the neurosurgeon on your case took pity on her and let her in."

"Dr. Beaulieu?" he asked.

"No, it was a man. Anyway, she smelled garlic on your breath. She connected you with the Wyoming case, told Dr. Beaulieu, and the rest is history. Saved your life, son," he added. "You were dying and they didn't know why. I assume your blond friend hit you on the head and shot you so that they wouldn't think of looking for poison until it was too late."

"I don't remember any of this."

"I guess not. I had Carlie call you at your apartment because Rourke couldn't risk having his number show up on your phone, assuming that it was bugged by Helm's men. Lanette answered it. She told Carlie that you'd be a long time dying and she'd have to watch you suffer. Almost came true."

"Almost." His heart lifted like a bird. Carlie had lied. She'd been with him all the way, all the time. She did care. Cared a lot.

"So just get well, will you? We've got everything covered down here."

"Okay." He drew in a breath. "Thanks, Cash."

"You'd do it for me."

"In a heartbeat."

He hung up the phone and closed his eyes. He should call Carlie. He wanted to. But that was when the pain meds they'd been shoveling into him took effect. He went to sleep.

CARLIE OPENED THE DOOR. Just as she did it, she realized that she shouldn't have done it. She had no weapon, her phone was in her coat, she was vulnerable. Just like when she'd answered the door and Fred Baldwin had carried her off.

Her father stared back at her with set lips. "How many times do I have to tell you to make sure who's at the door before you answer it?" he asked.

She smiled sheepishly. "Sorry, Dad." She stared at him. "Why did you knock?"

He grimaced. "Forgot my keys."

"See? It's genetic," she told him. "You lose your keys, I lose my phone. It's catching, and I got it from you!"

He chuckled. "Heard from Carson?"

"He's sitting up in bed yelling at people," she said.

He let out a relieved whistle. "I wouldn't have given a nickel for his chances when I saw him," he replied. He smiled. "I wouldn't have told you that. You still had hope. I guess they've got some super neurosurgeons in that hospital."

"It wasn't the head injury," she said. "Or the gunshot wound. It was poison. She put malathion in his coffee."

"Good Lord!" he exclaimed. "That's diabolical!"

"Yes. I hope they catch her," she said doggedly. "I hope they lock her up for a hundred years!"

He hugged Carlie. "I can appreciate how you must feel."

She hugged him back. "Carson sent me home," she said, giving way to tears. "I think I made him mad by just going up there."

He grimaced. "Maybe he's trying to be kind, in

his way, Carlie. You know he's probably never going to be able to settle in some small town."

"I know. It doesn't help."

She drew back and wiped her eyes. "How about some coffee and cake?"

"That sounds nice."

"Did you just try to call me?" she added on the way.

"Me? No. Why?"

"Just a wrong number, I guess. Somebody phoned and hung up." She laughed. "I'm probably just getting paranoid, is all. I'll make a pot of coffee."

TWO DAYS LATER, Carson was out of the hospital. He was a little weak, but he felt well enough to drive. He went to his apartment first, looking for the missing cell phone. He knew he wouldn't find it. He hoped they could catch Lanette before she managed to get out of the country. She probably had several aliases that she could refer to if she was as competent at her job as he now believed she was.

A contract killer, and he'd been dating her. All the while she'd been hell-bent on killing Carlie's father. He felt like an idiot.

He drove down to Jacobsville to Cash Grier's office. As soon as he opened the door, he looked for Carlie, but she wasn't at her desk. He went on in and knocked at Cash's door.

"Come in."

He opened the door, expecting Carlie to be taking dictation or discussing the mail. She wasn't there, either.

"You look like hell," Cash said. "But at least you're still alive. Welcome back."

"Thanks. Where's Carlie?" he asked.

"Bahamas," he replied easily.

He frowned. "What's she doing in the Bahamas?"

"Haven't a clue," Cash said heavily. "She and Robin took off early yesterday on a red-eye flight out of San Antonio. She asked off for a couple of days and I told her to go ahead. She's had a rough time of it."

"I tried to call her. I didn't get an answer."

"Same here. I don't think her cell phone is working. Her father's still looking for it. She said she left it in her coat pocket, but then they noticed there's a hole in the pocket. Probably fell out somewhere and she didn't notice. She was pretty upset over you."

"I heard." He was feeling insecure. He thought Carlie cared. But she'd gone to the Bahamas with another man. He'd heard her speak of Robin with affection. Had he chased her into the arms of another man with his belligerent attitude? He should have called her father when he couldn't reach her, called the house phone. The damned drugs had kept him under for the better part of two days!

"Why did she go to the Bahamas with a man?" he asked shortly.

Cash frowned. "I don't know. She and Robin have always been close, from what I've heard. And he took her to the Valentine's Day dance." He hesitated. "It didn't seem like a love match to me. But..."

"Yes. But."

Cash could see the pain in the other man's face. "I'm sorry."

"So am I." He managed a smile. "I'm leaving."

"Today?"

He nodded. "I'm going home. I have some ghosts to lay."

Cash got up, went around the desk and extended his hand. "If you ever need help, you've got my number," he told the younger man.

Carson returned the pressure. He smiled. "Thanks."

"Keep in touch."

"I'll do that, too." He glanced out at the empty desk where Carlie usually sat.

"What do you want me to tell her?" Cash asked.

Carson's face set into hard lines. "Nothing. Nothing at all."

CARLIE STOOD UP with Robin and his fiancée, Lucy Tims, at their secret wedding in Nassau.

"I hope you'll be very happy," she told them, kissing both radiant faces.

"We will until we have to go home and face the music," Robin chuckled. "But that's not for a few days. We're going to live in paradise until then. Thanks so much for coming with us, Carlie."

"It was my pleasure. Thanks for my plane ticket," she added gently. "I sort of needed to get away for a little while."

"Stay for a couple of days anyway," Robin coaxed.

She shook her head. "Overnight was all I can manage. The chief won't even be able to deal with the mail without me," she joked. "I'm going back tonight. You two be happy, okay?"

"Okay." They kissed her again.

She didn't want to say, but she was hoping that

Carson might come to see her when he was out of
the hospital. It was a long shot, after his antagonis-
tic behavior, but hope died hard. She went home and
wished for the best.

SHE MISSED HER cell phone. She knew it had probably
fallen through the hole in her pocket and it was gone
forever. It was no great loss. It was a cheap phone and
it only had a couple of numbers in it, one was her father and the other was Cash Grier.

But it was like losing a friend, because Carson
had carried it around with him before he brought it
to her. It had echoes of his touch. Pathetic, she told
herself, cherishing objects because they'd been held.

It had been several days. She was getting used to
the idea that Carson was gone for good. Chief Grier
had told her that Carson had come by the office on
his way out of town. But he hadn't had a message
for Carlie. That was all right. She hadn't really expected one.

She disguised the hurt on the job, but she went
home and cried herself to sleep. Wolves couldn't be
tamed, she reminded herself. It was useless to hope
for a future that included Carson. Just useless.

ROURKE WAS BAILED out by Jake Blair. They had a good
laugh about his imminent prosecution for breaking
and entering, possession of narcotics and possible
conspiracy.

They laughed because Rick Marquez and the San
Antonio assistant D.A. working the case finally had
enough evidence to arrest Matthew Helm. It made
headlines all over the country, especially when

Rourke gave a statement to the effect that Mr. Helm had ordered him to plant narcotics on Calhoun Ballenger's son Terry and that Charro Mendez had supplied them.

There was an attempt to extradite Mendez to stand trial in the U.S. on drug charges, but he mysteriously vanished.

Helm wasn't so fortunate. He, his senior campaign staff and at least one San Antonio police officer were arrested and charged with crimes ranging from attempted murder to theft of police evidence and narcotics distribution.

It came as a shock when Marquez released a statement heralding Fred Baldwin as a material witness in the case. Fred, who was turning state's evidence, was being given a pardon by the governor of the state in return for his cooperation.

That news was pleasing to Eb Scott, whose kids had become great playmates of the big, gentle man who lived with them while Helm was under investigation. Eb wanted to give Fred a job, in fact, but Cash Grier beat him to it. Fred was wearing a uniform again, having been cleared of all charges against him in Chicago, his record restored, his reputation unstained, his former partner now under investigation for police corruption.

He was Jacobsville's newest patrol officer, and his first assignment was speaking to children in grammar school about the dangers of drugs. He was in his element. Children seemed to love him.

Carlie went about her business, working diligently, keeping up with correspondence for the chief. But the sadness in her was visible. She'd lost that impish spark that had made her so much fun to be around. Her father grieved for her, with her. He understood what she was going through as she tried to adjust to life without Carson, without even the occasional glimpse of him in town. He was long gone, now.

AUTUMN CAME TO Jacobs County. The maples were beautiful and bright, and Carlie was filling her bird feeders for the second time, as the migrating birds came from the north on their way to warmer climates. Cardinals and blue jays were everywhere. The male goldfinches were losing their bright gold color and turning a dull green, donning their winter coats.

Carlie was still wearing her threadbare one with the hole in the pocket sewn up. Her phone had miraculously reappeared, brought in by a street person who found it and traded it to a soup kitchen worker for a sandwich. The worker had turned it in to police, who returned it to Carlie. She had the phone in her pocket even now. It was safe enough with the hole mended.

The birds usually stayed nearby while she filled the feeders, but they suddenly took off as if a predator was approaching. It was an odd thing, but she'd observed it over the years many times. Sometimes, for no apparent reason, birds just did that. Flew up all together into the trees, when Carlie saw nothing threatening.

This time, however, there was a threat. It was standing just behind her.

She turned, slowly, and there he was.

She tried valiantly not to let her joy show. But tears stung her eyes. It had been months. A lifetime. She stood very still, the container of birdseed held tight in her hands, her eyes misting as she looked at him.

He seemed taller than ever. His hair wasn't in a ponytail. It was loose around his shoulders, long and thick and as black as a grackle's wing. He had something in a bag under one arm. He was wearing that exquisite beaded jacket that was so familiar to her.

"Hello," he said.

"Hello," she said back.

He gave her coat a speaking look. "Same coat."

She managed a smile. "I was going to say the same thing."

He moved closer. He took the seed canister out of her hands and placed it on the ground. He handed her the bag and nodded.

She opened it. Inside was the most exquisite coat she'd ever seen in her life, white buckskin with beading, Oglala Lakota colors of the four directions, in yellow, red, white and black patterns on it. She gasped as she pulled it out of the bag and just stared at it.

He held out his hand. She took off her ratty coat and gave it to him to hold while she tried on the new jacket. It was a perfect fit.

"It's the most beautiful thing in the world," she whispered, tears running down her cheeks.

"No, Carlie," he replied, dropping her old coat on top of the birdseed canister. "You're the most beautiful thing in the world. And I've missed you like hell! Come here…!"

He wrapped her up against him, half lifting her so that he could find her lips with his hard, cold mouth. He kissed her without a thought for whoever might see them. He didn't care.

He was home.

She held on for dear life and kissed him back with all the fear and sorrow and grief she'd felt in the months between when she thought she'd never see him again. Everything she felt was in that long, slow, sweet kiss.

"I love you," she choked.

"I know," he whispered into her mouth, the words almost a groan. "I've always known."

She gave up trying to talk. It was so sweet, to be in his arms. She was probably hallucinating and it wasn't real. She didn't care. If her mind had snapped, it could stay snapped. She'd never been so happy.

Eventually, he stood her back on her feet and held her away from him. "You've lost weight."

She nodded. She studied him. "You look...different."

He smiled slowly. "At peace," he explained. "I had to go home and face my demons. It wasn't easy."

She touched his hard face. "There was nothing you could have done to stop it," she said softly.

"That's what his own brother said. I made peace with his family, with her family."

"I'm glad."

"I had my cousin make the jacket. I'm glad it fits."

She smiled. "It's beautiful. I'll never take it off."

He pursed his lips. "Oh, I think you might want to do that in a week or so."

"I will? Why?"

He framed her face in his big, warm hands. "I'm not wearing clothes on my honeymoon. And neither are you."

"How do you know what I'll be wearing?" she asked, brightening.

"Because we'll be together." The smile faded. "Always. As long as we live. As long as the grass grows, and the wind blows, and the sun sets."

Tears rolled down her cheeks. "For so long?" she whispered brokenly.

"Longer." He bent and kissed away the tears. "I would have been here sooner, but I stopped by to talk to Micah Steele."

"Micah?"

He nodded. "I still have to do an internship. I'm arranging to do it here. Afterward, a year or two of residency in internal medicine, here if possible, San Antonio if not. Then I'll move into practice with Lou and Micah."

She was standing very still. She didn't understand. "You're going to medical school?"

He laughed softly. "I've already been to medical school. I got my medical license. But I never did an internship so I couldn't, technically, practice medicine." He smoothed her hand over his chest. "I did keep my medical license current. I guess I realized that I'd go back to it one day. I have some catching up to do, and I'll have to work late hours, but—"

"But you want to live here?" she asked, aghast.

"Of course," he said simply. "This is where your tribe lives, isn't it?" he teased.

Tears were falling hot and heavy now. "We're going to get married?"

He nodded. "I'm not asking, by the way," he said with pursed lips. "We're just doing it."

"Oh."

"And I don't have a ring yet. I thought we'd go together to pick them out. A set for you, and a band for me."

"You're going to wear a ring?" she asked.

"It seems to go with the position." He grinned.

She hesitated, just for a second.

"You're thinking of my reputation with women. I took them home, kissed them at the door and said good-night," he said, reading her apprehension. "It was a nice fiction, to keep homebodies like you from getting too interested in me." He shrugged. "I haven't had anybody since I was widowed."

She pressed close into his arms, held on for dear life. "I would have married you anyway."

"I know that."

"But it's nice that you don't know a lot more than I do…"

"And that's where you're wrong," he whispered into her ear. "I'm a doctor. I know where ALL the nerve endings are."

"Gosh!"

"And the minute your father pronounces us man and wife, I'll prove it to you. When we're alone, of course. We wouldn't want to embarrass your father."

"No. We wouldn't want to do that." She pressed close into his arms, felt them fold around her, comforting and loving and safe. She closed her eyes. "You didn't say goodbye."

His arms contracted. "You went to the Bahamas with another man."

She jerked back, lifting horrified eyes. "No! I went to be a witness at his wedding to Lucy Tims!" she exclaimed.

He grimaced. "I know that, now. I didn't at the time. I tried to call you, but I never got an answer."

"I lost my phone. Some kind person turned it in at a soup kitchen in San Antonio."

He sighed, tracing her mouth with a long forefinger. "A comedy of errors. I felt guilty, too. I'd sent you packing without realizing that you'd saved my life. I was still confused from the blow on the head and the drugs. I was worried that you'd be on the road alone in the dark." He leaned his forehead against hers. "Lanette was still on the loose. I was afraid for you. I should never have let you leave the hospital in the first place—"

"I was okay," she interrupted. "Cash Grier had people watching me all the time. Dad, too. Just in case."

"I hurt you. I never meant to." He closed his eyes as he rocked her in his arms. "I wasn't sure, Carlie. I had to be sure that I could settle down, that I could give up the wild ways. Until I was sure, I wasn't going to make promises."

She drew away. "And are you? Sure, I mean?"

He nodded. "That's why I went home." He smiled. "Cousin Bob Tail says we're going to have three sons. We have to name one for him."

"Okay," she said, without hesitation and with a big grin.

He laughed. "He wants us to name him Bob. Just Bob."

"I wouldn't mind." She searched his black eyes. "Our sons. Wow."

"Just what I was thinking. Wow." He chuckled. "I haven't been playing online for a while."

"Neither have I," he confessed. "I missed you so much that I really wanted to. But I had to be sure, first." He sighed. "I guess if push comes to shove I can make an Alliance toon and we can run battle-grounds on the same side."

"Funny, I was just thinking I could make a Horde toon for the same reason."

He smiled. "We're on the same side in real life. That's enough."

"So," she asked, her green eyes twinkling, "when are we getting married?"

"Let's go and ask your father when he's free," he said.

She slid her hand into his and walked back into the house with him. Her father didn't even have to ask. He just grinned.

THEY WENT TO Tangier for their honeymoon. Carlie was horrified at the expense, but Carson just laughed.

"Honey, I've got enough in foreign banks to keep us going into our nineties," he said complacently. "I work because I enjoy working. I could retire tomorrow if I felt like it. But I think practicing medicine will occupy me for many years to come. That, and our children."

"You told Rourke you wanted to be an attorney," she recalled.

"Yes, well, if you tell somebody you gave up law they don't care. If you tell them you gave up medicine, that's a whole other set of explanations I didn't want to make. As it happens, I did a double major in undergraduate school in biology and chemistry, but

I minored in history and anatomy. History and law do go together."

"I wouldn't know. Will it matter to you that I haven't been to college?"

"You're kidding, right?" he teased. "You can speak Lakota and you know who Crazy Horse's mother was. That's higher education enough to suit me."

"Okay. Just so you're sure," she laughed. "And you don't mind if I go on working for the chief?"

"He'd skin me if I tried to take you away," he said with a sigh. "He'd never find a stamp or a potato chip, and some new girl would surely find out about the alien files he's got locked up in his office and call the Air Force. So, no, you can go on working. I intend to."

She smiled. "Dr. Farwalker. Sounds very nice."

"I thought so myself."

TANGIER WAS AN amazing blend of old and new. There were high-rise apartment buildings near the centuries-old walled marketplace. Carlie found it fascinating as they drove through the city at night in the back of a taxicab.

It had been a very long flight, from San Antonio to Atlanta, Atlanta to Brussels, Brussels to Casablanca, Casablanca to Tangier. They'd arrived in the dead of night and Carlie was worried sick about being able to find a way to get into the city as they waited endlessly to get through passport control and customs. But there were cabs sitting outside the main building.

"Told you so," he chuckled.

"Is there any foreign city you haven't been to?" she wondered.

"Not many," he confessed. "You'll love this one.

I'll take you around town tomorrow and show you where the pirates used to hang out."

"That's a deal."

CARLIE WAS SO tired by the time they got into the hotel, registered and were shown to their room that she almost wept.

"Now, now," he said softly. "We have our whole lives for what you're upset about missing. Sleep first. Then, we explore."

She smiled shyly. "Okay."

He watched her undress, with black eyes that appreciated every stitch that came off. But when she was down to her underwear, he moved close, pulled out a gown and handed it to her.

"First times are hard," he said gently. "Go put on your gown. I'll get into my pajamas while you're gone. Then we'll get some sleep before we do anything else. Deal?"

She smiled with relief. "Deal. I'm sorry," she started to add.

He put his fingers across her lips. "I like you just the way you are," he told her.

"Hang-ups and all?"

He smiled. "Hang-ups and all."

She let out the breath she'd been holding and darted into the bathroom, chiding herself for her wedding night nerves. It was natural, she supposed, despite the fact that most people had the wedding night long before the wedding. She and Carson must be throwbacks, she decided, because he'd wanted to wait as much as she had.

The lights were out when she came back into the room. The shutters were open, and moonlight filtered across the bed, where Carson was sprawled under the sheet. He held out his arm. She darted into bed and went close, pillowing her cheek on his hard, warm chest.

"Oh, that feels good," she whispered.

"I was about to say the same thing. Happy?"

"I could die of it."

"I know exactly what you mean." He closed his eyes, tucked her close and fell asleep almost at once. So did she. It had been a very long trip.

SHE WOKE THE next morning to the smell of coffee. She opened her eyes. Carson was sitting on the side of the bed in his pajama bottoms holding the cup just over her head.

"What a wonderful smell," she moaned.

"Sit up and have a sip. They serve a nice buffet breakfast downstairs, but I thought you might like coffee first."

"I would." She sat up, noticing at once how much of her small breasts were visible under the thin gown. He was looking at them with real interest, his eyes soft and hungry.

The way he looked at her made her feel beautiful. Exciting. Exotic.

"Tangier," she murmured, putting the cup down on the side table. "It makes me feel like I should be wearing a trenchcoat or something." Breathlessly, she slid the straps of the gown down her arms and let them fall.

Carson's expression was eloquent. He didn't even hesitate. He moved across the bed, putting her down on it, while his mouth opened and fed on her firm, soft breasts.

She arched up, shyness vanishing in the heat of sudden passion. She felt his hands go down her back, sliding fabric out of the way. She felt him move and then his body was moving on hers, bare and exciting.

He eased between her legs, his mouth poised over hers. He teased her lips while his body teased hers. He was smiling, but there was heat and passion in the smile. "Lift up," he whispered. "Seduce me."

"Gosh, I don't have…the slightest idea…I'm sorry…I…!" A tiny, helpless moan escaped her as his hand moved between them. "Carson, oh, gosh!"

"Yes, right there," he murmured at her lips. He chuckled softly. "It feels good, doesn't it? And this is just the beginning."

"Just the…?" She cried out again. Her body arched, shivering. What he was doing was shocking, invasive, she should be protesting or something, she should be… "Carson," she sobbed against his mouth. "Please…don't stop!"

"Never," he breathed against her lips. "Move this leg. Yes. Here. And that one. Now lift. Lift up, baby. Lift up…that's it…yes!"

There was a rhythm. She'd never known. In all her reading and covert watching of shocking movies, she'd never experienced anything like this.

It was one thing to read about it, quite another to do it. He knew more about her body than she did, apparently, and used that knowledge to take her to places she'd never dreamed about. The sensations piled upon themselves, growing and multiplying, until she felt as if she had the sun inside her and it was going to explode any second. The tension was so high that it was like being pulled apart in the sweet-est sort of way.

She dug her nails into his hips as he strained down toward her, his powerful body arched above her as he drove down one last time.

She heard herself sobbing as she fell and fell, into layers of sweet heat that burned and burned and burned. It was like tides, rippling and falling, over-whelming and falling, crushing and falling, until fi-nally she burst like fireworks and shuddered endlessly under the heavy, hard thrust of his body.

She heard him cry out at her ear, a husky sound that was so erotic, she shivered again when she felt his body cord and ripple and then, quite suddenly, relax.

He was heavy. His skin was hot, damp. She held him, smoothed the long, thick hair at his back, lov-ing him.

"Everybody says it hurts the first time," she mur-mured.

"Oh? Did it?"

She laughed secretly. "I don't know."

He chuckled, the sound rippling against her hard-tipped breasts. He moved on her, feeling her instant response. He lifted his head and looked into her wide, soft eyes. "You will never get away," he promised her. "No matter how far, how fast you run, I will find you."

"I will never run," she said with a sigh. "Every-thing I want or love in all the world is right here, in my arms."

He bent and kissed her eyes shut as he began to move. She shivered gently.

"How long do you want to wait?" he whispered at her mouth.

"How…long? For…what?" she gasped, moving with him.

"To make a baby," he whispered back.

Her eyes opened. She shivered again. The look on her face was all the answer he needed. He held her gaze as he moved, tenderly, enclosing her in his legs, bending them beside her, so that they were locked together in the most intimate position she'd ever experienced.

"Oh…my…goodness," she said, looking straight into his eyes.

His hands framed her face. His was strained, taut, as he moved expertly on her body.

"I can't bear it," she managed to say.

"Yes, you can," he whispered. His eyes held hers. "I love you. This is how much…"

He shifted, and she cried out. The pleasure was beyond words, beyond description. She held on and sobbed with each slow, deep, torturous movement of his hips as he built the tension and built it and built it until she exploded into a million tiny hot pieces of sheer joy.

He groaned, almost convulsing, as the pleasure bit into him. "Never," he whispered hoarsely. "Never, never like this!"

She couldn't even manage a word. She just clung to him, enjoying the sight of the pleasure in his face, in the corded muscles of his body, in the sweet agony that echoed in the helpless movements of his hips.

Long after they felt the last ripple of pleasure, they

clung to each other in the bright stillness of the morning, unable to let go.

"I think I dreamed you," he whispered finally.

"I know I dreamed you," she replied at his ear, still holding tight.

He rolled over so that she was beside him, but still joined to his body.

"I didn't know it felt like this," she confessed shyly. "I feel hungry now in a way I didn't before."

He smiled, brushing his mouth over hers. "You can't miss what you've never had."

"I guess so." She drew in a breath and looked down.

He smiled to himself and pulled away, letting her look. Her eyes were as wide as saucers when he moved away.

"Show-and-tell," he teased.

She blushed. "Men in racy magazines don't look like that," she whispered. "I only saw one and he was, well, he was..." She cleared her throat. "He wasn't that impressive."

He chuckled. He pulled her to her feet, enjoying her nudity. "I have an idea."

"You do? What?" she asked, looking up at him with a smile.

"Let's have a shower, and then breakfast and go look for pirates."

"I would like that very much."

He led her toward the bathroom.

She hesitated at the door.

He raised an eyebrow.

"What you said." She indicated the bed. "Was it just, I mean, did you really mean it?"

He pulled her close. "I want children very much, Carlie," he said softly. "They'll come when it's time for them to come." He smiled. "If it's this year, I don't mind at all. Do you?"

She laughed and hugged him close. "Oh, no, I don't mind!"

"Then let's have a shower and go eat. I'm starving!"

LIFE WITH CARSON was fascinating. They found more in common every day. They moved into a house of their own and Carson went to work at Jacobsville General as an intern. It was long hours and hard work. He never complained and when he got home, he told Carlie all the interesting things he'd learned that day. She never tired of listening.

Fred Baldwin had coffee with her when he started out on his patrols. He'd turned into a very good cop, and he'd have done anything for Cash Grier. He'd have done anything for Carlie, too. He told her that her father was going to have to share her with him because he didn't have a daughter of his own. She'd almost cried at the tenderness in his big brown eyes.

Lanette had been found, but not in a condition that would lead to trial. She took a flight to a small South American country that had no extradition treaty with the United States, but had the misfortune to run into the brother of a man she'd killed for money. Since she had no living family, they buried her in an unmarked grave in South America.

Matthew Helm was arrested, prosecuted and convicted on so many felony counts that he'd only get out of prison when he was around 185 years old. Or so the jury decided.

His cohorts went with him. The wife of the murdered assistant district attorney was in the courtroom when the sentence was pronounced.

Calhoun Ballenger won the special election and went to Washington, D.C., with his wife, Abby, as the junior United States senator from the grand state of Texas. Terry, having just graduated from high school, was off to college with his two brothers, Ed and Matt.

Calhoun had given Fred Baldwin a musical watch that played an Italian folk song when he learned about Fred's role in preventing the potential criminalization of his son Terry. Fred wore the watch to work every day.

Charro Mendez was still on the run. But people across the border were watching and waiting for his return.

Two months after Carlie and Carson were married, she was waiting for him at the front door when he came home from a long day at the hospital. She was holding a small plastic device in her hands. She handed it to him with an impish grin.

He looked at it, read it, picked her up and swung her around in his arms, kissing her the whole while and looking as if he'd won the lottery.

Seven months later, a little boy was born at Jacobsville General Hospital. They named him Jacob Allen Cassius Fred Farwalker, for his father, his grandfather and his two godfathers. Officer Fred Baldwin held him while he was baptized. He cried.

* * * * *

Don't miss Diana Palmer's next
HQN in the summer of 2015—UNTAMED—
the romance of Rourke and the woman
who finally tames the rogue warrior!

HQN

www.HQNBooks.com

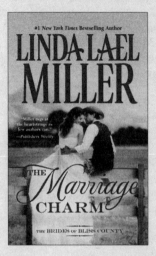

Look for the pulse-pounding new thriller from

ELIZABETH HEITER

Eighteen years ago, FBI profiler Evelyn Baine's best friend, Cassie Byers, disappeared, the third in a series of unsolved abductions. Only a macabre nursery rhyme was left at the scene, claiming Evelyn was also an intended victim. After all these years of silence, another girl has gone missing, and the Nursery Rhyme Killer is taking credit. Is Cassie's abductor back, or is there a copycat at work?

Evelyn has waited eighteen years for a chance to investigate, but when she returns to Rose Bay, she finds a dark side to the seemingly idyllic town. As the place erupts in violence and the kidnapper strikes again, Evelyn knows this is her last chance. If she doesn't figure out what happened to Cassie eighteen years ago, it may be Evelyn's turn to vanish without a trace.

Available now, wherever books are sold!

Be sure to connect with us at:

Harlequin.com/Newsletters
Facebook.com/HarlequinBooks
Twitter.com/HarlequinBooks

MIRA®

www.MIRABooks.com

MEH1738

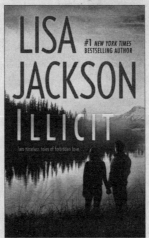

REQUEST YOUR
FREE BOOKS!

2 FREE NOVELS
FROM THE ROMANCE COLLECTION
PLUS 2 FREE GIFTS!

YES! Please send me 2 FREE novels from the Romance Collection and my 2 FREE gifts (gifts are worth about $10). After receiving them, if I don't wish to receive any more books, I can return the shipping statement marked "cancel." If I don't cancel, I will receive 4 brand-new novels every month and be billed just $6.24 per book in the U.S. or $6.74 per book in Canada. That's a savings of at least 22% off the cover price. It's quite a bargain! Shipping and handling is just 50¢ per book in the U.S. and 75¢ per book in Canada.* I understand that accepting the 2 free books and gifts places me under no obligation to buy anything. I can always return a shipment and cancel at any time. Even if I never buy another book, the two free books and gifts are mine to keep forever.

194/394 MDN F4XY

Name _____ (PLEASE PRINT) _____

Address _____ Apt. # _____

City _____ State/Prov. _____ Zip/Postal Code _____

Signature (if under 18, a parent or guardian must sign)

Mail to the Harlequin® Reader Service:
IN U.S.A.: P.O. Box 1867, Buffalo, NY 14240-1867
IN CANADA: P.O. Box 609, Fort Erie, Ontario L2A 5X3

Want to try two free books from another line?
Call 1-800-873-8635 or visit www.ReaderService.com.

* Terms and prices subject to change without notice. Prices do not include applicable taxes. Sales tax applicable in N.Y. Canadian residents will be charged applicable taxes. Offer not valid in Quebec. This offer is limited to one order per household. Not valid for current subscribers to the Romance Collection or the Romance/Suspense Collection. All orders subject to credit approval. Credit or debit balances in a customer's account(s) may be offset by any other outstanding balance owed by or to the customer. Please allow 4 to 6 weeks for delivery. Offer available while quantities last.

Your Privacy—The Harlequin® Reader Service is committed to protecting your privacy. Our Privacy Policy is available online at www.ReaderService.com or upon request from the Harlequin Reader Service.

We make a portion of our mailing list available to reputable third parties that offer products we believe may interest you. If you prefer that we not exchange your name with third parties, or if you wish to clarify or modify your communication preferences, please visit us at www.ReaderService.com/consumerschoice or write to us at Harlequin Reader Service Preference Service, P.O. Box 9062, Buffalo, NY 14269. Include your complete name and address.

DIANA PALMER

77977	LONG, TALL TEXANS VOLUME III: ETHAN & CONNAL	___ $7.99 U.S.	___ $8.99 CAN.	
77976	LONG, TALL TEXANS VOLUME II: TYLER & SUTTON	___ $7.99 U.S.	___ $8.99 CAN.	
77975	LONG, TALL TEXANS VOLUME I: CALHOUN & JUSTIN			
77941	WYOMING TOUGH	___ $7.99 U.S.	___ $8.99 CAN.	
77910	WYOMING STRONG	___ $7.99 U.S.	___ $8.99 CAN.	
77854	PROTECTOR	___ $7.99 U.S.	___ $8.99 CAN.	
77762	COURAGEOUS	___ $7.99 U.S.	___ $9.99 CAN.	
77727	NOELLE	___ $7.99 U.S.	___ $9.99 CAN.	
77724	WYOMING BOLD	___ $7.99 U.S.	___ $8.99 CAN.	
77696	WYOMING FIERCE	___ $7.99 U.S.	___ $9.99 CAN.	
77666	MERCILESS	___ $7.99 U.S.	___ $8.99 CAN.	
77631	NORA	___ $7.99 U.S.	___ $9.99 CAN.	
77570	DANGEROUS	___ $7.99 U.S.	___ $9.99 CAN.	
77283	LAWMAN	___ $7.99 U.S.	___ $7.99 CAN.	

(limited quantities available)

TOTAL AMOUNT	$_____
POSTAGE & HANDLING	$_____
($1.00 FOR 1 BOOK, 50¢ for each additional)	
APPLICABLE TAXES*	$_____
TOTAL PAYABLE	$_____

(check or money order—please do not send cash)

To order, complete this form and send it, along with a check or money order for the total above, payable to Harlequin HQN, to: **In the U.S.:** 3010 Walden Avenue, P.O. Box 9077, Buffalo, NY 14269-9077; **In Canada:** P.O. Box 636, Fort Erie, Ontario, L2A 5X3.

Name: _____

Address: _____ City: _____

State/Prov.: _____ Zip/Postal Code: _____

Account Number (if applicable): _____

075 CSAS

*New York residents remit applicable sales taxes.
*Canadian residents remit applicable GST and provincial taxes.

HQN™

www.HQNBooks.com

PHDP0215BL